DATE DUE			
Jun 21 '76			
Dec 13 77			
May 10			
Dec 6 78			
Apr 26 79			
Apr 26			
Nov 20 80			

WITHDRAWN

Consumer Behavior

Consumer Behavior

A Cognitive Orientation

Rom J. Markin, Jr.

Director of the Bureau of Economic and Business Research
and Professor of Business Administration,
Washington State University

Macmillan Publishing Co., Inc.
New York

Collier Macmillan Publishers
London

Macmillan Publishing Co., Inc.
866 Third Avenue
New York, New York 10022

Collier-Macmillan Canada, Ltd.

Library of Congress Cataloging in Publication Data

Markin, Rom J.
     Consumer behavior.

     Includes bibliographical references.
     1. Consumers. 2. Consumption (Economics)
I. Title.
HB801.M295   658.8'34   73–7346
ISBN 0–02–376110–5

Printing: 1 2 3 4 5 6 7 8   Year: 4 5 6 7 8 9 0

This book is dedicated
to a singular wife,
two sons,
and an only daughter.

Preface

This work is basically a textbook for students in the first course in consumer behavior. It assumes little prior preparation, although in most instances students will have had an introduction to some one or several behavioral or social science subjects like psychology, sociology, social psychology, cultural anthropology, and economics. Furthermore, some background in business subjects is anticipated; most students will have had at least an introduction to business course and a principles of marketing course. In almost all instances, the basic points from these fields have been introduced and reviewed in this text before we use them in an understanding of consumer behavior's distinctive eclectic approach.

The book has two major objectives. The first is to treat in a balanced way as much of the discipline as is pedagogically sound and possible. The second is implicit in the first: to do so within the framework of a systematic and integrated treatment. I have sought to provide the reader with what he needs to know about the range and shadings of research on each particular topic and to discuss research studies in connection with specific points in the body of the text. The material is extensively documented.

My treatment of the field is primarily cognitive and includes the consumer's ability to seek, extract, and process information in the interest of consumer problem-solving. Emphasis is on consumer decision processes as a series of activities related to the purchase and consumption of goods, namely, problem recognition, search, evaluation, commitment, and postpurchase consideration. All of these factors involve information-processing activities. Thus, information processing is seen as applied to many phenomena often treated quite separately in the literature of consumer behavior, among them attitude change, socialization, role behavior, motivation, and so forth. The treatment is holistic rather than reductive-functional. This means simply that consumer behavior as a dependent variable is not treated as the singular result of some one or two independent variables such as motivation or perception. Instead, in a holistic fashion, consumer behavior is the result of a congeries of factors, many of which operate in an interactive and interdependent fashion.

The organization of the book proceeds from the general and historical to the most modern thinking regarding theory development and business practice. Four chapters constitute the introduction. The role of marketing theory and business strategy is demonstrated to peg the necessity of understanding consumer behavior. Furthermore, the necessity for understanding and studying consumer behavior emerges from the reaction of neglected, mistreated, and often exploited consumers, underscoring even more the vital role of social issues such as consumerism in the field of consumer behavior. Part I sketches rather comprehensively the more relevant issues and concepts in consumer behavior and concludes with a survey and critique of several "models" of consumer behavior. The author's own "holocentric model" is developed in this section.

Part II, "Intrapersonal Dimensions of Consumer Behavior," develops the fundamental mechanics and structure of cognitive activity. As used here, cognition is that complex phenomenon of thinking, reasoning, and memory that relates to the extraction of information from the environment and the way in which such information is processed and used for both utilitarian and symbolic problem-solving. Specific concepts treated and analyzed are cognition, motivation perception, learning, and attitudes.

Part III emphasizes the facilitating variables, or the mediating role, of communication and personality and their impact on consumer decision processes.

Part IV is an extensive excursion into social influence and its impact upon consumer behavior. The treatment of interpersonal variables draws heavily from our emphasis on cognition, the perceptual feature of social interaction, and considers the concepts of social rewards and the social exchange-transaction basis of consumer interaction. Here the focus is upon socialization, group processes and social class, family influences, life style and life cycle concepts, and most important the cultural-social matrix of consumer behavior.

Part V looks at the many dimensions of the consumer decision process. Consumer behavior is not a single act but a whole series of related activities. The major theme—namely, that consumer behavior is an exercise in decision making or problem-solving under conditions of uncertainty—is continued throughout these chapters.

The one chapter in Part VI takes a brief look at what conceivably is in store for consumer behavior theory in the future. We examine the directions being taken by the discipline and attempt to chart what course it is likely to take in the years ahead.

It should be pointed out that a careful effort is made to integrate material from various sections of the book into a cohesive unit or total action system. The consumer is treated as a biological-social-psychological organism. He is not an economic man—a calm, dispassionate rationalizer or prowling computer; nor is he a Freudian symbol-driven, stimulus-response mechanism behaving according to the urgings of his psychological drive state. Neither is he the mindless, faceless creature hidden in the lonely crowd, seeking to win friends and approbation from his fellowmen by manifesting behavior that conforms to someone else's norms and folkways. The consumer is, instead, a person endowed with all the characteristics and foibles endemic to the human condition.

Many friends and colleagues have contributed to this effort. My own colleagues at Washington State University have helped to shape my thinking on many concepts; and with their insight, our discussions have led me to considerably greater understanding. Their presence alone is an important intellectual stimulus. I am particularly grateful for the encouragement of Dr. Chem Narayana, Dr. James Horrell, and Dr. Charles Lillis. I am especially indebted to the many authors whose ideas are incorporated into this work. My gratitude is extended also to my students in B.A. 367, "Consumer Behavior," who indulged me considerably throughout the formation and shaping of my own ideas. Two graduate research assistants are due special mention for their contribution—Mr. Larry Hunt and Miss Pattie Ireland. Dr. V. Parker Lessig of Kansas University read and criticized the entire manuscript, and his always perceptive suggestions strengthened the text in both content and organization. Miss Breta Smith typed the entire manuscript with devotion and commitment and for her effort, patience, and attention to detail I am indebted.

Finally, to my wife, who gave unstintingly of her encouragement, understanding, and love—out of which all things flow—I am most grateful.

In the final analysis, in spite of so much help the responsibility for the effort is mine and no disclaimer of this responsibility is implied.

R. J. M.

Contents

Part I

Introduction

1

Marketing Theory, Strategy, and Consumer Behavior

In every field or discipline there always appear to be a few simple questions that are highly embarrassing because the debate that forever swirls around them seemingly leads only to perpetual failure and ultimately makes ardent fools of the most expert. "Why do customers buy goods?" is an example of just such a question in marketing. This question, so essential and relevant to market planners, researchers, academicians, and practitioners, has brought forth a host of responses—most of which continue to embarrass and to make fools of the expert. The embarrassment results in part because the responses are often inadequate, lacking in conceptual foundations, or based upon faulty and illogical premises or, more frequently, are simply unspecific and ambiguous. Too often the responses are not answers at all. Instead they are extensions of the basic questions—for example: "Why do some persons prefer Brand X to Brand Z?" "Why do some customers manifest greater loyalty to Store B than to Store A?" "How might marketers meaningfully identify and classify market segments?" "Why, why, why?" Why do men of science always seem to want the answer to some question beginning with "Why"? The answer, of course, is that men of science, whether they be marketers, physicists, ecologists, or entomologists, are always obsessed with the desire to understand their environment, or what to them appears to be some illusory and complex set of phenomena with which they must deal effectively. In the case of marketers, this environment, or a large part of it, is necessarily a class or set

3

of phenomena that, for the sake of convenience, is labeled *consumer behavior. Consumer behavior is the indispensable condition upon which all market planning and market strategy must be predicated.* Furthermore consumer behavior, the essence of which is "Why consumers do what they do," is the most dynamic, indeterminate, stochastic, and unpredictable factor with which marketers must contend. There is only one constant regarding consumer behavior and that is change. Because consumers do change. They are not the routinized, habitual, programmed, imprinted automatons that many marketers and businessmen would have us believe. If they were, markets would be sodden trading places of inertia. Brand and market shares would be locked into a state of impermeability. And the failure rate of new products, and that of new firms, would be considerably less than 50 to 98 per cent for the former and 20 to 50 per cent for the latter.

This, then, is a book about marketing and therefore it is a book about consumer behavior, because the two terms or concepts are inextricably bound together. To illustrate, marketing broadly conceived is a set of human activities directed at facilitating and consummating exchanges. The core of modern marketing is customer orientation and market segmentation. The marketing concept emphasizes a basic reorientation of the company from looking inward toward its products to looking outward toward its customers. This point of view suggests further that in defining a basic need category the company must recognize the existence of many market segments within every market; that it must recognize, furthermore, that each market segment has, perhaps, different demand characteristics, many of which are not just demographic or economic but most of which are behavioral, that is, result from different perceptions, cognitions, and motivations; and that these behavioral differences emerge from different socializing experiences, different life styles, different group affiliations, and different subcultural orientations.

Our concern, then, is with how the marketer utilizes behavioral information in order to do a better marketing job, that is, to perform the business activities that direct the flow of goods and services from producer to consumer or user. And what we sometimes label as *consumer behavior* is only the total reaction of the human organism to any attempt to get him to accept an idea or to undertake an action of any kind proposed by others.

Consumer behavior changes rapidly. And it may come as some surprise that marketers, like others, do not always appreciate the new. Often they are afraid of it. Too frequently, as Dostoevski put it, "taking a new step, uttering a new word is what people fear most." In the case of consumer behavior, the experience of the new is rarely without some forebodings and misgivings. In the case of drastic and significant change, the uneasiness is deeper and more lasting.[1] So although some

---

[1] For an explanation on this theme, see Eric Hoffer, *The Ordeal of Change* (New York: Harper and Row, Publishers, 1963).

marketers might prefer a more stable universe, the truth is that they must cope with the dynamic and changing nature of consumer behavior. They must seek to find better answers to the riddle and mystery surrounding consumer behavior and product choice. Why? Because all the firm's activities—its planning, scheduling, budgeting, and controlling activities—are related to the master that it allegedly serves: its customers and potential customers. Notice that it was said, "all the firm's activities," not just marketing or sales but *all:* production, finance, and marketing. Therefore, from the point of view of marketing, all marketing activities must begin and end with some statement or understanding, either implicit or explicit, of consumer behavior. The firm, and especially the marketing operations of that firm, must be linked to the marketplace. In short, the firm must take its marching orders from the market. To accomplish this, it must develop better answers to the questions relating to consumer behavior. And to accomplish the latter marketers must learn to appreciate and cultivate the use of theory as a basis for the formulation of marketing strategy.

The Development and Use of Theory

To understand human behavior, we must have better theories of behavior, generally. To understand consumer behavior, we must develop better theories of this specific kind of behavior. To understand the behavior of the business firm, the marketplace, competitive reaction and retaliation, the economy, and the political system, there must be developed better theories of these phenomena. Thus our purpose here is to develop more fully the meaning, relevance, and usefulness of theory as a basis for management decision-making and problem-solving.

WHAT IS THEORY?

Theory, broadly conceived, is an explanation.[2] It may be an explanation based upon thought or introspection, or it may be an explanation based upon combined empirical observation and reasoning. Our theories of consumer behavior fall into both classes. For example, a simple economic explanation (theory) of consumption states that consumption is a function of income. Such a theory lends itself to empirical, or direct, observation. On the other hand, another explanation of consumption or consumer behavior states that consumption, i.e., the purchase and use of goods, is a part of the individual's goal-striving or self-actualizing behavior. This explanation is, at this juncture at least, largely conjectural and not easily verified by direct observation.

This latter explanation leads to another important aspect of theory, namely, that a theory is usually a hypothesis or set of hypotheses pro-

[2] For more on this subject, see Reavis Cox, Wroe Alderson, and Stanley Shapiro, eds., *Theory in Marketing* (Homewood, Ill.: Richard D. Irwin, Inc., 1964).

posed as an explanation. The hypothesis may amount to a reasonable guess and have yet to be verified. Many of our theories of consumer behavior fall into this particular classification. The task of science and men of science is to know. The method used to discover knowledge is the scientific method, which entails the formulation of a hypothesis. A hypothesis is a tentative explanation for a certain group of facts, admittedly unproved but accepted for the time being as highly probable. From observation or reasoning related to the phenomena or behavior in question, given focus by the hypotheses, theories are formulated. In such cases theory is used to mean an explanation that has been tested and confirmed as a general principle explaining a large number of related facts, occurrences, or other phenomena in nature.

When using the term *theory* what is usually meant is a straightforward, explicit, and coherent organization of variables and relationships that may possess both empirical and potential foundations and is addressed to gaining understanding, prediction, or control of an area or phenomenon.

The study of consumer behavior as a part of a larger system of action and behavior, marketing, is both a discipline and a science. As a discipline, the field of consumer behavior has techniques that supply answers to certain questions. In addition to techniques, consumer behavior as a field of study has theories that, in a broad sense, supply the criteria by which answers are judged.[3] This book is concerned with both the techniques and the theories of consumer behavior as they might affect marketing behavior and practice.

THE ROLE OF THEORY

Theory has come increasingly to occupy a featured role in business administration. The businessman uses theory because in an increasingly complex and dynamic world he needs ways of thinking about his responsibilities that tend to make them more manageable and, in turn, will allow him to relate his experience in past situations to his contemporary problems. Equally importantly, however, theory is valuable to students who look at marketing as observers rather than as participants because it enables them to order, classify, and manage what they perceive in more understandable terms. In both cases, the desire is to improve the understanding of a given system.

Theory, as a generalized explanation of a set of phenomena, serves the following objectives for both the marketing practitioner and the student of marketing:

1. Description.
2. Explanation.
3. Prediction.

[3] See Michael H. Halbert, "The Requirements for Theory in Marketing," in Cox, Alderson, and Shapiro, op. cit., pp. 17–36.

DESCRIPTION. At least in part, theory supplies a descriptive framework for complex phenomena. The beginning of analysis and understanding is often simple description.

EXPLANATION. Theory supplies tentative explanation. To understand how a given thing works often is useful in terms of how a general class of things is likely to work. Explanation leads to understanding; and understanding quite frequently leads to greater manageability.

PREDICTION. As a manager, the marketer is forced to make decisions under conditions of uncertainty and risk. Description and understanding that stem from theory construction and development can often lead to a greater assessment of the relative probabilities of various outcomes and, in turn, enhance the ability of the decision maker to anticipate the future. Without theory, prediction is sheer guess and conjecture.

To create a theory is to create a testable hypothesis. *Testable,* in this context, means falsifiable by comparison with empirical evidence. Eventually all theories must be squared with objective reality.

MARKETING BEHAVIOR

Our theories of consumer behavior affect the behavior and operation of the business firm. A *business firm* may become a *marketing firm* depending upon how it sees its role in relationship to consumers.

To discuss the role of theory in marketing is really to say something about the mode or style of managing marketing functions.[4] Churchman classifies managers in terms of three sets of characteristics related to management's perceptions about theory:

1. Theorizer—A management based on the assumption that reality is rational (predictable) and hence the task of the manager is to remove the randomness and obscurity of his own thinking in order to become as much like reality as possible.
2. Generalizer—A management based on the assumption that reality is non-rational, but that the task of the manager is to construct a strong structure within which the raw inputs from reality may be given the fullest possible weight.
3. Particularizer—A management based on the assumption that reality is irrelevant, and that the task of the manager is to permit maximum flexibility of decision making so as to meet the requirements imposed by the data.[5]

Given the underlying theoretical predicates, contemporary marketing practice strongly suggests the endorsement of at least a generalizing

[4] See C. West Churchman, "Marketing Theory as Marketing Management," in Cox, Alderson, and Shapiro, op. cit., pp. 313–321.

[5] Ibid., p. 316.

marketing manager—one who plans in advance what needs to be done. Hopefully such planning will also be oriented around some theoretical focus, that is, a marketing manager should know how to ask questions. Increasingly, the management style that is becoming more characteristic of today's marketing manager is that of the planner—and one whose plans are based upon theories. His theories relate not only to his own controllable operation but pertain as well to what he perceives as his uncontrollable external environment.

The Marketing Concept

To understand more fully the theoretical basis of the behavior of today's marketer, we need to understand the concepts or assumptions upon which much of his behavior is based. The *marketing concept* is the foundation stone of the marketer's behavior and his philosophic outlook. The marketing concept rests fundamentally upon two basic theories or ideas. Foremost among these is the idea that all company planning, policies, and operating procedures should be oriented toward the consumer: the firm takes its marching orders from the market. The second basic premise of the marketing concept is that profitable sales volume is the major operating goal of the firm, that is, that every alternative considered in relationship to the decision processes of the company should be analyzed in terms of costs and benefits and that the alternative making the greatest contribution to profit and overhead should be chosen.

These two considerations are tied together in many business organizations or marketing firms via management's belief that the best way to attain profit maximization is through supplying what the customer wants.

During the mid 1950s the marketing concept was hailed as a new business philosophy.[6] From this philosophy and its underlying theory emerged a new theory of marketing management.

MARKETING STRATEGY

As a theorizer and a generalizer, i.e., one who plans in advance what needs to be done based upon theoretical considerations, the marketing manager's principal responsibility is that of creating and implementing a *marketing strategy*. A marketing strategy is a comprehensive plan of action that attempts to coordinate the efforts of the marketing-oriented firm with its task. The essence of strategy is its dynamic nature. Strategy suggests movement and countermovement in pursuit of predetermined objectives. Thus, the marketing concept gives some

---

[6] For example, see Fred J. Borch, "The Marketing Philosophy as a Way of Business Life," *The Marketing Concept: Its Meaning to Management,* Marketing Series, No. 99 (New York: American Management Association, 1957), pp. 3–5. Also see Bernard J. LaLonde, "Evolution of the Marketing Concept," in Stephen A. Greyser, ed., *Toward Scientific Management* (Chicago: American Marketing Association, 1964), pp. 333–343.

theoretical underpinning to the behavior of the marketing firm. The marketing concept dictates *consumer orientation* and *profitability.* Strategy is the manifestation of the firm's efforts to achieve these dual objectives. It further implies a sequence of decision rules to enable the firm to meet these goals and objectives. The purpose of the marketing-oriented business firm is clearly to create satisfied customers.[7]

Marketing strategy as a major comprehensive plan is of necessity constructed around a series of subplans or variables. The marketing firm exists within a larger social, economic, political, and legal framework that tends to circumscribe the firm's behavior. For example, the individual firm can seldom control the level or nature of demand for its products, and it cannot effectively control the social, political, or legal climate within which it must operate. In short, the marketing firm cannot control or manage its environment, but it can and does attempt to manage its own affairs. The firm attempts to accommodate to external environmental forces via its marketing strategy. The strategy consists of a continuous readjustment, combining and permuting these four elements:

1. Products and services.
2. Promotion and selling.
3. Place and location decisions.
4. Pricing.

There are two principal components of every marketing strategy. The first, and perhaps the most important component, is the bundle of decisions about the selection of the market target group. The second component is the development of the marketing mix. This latter component is made up of the set of policies in each of the four decision areas listed by which the firm hopes to convince potential customers to buy its products.[8]

Almost every decision in marketing is affected by the quality of the information that surrounds that decision. Decisions related to market targets must be predicated on *information* regarding market opportunities. This information and how it is interpreted is affected by our notions and theories regarding customer needs, life-style motivations, and so on. Concomitantly, the decisions relating to the market mix must all be treated within a framework of both behavioral and economic considerations. Marketers soon learn that information and explanations relating to human behavior are complex and confusing. Economists have provided an approach to this type of understanding, and the behavioral sciences broaden that approach so that the human beings described are realistic ones and behave as the real humans we know behave.

[7] For more discussion on this point, see John E. Wakefield, "Make Your Company Marketing Conscious," *Business Management* (October 1965), pp. 82–84.

[8] Leonard S. Simon and Marshall Freimer, *Analytical Marketing* (New York: Harcourt Brace Jovanovich, Inc., 1970), p. 4.

Markets and Marketing

Even the novice would recognize that there is a strong relationship between marketing as an activity and markets as places or areas where such activities take place. Yet the real relationship between marketing and markets is often overlooked. Marketing is not the study of markets. It is, instead, the study of specific kinds of market activities. Furthermore, the kind of marketing activities engaged in in a given economic system will depend to a great degree on how that economic system structures its markets and circumscribes its market activities. Let us look more intently at the nature of markets and marketing and their relationship.

MARKETING DEFINED

Marketing is a complex set of economic and social-psychological phenomena. It interfaces with many disciplines such as production, finance, and distribution economics. It involves millions of people, many thousands of firms, and an infinite variety of products, and it generates countless billions in revenue and expenses, some profits, and lots of occasions for decision making. There is a vast literature on the theory and practice of marketing. Yet we are constantly asked to define the subject in one or two sentences. Not surprisingly, in the face of all this demand there is no shortage of supply. For example, here are several popular and accepted definitions (in each definition, italics were supplied by this author):

> Marketing—the performance of business activities that direct the flow of goods and services from producer to *consumer* or *user.*[9]

> Maketing is traditionally viewed as the business function . . . of finding *customers.*[10]

> Marketing is a total system of interacting business activities designed to plan, price, promote and distribute want satisfying products and services to *present and potential customers.*[11]

> Marketing—the art of selling or purchasing in a *market.*[12]

The reader will observe that each of the four definitions includes either markets as abstractions or customers, who constitute markets. Each definition also alludes to a set of activities or functions, and in the

[9] Ralph I. Alexander and the Committee on Definitions of the American Marketing Association, *Marketing Definitions* (Chicago: American Marketing Association, 1960), p. 15.

[10] Philip Kotler, *Marketing Management* (Englewood Cliffs, N.J.: Prentice-Hall, Inc. 1967), p. 3.

[11] William J. Stanton, *Fundamentals of Marketing,* 2nd ed. (New York: McGraw-Hill Book Company, 1967), p. 5.

[12] *Webster's Third New International Dictionary* (Springfield, Mass.: G.&C. Merriam Co., 1965), p. 1383.

Stanton definition marketing is described as a "total system of interacting business activities."

The major purpose of this discussion has been to point out the importance of markets and consumer orientation to marketing. What is more, marketers, if they are truly customer oriented, must become better aware of the nature of markets and market opportunities. It must be added that this admonishment transcends a tendency to mouth such bromides as "The customer is king," and "Without customers we wouldn't really be in business."

MARKET OPPORTUNITY

Businesses come into existence, survive, and prosper as a result of perceiving a market opportunity and developing and promoting a stream of want-satisfying commodities for that market.

Thus the market opportunity concept is really just another way of looking at a more traditional marketing problem, namely, discovering, analyzing, and interpreting the significance of markets.[13]

MARKETS DEFINED

There are several ways of looking at the concept of a market. Markets are sometimes viewed as physical places. The downtown central business district is a market. Wall Street in New York is a financial market. Some of the early public markets were the Lexington Market of Baltimore, the Faneuil Hall Market of Boston, and the Catherine Market of New York City. It is certainly true that one aspect of certain kinds of markets is their physical location. Yet markets are more than physical locations. *A market is an area in which the minds of buyers and sellers meet and operate.* Two major qualifications or explanations should be offered in connection with this definition. First, "market as an area" does not imply necessarily a physical space; rather it is meant to imply both physical and psychic space. A particular market may be quite diffused: buyers and sellers may be separated by miles or thousands of miles, but they can interact via communication devices. Second, markets denote interaction. What is more, they denote interpersonal behavior. That is, the market must contain both buyers and sellers interacting in a situation in which Buyer A's behavior affects Seller B's behavior and vice versa. Such is the nature of market dynamics.

A LOOK AT MARKETS

All markets, viewed from the demand or buyers' side, are composed of three major elements or characteristics:

1. Markets are comprised of people (only people buy goods and services)

---

[13] For an extended treatment of the market opportunity concept, see Rom J. Markin, *Retailing Management: A Systems Approach* (New York: Macmillan Publishing Co., Inc., 1971), Chapter 5, pp. 97–118.

2. With purchasing power, *and*
3. A willingness to spend and consume.

Thus markets are determined by numbers of people, size of families, the composition and structure of population, households and household formation, and so on. There is a basic economic dimension to markets. For example, how much money the market participants have, what its source is, whether it is sustaining, and so on. Finally, there are a host of social-psychological market considerations. For instance, what percentage of income is spent rather than saved? What goods are demanded, when, and how often? And most importantly, what affects a consumer's propensity to consume or willingness to buy and WHY? So here we are again faced with the necessity of knowing more about consumer motivation and behavior.

Because most of you who are reading this book in the mid-1970s will soon be earning your livelihood in the markets of the late 1970s and beyond, our discussion of markets will focus on the changing dimensions of the markets of the future. Where are we going? What is happening? What changes in market characteristics bode well for the future success of your marketing ventures?

POPULATION. The United States entered the decade of the seventies with a population of approximately 202 million. By 1980, by conservative estimate, our nation's population will have swelled to 235 million. Thus, the projected 1980 figure represents an increase of 3 million persons in each year of the decade.[14] A large and important segment of this population bulge will be among young adults. In the early 1970s the last wave of teen-agers from the post-World War II baby boom will reach adulthood. By 1980, the 20–29 age group will be up to 40 million from the 1970 figure of 25 million. This represents an increase of 60 per cent. There will thus be many new adults who will be getting married, starting new families, and looking for places to live.

Nearly three out of four of these new families are expected to live in cities, adding even more to the crowded and congested nature of urban areas. Farm population will continue to decline.

Most of the new adults will not be heading, however, to the already congested cities of the eastern United States. People in increasing numbers are moving west and south. Florida and Arizona are the states expected to grow fastest, and according to projections, a lot of people are going to be migrating to new centers and filling up the empty spaces. Such states as Alaska, Nevada, New Mexico, Utah, Wyoming, and Washington will be the locus of much immigration. California will continue to witness an increasing population, but overall the trend to redistribution of the country's population away from the older, established centers will continue. The decade of the 1970s will be the decade of the "young marrieds" and one during which the "youth culture" will con-

[14] These projections are the author's, based upon U.S. Bureau of the Census data, 1970.

tinue to have considerable force in terms of group norms, folkways, and adolescent life styles.

A new baby boom in the 1970s in spite of lower fertility rates, will bring a new teen-age bumper crop in the 1980s and 1990s. Our society is not likely to lose its youth orientation for some time to come.

Figure 1-1 summarizes the preceding generalizations regarding population by depicting population growth by age groups for 1970–1975 and 1980.

Before we proceed further, however, some caution may be warranted. Demography is one of the most mechanical of the social sciences. Yet in many instances its predictions are dismal. Almost all population predictions have been wrong, with few exceptions. Sometimes these predictions are not just a little wrong but grossly wrong. Not many anticipated the huge bulge in fertility between 1947 and 1961, and not many anticipated the enormous decline in fertility that we are currently experiencing. In demographics, you can get enormously puzzling parametric changes almost overnight. For example, in the first nine months of 1971 Americans were having babies at a rate of 2.39 children for each family. Through September, 1972, the rate had fallen below the "replacement rate" of 2.1 babies per family to the all-time low of 2.08 children per family. Should this rate be continued for a prolonged period of time, the American population would actually decline.

Among the causes of this lower birthrate can be cited the tendency

Figure 1-1

Population Growth by Age Groups

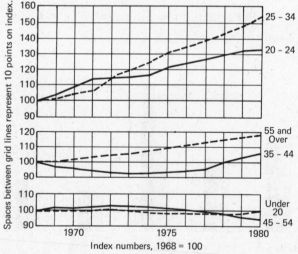

Index numbers, 1968 = 100

Source: U.S. Department of Commerce

of more women to work, to marry later in life, and to postpone having children.

One additional important factor might be mentioned regarding population and population characteristics: during the decade of the 1970s and on through the 1980s, people will be going to school longer, and many persons will even continue formal learning while actually pursuing professional careers. Training programs will be initiated by more companies, and many companies will encourage, and perhaps even help to finance, outside schooling. Some of the schooling will take place at night, some will occur during employee sabbaticals, and some even on company time.

One other interesting comment of note. The university of the 1980s will no longer be a rural enclave or youth palace. It will more likely become a dynamic urban center of learning for lifelong attendance by managers, professionals, and all those interested in participating at a high level in a knowledge-oriented society.

Better-educated consumers, in turn, will mean increasingly aware and sensitive consumers, who will have far-reaching consequences on marketing behavior and strategy.

INCOME. The Gross National Product, a measure of the value of all goods and services produced in the United States for a one-year period, reached nearly $1 trillion in 1970, and by 1980 this measure will be likely to increase to $2 trillion. By 1980, more than half the families in the United States should have incomes over $10,000.

U.S. families and income recipients will witness a rather massive increase in disposable personal income during the 1970s. Disposable

Figure 1-2

U.S. Population by Educational Levels

Millions of Persons 25 Years and Over

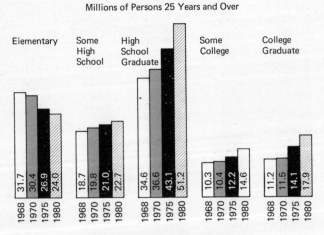

Source: U.S. Department of Commerce

personal income (DPI) is a very important barometer of marketing activity—it is of utmost significance in the analysis of variations in total consumption over periods of time and the nature of demand and market opportunity for various categories of consumption at any particular period of time.

Disposable personal income is the wherewithal that supports consumer expenditures. Personal consumption expenditures traditionally run about 92 per cent of disposable personal income. This figure should hold at about that same level during the decade of the 1970s. However, any small shift in the tendency to spend versus save can have a marked effect on consumption expenditures and thus on the market opportunity for marketers.

Figure 1-3 summarizes the changes forecast in discretionary income to 1980 and discretionary income as a percentage of personal income to 1980.

In addition to the quantitative changes in disposable income and personal consumption expenditures in the United States, another far-reaching and significant change has taken place in the distribution of income shares. In the first three decades of this century, the United States began to develop its first so-called mass market. In 1900, almost half of the family units in the United States had less than $2,000 of income in 1960 prices. During the 1920s the most significant market development was the creation of a sizeable "lower-middle" income class

Figure 1-3

Discretionary Income in Billions of Dollars

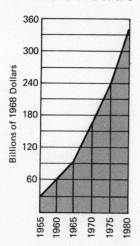

Sources: U.S. Department of Commerce; The National Industrial Conference Board, 1970.

Discretionary Income as Per Cent of Personal Income

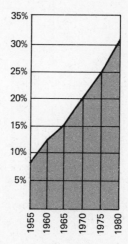

Sources: U.S. Department of Commerce; The National Industrial Conference Board, 1970.

based on family units in the $2,000–$4,000 income class. By 1954, over 40 per cent of all family units had an after-tax income between $4,000 and $7,500, and their income was about 40 per cent of the total. Currently, about 16 per cent of all families in which the head is under thirty-five have earnings of over $10,000 per year. But by 1975, that percentage will have increased to an estimated 35 per cent. In absolute numbers, we now have roughly 2 million families in the indicated age bracket; ten years hence there will be over three times as many.

Contributing to this development, (1) young families will become half again as numerous as they are now, and (2) the configuration of the prevailing income distribution curve will change. Today many relatively young families are clustered in the $7,000–$10,000 income category. Given the overall improvement in earnings expected in the course of the next ten years, many families will be found in the upper income brackets. Figure 1-4 shows relative changes in families by income groups for the year 1966, contrasted with forecasted figures for 1980.

In summary, the general improvement in economic fortunes (in conjunction with population growth) will make for a pronounced increase in the number of young higher-income families. By 1975, young and affluent homes—in which the head is under thirty-five and the income exceeds $10,000—will account for an estimated 15 per cent (based upon 1970 dollars) of total buying power.[15]

On the other hand, the poor as a percentage of the population will shrink as rising incomes pull more and more people above the poverty

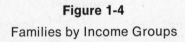

Figure 1-4

Families by Income Groups

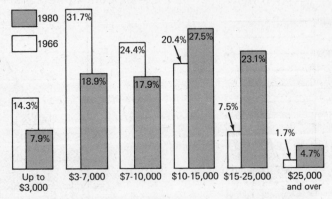

Sources: U.S. Department of Commerce; The National Industrial Conference Board.

[15] Fabian Linden, "Family Formation," *The Conference Board Record,* Vol. 4, No. 2 (New York: The National Industrial Conference Board, 1967), pp. 38–40.

line. The income pyramid, characteristically narrow at the top and wide at the bottom, may someday soon be turned upside down.

THE PROPENSITY TO CONSUME. Income and population are the two major quantitative determinants of consumption, so they would, in turn, be major factors in the analysis of market opportunity. However, there is a slippery, complex, qualitative dimension to every market opportunity, and this, of course, is the willingness to buy or the propensity to consume. This qualitative dimension, which is the major focus of this book, is rooted in the psychology of consumer behavior: consumer motivations, expectations, and aspirations as affected by changing cultural and societal norms and values. Consumer behavior is by far the most illusory dimension of market opportunity or demand.

The consumer's willingness to buy goods in various amounts is affected by his need or demand for goods. Consumers buy goods to solve problems, to make them more socially acceptable, and to attain a particular life style. Consumers buy goods for their symbolic significance rather than simply for their utility. The esteem in which consumers hold goods, that is, the role and value imputed to goods by consumers, is largely a function of the way society and individual cultures value goods. Thus the Kwakuitl Indians consider it desirable not to accumulate goods but to give them away in the *potlatch*—a roisterous celebration. This lack of acquisitive behavior is not surprising to anthropologists—from their research they have learned that what is correct behavior in one culture is not necessarily at all correct in another.

The decade of the 1970s will see some marked differences in the way people live, and these changes in life style will reflect a changing emphasis in societal and cultural values. The newly acquired values of peace, brotherhood, service, and commitment will have rubbed off on much of the silent majority. Furthermore, these new values will, to some extent, affect consumers' attitudes and values regarding consumption. For example, there is likely to be a decreasing emphasis on conspicuous consumption. For many years the prevailing consumer ethic has been based upon a strong set of attitudes regarding work, success, and consumption known as the *Protestant ethic*.

An ethic is a set of norms or values that forms the basis of behavior. The Protestant ethic, or the Puritan ethic, as it is sometimes called, has for many years formed the basis of what might be called America's core culture. Thus to understand American core culture behavior it is necessary to understand something about Puritan values and the resulting Protestant ethic. There are four basic tenets to the Protestant ethic that have special reference to the ownership of goods and consumption, and thus consumer behavior, which might be described thus:

1. It is man's duty to know how to work and how to work hard.
2. Success in work is evidence of God's favor.

3. The measure of success is money and property.
4. The way to success is through industry and thrift.[16]

Two essential propositions support the tenets of the Protestant ethic. The first of course is that hard work is vital to success and God's favor; that is, both earthly success and happiness are a function of man's work orientation. However, the second essential proposition is that work is a *means* to an *end,* the end being the acquisition of money and property. Property at an earlier time meant land, but it soon also came to mean *goods.*

Many of our consumption patterns and forms of consumer behavior can be traced to remnants of these older cultural values. For example, much of our society's emphasis on material achievement affects individual attitudes about motivation. The United States is often characterized as a nation obsessed with achievement motivation, or we are characterized as the acquisitive society marked by an unusually high incidence of conspicuous consumption. In short, goods and property are perceived as symbols of a man's success and, in turn, as symbols of his cleverness and ingenuity, and therefore as a measure of his esteem.

In some part at least, the Protestant ethic is responsible for the rationale of much of America's economic activity. In no small way the Protestant ethic is responsible for our consumption-oriented production activity. As a nation, we have virtually become obsessed with producing more and more, which in turn leads to higher and higher levels of consumption. As long ago as 1929, one business writer was talking and writing about "consumption engineers," i.e., those who would engineer, teach, or program buyers to buy and consume more and more.[17] At about the same time the beginnings of planned product obsolescence and the "throwaway culture" syndrome were also being extolled. One writer, calling his philosophy "the progressive obsolescence basis of consumption," stated, "What waste to educate and train artists, inventors, chemists, and engineers and workmen to create beautiful, efficient, new things if people reply smugly that they are satisfied with what they have."[18] The logic was that even if you didn't need or want the new goods, it would be in the best interest of a high-level consumption-oriented society for you to buy them. *Even if it meant cluttering up our streets and countryside with garbage and poisoning our rivers and our atmosphere with the pollutants of a rampant, unconcerned, slavish addiction to goods.*

[16] Perry Miller and Thomas H. Johnson, *The Puritans* (New York: American Book Company, 1938), p. 1.

[17] Earnest Elmo Calkins, "The New Consumption Engineer and the Artist," in J. George Frederik, ed., *A Philosophy of Production* (New York: The Business Bourse Publishers, 1930), pp. 107–133.

[18] Charles Abbott, "Obsolescence and the Passing of High Pressure Salesmanship," in J. George Frederik, ed., *A Philosophy of Production* (New York: The Business Bourse Publishers, 1930), p. 159.

There is evidence of the decay of the Protestant ethic and the emergence of a new counterculture. A counterculture is a value system that stands opposed to the value system of the older core culture. Much of the counterculture activity has been centered around the youth of America—those under thirty years of age. Several of their underlying values are peace, brotherhood, cooperation, and service. The old culture tended to stress scarcity and the value of physical goods. The new counterculture is based upon the assumption that important human needs are easily satisfied and that the resources for doing so are plentiful. Competition is deemed unnecessary. The overaddiction to acquisition of physical goods not only is damaging to the well-being of the individual but leads to a lack of concern for the environment and for those living in deprived minority cultures.[19] Whereas the old culture stresses *physical goods*, the new culture is more likely to stress *metaphysical goods*, such as awareness, sensitivity, belongingness, love, altruism, and the value of non-work-oriented leisure.

In the twentieth century man's life expectancy has increased eighteen years and his working life only nine years, leaving a bonus of nine extra years for leisure. Women have gained eight years of playtime. If our average annual increase in productivity remains constant at 3 per cent, we are in store for a shorter work week and earlier retirement. By 1990 for instance, the United States could maintain the same Gross National Product with a twenty-hour, four-day week, or a forty-hour week with retirement at the age of thirty-eight. Either way, this indicates a revolution in leisure time that, along with other socioeconomic and cultural changes, portends a change in America's propensity to consume.

The Rise of Consumerism

Consumerism has at least two very special meanings. On the one hand it denotes the underlying value system that guides much of our economic and productive enterprise, namely, the emphasis given to consumer orientation within the market system. On the other hand, more lately it has come to mean the social and economic movement of consumers dissatisfied, disillusioned, and disenchanted with the efforts and activities of manufacturers, marketers, and resellers. It is *consumerism* as an economic and social movement that will guide the efforts of marketers in the future. The movement itself is the result of a great disparity, namely, the variance between what is promised by marketers and what is actually delivered by them. So although the marketer may mouth the phrase "The customer is king," he may at the same time continue to produce shoddy goods that he misrepresents through false and misleading advertising, using blatant and offensive

[19] For more related to these ideas, see William Lazer, "Marketing's Changing Social Relationships," *Journal of Marketing*, Vol. 33 (January 1969), pp. 3–9 at p. 9.

appeals. And he may profess "consumer sovereignty" and still price his merchandise at unconscionable levels and fail to listen to the complaints and entreaties of his disgruntled customers. Consumerism is the ideology of the militant consumer—the consumer who demands good products, fair prices, and meaningful and relevant promotion. And furthermore it includes the right of the consumer to be heard and considered in relationship to his grievances and complaints. Consumerism is a protest against sham, deceit, greed, and overzealous marketing.

Consumerism is concerned with some aspects of our social values, especially to the extent to which they are shaped and influenced by Madison Avenue. Galbraith has stated the case for consumerism by commenting that "the further a man is removed from physical need, the more he is open to persuasion—or management—as to what he buys. That is, perhaps, the most important consequence for economics of increasing affluence."[20] And the persuasive influence of advertising and selling is so effective that specific demand is brought "under substantial control" and also "provides in the aggregate a relentless propaganda on behalf of goods in general."[21] Thus consumer sovereignty, even limited consumer sovereignty, is denied and the so-called marketing literature represents merely a self-serving rationalization for the rising importance of marketing strategy under declining market discipline.

But can such a situation be? Do marketers and manufacturers hold such power via manipulation and Madison Avenue? As we shall learn in subsequent chapters, the argument is perhaps overdrawn, but the existence of *consumerism* as a protest movement is dramatic testimony of the consumer's dilemma and his determination to be heard and responded to.

CAVEAT VENDITOR

The consumer traditionally has been cast in the role of sovereign. His sovereignty is based upon his economic purchasing power and his capacity to determine the fate of merchants by casting his dollar votes in the marketplace. Such sovereignty has given the consumer the power of life and death over businesses in the marketplace. However, in the years to come, the consumer is slated for promotion to dictator. He will exercise a greater amount of power not only through his purse but by the expression of his imperious will through the courts, the legislatures, and government agencies at the local, state, and national levels.

Such a revolution brought about by the demanding consumer is signaled by the transformation of the slogan *caveat emptor*—"let the buyer beware"—into *caveat venditor*—"let the seller take care."

For many years, consumers have been frustrated and driven to a new level of militant agitation by the appalling amounts of deceit, in-

---

[20] J. K. Galbraith, *The New Industrial State* (Boston: Houghton Mifflin Company, 1967), p. 202.

[21] Ibid., p. 209.

eptness, and inefficiency that confront them. Consumers are fed up with telephones that won't work, television and automobiles that cost fortunes to repair, and toys that cannot be assembled, do not last, and are unsafe for children. Consumers have discovered that they can help themselves and society by complaining more about slapdash service and shoddy goods. And when it comes to complaining, not all Americans are members of the silent majority.

Many consumers realized that shoddiness and ineptness were not an integral part of U.S. enterprise when, in July of 1969 while watching TV they saw two men landed on the surface of the moon and later brought back to earth—the whole fantastic, mind-boggling technical feat accomplished without a hitch or apparent flaw. After that experience consumers, or at least some of them, would never again be content with all the malfunctioning kitchen appliances, the undependable automobiles, the overdue commuter trains, or any of the other countless products that function poorly, unsafely, or not at all.

Consumers in the years ahead will be exercising considerably more clout in many respects. They are better educated and better informed, with a greater sense of awareness and righteousness. This will make them more discerning in their choices and in their overall demands.

Consumers have now, and will have to an increasing extent in the future, greater aid and benefit from "truth-in-packaging," "truth-in-lending," and "truth-in-advertising" laws and governmental consumer protection agencies.[22]

Consumers are finding themselves with an increasing number of new powerful advocates defending their interests. These include presidential advisers, vote-conscious legislators, and other self-appointed watchdogs and crusaders for consumer interests.

To meet these new rules of consumerism and competition, businesses will have to cater increasingly to consumer needs—not those phonied up and created by the behemoths of Madison Avenue, but the consumer's real, meaningful, and relevant needs and wants. If old products are obsolete, marketers will have to create new ones. If old services are less than satisfactory, marketers will have to provide new kinds of service. And finally, if old ways and old values relating to ways of doing business displease, new ways will have to be found— new consumer-oriented ways!

The New Social Responsibilities of Marketers

The social responsibilities of business organizations are changing. At an earlier time in our economic and business history, the pursuit of the profit motive was deemed not only desirable but beneficial to society as a whole. Each man's or each company's greed was allegedly to redound to the benefit of society as a whole. Adam Smith, in *Wealth of*

[22] See "Who Speaks for the Consumer Now?" *Changing Times: The Kiplinger Magazine* (July 1967), pp. 41–44.

Nations (1776), proclaimed the principle of the "Invisible Hand": every individual in pursuing only his own selfish good was led, as if by an invisible hand, to achieve the best good for all. Thus any interference with free competition by government was almost certain to be injurious. As we know so well now, the concept of the "invisible hand" operates only in markets characterized as perfectly competitive. And perfect competition does not really exist. Therefore, to make a profit is no longer sufficient or adequate motivation to justify the existence of a business enterprise. Furthermore, the dual objective of marketing organizations, i.e., to serve customer needs and to make a profit, is ambiguous and not clearly understood. The result of this confusion is that the firm is often in a state of schizophrenic conflict. How can the firm serve two masters, profit and consumers? Unfortunately, too often it subordinates its service and social responsibilities to the pursuit of its profit objectives. Many executives of marketing organizations forget that the primary objective of the firm is the long-run maximization of profit, given an initial level of investment. This fundamental decision rule, if it is properly constrained by the legal, moral, and social dictates of society, is a singularly effective criterion for management decisions.

Marketers must increasingly, during the decade of the 1970s and beyond, look toward the development of better models for ethical and social responsibilities in business.[23] Such models will necessarily be concerned with the "rightness" of certain actions and behavior and will seek standards derived from the culture, from various institutional processes and structures, and from the expectations nurtured among the economic and societal participants.

Business and marketing organizations must play a leading role in solving the social problems of the period. Marketers will meet social demands not by abandoning the profit motive but by finding ways to fill social needs profitably. Profit may come to be increasingly defined as the "cost of the future." Such a measure of profit in turn becomes a measure of social value. If socially desirable services are unprofitable, then what is needed is not for marketers to perform them at a loss but for government and society to change the ground rules in such a way as to bring the profit mechanism to bear.

Perhaps instead of asking, "What are the social responsibilities of marketing?" the question might better be "What workable guides are available to help a marketing executive to evaluate alternative courses of action in a specific concrete situation?"[24] Generally speaking, in each specific concrete situation and for each individual firm, the best contribution that any marketer or business can actually make to overall society is to perform its service or produce its product—as efficiently, abundantly, and successfully as possible.

[23] For an outline and discussion of such a task, see Robert Bartels, "A Model for Ethics in Marketing," *Journal of Marketing*, Vol. 31 (January 1967), pp. 20–26.

[24] James M. Patterson, "What Are the Social and Ethical Responsibilities of Marketing Executives?" *Journal of Marketing*, Vol. 30 (June 1966), p. 12.

Marketers must attract and hold not only minority persons, but they must also appeal to the growing wave of young white people whose commitment to making a profit does not eliminate or transcend their commitment to using some of that profit for broad social purposes.

With this much said, it remains a contemporary wisdom that the success of a business, or its social contribution, can no longer be measured by the balance sheet alone. Businesses operate not in a vacuum but in a social and physical environment, and each increasingly will be required to give appropriate concern to the total environment. Thus marketers and other businessmen will no longer be permitted, for example, to pollute the air or water in order to make steel or cement, or to ignore the social effects of false and misleading advertising, or to produce products that are unsafe in use or that perform poorly or not at all. Marketing must and will become more *humanistic;* that is, it will become a system of business activities and actions in which human social interests predominate. Marketing theory and strategy must reflect an increasing awareness of these human and social interests through a more concerted and deliberate *consumer orientation.*

In the remaining two chapters of Part I, we shall look at an expanded treatment of consumerism and its impact on consumer behavior and market planning and strategy. In Chapter 3, we shall outline some of the major problems in the study of consumer behavior and develop something of an overview for the remaining part of the book.

Questions for Study, Reflection, and Review

1 How is consumer behavior related to market planning and market strategy?

2 What is a theory?

3 Describe the three principal objectives of theory.

4 Discuss two fundamental ideas upon which the marketing concept is based.

5 How does a firm's environment affect the marketing strategy of that firm?

6 Discuss the three major characteristics of a market and how they relate to the marketing concept.

7 Describe the anticipated changes in population and income and explain the effect of these changes on marketing activities.

8 How is consumer willingness to buy affected by consumer motivations and want structures?

9 Discuss the basic tenets of the Protestant ethic and their relationship to the ownership of goods, consumption, and consumer behavior.

10 What have been some of the important factors responsible for the increase in consumerism, and what are the potential effects of consumerism on marketing?

2

Consumerism:
Militant Consumer
Behavior

Introduction

A relevant generalization developed in the previous chapter is restated at this point, namely, that marketing theory is basically a set of explanations and descriptions for the purpose of forming the under-pinnings, or the principles and methods, of marketing as both a science and an art. From this theory emerges a set of practices, policies, and procedures. In marketing, the formalized embodiment of a firm's theoretical beliefs and its value orientations emerge in the form of a *marketing strategy*. As defined earlier, the marketing strategy is the firm's comprehensive, dynamic plan of action—a statement of desired operations (goals) and a statement of tactical maneuvers (alternatives and contingencies).

Furthermore, the thesis of marketers is that their strategies are consumer oriented; that is, the firm is supposed to take its marching orders from the market. This professed theme of marketers is said to revolve around their concern for the customer and his satisfaction.

The literature of marketing reflects this concern. For example:

> The market concept point-of-view is that *all* the activities of the company should be directed to satisfying customers at a profit.[1]

[1] E. Jerome McCarthy, *Basic Marketing: A Managerial Approach* (Homewood, Ill.: Richard D. Irwin, Inc., 1971), p. 31.

24

The marketing concept is defined as a managerial philosophy concerned with mobilization, utilization and control of total corporate effort for the purpose of helping customers solve selected problems. . . .[2]

The marketing concept underscores the importance of the market rather than marketing.[3]

Thus one would conclude that consumer orientation *is* or *ought to be* the principal tenet on which all marketing strategies rest. Yet the behavior of many marketers would belie this conclusion. Furthermore, such a conclusion hardly seems warranted in light of much consumer reaction to the efforts of marketers. There is a great deal of consumer behavior that indicates that not all consumers are convinced that they are the beneficiaries of the efforts of firms whose actions and conduct are supposedly guided more by consumer interests than by an avaricious, rapacious, and exploitative self-interest. The presence of *consumerism* as a social and economic movement composed of dissatisfied, disillusioned, and disenchanted consumers is dramatic testimony of their disbelief. The ideology of consumerism posits that there is a great variance between what some marketers espouse on the one hand and what they practice in the marketplace on the other.

Consumerism, therefore, is the manifestation of militant consumer behavior. And what is more it is a cue that something may be wrong. Furthermore, the widespread presence of a militant consumer movement reflects the cognitions and perceptions of an increasingly large number of consumers.

Consequently, although militant consumer behavior as typified by consumerism is probably indicative of the attitudes and behavior of only a small proportion of the total consuming population, it is for several reasons a worthy focus for our interest in this chapter.

First, consumerism is a signal that *all* consumers are not docile, happy, well-satisfied customers of the marketplace.

Second, the militant consumer is an unsatisfied consumer and, therefore, is probably worthy of special effort and attention from marketers.

Third, militant consumers are usually characterized as the active, vocal, semiorganized, participative *critics* of marketing systems and firm behavior.

For these explicit reasons, we will focus our attention in this chapter on matters relating to consumerism, or consumer movements, with the realization that the militant consumer who comprises such movements is a vocal critic of marketing. One can learn a great deal about both the strengths and weaknesses of a system by examining and paying heed to the antagonists and critics of that system.

[2] Robert L. King, "Interpretation of the Marketing Concept," in Steven J. Shaw and C. M. Gittinger, eds. (New York: Macmillan Publishing Co., Inc., 1963).

[3] Wroe Alderson and Paul Green, *Planning and Problem Solving in Marketing* (Homewood, Ill.: Richard D. Irwin, Inc., 1964), p. 5.

This chapter, therefore, will be devoted to a discussion and analysis of marketing performance and the growth and development of consumer movements, with a review of consumer-oriented legislation, the increasing concern of business with social responsibilities, and the broader implications of consumerism.

THE COST OF MARKETING

Marketing activities are not free. Almost nothing produced by our system is. Marketing costs vary from good to good, but it would be a reasonable estimate to state that of every dollar spent by consumers in the marketplace, approximately fifty cents go to pay for the performance of marketing functions.

So although it is probably true that marketing does help to deliver a higher standard of living,[4] it does not do it without costs.[5] The widespread acquisition of goods, the near-obsession of many to have more and more, mechanization and the increasing emphasis on technology, and the fetish of growth and size are not without costs. We, as individuals, pay for these goods. And, furthermore, there are vast social costs that must be considered. Our society and our environment, as has been shown, reflect the damage and abuse brought about by our increasing attention to the production and consumption of goods.

So although it is probably true that we all own more goods, we may be paying a needlessly high cost for this ownership. And so, too, although our marketing system is envied and emulated, our value systems are often ridiculed and rejected. America is too often regarded as the acquisitive society characterized by greed and avarice, with too little attention paid to the costs related to such acquisition. We are too often reminded that a standard of living is not simply how many goods or appliances we own but that it relates also to the quality of our life and our environment.

W. A. Weisskopf has suggested that abundance is a "threat to the system because, with its establishment, the entire meaning and purpose of the system would vanish."[6] In his autobiography, maverick and outspoken actor Sterling Hayden wrote:

> What does a man need—actually need? A few pounds of food each day, heat and shelter, six feet to lie down in—and some form of working

[4] This idea was a very popular and fashionable one during the mid and late 1940s. For example, see P. M. Mazur, "Does Distribution Cost Enough?" *Fortune*, Vol. 36, No. 5 (November 1947), p. 138.

[5] Marketing costs were widely discussed during the 1940s and 1950s but as a general topic do not receive widespread attention today. For specific examples of these earlier studies, see P. D. Converse, "The Total Cost of Marketing," *Journal of Marketing*, Vol. 10, No. 4 (April 1946), p. 389; and P. W. Stewart and J. F. Dewhurst, *Does Distribution Cost Too Much?* (New York: Twentieth Century Fund, 1939), p. 13.

[6] W. A. Weisskopf, N. Raghaven, et al., *Looking Forward: The Abundant Society*. A paper published by the Center for the Study of Democratic Institutions, 1966.

activity that will yield a sense of accomplishment. . . . But we are brain-washed by our economic system until we end up in a tomb beneath a pyramid of time payments, mortgages, preposterous gadgetry, playthings that divert our attention from the sheer idiocy of the charade.[7]

Such a declaration of need differs markedly from more generally prevailing attitudes. For example, during the last decade the average American family's earnings rose, even after accounting for inflation, from $6,900 to $9,400. And accordingly, consumers rushed to buy items ranging from clothes to clothes dryers. Many, if they already had one, bought another.

As a result, more families now have two cars than have none. As many families have television sets as have toilets. In slightly more than five years, the number of families with color television has jumped to nearly 40 per cent. The proportion of the nation's 63 million families with basic appliances—refrigerators, radios, ranges, and electric irons—has gone over the 99 per cent mark. Nearly 86 per cent of all American families have automatic electric coffeemakers. Nearly 47 million home hair dryers have been sold since 1961. Twenty-two million electric carving knives buzz and chew their way through America's meat-dish dinners. The average family now has five radios, compared with three in 1960. Consumer spending for such items as appliances and stereo systems has soared from $7.6 billion in 1960 to $13.9 billion in 1970. Finally, among families with incomes over $15,000, more than 96 per cent have at least one car and 63 per cent have more than one.

What is more, many people do not consider these items to be luxuries at all. A Seattle housewife, commenting on a recent purchase, said, "The perfect example is our refrigerator." When it was purchased, a persistent salesman persuaded her to buy a $25 automatic ice maker as a featured accessory. "We really didn't want it. We really didn't need it. But now, it's just so neat to reach in and not mess around with a tray of ice when you only want a couple of cubes."[8] The same family, when the old second car broke down, perceived as the obvious remedy a small economy car. What did they purchase? A full size $3,500 station wagon. The wife commented, "We needed something big enough to pull the boat."[9]

It can thus be seen that there are widespread, but differing, opinions as to what constitutes an adequate standard of living. And there is increasing evidence to suggest that America, in relation to its current crises that focus on poverty amid widespread affluence, on the good life tainted by dirty water and foul air, and on more and more goods causing more and more stresses and problems, may be rethinking its attitudes about goods and consumption. Marketing and attempts to

[7] Sterling Hayden, *Wanderer* (New York: Alfred A. Knopf, Inc., 1963).

[8] Jack Rosenthal, "Necessities or Opulence?" *The Spokesman Review,* Spokane, Wash. (December 13, 1970), p. 12.

[9] Ibid.

study consumer behavior may both have some instrumental role in what one writer has called the irony of American history:

> The prosperity of America is legendary. Our standards of living are beyond the dreams of avarice of most of the world. We are a kind of paradise of domestic security and wealth. But we face the ironic situation that the same technical efficiency which provided our comforts has also placed us at the center of the tragic developments in world events. There are evidently limits to the achievements of science; and there are irresolvable contradictions both between prosperity and virtue and between happiness and the "good life" which had not been anticipated in our philosophy. The discovery of these contradictions threatens our culture with despair. . . . We are therefore confronted for the first time in our life with the questions:—whether there is a simple coordination between virtue and prosperity; and whether the attainment of happiness either through material prosperity or social peace is a simple possibility for man, whatever may be his scientific and social achievements.[10]

Evidence suggests, though not overwhelmingly, that our value system may be beginning to catch up with our economic and marketing systems. One writer appeared to have a prophetic glance of the future when in 1961 he wrote that:

> The desire of the consumer for additional goods and a high standard of living might decline. People would then come to spend less time and effort augmenting their incomes. . . . Many commentators claim that the contempt for material goods is already more widely spread than is generally realized and that a real revolution in this field can be expected within a relatively short time.[11]

What all this expresses, of course, is that consumers, or some of them, are beginning to understand Thoreau's principle that what a man owns also owns him.

Some consumers are rebelling and no longer wish to be "slaves to goods." Their rebelliousness, in part at least, stems from the ugly and distasteful experiences that are associated with their acquisition and maintenance of an inventory of goods and services.

THE CONSUMER'S DILEMMA

The consumer's dilemma is that he wants goods. *He needs goods.* But the fact is that technology is spawning such a torrent of new and improved goods, marketing is creating such complicated packages and deals, and advertising is so misleading, uninformative, and riddled with half-truths, that it is difficult for the consumer to choose wisely and to be an effective decision-maker. As E. B. Weiss put it, "Just as a rational voting procedure is necessary to a free political system, so a rational

[10] Reinhold Niebuhr, *The Irony of American History* (New York: Charles Scribner's Sons, 1962), p. 9.

[11] Robert Theobald, *The Challenge of Abundance* (New York: Clarkson N. Potter, Inc., 1961), p. 32.

shopping system is necessary to a free market."[12] But much of the shopping, buying, consuming, using system is no longer rational. A rational marketing process implies reason, order, and sensibleness. It further implies sound knowledge on the part of consumers and full and fair disclosure of information by sellers. Today, however, marketplace complexities require the consumer to be an electrician, a safety and mechanical engineer, a nutritionist, chemist, a lawyer, and a mathematician in order to deal with complicated and confusing fractional-ounce packages, cents-off deals, trading stamps, coupons, trade-in allowances, and credit terms. Consumers are finding it harder to cope with the increasing sophistication of marketing strategies, product proliferation, and communication through seller-dominated channels. Polls have shown that seven out of ten Americans believe that further legislation is needed for consumer protection.[13] Such beliefs are widely held for the following reasons.

PRODUCTS. It has been pointed out that the technology responsible for our great American conveniences has a concomitant disadvantage of providing, with each mechanical moving part, something that can stop working. Most machinery has gotten too complicated, and as a consequence the do-it-yourself fixer has been frustrated. Products are programmed to wear out faster so that they will have to be replaced more frequently—a process euphemistically called "creative destruction." Stories about product failures and deficiencies are legion.

Senator Philip Hart concluded from his hearings on automobile repairs that a third of all of them are unsatisfactory and that nine out of ten cars more than five years old have things wrong with them that pertain to safety. All this, despite the fact that Americans spent $8.8 billion in repairs last year ($138 for each of the 64 million cars).[14] New automobiles are a frequent source of consumer complaints. Knobs, handles, and switches fall off. Windows and doors leak profusely. Hydraulic accessories seldom work.[15]

The technology that produces the automobile is largely the same as that that produced the F-111 swing-wing jet and that creates and manages our total transportation and communication network. A busy signal may no longer mean that the phone is in use. Instead, it may more exasperatingly mean that the circuits are no longer sufficient to handle the crush of calls. In the first half of 1969 the New York Public Service Commission received more than forty-three hundred complaints about telephone service.[16] Subways and trains in major cities, when

[12] E. B. Weiss, "The Corporate Deaf Ear," *Vital Speeches of the Day,* Vol. 35, No. 7 (January 15, 1969), pp. 205–207.

[13] "And Now, A Message from the Consumer," editorial in *Fortune,* Vol. 80, No. 6 (November 1969), p. 103.

[14] David Sanford, "Nothing Works Anymore," *The New Republic,* Vol. 162, No. 7 (February 14, 1970), p. 22.

[15] "America the Inefficient," *Time* (March 23, 1970), p. 72.

[16] Sanford, op. cit., p. 22.

running at all, are not on time. Even the basic service of mail distribution is subject to the most abusive criticism. A letter from Seattle with an air mail stamp, zip code, and all the rest took nine days to reach Washington, D.C.[17]

Consumers are frustrated by toasters that won't toast, razors that don't shave, and television sets without audio or picture, but even more serious is the fact that in attempting to use many items they subject themselves to extreme hazards. Cranberries are contaminated, as are some tuna, poultry, and much meat. Other products injure, shock, or maim. At one time, even a child watching color television was subject to an overdose of radiation if he sat too close to the receiver.

One appliance executive has commented that "the public is staging a revolt of rising expectancy. Customers today expect products to perform satisfactorily, to provide dependable functional performance and to be safe. This threshold of acceptable performance is steadily rising."[18] All too often the complexity and malfunction potential of many products has also been rising.[19] The end result has been an increase in the level of dissatisfaction with quality and with grossly inadequate service facilities.[20] Nor is the situation solely confined to goods and services, because another result of rapidly rising retail sales is to overburden retail and manufacturing facilities. Such a situation tends only to exacerbate the consumer's dissatisfaction with deteriorating quality and service for nearly the entire range of mass-merchandised goods.

ADVERTISING AND PROMOTION. One of the hallmarks of a rational and effective market or shopping system is adequate and informative communication. The consumer, as purchasing agent, is an information seeker. Consumers need information to enable them to make wise purchase decisions. They need to be informed about product features and characteristics. They need to know about product availability and wearability. So in order to gain something approaching near optimal satisfaction from purchases, consumers need information to guide them in the marketplace and they need information that will enable them to obtain full satisfaction and use from the product once it is purchased. Advertising and promotion are supposedly intended by sellers to provide such information. Yet too frequently advertising messages are hardly more than inane jingles and meaningless slogans, the informative value of which is negligible. Furthermore, much too frequently advertising and promotional methods are either tainted with deceit or are flagrantly false and deceptive. Massively documented instances of such

---

[17] Ibid.

[18] Robert C. Wells, quoted in James Bishop and Henry W. Hubbard, *Let the Seller Beware* (Washington, D.C.: The National Press, 1969), p. 14.

[19] "Rattles, Pings, Dents, Leaks, Creaks—and Costs," *Newsweek*, Vol. 45 (November 25, 1968), p. 93.

[20] See "Staff Report on Automobile Warranties" and "Report of the Task Force on Appliance Warranties and Services," Federal Trade Commission, Washington, D.C., January 1969.

practices are not necessarily the exception to advertising and promotional policies. Several such examples follow.

One large and successful sewing-machine manufacturer recently engaged in a promotion by direct mail, wherein they informed each respondent that he had won a sewing machine. All he had to do was purchase a five-year service contract, the price of which greatly exceeded the cost of the machine. For those unwary customers who did purchase, the company immediately proceeded to sell these contracts to loan companies (as loan contracts and not service policies). The company thus abandoned its obligation to provide any service.

Another instance involved a vacuum cleaner company in what is labeled a chain-referral scheme. One frequently used ploy involves the sale of a vacuum cleaner priced at $250, a needlessly high price. The purchaser is persuaded to sign a contract that commits him to make a down payment of $19.90. He is also told that he can pay off the balance by earning credit, which he allegedly can do by giving the salesmen names of people willing to buy the cleaner. For each friend who buys, the original buyer earns a credit of $25.00. However, in some instances, each prospect must also bring in ten more names and so on, in order for the first victim to get his refund or credit. Actually, no more than 10 per cent of the families buying the high-priced vacuum cleaner received more than three bonuses or $75.[21]

All too frequently, promotions are only blatant attempts to befuddle an already ill-informed and confused customer. To illustrate:[22]

> *"Bait" Sales.* A refrigerator is advertised at cut-rate prices—but no mention is made that only one or two of this model are on sale at this price. When the customer shows up he is told they are out of stock and an attempt is made to switch him to a higher-priced model.
>
> *Phony Sales.* Furniture, used cars, and major appliances are advertised at "50 per cent off the regular price," when a store never sold the goods at the higher price.
>
> *T. O. Selling.* Customers who visit promotion-minded stores are shuttled from salesperson to salesperson (turned over) with the thought that sooner or later their resistance will weaken and they will commit to buy.
>
> *Unsolicited Goods.* Unordered books and magazines may be sent through the mail, followed by letters demanding payment.
>
> *Contests.* Customers often receive cards saying, "You have already won." The prize is inconsequential and usually intended as a further come-on. Usually, only about 10 per cent of the prizes advertised and ostensibly offered are ever awarded.[23]

[21] "The Post Office Protects Consumers Against Fraud," *Consumers Bulletin,* Vol. 50, No. 11 (November 1967), p. 19.

[22] See "Rush to Protect Consumers," *U.S. News & World Report,* Vol. 68, No. 5 (February 2, 1970), p. 46.

[23] Joyce C. Wilson, "The Concerned Consumer," *Better Homes and Gardens,* Vol. 48, No. 3 (March 1970), p. 6.

Vanishing Deposits. Newspaper and magazine readers mail in deposits or advance payments with an order for some novelty item. However, they get neither the product nor their money back.

Far too little that is disseminated by advertisers is really believable, yet, unfortunately, the consumer is often gullible. Not only are some consumers gullible, but they are woefully confused. They are subjected to contradictory cues from advertising and substantiated reports.

How should housewives react when they read the testimony presented before a Senate subcommittee that most dry, ready-to-eat cereals, the breakfast mainstay of millions of Americans, are "empty calories" providing few of the nutrients we need every day. Such information does not square with the usual claims made by breakfast cereal manufacturers.[24]

Bread, the staff of life, the "wonder food," with "wholesome" characteristics, allegedly enriched with vitamins and minerals, became suddenly suspect when a Texas nutrionist experimentally fed sixty-four laboratory rats nothing but bread called "enriched" by common bakeries. Within ninety days, he discovered that forty of the rodents had died of malnutrition and the survivors were severely stunted.

Mouthwashes are promoted as essential to health and social well-being. They are highly touted as killers of the germs that cause colds and bad breath. Yet the Federal Trade Commission reports that most mouthwashes are no more effective in killing germs than warm salt water.

The Federal Trade Commission informed the three largest makers of enzyme detergents that their advertising claims were false and misleading. Yet consumers have been led to believe that "stains are locked into fabric fibers. But ——— enzymes act like little keys to unlock stains."

Perhaps the epitome of false advertising and sleazy, fraudulent selling is represented by the Shell Oil Company's "Platformate" promotion and the Holland Furnace Company case that took the FTC thirteen years to prosecute.

Consumer Bulletin charged the Shell Oil Company with a bit of deception in its "Platformate" advertising. The magazine alleged that Shell's TV commercials and newspaper advertising did not reveal that "Platformate," or its equivalent, was present in practically all gasolines sold for automobile use and that the kind of gasoline that was made without Platformate, as used in the test, was not available for purchase by ultimate consumers. Shell's obvious intention was to convince buyers that Super Shell would give them better mileage than the other brands of gasoline they might have been using. Shell's reply was rather anemic. They argued that the ads never said Shell was the only gasoline that used Platformate.[25]

The Holland Furnace case further exemplifies the inadequacies of our present laws and enforcement agencies, the gullibility of consumers,

---

[24] "What's Behind Those Breakfast-Cereal Headlines?" *Good Housekeeping,* Vol. 175 (November 1970), p. 215.

[25] Quoted in Richard H. Buskirk, *Principles of Marketing,* 3rd ed., (New York: Holt, Rinehart & Winston, Inc., 1970), p. 162.

and the irresponsibility of some business firms. Often misrepresenting themselves as safety inspectors or furnace engineers, Holland's salesmen would frequently partially disassemble a furnace. Then, stating that it was a safety hazard, they would refuse to reassemble it. Of course, a Holland Furnace Company salesman then appeared on the scene to sell a new furnace and to buy the old furnace (often still in good shape) for "junk." Using scare tactics such as this, as well as through other questionable techniques, company salesmen were able to victimize unsuspecting homeowners for over thirty-five years.[26] The case finally resulted in a $100,000 contempt-of-court charge against the company in 1965.[27]

Thus, from the sellers' point of view, advertising and promotion are often deliberately used as methods to confuse, bewilder, and trick consumers. It is a situation in which a part-time, uninformed buyer faces a full-time, professional seller. Is it any wonder, then, that the consumer often feels that he is at a disadvantage in dealing with the seller?[28]

PRICING AND CREDIT. Pricing and credit are further means of beguiling and befuddling consumers. Together with promotion and advertising, pricing and credit are used to lure customers into the store and commit them to twelve, fifteen, or eighteen easy payments. Many prices are deliberately deceptive. An item advertised as a special for $5.95 may regularly sell at that price. New automobiles have patently false and inflated window sticker prices. The astute customer knows that this price is overinflated and that, in order to get a proper deal, he must bargain vigorously. However, the myriad consumers who, because of temperament or training, are reticent and averse to bargaining are likely to pay the full sticker price. Such customers are referred to in the trade as "pigeons." Large ticket items are almost always marked with overinflated prices. A sweeper marked at $195, with a $50 trade-in allowance for the customer's old broom, is not an unusual pricing and promotion gimmick.

The use of leader pricing, often a legitimate pricing practice in supermarkets, is, nonetheless, frequently abused. Such price specials are often available in only limited amounts and may be made available for only a small fraction of the selling day.

Cents-off specials on a package are almost always deceptive. Cents off what price? The customary price? Whose customary price? The cents-off label is a seductive selling device, but it is not a price guide to value. It is a promotional device designed to make you think you are

[26] Warren G. Magnuson and Jean Carper, *The Dark Side of the Marketplace* (Englewood Cliffs, N.J.: Prentice-Hall, Inc., 1968), p. 23.

[27] "Multi-Million Dollar Floodgate," *Forbes,* Vol. 105, No. 9 (May 1, 1970), p. 28.

[28] See Richard H. Holton, "Government-Consumer Interest: Conflicts and Prospects (The University Point of View)," *Changing Marketing Systems* (Chicago: American Marketing Association, 1967), pp. 15–17.

getting a bargain.[29] The sponsors of the truth-in-packaging legislation proposed to prohibit the use of cents-off claims on labels. However, the bill finally passed by Congress in 1966 failed to go that far. It empowered the government to regulate such labels only when that became necessary, as Congress put it, "to prevent the deception of consumers or to facilitate value comparisons."[30]

One of the consumer's further dilemmas in regard to pricing is that he really does not know *how* much he is paying for some commodities, especially food store items. He knows, of course, that a small package of sesame seeds costs 30¢, a can of beans costs 49¢, and a small frozen package of chives 69¢. But what consumers really do not know is how much items cost per ounce, per pound, per quart, or per foot. The reason, of course, is that many retailers have resisted strongly all efforts and suggestions that they display *unit pricing information.* Unit pricing is a system whereby items would be priced as items but the price would also be stated as so much per ounce, pound, or quart. With unit pricing, consumers could figure out whether an 8-ounce bottle of salad dressing that sells for 87¢ is more expensive than a 14-ounce bottle selling for $1.20. They would quickly see that the smaller size is priced at 12¢ an ounce and the larger at 8¢.[31] The more typical situation is one in which the shopper is comparing two cans of beans. One is a 16-ounce can selling two for 57¢, or 29¢ each. The larger can is 28 ounces for 35¢. Which is the better buy? In this case, the small can cost 42 per cent more than the larger can, but the customer would have to have a slide rule to make the determination. The result of unit pricing would be a more informed buyer. For example, the package of sesame seeds mentioned earlier is a 2-ounce package selling for 30¢, which means that sesame seeds so purchased cost $2.40 a pound, about as much as sirloin steak. The 69¢ jar of frozen chives has a net weight of ⅛ ounce, which means that such an item equals $88.32 a pound—more than the most expensive red caviar.[32]

One consumer crusader has argued that if consumers knew what they were really paying for a product, the average housewife could save ten cents on every shopping dollar.[33] However, the food industry argues that unit pricing would cost up to $300 million a year, thus adding significantly to food prices. One chain group is experimenting with a "mini-minder," a wallet-sized card that allows a shopper to calculate the unit price himself.[34]

[29] "Those Exasperating Cents-off Labels," *Consumer Report,* Vol. 35 (1967), pp. 508–510.

[30] Ibid., p. 509.

[31] "$1.20 Divided by 14 Ounces Is What?" *Forbes,* Vol. 105, No. 7 (April 1, 1970), p. 55.

[32] "New York Leads the Consumer Crusade," *Business Week* (January 31, 1970), p. 51.

[33] "$1.20 Divided by 14 Ounces Is What?" op. cit., p. 55.

[34] "New York Leads the Consumer Crusade," op. cit., p. 52.

Some governmental and industry changes have been made recently in such areas as cents-off and unit pricing. In the area of unit pricing some firms have voluntarily adopted the practice, yet many continue to resist. Interestingly enough, tentative evidence suggests that in those stores that display unit pricing information only 4 or 5 per cent of the shoppers use it and that these are persons in the upper-middle socio-economic class. Given the cost added to food commodities by unit pricing, perhaps the less economically well-off consumer who does not use unit pricing is subsidizing the higher-income user, who in actuality needs it less.

Finally, some brief word must be said about credit and its impact on consumerism. Without doubt, the increased consumer awareness of credit abuses created by the hearings and news stories in connection with the truth-in-lending legislation did much to add to the agitation of increasingly militant consumers. Such abuses involved scandalous tales of usury, garnishment, harassment, and overcommitment. Credit terms, in true equivalent annual interest rates, were often as high as 36 per cent or more per year. Even today, after the passage of truth-in-lending laws, some installment contracts involving revolving credit may legally charge interest at the rate of 18 per cent a year. Consumers are increasingly recognizing that such interest rates on contracts running for two or three years mean simply that they are paying for goods not once but twice or three times.

INFORMATION VERSUS MISINFORMATION. Consumerism is a demand for full and accurate information. Such demands have been the basis for auto and tire safety legislation, the truth-in-packaging bill, and the truth-in-credit regulations. Yet all too frequently firms make no distinction between information and misinformation, and unfortunately in many instances outright attempts at providing misinformation are practiced. Even federal attempts at providing standards for rating products perform the function of indirectly misleading through misinformation. For example, a housewife buys a food product labeled "U.S. Grade A" assuming that this is the best quality. Too often, however, it is only a medium or fair grade and quality. The same housewife who buys apples packed as "U.S. No. 1" is probably not aware that these are usually a lower grade and that there are two higher grades called "U.S. Fancy" and "U.S. Extra Fancy." By the same token, if a housewife buys Cheddar cheese labeled "Grade A" she is really getting the lower of the two grades normally sold in retail stores. The higher grade is "Grade AA."[35]

Private firms do little better in terms of developing product standards and grade labeling. Consumers are invariably confused as to the distinction among good, better, and best product lines. Price line distinctions are almost always hazy and confusing to customers, and their sole means of differentiation is usually to rely on price distinctions as

---

[35] Weiss, op. cit., p. 205.

a criterion for quality differences. Consumers today almost invariably believe that adequate information should mean information that goes beyond the right not to be deceived and provides the data and knowledge that will lead to purchase and consumption satisfaction. Such information is deemed essential to consumer welfare.[36] Two basic, but polarized, views regarding consumer information have emerged. One, espoused by Bauer and Greyser, contends that the buyer, exercising due caution and awareness, should be guided by his judgment of the manufacturer's reputation and the quality of the branded product. The other emerging perspective holds that consumer information should be provided by impartial sources and that such neutral media should reveal both product and firm performance characteristics.[37] Consumerism is largely a rejection of the Bauer and Greyser contention—the more contemporary point of view being that paternalism is a legitimate and worthwhile policy and that consumers need to be protected not only from business firms but, to some extent, even from themselves.

THE LOW-INCOME CONSUMER. In many respects, the militant and minority poor have tended to act as the catalyst in the consumer movement. Their acts of civil disobedience, sit-ins, and even riots have focused upon gouging and unscrupulous merchants in the ghetto areas. Their rage and anger were often vented by looting and burning the premises of merchants who overcharged, deceived, and preyed upon the captive victims of what seemingly was a hopeless system of high prices, shoddy goods, usurious interest, and other forms of abuse.

The civil rights movement has created a new profile of high visibility for the low-income consumer. Such consumers have suffered greatly from fraud, excessive prices, exorbitant credit charges, and poor-quality merchandise. The poor have been seen as victims of their own poverty and ignorance. And the same efforts that improve the welfare of middle-income consumers have often been doomed to failure in the case of low-income ghetto residents.

The low-income consumer has little opportunity for trial and error and other forms of consumer experimentation. Because of their low income they cannot learn through experience and they cannot take advantage of price specials, sales, or quantity purchases. Economy is truly the luxury of the rich. Low-income consumers are not aware of the advantage of comparative shopping, for they are not mobile. Few such families own automobiles or have the money for transportation out of the central city that would enable them to engage in comparative shopping. They are poorly educated and often have language and cultural barriers that impede effective communication and thereby affect

---

[36] *Freedom of Information in the Market Place* (Columbus, Mo.: F.O.I. Center, 1967).

[37] Raymond A. Bauer and Stephen A. Greyser, "The Dialogue That Never Happens," *Harvard Business Review*, Vol. 45 (November–December 1967), p. 2.

their shopping prowess. Thus their lack of education and available knowledge impedes obtaining good buys even if they were available. Their ignorance makes them ready victims for unscrupulous dealers and operators. Such consumers seldom have any awareness of their rights and liabilities in postsale legal conflicts. Finally, the low-income consumer does not really appreciate the necessity of seeking better value for his money and effort and, because of the wretchedness of his existence, he often lacks the motivation to seek improvement in his consuming situation.[38]

The low-income consumer environment has thus become an infectious breeding ground for deceit, exploitation, and outright fraud. It is a rather sad commentary that marketers and researchers in consumer behavior in particular, and society in general, have only recently become sensitized to the necessity of focusing some study on and possibly offering some assistance to this badly disadvantaged segment of our society.[39]

The History, Meaning, and Development of Consumerism

There are about as many definitions of consumerism as there are writers on the subject. For example, consumerism has been defined or described in the following ways:

> Consumerism expresses itself in efforts to bring pressure on business firms as well as government to correct business conduct thought unethical.[40]

> The most common understanding of consumerism is in reference to the *widening* range of activities of government, business and independent organizations that are designed to protect individuals from practices (of both business and government) that infringe upon their rights as consumers.[41]

> Consumerism means that the consumer looks upon the manufacturer as somebody who is interested but who really does not know what the consumers' realities are.[42]

Finally, another set of authors has defined consumerism as:

---

[38] See Lewis Schnapper, "Consumer Legislation and the Poor," *The Yale Law Journal*, Vol. 76 (1967); and Gerald Leinwald, ed., *The Consumer* (New York: Washington Square Press, 1970).

[39] David Coplovitz, *The Poor Pay More* (New York: The Free Press, 1963). Also, Fred C. Allvine, "Black Business Development," *Journal of Marketing*, Vol. 34 (April 1970), pp. 1–7.

[40] David W. Cravens and Gerald E. Mills, "Consumerism: A Perspective for Business," *Business Horizons* (August 1970), p. 21.

[41] George S. Day and David Aaker, "A Guide to Consumerism," *Journal of Marketing*, Vol. 34 (July 1970), p. 13.

[42] Peter Drucker, "Consumerism in Marketing," a speech to the National Association of Manufacturers, New York, April 1969.

the organized efforts of consumers seeking redress, restitution and remedy for dissatisfactions they have accumulated in the acquisition of their standard of living.[43]

Regardless of which definition is accepted, the underlying theme becomes evident. Consumerism is related to several major issues— consumer choice, consumer information, consumer protection, and consumer representation—and all these things embody the consumer's organized and deliberate efforts to promote his interest.[44]

Consumerism, a movement largely associated with the past decade, takes as its creed and manifesto the so-called consumer's bill of rights. These rights, first articulated as such by John F. Kennedy, include the following:

1. The right to safety—to be protected against the marketing of goods which are hazardous to health or life.
2. The right to be informed—to be protected against fraudulent, deceitful or grossly misleading information, advertising, labeling or other practices, and to be given the facts he needs to make an informed choice.
3. The right to choose—to be assured, wherever possible, access to a variety of products and services at competitive prices; and in those industries in which competition is not workable and government regulation is substituted, an assurance of satisfactory quality and service at fair prices.
4. The right to be heard—to be assured that consumer interests will receive full and sympathetic consideration in the formulation of Government policy, and fair and expeditious treatment in its administrative tribunals.[45]

Thus to promote the fuller realization of these consumer rights, consumers have organized and voiced their grievances.

HISTORY AND EXPLANATIONS

During the 1960s there had been an uproar concerning consumerism; in fact, the 1960s have often been called the "Decade of the Consumer."[46] But this title is a little misleading, for it implies that consumerism is only a modern-day development, whereas, in reality, the consumer movement has a history that spans approximately eighty years. During this time there have been three distinctive periods in which a consumerism type of activity has peaked in intensity: the very

---

[43] Richard H. Buskirk and James T. Rothe, "Consumerism—An Interpretation," *Journal of Marketing,* Vol. 34 (October 1970), p. 62.

[44] James E. Kenny, "The New Consumerism," *America* (March 14, 1970), p. 270.

[45] *Message from the President of the United States* Relative to Consumers Protection and Interest Program, Document No. 364, House of Representatives, 87th Congress, 2nd Session, March 15, 1962.

[46] See "The 'Year of the Consumer'," *Consumer's Bulletin* (January 1967), p. 31; and "The Irate Consumer," *Newsweek* (January 26, 1970), p. 73.

early 1900s, the late 1920s and early 1930s, and the 1960s to the present.

A most important question is "What were the causes for consumer unrest at these particular times?" To some extent, each of these three periods of consumer unrest occurred during times in which real income for a major part of the population was in a decline.

For several decades prior to the twentieth century, American consumers enjoyed substantial increases in their real income as prices fell or remained constant. However, at the turn of the century financial uncertainty triggered by the discovery of new gold and refining methods set in. The dubious state of the gold structure resulted in an outflow of capital through the purchase of foreign investments. The loss of capital, together with the bankruptcy of several railroads, placed a heavy strain on the banks, many of which eventually failed. The earlier trend of falling or stable prices was thus reversed in 1897. As a result of rising prices, many people, especially those on fixed incomes, became most resentful of the thriving trusts and the burgeoning labor union movement.[47] The consumer also looked very critically upon business and its products. Between 1879 and 1905, more than a hundred bills were introduced in Congress to regulate the interstate production and marketing of food and drugs.[48] The pressures of rising prices also fostered organizations such as consumer leagues that worked toward making consumers more conscious of their responsibilities as buyers.

The early 1930s, of course, was a time of deep and serious depression. Incomes rapidly declined after the stock market collapse, but consumer prices also receded. However, prices began to move steadily upward around 1935. Consequently, in protest against increases in meat prices, Detroit housewives began a meat buying strike that quickly spread to other cities. These strikes, in turn, led to a series of consumer-business confrontations on the high cost of living.[49]

In the early 1960s prices rose very gradually at the rate of about 1 per cent a year. However, inflationary pressures were increasing during the mid 1960s, and by 1970 prices were rising faster than at any period since the inflation of the 1950s. The most dramatic price movement came in food. Retail prices of foods rose 7 per cent from the first quarter of 1965 to the second quarter of 1966.[50] Such increases became readily evident to housewives, and in October, 1966, angry and militant consumers began to picket supermarkets in Denver. Similar supermarket protests quickly spread to the East and West. Shortly after this rash of outspoken public concern a flood of consumer legislation ap-

---

[47] Robert O. Hermann, "Consumerism: Its Goals, Organization and Future," *Journal of Marketing*, Vol. 34 (October 1970), p. 56.

[48] Ralph M. Gaedeke, "The Movement for Consumer Protection: A Century of Mixed Accomplishments," *Business Review* (Spring 1970), p. 32.

[49] Hermann, op. cit., p. 57.

[50] See "What's Happening to the Cost of Living?" *Nation's Business*, Vol. 57, No. 7 (July 1969), p. 67; and "Why Americans Are Buying Less," *Time* (October 3, 1969), p. 90.

peared. Despite record incomes and employment, U.S. consumers were having trouble finding the money to make ends meet. And thus their economic stress found quick outlet in the form of consumer protests. The decline in real purchasing power is, however, only one factor that instigates consumer unrest. There are, at the same time, other causes that have tended to accelerate the consumer movement. For example, another interesting parallel that could be drawn between each of the three peak periods of consumer unrest is the publication of one or more books that aroused public consternation and demands for redress, restitution, and correction of conditions. The early 1900s has been referred to as the muckraking era. For instance, one such book, *The Jungle* (1906) written by Upton Sinclair, described the filth and total lack of sanitary conditions in the meat-packing industry. Sinclair's exposé gave full impetus to the consumer movement, which to that point had been mild and unaggressive. Furthermore, Sinclair's book was also largely responsible for the passage by Congress of the first Pure Food and Drug Act.

Similarly, in the 1930s the new drive for consumer protection followed the publication in 1927 of Stuart Chase and F. J. Schlink's book *Your Money's Worth*. The authors depicted the consumer as an Alice in Wonderland, where producers made bright promises and conflicting product claims. Another such book, entitled *100,000,000 Guinea Pigs* (1933) written by Arthur Kallet and F. J. Schlink, added even more impetus to the movement and led to the passage of more food, drug, and cosmetic legislation.

Finally, the 1960s saw the publication of such books as Jessica Mitford's *The American Way of Death* (1963) (the mortuary business), *The Silent Spring* (1962) by Rachel Carson (the indiscriminate use of insecticides), *The Quiet Crisis* (1963) by Stewart Udall (our vanishing natural resources and our inadequate conservation policies), and *The Health Hucksters*, a follow-up on *The Bargain Huckster* by Ralph Smith (market trickery and deception practiced by various industry lobbies). Other influential books have been *Overcharge* (1967) by Senator Lee Metcalf (private electric utilities), *Monopoly* (1968) by Joseph C. Goulden (American Telephone and Telegraph), *The Mortality Merchants* (1968) by G. Scott Reynolds (life insurance), *The Dark Side of the Marketplace* (1968) by Senator Warren G. Magnuson (consumer exploitation by large and small businesses), *God's Own Junkyard* (1964) by Peter Blake (the man-made mess we call America), and Ralph Nader's *Unsafe at Any Speed* (1965), which deals with the unsafe nature of American-produced automobiles, especially GM's Corvair.

As in the past, these books exposed abuses and quickly crystallized the vague but widespread discontent of consumers into a more earnest and militant form.

Not to be overlooked as significant factors in the development of consumerism or the consumer movement are consumer attitudes. Consumers are known to react to developments as either good or bad because of their perceived consequences.[51] This condition related to the consumer movement would suggest that the extent of consumer unrest or vocal discontent depends on how people perceive the events occurring around them. It is thus very plausible that attitude has a history in the consumer movement—a rising level of expectations, business exposés, a damaged and deteriorating environment, the revolt against the intimate yet impersonal and demeaning, unaesthetic partnership of man with his technology and machines can all be interpreted as affecting consumer attitudes and, thus, the consumer movement.

So, income pressures, exposés, and changing attitudes are all seen as forces affecting the consumer movement. During the 1930s the movement gained momentum and expanded its scope to include not only consumer protection but also consumer education, more consumer representation, and a demand for better and more information. During this time the first major consumer testing and regulating agencies were established. In 1929 Consumers Research, Incorporated, was organized and in 1936 Consumers Union was formed. These agencies are sometimes credited as being the mainstay of the movement through their writing of its philosophy, their guidance of its course of action, and their formulation of its objectives.[52]

WHAT THE MOVEMENT HAS ACHIEVED

Consumerism as a social and economic protest movement has produced a large number of meaningful results. It is perhaps fair to say that though its success rate is certainly well below the 100 per cent level, the movement nonetheless has gone a long way toward creating a better buying and consuming atmosphere for the consumer. The movement has advanced the cause of consumer rights by providing safer goods, by providing more information, and by adding to the consumer's fund of alternatives so as to promote the consumer's right to choose, and, finally, the movement has created a new sensitivity on the part of business and government, impressing them genuinely with the consumer's right to be heard.

Consumerism, as a social and economic protest movement, has succeeded in bringing about these achievements through the combined efforts of consumer groups, government, and business-sponsored initiative.

CONSUMER GROUPS. Consumer groups have been the vocal vanguard of the consumer movement. Although attempts to organize a national consumer movement have met with mixed success, local, regional, and statewide organizations have flourished. In the early

---

[51] George Katona, "Long Range Changes in Consumer Attitudes," in *Dynamic Aspects of Consumer Behavior* (Ann Arbor, Mich.: Foundation for Research in Human Behavior, 1963), p. 97.

[52] "The Consumer Movement," *Business Week* (April 22, 1939), p. 42.

1970s, there were twenty-nine state consumer organizations and local organizations in ten major cities or counties. The most active organizations were the Louisiana Consumer League and the Arizona Consumers Council, which has chapters in Tucson, Phoenix, and Flagstaff. In some instances, such state and regional chapters have been successful in obtaining legislation on specific issues. These local and regional efforts are usually dependent on part-time, unprofessional, and volunteer staff aid, thus compounding the difficulty of maintaining continuing programs. However, such groups have proved useful in providing the needed group support for consumer-oriented representatives in both state and local governments.[53]

Usually the members of these organizations are just diverse individuals; however, organizations with consumer interests (labor unions, women's church and civic clubs, and college home economics departments) also participate. And although the size of such groups is usually small, they attain their effectiveness by testifying at hearings, by issuing statements on pending legislation, and by talking to merchants and business associations about eliminating consumer grievances. Educating the public is their broad but common aim. Today's consumer organizations are dealing with a host of problems—medical care, taxes, better control of product quality, informative labeling, ethical sales practices, and safety standards for products from toys to automobiles.[54]

Two new national consumer-oriented groups were founded in the late 1960s. The United National Consumers Association, Inc., known as TUNCA, now has several chapters and members in a large number of states. The other, the Consumer Federation of America, is a national federation of organizations with consumer interests, including such organizations as labor unions, state and local consumer organizations, the National Council of Senior Citizens, and the National Consumers League.

The consumer movement has spawned two of its own communication and information-producing organizations. These are Consumers Union and Consumers Research. Both these organizations are nonprofit firms that endeavor to create the philosophy on which the consumer movement rests and to fuel its causes via written editorial stories in their publications. Furthermore, they aim to produce objective information about the products consumers most frequently buy. For example, Consumers Union undertakes to inform consumers about such diverse matters as interest rates, guarantees and warranties, life insurance, product safety, and other factors. Consumers Union boasted a membership of 1.6 million people in 1970 with an annual budget of $10 million. Such financial strength and such a membership base afford the organization considerable clout in terms of the overall consumer movement.

[53] Hermann, op. cit., p. 58.
[54] "Who Speaks for Consumers Now?" *Changing Times* (July 1967), p. 44.

BUSINESS. The response of business to the demands of consumerism has not always been positive. Business reactions have run the entire gamut from (1) "Deny everything," (2) "Pass the buck," (3) "Discredit the critics," (4) "Hire a public relations man," (5) "Defang the legislation," and (6) "Launch a fact-finding committee," through (7) "Actually do something." Our efforts here will focus briefly on Number 7, and we shall reserve our judgment on the other range of responses for a later section.

The response of individual business firms has been varied and diverse. Their efforts have ranged through such actions as providing more and better product information, toning down the rhetoric of sales and advertising promotions, rewriting product warranties and guarantees, experimenting with unit pricing, abandoning trading stamps and centers, and discontinuing price specials intended as bait only. Manufacturers and retailers both realize that they are under closer scrutiny than they have ever been. Arjay Miller, Ford Motor Company executive, put it this way:

> The corporation must go beyond its traditional role of business enterprise and seek to anticipate, rather than simply react to, social needs or problems. This may require the establishment of a long range planning function to make sure a firm will be able to respond to what society wants it to do. It may involve not only changed "product," but also changed internal organization.[55]

This sort of thinking, permeating many business organizations, is the stimulus for a host of changed consumer-oriented corporate practices. For example, some firms are considering reorganizing in such a manner that consumers really are viewed as the center of the corporate universe. A separate division for consumer affairs is envisioned in which consumer complaints, better product design, and information would be the central focus of concern. Other firms are reexamining all corporate practices that might be perceived as deceptive.

Some firms are acknowledging the validity and presence of the aroused consumer by implementing simple but effective systems of two-way communication. One such plan, that of R.C.A. Whirlpool, involved the installation of a "cool line" telephone service whereby consumers could dial the firm direct to register their complaints about the firm's products or other problems related to dealers or service.

There has been some movement, too, toward collective action by business firms in regard to consumerism.[56] In 1967, the Grocery Manufacturers Association commissioned a study by the McKinsey Company to try to obtain new ideas. Options that were rejected included a massive public relations campaign and an expensive continuing opinion survey

[55] From a speech delivered at a Universty of Illinois symposium, April 21, 1967.

[56] David S. R. Leighton, "Consumerism in the 1970's, *Akron Business and Economic Review*, Vol. 3, No. 3 (Fall 1972), pp. 22–25.

to find out what really does concern the consumer. Finally, the idea of a Consumer Research Institute was adopted. The Grocery Manufacturers agreed to support this plan, which now has more than a hundred members, including manufacturers, media, advertising agencies, distribution organizations, and research and management consulting firms. The Institute's purpose, simply stated, is to sponsor and/or conduct research in any area of marketing practice that may be the subject of consumer concern, for the purpose of shaping and affecting public policy.[57]

The continuing concern of businessmen regarding demands for consumer protection is further indicated by the establishment of a consumer-information service by the National Association of Manufacturers, known as Techniques in Product Selection (TIPS), and a program of cooperation between the Association of Better Business Bureaus and federal departments and agencies that affect consumer-business relationships. Although such programs are, no doubt at least in part, public relations efforts to mollify consumers who desire better information and protection, they do help to establish the claim of concern. Other responses and suggestions from business have been a Consumer Index of Buying Satisfaction to provide both the regulators and the regulated with something better than letters of complaint as a clue to consumer unhappiness. General Foods has set up a Center for Applied Nutrition, which is charged with research into problems of nutrition and hunger.[58]

GOVERNMENT. Government at all levels has been particularly sensitive and responsive to the consumer movement. John F. Kennedy, Lyndon B. Johnson, and Richard M. Nixon have each recognized the political popularity of such a movement. Each has had a special assistant on consumer affairs, and it has recently been suggested that a new consumer agency, or even a Cabinet post concerned with consumer affairs, be established.[59] Government is involved with consumerism on a rather grand scale. For example, in 1961 the government was involved in 113 consumer protection or advancement projects that employed 23,917 people at a cost of $315 million. By 1967 the number of people devoted to this work had risen to 31,474 and the expenditure had risen to $725 million.[60] By the early 1970s such efforts were the concern

[57] It is interesting to note that when the American Marketing Association voted in 1972 for mandatory unit pricing, this position was opposed by the Consumer Research Institute.

[58] Ibid., p. 100.

[59] "Consumer Power Grows in Congress," *Business Week* (July 11, 1970), p. 20. See also Willis Park Rokes, "Nixon vs. the Consumer," *The Nation*, Vol. 207, No. 19 (December 2, 1968), p. 583.

[60] Arthur C. Tatt, "Let's Take the Politics out of Consumerism," *Nation's Business*, Vol. 57, No. 1 (January 1969), p. 82.

of thirty-three federal agencies, staffed by 65,000 employees, administering over 250 consumer programs costing nearly a billion dollars.[61]

The states, too, are often champions of consumer-oriented actions and causes. As of 1970 thirty-four states had consumer fraud bureaus in their attorney general offices. Nine states have consumer councils, and six cities have consumer protection offices.

New York, for example, is contemplating the creation of a new Board of Consumer Protection within its executive branch. Tennessee is considering a comprehensive consumer protection act, as is Massachusetts, one of the country's most consumer-conscious states. In California a recently introduced bill would enable the state's fifty-eight counties to have their own offices of consumer affairs.[62]

In addition, a host of laws relating to consumer affairs has been passed in recent years, including the Wilderness Act of 1964, the Water Quality Standard Act of 1965, the Wholesome Meat Act of 1967, the Air Quality Act of 1967, acts creating national parks and recreation areas in 1968, and the new Truth-in-Lending Law, which took effect in 1969.

Some of this legislation was passed in the face of formidable opposition. For example, the National Traffic and Motor Vehicle Act took on virtually the entire automobile industry, the Fair Packaging and Labeling Act was passed over the strenuous objection of the mammoth food industry, and the Consumer Credit Protection Act was resisted by the banking and finance industries, as well as nearly all retail organizations that grant credit.

Consumers are witnessing a rising level of expectations regarding government's role in the consumer movement and government appears to be responding readily. Currently, there are in excess of a hundred bills dealing with consumer interests before Congress. And government's role in the consumer movement can be expected to increase. Several positive steps that have been recommended for government include an expanded and revitalized role for the Federal Trade Commission, further studies of warranties and guarantees, a truth-in-advertising bill, and legislation to give private citizens the right to bring actions in a federal court to recover damages. Such "class action" suits mean that, instead of each individual suing for damages for faulty merchandise (say a $350 automatic washer), any number of purchasers of similar products could join in a single action. Thus they would save money on legal fees and possibly have more force in court. As the bill currently is written, such class action could be brought only after the new consumer protection division had investigated complaints about the faulty merchandise and had either been able to get the company to change its ways or had

[61] Howard Frazier, "Consumer Protection," *Vital Speeches of the Day*, Vol. 36, No. 9 (February 15, 1970), p. 265.

[62] "New York Leads the Consumer Crusade," *Business Week* (January 31, 1970), p. 51.

won a court trial.[63] Such a move would be a powerful weapon in the hands of aggrieved consumers. Other impending bills would establish a permanent consumer protection office within the White House; would establish a consumer protection division within the Justice Department; would beef up the 1966 Fair Packaging and Labeling Act; would expand the Federal Hazardous Substances Act; and would set up some kind of federal standards body that would develop standards of quality, size, and form and definitions of identity to be designated as U.S. "official" standards that would have standing in international markets.

Also in the works are plans for releasing to the public the results of government tests conducted on a wide range of consumer products by such agencies as the Defense and Agriculture departments and the Food and Drug Administration. For example, the Veterans Administration recently released its findings on the performance of hearing aids.[64]

Thus it would appear likely that the coming years will see the adoption of much additional consumer legislation by federal, state and local governments. More consumer education services will be launched by business groups. Consumer associations, too, will lobby more aggressively. And it is likely that we can expect more pressure on federal agencies to enforce existing laws with greater vigor.

Consumerism: Its Broader Implications and Meaning for Business

Consumerism, in terms of its broader meaning, is concerned with a great deal more than the individual welfare of consumers in the marketplace. One writer has indicated, and quite rightly so, that the ultimate and final challenge of consumerism to business and to marketers is "toward ending hunger and malnutrition . . . toward alleviating pollution of the air and water and soil . . . toward educating and training the disadvantaged . . . toward solving these and other problems of a society rather than strictly those of an industrial nature."[65]

Today consumerism is becoming increasingly concerned with the quality of the physical environment and the impact of marketing practices and technology on the ecology. Ecology is the systems approach to nature, the study of how living organisms and the nonliving environment function together as a whole or an ecosystem. Such an understanding gives meaning to the idea that one man's goods are somebody else's garbage; that there is no such thing as no-return containers—they do return *somewhere*. It is a recognition that has

[63] David Sanford, "Giving the Consumer 'Class,' " *The New Republic*, Vol. 161, No. 4 (July 26, 1969), p. 15.

[64] "Rush to Protect Consumers," *U.S. News & World Report*, Vol. 68, No. 5 (February 2, 1970), p. 46.

[65] Aaron S. Yohalem, "Consumerism's Ultimate Challenge: Is Business Equal to the Task?" Address before the American Management Association, New York, November 10, 1969.

finally emerged from our long-standing concern with built-in obsolescence and all the attendant problems that contribute to pollution in a
"disposable society" and a "throwaway culture."[66]

THE NEW CONSUMERISM

Today the consumer movement increasingly has a scientific concern with atomic energy, ecology, medicine, chemistry, environment,
conservation, economics, manufacturing, advertising, and all those promotional and selling activities that are subsumed under the term
marketing. Development in these many areas is at the point of critical
mass, and consumerism is the explosion. Consumerism is concerned
with today and also with the impact of consumption on the coming
tomorrows. It is, as one spokesman for the movement has said, "[the]
conscience and responsibility contending with tunnel vision. It would
be an impossible undertaking if it were not for the fact that every
citizen is a member. If it succeeds in its mission, it may well accomplish a great deal that politics has not been able to reach."[67]

An example or two of what happens when we don't think as a
collective consciousness, when we abandon the ecological and systems
framework for our myopic and tunnel-visioned selfishness, are dramatic
and enlightening.

Whereas the U.S. population increased 13 per cent during the
1960s, our material consumption of goods and services jumped 60 per
cent, thus loading the landscape with more and more beer cans, junked
autos, and other garbage.

Marketers who have historically viewed a rising population as an
expanding marketing opportunity are going to have to begin thinking
otherwise. The idea of an ever-expanding economy fueled by population growth is tightly entrenched in the minds of marketers. Each new
baby is viewed as a potential customer to stimulate an ever-growing
economy. Marketers often gleefully rejoice at the thought that each
American baby will consume in a seventy-year life span, directly or
indirectly: 26 million gallons of water, 21,000 gallons of gasoline,
10,000 pounds of meat, 28,000 pounds of milk and cream, $5,000 to
$8,000 in school building materials, $6,300 in clothing, and $7,000
worth of furniture.[68] Each American child is fifty times more of a
burden on the environment than each East Indian child.

The result of mass marketing is massive filth.[69] Every year Americans junk 7 million cars, 100 million tires, 20 million tons of paper,
28 billion bottles, and 48 billion cans. To collect our garbage costs

---

[66] Day and Aaker, op. cit., p. 14.

[67] Howard Frazier, "Consumer Protection," *Vital Speeches of the Day,* Vol. 36,
No. 9 (February 15, 1970), p. 266.

[68] Robert and Leona Reinow, *Moment in the Sun* (New York: The Dial Press,
1967), pp. 54–55.

[69] "The Leisurely War on Filth," *The New Republic,* Vol. 162, No. 8 (February
21, 1970), pp. 9–10.

$2.8 billion a year. The United States, although the most affluent country in the world, is also the most effluent—we produce 50 per cent of the world's industrial pollution. Each year, U.S. firms discard 165 million tons of solid waste and pour 172 million tons of smoke and fumes into our atmosphere. The country's 83 million cars cause 60 per cent of the air pollution in cities.[70]

But what is the point? The point is that our marketing systems and the business philosophy and attitudes that underlie them are about to change. Our interest in consumers must reflect the new ethic of consumerism, and our study of consumer behavior must be concerned with both humanism and ecology. Marketing and consumer behavior philosophy is changing. We are faced with the prospect of a consumer-oriented economy in which the individual is regarded as having a natural inclination toward excellence and self-improvement and the improvement of his overall environment. There are traditional forces, described most eloquently by an early champion of the consumer movement, Mrs. Esther Peterson, that may attempt to subvert this ideal. Speaking of the "consumption-directed economy," she said,

> In a consumption-directed economy, anything would be permissive. Deceptive and false advertising would be perfectly okay as long as it made people buy. Planned obsolescence as a means of increasing consumption would be the rule rather than the exception. In this kind of a system, skill, craftsmanship, and quality are unimportant. All that is important is that there be many things to buy and that they be bought. This system frowns on frugality and financial planning and promotes over-extended credit buying.[71]

Unfortunately, businessmen and marketers may not be ready yet to embrace the philosophy of the consumer-directed economy.

MARKETERS: ECONOMIC OR SOCIAL MAN?

Much of the businessman's dilemma can be traced to the conflict between economic and social man—a confrontation that stems from the marketer's concern with making a living on the one hand and living with his fellows on the other, or, in short, the problems that surround the paradox of "making a living" versus "making a life." Those who are primarily economically oriented see life differently than those who are socially oriented. Those with more balance are likely to be torn by conflicting beliefs.[72]

It is easy to overdraw a generalization, including the contrast between economic and social values. But Table 2-1 gives a fairly adequate shorthand definition.

[70] See Leonard Hall, "What Price Tomorrow?" *American Forests*, Vol. 76, No. 1 (January 1970).

[71] Quoted in "Can Betty Furness Help the Consumer?" *Consumer Reports*, Vol. 32, No. 5 (May 1967), p. 256.

[72] See David P. Eastburn, "Economic Man vs. Social Man," *Business Review*, Federal Reserve Bank of Philadelphia (October 1970), pp. 3–6.

TABLE 2-1

Economic man	Social man
Production	Distribution
Quantity	Quality
Goods and Services	People
Money Values	Human Values
Work and Discipline	Self-realization
Competition	Cooperation
Laissez-faire	Involvement
Inflation	Unemployment

Source: David P. Eastburn, "Economic Man vs. Social Man," *Business Review*, Federal Reserve Bank of Philadelphia (October, 1970), p. 3.

As can be seen, marketers and businessmen are too often too deeply steeped in the values of economic man to appreciate the values of social man as reflected in consumerism and the consumer movement. Economic man often is the mirrored reflection of the "establishment." His value system runs to production, mass marketing, the outpouring of goods, and the regulation of industry by competition alone or laissez-faire economic principles.

Such a value system and attitude set has programmed marketers and businessmen to possess a reflexive resistance to almost all consumer-oriented legislation and has placed marketers in the unedifying role of contending against legislation that the general public has viewed as liberating, progressive, and necessary.[73] Furthermore, the ethics and values of economic man, as embodied in marketers, has created a conditioned response that rejects nearly all change: A marketer may welcome new things in his business but not necessarily in vocal protest movements or in his relationship to his government and overall society. Economic man is an uncertainty avoider and too much change means too much uncertainty.

It is high time for marketers and businessmen to move from the defensive to the offensive, to become more aware and sensitive to the needs of society as voiced by social man in a consumer-directed economy. It is time for marketers to begin pushing the boundary line the other way between the public and private sectors. As one writer stated, "this would be a healthy thing for our economy and a formidable hedge against a future in which we must grapple with the social and economic 'fallout' of technological advances."[74]

There is a growing realization that the market, which is supposed

[73] Theodore Levitt, "Why Business Always Loses," *Harvard Business Review*, Vol. 46, No. 2 (March–April 1968), p. 81.

[74] George Champion, "Creative Competition," *Harvard Business Review*, Vol. 45, No. 3 (May–June 1967), p. 67.

to be the reflection of the way in which people spontaneously value their individual wants and efforts, is a rather poor guide to the best means of satisfying the real wishes of consumers. Why? Because market prices generally fail to measure the social costs or the social benefits of consumption, and in our society these are growing constantly more important.[75]

In the future, the overall price of goods will very likely be determined in such a way as to include the costs of their production, marketing, and disposal without damage to the environment.

Society, marketers, and individual consumers would all stand to reap the rewards of sociocommercial enterprise. Marketers, especially, must pay increasing heed to the Jeremiahs of consumerism, who are crying, "I am a human being; do not fold, bend, mutilate, violate, or pollute me!"

Therefore, our study of consumer behavior in the subsequent chapters must reflect these new attitudes and these new demands of consumers. We will analyze and explore the various sociopsychological dimensions of consumer behavior, not so that we can acquire a bag of tricks for fooling and manipulating an adversary but, instead, so that we can acquire a better understanding of consumer needs, wants, and motivations and thus better serve the aims of a consumer-directed economy.

Questions for Study, Reflection, and Review

1 What are some of the reasons that consumerism is an important focus for study?

2 Explain what is meant by the consumer's dilemma.

3 Describe the consumer's major problem with regard to determining the actual value of an item.

4 Contrast the two basic views that have emerged regarding consumer information and relate them to consumerism.

5 What are some of the disadvantages encountered by the low-income consumer in the purchasing situation?

6 Describe the consumer's bill of rights and explain what these rights mean.

7 Discuss the similarities among the three time periods that were characterized by consumer movements.

8 Discuss some of the activities being undertaken by consumer groups, businesses, and government in response to consumerism.

9 Discuss the primary concern of the new consumerism and its potential effect on marketing activities.

10 How does economic man differ from social man in terms of his value orientation?

[75] Andrew Shonfield, *Modern Capitalism: The Changing Balance of Public and Private Power* (New York: Oxford University Press, 1965), p. 227.

3

A Conspectus of
Consumer Behavior

Introduction

One of the oft-quoted bits of conventional wisdom is that a "little knowledge is a dangerous thing." The danger of a little knowledge is, of course, that the possessor of that knowledge will not use it to acquire more knowledge but will instead tend to behave as if he understood a great deal more about a subject or phenomenon than he really does. To proceed in such a fashion can truly be dangerous.

Yet, another problem arises. In order to acquire an understanding of complex phenomena, one must invariably begin his immersion into the subject slowly. We start by learning simple generalizations and by exploring elementary and fundamental concepts. Hence, the title of this chapter is no accident: it is a deliberate attempt to describe exactly what this chapter is all about. A *conspectus* is a general or comprehensive view presented in the form of a survey or digest. It is, in its most summary form, an outline or a digest. Hence, a conspectus of consumer behavior is a summary outline or digest of the field of consumer behavior.

Therefore, this chapter has as its main objective the development of a rather broad, general framework. It will be a survey of consumer behavior. And as a survey, it will discuss the more relevant and essential aspects of the topic of consumer behavior in order to give the reader an overview of the field. Thus, we shall look first at the whole, taking what is sometimes called the macro point of view. We shall then proceed to break down this whole into a series of parts. It is hoped that this approach will give some initial insight into consumer behavior and will form the backdrop against which more sophisticated concepts can be explored and explained in subsequent chapters.

Throughout the sections of this chapter, some of the essential and more fundamental concepts are explored. We shall look again briefly at the role of consumer behavior in marketing strategy. The discussion will then move to the analysis and implications of some contemporary consumer phenomena affecting marketing and our study of consumer behavior and will move subsequently to the topic of the images of man that affect consumer behavior analysis. The chapter will conclude with a discussion of consumer decision processes.

Consumer Behavior and Marketing Strategy

From the point of view of both the practitioner with his interest in strategy formulation and the theoretician with his interest in the development of testable hypotheses, theory formulation, and the ultimate construction of a science of marketing, consumer behavior is the key concept of marketing. The widespread adoption of the marketing concept, with its fundamental predicate of consumer orientation, demands more attention to customer-centered marketing problems and a better understanding of consumer behavior phenomena. In short, it is the consumer around whom a marketing strategy or program is built. The consumer, as we have seen, is to be served, not manipulated. His wishes and cravings are to be discovered and sounded out, not structured and artificially altered to meet the needs of the company. The consumer and the market are viewed as an end rather than a means. Consumer behavior thus becomes the single most important determinant of marketing strategy.

The marketing manager's task is to develop, formulate, and implement strategy.[1] Strategy is the movement and countermovement in pursuit of goals and objectives. Given the link between firm and marketplace, every decision made in the firm is analyzed and evaluated in terms of its eventual effect on consumer reaction or behavior. Strategy must not be viewed as a ruse or a deception. Instead, it is a dynamic series of actions whereby the firm adapts and reacts to the competitive conditions of the marketplace.

ELEMENTS OF STRATEGY

Broadly conceived, strategy formation begins with an analysis of needs or wants. The firm ought to base its entire marketing plan on how it perceives consumer behavior in the marketplace. Thus, the primary point of view in the marketing concept is consumer orienta-

---

[1] For an excellent discussion of strategy, see James Myers, et al., *Managerial Analysis in Marketing* (Glenview, Ill.: Scott, Foresman and Company, 1970), especially Chapter 6, pp. 283–323.

tion. A marketing strategy is a comprehensive plan of action that involves the adjustment and accommodation of the controllable elements of a firm's marketing mix—that is, price, promotion, product, and place —to the ever-changing elements of the environmental conditions in which the firm must operate, such as law, costs, structure, competition, and demand. Every aspect of the marketing strategy has behavioral implications.

Prices are cues that signal customers about quality and value.[2] Products, for the most part, have a vast symbolic significance that far transcends their basic functional significance.[3] Promotion in the form of mass advertising[4] and personal selling[5] involves more than the simple transmission of information. Stores are more than just warehouses where merchandise is collected and disseminated. They acquire instead anthropomorphic characteristics[6]—personalities that are warm, inviting, and friendly or cold, haughty, impersonal, and repelling, depending upon the perception of given consumers.

The marketing manager, like others charged with managerial responsibilities, must plan, organize, and control the elements for which he is assigned responsibilities. By planning he decides in advance what needs to be done; he anticipates market and consumer behavior and acts accordingly. By organizing he marshals resources and establishes proper relationships and priorities; he sequences behavior. By controlling he sets standards, compares planned performance with actual performance, and takes corrective action.

The marketing strategist recognizes that there are elements that affect his management and strategy considerations over which he has little or no control. But he recognizes at the outset that the success or failure of his marketing plans rests ultimately with the consumer or market for which his strategy has been designed. Consequently, most strategy formulations are based upon the assumption that consumer behavior can be either (1) analyzed and understood, or (2) analyzed, understood, and modified. Both assumptions strongly dictate that the marketing manager know and understand what affects consumer behavior, that is, how consumers learn; who makes buying decisions; how consumer impressions, opinions, attitudes, and images are modified by group influences; how consumers acquire and process market information; why some consumers are more susceptible to persuasion than

[2] Benson P. Shapiro, "The Psychology of Pricing," *Harvard Business Review*, Vol. 46, No. 4 (July–August 1968), pp. 14–18.

[3] S. J. Levy, "Symbols by Which We Buy," Proceedings of the American Marketing Association (1959), pp. 409–416.

[4] Harper W. Boyd, Jr., and Sidney J. Levy, *Promotion: A Behavioral View* (Englewood Cliffs, N.J.: Prentice-Hall, Inc., 1967), pp. 43–47.

[5] Franklin B. Evans, "Selling as a Dyadic Relationship—A New Approach," *American Behavioral Scientist,* Vol. 6 (May 1963), pp. 76–79.

[6] Pierre Martineau, "The Personality of the Retail Store," *Harvard Business Review,* Vol. 36, No. 1 (January–February 1958), p. 47.

others; and how firms can successfully communicate their marketing programs to the consumer. Thus, once again, the principal reason for studying consumer behavior is that such knowledge can lead to better market performance by the business firm and ultimately redound to the improvement of general social welfare.

PROPOSITIONS REGARDING CONSUMER BEHAVIOR

In any survey of consumer behavior it would seem only fitting that at some juncture a few basic but critical propositions regarding consumer behavior be presented for consideration. Invariably it is around such propositions that many of our inquiries into consumer motivation and behavior are built, and such propositions often become the essential and vital basis toward which theories of consumer decision processes are oriented and upon which marketing strategies are structured and implemented. The following are offered as such basic and vital propositions.

1. The Dynamic State of the Organism. *The human organism is a constantly active and dynamic entity.* As humans, consumers are in a near-constant state of arousal. The U.S. consumer is not necessarily guided in his consumer behavior by an urge to reduce tension. He seeks it. He looks for goods and services that offer him a heightened sense of satisfaction. He wants an "exciting experience" or an "exciting house" in an "exciting neighborhood filled with 'exciting' people." The dynamic state of the consumer expresses itself in the fact that the consumer wishes to know, to have, and to become. His prepurchase, purchase, and postpurchase behavior attempt to unify and integrate the purchase idea or situation with his own life style and cognitive structures. The consumer is constantly active because his existence confronts him with the necessity to act. The consumer's existence creates a need for goods and services as solutions to problems. To exist is to have problems, and to have problems generates the need to search and create solutions for these problems.

Finally, as an energy system containing tensional forces, a great part of the consumer's activity is related to tension management. The consumer wishes to manage and control his tensions, which emerge as drives, motivations, needs, and wants. Tension is a state that exists between one inner personal region relative to another inner personal region.[7] An inner personal region is simply another way of describing the organism's need-value system. When one dimension of the need-value system is satisfied or rewarded, another dimension is likely to be unsatisfied. Thus, many consumers discover that satisfaction and pleasure come to him who ceaselessly bestirs himself in the pursuit of objectives that in total are not fully attained.

[7] See Harold H. Kassarjian, "Consumer Behavior: A Field Theoretical Approach" in Robert L. King, ed., *Marketing and the New Science of Planning* (Chicago: American Marketing Association, 1968), pp. 285–289.

2. Human Versus Rat Psychology. *The consumer psychologist's interests and the basis for his research and generalizations stem from human behavior. We reject the concept of species equivalence.* This proposition actually requires very little elaboration. There are fields of psychological endeavor relating to physiology, perceptual-motor systems, and stimulus-response and operant-conditioning psychology, in which experiments conducted among lower animal forms such as rats, pigeons, and monkeys are sometimes generalized to higher-level organisms. However, the consumer psychologist takes as his subject for investigation and inquiry the human organism. No attempt to generalize about consumer behavior and consumer decision processes based upon lower animal experiences will be made in this book.

3. The Interdisciplinary Approach. *There is no single science of human behavior.* Consumers are complex and sophisticated entities. Thus, there is no single way to approach the study of human behavior in general or consumer behavior in particular. Consumer behavior studies are based upon concepts and methodologies borrowed from such disciplines as economics, statistics, sociology, psychology, social psychology, and cultural anthropology. The consumer is a biopsychosociological being affected by many diverse and ambiguous stimuli. His behavior remains to be explained in terms of psychological, sociological, and cultural factors as well as biological and physiological phenomena.[8]

4. The Contaminated Nature of Consumer Behavior. *Consumer behavior is not a neat or tidy subset of human or social behavior.*[9] To attain such a feat as that suggested by McNeal (see footnote 9) would be an Olympian task indeed. Consumption in a sophisticated, affluent society takes on large, significant, *symbolic* implications. Consumer behavior is an integral part of the social behavior of the individual, and therefore we can no more isolate consumer behavior from its social setting than we can isolate worker motivation from that of the work environment. Thus to know something about consumer behavior we need to study consumers as functioning, witnessing, experiencing agents within a larger framework of behavior and analysis. The consumer's behavior is significant only so long as it exists as a part of this larger fabric or framework. Change the framework—that is, alter the consumer's life style, rearrange and redistribute the groups to which he belongs, or move him along the continuum of his life cycle—and you will likely witness profound changes in his behavior. McNeal's proposition denies the Gestalt or field theoretical perspective regarding

[8] For more on the subject, see George Katona, "What Is Consumer Psychology?" *American Psychologist,* Vol. 22 (March 1967), pp. 219–226.

[9] This proposition is in marked contrast to that of another writer, who states almost the opposite: see James U. McNeal, *Dimensions of Consumer Behavior,* 2nd ed. (New York: Appleton-Century-Crofts, 1969), p. 8. The statement of McNeal's is "Consumer behavior is only one type of human behavior and can be isolated and studied with only small concern for the many other kinds of human behavior."

consumer behavior that asserts that all analysis of consumer decision processes must begin with the entire situation as a whole and then move to a differentiation of the relevant parts.[10]

5. The Entropic Nature of Behavioral Change. *There exists a statistical tendency for things to change.* Entropy is nature's statistical tendency to disorder or change.[11] All systems are subject to entropy—that is, they run down, decay, and degenerate. Behavioral systems are no exception. As we have seen, human beings are not isolated systems. Instead, they take in food, which generates energy, from the outside, and in so doing become a part of a larger world, the source of their vitality. Furthermore, and most importantly, is the fact that consumers take in information through their sense organs and they act on the information received. Thus generalizations regarding consumer behavior may be constantly subject to change. The environment of consumer behavior is constantly changing—incomes rise and fall, education increases, demographic changes occur that change the structure and the function of population and market segments. Thus, because of the dynamic and constantly active nature of the human organism, our generalizations about this organism must be, in turn, constantly active and dynamic—hence, changing!

6. Perceived Risk, Risk Avoidance, and Expectations. *Consumers' behavior is to some great extent related to their expectations. However, all consumer decision processes are surrounded by a degree of perceived risk, and some decisions are surrounded by such a high degree of risk that consumers, to avoid such risks, may forego purchasing or delay purchasing to seek more information or to reorder priorities and reappraise expectations.*[12] Such a profound and complex proposition demands a well-reasoned and lengthy explanation. Such a treatment is provided later, in Chapter 18. It suffices to say at this juncture that products and services are all evaluated in terms of their functional and symbolic utility. Because we aspire to given ends, and means are limited, all decision processes generate varying degrees of anxiety. The level of anxiety is related to the degree of risk or the perceived probability that the product or service will fail to deliver what we expect it to deliver. It is from this proposition that such consumer behavior as *search, evaluation, budgeting,* and *postpurchase behavior* are analyzed.

7. Consumer Planning Horizons. *The planning time, or the time that elapses between perceived need* (awareness) *and actual purchase, is for most goods relatively short.* The typical consumer does not postpone or forego gratification for any prolonged period of time, given, of course, his needs-wants hierarchy and his ability via income to fulfill

---

[10] See again Kassarjian, op cit, p. 289.

[11] Norbert Weiner, *The Human Use of Human Beings* (New York: Avon Books, 1967), especially Chapter 11, pp. 41–67.

[12] An elaborate treatment of such factors can be found in Jagdish N. Sheth and M. Venkatesan, "Risk Reaction Processes in Competitive Behavior," *Journal of Marketing Research,* Vol. 5 (Chicago: American Marketing Association, August 1968), pp. 307–310.

these needs. The planning period or horizon for small items such as convenience goods is almost nonexistent and can be described as spur-of-the-moment or precipitous. Even for big ticket items such as boats, automobiles, major appliances, and new homes, the planning horizon is not likely to exceed one year.[13]

Such a proposition is consistent with earlier ones relating to the dynamic nature of both the environment and the individual. Consumers are constantly confronted with new problems that demand new products and services as solutions. It really does not follow that because planning horizons are relatively brief, consumers act without deliberation or that consumer behavior is "irrational."

8. The Consumer's Quest for Variety. *Consumer tastes, attitudes, values, and perceptions do change and such changes generate the need for variety.* In a high-level, consumption-oriented society this demanded variety may call for an ever-increasing and expanding mix of goods. However, in a "consumerism"-oriented society, the constant attention to further acquisition of goods may become dull and unexciting or even threatening in terms of survival. In such a case, variety may mean an increased opportunity to choose a better quality of environment by way of clean air and water, more leisure time, or more art and other aesthetic products, as opposed to continually increasing amounts of consumer goods.

Images of Man Affecting Consumer Behavior Analyses

Many of the inquiries and analyses into consumer behavior are affected or conditioned by what might be most descriptively called our images of man. Our research methodologies, especially our efforts to build "models" of consumer decision processes, are based either explicitly or implicitly upon certain intuitive and preconceived notions regarding what we consider to be the basic nature of man or what constitutes the basic essence of man's behavior.[14]

IMAGE AS PERSPECTIVE

Rather than as stereotypes, the real value of images is the perspective that they create or the point of view that they provide.[15] A perspective is an ordered view of one's surroundings—his physical and psychological space. One's perspective is what he takes for granted about the objects and events that transpire within this space or field.

[13] Eva Mueller, "A Look at the American Consumer," in R. A. Scott and N. E. Marks, *Marketing and Its Environment* (Belmont, Calif.: Wadsworth Publishing Co., Inc., 1968), pp. 124–136.

[14] Models of consumer behavior are examined in the next chapter. The distinction between *models* and *images* is purely arbitrary and therefore definitional. Images will be defined in this section and a full treatment of models will be presented in Chapter 4.

[15] The pioneering and classic work in stereotyping was done by Walter Lippmann, *Public Opinion* (New York: Harcourt Brace Jovanovich, Inc., 1922).

It is an order and image of things witnessed, expected and perceived, the range of which includes what is plausible and what is possible. An image as a perspective constitutes the matrix through which one perceives his environment.[16] Therefore, in the pages that follow, we shall look at some of these images of man and use them as a perspective. All such images have certain common characteristics: they describe some basic behavior and its preceding motivation, basic needs, and common situations, and they optimistically assume that "this is what man is really like." The researcher then usually proceeds to build his study on such an image and necessarily proceeds to ignore aspects of behavior not previously incorporated into his image.[17] As a result we have concepts or images of economic man, Pavlovian or stimulus-response man, Freudian man, sociological man, and others.[18] Some of these we shall explore in the following pages.

Economic Man

A large and significant part of consumers' behavior is constrained and affected by economic considerations. As a matter of fact, in many parts of the world a preponderant part of man's behavior is oriented around his quest for funds with which to buy the basic necessities of life. Man in such situations becomes obsessed with consumption, because he has an opportunity to engage in so little of it. Scarcity has confronted man throughout the ages, and his reaction to this scarcity affects nearly all acts of consumption and preconsumption endeavors, in both impoverished as well as more affluent societies. Economics deals with the allocation of scarce resources as means to alternative uses or ends. Or more comprehensively:

> Economics is the study of how men and society *choose,* with or without the use of money, to employ *scarce* productive resources to produce various commodities over time and distribute them for consumption, now and in the future, among various people and groups in society.[19]

Because of the concern of economics with consumption, allocation, and rationing, a potent and prevailing image of consumers as economic men has emerged. The image of the consumer as an economic man rests on several basic assumptions. The needs and wants of consumers are considered to be virtually unlimited. Man's capacity to want is

[16] T. Shibutani, "Reference Groups and Social Control," in *Human Behavior and Social Processes*, A. M. Rose, ed. (Boston: Houghton Mifflin Company, 1967). See especially Chapter 7.

[17] See Arthur J. Kover, "Models of Man as Defined by Market Research," *Journal of Marketing Research,* Vol. 4 (May 1967), pp. 129–132, especially p. 129.

[18] Philip Kotler, "Behavioral Models for Analyzing Buyers," *Journal of Marketing,* Vol. 29 (October 1965), pp. 37–45.

[19] Paul A. Samuelson, *Economics: An Introductory Analysis,* 5th ed. (New York: McGraw-Hill Book Company, 1961), p. 6.

limited only by his imagination, but his ability to supply his wants is constrained by his economic position, i.e., his earnings and his stock of assets. Given the image and concept of economic man, consumption is almost solely a function of income, either present income or expected future income. Economic man as a consumer must ration. He cannot have all that he desires, so he must, given his budget constraints, decide how much of his income he is willing to spend for various categories of consumption—housing, clothing, food, entertainment, and savings —and he must choose from among various competing items in each of these categories. The concept of economic man rests essentially on the principle of utility, or satisfaction. Utility is the ability of a thing to satisfy a want or need. Economic man is construed as an all-knowing, omniscient, hedonistic calculator who is capable of perceiving his needs correctly, measuring these needs against his income and wealth, and choosing a total bundle of goods and services that will deliver to him optimum satisfaction. Such a view rests on the principle of marginal utility, which asserts that the consumer will continue to buy a product until the satisfaction from acquiring one more (or marginal) unit per dollars worth of that product, just equals the marginal utility per dollars worth of any other product for a given period of time. If that sounds confusing, look at the proposition in terms of this equation:

$$\frac{MU_1}{P1} = \frac{MU_2}{P2} = \frac{MU_3}{P3} = \cdots = \frac{MU_n}{Pn}$$

This equation shows that the utility or satisfaction received from the last dollar spent on any one product is equal to the utility received from the last dollar spent on any other product. It can also be shown that if

$$\frac{MU_i}{Pi} < \frac{MU_j}{Pn}$$

then the satisfaction received from the last dollar spent on i is not as great as the satisfaction received from the last dollar spent on j. This would indicate that the consumer can increase his overall level of utility by reallocating his expenditure and spending more for j and less for i. As a result, there is no equilibrium until an equality between ratios is established.

Such an image of man's behavior regarding purchase and consumption behavior is based upon classical utility theory and it rests upon two rather shaky assumptions. Each consumer is credited with the ability to measure the utility to be derived from each commodity he consumes, and given his total rationality, he will select from all possible goods within his budget constraint that combination of goods and services that will provide the greatest total utility by equating marginal utilities spent for all goods.

The concept of utility theory and equilibrium is often presented in the form of what is called the indifference curve model. The equation on page 59 actually describes what happens as we move along the indifference curve toward consumer utility maximization. The consumer attempts to move to the highest indifference curve, limited by qualifying factors such as income and product price. The consumer is visualized as substituting one good for another until the highest level of equilibrium is achieved. Having reached this equilibrium point, he is spending his income in such a way that the last dollar spent on each kind of good results in the same additional satisfaction or marginal utility. Four basic assumptions are needed for indifference analyses.[20] First, the consumer must be able to identify preferences for all the pairs of alternatives presented during his decision processes. Second, he can and must choose only one of these possibilities for every pair of alternatives. Only by doing this can he obtain a determinate solution. Third, the consumer is expected, somewhat unrealistically, to be consistent in his choices. And fourth, being rational, a consumer must try to maximize his total satisfaction.

SHORTCOMINGS OF THE IMAGE OF ECONOMIC MAN

Man isn't equipped to behave in the manner described by economists. Microeconomic concepts such as marginal utility are interesting theoretical concepts and have served a useful function in terms of the continuing development of tools and methodologies in abstract economic thinking. But as a basis around which to build a useful theory of consumer behavior, the economic image of man is woefully deficient.

The major deficiency is that utility is not measurable. Consumers can rank one product over another, but they cannot measure in any sense whatsoever the utility or satisfaction derived from a particular product. Hence, the question of intrapersonal utility measurement becomes moot if not hopeless.

Consumer rationality as seen by the economist is also open to serious questioning. From the economist's point of view, consumers are rational by definition; that is, economists endow consumers with perfect knowledge, and with perfect knowledge why wouldn't everyone be rational? The point is that consumers probably are rational, or have what has more lately been called *bounded rationality*, but they are not omniscient, and therefore their judgments and decisions are on occasion likely to be faulty.[21]

Another deficiency in the image of economic man is that it is assumed that he attempts to maximize his consumption utility and satisfaction. Recent research into organizational and individual decision-making has indicated that "satisfactory" alternatives are generally the goal rather than "optimal" achievements.

[20] See Marguerite C. Burk, "Survey of Interpretations of Consumer Behavior by Social Scientists in the Postwar Period," *Journal of Farm Economics*, Vol. 49 (February 1967), pp. 1–31.

[21] We shall treat the concept of rationality more extensively in subsequent sections.

The *satisficer,* as he is sometimes called, is one who seeks some normal return on his investment. He may price and produce in accordance with some policy goals related to a target rate of return, or because of fear of attracting competitors or inviting government regulation or intervention, he may seek what to him or his company is a satisfactory profit or return on investment. Consumers too often seek only satisfactory solutions to problems, and therefore they would be called satisficers rather than maximizers.[22]

Finally, the most damaging and unrealistic aspect of the economic image of man is that it does not attempt to deal with important problems like changes in taste, in culture, or in a whole host of sociopsychological factors. No realistic image of consumer behavior could be built on a concept that ignores tastes and preferences. However, the classical microeconomic theory of consumption cavalierly dismisses these determinants of behavior in the well-known and overused qualification "all else being equal."

Psychological Man

Psychology is the study of human and animal behavior. Thus consumer behavior as a part of human behavior is a worthy and legitimate field of inquiry for the psychologist. And it would seem only logical that our inquiries into the nature of consumer decision processes would be guided by an image or concept based upon man as a psychological organism. However, psychologists, in one sense at least, are not the single-minded creatures that economists are. The economists are generally well agreed as to the basic principles of behavior of economic man, i.e., perfect knowledge, complete rationality, the search for marginal utility, and maximizing behavior. However, there are a multitude of general principles, points of view, and basic methodologies that surround the psychologist's reasoning regarding man's social, biological, and psychological activity. Therefore one finds not one image of psychological man as a basis for consumer behavior analysis but several. And these images are based upon differences that stem from what are called the various fields of psychology. We shall examine these fields briefly at this juncture.

MAJOR FIELDS OF PSYCHOLOGY

Psychology is a broad science and includes many areas of inquiry. Psychological studies range from posthumous personality analyses of world figures to the study of the visual activity of hooded rats. The three major fields of psychological study are listed and briefly described.

CLINICAL PSYCHOLOGY. Clinical psychology deals with normal and abnormal behavior and with the individual's psychological adjustment to himself and his environment. Clinical psychology deals essentially

[22] See J. G. March and H. A. Simon, *Organizations* (New York: John Wiley & Sons, Inc., 1958).

with learned or acquired drives as opposed to the innate drives that are the chief concern of experimental psychology. Much of the inquiry of clinical psychology relates to the socialization processes of the individual whereby the conflicts that arise between human biological drives and the norms and folkways of society are studied and investigated.

EXPERIMENTAL PSYCHOLOGY. Experimental psychology is often disparagingly referred to as "rat psychology" and more politely as "laboratory psychology." This field deals with relationships between variables observed under strictly controlled laboratory conditions. Studies in this area are often oriented around the effect of some identifiable variable such as age, sex, size, weight, and so on, or some experimenter-induced factor such as stress, heat, light, sound, and so on, on some dependent variable in animal behavior. Experimental psychology is fundamentally concerned with drives and motives that stem from basic biological conditions, such as sexual drive, thirst, hunger, cold, heat, and so on.

PSYCHOANALYSIS. Psychoanalysis is a field of psychology that is concerned with the impact of unconscious motivation on human behavior. In this method of analysis, the patient tells the psychoanalyst what he is thinking and feeling without consciously controlling his thoughts. This procedure is called *free association*.

Psychoanalysis stresses the impact of childhood maladjustments, rejection, loss of love, and society's taboos on free and unlimited sexual gratification on personality disorders.

There are, of course, other fields or schools of thought relating to psychological inquiry, but the three mentioned are the most important from the point of view of our interest in consumer behavior. Before departing from this section, it should be pointed out that there is a difference between fields of psychology and methods of psychology. Methods are the ways in which psychologists attempt to generate principles that can be used to explain, predict, and control behavior, and they include such techniques as experiments, observation, introspection, case histories, and surveys.[23]

Reductive-Functional Versus Holistic Psychology

In the interests of efficiency, we shall divide the field of psychology into two polar positions. After having described each of these conceptions of psychology, we shall describe one or two of the major schools of psychology within each of these polarized categories. Very briefly, the reason for such an effort is as follows: the problem rests in the basic assumptions that these two types of theories make about some important characteristics of sociopsychological phenomena and, there-

---

[23] For a more comprehensive discussion of this topic, see Ernest R. Hilgard and Richard C. Atkinson, *Introduction to Psychology*, 4th ed. (New York: Harcourt Brace Jovanovich, Inc., 1967), pp. 10–20.

fore, about consumer behavior. A *functionalist* assumes that these characteristics are reducible to a set of small molecular, discrete, and isolatable variables and that the unique relationships existing among these variables are discernible. A *holist* assumes, contrariwise, that these characteristics are *organized, conceptual,* and *nonreducible* in nature and therefore must be examined as a complete, phenomenalistic, holistic *totality.*[24]

REDUCTIVE-FUNCTIONAL PSYCHOLOGY

Reductive-functional psychology is an endeavor to see human beings in terms of forces, drives, conditioned reflexes, and so on. There are three basic assumptions that underlie nearly all reductive-functional psychological approaches. The first is that human behavior is determined by variables that are potentially discoverable. Such things as spontaneous human activity are largely denied by this point of view. All acts of behavior are said to be traceable to physiological conditions within the organism.

A second assumption of the reductive-functionalist is that the most beneficial, efficient, and productive approach to the discovery of insight and generalizations regarding consumer behavior is the exploration of the relationship between independent environmental variables and dependent response variables in the organism's response patterns; in other words, the stress is on cause and effect relationships between independent and dependent variables, and the environmental conditions relating to the organism are the major sources of independent variables that affect the dependent variables. This makes for a kind of functional input-output relationship.

The third and final assumption is that functional relations are reducible to physiological entities that are directly observable and not hypothetically inferred as a result of introspection. Where possible, these physiological entities are reduced to biochemical and eventually physical terms. Thus, reductive-functionalists are *behaviorists* in the sense that they restrict psychology to objective observation, ignoring introspection and consciousness.[25]

PAVLOVIAN AND FREUDIAN MAN

Two prominent points of view regarding human behavior that are essentially reductive-functionalist are those about Pavlovian man and Freudian man. Pavlovian man is seen as an organism with a bundle of drives, needs, instincts, and conditioned reflexes and as an object that reacts to a kind of input-output conditioning or learning situation. Freudian man is seen as a bundle of tensions, anxieties, and stresses,

[24] This approach is suggested in Robert E. Lana, *Assumptions of Social Psychology* (New York: Appleton-Century-Crofts, 1969). See especially Chapters 4 and 5 and pp. 154–156.

[25] See John B. Watson, *Behaviorism* (New York: The Peoples Institute Publishing Company, 1925).

most of which manifest themselves subconsciously and reflect such factors as hidden or suppressed guilt, sexual suppression, and other libidinous influences. Each conception is briefly discussed.

PAVLOVIAN MAN. This conception of human behavior has been generalized from the work of such psychologists as the Russian Ivan P. Pavlov and the American B. F. Skinner. The classic experimental work of Pavlov involved ringing a bell just prior to feeding a dog.[26] As a result of repeated bell ringing and feeding, Pavlov soon found that the dog salivated when the bell was rung whether or not the food was supplied. He concluded, as do many learning-theory psychologists, that learning is largely an associative process.

B. F. Skinner, a strict behaviorist who made important contributions to learning theory by way of his work in operant conditioning, has reemphasized the role of association and especially reinforcement as a primary determinant of behavior.[27] The theories of both Pavlov and Skinner emphasize the input-output or cause-effect basis of behavior, stressing the critical nature of stimulus-response mechanisms.

Buying and purchase behavior, as social behavior, generally is thus viewed as a largely mechanistic set of learned responses to invoked stimuli. In other words, consumer behavior is a bundle of conditioned responses in an associative context. Such a Pavlovian view, which stresses the stimulus-response configuration, rests upon four central and fundamental concepts:

1. Drive.
2. Cue.
3. Response.
4. Reinforcement.

Drive. A drive is a strong internal stimulus that impels action. A drive may be severe physical pain or a strong emotional inclination or wish. Drives are the internal manifestation of man's energy system and relate closely to his tension mechanisms.

Cue. Cues are weaker stimuli in the environment and/or in the individual that determine when, where, and how the subject responds and which response he makes. Cues enable us to differentiate our pattern of responses.

Response. A response is an organism's reaction to a configuration of cues. By *response*, psychologists mean any pattern or act of behavior of an organism to its environment. Thus, responses may be actions, emotions, or thoughts, as well as such kinetic things as muscular and glandular changes.

Reinforcement. If the experience is rewarding or satisfying, a

---

[26] Ivan P. Pavlov, *Conditional Reflexes*, trans. G. V. Anrys (London: Oxford University Press, 1927).

[27] B. F. Skinner, *The Behavior of Organisms: An Experimental Analysis* (New York: Appleton-Century-Crofts, 1938).

particular response is reinforced, that is, strengthened, and there is a tendency for it to be repeated when the same configuration of *cues* appears again.

Thus in classical conditioning, learning occurs when a new stimulus elicits behavior similar to that originally produced by an old stimulus or, in the case of instrumental learning, when the person learns to respond in the same way again as a result of what happened after the last response was made.[28]

Marketers often base their advertising and promotional efforts on classical learning precepts. For example, consider the man with an upset stomach. He has a pain that manifests itself in the form of a *drive*. Having been previously exposed to advertisements that project the curative powers of Pepto-Bismol, observing that this product is available in his medicine cabinet, and, further, having read the promises on the label, he has the necessary *cues*. The subject's response consists of pouring the necessary dosage, taking the medicine, and awaiting the results. If his aching stomach is relieved, the product—or the goal object, as it is called—is perceived to be satisfactory, and the learning theorist would then predict that the next time the subject has an upset stomach he will probably take Pepto-Bismol again.

Such a Pavlovian view of consumer or general social behavior is exceedingly simpleminded and overly mechanistic. It ignores the complex and sophisticated nature of man's intricate cognitive structure.

FREUDIAN MAN. The theories about Freudian man rest upon the work of the Austrian physician Sigmund Freud. Freud's basic view concerning man was that he was an energy system obeying the same physical laws that regulate the soap bubble and the movement of the planets.[29] His insights regarding nervous disorders led him to develop what he called a dynamic psychology. A dynamic psychology is a study of the transformation and exchange of energy within the personality. The personality was divided by Freud into three functional dimensions that he called the id, the ego, and the superego.

The id. The main function of the id is to release quantities of energy. The id fulfills the primordial or basic principle of life that Freud called the pleasure principle. The goal of the pleasure principle is to rid the person of tension or, at least, to reduce the amount of tension to a reasonably low level and keep it as low as possible. The id is not controlled by the laws of reason or logic, and it does not possess values, ethics, or morality. The id is compulsively driven by one basic goal and that is to obtain satisfaction for instinctive needs in accordance with the pleasure principle.

[28] We shall engage in a much more exhaustive analysis of learning theory in Chapter 9.

[29] Material here is based to a considerable degree upon an earlier work of this author. See Rom J. Markin, "Consumer Motivation and Behavior: Essence vs. Existence," *Business and Society*, Vol. 10, No. 2 (Spring 1970), pp. 30–36.

The ego. The organism, in order to cope with reality, needs a mechanism other than the id to harmonize his behavior and personality. This psychological subsystem Freud called the ego. The ego in the well-adjusted personality acts very much like a thermostat or any other servomechanism. It enables the personality to maintain some sort of equilibrium between its external environment and the impulsiveness of the id. The ego performs the executive functions of personality, especially those functions relating to goal determination, review, and evaluation of alternatives and decision making.

Whereas the id impulsively pursues the pleasure principle, the ego is governed by the reality principle. The goal or objective of the reality principle is to delay the discharge of energy until the actual or true object that will satisfy the need has been discovered and produced.

The superego. The third dimension of personality, according to Freud, is the superego, and its role is that of serving as the moral and judicial branch of personality. The superego represents the ideal rather than the real, and the goal of the superego is to strive for perfection rather than pleasure or reality. The superego becomes the person's moral code, which develops out of the ego as a result of the child's assimilation of his parents' standards regarding what is good and virtuous and what is bad and sinful.

The basic components of the superego are the ego ideal and the conscience. The ego ideal is analogous to the child's conception of what his parents consider to be morally good. Conscience, on the other hand, is analogous to the child's conception of what his parents feel is morally bad, and these notions are established through experiences with punishments.

Having discussed the structure and function of the personality in terms of Freud's division of the psyche into the id, the ego, and the superego, we now direct our attention to some other dimensions of Freud's dynamic psychology.

Freudian pansexualism. Freud believed that the basic energizing forces affecting man's behavior were largely unconscious. He was obsessed with the idea of psychology as a deterministic science; that is, he believed that all events are the inevitable result of antecedent conditions and that the human being, in apparent acts of choice, is the mechanical expression of his heredity and his past environment.

Freud was somewhat narrow-minded about man's nature. He was a pansexualist who thought that man's life centered around his basic desire for sexual gratification. He reasoned that society's taboos on free and unlimited sexual gratification, as they affected the superego, and the superego's punishment of the ego for curbing these desires resulted in most of man's frustrations and anxieties and hence much of his behavior.[30]

---

[30] For a concise and literate treatment of Freudian psychology, see Calvin J. Hall, *A Primer of Freudian Psychology* (New York: New American Library, 1955).

Freud argued that the direct expression of sexually aggressive instincts is transferred into apparently nonsexual and nonaggressive forms of behavior. He believed that a person, in seeking objects, is always looking for his first love in the substitute object. Failing to find a completely satisfactory substitute, he either continues the search or reconciles himself to something that is second best. When a person accepts a substitute, he is said to be compensating for the original goal object.

Thus, the Freudian takes sex as the single, foremost, and dominant derivative of the human behavior equation. Many marketers have adopted Freudian ideas and assumptions and incorporated them into programs and strategies for consumers. The essential underlying assumption of such programs or strategies is that customer behavior is triggered by subconscious motivations stemming from heavily laden sexual overtones. As a result it has been suggested from one time or another that:

"A man buys a convertible as a substitute mistress."

"A woman is very serious when she bakes a cake because unconsciously she is going through the symbolic act of giving birth."

"Many people reject prunes because they remind them of death."

"Men who wear suspenders are reacting to an unresolved castration complex."[31]

But what of the predictive powers of these generalizations? Does this mean that these attitudes characterize all consumers in regard to these products? The answer is an emphatic No! Even Freud did not believe his psychology to be a predictive science. It could only be what he considered a postdictive science in the sense that it can look back and perhaps unearth the causes that produced a given result. Freud commented on this problem by stating:

If we proceed the reverse way, if we start from the premises inferred from the analysis and try to follow these up to the final result, then we no longer get the impression of an inevitable sequence of events which could otherwise not be determined. We notice at once that there might have been another result, and that we might have been just as well able to understand and explain the latter. The synthesis is thus not so satisfactory as the analysis; in other words, from a knowledge of the premise we could not have foretold the nature of the result.[32]

This is a critically important conclusion and one that marketers and consumer psychologists had best recognize. It means, of course,

---

[31] For a look at other Freudian-based conclusions regarding consumer behavior, see Ernest Dichter, *Handbook of Consumer Motivations* (New York: McGraw-Hill Book Company, 1964).

[32] Sigmund Freud, "The Psychoanalysis of a Case of Homosexuality in a Woman," in *Collected Papers*, Vol. 2 (London: The International Psychoanalytical Press, 1933), p. 226.

that it is doubtful at best if we can generalize about overall consumer behavior on the basis of the premises and findings of Freudian investigation and analysis. Furthermore, as we shall learn, many of the basic premises of Freudian psychology are open to serious question.

HOLISTIC PSYCHOLOGY

To repeat, the reductive-functional psychologist assumes that behavior is reducible to the terms of physiology and physics, and he underscores the deterministic and cause-effect basis of behavioral analysis. On the other hand, the holist assumes that behavior is cohesive, organized, conceptual, and nonreducible in nature and therefore must be examined and analyzed as an integrated totality. Emphasis on cause and effect stresses the connections between conditions internal and external to the individual and the broad effect of these conditions on the general state of the organism.

The holistic approach in psychology does not, therefore, deny the validity of the reductive-functionalist approach based upon conditioning, the formulation of drives, and the analysis of distinct mechanisms on a physiological basis. Instead, holistic psychology holds that one can never explain or understand any living, acting human being on that basis. The holists argue that the harm arises when the image of man, the presuppositions that we make about man himself, focuses exclusively upon such features. The holists are adverse to too great an abstracting: the more accurately and completely one can describe a given mechanism, the more likely, they argue, one is to lose the significance of the living organism. The reductive-functionalist would say the person has meaning in terms of the psychological mechanism (drive, instinct, reflex), whereas the holist would argue that the mechanism (drive, instinct, reflex) has meaning solely in relationship to the person.[33]

The thrust of holistic inquiry and analysis is that it seeks to understand the nature of the man who does the experiencing and to whom the experiences occur.

Holistic psychology is concerned with the experimental study of human beings in their social and cultural settings. Through training and experience, the holistic psychologist is encouraged to raise his sights from strict psychological concerns and to include in his perspective the larger matrix of the social world—a world that imprints its inhabitants with patterns of behavior, attitudes, group norms, and cultural and social values—experiences that affect the behavior of individuals and influence their modes of interacting. Such a broadened perspective means that the holistic psychologist comes to realize that psychological processes must be examined in the light of the host of social influences that contribute to the development and ultimate style

---

[33] For a more complex treatment, see Karl Jaspers, *Way to Wisdom: An Introduction to Philosophy* (New Haven, Conn.: Yale University Press, 1966). See especially Appendix I, p. 147.

of human personalities. Because the holist psychologist is as interested in social and cultural settings for behavior as in individual organisms, he conducts his experiments with both social context and individual in mind.[34]

Finally, *holistic psychology* is in many respects a term that demarcates an attitude, an approach to the study of human beings, rather than a special group or school. It is doubtful whether it makes sense to speak of a holistic psychology in contradistinction to other schools. It should be pointed out that it is not so much a system of analysis as an attitude or point of view toward analysis and experimentation, not a set of new techniques so much as it is a concern with the understanding of the structure of the human being and his experience that must underlie all techniques. It is an endeavor to clear our minds of the mechanistic presuppositions that so often cause us to see, in the subject of our investigation, only our own theories or the dogmas of our own systems —the effort to experience instead the phenomenon in its full reality as it presents itself. Such is the central tenet of holistic psychology.[35]

GESTALT PSYCHOLOGY. Gestalt psychology is one of the foremost and earliest schools of holistic psychology. Gestaltists are concerned with the organization of mental processes. *Gestalt* is a German word (pronounced guh-SHTAHLT) that means "pattern" or "form."

Max Wertheimer founded Gestaltism in Germany in the early 1900s. In the early 1930s, Wertheimer and several of his associates— Wolfgang Kohler, Kurt Koffka, and Kurt Lewin—moved to the United States, where they promoted and led the Gestalt movement.

Gestalt psychologists believe that human beings tend to perceive organized patterns, not single individual parts that are merely added up. Furthermore, they posit that the relationship between different parts of a stimulus, which we perceive as a whole or a pattern, gives us our meaning. Gestalt psychology emphasizes the role of social perception—i.e., the way in which humans organize, interpret, and order sensory stimulation—as an important determinant of behavior. Koffka set the tone for what has been one of the principal emphases of Gestalt, namely, that the interaction among many psychological elements is of central importance in the understanding of human activity.[36] Thus the task of Gestalt psychology is to discover the interactional units or wholes composed of separate facts that would constitute the full explanation of any phenomenon. Presumably then, Gestalt psychology attempts to

[34] William W. Lambert and Wallace E. Lambert, *Social Psychology* (Englewood Cliffs, N.J.: Prentice-Hall, Inc., 1964). See Chapter 1, especially pp. 1–3.

[35] A. W. Combs and D. Snygg, *Individual Behavior: A Perceptual Approach to Behavior*, rev. ed. (New York: Harper and Row, Publishers, 1959). See pp. 20–28.

[36] K. Koffka, *Principles of Gestalt Psychology* (New York: Harcourt Brace Jovanovich, Inc., 1935).

fuse science and life the way they are not fused in physics, mathematics, or other "hard" scientific disciplines.

The Gestalt psychologist is interested in behavior but not in the same way as other psychologists, especially reductive-functionalists. As we have seen, the ultimate solution for the behaviorist or the stimulus-response psychologist lies in the eventual reduction of behavioral terms to those of physiology and related disciplines. For the Gestalt psychologist, the observed behavioral event is the unit of study itself. He sees such a behavioral event as what he calls a molar unit. It is not necessarily reducible to other terms for its full explanation.

In line with this approach to psychology, studies using the Gestalt method or point of view begin with a description of the whole situation —the field—and proceed to a detailed analysis of various aspects of the situation: "At no time are aspects of a field viewed as isolated elements."[37] This idea of wholeness pervades all the holistic psychologies, including field, cognitive, and Gestalt theories. Edna Heidbreder states that:

> Gestalt psychology attempts to get back to naive perception, to immediate experience undebauched by learning; and it insists that it find there not assemblages of elements, but unified wholes.[38]

Gestalt psychology begins and ends with molar behavior. And because it is a nonreductive approach to understanding human activity, the more complex types of human activity, such as reasoning, loving, attitude formation, and decision making, are more easily incorporated within its scope than within the framework and methodology of reductive-functional psychology.

The Gestalt approach to psychology is further characterized in terms of its consideration of what is called the behavioral environment and what later came to be called the psychological field. The behavioral environment is the prevalent condition for the organism at the time some behavior takes place. The behavioral environment includes geographical as well as psychological space, and the Gestaltist argues that aspects of the human mind not only mediate between the external stimulus conditions of the environment and behavior but also shape much, if not all, of what we perceive as the nature of the basic, uncontaminated geographical environment.

Gestalt psychology further proposes that group behavior of human beings involves reaction patterns that are specific only to group situations. These patterns constitute a group's Gestalt; that is, the various members are interdependent, and they should be analyzed as such. The cohesion of the group is the same as the strength of its Gestalt

---

[37] Morris L. Bigge and Maurice P. Hunt, *Psychological Foundations of Education* (New York: Harper and Row, Publishers, 1962), p. 348.

[38] Edna Heidbreder, *Seven Psychologies* (New York: The Century Company, 1933), p. 331.

character. The group is said to follow Gestalt principles of individual behavior, and the sociological consequences of this behavior can be explained by or reduced to these principles of individual behavior. Therefore an interactive, interpersonal, and interdependent field of behavior is established. The individual operating within the group situation is preserved as an autonomously functioning unit, but his psychological or behavioral field is influenced by the sociological group situation.[39]

There have been other notable contributors to Gestalt and other aspects of holistic psychology. Kurt Lewin did much to pioneer what has become a separate science of interpersonal relations, or social psychology.[40] The most lasting and perhaps fundamental of Lewin's concepts is that of the life space or psychological field. The life space, according to Lewin, affects all aspects of behavior—loving, thinking, analyzing, buying, consuming. The life space consists of a matrix of facts, attitudes, and cognitions that exist psychologically for each and every individual at some particular point in existence. The psychological field as viewed by Lewin is the totality of the individual's world as he himself perceives it. Thus, it is the individual's perception of himself in his environment.[41]

Two other holistic psychologists are David Krech and R. S. Crutchfield, whose major effort to organize and explain a vast body of socio-psychological phenomena by a series of clearly stated principles has done much to integrate and consolidate social behavior phenomena into a meaningful holistic framework.[42] Their work has focused upon man as a social being, and they submit that psychologists must develop such a point of view if they are to understand him at all. Their position follows from the field position that behavior is best understood when the tensions, stresses, anxieties, motives, and so on, operating on the individual at a particular time are discovered.

The work of S. E. Asch, whose series of now famous experiments on the influence of social pressure on conformity of judgments in a group situation, has convincingly demonstrated the holistic nature of many behavioral phenomena.[43] T. M. Newcomb, whose work was with the concept of attitude, is another noteworthy contributor to holistic

[39] Wolfgang Kohler, "Gestalt Psychology Today," in *Documents of Gestalt Psychology*, Mary Henle, ed. (Berkeley, Calif.: University of California Press, 1961).

[40] Kurt Lewin, *A Dynamic Theory of Personality* (New York: McGraw-Hill Book Company, 1935).

[41] Harold H. Kassarjian, "Consumer Behavior: A Field Theoretical Approach," in *Marketing and the New Science of Planning*, Robert L. King, ed., (Chicago: American Marketing Association, 1968), pp. 285–289.

[42] D. Krech and R. S. Crutchfield, *Theory and Problems of Social Psychology* (New York: McGraw-Hill Book Company, 1948).

[43] S. E. Asch, *Social Psychology* (Englewood Cliffs, N.J.: Prentice-Hall, Inc., 1952).

psychology.[44] Newcomb was convinced that attitudes played an important role in the understanding of social behavior inasmuch as they predisposed the individual to act, to think, and to perceive under particular kinds of psychological field conditions. Newcomb's work laid the basic groundwork for considerable research involving holistic systems that focused upon communication concepts and networks.

From Essence to Existence

In the preceding pages we have viewed some rather extreme variations in the interpretations of man's behavior. Throughout history, mankind has been assumed to be perfectly rational or totally irrational; largely kind or innately cruel; mean and aggressive or basically loving, cooperative, and benign; a mechanistic robot or a sensory-data-gathering and information-processing superman. What is intriguing about these contrasting images of man is that each was put forth by profound and reasonable people as sufficient explanation of man's complex nature or essence. It is important to recognize that one's presuppositions always limit and constrict what one sees in a problem, experiment, or phenomenon. Hence, the reductive-functional school of psychology is largely based upon an essence philosophy; that is, the central concept is that there is some basic mainspring or fundamental cause (essence) of human behavior. In effect, what this means is that the reductive-functionalist takes his presuppositions about man's essence and then generalizes about man's behavior or existence, and this generalization, in light of current holistic thinking, is wrong and leads to what may be very specious results.[45] The philosophy of existentialism represents much of this new thinking of holistic psychology.[46] Probably the foremost argument of existentialism is that a man's existence comes before his essence. A man can be nothing but what he is. His behavior is not the result of his inner essence—his drives, his instincts, and his reflexes —or what he is; rather he is what he is as a result of how he behaves or exists. Stated another way, man makes his own nature or essence out of his existence. There are several pivotal concepts in existential philosophy and psychology. Let us discuss these briefly and then examine how these concepts might affect and shape our attitudes regarding consumer behavior in the marketplace.

One of the key concepts of existentialism is ontological. Man *is*. Therefore this is the singular and foremost fact regarding man.

[44] T. M. Newcomb, *Social Psychology* (New York: Holt, Rinehart & Winston, Inc., 1950).

[45] The material here has been previously published by the author. See Rom J. Markin, "Consumer Motivation and Behavior: Essence vs. Existence," *Business and Society*, Vol. 10, No. 2 (Spring 1970), pp. 30–36.

[46] There are several good primers on existential philosophy that are not beyond the comprehension of any interested reader. See, for example, William Barrett, *Irrational Man* (Garden City, N.Y.: Doubleday & Company, Inc., 1958); and Marjorie Green, *Introduction to Existentialism* (Chicago, Ill.: Phoenix Books, University of Chicago Press, 1948).

BEING AND BECOMING. Man *is,* but he is also becoming. Becoming is a process of growth and development. Man is in the process of becoming someone.

DASEIN. Man exists in an interdependent state with his environment. Thus, his behavior is holistic and must be analyzed as a molar unit of activity. *Dasein* means "being there" or "existence" in German. To understand man's behavior you must understand his world or *dasein.* A Gestaltist would call *dasein* the *life space,* and the marketing concept that appears closely analogous to *dasein* is that of *life style.*

EITHER/OR DECISIONS. In his efforts to become, man makes decisions. Man *is* his decisions and his decisions constitute the critical turning points in his life.

FREE CHOICE. Man can choose. He can or he cannot. He is aware of his fate and can choose what is to be his own reaction to it. He exercises choice as a result of his own cognitive processes and not because of unseen, unconscious, deterministic forces.

NON BEING. Non being is a situation in which one ceases to become. It results when man refuses to exercise his will.

ANXIETY AND GUILT. The fact that man has freedom of choice and could conceivably, as a result of wrong decisions, impair his possibility of becoming makes him anxious. Some individuals have denied their possibility of becoming or the fulfillment of their potentialities, and therefore their anxiety has been replaced by guilt.

The ideas of existentialism are today having a profound effect on man's thinking and presuppositions about man. Thus, from holistic and existential thinking is emerging a body of thought, a discipline, concerned with the causes and ramifications of human behavior.

Existential Concepts of Motivation and Behavior

Reductive-functional psychologists such as Freud reduced all motives to basic drives, whereas the holists, especially the existentialists, believe in the interactive and interdependent nature of drive states. Whereas Freud believed that most behavior was sexually motivated and resulted in regressive manifestations, the principal energizing force of human behavior from the point of view of existentialism is a single unifying force; a striving for movement or a striving from a perceived negative condition toward a positive condition; from a feeling of inferiority to superiority, perfection, totality. In relationship to the ceaseless striving onward, or becoming, another important aspect of existential psychology is that the individual receives his specific direction from an individually unique goal or self-idea, which, though influenced by biological and environmental factors, is ultimately the creation of the individual. This concept is closely related to the idea of self-image.[47] Thus, our self-image is affected by our goals and our goal attainment is, to a degree, affected by our self-image.

The goal-striving behavior of a subject becomes the key to understanding that individual. For the investigator, such behavior is a working hypothesis. Consequently, all the psychological processes of the individual form a self-consistent organization toward goal achievement much like a play, constructed from the beginning with the finale in view. This self-consistent personality structure is what Adler called the style of life.[48] This is the consistent movement of the individual toward his goal. In effect, what all this means is that we must know more about man's existence. If we know the characteristics of his life style— that is, the way he exists, his yearnings and strivings, his goals, and the accomplishments or conquests he wishes to achieve—then we may begin to learn something about the nature of man's motivation and behavior.

Stemming from the existential point of view is a different set of axioms regarding behavior. Man does not avoid tensions, or necessarily wish to reduce them, as long as they remain balanced and consistent with his life style. Man is a tension manager who seeks out tensions and excitements via his process of becoming. He looks for means, in his search for fictional goals and problem solving, of enhancing his experiences and of adding to his life's glamour and excitement. He wishes to strive and become, and the impediments that get between him and his goals cause him anxiety. Motivation, therefore, can be viewed in the light of growth motives that call for the maintenance of tension or excitement in the interest of distant and often unattainable goals.

THE EXISTENTIAL CONSUMER

Are consumers existential? Do existentialism and its concepts shed any light or offer any insight to help explain, predict, alter, or influence consumer behavior? The answer would appear to be affirmative. The existential concepts of motivation and behavior certainly appear more logical, and thus more realistic, than does the reductive-functionalist Freudian model that centers on hidden motives and semiconscious or unconscious "mechanisms." Yet customer behavior is too often analyzed around Freudian or neo-Freudian concepts.

Existential psychology, on the other hand, is concerned with the individualizing manner, which places special emphasis on the life-style concept. This really makes existential psychology something of an ideographic science. The term *ideographic* pertains to laws that are particular to the individual case, whereas *nomothetic* formulations are laws of general validity. Existential psychology has also developed some important *nomothetic* principles: the concept of compensation, the

[47] See C. G. Jung, *The Undiscovered Self* (Boston: Little, Brown and Company, 1957).

[48] Heinz and Rowena Ansbacher, eds., *The Individual Psychology of Alfred Adler* (New York: Harper and Row, Publishers, 1956).

striving for superiority or becoming, the idea of social interest, and most importantly, the role of stress and anxiety in decision making or choice. However, the important point to recognize is that the emphasis rests, in the final analysis, on the ideographic aspects such as style of life, the opinion of self or the self-idea, and the individual goal.

What nomothetic generalizations might then be postulated regarding consumer behavior from the ideographic principles derived from studying existentialism? The answer is several. First of all, our model of consumer behavior would have as its central hypothesis that consumer behavior is problem-solving behavior. The problem solving is inextricably bound up with and a part of the individual's life style or *dasein. Therefore, the purchasing and acquisition of goods are important means in the individual's becoming process.*

In the affluent United States, some portion of consumer behavior can be characterized as existential or self-actualizing. In existential terminology this is called *propriate striving.*[49] The proprium is, in effect, the individual's personality, but more specifically, it is those aspects of personality that create inward unity. Thus, propriate striving, from the standpoint of consumer behavior, is that prepurchase, purchase, and postpurchase behavior on the part of the individual that attempts to unify and integrate the purchase with his own life style. Anxiety often surrounds propriate-striving purchase behavior. This anxiety arises because of man's knowledge that he may fail and attain less than that for which he strives. *In effect, the more anxious the consumer is about a given purchase, the greater the perceived risk surrounding the purchase.*[50] If a consumer buys a product and later has doubts as to how well, in light of alternative products or alternative goals, this product serves his concept of self or propriate striving, then the individual is likely to have guilt. This postdecision purchase phenomenon has been discussed before. According to Leon Festinger, "dissonance" occurs if, after a decision, a person is faced with doubt that he made the right choice.[51] If the consumer has doubts about his choice, and inasmuch as these doubts manifest themselves as ontological guilt resulting from his failure to achieve what he perceived or thought he should, then dissonance arises and we have now something that has been lacking before, an explanation for it—albeit an existential explanation.

In summary, consumer behavior might very well be viewed within the framework of heuristic problem-solving. The consumer's behavior is goal directed and, therefore, purposive. His goal is often nonspecific —he is open to recommendation and suggestion—thus learning and communication are important to the consumer in his propriate-striving

---

[49] Gordon W. Allport, *Becoming: Basic Considerations for a Psychology of Personality* (New Haven, Conn.: Yale University Press, 1955), pp. 41–58.

[50] The concept of perceived risk and consumer decision making is explored at great length in Chapter 18, p. 521.

[51] Leon Festinger, *A Theory of Cognitive Dissonance* (Evanston, Ill.: Row, Peterson and Company, 1957), pp. 26–32.

consumer behavior. The consumer cannot be controlled or manipulated in any mechanistic sense. Consumer behavior is largely directed along the lines of search and discovery; therefore he develops certain rules of thumb that he uses as guidelines to shape his behavior. The existential consumer learns to rely on dependable modes of reducing tensions, but he is constantly sloughing off old habits and taking risks in searching out new means of problem solving and becoming.

The existential consumer looks for principles or devices that contribute to the reduction of tension in the search for a solution. He is considerably more of a satisficer than a maximizer. He looks for solutions that are satisfactory and consistent with his cognitive structure. He is a decision maker under conditions of uncertainty. In looking for satisfactory solutions, he thus attempts to unify and bring into balance the variables of his decision model.

The existential consumer's behavior is manifesting itself in today's marketplace in many important ways, and it would appear that the image of the existential consumer and the associated rationale regarding consumer motivation and behavior ought to bear directly on our research and practice in marketing.

In the next chapter we shall have a look at how our images, perspectives, and suppositions about human behavior become incorporated into so-called models of consumer behavior.

Questions for Study, Reflection, and Review

1 Describe the managerial responsibilities of a marketing manager and the assumptions upon which his strategy formulation is based.

2 Describe how the dynamic nature of the consumer affects his problem-solving behavior.

3 Discuss the relationship between consumer behavior and its social setting.

4 Discuss the concept of images and how they affect the way we view consumer behavior.

5 Discuss the major shortcomings of the image of economic man as a perspective for consumer behavior.

6 Compare and contrast the reductive-functionalist view of psychology and the holistic view of psychology.

7 Explain the four fundamental concepts upon which the Pavlovian view of man is predicated.

8 Comment on the nature of marketing that is based upon Freud's pansexualism.

9 Discuss the basic principles of Gestalt psychology.

10 Describe the fundamental concepts upon which existentialism is based.

4

Models of
Consumer
Behavior

Much of what we have said thus far has simply been a prologue for those ideas and concepts that are to be presented in this and subsequent chapters. For example, Chapter 1 developed and expounded on the relationship between marketing theory and strategy and consumer behavior. Chapter 2 treated the phenomenon of consumerism as a form of militant consumer behavior and thus dramatically emphasized the need for marketers to take heed of the clarion calls of dissatisfied and disgruntled consumers. Chapter 3 dealt with a general overview of consumer behavior but focused intently on the concept of image, emphasizing the important point that our images of man, whether they be economic, sociological, psychological, or otherwise, are likely to become imprinted as a part of our overall cognitive structures. These images of man are, therefore, most likely to become the foundation upon which our theories, and what we shall call in this chapter our models, of consumer behavior are built.

Thus, in this chapter our attention is turned to the examination of various alternative models of consumer behavior. We shall be concerned with both the structure and the function of these models, and furthermore, we shall be concerned with basic images or perceptual concepts around which they are constructed. We shall explore briefly such concepts as the meaning of cause and effect, the nature and implication of determinism, and the definition of rationality and rational consumer behavior. And finally, we shall commit ourselves to some formal explanation and definition of the term *consumer behavior*.

The Nature and Use of Models

Model is a word of great contemporary popularity. It is fashionable today whether in engineering or consumer behavior to talk about models or to talk about building a model of some process or structure. Models are abstractions of reality that offer us a means of dealing with and manipulating complex processes in simple ways. Models are images or reproductions of something, often on a smaller scale or in a less complex form. We are all familiar with certain kinds of models—the scale-model airplane or automobile, the blueprint or scale mockup of a model city. There are other kinds of concepts that can be called models. The profit-and-loss statement and the financial balance sheet are kinds of models. There are also verbal models, for example:

Consumption is a function of income.

And there are quantitative models, for example:

$$E = \frac{\dfrac{\Delta q}{q}}{\dfrac{-\Delta p}{p}}$$

which many will recognize as the formula for measuring price elasticity of demand. Even such a phenomenon as a test market is, broadly conceived, a model.

Thus, "A model can be defined as a representation of reality that attempts to explain the behavior of some aspect of it."[1]

Roughly speaking, models are theories or theoretical constructs. The term *model* is much more popular today than the term *theory*, which has come to connote all too frequently things that are fuzzy, ambiguous, and often impractical. Thus the word *model* is frequently used synonymously with *theory* on the assumption that models are practical, realistic, and meaningful, and theory is not.[2] On the contrary, however, we cannot build models of anything unless they are built around solid, sound, and meaningful principles and theory. If our theories won't hold water, our models aren't likely to be successful either.

[1] David W. Miller and Martin K. Starr, *Executive Decisions and Operations Research* (Englewood Cliffs, N.J.: Prentice-Hall, Inc., 1960), p. 115.

[2] Peter Langhoff, "The Setting: Some Non-metric Observations" in *Models, Measurement and Marketing*, Peter Langhoff, ed. (Englewood Cliffs, N.J.: Prentice-Hall, Inc., 1965), p. 13.

WHAT MODELS DO

Models, then, can be either simple or complex structures, but they invariably have one central purpose and that is to help man think rationally.[3] They do this by enabling him to take a complex process or phenomenon, in itself too large for analysis or manipulation, and to reduce it to what the analysts believe to be a series of meaningful variables. Most often the analysts divide these variables into at least two categories, independent and dependent variables. The independent variables are those that affect, influence, or bring about change in the dependent variables.

What this really amounts to is a confession of sorts, namely, that what we previously called images of man and theories of consumer behavior are nothing more than models of man and models of consumer behavior. Economic man, sociological man, and psychological man are really just models of behavior whose basic independent variables are respectively economic, sociological, and psychological.

In addition to generally helping man think more rationally about complex phenomena such as consumer behavior, models serve a variety of particular purposes. First of all, a model, because it is often an abbreviated version of a larger statement or configuration, can be an important tool for conveying a vast amount of information. Much information can, therefore, be conveyed with a high degree of both precision and efficiency. Second, models permit us to observe and measure a whole host of characteristics, and through continued observation and measurement, the hallmark of science itself, we gain a deeper and fuller understanding of our subject. Third, the use of models permits us to determine which variables in our model are really the important ones, because the construction of a model is very often followed by testing to verify its relationship to the world. In this respect, models are tantamount to theory in that they permit us to describe, explain, and predict the behavior of complex phenomena. Finally, model building and testing ultimately lead us to the point where we gain insight not only into the nature of the variables involved but into their complex interactions.

All marketers have models of consumer behavior. Most of these "models" are only vague, implicit, and intuitive impressions about what makes customers "tick." The models that are needed, however, and that are explored in this chapter, are explicit, complex, schematic, and verbal statements relating to a set of variables that are offered as explanations and descriptions of consumer behavior as a sequence or series of decision processes. Before introducing and discussing these models, however, we shall first explore some basic ideas upon which our understanding and building of models must be predicated.

[3] C. West Churchman, "Reliability of Models in the Social Sciences," *Models, Measurement and Marketing*, Peter Langhoff, ed. (Englewood Cliffs, N.J.: Prentice-Hall, Inc., 1965), p. 24.

Determinism and Causality

Almost all models of consumer behavior are models that, in effect, are input-output configurations, and they assume certain kinds of causality or determinism. Thus a simple model of consumer behavior might look som..thing like the following:

$C_B = f(P, E)$ where:
C_B = consumer behavior
f = sign that denotes function
P = personality
E = environment

Note that this is not an equation and it does not state precise relationships. It is instead a rather innocuous statement that says: Consumer behavior is a function of the personality of the individual in relationship with his environmental circumstances. The statement leaves more to the imagination than is stated explicitly. It does not specifically state that consumer behavior is caused by personality and environment, yet there is a strong implication that this is the case. In the physical sciences such direct cause and effect relationships are often noted. But in the social and behavioral sciences, the object usually under investigation is the human being. Because man is subject to such a host of influences, all working concomitantly, and because it is so difficult to isolate or hold constant certain variables while others are allowed to continue to exert their influence, such direct cause and effect relationships are not often discovered.

Our interest in cause and effect stems from the very essence of the scientific method. Learned men from the beginning of history have sought the meaning of cause and effect relationships, and through time our beliefs and attitudes regarding cause and effect have undergone considerable change. Galileo believed that the presence of a cause was always followed by its effect, and thus his view of causality was that of necessary production.[4] And when the cause is removed, the effect disappears. This has been and continues to be a widely held view regarding cause and effect.[5]

Man's near-obsession with following a line of reasoning based upon cause-effect relationships stems at least in part from his beliefs regarding determinism. Determinism is the doctrine that all events are the inevitable result of antecedent conditions and, in the case of human behavior, that the human being, in acts of apparent choice, is the mechanical expression of his heredity and his past environment. Most modern behavioral and social scientists reject at least the latter part of

[4] Galileo, *Dialogo sopra i due massimi sistemi del mondo In Opere*, Vol. 7 (Florence: Edizione Nazionale 1890–1909).

[5] The points of view regarding cause and effect discussed here are contained in a much more elaborate treatment in Robert E. Lana, *Assumptions of Social Psychology* (New York: Appleton-Century-Crofts, 1969), pp. 6–42.

this statement. However, as scientists, we must all come to grips with the elementary issue surrounding determinism, namely, that *every event has a cause*. Such a dictum holds that nothing may arise from nothing or pass into nothing and that nothing occurs in an irregular, lawless manner: "Everything is determined in accordance with laws by something else."[6] These laws, however, may not be, and in the case of human beings are not likely to be, the same "laws" that govern the planets or the soap bubble.

In the behavioral sciences, at least, the more modern and widely held view concerning cause and effect is that espoused by Braithwaite. Essentially, he says that to want to do something is associated with cause and the something done, with effect.[7]

Such a viewpoint frees man forever from the bogey of determinism. Although it may be true that "every event has a cause," the *causes* that we acknowledge as those moving a billiard ball are not the same as the *reasons* attributed to human behavior in apparent acts of choice. The explanation is put quite well as follows:[8]

> There are human actions whose explanations require citing a reason. Now if we say of such actions that they too are covered by the dictum "Every event has a cause," we must be very careful to notice what the "cause" means here. It means that someone had a reason for what he did, and thus it is he who is responsible for his action. But if it is he who is responsible, then he was not made to act as he did by an external force as the determinist claims.

Goal-Oriented Behavior

Hopefully, our exercise has led to an important point of view, namely, that cause and effect in consumer behavior will be explored along the lines suggested by Braithwaite, that a consumer's goals constitute sufficient *cause* for his actions and behavior and that such actions and behavior become the *effects* of his causes. Mittelstaedt has observed that the cause of behavior can be viewed as preceding the event, which is a deterministic position, or following it, in which case the behavior is goal seeking.[9]

Such an assertion is not necessarily a reflection of the modern view regarding determinism but is, instead, more closely aligned to the idea of determinism as viewed by Galileo, namely, that the presence

[6] M. Bunge, *Causality* (Cambridge, Mass.: Harvard University Press, 1959), p. 26.

[7] R. B. Braithwaite, *Scientific Exploration* (New York: Harper and Row, Publishers, 1960), p. 339.

[8] Elmer Sprague, *What Is Philosophy?* (New York: Oxford University Press, 1961), p. 92.

[9] Robert A. Mittelstaedt, "Criteria for a Theory of Consumer Behavior," in *Consumer Behavior: Contemporary Research in Action*, Robert J. Hollaway, Robert A. Mittelstaedt, and M. Venkatesan, eds. (Boston: Houghton Mifflin Company, 1971), p. 11.

of a cause is always followed by an effect and thus that causality means "necessary production." This point of view is more in keeping with the contemporary point of view regarding causality. A deterministic cause is any event that is necessary and sufficient for the subsequent occurrence of another event. On the other hand, a probabilistic cause is defined as any event that is necessary but not sufficient for the subsequent occurrence of another event.[10]

Thus, relationships among variables in consumer behavior models can be either deterministic or probabilistic and, furthermore, the relationship need not necessarily imply causality. Very few relationships in marketing are of one-way causality. Instead, there is usually a two-way causality. For example, in the immediate short run many relationships normally are one-way causalities. However, in the longer run, because of feedback, the relationships typically evolve into at least two-way causality.

Goal-seeking activity is the principal subject of this work. The consumer seeks goals. As a matter of fact, he has a hierarchy of goals that constitute the *reasons* or *causes* for his behavior. His goal-striving behavior is sociopsychological. Man is an energy system comprised of many dimensions, physical and psychical. His goals are the product of his personality, his life style, his self-image, and his individual and unique striving. Too, his goals are, in part, the product of his culturally determined existence. His goals are his rationally sought objectives. Thus, behavior is caused. The consumer's goals are necessary and sufficient *cause* for behaving. And, further, behavior, the attainment of goals, leads to the removal of causes and motivations.

THE MEANING OF RATIONALITY

There is one more major concept to be explored before we proceed further, and that is: What do we mean by rational behavior? Do consumers act rationally? We often hear people say that consumers are fickle and that many of their decisions are made emotionally or irrationally. Is such the case? Perhaps! But perhaps our difficulty in answering these questions lies more in our lack of understanding of the terms than in the real difficulty of the question. We can probably thank the economists for at least a part of our difficulty, for they have traditionally posited a situation wherein man needed to be omniscient—to have "perfect knowledge"—in order to make rational choices. We all know that no man has perfect knowledge. This has led some to argue that if perfect rationality is a function of perfect knowledge, then imperfect knowledge must mean imperfect rationality, or even irrationality.

Models of rationality are usually built upon a system of rather stringent propositions such as:

[10] The definitions of deterministic causation and probabilistic causation follow those in Russell Ackoff, et al., *Scientific Method: Optimizing Applied Research Decisions* (New York: John Wiley & Sons, Inc., 1962), Chapter 1.

1. Goals and objectives must be known.
2. There must be a set of alternatives from which to choose.
3. The effect of each alternative on the decision maker's degree of goal attainment must be discernible.
4. There is a payoff representing the utility to the decision maker of each alternative.
5. Knowledge about the prevailing state of nature or information as to what will be the effect of choosing either alternative must be available.[11]

Now it is rather evident that such a decision-making situation as the one described in this list would be quite rare. The decision maker's knowledge, which may not be complete, would indeed be clear and voluminous. His preferences would be well ordered and stable and he would be possessed with an Olympian calculating skill. As a theoretical model of total and perfect rationality, such a set of axioms is indeed desirable. But they are not necessary for *rationality* to prevail.

Rational behavior on the part of consumers does not mean the fulfillment of all of the conditions just described. Consumers do not necessarily seek an optimum choice in the realistic decision problems facing them. They seek, instead, satisfactory solutions to their problems, given limited time, money, and energy. They often recognize that the best decision at one point of time may not be the best at a later date. Consumers also recognize that, given any goal that necessitates a decision, they have an enormous range of choices. An examination of all possible choices would simply be too inefficient. Finally, there are too many factors and conditions that lie outside the control of the consumer decision-maker that are likely to affect the outcome of his decisions.[12] Thus, the consumer is rational and his rationality is characterized as bounded rationality.[13] According to this principle, human beings seldom make a concerted effort to find the best action in a decision problem. Instead, they perceive and select a number of possible outcomes from the available strategies that in light of their own goals and decision criteria, are good enough. In other words, human beings act like human beings and not like superhuman, omniscient, all-powerful organisms created by a "super science" like economics. To paraphrase John Maurice Clark, people simply don't have such an irrational passion for dispassionate rationality.

Thus, rational consumers are all those who look for principles or devices that contribute to the reduction of the average search time for problem solutions. Such consumers are *satisficers* rather than *maximiz-*

---

[11] See Herbert A. Simon, "A Behavioral Model of Rational Choice," *The Quarterly Journal of Economics,* Vol. 69 (February 1955).

[12] George Katona, "Rational Behavior and Economic Behavior," *Psychological Review,* Vol. 60 (1953), pp. 307–318.

[13] *Bounded rationality* is a term popularized by Herbert A. Simon. See James G. March and Herbert A. Simon, *Organizations* (New York: John Wiley & Sons, Inc., 1958).

ers. They look for solutions that are satisfactory and consistent with their cognitive structures and life styles.[14] Maximization is out of the question, because the consumer "knows" he does not have all the relevant information necessary for maximization. He is a decision maker under conditions of uncertainty. Because he is looking for "satisfactory" solutions, he attempts to unify and to maintain balance among the various components of his decision model. There may be irrational consumers, but to the extent that there are, they can be found in large numbers only in the mental institutions of America.

What Is Consumer Behavior?

Before proceeding to our discussion and analysis of alternate models of consumer behavior, we must define exactly what we mean by *consumer behavior.* Not surprisingly, there is a considerable difference of opinion surrounding the meaning and use of this term. Almost every writer on the subject has his own views about what the term should mean. There are those who insist that consumer behavior is the act or set of actions that result from a decision process. There are those who look upon consumer behavior as being synonymous with consumer decision processes.

In any event, this book is about consumer behavior, and we define consumer behavior as a host of complex activities and actions, some physical and some mental. Our concern is with such consumer decision processes as the prepurchase activity of problem recognition, awareness, attention, search, and evaluation and with such final acts of choice as acceptance, rejection, or postponement. Our definition also acknowledges a concern with postpurchase phenomena, such as cognitive dissonance and all those activities related to dissonance reduction.

Furthermore, our definition suggests that we are interested not only in the objective observation that characterizes the strict behaviorist but in all subjective phenomena, such as mood, introspection, attitude, self-theory, and cognitive structures, that are likely to affect the consumer's choice of goals, decision processes, and solutions. Finally, our definition is not so restrictive as to limit our concern only to consumers: because we recognize the role of social and group interaction, we are interested in the behavior of influencers and opinion leaders.

Alternate Models of Consumer Behavior

In the following pages several models of consumer behavior are discussed and analyzed in some detail. Mostly these are comprehensive models or frameworks designed by their creators for the purpose of enabling them to think more rationally about consumer behavior

---

[14] Consistency is viewed as the key criterion for rationality by many. See C. West Churchman, *Prediction and Optimal Decision* (Englewood Cliffs, N.J.: Prentice-Hall, Inc., 1961), especially Chapter 8, "Rational Behavior," pp. 219–250.

processes, to convey information, and to observe and hypothesize about the structure and function of consumer decision processes. These models are comprehensive to the extent that each model is described and explained in considerable depth, even though the actual mechanism offered as the explanation for behavior or decision processes may be limited in scope and consist of only two or three major determinants.

In many ways the models explained here, with the exception of the author's own model presented toward the end of this chapter, are classic in the sense that they have served as standards and guides for nearly all those who aspire to "model" consumer behavior. Three major models of consumer behavior have been selected for analysis and discussion. In addition the author's own model, a somewhat different approach to model building, is presented in considerable detail. There has been a propensity in recent years to develop models of consumer behavior, an effort that no doubt reflects the practitioner's and the researcher's perennial urge to discover an all-encompassing theory of consumer behavior. Tucker continues to remind us of our search for "foundations for a theory of consumer behavior" or the golden key that would unlock all the abstruse mysteries of man in the marketplace.[15] Thus, we continue to build and shop for models because we, quite correctly, feel that there are questions that are still unanswered, hypotheses that remain to be tested, and relationships that have not yet been explored.

There are many criteria by which consumer behavior models may be analyzed and evaluated. For example, consumer behavior models may be

1. Partial-comprehensive.
2. Normative-descriptive.
3. Macro-micro.
4. Deterministic-probabilistic.
5. Static-dynamic.
6. Hypothetical-concrete.

These terms are either self-explanatory or, as in the case of deterministic versus probabilistic, have already been defined earlier in our treatment. But to illustrate, the Howard-Sheth Model, soon to be discussed, is a dynamic, descriptive, comprehensive, hypothetical, and micro model. Most of the stochastic models, such as the Markov model or the learning models, are probabilistic, partial, macro models.

In the past, several approaches have been taken in the building of consumer behavior models. One major approach in this regard considers only the consumer's overt behavior. The objective of this approach is to find the pattern and form of this behavior. In general, the models that have taken this approach are mainly stochastic models, such as the Markov analysis models, the diffusion process models, and

[15] See W. T. Tucker, *Foundations for a Theory of Consumer Behavior* (New York: Holt, Rinehart & Winston, Inc., 1967).

the learning models. It should be pointed out that models based upon this approach usually suffer certain inherent deficiencies; namely:

1. Even though they may help in predicting the consumer's behavior they do not provide any insight as to the reasons and determinants of behavior.
2. All consumers tend to be heterogeneous; these models base their assumptions on aggregate data.
3. There can be many alternative models that may describe and explain the same set of data.[16]

The second major approach taken by model builders is not only to consider the consumer's overt behavior but to relate it to some factors that affect it. This approach has attracted considerable attention in the model-building literature. Examples of such efforts relate to "heavy" versus "light" users, "buyers" versus "nonbuyers," and "brand loyalty" versus "brand switching" behavior. Given this phenomenon of buyer behavior, each model emphasizes different types of variables. Some models relate socioeconomic variables to overt consumer behavior, some relate economic planning to expectations, and a large number of models consider mostly psychological factors, such as perceptions, attitudes, and preferences.

Evidently the second approach to model building is much more informative than the first approach because it indicates the probable determinants of the behavior in addition simply to describing it.

A third major approach to model building is to consider the entire process that leads from determinants and causes to a specific behavior. The Nicosia model is one example of such an approach and the holocentric model another. The common procedure adopted in this approach is to start with a general theory or theories to describe the underlying process of the model. Then the model builder applies this general theory to the specific situations of consumer behavior and explains the typical characteristics of these situations in the light of the theory. Such models are often labeled as behavioral process models because they attempt to give a detailed picture of the behavioral process of the consumer's actions. These models, as we shall soon see, are not limited to any one group of variables or one scientific discipline; instead, they integrate ideas from several areas and allow the investigating and describing of many interacting variables.

In the immediate pages to follow, we shall examine the consumer behavior models of Andreason, Howard and Sheth, and Nicosia. Other meaningful models have also been developed, but they will not be discussed here. The models selected for our discussion are generally representative of the wider range of available models. This author's "model" of consumer behavior is presented at the end of the chapter.

---

[16] For a more detailed discussion, see Donald G. Morrison, "Testing Brand-Switching Models," *Journal of Marketing Research,* Vol. 111 (November 1966), p. 401.

THE ANDREASON MODEL

Alan R. Andreason has built a general model of consumer behavior that focuses essentially on the role of attitude formation and change given the capacity and inclination for information processing on the part of consumers.[17] The central idea of the Andreason model is that consumers formulate attitudes about products and that these attitudes then predispose consumers favorably or unfavorably toward products in given purchase situations. The key to consumer behavior then, according to Andreason, is to determine the state of the individual's various attitude subsystems, and he suggests five principal formative factors for this process: (1) information and feelings gathered from past want-satisfaction experiences; (2) information gathered in the past but unrelated to the immediate want-satisfying effort; (3) group affiliations (specifically, the individual's perception of the beliefs, norms, and values of "significant others"); (4) attitudes toward related objects in the relevant attitude cluster; and (5) the individual's personality. Thus Andreason posits that attitude change may be brought about by (1) further or different want-satisfying experiences; (2) exposure to further or different information; (3) changes in group affiliation; (4) changes in attitudes toward other cluster objects; and (5) changes in personality.

The structure of the Andreason model is shown schematically in Figure 4-1. In essence, this figure shows the independent variables (information and attitudes) and the dependent variable (behavior, i.e., selection, search, and no action). The flow of influence is shown by the solid and dotted lines. Information is shown as emanating from four sources: (1) advocate impersonal sources, (2) independent impersonal sources, (3) advocate personal sources, and (4) independent personal sources. This information is processed through a mechanism labeled *filtration* by Andreason. Such a mechanism would normally be called our perceptual processes. His filtration concept is simply an acknowledgment that information almost never reaches our intellect, nor is it processed without being contaminated by our own existing cognitive and perceptual mechanisms.

Thus, after being filtered, information is said to interact with such factors as personality, feelings, disposition, beliefs, direct experience, and other factors; and the resultant attitude and its valence are then said to condition or affect behavior. Valence is a measure of the degree to which feelings, beliefs, or dispositions are favorable or unfavorable toward an attitude object as measured on an arbitrary scale from -1 through zero to $+1$. Andreason defines the point of decision as the point at which the disposition component of the attitude subsystem has a maximum positive valence, or $+1$. Consequently, the key to consumer behavior lies with these attitudes and the extent to which they can be

[17] Alan R. Andreason, "Attitudes and Customer Behavior: A Decision Model," in *New Research in Marketing*, Lee Preston, ed. (Berkeley, Calif.: Institute of Business and Economic Research, University of California, 1965), pp. 1–16.

Figure 4-1

Andreason Model of Consumer Behavior

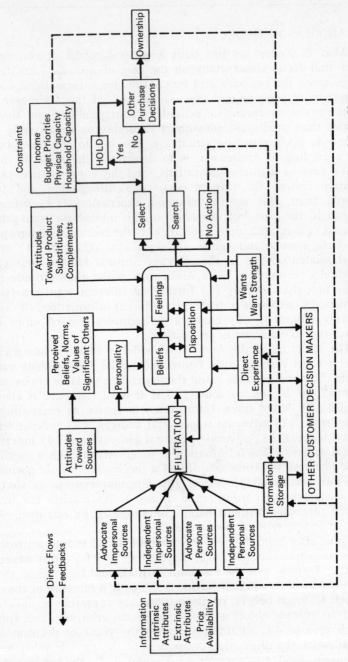

Source: Alan R. Andreason, "Attitudes and Customer Behavior: A Decision Model," in *New Research in Marketing*, Lee Preston, ed. (Berkeley, Calif.: Institute of Business and Economic Research, University of California, 1965).

changed. Attitudes, within the Andreason scheme, are changed by information, and information is broadly defined as all environmental or internal stimuli that contain meaning for the individual.

The Andreason model has stimulated much research and discourse on the complex question of consumer behavior. The model's principal contribution has probably been its emphasis on attitude as a determinant of consumer behavior. The Andreason model is somewhat deterministic and stimulus-response oriented—what was called earlier a reductive-functional model. Let us explore these statements in greater depth.

In a deterministic system, an event is seen as resulting from a direct cause. Andreason however, emphasizes the intervening variables, such as past experience, personality, other attitudes, significant others, and so on. All these factors act to condition or affect attitudes, which in turn affect behavior. The lines of causality, then, would look something like this:

$$\text{Information} \longrightarrow \text{Attitudes} \longrightarrow \text{Behavior}$$

Thus, the Andreason model is an elaborate stimulus-response configuration. However, it is a stimulus-response scheme that posits that the response is mediated by a series of intervening variables. In the Andreason model, the stimulus is defined as the information (which in turn is defined as almost everything, i.e., experience, perceptions, cognitions, and so on). The intervening variables are beliefs, dispositions, and feelings, and the response is defined as overt action. It should be pointed out that one difficulty with this view is that the stimulus (information), because it is all-inclusive, is at one and the same time a part of the intervening variables. For example, perceptions as information may be nothing more than beliefs and feelings. Is it to be construed then that the intervening variables are really only stimuli, or are they both stimuli and intervening variables?

Andreason's scheme is reductive in the sense that his model focuses only upon one central determinant of behavior, namely, attitude. Certainly, the role of attitude in all forms of human behavior is well recognized, but to make attitudes the *deus ex machina* of all consumer behavior is to vastly overwork and overrate the role of attitudes. Andreason's model focuses mainly upon structured relationships, but he is not explicit about the interrelationships among these variables. Any scheme can mean whatever its author wishes it to mean, and in the case of the Andreason model, one must question the extent to which it is a positive and accurate description of what really transpires, rather than a description of what the author thinks is the true state of affairs. What an author usually sees in a model is the reflection of what he himself put there.

THE HOWARD-SHETH MODEL

Perhaps no model of consumer behavior has been built so painstakingly over such a prolonged period of time and has undergone such rigorous modification and rethinking as has the Howard-Sheth model.

An effort to build a model that deals with overt behavior as well as with constructs that fall short of behavior, and an attempt to pinpoint the variables affecting consumer behavior and to treat the interactions among these variables, has been the general goal of at least one of these model builders since the very early 1960s. Howard was commissioned by the Ford Foundation in 1960 to undertake such a task, and his work, aided and complemented by the notable contributions of Jagdish Sheth, has continued to mature and bear considerable intellectual fruit.[18]

The Howard-Sheth model is a model of consumers' rational choice decisions. Howard and Sheth's viewpoint of rationality is compatible with that developed in the early pages of this chapter, namely, that the consumer is rational within the limits of his cognitive, learning, and information-processing capabilities. The Howard-Sheth model is basically a stimulus-response learning model, though admittedly a very well-reasoned and elaborate one. Their model rests on a set of hypothetical constructs that are the result of an amalgamation of Hull's learning theory, Osgood's cognitive theory, and Bulyne's theory of exploratory behavior.[19]

Howard and Sheth's theory of consumer behavior consists of four sets of abstractions that they call constructs or variables. These are (1) input variables, (2) output variables, (3) hypothetical constructs, and (4) exogenous variables.

The input and output variables are the less abstract of the four constructs. The input variables are essentially the stimuli from the buyer's environment (see Figure 4-2). The environment is classified as either social (the buyer's social environment) or commercial (communications from marketing firms).

The output variables are (1) attention, (2) brand comprehension, (3) attitude, (4) intention, and (5) purchase. These output variables are given the same names as some of the hypothetical constructs that will be discussed later. The basic difference according to the creators of the model is that the hypothetical constructs are "more inclusive in meaning and richer in speculation" than the output variables in this chart.[20]

The hypothetical constructs of the model are considerably more abstract, more introspective in origin, and not operationally well de-

[18] See his earlier works in *Marketing: Executive and Buyer Behavior* (New York: Columbia University Press, 1963) and *Marketing Management* (Homewood, Ill.: Richard D. Irwin, Inc., 1963).

[19] Clark L. Hull, *A Behavior System* (New Haven, Conn.: Yale University Press, 1952); Charles E. Osgood, "A Behavioristic Analysis of Perception and Language as Cognitive Phenomena" in *Contemporary Approaches to Cognition* (Cambridge: Harvard University Press, 1957), pp. 75–118; and D. E. Bulyne, "Curiosity and Exploration," *Science*, Vol. 153, No. 3731 (July 1, 1966), pp. 25–33.

[20] John A. Howard and Jagdish N. Sheth, *The Theory of Buyer Behavior* (New York: John Wiley & Sons, Inc., 1969), p. 31.

Figure 4-2

Howard-Sheth Model of Consumer Behavior

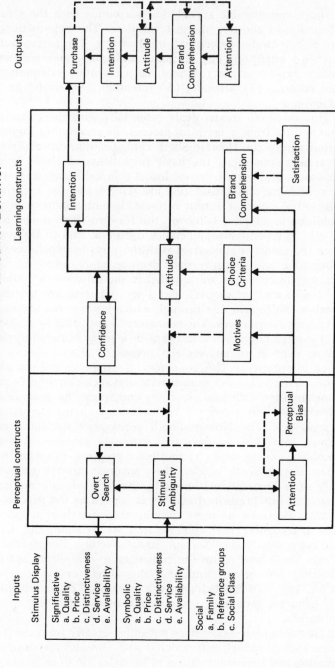

Solid lines indicate flow of information; dashed lines, feedback effects.

A simplified description of the theory of buyer behavior.

Source: John A. Howard and Jagdish N. Sheth, *The Theory of Buyer Behavior* (New York: John Wiley & Sons, Inc., 1969), p. 31.

fined. In short, considerable speculation surrounds both the structure and the function of the hypothetical variables. The hypothetical constructs are of two kinds: perceptual and learning. The perceptual constructs are (1) attention, (2) stimulus ambiguity, and (3) search. The learning constructs are (1) motives, (2) brand comprehension, (3) choice criteria, (4) attitude, (5) intention, (6) confidence, and (7) satisfaction.

The Howard-Sheth model deals essentially with the adaptive behavior that results from a learning process. By examining Figure 4-2, one can find within the Howard-Sheth configuration, especially in the learning-variable constructs, the basic ingredients of Hull's learning-theory approach. Motives are *drives;* brand comprehension and attitude are *cues;* confidence and satisfaction are *reinforcements;* and then, of course, the entire range of output variables is tantamount to *response.*

In addition to adaptive behavior, the Howard-Sheth model focuses upon the role of repetitive brand-choice decisions, and in light of this orientation, the model is concerned with the ways in which consumers store information and routinize their decision processes.

Certain characteristics are imputed to the consumer's actions. He is endowed with a set of motives and a set of alternative brands and, finally, with a choice criterion through which his motives are matched with the various alternatives. The consumer is not made to consider all brands but instead only an "evoked set," or a set of brands individually perceived or deemed to possess the necessary characteristics to be satisfactory alternatives. The consumer is characterized as actively seeking information from his commercial and social environment, and, again in accordance with basic learning constructs, he *generalizes* his experiences from past purchase ventures to contemporary decision-making processes. The Howard-Sheth consumer's decisions can be broken down into three stages: (1) extensive problem-solving, (2) limited problem-solving, and (3) routinized response behavior. According to the Howard-Sheth model, the consumer always reduces the complexity of a buying situation with the help of information and experience, and this prescribed activity is labeled as the *psychology of simplification.* However, as most stimulus-response theorists sooner or later come to recognize, man is never in a steady state, and decisions that were once satisfactory become unsatisfactory. Recognizing this, Howard and Sheth now cause the consumer to *complicate* his buying by considering new brands and new alternatives or by perceiving a different set. They call this behavior the *psychology of complication.* In turn, this behavior generates a new round of the simplifying activity described earlier.

The Howard-Sheth model does not differ greatly from the Andreason model. It is a reductive-functional and stimulus-response model. The mediating and important causes of behavior are to be found within the perceptual and learning constructs. The triggering stimuli are to be found among the input variables. It is reductive-functional in the sense that it reduces the consumer's decision process to a basic determinant (learning) or an independent variable and it attempts to describe the functional relationship between this independent variable and a dependent variable (behavior). The following flow of relationships illustrates the stimulus-response nature of the model:

Inputs $\longrightarrow$ Intervening Variables $\longrightarrow$ Outputs

The stimuli, or inputs, are communicative messages, or information, from the commercial and social environment; the intervening variables are essentially the person's cognitive and perceptual concepts; and the output is behavior, including attitudes or mind sets. Thus the stimulus-response mechanism is used to explain the consumer's adaptive behavior in repetitive brand-choice decisions. And stimulus-response advocates have to be constantly reminded that if man as an adaptive organism lived only according to the rules of conditioned reflexes suggested by stimulus-response mechanisms, he would inexorably "tend to sink into an invariable routine of self reinforcing reflexes, leading to (his) ultimate destruction by inflexibility."[21]

The structure of the Howard-Sheth model is interesting and focuses upon what are undoubtedly important determinants of consumer behavior, namely, communication, learning, attitudes, perception, and cognition. Its most glaring deficiency is the deficiency of all models of human behavior: its inability to specify how independent variables interact with dependent ones and what the nature of the interaction process is and to point out the interactive, interdependent nature of almost all variables related to behavior.

Our thinking and research regarding consumer behavior has been enlivened and enriched by the model conceived and constructed by Howard and Sheth. Their continuing work along the lines of learning theory and adaptive behavior are bound to bring forth even more insight regarding the profoundly complex phenomena that we label consumer behavior.

The Nicosia Model

The Nicosia model represents a considerable departure from the more or less traditional reductive-functional approach to consumer behavior and to model building in this field. This model attempts to describe a consumer decision process over a multidimensional space around a sophisticated, complex, interactive network of relationships.[22] Two essential characteristics distinguish Nicosia's efforts from most earlier attempts at model building. First, the Nicosia scheme incorporates a network of circular relations. These circular relations center

[21] W. R. Ashby, "Simulation of a Brain," in *Computer Applications in the Behavioral Sciences*, H. Borko, ed. (Englewood Cliffs, N.J.: Prentice-Hall, Inc., 1962), pp. 452–467.

[22] See Francesco M. Nicosia, *Consumer Decision Processes* (Englewood Cliffs, N.J.: Prentice-Hall, Inc., 1966), especially pp. 153–191.

around the interactions of human beings. Broadly defined, such interaction refers to the fact that the response—gesture, word, movement—of one individual is the stimulus to another, who in turn responds to the first. Nicosia views such interaction as transpiring between firms, via their communicative activities, and customers. Hence, the firm's behavior affects customers, and customer reactions and responses in turn affect the behavior of the firm.

A second major feature of the Nicosia model is that it is a holistic model, or what he calls an "extended" view. "The extended view . . . conceptualizes consumer *behavior as a* decision process, rather than *as the result* of a decision process. It is extended with respect to both the process morphology (structure) and dynamics (function)."[23] In other words, Nicosia does not attempt a wholesale "reduction" of the consumer decision processes to one or two variables and offer them as the independent variables in his behavioral equation. Instead, he views the structure of consumer behavior as pluralistic and forgoes the usual effort to search for and pinpoint a basic behavioral determinant. Within such a scheme the final act, that is, purchasing, is viewed as an integral part of the overall total process. Such a view sees behavior as *"circular systems-like relations,"* as an adaptive system.[24] Nicosia's model was one of the first to apply mathematical and computer-simulation techniques to consumer decision processes.[25] The natural starting point, or origin of action, in his model begins when a firm attempts to communicate with a consumer regarding a new product being introduced and an entire round or hierarchy of responses is triggered. For example:

> the structure would consist of the flow: the firm, its advertisement, the consumer's possible response to it, the interaction between the advertisement and the consumer's predispositions operating or evoked at the time of exposure, the possible formation of an attitude, the possible transformation of this attitude into a motivation, the possible conversion of this motivation into an act of purchase, and then back to the consumer's predispositions, *and* to the firm.[26]

All this is presented in the comprehensive scheme or model shown in Figure 4-3. The model is composed of four fields, which together constitute a summary flow chart. Field One constitutes the flow of the firm's message to the consumer. As can be seen from Figure 4-3, Field One is comprised of two subfields, (1) the firm's attributes and (2) the consumer's attributes. Essentially, this flow involves an elaborate communication process with all the normal attendant problems relating to

[23] Ibid., p. 142.

[24] Ibid., p. 146.

[25] For another interesting approach using these techniques, see Arnold E. Amstutz, *Computer Simulation of Competitive Market Response* (Cambridge, Mass.: The M.I.T. Press, 1967). See especially Chapter 8, "A Model of Consumer Behavior," pp. 153–246.

[26] Nicosia, op. cit., p. 154.

Figure 4-3

The Nicosia Model

The Comprehensive Scheme: A Summary Flow Chart

Field One: From the Source of a Message to the Consumer's Attitude

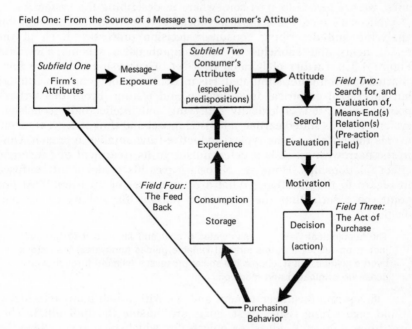

Source: Francesco M. Nicosia, *Consumer Decision Processes* (Englewood Cliffs, N.J.: Prentice-Hall, Inc., 1966), especially pp. 153–191.

the encoding and decoding of messages; with all the behavioral implications of communication relating to cognitive compatibility, selective exposure, retention, and perception; and with all the interpersonal or group dynamic problems stemming from group culture, group interaction, roles, norms, personality, and self-theory. In short, the effectiveness of communication in Field One is likely to hinge upon the old concept of starting where the audience is. To the extent that messages are compatible with the existing belief systems of the audience and to the extent that they address an established need at the time they are sent, they are likely to be effective. The result is a favorable attitude, which then predisposes the consumer to engage in a continuing act of problem solving characterized by search and evaluation. This aspect of the model is designated as Field Two. Emanating from these actions is a desire that impels the action characterized as *decision*. Decision, or choice, always involves at least two alternatives—to buy or not to buy— and such choices are fed back into both the consumer's attitudes in Subfield Two and the firm's attitudes in Subfield One.

Nicosia is quick to point out that the interactions that occur in his model can occur simultaneously or in sequence. Action, or analysis, can be initiated at any juncture within the model. Hence it can begin with the firm, the consumer's attitudes, a purchase, a failure to purchase, or the feedback mechanism. Because everything cannot be described at once, we are forced to start somewhere in describing the system.

Nicosia's model is a most advanced and sophisticated scheme for analyzing and describing consumer decision processes. Each of the major fields and subfields of his comprehensive scheme shown in Figure 4-3 is further elaborated in a set of subsystems that are flow-charted and computer-simulated. His model has undergone some limited but successful empirical investigation and testing. From this writer's point of view, it is a logically satisfying and intellectually consistent system. It is, as stated earlier, a holistic model and thus to a great extent avoids the pitfalls of the typical reductive-functionalist approach. Only in the narrowest sense is it deterministic in its treatment of cause and effect relationships. However, Nicosia leaves his reader a bit confused in regard to the question, "What are the causes of an event?" At one point, he asserts that the causes, or reasons for behavior, are teleological.[27]

> The teleological view . . . postulates a goal and imputes it to the subject. It postulates that this internal variable guides (motivates) the actor's overt activities, but it ignores the social processes (stimuli) through which goals are originated and modified.

This is an unusual statement and one with which many teleologists would take strong issue. First, goals are outside the individual. They are things, concepts, ideas, or objects for which men strive. They become internalized as the result of a socialization process. Man literally learns to strive for the things that his culture and his group esteem. Thus, goals originate and are modified by elaborate social processes; they are outside the individual in the sense that they are not part of one's genotype but are, instead, a function of one's environment and related to the whole question of aspirations and expectations.

All in all, the Nicosia model is a significant step toward the future—a future that holds the promise of the discovery and development of an encompassing and comprehensive theory of consumer behavior. It is a theory that is adaptable to mathematical manipulation, testing, and analysis by computer simulation. Such theories hold out the promise of much discovery and continuing insight into consumer decision processes.

A Holocentric Model of Consumer Behavior

In the models just reviewed, with the exception of the Nicosia model, the emphasis has been on a set of reductive-functional processes; that is, behavior has been treated as an output, or as a dependent

[27] *Teleology:* The theory or study of development as caused by the purposes that things serve.

variable, and the independent variables have been such reduced-form schemes as attitude, learning, perception, or some other single determinant. Almost without exception, a direct cause of the event—the determinant of behavior—is treated as preceding the event. Hence, the usual treatment of consumer behavior is oriented around the familiar and near-classical stimulus-response mechanism, and almost all models have fallen victim to this approach.

As earlier stated, however, the holist's approach to behavior analysis is a concern with the total *wholeness* of behavior. The model that is about to be presented is a *holocentric* model. A word or two of clarification would appear to be warranted. A holocentric model of consumer behavior is one that recognizes the interactive and inter-stimulative nature of behavioral processes. The basic premise of the model is as follows: *The holocentric model of consumer decision processes posits that although some feature or factors affecting behavior may appear dominant and may strongly affect certain individuals, that factor(s) always operates in conjunction with all other factors present.*

Holocentric implies two things: wholeness and centeredness. The wholeness aspect is emphasized in the previous statement. The centeredness dimension posits that the consumer is the basic unit of analysis in our model and thus the consumer is placed at the center of the system. All mechanisms evolve from and relate to the consumer. Such a view follows Kant's emphasis, which tends to perceive the central position of the total (whole) organism as the author of all attempts to order the universe. Our holocentric model stresses man's processes, which of necessity cannot be reduced to principles separate from his nature.[28]

Therefore, our model is holistic and not reductive; it does not view man as a soap bubble to be reduced to the laws of physics. He is not a simple organism whose behavior can be reduced to simple reflexes brought about by conditioning. His reactions are not simple physiological responses to innate biological cravings, but he is instead *a man* with all that is entailed in such a statement. As one set of writers put it, "applications of rat psychology notwithstanding, consumers are human and their behavior is obviously a reflection of their human qualities."[29]

The typical approach or model would probably look something like this,

Cognition, Perception, and Learning———➤Behavior

[28] See Robert E. Lana, *Assumptions of Social Psychology* (New York: Appleton-Century-Crofts, 1969), p. 75.

[29] Montrose S. Sommers and Jerome B. Kernan, "Consumer Behavior in Retrospect and Prospect," in *Explanations in Consumer Behavior*, Montrose S. Sommers and Jerome B. Kernan, eds. (Austin, Tex.: The Bureau of Business Research, The University of Texas, 1968), p. 5.

whereas the holocentric model of consumer behavior views the causes or reasons for behavior as following, rather than preceding, the event. Recognizing that all events have a cause, but recognizing further than causes are only reasons, the holocentric position would look more like this:

Goals———→Behavior

Or, again to be more explicit, our behavior is caused by the goals for which we strive. Now admittedly, our goals are socialized; therefore, social interaction and culture affect the way in which goals are specified, and such specification would affect the particular kinds of behavior manifested. *To affect something, however, is not necessarily to cause it.* Furthermore, as individual cognitive, reasoning, and data-gathering and -processing humans, we internalize our goals via a series of intrapersonal processes such as the formation of belief systems, perceptions, and attitudes; but again, these intrapersonal processes are subject to the interaction and interstimulation of other significant factors.

The goal-striving aspect of the model is one of its central and dynamic features. It legitimates the oft-stated assumption that consumer behavior is problem-solving behavior. A problem, by definition, exists when there is a *goal* to be attained and uncertainty exists as to how best to attain the goal. All of the activity related to goal determination such as attention and awareness, all the activity related to treating and handling uncertainty, and all the activity related to the actual problem of choice determination is consumer behavior when it is related to the acquiring of economic goods. And, of course, all the factors that affect these processes are within the purview of consumer behavior analysis.

The holocentric model is offered as a framework for the study of consumer behavior, reflecting what one writer on the subject has described as the penchant of consumer behavior analysts for "model shopping."[30] It is simply another way of looking at consumer behavior; a perspective involving a somewhat different point of view with a different set of logical and theoretical assumptions. It represents a combination of concepts and logic that is both Lewinian and existential.

The model is shown in its schematic form in Figure 4-4. Although the model is holistic, it is viewed as a system of sets and subsystems. The sets are ordered by neither time nor rank but are instead a way of conceptualizing the processes that relate to consumer behavior. Neither the sets nor the concepts contained therein are observable "things." Instead, they are names of things or processes that, given the current state of theory development, appear to be logically defensible. Physicists have postulated what are known as black holes, which they reason are collapsed stars whose mass becomes infinitely dense yet occupies no

---

[30] W. T. Tucker, *Foundations for a Theory of Consumer Behavior* (New York: Holt, Rinehart & Winston, Inc., 1967).

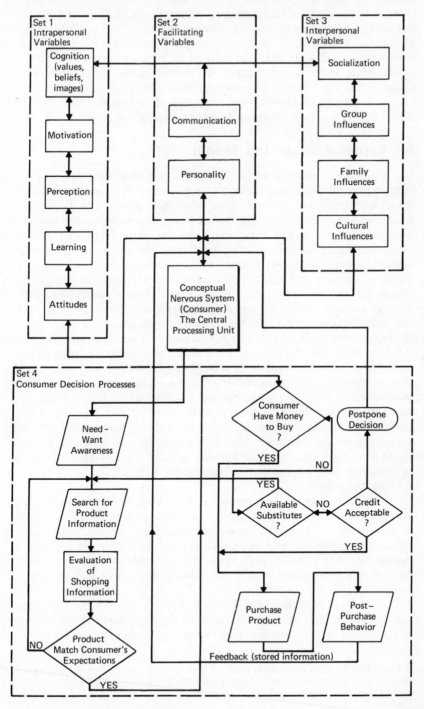

Figure 4-4

A Holocentric Model of Consumer Behavior

Set 1
Intrapersonal Variables

Cognition (values, beliefs, images)

Motivation

Perception

Learning

Attitudes

Set 2
Facilitating Variables

Communication

Personality

Set 3
Interpersonal Variables

Socialization

Group Influences

Family Influences

Cultural Influences

Conceptual Nervous System (Consumer) The Central Processing Unit

Set 4
Consumer Decision Processes

Need – Want Awareness

Search for Product Information

Evaluation of Shopping Information

Product Match Consumer's Expectations

NO

YES

Consumer Have Money to Buy ?

YES

NO

Available Substitutes ?

YES

NO

Credit Acceptable ?

YES

Postpone Decision

Purchase Product

Post– Purchase Behavior

Feedback (stored information)

space. The gravitational pull of such black holes becomes so intense that no light or other radiation can escape from it. Thus the star cannot be detected by any means. Sound absurd? Yes, but the logic of physics and Einstein's general theory of relativity support such a contention. So if physicists can have black holes, why cannot consumer behaviorists have "black boxes," or unobservable areas such as the mind of the consumer, that are analyzed and explained both on the basis of empirical observation and logical inductive and deductive reasoning? To gain a continuing understanding we must.

An Explanation of the Model

Consumer behavior is viewed as the set of interacting and inter-stimulating physical and mental activities and the resultant action of those who purchase and consume economic goods. The heart of the model, depicted in Figure 4-4, is Set Four, which is labeled Consumer Decision Processes. The consumer's actions stem from and arise out of the nature of his goal-striving existence. The consumer is an energy system, almost constantly active, seeking, striving, and aspiring to new levels of activity and tension management. As a matter of fact, consumer decision processes are nothing more than a special category of human activity related to tension management. Tension arises within the individual when he becomes aware of deficiencies or discrepancies that exist between his present stock of goods or services and his desired stock or aspiration levels. Thus we strive or behave in order to attain goals. Our goals are sometimes only dimly envisaged, but as a result of new information, or as a result of some change or alteration in our psychological field, the goal reaches a threshold limit and triggers the ensuing efforts related to tension management that take the form of such activities as search, shopping, evaluation, postponement, purchase, and postpurchase behavior. Man is his choices, and past acts condition us to varying extents to subsequent acts of choice. Hence, behavior is feedback and affects our psychological field or our total cognitive mental processes.

Set One, labeled Intrapersonal Behavior, is really just another way of visualizing the concept of "psychological field."[31] Psychological field is a set of psychical processes comprised of cognition, perceptions, and attitudes, and the psychological field of each individual is unique to that specific individual. Hence, the psychological field is each man's perspective or ordered view of his world and his environment.

Set Two is called Facilitating Process Variables and reflects nothing more than the dynamic state of the organism. "If the consumer is a problem solver, then he chooses among alternatives on the strength

---

[31] Kurt Lewin, "On the Structure of the Mind," in *A Dynamic Theory of Personality*, Kurt Lewin, ed. (New York: McGraw-Hill Book Company, 1935), pp. 43–66.

of what he knows [or has learned] about them. In this sense, information [which is communicated] becomes a critical factor in the consumer's choice processes. It determines which alternatives he perceives and how he perceives them."[32] Learning, then, simply reflects the organism's dynamic tendency to acquire adaptive modes of tension management; and communication is the means by which information is transmitted and processed both within the individual and between the individual and his environment.

Set Three is called Interpersonal Variables. These constitute the societal, cultural, and environmental context within which the consumer exists and operates. They reflect the interpersonal relations and the socialization process that affect all consumer behavior, but the extent to which they affect a given act is a function of the extent to which they are operating the instant the event occurs.

Thus, the holocentric model stresses the centrality of some aspects or reasons for behavior, but it also emphasizes the wholeness and the interactive and interdependent nature of behavioral events. It focuses upon goals and aspirations as the reasons for behavior. The model stresses and emphasizes Lewin's assertion that:

1. Aspirations are not static; they are not established once for all time.
2. Aspirations tend to grow with achievement and wane with failure.
3. Aspirations are socially and culturally influenced. The performance of other members of the group to which one belongs and his reference groups influence the subject's aspirations.[33]

The model stresses that consumer behavior must be analyzed and explained in terms of individually patterned totalities. Clawson writes that "They are individual because attention is centered within a specific person and on the way in which these desires affect his behavior. They are patterned because the person's behavior possibilities all seem as a unified system of choices related to one another in a definite fashion."[34]

The holocentric model recognizes that present behavior is both future facing and past reflecting. Aspirations are affected by expectations and perceptions that flow from both the future and the past. Consumer behavior

can be regarded as a series of events in which the conditions of one time period are the primary determinants of the activities and conditions of the next time period. It can be conceived as a goal sequence in which an apparent goal becomes a stepping stone to some further goal, each

[32] Sommers and Kernan, op. cit., p. 5. The items in brackets were added by the author for explanatory purposes.

[33] Kurt Lewin, et al., "Level of Aspiration," in *Personality and Behavior Disorders*, J. M. Hunt, ed., Vol. 1 (New York: The Ronald Press Company, 1944), pp. 333–378.

[34] Joseph Clawson, "Lewin's Vector Psychology and the Analysis of Motives in Marketing," in *Theory in Marketing*, Reavis Cox and Wroe Alderson, eds. (Chicago, Ill.: Richard D. Irwin, Inc.), p. 42.

chosen in turn because it represents the greatest of pleasures or the least of pains. There is no great intellectual effort involved in imagining causal effects that flow backward from the future, forward from the past, inward from the surrounding world or outward from some deep organic process.[35]

However, the holocentric position would agree with Lewin's argument that all factors affecting behavior—that is, intrapersonal ones such as culture or family influences—may be taken into account in explaining behavior only to the extent that they make a difference to the consumer at the moment in question; that is, these factors must be operative in the consumer's psychological field at the time specific behavior is underway. Thus, it is not the observer of consumer behavior who can pinpoint behavioral determinants, but it is the consumer who decides what is important, what will be perceived, how he will be influenced, from whom he shall receive information, and to whom he will listen and respond. The consumer is *free* to choose and free to *react* to his own individual and unique destiny. In one sense the consumer is a central processing unit. In a manner analogous to the computer, the consumer's terminals are communications and purchase behavior. His programs or compilers are written by the inter- and intra-personal variables, translated into machine language by learning and personality.

Before the conclusion of this chapter, an important disclaimer must be made. In the final analysis no model should be adjudged good or bad on the basis of whether or not it is reductive-functional or holistic. Models are good or bad only in terms of how well they fulfill their purposes. The various models discussed in this chapter have all made important contributions to our understanding of consumer behavior. Models are useful devices for describing, understanding, and predicting phenomena. However, it would appear that consumer behavioralists all too frequently have a penchant for labeling any scheme that appears to interrelate some variable with behavior as a "model." Instead of extolling or deprecating a model because it is reductive-functional or holistic, a better approach is to examine each model in detail with the emphasis on explaining specifically why the model is weak or strong rather than simply trying to attach a label to the model.

It is unfortunate but true that our consumer behavior models have had little influence on consumer research.[36] As a matter of fact, it is rare to find a published study that has utilized, been based upon, or even been greatly influenced by any of the models mentioned.

Hopefully, in the future we shall submit our models to more rigorous empirical testing, and as we do, such tests will involve a mixture of the following elements.

---

[35] Tucker, op. cit., p. 1.

[36] David T. Kollat, Roger D. Blackwell, and James F. Engel, "The Current Status of Consumer Behavior Research: Developments During the 1968–1972 Period," an unpublished paper presented at the annual meeting of the Association for Consumer Research, Chicago, Illinois, November 1972.

1. To what extent does the model predict correctly the direction of individual relationships among variables?
2. To what extent do the data fit the model?
3. To what extent are the results of the test similar to those of other work on the same or competing models?
4. To what extent does a model predict importance of the variables better than a competing model?[37]

In short, our knowledge regarding consumer behavior has not been at all adequately synthesized into most of our models of consumer behavior.[38] Consumer behavioralists do not agree on the criteria for accepting a model as a true representation of a consumer behavioral process system. It is also possible that consumer behavior models have not generated a great amount of interest on the part of marketers because model builders have not taken the initiative to show how their models will contribute to better decision-making by managers.

In some respects consumer behavioralists have demonstrated their own brand of professional arrogance by their concerted attempts to model the complex and intricate phenomena of behavior. Almost no other social or behavioral science attempts such heroic schemes. Social psychologists, cultural and social anthropologists, sociologists—all have eschewed attempts directed toward general models of behavior.

It would appear that at least one more important question should be raised in conjunction with our overall discussion of models: For whom are we attempting to model such behavior? Given the usual relationship between marketing and consumer behavior, the most likely response to this question would undoubtedly be *the marketing decision-maker*, a highly defensible position. However, the holocentric model is essentially a *pedagogical* model—a means of relating to the student of consumer behavior, whether he be in the classroom or the marketplace, the many complex, interrelated, and interdependent variables affecting buying and consumer decision processes. The holocentric model strives to describe these variables and their relationships. From description and analysis flows understanding. Ultimately such understanding, from the standpoint of both the student and the practitioner of marketing, leads to a capacity for better prediction and control.

Thus, our holocentric model with its attendant point of view shall constitute the basic framework of our continuing analysis of consumer behavior. We shall proceed now to an examination by parts of the components of this model. Throughout this examination and analysis, however, we shall be ever mindful that we are examining only parts of individually patterned totalities.

[37] Suggested by the work done by John U. Farley and L. Winston Ring, "An Empirical Test of the Howard-Sheth Model of Buyer Behavior," *Journal of Marketing Research,* Vol. 7 (November 1970), pp. 427–438.

[38] Tanniru R. Rao, "Toward a Synthesis of Buyer Behavior Research," proceedings of the fourth annual meeting of the American Institute for Decision Sciences, New Orleans, Louisiana, November 1–4, 1972, pp. 190–196.

Questions for Study, Reflection, and Review

1 What are the various functions of models?

2 Define *determinism* and discuss its implications for human behavior.

3 Discuss the activity of goal seeking on the part of the consumer in terms of a cause-effect relationship.

4 Discuss the concept of bounded rationality with respect to consumer decision processes.

5 What are some of the criteria on which models of consumer behavior may be evaluated?

6 Describe the three major approaches to the building of models of consumer behavior.

7 What is the basic concept upon which the Andreason model of consumer behavior is predicated?

8 Discuss the role of learning in the Howard-Sheth model.

9 What are the primary contributions rendered by the Nicosia model?

10 What are the two major aspects of the holocentric model of consumer behavior?

Part II

Intrapersonal Dimensions of Consumer Behavior

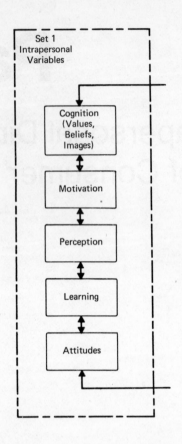

Set 1
Intrapersonal
Variables

Cognition
(Values,
Beliefs,
Images)

Motivation

Perception

Learning

Attitudes

5

The Impact of Cognitive Organization and Function

Introduction

Within this chapter it will be our task to sketch the relevant dimensions of a psychology of cognition. Much of our effort will be concerned with developing and positing some relevant definitions; but more importantly, our work will focus upon an exposition of cognitive concepts or structure and the implication of their function in certain dimensions of consumer behavior. The early treatment of the chapter is concerned with this conceptual development. Hence, we shall explore in great detail certain cognitive structures, namely, such phenomena as value theory and decision making; the role of attitudes, opinions, and beliefs; self-concepts, images, and cognitive style; and the meaning and significance of cognitive consistency. Our treatment shall also investigate in a summary fashion such functional cognitive activities as motivation, aspirations, and expectations, or the entire cluster of mental activities known as arousal. Furthermore, our treatment in this chapter will also introduce the reader to the concepts of perception and learning and their impact upon consumer decision-making.

A more simpleminded treatment of consumer behavior might very well ignore the entire area of cognitive phenomena. It would do so, however, at the expense of a much richer conceptual investigation and treatment. Those of us who call ourselves consumer behaviorists or consumer psychologists have realized from the outset that our subject is a complicated mass of ultrasophistication. Simpleminded theories of consumer behavior simply do not suffice to describe, explain, or predict the actions of consumers. All too frequently our theories have sprung up in a sort of either/or fashion from the armchair of speculation or from the laboratory of direct measurement and observation. As a consequence our consumer models are either man-gods—mystical, sophisticated, and omniscient—or little more than machines locked in endless repetitive conditioned acts of behavior.

Admittedly, cognitive psychology and cognitive approaches to consumer behavior are somewhat speculative in character. By necessity the approach centers upon mental activity that is itself not directly observable. Who has ever seen thinking or witnessed a motivation manifesting itself or seen someone's learning curve affecting his consumer behavior in the marketplace? Yet, it is possible for us to develop operational theorems and testable hypotheses based upon an introspective analysis of these phenomena.

Cognitive psychology, then, is an attempt to look into the mythical and mystical "black box" of the consumer's mind. It is an approach that attempts to analyze and map mental, as opposed to physical, behavior.[1]

The Meaning of Cognitive Psychology

Cognitive psychology might well be better understood if we look first at its counterpart, behaviorist psychology. The reader will recall that several reductive-functional or behaviorist models were examined in Chapter 4. Perhaps at this juncture we might best review the basic assumptions and logic of behaviorist psychology—oftentimes also referred to as stimulus-response psychology or objective psychology— and from this examination move toward a more comprehensive treatment of our subject matter of this chapter, cognitive psychology.

ELEMENTS OF BEHAVIORISM

The behaviorist psychologist has a theoretical orientation far removed from that of his cognitive counterpart. The behaviorist view focuses on publicly observable responses and their so-called environmental instigators and reinforcers. These elements become the proper objects of investigation in psychology. The behaviorist denies, or at least ignores, any element of consciousness as being both highly resistive to scientific inquiry and not very relevant to the real purposes of psychology as a "science."[2]

Behaviorism as a science rests essentially on a single mechanism,

[1] Heinz L. Ansbacher and Rowena R. Ansbacher, *The Individual Psychology of Alfred Adler* (New York: Harper and Row, Publishers, 1956), p. 6.

[2] A lengthier and more detailed treatment of this topic can be found in Richard C. Anderson and David P. Ausubel, *Readings in the Psychology of Cognition* (New York: Holt, Rinehart & Winston, Inc., 1966). See especially pp. 3–17.

that is, operant and classical conditioning. It emphasizes rote, instrumental, and discrimination learning. With this methodology behavorists attempt to deduce generalizations from the directly observed responses of their subjects. Introspection has no place in behaviorist psychology. Behaviorism places a heavy emphasis on its assumption that development is essentially an organismic process. This organismic approach to the analysis of behavioral events centers around certain formal features of the organism as a living system, such as genetic endowment, and upon the nature of the formal changes that occur in this living system.[3]

Several other main features of behaviorism are that it focuses upon a molecular form of analysis; it posits a genetic bias, inasmuch as it emphasizes that genetic endowments are regarded as more fundamental than events that occur later. Finally and most importantly, our brief synopsis of behaviorism must include the statement that behaviorism tends to assume that behavior is activated by specific primary or derived needs and that no learning occurs without the reduction or elimination of these needs.

But what about the implications of these propositions regarding behaviorism for social behavior in general or consumer behavior in particular? The basic implication is that man is a machine that can be conditioned to do or accept almost anything deemed desirable. And the way to condition him is through behavioral technology. B. F. Skinner, behaviorism's most prominent and influential proponent, argues that man can be mechanistically conditioned to want what the group wants.[4] Behavioral technology is, to his mind, a developing science of control that aims to change the environment as a means of changing people and to alter action rather than feelings. Central to Skinner's approach is a method of conditioning that has been used with uniform success on laboratory animals: giving rewards to mold the subject to the experimenter's will.[5]

Skinner's latest proposition—one advocated also by other members of the behaviorist tradition—is that man can no longer be indulged in his freedom of choice, so his freedom must be replaced with control. Thus, Skinner and the behaviorists contend that actions are determined by the environment or that behavior is shaped and maintained by its

[3] Seymour Wapner, "An Organismic-Developmental Approach to the Study of Perceptual and Other Operations," in *Cognition: Theory, Research, Promise*, Constance Sheerer, ed. (New York: Harper and Row, Publishers, 1962), pp. 6–44.

[4] A fictionalized version of Skinner's work can be found in his now classic work, *Walden II* (New York: Macmillan Publishing Co., Inc., 1948). A more up-to-date treatment can be found in his latest book, *Beyond Freedom and Dignity* (New York: Alfred A. Knopf, Inc., 1972).

[5] Behaviorists are enamored of the concept of species equivalence or isomorphism, that is, the idea that conclusions based upon observations stemming from lower animal behavior can be generalized to higher forms of organisms, especially human beings.

consequences. By altering and adjusting the environment we can alter, adjust, and manipulate its societal members—consumers being no exception. Consequently, if marketers were only to offer the right rewards to customers, they, in turn, would be rewarded with perpetual patronage and continually rising sales. However, as is so often the case, the conditions of the marketplace differ markedly from those of the laboratory, and consumers, as most businessmen know, are not easily conditioned.

ELEMENTS OF COGNITIVE PSYCHOLOGY

Our brief review of and excursion into the behaviorist tradition has served at least this important function: it has instructed us as to what cognitive psychology is *not*. Let us look now more positively at what cognitive psychology *is*.

COGNITION DEFINED. *Cognition* relates to a cluster of psychological activities, which are a central part of behavior. *Cognition* refers to the set, cluster, or constellation of knowledge, attitudes, and perceptual states that make up a particular individual's total and integrated belief system. *Cognition* has the same root as *recognize*, which means "be aware of," and *cognizant*, which means "apprised of." *Cognition* is concerned with *knowing* and how we come to know.

Cognitive theorists take almost precisely the opposite point of view from that of the behaviorists. Cognitive psychologists regard differentiated and clearly articulated conscious experience as the foundation for providing the most significant data for a science of psychology. Cognitivists are, therefore, concerned with such phenomena as knowing, meaning, understanding, perception, learning, and motivation.

The term *cognition* is used in widely varying ways; for example, Scheerer referred to cognition as a centrally mediated process representing internal and external events: "It takes the form of phenomenal organization which is centrally imposed between the source of stimulation and the behavior adjustment."[6] Festinger identified the cognitive elements as the things a person knows about himself, his behavior, and his surroundings.[7] More recently, Neisser stated that cognition refers to the processes by which any sensory input is transformed, reduced, elaborated, stored, recovered, and used.[8] Neisser's definition is most popular with those who work with cognition in an information-processing–decision-making context. Overall, however, cognition seems to distill down in meaning to what is known, or knowledge acquired through personal experience.

[6] Martin Scheerer, "Cognitive Theory," in *Handbook of Social Psychology,* G. Lindzey, ed., Vol. 1 (Reading, Mass.: Addison-Wesley Publishing Co., Inc., 1954), p. 99.

[7] Leon Festinger, *A Theory of Cognitive Dissonance* (Stanford, Calif.: Stanford University Press, 1957), pp. 18–24.

[8] U. Neisser, *Cognitive Psychology* (New York: Appleton-Century-Crofts, 1967), p. 10.

AN EXPANDED VIEW OF COGNITION

Now, however, let us move beyond a definition of cognition and explore something of the scope and the conceptual implications of the phenomenon. Cognition and cognitive psychology are intensely concerned with such ideas as concept formation, thinking, and the acquisition of knowledge. Within the cognitive school the emphasis is on mentalistic concepts of behavior and on the position that such conscious experiences as knowing, learning, perceiving, and so on are the most significant data on which to base a science of psychology or behavior. Cognitive events are defined in terms of differentiated states of consciousness, and these states exist in terms of such concepts or organized systems as images, idealized selves, personality structure, and other perceptual states. Cognitive theories are, in terms of our previous language, holocentric systems; that is, they focus upon a molar analysis in which some factor affecting behavior may appear dominant and may strongly affect certain individuals; however, this factor(s) always operates in conjunction with all other factors present. Finally, the cognitive theorists hold a unique and differing view from that of the behaviorists regarding learning. Learning, from the cognitive point of view, occurs as a result of adaptive problem-solving and may or may not involve tension reduction. The cognitive model implies that learning is the organism's basic device for tension management.[9] More will be said about learning later.

COGNITIVE STRUCTURES. Another term used frequently by cognitive theorists is *cognitive structure*. All of us possess cognitions—that is, bits of knowledge—and it would appear also that our cognitions are organized into meaningful clusters or units of information. As a matter of fact, cognitive structures are defined as organized subsets of the attributes an individual uses to identify and discriminate a particular object or event.[10] When a man buys a suit of clothes, his cognitive structure provides him with a suitable frame of reference or decision matrix by which to identify, discriminate, and judge colors, fabrics, styles, brands, and even the store from which the suit might be purchased. Cognitive structures are thus ideas or sets of ideas (opinions, beliefs, and attitudes) maintained by a person and available to conscious experience.

There are several other dimensions of cognitive structure to be explored. What about, for instance, the relationships that exist among our cognitive structures? To what extent do cognitions or ideas about one object or event affect our feelings, attitudes, or behavior toward other objects or events? Such questions create the necessity for identify-

[9] The roots of this proposition can be traced to Allport. See Gordon W. Allport, *Personality: A Psychological Interpretation* (New York: Holt, Rinehart & Winston, Inc., 1937).

[10] R. B. Zajonc, "The Process of Cognitive Tuning in Communication," *Journal of Abnormal and Social Psychology*, Vol. 61 (1960), pp. 159–167.

ing and describing the properties of these relationships. A detailed analysis of cognitive structure is beyond the scope of our treatment here. However, one researcher, W. A. Scott, has examined cognitive structure in great detail and has identified three major structural properties of cognition: differentiation, relatedness, and integration.[11]

Differentiation refers to the distinctiveness of the elements or units that contribute to the set of ideas maintained by a person. Consumers, for example, may have a complex, sophisticated set of ideas that constitute their cognitive structure. Or they may have a woefully deficient set of ideas and hence possess little differentiation. These consumers belong to a rather large group of consumer decision-makers aptly characterized as chronic know-nothings.

Relatedness refers to types of relations among cognitive structures such as similarity, association, and proximity, and it also refers to the influence of one element on another. To strike an example in terms of consumer behavior, brand choice is often considered a function of the consumer's attitudes toward the brand (a cognition). If a consumer has a given positive cognition (attitude) toward a family brand, say, Ford, then relatedness in terms of similarity, association, and proximity may imply that a new Ford product, say, Mustang, would have a high probability of general acceptance by those holding these cognitive clusters.

Integration pertains to the extent of assimilation and connectedness among the various parts of the cognitive structure. The consumer who possesses a well-integrated cognitive structure is aware of these relations and is capable of manipulating them to the ends of search, evaluation, and overall information-processing and decision-making. *Cognitive structure* in all its ramifications implies a complex network of ideas consisting of various subunits or parts related either tightly or loosely to one another. Cognitive structure and function form the process whereby persons, consumers being no exception, deal with a complex environment in a meaningful and rational way.

COGNITIVE FUNCTIONS. Our cognitive structures and processes have two basic functions in behavior. (1) They are *purposive* in that they serve the individual in his attempt to achieve satisfaction of needs; that is, as previously stated they facilitate dealing with a complex environment in meaningful (from the point of view of the individual) ways. (2) Cognitive structure and processes are *regulatory* in that they determine in large measure the direction taken in the consumer's steps toward his attempt to attain the satisfaction of his initiating needs. It is the consumer's cognitions that cause him to particu-

[11] See W. A. Scott, "Cognitive Structure and Social Structure: Some Concepts and Relationships," in *Decisions, Values and Groups,* N. F. Washburne, ed., Vol. 2 (New York: Pergamon Press, Inc., 1962), pp. 86–118; and also W. A. Scott, "Conceptualizing and Measuring Structural Properties of Cognition," in *Motivation and Social Interaction,* O. J. Harvey, ed. (New York: The Ronald Press Company, 1963), pp. 266–287.

larize both his motivation and his perceptions. Cognitions are unique to each and every individual. The cognitive map of the individual is a partial, personal, subjective construction in which certain objects, selected by the individual for a major role, are perceived and interpreted in a highly individual manner.

COGNITIVE PROCESSES. *Cognition* is a broad generic term that refers to a host of mental processes or phenomena. It is, in another sense, a kind of logical framework or set of propositions out of which flows our subsequent analysis of cognitive processes such as learning, motivation, and perception. Each of these topics, as they relate to consumer behavior and consumer decision processes, will be treated at length in separate chapters. However, a summary treatment of these topics will be given at this juncture: first, to introduce the concepts and, second, to dramatize rather conclusively the cognitive implications that are an integral part of learning, motivation, and perception.

As we shall learn subsequently, the human organism, and especially the focus of our inquiry, the consumer, is a sensory-processing and data-gathering organism. His behavior stems from his goal striving and his aspirations. He is not so much driven to acts of choice as a result of inner drives or needs as he is pulled to acts of choice by his goals and aspirations. Consumers *learn*—they modify their behavior over time. What was sufficient cause or *motivation* for behavior in one situation may for numerous reasons no longer be interpreted or *perceived* as sufficient justification for action or similar action in a subsequent situation. Thus, it can be seen that motivation, learning, and perception lie at the core of consumer cognitive processes.

LEARNING. The cognitive school is quick to recognize that there are several different kinds of learning and that consumers adapt their learning to the nature of the problems with which they are confronted. Some problems are quite simple, easily structured, and routine. In such instances, consumers engage in a kind of perfunctory, routine, or *limited problem solving*. In other instances, problems are complex, ill structured, nonlinear, and stochastic. The consumer is forced to undertake complex cognitive reorganization, characterized as *extensive problem-solving behavior*.

Consumers learn adaptive behavior. Some of such learning could even be of the stimulus-response or operant-conditioning kind. Most learning, however, is far beyond such simplistic approaches. Most frequently consumer learning requires that information be reorganized and reintegrated into the cognitive structure. This process is usually followed by further reorganization and transformation, resulting in new combinations of cognitive constructs. From the standpoint of consumer behavior, learning is meaningful when the cognitive structure is composed of a patterned organization of conceptual traces. Such traces are nothing more than memory or stored experiences, hypothetical bits of information or cognitions used to account for the continuing representation of past experience in the cognitive structure.[12] This would mean that as new information enters the cognitive field, it interacts with and is assimilated and integrated into a relevant, more comprehensive conceptual system. Such a procedure tends to accelerate and facilitate the learning process and the retention of information by anchoring it to related materials.[13]

Much consumer learning can be characterized as a categorizing, classifying, and sorting process. Bruner, Wallach, and Galanter posit that such learning can be regarded as a problem of identifying recurrent regularities in the task environment.[14] Consumers have many "models" of regularity, or given a problem-solving–learning situation, they are forced to develop such models. In either event, the consumer's task is to identify the recurrent regularities and relate them to the model.[15] Unquestionably, learning does play an important role as a determinant of or a variable in consumer behavior. We shall examine the total extent of that role later.

MOTIVATION. Within the cognitive framework, the concept of motivation as impetus to behavior takes on rather special meaning and significance. Cognitivists speak of motivation as the reasons that bring about behavior. They are not at all enamored of the idea of motivation as internal mechanisms related to inner drives, needs, or reflexive actions. Within the cognitive context, motivation has meaning and significance in the sense that man has "needs," but related to the concept of cognition these needs pertain to the "need to know" or the implicit assumption of the need for cognition and the need for cognitive structure. Some cognitivists, namely, Cohen, Stotland, and Wolfe, have gone so far as to make this assumption explicit by defining need for cognition as the urge and desire to structure relevant situations in meaningful and integrated ways.[16]

Motives are usually conceived of as active, strong, driving forces that exist to reduce a state of tension and to protect, satisfy, and enhance the individual and his self-concept.

The concept that motivation is tension and that all acts that lead to reinforcement reduce tension is largely rejected by the cognitivists. Instead, cognitive theory contends that although tension or drive re-

[12] For more detail on this subject, see David P. Ausubel, "Cognitive Structure and the Facilitation of Meaningful Verbal Learning," *Journal of Teacher Education*, Vol. 14 (1963), pp. 217–221.

[13] Marvin E. Shaw and Phillip R. Costanzo, *Theories of Social Psychology* (New York: McGraw-Hill Book Company, 1970), pp. 178–181.

[14] J. S. Bruner, M. A. Wallach, and E. H. Galanter, "The Identification of Recurrent Regularity," *American Journal of Psychology*, Vol. 72 (1959), pp. 200–209.

[15] The Howard-Sheth model described in Chapter 4, especially in terms of its learning implications, is built upon such a conceptual foundation.

[16] A. R. Cohen, E. Stotland, and D. M. Wolfe, "An Experimental Investigation of Need for Cognition," *Journal of Abnormal and Social Psychology*, Vol. 52 (1955), pp. 291–294.

duction may be satisfying under some circumstances, it is just as often the case that the person seeks drive intensification.[17]

Scheerer has argued convincingly that capacity fulfillment may be a more important reason, cause, or motivation for behavior than tension reduction.[18] His contention is that (in seeking a personalized goal) the individual is in effect creating a tension for himself. Such goal attainment, in and of itself, thus becomes satisfying—not so much because it leads to tension reduction or is reinforcing but because it leads to the cognitive enrichment that results from the successful attainment of desired goal objects. Cognitive-oriented motivation leads to personal satisfaction in the sense of an enriched cognitive structure (insight) and to a changed, perhaps even more integrated or differentiated state of the person.

Such a view regarding motivation is widely held by cognitive theorists and is similar to the capacity fulfillment or self-actualizing position of Maslow discussed briefly in Chapter 2.[19] Furthermore, a cognitive interpretation of motivation would support the contention that behavior stems from the individual's desire for a well-integrated, related, and differentiated cognitive structure.

PERCEPTION. Perception is another sophisticated and complex cognitive process. In the cognitive tradition, perception is viewed as the way in which the individual orders, structures, and interprets what he receives through his senses. What this means, of course, is that we mentally interpret or decode all those sensory stimulations that reach our central nervous system; thus perception is the representation of objects or events that results from the organization of stimuli. This organization and interpretation, which we call perception, is affected by two major sets of variables: structural variables and functional variables.[20] The structural variables are those contained within the physical stimuli, such as intensity, frequency, and so on. The functional variables are those contained in the perceiver, such as needs, moods, past experience, and so on.

Perception profoundly affects our learning processes. As a matter of fact, perception itself is a process involving a great deal of categorizing, classifying, and sorting—activities mentioned earlier as falling within the context of learning.[21] In a perceptual situation, the con-

---

[17] See Rom J. Markin, *The Psychology of Consumer Behavior* (Englewood Cliffs, N.J.: Prentice-Hall, Inc., 1969), pp. 57–59, especially p. 58, "The existential man is not necessarily guided in his consumer behavior by an urge to reduce tension. He seeks it."

[18] Scheerer, op. cit., pp. 91–142.

[19] Abraham H. Maslow, "Higher and Lower Needs," *Journal of Psychology*, Vol. 25 (1948), pp. 433–436.

[20] D. Krech and R. S. Crutchfield, *Theory and Problems of Social Psychology* (New York: McGraw-Hill Book Company, 1948).

[21] J. S. Bruner, "On Perceptual Readiness," *Psychological Review*, Vol. 64 (1957), pp. 123–152.

sumer is stimulated by some appropriate input (goal object, sales event, special promotion, or window display) and responds to it by relating it to an internalized category of earlier perceived and now cognized objects or events. The consumer's reaction to this new stimulus would at this juncture be indeterminate but would be affected by his perceived needs, the desirability of the object or event, his current motivations, his mood and total emotional state, his economic well-being, and so on.

Because perception entails inference and the categorizing of sensory inputs, it therefore rests upon a decision process. Individuals willfully choose the proper categories in which to file information. Perception is not a passive reception and automatic interpretation of stimuli but is instead an active and dynamic process by which incoming data is selectively related to the existing cognitive map of the individual. Therefore, it is the matching with and sorting of the sensory inputs in relation to the organization of already-existing cognitive elements that condition and give meaning to the thing perceived. From the point of view of consumer behavior, perception depends upon a decision process; that is, what is perceived is selectively filtered from his environment by the consumer. Such a process involves the use of discriminatory cues that assign sensory inputs to categories. The use of cues entails inference, which leads to the placement of objects in categories. Finally, some categories are more developed than others and hence are more accessible.

The Information-Processing Approach

What we have learned thus far in our treatment of cognitive psychology is that the consumer as an individual human organism possesses unique characteristics, namely, that he is a thinking, reasoning, and problem-solving creature and that he seeks goals and satisfaction in terms of his own capacity fulfillment and cognitive environment. Man needs knowledge just as he needs food, and the phrase "food for thought" might be changed to "thought for food." Consumers need to know. They need to know about themselves and about goods and the stores and trading centers that sell goods. And, not surprisingly, consumers have long known that knowing about goods can lead to increased knowledge about themselves.

Thus, with this brief and still relatively elementary understanding of such cognitive phenomena as learning, motivation, and perception, we are ready now to attempt some synthesis of these concepts into a description of behavior based upon information processing as a means of human problem-solving.

Consumer behavior has already been defined as a problem-solving activity. Problems emerge relating to assortment deficiencies of varying kinds. In any event goods are used up or become obsolete. The need for goods arises out of the consumer's existence. He needs goods to fulfill the dictates of his needs-wants hierarchy, and the seeking of these goods becomes a kind of goal-striving and, hence, problem-solving activity.

In a very simple sense, the problem-solving process of consumers is a search for some solution to a perceived problem among a very large number of possible solutions. Thus, the possible solutions must be examined in some particular sequence, and if they are, then certain possible solutions will be examined before others. The particular decision strategy that induces the order or priority of search and information processing is related to cognitive, motivational, and perceptual phenomena.[22] Consumers solve problems and process information in keeping with their cognitions. Problems and information processing are affected by the perceptual and motivated states of the individual. The consumer's perceptions and the individual manner in which sensory stimuli are ordered and interpreted enable him to rearrange his priorities and restructure his cognitive sets and networks, conditioning him to respond to information and communication in a highly selective fashion.

The consumer's motivations impel him to act, respond, or ignore marketing phenomena. Consumer motivations are pulls or attractions related to his goal seeking, his aspirations, and his expectations, rather than solely drive or tension-reducing mechanisms.

Information processing serves one basic need, the need to know, and involves meaningful learning. The consumer discovers that certain products deliver more satisfaction than others. He learns to store vast quantities of meaningful information, and although the consumer's capacity for storage is nearly unlimited, his ability to *retrieve* large quantities of information is rather seriously limited. One writer suggests "that as a general rule, most everything we experience tends to be *forgotten*. Only as an exception is an item of information long retained ready at hand."[23] Nonetheless, we continue to solve problems, and the insight gained in one problem-solving situation can and often does lead to the structuring or solution of a subsequent problem. Such effective use of previous learning is an illustration of positive transfer and is the desired outcome of information processing.[24] Consumers, throughout their information processing and problem solving, encounter numerous *detours*. Nearly all problems contain some form of detour. If the path to the goal were unambiguous and direct, there would seldom be a problem. However, because paths to goals are littered with uncertainty and risk, consumers deliberate and frequently back off and detour to another route, which may lead to another decision.

What this means is that consumers become heuristic problem-

[22] See Allen Newell, J. C. Shaw, and Herbert Simon, "Elements of a Theory of Human Problem Solving," *Psychological Review*, Vol. 65 (1958), pp. 151–166.

[23] Walter R. Reitman, *Cognition and Thought* (New York: John Wiley & Sons, Inc., 1965), pp. 206–207.

[24] Rudolph W. Schulz, "Problem Solving Behavior and Transfer," *Harvard Education Review*, Vol. 30 (1960), pp. 61–77.

solvers. They learn shorthand, abbreviated rules-of-thumb for processing information; and given their desire to use heuristic approaches, consumers are more likely to be interested in optimal solution procedures than in optimal solutions. Consumers look for principles that contribute to the reduction in the average time spent searching for a solution.[25]

To summarize, the information-processing approach to the study of consumer behavior follows the consumer's plans and goals as he seeks, does, and creates things, manipulating objects and information to attain his ends. However, one caveat is in order. Consumers are not performance machines—that is, they are not simply problem solvers; instead they are organisms that *learn* to solve problems, who improve upon their problem-solving abilities.

We may conclude our treatment of information processing and problem solving with the following relevant generalizations:

1. Problem solving of necessity entails the use of strategies (plans or patterns) of search behavior when the slightest complexity prevails. The greater the *cognitive strain* imposed by problem constraints such as time, information retention, and recall activities, the simpler are the search rules. The problem solver may minimize cognitive strain in part by choices of strategies.
2. Problem solving behavior is adaptive. Individuals start with a tentative solution, search for information, modify the initial solution and continue such processes until there is some balance between expected and realized behavior.
3. In even the most restricted problem solving situation, the problem solver's personality [cognitions, perceptions, and motivations] and his aversion or preference for risk enter into his choice of strategies, his use of information, and his ultimate solution.[26]

Cognitive Concepts as Behavioral Determinants

Our coverage to this point has emphasized the structural and functional aspects of cognitive psychology, and we have explored several dimensions of various cognitive phenomena, such as learning, perception, and motivation. Our treatment has also emphasized the information-processing–decision-making aspects of cognitive mental processes. We need now to explore some ideas related to cognitive activity. Inasmuch as cognitions pertain to knowledge or lists of information and because we assume that what we know affects what we do, it becomes incumbent upon us to investigate what we know, to analyze our cognitions and our cognitive structures.

There are hundreds of cognitive concepts that might be explored

[25] A. Newell, J. C. Shaw, and H. A. Simon, "The Process of Creative Thinking," *The Rand Corporation Paper*, P-1320 (August 1958), pp. 3–9.

[26] Marcus Alexis and Charles Z. Wilson, *Organizational Decision Making* (Englewood Cliffs, N.J.: Prentice-Hall, Inc., 1967), pp. 73–74. The bracketed items in the third generalization were supplied by the author.

as possible determinants of consumer behavior. Many of these concepts are well recognized and are developed in the literature. Others are more tentative and their effect on behavior is less certain. Several of these concepts will be explored in this section. Other cognitive concepts, because of their significance to and greater role in consumer behavior analysis, will be treated in separate chapters. In this section, we shall examine values, self-concepts, images, and cognitive styles. An introductory treatment of the concept of cognitive consistency is also presented.

PERSONAL VALUES AND CONSUMER BEHAVIOR

Our values constitute the basic foundation of our cognitive structures. Cognitions consist of what we know and believe and how we behave in accordance with these beliefs and knowledge. Our personal values carry expectations about our own behavior and the behavior of others. Values, like attitudes, define what is expected and what is desired. We shall reserve our treatment of attitudes and their role in consumer behavior for a later chapter. However, it must be pointed out that attitudes and values, although certainly interrelated, are usually treated as being distinctive and that convention will be honored herein. Individuals usually hold many more attitudes than values. For example, a given consumer has tens of thousands of beliefs and hundreds of attitudes but perhaps as few as a dozen values. To illustrate, a consumer may *value* thrift. As a consequence the careful spending of his resources becomes an integral part of his belief system and this, in turn, is transmitted into negative attitudes regarding the credit purchase of certain commodities. Opinions are verbalized attitudes. So with this terse attempt at differentiation, let us proceed. Marketers and others interested in market behavior and consumer actions are interested in the role of values. The concept of personal values has proliferated into a host of meanings—attitudes, opinions, beliefs, interests, preferences, valences, and so on are but a few. The major cleavage in the use of the term *value* is between those who focus on the person and his aspirations on the one hand and those who apply the term to properties of the object of choice on the other.[27] Our treatment emphasizes the role of value from the point of view of the person and as a factor or concept that does *predispose* him to certain behavior.

A definition of value that adequately stresses such a position has been supplied by Clyde Kluckhohn: "A value is a conception, explicit or implied, distinctive of an individual or characteristic of a group, of the desirable which influences the selection from available modes, means, and ends of action."[28]

[27] M. Brewster Smith, "Personal Values in the Study of Lives" in *Social Psychology and Human Values,* selected essays by M. Brewster Smith (Chicago: Aldine Publishing Company, 1969), pp. 97–116.

[28] Clyde Kluckhohn, "Values and Value Orientations in the Theory of Action" in *Toward a General Theory of Action,* T. Parsons and E. A. Shils, eds., (Cambridge. Mass · Harvard University Press), p. 395.

The real core of Kluckhohn's definition, which I would stress in terms of our orientation, is its focus on *conceptions of the desirable that are relevant to selective behavior.*

Values thus become a very special kind of attitude or *standard* by which choices are evaluated. But from whence do such standards come? The definition of values as standards suggests certain requirements pertaining to behavior. Several such types of requirement can be distinguished in a preliminary way.[29]

SOCIAL REQUIREMENT. Many of our values as standards possess a kind of social requirement. We behave as if he, she, they, or the gods are requiring something of us. Many of these values are inculcated in us as a result of a long socializing process, and thus socialization and the impact of family, culture, and groups shape and affect our personal values as standards.

PERSONAL REQUIREMENT. Out of social requirement emerges what might be called personal requirement, and this type of standard or value relates to the way in which and the extent to which people internalize social values. It relates to the idiosyncratic nature of behavior, namely, that we consciously evaluate social norms or standards and adopt those that are compatible with our individual cognitive styles. Such values, relating to what a person feels himself to be and what he stands for, become a part of the individual's *self.* As one measures oneself and one's behavior against these standards, his self-esteem rises or falls.

CONSUMER VALUES AND BEHAVIOR. A complete treatment, one that would trace the role of consumers' core values and their impact on such behavior as buying and consumption, is beyond the scope of our introductory treatment here. However, if only briefly, let us look at some major value orientations of American consumers. Values can be classified into numerous categories, such as religious, economic, aesthetic, cultural, educational, and so on. Naturally there are numerous schemes for classification, but classification schemes aside, what are some of the standards of requirement that seem to guide consumers in their behavior? First of all, Americans in general value goods. Both social requirement and personal requirement exist in the acquisition of goods.[30] The social requirement of goods ownership is often emphasized in the literature and even lampooned as a distinctive flaw in the American character.[31] Nonetheless, Americans as consumers are fond believers in a well-stocked inventory of goods and their consumption. Whether we are talking about aesthetic, religious, educational, or

[29] See Fritz Heider, "Attitudes and Cognitive Organization," *Journal of Psychology,* Vol. 21 (1946), pp. 107–112.

[30] Richard Henry Tawney, *The Acquisitive Society* (New York: Harcourt Brace Jovanovich, Inc., 1920).

[31] Thorstein Veblen, *The Theory of the Leisure Class* (New York: The Modern Library, Inc., 1918).

familial values, the role of goods within these value orientations must not be underemphasized. We build elaborate homes and stock them with numerous products and gadgets for the purpose of providing the right shelter and atmosphere for our families. Americans extol the value of education not so much because it makes one more knowledgeable, better adjusted, or more humanitarian, but usually because they believe it will increase one's learning capacity and thus facilitate the individual's acquisition of goods.

Even such sacrosanct areas as religion are infused with a goods-laden value orientation. Christmas, Easter, and Thanksgiving are religious events, but they are also the occasion for near-hysterical levels of goods purchasing, consumption, and gift giving. It seems a reasonably safe position to assume that American consumers value goods and that their core values all have, to differing degrees, a consumption orientation. In keeping with our earlier-stated definition, such a goods-infused value orientation—that is, belief in the desirability of owning and consuming goods—has an influence on the choices, modes, means, and ends of action for consumers.

Finally, it must be pointed out that a value or set of values is not itself a motive but that in relation to other facts it can and often does generate motivation. For example, in the case of consumer behavior, a discrepancy between an evaluated state of affairs and what is optimal for the person may give rise to motivation. Such an observation shows the necessity to identify the value standards that consumers have adopted, whatever they may be, and then to inquire how their appreciation or engagement, or its lack, is motivationally relevant.

IMAGE AS A COGNITIVE CONCEPT

Our mental processes and our subsequent physical acts are affected by our cognitions; that is, our knowledge affects our behavior. Cognition or knowledge consists of ideas, conceptions, perceptions, attitudes, opinions, values, and beliefs. We often lump all of these things into a category that we call knowledge. Knowledge, however, is not necessarily a good word to adopt. Perhaps a better word would be *image*, because an image is our own personalized, internalized, and conceptualized understanding of what we know. An image is not necessarily objective knowledge. Rather, it is subjective knowledge. *Knowledge* carries the implication of validity and truth. *Image* connotes what I believe to be true or what you as an individual person believe to be true. Image, therefore, is a cognitive concept much like value. However, it is important to point out that image is a phenomenon that relates to what we believe as opposed to what we know.

Our image of the world as a total mental configuration consists of cognitive sets or constructs that relate to what we think we know. An interesting theory of human behavior has been predicated upon the concept of image.[32] The theory in its simplest form states that behavior

[32] See Kenneth E. Boulding, *The Image* (Ann Arbor, Mich.: The University of Michigan Press, 1956).

depends on the image—the sum of what we think we know and what makes us act the way we do. As you will recognize, such a theory is nearly parallel to our theory of cognitive psychology as developed to this point. Thus, our earlier statement that consumers behave in accordance with what they know, what they think they know, and what they think they ought to know is contained in the image as a cognitive concept. Thus, consumer behavior stems from consumer images. Consumers' images are affected by information. The information that reaches consumers consists of experiences, and the meaning of a message is the change that it produces in the image.[33]

   CONSUMERS' IMAGES. Consumers have a tendency to create many images, and these images in turn affect consumers' behavior, attitudes, values, and predispositions. Reynolds has stated that "An image is . . . the result of a . . . complex process. It is the mental construct developed by the consumer on the basis of a few selected impressions among the flood of total impressions; it comes into being through a creative process in which selected impressions are elaborated, embellished and ordered."[34] Thus, images are systems of influences that may or may not be related to knowledge in the more literal context of cognition. Consumers create images of stores, products, brands, packages, salesmen—almost anything and everything with which they come into contact in the marketplace. These images amount to the sum total of impressions that manifest themselves in relation to objects encountered by consumers. It is not what consumers know as objective fact but what they think or "feel" subjectively about a product, brand, or store that causes their selective behavior.

Thus, a product, store, or brand image is the buyer's mental picture of how a particular product, a given store, or a designated brand differs from other products, stores, or brands. A given image is what buyers "see" and "feel" when the product milk or prunes come to mind, when the brand name Ivory is called to their attention, or when Marshall Field, Frederick and Nelson, or Dayton's Department Store is mentioned in their presence.[35]

Images contain a great deal of plot value; that is, many people feel that certain things ought to go together, and by association and inference they put them together. A product is judged to be superior because of its unique package; a brand is judged to be suitable and acceptable because it is highly promoted or is endorsed by a well-known sports personality. For example, it has been shown that images based upon a limited amount of information in advertisements bear

---

[33] Adapted from ideas presented by Boulding, ibid., p. 7.

[34] William H. Reynolds, "The Role of the Consumer in Image Building," *California Management Review*, Vol. 7 (Spring 1965), p. 69.

[35] See Rollie Tillman and C. A. Kirkpatrick, "Brand Image," in *Promotion: Persuasive Communication in Marketing*, Tillman and Kirkpatrick, eds. (Homewood, Ill.: Richard D. Irwin, Inc., 1968), pp. 198–199.

a close resemblance to images based upon detailed information and long-standing familiarity.[36] Thus, in recent years marketing practitioners and academicians have become increasingly interested in the area of images. The main thrust of this interest has been in research on product images, brand images, store images, and company images.[37]

CONSUMERS' SELF-IMAGE. The images we have been discussing are internal images, but they focus outwardly on objects, such as stores, products, brands, and so on. Yet, consumers create another kind of image that affects their behavior, their values, their attitudes, and their predispositions. These images are somewhat different from the others in that they are *self*-images. Each of us has a unique view of himself, and such a view is called a self-concept. Such a self-concept or self-image is a view of the self in relation to others.[38] We are, all of us, it seems, not one person but several. We are the person we think we are, we are the person other people think we are, and we are the person we really are.[39] (This latter self, however, is particularly hard to nail down.) A self-image is what one is aware of, one's attitudes and feelings, perceptions, and evaluations of oneself. This self-image represents a totality. The self-image becomes something to be safeguarded and protected and, if possible, to be made still more valuable. Viewed from such a perspective, is it any wonder that so much of our behavior is ego- or self-oriented in the sense that it is ego-defensive and self-enhancing?[40] One writer has been so bold as to state that the basic purpose of all human activity is the protection, the maintenance, and the enhancement of the self-concept or self-image.[41] One thing does appear rather certain: an individual's evaluation of his self will greatly

[36] Pierre Martineau, *Motivation in Advertising* (New York: McGraw-Hill Book Company, 1957), p. 164.

[37] For an extensive view of the work done in relation to images, see *Images and Marketing: A Selected and Annotated Bibliography* (Chicago: American Marketing Association, 1971), compiled and edited by Robert G. Wyckhum, William Lazer, and William J. E. Crissy.

[38] M. Brewster Smith, "The Self and Cognitive Consistency," in *Social Psychology and Human Values*, M. Brewster Smith, ed. (Chicago: Aldine Publishing Company, 1969), pp. 148–155.

[39] The source of this idea is William James, *Principles of Psychology*, Vol. 1 (New York: Holt Publishing Co., 1890).

[40] Self-psychology is a rapidly growing and expanding field of inquiry in the behavioral sciences. Self-psychologists are often called *personologists,* meaning those whose focus is upon the person and his environment-related problems. Such inquiries are often directed toward such phenomena as identity, anxiety, and the search for meaning. See, for example, C. G. Jung, *The Undiscovered Self* (Boston: Little, Brown and Company, 1957); Abraham H. Maslow, *Toward a Psychology of Being* (New York: Van Nostrand Reinhold Company, 1968); and Rollo May, *Man's Search for Himself* (New York: W. W. Norton & Company, Inc., 1953).

[41] S. I. Hayakawa, *The Semantic Barrier* (Providence, R.I.: Walter V. Clark Associates, Inc.), a speech by Hayakawa at the 1964 Conference of Activity Vector Analysis at Lake George, New York.

influence his behavior, and thus the more valued the self the more organized and consistent becomes his behavior.[42]

The self-concept is formed cognitively through one's social experience and as a result of evaluational interactions with others. The self-concept is an integral part of one's personality, and it is unique in that it includes all aspects of personality that comprise inward unity. Important wants and goals emerge that have to do with the enhancement and defense of the self. And the self becomes, then, a nucleus around which the many diverse wants and goals of the individual become organized.

SELF-IMAGE, CONSUMER BEHAVIOR, AND THE SYMBOLIC NATURE OF GOODS. What all this leads to is the generalization that much of our acquisition and use of goods is really related to our self-identity, our self-enhancement, our self-extension, and our self-esteem; that is, we buy goods to enhance or complement our own self-images, and therefore at the heart of consumer activity lies the urge to match our self-images with the image of a product, a brand, a store, or a company.

Such a train of thought leads to the proposition that consumer goods are really *social tools* or symbols that serve as a means of communication between the individual and his significant references.[43] Goods as symbols are, therefore, self-enhancing inasmuch as their purchase and use (1) sustain and buoy the individual's self-concept—that is, are viewed favorably by those around him; and (2) have mean value as well as end value—that is, can be used as a means for causing desired reactions from other individuals.

In summary, all economic goods have a high symbolic character, and making a purchase involves, at least implicitly, making an assessment of this symbolism, of deciding whether or not a given good as a symbol is congruent with our perceived sense of self or our self-image. The good as a symbol is judged suitable and is purchased, used, and enjoyed when it joins with, adds to, or reinforces the way a consumer thinks about himself.

[42] Edward L. Grubb and Harrison L. Grathwohl, "Consumer Self-concept, Symbolism and Market Behavior: A Theoretical Approach," *Journal of Marketing*, Vol. 31 (October 1967), pp. 22–27. For some specific discussion relating to self-image and brand preference, see Al E. Birdwell, "A Study of the Influence of Image Congruence on Consumer Choice," *Journal of Business*, Vol. 41, No. 1 (January 1968), pp. 76–88; Ira J. Dolick, "Congruence Relationships Between Self Images and Product Brands," *Journal of Marketing Research*, Vol. 6 (February 1969), pp. 40–47; and Joseph Barry Mason and Morris L. Mayer, "The Problem of the Self Concept in Store Image Studies," *Journal of Marketing*, Vol. 34, No. 2 (April 1970), pp. 67–69.

[43] The concept of goods as symbols has been widely researched and documented in the literature. For example, see Sidney J. Levy, "Symbols by Which We Buy," in *Advancing Marketing Efficiency*, Lynn H. Stockman, ed. (Chicago: American Marketing Association, 1959), pp. 409–416; Montrose S. Sommers, "Product Perception and the Perception of Social Strata," in *Toward Scientific Marketing*, Stephen A. Greyser, ed. (Chicago: American Marketing Association, 1969), pp. 266–279.

Cognitive style—the patterned totality of thoughts, feelings, and actions—is the reflection of the individual's personality, his roles, and his images. It is, in short, a complex and sophisticated set of mental processes, including his knowledge, that is, what he knows and what he thinks he knows. From this base stems a most profound and yet elementary derivative of consumer behavior.

As a class of cognitive structures, the self-concept has properties of stability, differentiation, and importance that should weight it heavily when it is out of balance with other types of cognitions. Individuals, it appears, seek cognitive consistency or balance, and when one bit of knowledge (cognition) is inconsistent with another bit of knowledge (cognition), cognitive dissonance is said to arise.[44]

Consumers attempt to achieve cognitive consistency in relation to self-concepts by choosing goods that are congruent with their own perceived selves. A given act of decision binds the self to a particular course of behavior. Therefore, it could well occur that given the tendency to think well of oneself, the consumer may be inclined to act more satisfied with a given product selection than he actually is. To admit having made a poor choice is tantamount, in some cases, to admitting a flaw in an idealized self-image.

Cognitive Propositions and Consumer Behavior

One of the most ambitious and comprehensive attempts to mold a theory of cognitively oriented behavior is that of Krech and Crutchfield.[45] Their theory is composed of a set of basic propositions based upon principles of cognitive psychology. Their set of propositions constitutes perhaps the most explicit and precise statement of cognitive theory in existence today. We shall use their propositions in a brief outline of consumer behavior based upon fundamental principles of cognitive psychology. Krech and Crutchfield's propositions were grouped into those dealing with the dynamics of behavior, with cognitive processes, and with the reorganization of cognitive processes. Their order of presentation is used in this work.

THE DYNAMICS OF BEHAVIOR

The first set of propositions deals with the dynamics of behavior and is concerned with generalizations about and principles of motivation, that is, what brings about behavior and action. The propositions are rather self-explanatory. However, a brief explanation of each proposition as it relates to consumer behavior will follow the statement of each proposition.

[44] Cognitive dissonance and other theories related to cognitive consistency will be explored in Chapter 6.

[45] D. Krech and R. S. Crutchfield, *Theory and Problems of Social Psychology* (New York: McGraw-Hill Book Company, 1948); page numbers for the propositions are listed following the statement of each proposition.

Proposition I. The proper unit of motivation analysis is molar behavior, which involves needs and goals (p. 30).

This statement follows from our earlier discussion and from the development of the holocentric model of behavior in Chapter 4. Consumer behavior is, in its simplest sense, based on consumers' goals, wants, needs, aspirations, and desires. Consumer behavior is goal striving and problem solving, and consumer goals arise from the sociocultural context of the consumer's existence. Thus, roles, life styles, the influence of family, life cycle, and the socialization process all bear on the consumer's motivation.

Proposition II. The dynamics of molar behavior result from properties of the immediate psychological field (p. 33).

Rather than search around in the distant past for an explanation of consumer motivation, cognitive psychology stresses the immediacy of motivation as it arises out of the nature of the goals currently sought and thus out of the problems currently facing consumers. The solution for a future problem will not necessarily be a viable solution today. Why? Because the psychological field of the consumer will probably change, or his problem will be different.

Proposition III. Instabilities in the psychological field produce tensions whose effects on perception, cognition, and action are such as to tend to change the field in the direction of a more stable structure (p. 40).

Such instabilities may come about as a result of the consumer's recognition of a deficiency or inadequacy in his assortment of goods, or they may come about as a result of conflicting cognitions that induce cognitive dissonance. Such instabilities in the psychological field may lead to an effort to reduce tension, or they may trigger a desire for increased levels of tension. In any case, the consumer structures his behavior—search, evaluation, choice, utilization—in such a way as to manage his overall tension system.

Proposition IV. The frustration of goal achievement and the failure of tension reduction may lead to a variety of adaptive or maladaptive behavior (p. 50).

The consumer, as pointed out earlier, is not a performance machine; that is, he does not simply solve problems. Rather, he learns to solve problems; sometimes he learns by complicated and sophisticated processes that lead to insight. Other times he learns by detour and transfer processes and/or by simple trial and error. He does, as the proposition suggests, often fail to find a satisfactory solution to his problem.

Proposition V. Characteristic modes of goal achievement and tension reduction may be learned and fixated by the individual (p. 66).

Consumers solve essentially two types of problems. Some are routine, recurring, and rather mundane and often involve goods of small unit value with little symbolic significance. For such cases, the consumers routinize their solution procedures and make what amounts to programmed decisions. The other type of consumer problem is not well structured, arises infrequently, and involves goods of high unit value and products of considerable symbolic significance. Such problems generate nonprogrammed solution procedures; that is, they are more cognitive in the sense that they manifest rather extensive search patterns and ideation.

COGNITIVE PROCESSES

All behavior of individuals, certainly the behavior of individual consumers, is shaped by their own private view of the world. Such a generalization necessitates describing the social world as perceived by the individual and analyzing his cognitive structure and the network of cognitive concepts that inhabit his psychological field.

Proposition I. The perceptual and cognitive field in its natural state is organized and meaningful (p. 84).

Consumers have a tendency to formulate integrated impressions and images of objects such as products, brands, stores, and companies. They also form integrated images of themselves that together are called the self-image or self-concept. Such images and impressions form the basis of much consumer behavior.

Proposition II. Perception is functionally selective (p. 87).

Consumers organize into meaningful patterns what they "see" by way of sensory stimulation. Thus, consumers selectively perceive or filter out of the environment those things that are relevant to their task and goals.[46] Essentially, this proposition means that any given perception has meaning only in relation to the cognitive structure in which it is embedded.

Proposition III. Objects or events that are close to each other in space or time or resemble each other tend to be apprehended as part of a common structure (p. 102).

Consumers tend to view not parts of things but, in the Gestalt tradition, organized "wholes." Thus, consumers associate and draw inferences from their perceived and cognitively structured associations. This process can sometimes add both halo and plot effect to a given marketing phenomenon, but it can also have detrimental and negative effects, as when a store is rejected as high-priced because of its location in a high-priced or high-rent district, or when a store is judged unfriendly because of one imperious saleslady.

[46] Perception and selective perception will be discussed at much length in Chapter 8.

COGNITIVE REORGANIZATIONS

Our cognitions do change over time. Consumers do not remain locked in an indelible pattern of behavior based upon fixed, permanent cognitions, whether these cognitions are based on true, valid, and objective knowledge or on more subjective concepts, such as values, attitudes, beliefs, and images. Consumers' cognitive structures are constantly changing in response to their constantly changing experiences. These changes result from several factors, some of which are situational, such as learning. Other changes stem from changes in the physiological state of the consumer (he is hungrier, tireder, older, and so on). And finally, some changes result from the effects of dynamic factors related to the storage and retrieval of information (forgetting).

Proposition I. As long as there is blockage to the attainment of a goal, cognitive reorganization tends to take place; the nature of the reorganization is such as to reduce (or manage) the tension induced by the frustrating situation (p. 112).

Consumer behavior is largely adaptive behavior. When frustrated, the consumer continually bestirs himself in order to reduce the frustration, usually by reducing or eliminating its cause. Cognitive reorganization and adjustment are determined by several factors, including the strength of the need or the desirability of the goal, the consumer's characteristic mode of response, and his perception of the problem or the barrier impeding his chances of successful goal attainment. In common-sense terms, consumers change their minds when their needs or goals are very intense or when barriers to the goal are misperceived.

Proposition II. Cognitive structures, over time, undergo progressive changes in accordance with the principles of organization (p. 125).

The basic organizing principle of consumer cognitions is that of the self-concept or self-image. From the generalization that the basic purpose of all human activity is the protection, maintenance, and enhancement of the self-image, it would follow that as the consumer's perception of self changes a restructuring and reordering of all cognitive concepts would result. Major changes in the perception of self would thus lead to major cognitive reorganization. Minor changes in the perception of self would thus lead to minor or minimal cognitive reorganization.

Proposition III. The ease and rapidity of the cognitive reorganization process is a function of the differentiation, isolation, and rigidity of the original cognitive structure (p. 125).

In the case of consumers, cognitive reorganization depends upon such factors as the biological capacities of the person, the conditions and the context out of which flows the original cognitive structure, the needs and emotions of the individual, and a whole host of other considerations that are closely related to the phenomenon of personality, for example, the degree of commitment to a given value or belief. Complex and integrated cognitive structures are naturally more resistant to reorganization than are simple isolated structures.

The major outlines of cognitive psychology and its role in consumer behavior should by now be readily apparent. We conclude by summarizing the high points of the treatment, namely, that consumer behavior, which itself is a form of complex social behavior, can be understood only through an understanding and a consideration of the so-called mental phenomena, such as perception, learning, and motivation.

These are cognitive functions, and they lead to the formation of cognitive structures, such as ideas, attitudes, beliefs, values, and images. We analyze these functions and their resultant structures because we believe that consumer behavior is a function of what consumers know or what they think they know. The scope of our analysis is molar rather than molecular because it is impossible to understand unitary behavior by looking at parts unrelated to wholes. Cognition is seen as a central underlying and unifying aspect of consumer behavior because of the information-processing nature of consumer goal-striving and problem-solving. Learning is treated as the basic process of cognitive reorganization, and such training may stem from the consequences of tension-reducing inclinations. However, capacity fulfillment —the desire or urge (motivation) to do, to experience, to witness, to know—is, at the very least, an important motivational impetus or determinant of consumer behavior.

Questions for Study, Reflection, and Review

1 Discuss behaviorism with regard to its reductive-functional nature.
2 Discuss the basic premise upon which cognitive theories of behavior are predicated.
3 Contrast the cognitive view of learning with the behavioral view.
4 Relate the concept of motivation presented by the behavioral school with that of the cognitive school.
5 Discuss the function of the decision process with respect to perception.
6 Describe the process of the organization of priorities in consumer problem-solving activity.
7 Differentiate between the cognitive concepts of values, opinions, and attitudes.
8 Discuss the difference between knowledge and image and the function of each in purchase behavior.
9 Describe the relationship between a consumer's self-image and his purchasing behavior.
10 Discuss the effect of the self-image upon cognitive reorganization.

6

Cognitive
Consistency
and Consumer
Behavior

Introduction

In Chapter 5 we attempted to map the relevant dimensions of a psychology of cognition. Cognition, as stated previously, relates to a cluster of psychological activities that are a central part of mental behavior. The term itself refers to a set, cluster, or constellation of knowledge, attitudes, and perceptual states. Briefly put, cognition refers to a particular individual's total and integrated belief system. This means that cognitions are things a person knows about himself, his behavior, and his surroundings. However, in a broader sense cognitions are not only what a person knows, but they include also those things that people think they know. Cognitions, therefore, include such items as knowledge, values, attitudes, opinions, beliefs, and images. From our introduction to cognitive psychology we moved rapidly to a discussion of its implications for consumer behavior. Thus, we learned that our cognitions, broadly conceived, constitute a kind of framework out of which flows our behavior. Consumer perceptions, motivation, learning—in short, nearly all the determinants of behavior in general—are affected by cognition-related considerations. Thus, what a consumer does—what he buys, how he selects, processes, and perceives information, how he chooses, and how he evaluates products after he purchases them—is affected by his cognitions, by what he knows or thinks he knows. Having been introduced to cognitive concepts and processes, we are now ready to examine and consider the role of another cognition-related phenomenon—the role of cognitive consistency in consumer behavior. At the core of all cognition-related models or theories of behavior is the postulate that individuals strive toward attaining consistency among cognitions. For example, consumers strive for consistency among their values, beliefs, knowledge, images, and actions. Furthermore, it is argued that they strive for consistency among their generalized cognitions of themselves and objects or persons in their environment, psychological field, or frame of reference. It is additionally argued that inconsistency results in psychological discomfort and disturbance. As a result psychological tension, anxiety, and sometimes guilt tend to incline customers toward behavior that reduces such tension in their cognitive structure. A most interesting set of propositions! In this chapter we shall explore the ramifications of such propositions in the following manner: (1) by citing the early sources of this flourishing consistency theory; (2) by developing and sketching out several of the approaches that have emanated from consistency propositions; (3) by reviewing some of the problems and shortcomings of consistency approaches; and (4) by meaningfully relating several consistency theories to consumer behavior phenomena and suggesting where consistency theory fits within the larger framework of consumer behavior analysis.

Cognitive Consistency: The Outline of the Theory

Perhaps the progenitor of all cognitive consistency concepts is Fritz Heider, whose early work in cognitive organization laid the foundation for a series of subsequent treatments of the concept.[1] His idea, for example, that if person P likes other person O, and O likes object X, then P will also tend to like X was the basic building block of balance or consistency within cognitions. From this beginning Newcomb applied the theory to communicative arts, examined its motivational basis, and refined it in terms of role theory within the structure of his A-B-X model.[2]

Osgood and Tannenbaum attempted to quantify the links between cognitions and became increasingly concerned with a phenomenon that they called "cognitive congruity."[3]

Finally, another intrapersonal consistency approach that has received enormous space in the literature is the theory of cognitive dissonance proposed by Festinger.[4] To be sure, numerous significant others

[1] F. Heider, "Attitudes and Cognitive Organization," *Journal of Psychology,* Vol. 21 (1946), pp. 107–112.

[2] T. M. Newcomb, "The Prediction of Interpersonal Attraction," *American Psychologist,* Vol. 11 (1956), pp. 575–586.

[3] C. E. Osgood and P. H. Tannenbaum, "The Principle of Congruity in the Prediction of Attitude Change," *Psychological Review,* No. 62 (1955), pp. 42–55.

[4] L. Festinger, *A Theory of Cognitive Dissonance* (Stanford, Calif.: Stanford University Press, 1957).

have been involved in the development and refinement of cognitive consistency concepts, but those mentioned have surely played the most important role in the advancement of the theory. Our examination will focus on the concepts and points of view of these originators and developers of the concept.

THE ESSENTIAL ELEMENTS OF THE THEORY

The basic and essential elements of the concept of cognitive consistency are relatively simple. Each theorist, or each of the models, utilizes a set of polar adjectives and a mechanism or proposition. The polar adjectives already in use are extensive—consonant, dissonant; balanced, imbalanced; congruous, incongruous; symmetrical, asymmetrical; harmonious, inharmonious; and many others. Each pair of adjectives contains one word that describes cognitions that fit together consistently, and the other word describes cognitions that are inconsistent with one another.

The mechanism or essential proposition of the cognitive consistency concept is simply that inconsistency compels people to alter their cognitive system in such a way that it will become consistent or more consistent.

Inconsistent cognitions are said to arouse tension, strain toward symmetry, pressure toward congruity, or psychological dissonance. It must be admitted that there are wide variations among theories concerning the identification of cognitions that are psychologically inconsistent as well as the nature of the psychological state resulting from inconsistent cognitions and the kinds of behavior that lead to consistency.

Cognitive consistency may be related to either cognitive style or cognitive processes or, for that matter, both. In relation to cognitive style, for example, people may, when encountering new cognitions or pieces of knowledge or information, encode, restructure, distort, or learn them in a way that is consistent with their existing sets of cognitions. Additionally, people may have an incomplete set of cognitions about a behavioral system, and they may then infer the missing relations in such a way as to create closure, completeness, or consistency within their entire cognitive system. Such a use of and insistence upon consistency may be a trial-and-error way as part of a cognitive style for the scanning, processing, and storing of information.[5]

On the other hand, cognitive consistency may be sought or attained through cognitive processes. For example, a person who changes his feelings of attraction to another person or object as a result of being linked with that person or object is maintaining consistency within his cognitive structure not by encoding new information in a consistent or congruent fashion but by some process of changing or

[5] Jerome E. Singer, "Motivation for Consistency," in *Cognitive Consistency*, Shel Feldman, ed. (New York: Academic Press, Inc., 1966), pp. 49–50.

adjusting already existing cognitions to maintain or enhance a new level of consistency.

Finally, the basic notion of cognitive consistency is that inconsistent cognitions lead to behavior directed toward the achievement of consistency.

THE ALTERNATIVE TO CONSISTENCY

The extreme alternative to consistency is, of course, inconsistency.[6] And there is some evidence to suggest that total cognitive consistency is not the desired goal of people generally or of consumers in particular. We saw earlier that people may seek cognitive tension or excitement, essentially through the establishment of inconsistent cognitions. Whereas cognitive-consistency-seeking consumers would be characterized as having a strong drive toward stability, redundancy, familiarity, confirmation of expectation, and avoidance of the new, the unpredictable, and the uncertain, the cognitive-inconsistency-seeking consumer would be likely to manifest a tendency toward stimulus hunger, an exploratory drive, and a curiosity need. They would seek and take pleasure in the unexpected, the uncertain, and the unpredictable. Such a consumer, and there are probably many, would want to experience everything, show a tendency for behavior alternation, and revel in the reward and satisfaction of novelty.[7]

Thus, inconsistency conceivably can be as desired a state as consistency from the standpoint of consumers, and inconsistency may be sought to satisfy a number of conditions.

1. Under certain conditions, a consumer might well manifest or engage in behavior that is inconsistent because in so doing he maximizes his satisfaction from ultimate tension reduction. For example, a bizarre purchase may be made for the satisfaction that comes from willfully violating one's own consistent style.

2. Under certain conditions, the consumer seeks cognitive inconsistency in order to contain or mask conflicts of a different dimension. For example, given a mild depression, the consumer may go on a spending binge and indulge himself needlessly in order to change his frame of mind.

3. As previously mentioned, tension management, and not total tension reduction, is the usual goal of consumer behavior. Consumers may take a measure of their need for cognitive consistency by engaging occasionally in acts that they know to be inconsistent. Therefore, an optimal level of cognitive tension might well involve some ratio of consistent to inconsistent behavior.

There are other numerous ramifications of cognitive consistency concepts that we must at least tentatively explore. However, before

[6] See the discussion on rationality in Chapter 4.

[7] These ideas were suggested by William J. McGuire, "The Current Status of Cognitive Consistency Theories," in *Cognitive Consistency*, Shel Feldman, ed. (New York: Academic Press, Inc., 1966), p. 37.

proceeding further, let us examine several different models or theories of cognitive consistency. In our desire to attempt a broad coverage, we shall not neglect specifics and details, but for brevity's sake neither shall we allow any one of the models to detain us for long. We shall begin with Heider, proceed to Newcomb, and hence to Osgood and Tannenbaum. We shall dwell at length on Festinger's concept of cognitive dissonance, primarily because of the extraordinary interest it has generated in relation to marketing and consumer behavior.

Heider's Balance Theory

The forefather of nearly all cognitive consistency theories is Heider's P-O-X balance theory. This theory was first proposed by Heider in 1946 and was later amplified and refined in 1958.[8] Heider's balance model is a highly relevant model for consumer behavior analysis and an almost ideal starting point for a consideration of cognitive consistency as an important consumer behavior variable. Essentially, the balance model makes this assertion: A person tends to like the object he owns; or not owning the things he likes, he tends to want to own them. Ownership tends to bring the object into a structural unit with the self, and sentiments toward elements in the same structural unit tend to become uniform. As outlined earlier in our discussion of self-image, the balance prediction must assume that the individual likes himself, because it is with a positive feeling toward the self that a positive sentiment toward the newly owned object would come into balance.[9] Consumers who do not like themselves would find themselves in a state of cognitive imbalance if they sought ownership of a desirable object.

Heider's balance theory is concerned with the sentiments or feeling of a person P toward another person O and an impersonal object X belonging or associated with O. The major thrust of the theory is that separate entities, such as P-O-X, constitute a unit or a kind of Gestalt when they are seen as belonging together. When the total unit has the same dynamic character in all respects, a balanced state exists—there is equilibrium and no tendency to change.

However, when the various elements of the unit cannot coexist with stress, a tensional force is released, and this tensional force exerts a pressure to achieve a balanced state. Hence, imbalanced units lead to a kind of psychic disequilibrium, and this disequilibrium sets forces in motion to bring about a balanced state. According to Heider, the condition of unit formations—the extent to which they are balanced or unbalanced—is a function of perceptual organization, and therefore, the major unit-forming factors are conditions such as proximity, similarity, common fate, set, past experience, role, and personality.

[8] Heider, op. cit.; and *The Psychology of Interpersonal Relations* (New York: John Wiley & Sons, Inc., 1958).

[9] M. Brewster Smith, "The Self and Cognitive Consistency," in *Social Psychology and Human Values*, M. Brewster Smith, ed. (Chicago, Ill.: Aldine Publishing Company, 1969), p. 148–155.

Thus, things are seen as a unit if they are customarily or habitually seen together, or if they are together in space and time, or if they experience or undergo the same consequences. By and large, entities become a part of a set through the usual processes of association and socialization.

According to Heider's explanation two types of relations in the P-O-X system emerge: unit relations and sentiment relations. There are two dimensions to a unit relation: U and not U. Elements are seen as belonging together (U) or as not belonging together (not U). Unit formations are a critical part of Heider's theory. For example, if P, a customer, likes O, a salesperson, and dislikes X, Ford automobiles, the question of balance is of no great concern so long as O and X are seen as entirely separate entities. For example, the salesperson in question in our example sells Chevrolet automobiles. The U relationship was seen by Heider as positive and the not U relation as negative.[10] In addition to unit relations, Heider's model stresses sentiment relations, an important construct. Sentiment relations relate to a person's evaluation of something; they refer to such sentiments as liking, admiring, approving or rejecting, disliking, or condemning. As you can see, sentiment relations can also be either positive, which is designated L, or negative, which is designated DL.

Heider's balance theory formulation can be used to analyze both dyadic and triadic relations. For example, if P likes X where P is a consumer and X is a product, and P owns X, the dyad is balanced. However, if P owns X and dislikes X, then the dyad is imbalanced. To take a somewhat more sophisticated triadic example, consider that if P likes both O and X, and O owns X, there are two L relations and one U relation, and the triad is balanced. If P dislikes both O and X, and O owns X, the situation is also balanced because there are two negative DL relations and one positive (U) relation. However, if P likes O but dislikes his product, X, the triad is in an imbalanced state. Figure 6-1 may well facilitate our discussion and understanding at this point.

In Figure 6-1 we have consumer P in an interactive unit formation with salesperson O regarding product or goal object X. The relationship, as can be seen, is a balanced one, and the outcome would probably be a completed sale, a satisfied customer, and a pleased salesperson. It is a rather well-documented generalization in psychology that the attitudes and attraction of two people in an interactive situation can affect the evaluations of one or both of impersonal objects or events.[11]

---

[10] It was subsequently pointed out that it is desirable to distinguish between the opposite of a relation and the complement of a relation. Therefore, the not U relation has more recently been treated as neutral rather than negative. For an analysis of this view, see D. Cartwright and F. Harary, "Structural Balance: A Generalization of Heider's Theory," *Psychological Review*, Vol. 63 (1956), pp. 277–293.

[11] Heider, op. cit., pp. 107–112.

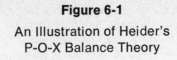

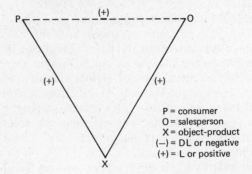

Figure 6-1

An Illustration of Heider's
P-O-X Balance Theory

P = consumer
O = salesperson
X = object-product
(−) = DL or negative
(+) = L or positive

Thus, for example, if P (one person) has a relation of affection for O (another person) and if O is seen as responsible for X (an impersonal object or event), then there will be a tendency for P to like or approve of X. If the nature of X is such that it would "normally" be evaluated as bad, the whole P-O-X unit is placed in a state of imbalance and pressure may arise to change it toward a state of balance. These pressures may work to change the relation of affection between P and O, the relation of responsibility between O and X, or the relation of evaluation between P and X.[12]

Thus our illustration serves to point out the dynamics of just these kinds of relationships. A salesperson who projects a cognitive style or image similar to the cognitive style or image of his customers is most likely to be effective in convincing those same customers of the merits of the goods being sold. Conversely, salespeople can "turn off" even the most enthusiastic of customers if the style, manner, or degree of aggressiveness is greatly out of balance with their customers. Too often consumers will forego a desired goal object if they must endure an unpleasant person in order to get it.[13] Such a situation is cognitively unpleasant and therefore imbalanced. The effects or consequences of such imbalanced states are several.

1. People seek or seem to prefer balanced states. If a customer doesn't like a given salesperson, he will tend to avoid that person. When such a situation occurs, the cognitions seem to be pulling in different directions, and this causes psychic disturbance, tension, or anxiety. Because such disturbances are generally considered undesirable, disturbance-inducing situations are avoided.

---

[12] Cartwright and Harary, op. cit., p. 283.

[13] For a more elaborate treatment of this idea, see F. B. Evans, "Selling as a Dyadic Relationship—A New Approach," *American Behavioral Scientist*, Vol. 6 (May 1963), pp. 76–79.

2. Given a particular relation, the tendency toward balance induces other relations that result in a balanced state. For example, if P likes O and P is a customer and O is a salesperson, then P would tend to like X, in this case another salesperson in the same store, or X products sold by O. Another example might be relevant. If P shops at O frequently where O is a given store, then P, given his continuing familiarity with O, would tend to be inclined to like store O increasingly. Association between familiarity and liking has been extensively and rather convincingly demonstrated.[14]

3. The major effect, of course, is that imbalanced states arouse pressure to change cognitive relations. Customers who do not like a given brand, change. If they do not like a salesperson or a store, they withhold their patronage and look for salespeople and stores that are more compatible. Given the tendency for seeking such balanced states, consumers are likely to devise new shopping strategies and to modify extensively their consumer decision processes.

Thus, Heider's P-O-X balance theory is an interesting starting point and a simple framework for analysis regarding the concept of cognitive consistency. His theory is simple and straightforward, and it provides a wealth of testable hypotheses. It is a conceptually rich construct. It should be noted that the relations posed by Heider are all-or-none in nature. One *likes* or *dislikes,* and therefore the *degree* of taste, sentiment, or affection is totally ignored. Such a shortcoming should not be minimized in an evaluation of the effectiveness of the theory as a framework for a sophisticated analysis of consumer behavior.

Newcomb's A-B-X Theory

Newcomb's A-B-X theory is quite similar to Heider's P-O-X theory. Heider's theory unquestionably contained the central idea upon which most theories of cognitive consistency are based. The A-B-X theory actually emerged in the late 1930s, but it was the mid 1950s that witnessed the serious formalization of the concept.[15] It is important to note early that Newcomb's theory is related to communicative acts—a kind of activity that is highly important in terms of marketing strategy and consumer behavior. The theory's central proposition is that there are certain logical relations among beliefs and attitudes held by any given individual. Certain of these relationships or combinations are psychologically unstable, and their instability results in behavior directed toward the attainment of greater stability. Newcomb's theory

---

[14] See F. E. Fiedler, W. G. Warrington, and F. J. Blaisdell, "Unconscious Attitudes as Correlates of Sociometric Choice in a Social Group," *Journal of Abnormal and Social Psychology,* Vol. 47 (1952), pp. 790–796.

[15] For the history of the concept, see T. M. Newcomb and G. Svehla, "Intrafamily Relationships in Attitudes," *Sociometry,* Vol. 1 (1937), pp. 180–205; and T. M. Newcomb, "An Approach to the Study of Communicative Acts," *Psychological Review,* Vol. 60 (1953), pp. 393–404.

has been applied to communicative acts between or among individuals as well as to acts and interrelationships within groups. His basic proposition rests on his assumption that communication performs the necessary function of enabling two persons to maintain a simultaneous orientation toward each other and at the same time toward the object of their communication.

The key elements upon which the A-B-X system is built are (1) communicative acts, (2) orientation, (3) coorientation, and (4) system strain.

A *communicative act* is the sending of information from a source to a destination or recipient. Information consists of stimuli associated with objects. Such information makes it possible to differentiate one object from another. The simplest act of communication consists of a situation in which one person (A) communicates or transmits information to another person (B) regarding something: an event, an object, a situation, or a person (X). A shorthand representation of this simple process is A to B re X, meaning A to B regarding X.

Orientation refers to the way people relate themselves to others or to events or objects. Orientation toward people is called *attraction* in Newcomb's model and orientation toward objects is called *attitude*. *Coorientation* refers to the interdependence of A's orientation to B and to X and, in Newcomb's framework, thus means that a given person can be oriented toward another person and an object at the same time and in the same context. For example, if A attributes to B a given attitude toward X and A himself holds an attitude toward X, A is said to be cooriented toward B and X.

The dynamics of Newcomb's system are built upon the concept of *system strain*. System strain is a propensity toward symmetry and is very similar to Heider's concept of system balance. If a discrepancy in a self-other orientation is discerned, or if such a discrepancy arises as a result of uncertainty regarding the other's orientation, then psychological tension arises and the tendency toward symmetry is set in motion.

Figure 6-2 should clarify several of these relationships and add measurably to our understanding of the theory.

In much of advertising, promotion, and personal selling, a sales message is delivered by some medium to an audience. The most general principle is to link the product with some person or thing highly valued by the consumer and by this means to cause the consumer to think highly enough of the product to buy it. It must never be overlooked that when people are living well above the subsistence level they begin to be interested in buying expensive symbols. The product can be made into a desirable symbol if it is placed in an appropriately suggestive setting and if a lot of money is spent to expose the result to a lot of people.

Symbols, in effect, become a means of self-enhancement. In Figure 6-2, individual A purchases and uses symbol X, which has intrinsic

Figure 6-2

An Illustration of Newcomb's A-B-X Theory

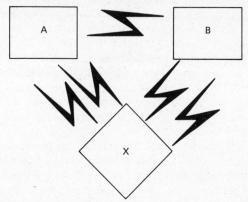

Source: Adapted from Edward L. Grubb and Harrison Grathwohl, "Consumer Self-concept, Symbolism and Market Behavior: A Theoretical Approach," *Journal of Marketing*, Vol. 31 (October 1967), pp. 22–27.

and extrinsic value as a means of self-enhancement.[16] By the use of symbol X, individual A communicates with himself and also with B. B may be a friend, an associate, a family member, or any significant other. Individual A is oriented to symbol X given his positive attitudes toward symbol X. A is oriented to B, because he is concerned about B's evaluation of A and A's choice of product. A is cooriented to both B and X because he has an attraction for B and a positive attitude toward X.

The model shown in Figure 6-2 is symmetrical. Such cognitive symmetry permits an individual to predict and anticipate the other's behavior. If A and B have similar orientations toward X, there is less need for either of them to translate X in terms of the other's orientation. Too, coorientation becomes less difficult.

Strain and asymmetry, however, do arise, and when they do the usual result is an increased amount of symmetry-directed communication. Such a reaction varies with a number of factors:

1. The degree of attraction between A and B.
2. The degree of perceived attitude discrepancy between A and B.
3. The certainty, strength, or commitment of A and B.
4. The importance of X as a goal object or symbol.
5. The relevance of X to the symmetry of the system.

---

[16] This example is from Edward L. Grubb and Harrison Grathwohl, "Consumer Self-concept, Symbolism and Market Behavior: A Theoretical Approach," *Journal of Marketing*, Vol. 31 (October 1967), pp. 22–27.

When strain or asymmetry does occur, Newcomb suggests several ways in which an individual can reduce strain. He might (1) reduce the strength of his attraction to B, (2) reduce the relevance of X, (3) reduce the perceived relevance of X to B, (4) reduce the importance of X, (5) reduce the perceived importance of X to B, (6) change his own attitudes, or (7) change his perception of B's attitude toward X. This is quite a number of possibilities. It should be added that all of these schemes for reducing strain and bringing about symmetry can be facilitated without communication. However, the process is likely to be enhanced by the use of communication processes. In consumer behavior and marketing, the role of communication as such a facilitating device could hardly be overstated.

Efforts to sell products are invariably communicative acts—the transmission of messages—in the mass media and sometimes in face-to-face conversation. The fact that a potential buyer can send messages to his would-be persuader in the second case, but cannot in the first case, makes a difference in the strategy of persuasion. Both strategies, however, fall within the domain of balance and symmetry theory.

A treatment of interactive elements such as is depicted in Newcomb's A-B-X theory "fits" in a rather loose way many familiar phenomena in the sphere of persuasion and attitude change. But the question is, What is it that fits? The answer is that lack of symmetry or balance is a force for change, and this theme is recurrent throughout the entire range of cognitive consistency concepts. Newcomb's model, although nearly identical to Heider's, adds the enriching concept of interpersonal communication. Thus, his analysis has clarified many aspects of the interpersonal situation and has provided a host of interesting and testable hypotheses concerning interpersonal behavior. Our treatment of his model should prove useful in our later analysis and treatment of communication, group dynamics, and other interpersonal behavior phenomena.

THE CONGRUITY PRINCIPLE

Our treatment of cognitive consistency concepts would be incomplete without at least some discussion of Osgood and Tannenbaum's congruity principle.[17] We shall return again to the congruity principle at the time when we explore the role of attitudes in consumer behavior. Therefore, our treatment of the concept will be necessarily brief at this juncture and is included now only because congruity is a notion central to cognitive consistency.

The congruity principle stems from Osgood and Tannenbaum's work that relates to prediction of attitude change when communication from an identifiable source urges a subject-person to adopt a particular

[17] C. E. Osgood and P. H. Tannenbaum, "The Principle of Congruity in the Prediction of Attitude Change," *Psychological Review*, Vol. 62 (1955), pp. 42–55.

attitude toward some goal.[18] Several important variables constitute the dynamic aspect of this principle, namely, the existing attitude toward the goal object, the existing attitude toward the source of the message about the goal object, and the evaluative nature of the assertion between source and goal object.[19] The congruity model attempts to predict both the direction and the amount of attitude change toward both the source and the goal object. A great part of the theory that underlies the congruity principle grew out of Osgood's work concerning the meaning of concepts and the measurement of meaning by use of the semantic differential scales.[20]

The basic idea of the congruity principle is quite similar to that of balance theory (Heider) and symmetry (Newcomb). Essentially, the congruity principle states that when two or more attitude objects (a communication source and a goal object) are linked by an assertion, there is a tendency for the evaluation of one or both of the objects to change so that the evaluations of the two objects are more similar. The principle also contends that changes in evaluation always occur in the direction of increased congruence within the person's frame of reference. For example, the principle suggests that if a well-received, positively evaluated salesperson praises a negatively perceived and evaluated product, there would be a subsequent tendency for the salesman to be evaluated more negatively and the product or goal object to be evaluated more positively. Or a well-liked, positively evaluated company that brings out a new low-priced and low-quality product will tend to bring about in the eyes of the subject a situation in which the company loses stature and the single product gains stature. An interesting proposition, to say the least! It must be pointed out that the issue of congruity arises only when two or more attitude objects are connected by an assertion. The most common assertions are descriptive; for example, "Camay soaps are mild." The two concepts involved here are Camay soap and mildness. If the subject evaluates both Camay and mildness positively, he is not apt to change. But if he evaluates soap as drying and harsh (negatively) and evaluates mildness positively, he tends to change because incongruity is present. Just such reasoning

[18] Attitudes, it should be remembered, are a subset of cognitions. Attitudes are basically learned predispositions to respond to an object or a class of objects in a consistently favorable or unfavorable way. We shall refine this definition considerably, however, in our subsequent efforts. For an excellent treatment of the relationship between cognitions and attitudes, see Martin Fishbein, "The Relationship Between Beliefs, Attitudes and Behavior," in *Cognitive Consistency*, Shel Feldman, ed. (New York: Academic Press, Inc., 1966), pp. 200–226.

[19] Osgood and Tannenbaum used the term *concept* to mean the thing toward which persons hold or project attitudes. I have used the term *goal object* because, in the case of consumer behavior, the attitudes under study are often those related to products, or goal objects, as they are often called.

[20] C. E. Osgood, "The Nature and Measurement of Meaning," *Psychological Bulletin*, Vol. 49 (1952), pp. 197–237; semantic differential scales will be treated in Chapter 10.

is the basis for the marketing of many products, for example, lotions for cleansing the face that contain no harsh soaps or drying ingredients: "Dove is one-quarter cleansing cream."

In addition to descriptive assertions, another kind of assertion is a statement of classification; for example, "Geritol is a geriatric product." Such a statement, even though it is one of classification, is not likely to be perceived neutrally. If the subject evaluates Geritol positively and geriatric products negatively, his overall evaluation of both the product and the other attitude object—geriatric products—regresses to the mean evaluation of both. The most complex and sophisticated assertions involve those in which a *source* makes a statement or assertion about an object. All assertions are classified as either associative (or positive) or disassociative (or negative). In essence, Osgood and Tannenbaum postulate that sources that are evaluated positively should support the things we as subjects support or in general reinforce our cognitions (attitudes, values, knowledge, and beliefs). By the same token, sources that we dislike or evaluate negatively should deprecate the things that we support and fail to reinforce the things we like. *Thus, what emerges from this argument is a tendency for congruency whereby the total pressure to change an evaluation of either the attitude or goal object or the source is equal to the difference between its polarization and the point of maximum congruence.*

Several important corollaries can be derived from the congruity principle, and they all have important bearing on various dimensions of consumer behavior. For example:

1. Changes in evaluation are always in the direction of equalization of the polarization of objects associated by an assertion. For example, some balance is struck by the consumer in terms of the desirability of owning a new car and the unpleasantness of committing himself to twenty-four or thirty-six "easy payments."

2. Given the tendency toward congruity, it is sometimes easier to move toward more rather than less polarization. Cognitive consistency is sometimes more easily attainable when the subject insists upon the differentiation of one cognitive evaluation from another. Evaluative frames of reference often tend to simplify, and such simplification leads to increases in gross polarizations. For example, two products may be nearly identical. Yet to facilitate making a decision about which product to purchase, the subject may impute greater differences to the products than actually exist.

3. The amount of attitude change in a given subject concerning a given object is an inverse function of the intensity of the initial attitude toward the subject. This requires a minimum of elaboration. The simple point is that attitudes, beliefs, and values to which we have a strong psychic commitment are not easily changed. Weakly held attitudes, values, and beliefs are more subject to change.

As an example, a pipe smoker who believes pipe smoking is essential to his image of himself in terms of his perceived role—professor, sportsman, and so on—is not likely to be persuaded that smoking is harmful and ought to be abandoned.

Thus, the congruity principle hopefully adds one additional layer of understanding to our overall treatment of cognitive consistency concepts. The congruity principle, because of its logical consistency and its ready testability, is an important theory for consumer behavior analysis. And it continues to serve a useful purpose in stimulating research and in describing variables that have been neglected by other theories and approaches.

The Theory of Cognitive Dissonance

The theory of cognitive dissonance is predicted upon the assumption that each individual strives toward consistency among his opinions, attitudes, and values. In addition, each individual strives toward consistency among his psychological attributes and the behavior that stems from them: "All of us, for example, have at one time or another experienced the discomfort of having someone point out to us during some discussion that we have made two or more contradictory statements."[21] This is an example of inconsistency among psychological attributes. We can also think of the case of an individual who feels one way and behaves another way. Take for example the student who strongly believes that cheating on an examination is wrong, yet when the opportunity to cheat arises, he does so. This individual's behavior is inconsistent with his belief about cheating. This type of inconsistency would also lead to cognitive dissonance.

Another basic assumption of the theory is that sets of cognitions can be clustered into elements: "Some of these elements represent knowledge about oneself: what one does, what one feels, what one wants or desires, what one is, and the like. Other elements of knowledge concern the world in which one lives: what is where, what leads to what, what things are satisfying or painful or inconsequential or important, etc."[22] Elements, then, consist of a set of cognitions that deal with a specific attitude, value, or belief.

Because dissonance is a direct result of an inconsistency between sets of elements, it is necessary to examine the relationship that can exist between pairs of elements. Elements can exist in either an irrelevant or a relevant relationship. Two elements can exist that have nothing to do with each other: "That is, under such circumstances where one cognitive element implies nothing at all concerning some other element, these two elements are irrelevant to one another."[23]

[21] Leon Festinger and Dana Bramel, "The Reactions of Humans to Cognitive Dissonance," in *Experimental Foundations of Clinical Psychology*, Arthur J. Bachrach, ed. (New York: Basic Books, 1962), p. 254.

[22] Festinger, op. cit., p. 9.

[23] Ibid., p. 11.

There is little to say about irrelevant elements because dissonance or consonance will not result from them. Relevant elements are elements that can cause dissonance. In other words, elements that logically follow from each other are consonant; if they *should* follow from each other and do not, they are dissonant.[24] The vagueness of this definition results from the words *follow from:* "Thus, the specification of the phrase 'follows from' involves specification of the operation by means of which one can say that for a given person, element A follows from element B."[25] As stated earlier, two elements may follow from each other because of logic. However, they may also follow from each other because of learning, experience, or certain sociological processes, such as small-group expectations or mores.

It is helpful to point out that dissonance can exist within a person's behavioral or environmental cognitive structure as well as between the behavioral and environmental cognitions. If an individual experiences dissonance between a behavioral and an environmental cognitive element, he can do one of two things: he may attempt to change his behavior so that it will be more consistent with his attitudes and opinions, or he may attempt to change his opinions and attitudes so that they will be more consistent with his behavior. However, if dissonance should exist between attitudes and opinions, the only change that can occur is among these environmental cognitions: "This, of course, is much more difficult than changing one's behavior, for one must have a sufficient degree of control over one's environment—a relatively rare occurrence."[26] Because environmental cognitions are more difficult to control and therefore change, most changes that do take place because of the existence of dissonance are in a person's behavioral elements.

DISSONANCE-AROUSING SITUATIONS

From this brief recapitulation of the theory of cognitive dissonance, it is easy to see that there are a number of situations in which cognitive dissonance can exist. The purpose of this section is to examine a number of these different situations.[27]

A large amount of the work in cognitive dissonance has been concerned with the dissonance that occurs after a decision between two or more alternatives has been made.[28] Each alternative has both positive and negative characteristics of which the individual is aware. After the decision has been made, all the negative characteristics of the chosen

[24] Ibid., p. 13.

[25] Ibid., p. 279.

[26] Ibid., p. 20.

[27] An extensive list of dissonance-arousing situations can be found in Festinger, op. cit., pp. 261–262.

[28] See, for example, J. W. Brehm, "Postdecision Changes in the Desirability of Alternatives," *Journal of Abnormal and Social Psychology*, Vol. 52 (1956), pp. 384–398; also, see D. Ehrlich, I. Guttman, P. Schonbach, and J. Mills, "Postdecision Exposure to Relevant Information," *Journal of Abnormal and Social Psychology*, Vol. 54 (1957), pp. 98–102.

alternative are dissonant with the act of choosing this specific alternative. Inversely, all the positive characteristics of the unchosen alternatives are dissonant with the fact that these alternatives have not been chosen. It is also believed that the more attractive the alternatives are, the greater the dissonance.[29] For example, if an individual had to choose between two automobiles that he felt were of equal quality and style, he would experience more dissonance than if he had to choose between what he felt were a superior and an inferior automobile.

Dissonance can also arise when an attempt is made to elicit overt behavior that is at variance with an individual's private opinion. For example, if an individual is offered a reward to make a certain statement or testimonial about a product that is the opposite of his belief, dissonance will occur. This type of dissonance, however, is not self-induced in the strictest sense. Some form of dissonance or inconsistency would be expected to occur in this type of situation.

Forced or accidental exposure to new information may also create dissonance. The new cognitive elements that result from the new information may be dissonant with present cognitions: "Thus, the theory predicts that persons . . . generally seek out consonant information and avoid information that would introduce new dissonant elements."[30] It has been assumed that individuals generally expose themselves to information that they find congenial with their existing attitudes and beliefs and avoid information that may be irritating or dissonant.

Cognitive dissonance can also be experienced when there is open disagreement in a group. The fact that some other individual, generally like oneself, holds a contrary opinion is usually uncomfortable to the individual. It has been found that attitudes that are in conflict with one or more reference groups are apt to be less intense than those that are in agreement with the reference groups.[31] It has also been hypothesized that the existence of dissonance will lead a person to seek social support of an attitude or belief.[32] In this case, opinion disagreement could result in the deterioration of a group, assuming that the individual's attitudes are strongly held. In this instance, the individual would search for a group whose attitudes and opinions are more like his own.

The Magnitude of Dissonance

Generally, the more attractive the rejected alternative, the greater will be the magnitude of the dissonance. Thus, it is possible for a person to make a decision and experience a great amount of dissonance,

---

[29] J. W. Brehm and A. R. Cohen, *Explorations in Cognitive Dissonance* (New York: John Wiley & Sons, Inc., 1962), Chapter 2.

[30] Ehrlich, Guttman, Schonbach, and Mills, op. cit., p. 98.

[31] S. S. Komarita and Ira Bernstein, "Attitude Intensity and Dissonant Cognitions," *Journal of Abnormal and Social Psychology*, Vol. 69 (September 1964), pp. 323–329.

[32] Festinger, op. cit., p. 217.

even after he is convinced that the decision was the best he could have made under the circumstances. In this situation dissonance will usually be greater because of the attractive characteristics of the unchosen alternative. The greater the number of attractive characteristics, the greater the amount of dissonance.

Another factor that will affect the magnitude of dissonance is the importance attached to a specific decision: "Other things being equal, the more important the decision, the stronger will be the dissonance."[33] For the most part, the importance of a decision depends on the individual. For example, the decision to move to a new and strange city may cause greater dissonance than a decision to buy one type of car instead of another, but for the individual who is accustomed to moving quite often this may not be true. It becomes obvious that an accurate measurement of dissonance is quite a difficult task. Because dissonance varies for different people, a great deal must be known about a person's cognitive structure and his cognitive style before an attempt is made to measure the magnitude of dissonance. However, for a given person dissonance generally increases as the importance he places on the decision increases.

Another major determinant of the magnitude of dissonance is the number of negative characteristics of the chosen alternative. Generally, the intensity of dissonance becomes greater as the number of negative characteristics increases. Consider the case of an individual with a fixed budget to spend on a certain item. If a more expensive item that was superior to the lower-priced item was available, he may be quite aware of the negative characteristics of the lower-priced item he had to purchase because of his budget. Under these circumstances the negative characteristics will increase the individual's dissonance, especially if the superior item does not cost a great deal more than the lower-priced item.

Another factor that may influence the magnitude of dissonance deals with the number of rejected alternatives. As the number of rejected alternatives increases, the greater will be the dissonance. As stated previously, each rejected alternative has some favorable characteristics of which the individual is aware. Therefore, the total number of favorable characteristics increases as the number of rejected alternatives becomes greater. Following this through, it is possible to think of the case of an individual having to choose among so many alternatives that he may delay or even decline making a decision. However, at this point psychological processes such as selective exposure or selective forgetting usually come into play, allowing the individual to make a decision based upon the information he has for only a few of the many possible alternatives.

Another variable that has an effect on the magnitude of dissonance is the degree of cognitive overlap that exists between the alternatives available. *Cognitive overlap* means the degree to which one

[33] Ibid., p. 37.

alternative is similar to another: "High cognitive overlap is generally loosely implied when we speak of two things being similar. Low degree of cognitive overlap is generally implied when we speak of two things being qualitatively different."[34] Generally, if two alternatives are quite similar, the degree of cognitive overlap will be great. This situation will be less dissonance-inducing because the cognitive elements will not be inconsistent with each other. On the other hand, if the cognitive elements are quite dissimilar, the amount of cognitive overlap will be very little. In this situation the magnitude of the dissonance will be greater because of the inconsistencies among the various cognitive elements related to the various alternatives.

Time is also a variable that may affect the magnitude of dissonance. The more recent the decision between alternatives, the greater will be the magnitude of dissonance because of the phenomenon of forgetting. It would seem that both the importance of the decision and the individual's own ability to retain details would determine how long he experiences a high degree of dissonance after a decision has been made. Another possibility may be that individuals quickly forget the details of a decision that causes dissonance. Although this hypothesis has not been empirically evaluated, it seems logical that individuals attempt to reduce tension through selective forgetting. It may even be true that high dissonance increases the forgetting process. Which process, the decision or the forgetting, is the cause or the effect is still not clear. It may be that they act as a dyad ⇌, each element affecting and interacting with the other.

Strongly held cognitions will also affect the magnitude of dissonance. Certain attitudes and values are stronger than others. Each individual possesses a hierarchy of attitudes and values, some of which will resist change to a much greater degree than others. Under these circumstances, a decision that violates a strongly held attitude would be expected to produce greater dissonance than a decision that violated a less important cognition. Why would an individual violate a strongly held cognition? One explanation may be that he is not aware of the violated cognition until after the decision has been made. For example, assume that an employer feels that honesty is the single most important trait of a good employee. After he has interviewed and hired a new employee, he learns that the employee falsified his application blank. Surely he would experience greater dissonance over this decision than he would over another decision that did not involve the question of honesty.

Finally, a generalization can be made concerning the limits of the magnitude of dissonance that can exist in a given situation: "The maximum dissonance that can possibly exist between any two elements is equal to the total resistance to change of the less resistant element."[35]

[34] Ibid., p. 41.
[35] Ibid., p. 28.

In other words, the maximum magnitude of dissonance depends upon the least strongly held element. These elements, a set of related cognitions, determine the extent of dissonance for any given situation.

MODES OF DISSONANCE REDUCTION

Because dissonance is a psychologically uncomfortable state it would be reasonable to assume that individuals attempt to reduce dissonance just as they attempt to reduce any other physical or mental discomfort. Previously, it was mentioned that the existence of dissonance was a motivating state that induced behavior just as hunger induced behavior to reduce hunger. This section deals with the various types of behavior intended to reduce dissonance.

Basically, there are three major ways to reduce dissonance. A person can reduce dissonance by changing one or more of the elements involved in the dissonant relations, by adding new cognitions that are consonant with already existing cognitions, or by decreasing the importance of the elements involved in the dissonant relations.[36] The different methods employed in a given situation will depend upon the degree of dissonance and the individual's control over the environment.

One means of reducing dissonance is opinion change. When an individual is confronted with an opinion that differs from his own, he will experience dissonance. Because dissonance is uncomfortable, the individual will either change his opinion or attempt to change the other individual's opinion. Several studies have attempted to relate the extent of disagreement and the degree of opinion change.[37] However, the studies have not offered conclusive results. In some instances greater disagreement results in greater opinion change, but at other times the greater the disagreement, the less the opinion change. Another study postulated that individuals tend to maintain consistency among their opinions on logically related issues.[38] This study revealed that a persuasive communication directed at a person's opinion also tends to change his opinions on logically related (even if unmentioned) issues in a consistent direction. The difficulty of opinion change cannot be underestimated, especially if it calls for an entire restructuring of a set of cognitive elements. As mentioned earlier, it may be easier for an individual to change his behavior than to restructure his cognitions.

Dissonance reduction may also be accomplished through exposure to new information. In order to reduce dissonance an individual will seek information that he perceives as likely to support his decision and will avoid information that will favor the unchosen alternatives. One research project showed that new car owners read significantly more

---

[36] Ibid., p. 264.

[37] C. Hovland and J. Pritzker, "Amount of Opinion Change as a Function of the Amount of Change Advocated," *Journal of Abnormal and Social Psychology*, Vol. 54 (1957), pp. 257–261.

[38] W. J. McGuire, "Cognitive Consistency and Attitude Change," *Journal of Abnormal and Social Psychology*, Vol. 60 (1960), pp. 345–353.

advertisements of the car they purchased than of other cars.[39] Because it was assumed that the advertiser would mention only the attractive features of the car, the study seemed to support Festinger's theory that after making a decision people tend to seek out consonant information. The study also showed that car purchasers who considered more than one car read more advertisements of their own car. Because it was pointed out earlier that dissonance increases as the number of rejected alternatives increases, the new car owners who considered many alternatives could be expected to be more conscious of favorable information concerning the car that they finally purchased. This type of dissonance-reducing activity is generally termed *selective exposure;* that is, the individual controls the type of information he is exposed to.

A person can also reduce dissonance by forgetting the favorable characteristics of the unchosen alternative or by remembering the unfavorable characteristics of the unchosen alternative. This technique, generally termed *selective recall,* may be quite effective in reducing postdecision dissonance. By forgetting the favorable details of the unchosen alternative, the individual will be satisfied that he has made the best choice among the relevant alternatives. On the other hand, remembering the unfavorable details of the unchosen alternative, the individual will also assume that his decision is the best possible given the relevant alternatives.

Another method of reducing dissonance is to change the behavioral cognitions: "When some of the cognitive elements involved in dissonance are cognitions about one's own behavior, the dissonance can be reduced by changing the behavior, thus directly changing the cognitive elements."[40] Festinger believes that it is easier for individuals to change a behavioral element than it is to change an environmental element. However, there are certain instances in which this generalization may not hold. The greatest resistance to change will come from the responsiveness of that behavioral element to reality: "Given this strong . . . responsiveness to reality, the problem of changing a behavioral element becomes the problem of changing the behavior."[41] In most cases, however, individuals are continually changing their behavior to coincide with the new information they are constantly receiving. If a person starts out to go to a ballgame and it then begins to rain, he may turn around and go home, modifying his behavior in light of the new situation. By modifying his behavior he has reduced his dissonance concerning other environmental cognitions.

A person can also reduce dissonance by establishing or imagining cognitive overlap: "the more the cognitive elements corresponding to the different alternatives involved in a decision are alike, the less is the resulting dissonance."[42] One method of establishing overlap is to

[39] Ehrlich, Guttman, Schonbach, and Mills, op. cit., pp. 98–102.
[40] Festinger, op. cit., pp. 264–265.
[41] Ibid., p. 25.
[42] Ibid., pp. 45–46.

assume that the cognitive elements corresponding to the different alternatives lead to the same end result. In this way the individual can be indifferent as to which choice he makes, thus reducing any dissonance resulting from the favorable elements of the unchosen alternatives.

The final dissonance-reducing technique to be discussed here is the defense mechanism of rationalization and repression. It has been hypothesized that rationalization and repression can be used to reduce dissonance just as easily as they are used to reduce other kinds of psychological discomfort and pain.[43] Most of the theory dealing with defense mechanisms considers the individual's perception of himself. Contrary to this situation, dissonance theory deals with what the individual is rather than what he ought to be. The individual's attitudes, values, and beliefs are assumed to be compatible with reality, and dissonance is a result of outward inspection rather than introspection.

Finally, there are a few limitations on the effectiveness of efforts directed toward dissonance reduction. Generally, the success of efforts to reduce dissonance depends upon the resistance to change of the dissonant cognitive elements as well as the availability of information or individuals who can supply cognitive elements that are consonant with the existing cognitions. Another factor that may affect efforts directed toward dissonance reduction is the degree of resistance to change of the less resistant element. In other words, dissonance reduction depends upon the degree of belief in a set of cognitive elements. If a cognition is held in high esteem, efforts directed toward dissonance reduction may have very little success.[44]

Marketing and Dissonance

From the viewpoint of marketing management, the relevant question is, How can cognitive dissonance be applied and used to explain or predict consumer behavior?

> Consider such questions as the following. Does dissonance relate to brand loyalty? Can marketers improve their position by helping consumers reduce any dissonance they might have developed? How does a salesman handle anticipated dissonance on the part of a potential customer? What can a salesman do in the pre-decision conflict period? How similar should alternatives be for the buyer? How many alternatives should be presented? Are impulse purchases apt to be dissonance producing? Does planning on the part of the buyer aid in the process of dissonance reduction?[45]

This list of questions is not intended to be exhaustive. Other important questions include: How does dissonance influence the repurchase rate? Do certain products create more dissonance than other products? What

[43] Festinger and Bramel, op. cit., p. 270.

[44] For a complete list, see Festinger, op. cit., pp. 265–266.

[45] Robert J. Holloway, "An Experiment on Consumer Dissonance," *Journal of Marketing,* Vol. 31 (January 1967), p. 39.

role does advertising play in dissonance reduction? Does dissonance occur even when the outcome exceeds expectancy? For instance, if a product exceeds the expected performance, does the buyer still experience dissonance? In a study by Engel and Light it was pointed out that dissonance occurs even when actual performance exceeds expected performance.[46] Another question is whether "puffy" advertising tends to create dissonance when product performance is less than promised performance. For the advertiser this is an extremely important consideration. It may be that advertising that oversells the product is actually reducing the possibilities of gaining a loyal (over time) customer.

Cognitive Dissonance and the Buying Environment

In order to analyze the theory of cognitive dissonance as it applies to consumer behavior, it will be helpful to investigate some buying situations. Table 6-1 lists some of the various dissonance-arousing factors and how they may be related to various buying circumstances.

It should be noted that the high dissonance and low dissonance conditions are a function of the individual's attitudes and values as well as the nature of the product and the conditions surrounding the purchase decision. The basic assumption upon which Table 6-1 is based is that several factors may simultaneously interact to increase or reduce dissonance. One factor "may be dissonance producing and two others may not be. Subsequently, the aroused dissonance may be reduced in a variety of ways. The buyer may change his evaluations, select supporting information, ignore conflicting information, distort his perceptions, or even return the item to the seller."[47]

Marketing Studies and Cognitive Dissonance

In his paper, "Are Automobile Purchasers Dissonant Consumers?", Engel proposed that marketing provided relatively little knowledge of the consumer's reactions and behavior once he had made his purchase decision. Engel considered the possibility that a dissonant consumer may turn to advertising to reinforce his purchase decision by seeking information to confirm his choice and proposed that if dissonance does in fact exist, the advertiser should direct a portion of his advertising to the needs of his recent customers. In order to test these assumptions he statistically surveyed a group of new car owners.[48] His

[46] James F. Engel and M. Lawrence Light, "The Role of Psychological Commitment in Consumer Behavior: An Evaluation of the Theory of Cognitive Dissonance," in *Application of the Sciences in Marketing Management,* Frank M. Bass, Charles W. King, and Edgar A. Pessemier, eds. (New York: John Wiley & Sons, Inc., 1968), p. 193.

[47] Holloway, op. cit., p. 40.

[48] For a thorough presentation of the survey, see James F. Engel, "Are Automobile Purchasers Dissonant Consumers?" *Journal of Marketing,* Vol. 27 (April 1963), pp. 55–58.

objective was to determine if (1) new Chevrolet owners seek consonant information (read more Chevrolet advertisements) and (2) if selective recall comes into action to reduce any dissonance that may exist. In order to do this Engel selected two groups of consumers who were matched with respect to social class, age, and income and differed only in that one group had purchased new 1962 Chevrolets, whereas the other group owned Chevrolets that were not new. Engel tested his first hypothesis by interviewing the subjects three days after a Chevrolet advertisement, placed by the manufacturer, appeared in the local newspaper. During the same time interval a local Chevrolet dealer ran a full-page advertisement featuring price. The data were gathered in two stages: unaided recall and recognition. The data for the unaided recall and recognition surveys are presented in Tables 6-2 and 6-3. Based on chi-square analysis Engel concluded, "There is no evidence in either [Table 6-2 or 6-3] to indicate that consumers turn to advertising claims

TABLE 6-1

Dissonance and Buying Situations[a]

Factors affecting dissonance	Buying situation	Conditions with high dissonance expectation	Conditions with low dissonance expectation
1. Attractiveness of rejected alternative	A high school graduate decides which of several pictures to order.	Three of the proofs have both attractive and desirable features.	One of the proofs clearly is superior to the rest.
2. Negative factors in chosen alternative	A man chooses between two suits of clothing.	The chosen suit has the color the man wanted but not the style.	The chosen suit has both the color and the style the man wanted.
3. Number of alternatives	A teacher shops for a tape recorder.	There are eight recorders from which to choose.	There are only two recorders from which to choose.
4. Cognitive overlap	A housewife shops for a vacuum sweeper.	A salesman offers two similarly priced tank types.	A salesman offers a tank type and an upright cleaner.
5. Importance of cognitions involved	A child buys a present for her sister.	The sister has definite preference for certain kinds of music.	The sister has no strong tastes for certain records.

[a] Source: Robert J. Holloway, "An Experiment on Consumer Dissonance," *Journal of Marketing*, Vol. 31 (January 1967), p. 40.

to help overcome postpurchase anxiety. In fact, it seems highly likely that Chevrolet purchasers were not dissonant with respect to product superiority."[49] However, Engel did find that many owners expressed concern as to whether or not they paid a competitive price. Engel went on to determine if selective exposure or selective recall played any part in preventing or reducing postdecision dissonance. In order to measure this, he prepared fifteen statements. The statements included both good and bad characteristics of the 1962 Chevrolet and the 1962 Plymouth. "It was hypothesized that Chevrolet owners, if dissonant, would readily embrace and agree with those statements alleging Chevrolet superiority, while disagreeing or offering no opinion on statements putting forth Plymouth excellence. No such pattern, of course, would

Factors affecting dissonance	Buying situation	Conditions with high dissonance expectation	Conditions with low dissonance expectation
6. Positive inducement	Parents decide to buy a photo-enlarger for their son.	The son already has hobby equipment and does not need the enlarger.	The son never has had a true hobby and needs something to keep him occupied.
7. Discrepant or negative action	A man purchases an expensive watch.	The man had never before paid more than $35 for a watch.	Fairly expensive watches had been important gift items in the man's family.
8. Information available	A housewife buys a detergent.	The housewife has no experience with the brand purchased—it is a new variety.	The housewife has read and heard a good deal about the product and has confidence in the manufacturer.
9. Anticipated dissonance	A small boy buys a model airplane.	The boy anticipates trouble at home because of the cost of the model.	The boy expects no trouble at home because of the purchase.
10. Familiarity and knowledge	A family buys a floor polisher.	The item was purchased without much thought.	The item was purchased after a careful selection process.

[49] Ibid., pp. 56–57.

TABLE 6-2

Percentages of Those Reading Chevrolet Advertisements as Disclosed by Unaided Recall*[a]

	Owners		Nonowners	
Readership	No.	%	No.	%
Not seen	51	58.0	76	77.6
Noted	9	10.2	11	11.2
Read some	11	12.5	6	6.1
Read most	17	19.3	5	5.1
Total	88	100.0	98	100.0

* Differences are significant at the 0.05 probability level.

[a] James F. Engel, "Are Automobile Purchasers Dissonant Consumers?" *Journal of Marketing,* Vol. 27 (April 1963), p. 56.

be expected from nonpurchasers."[50] The results showed that the opinions of the two groups (owners and nonowners) were almost the same. Engel concluded that "it seems unlikely that owners were misperceiving

TABLE 6-3

Percentages of Those Reading the Test Chevrolet Advertisement as Disclosed by Recognition Measurement[a]

	Owners		Nonowners	
Readership	No.	%	No.	%
Not seen	65	73.9	80	81.6
Noted	11	12.5	9	9.2
Read some	11	12.5	6	6.1
Read most*	1	1.1	3	3.1
Total	88	100.0	98	100.0

* Frequencies of "Read most" were deleted from chi-square analysis. Differences are not significant at the 0.05 probability level.

[a] James F. Engel, "Are Automobile Purchasers Dissonant Consumers?" *Journal of Marketing,* Vol. 27 (April 1963), p. 57.

[50] Ibid., p. 57.

the statements as a result of post-decision dissonance."[51] He went on to state that possibly the automobile purchase is more routine than previously believed.

Based upon Engel's independent variables (class, age, and income) his conclusion may be correct. However, a factor that was overlooked is that in 1962 the sales figures indicate that Chevrolet enjoyed a clear advantage over other makes. Bruce Straits pointed out that "If the Chevrolet owner sees nearly twice as many 1962 Chevrolets as the next popular make, this supports his purchase behavior and reduces dissonance."[52] Festinger states that social support is one of the most effective ways of eliminating dissonance.[53] In addition, Engel concludes that because new car purchasers did not reject dissonance-arousing information, they were not dissonant. Other studies, however, have shown that even after an individual has made a decision, he may still be interested in information that does not support his decision.[54] Owing to the interacting variables it is difficult to conclude that because new purchasers did not avoid dissonance-arousing information they did not experience dissonance.

Rather than studying the effects of a purchase decision, another study analyzed the behavioral and information processes of individuals who had been subjected to dissonance-arousing information.[55] In order to test the theory of cognitive dissonance these authors analyzed public reactions to the Surgeon General's report on smoking and health. The research design included a public opinion study three months after the Surgeon General's report had been released.

More specifically, the authors wanted to investigate the reactions of cigarette smokers to the dissonant information. Because cigarette smoking was linked to lung cancer and other illnesses, it was felt that this information was dissonant to cognitions concerning life and health. Furthermore, it was hypothesized that cigarette smokers would attempt to reduce dissonance by (1) changing their behavior pattern by either stopping smoking or changing to a less dangerous product, (2) denying or distorting the report by refusing to believe the evidence, (3) minimizing the importance of the issue, or (4) seeking information or social support that approved of smoking.

It was believed that dissonance theory would predict changes in behavior because the Surgeon General's report presented smokers with

[51] Ibid.

[52] Straits, op. cit., p. 63.

[53] Festinger, op. cit., Chapter 8.

[54] See, for instance, N. T. Feather, "Cognitive Dissonance, Sensitivity, and Evaluation," *Journal of Abnormal and Social Psychology,* Vol. 66 (1963), pp. 157–163; and J. S. Adams, "Reduction of Cognitive Dissonance by Seeking Consonant Information," *Journal of Abnormal and Social Psychology,* Vol. 63 (1961), pp. 74–78.

[55] Harold H. Kassarjian and Joel B. Cohen, "Cognitive Dissonance and Consumer Behavior," *California Management Review,* Vol. 8 (Fall 1965), pp. 55–64.

dissonant information. In view of this prediction the following question was asked: "Have you ever made a serious attempt to stop smoking? (If yes) Within the last year how many times would you say you have made an attempt to stop smoking?" The data for this question are presented in Table 6-4.

No significant difference was found between heavy smokers (one or more packages of cigarettes per day), moderate smokers (ten to nineteen cigarettes per day), and light smokers (less than ten cigarettes per day). Following this finding it was assumed that all smokers were too heavily committed to smoking behavior to be influenced by persuasive communication. In order to test the second part of the first hypothesis the subjects were asked if they had switched from one tobacco product to another. The results indicated that there had been very little switching, again indicating that smoking behavior is very resistant to change. In effect, the first hypothesis was not proved and the behavioral change predicted by dissonance theory did not occur.

The next step was to determine if perceptual distortion reduced the credibility of the report. The subjects were asked if the report on smoking and lung cancer had been definitely proved, probably proved, probably not proved, or definitely not proved. The data for this question are presented in Table 6-5.

The data lend support to the second hypothesis. That is, "The more a person smokes, the less he believes that the cigarette-cancer linkage is proven."[56] The conclusions drawn from this data were relevant for subjects with a high level of education as well as for those with a low level of education.

In order to test the third hypothesis—that is, the minimizing of the importance of the issue—subjects were asked to explain why some

TABLE 6-4

Percentage of Sample Stating They Made Serious Attempts to Stop Cigarette Smoking During the Previous Year[a]

No. of attempts	Heavy smokers (132)	Moderate smokers (50)	Light smokers (39)	Total smokers (221)
None	79.5	66.0	69.2	74.7
One	12.1	22.0	12.8	14.5
Two or more	8.4	12.0	18.0	10.8

[a] Harold H. Kassarjian and Joel B. Cohen, "Cognitive Dissonance and Consumer Behavior," *California Management Review*, Vol. 8 (Fall 1965), p. 59.

[56] Ibid., p. 60.

TABLE 6-5

Relationship of Smoking to Believability of Health Report[a]

Percentage saying linkage is	Heavy smokers (132)	Moderate smokers (48)	Light smokers (39)	Total cigarette smokers (219)	Pipe/ cigar smokers (37)	Non- smokers (240)
Proved	52.2	58.3	77.0	58.0	83.8	80.4
Not proved	40.9	37.5	20.5	28.8	13.5	10.8
Don't know	6.8	4.2	2.5	5.5	2.7	8.7

[a] Harold H. Kassarjian and Joel B. Cohen, "Cognitive Dissonance and Consumer Behavior," *California Management Review*, Vol. 8 (Fall 1965), p. 60.

reports conclude that there is a definite linkage between smoking and cancer whereas other studies do not draw the same conclusions. Among smokers there was a strong feeling that "many smokers live a long time; lots of things are a hazard; and, there are many hazards in life." Clearly, the smokers tended to minimize the importance of the issue. Furthermore, about 20 per cent of the sample reported that smoking was better than (1) taking pills, (2) being a nervous wreck, (3) drinking, and (4) excessive eating. In other words, the subjects were attempting to reduce dissonance by making this information more consonant with their total cognitive structure.

The authors conclude that "dissonance theory clearly opens up avenues for understanding why the consumer—or for that matter any individual, whether he is a buyer or seller, employee or manager—behaves as he does."[57] If it is assumed that consumers develop as strong a purchasing habit as smokers, then it may be safe to conclude that cognitive dissonance certainly exists. However, a great deal of study must be done in the areas of purchasing behavior, brand loyalty, and shopping habits. On the other hand, the two situations are quite different. For example, cognitions relating to health may be more strongly held than cognitions concerning products, brands, or stores. The cognitions relating to smoking and health may be much more resistant to change than cognitions relating to a certain brand or product. If this is the case, dissonance would not be expected to occur as a result of inconsistent information. In these situations price or quality may be more dissonance-arousing than discrepant information. In other words, product information may have to be substantiated in the marketplace before dissonance can be detected.

Dissonance theory would suggest that as the number of alternatives increased, the greater would be the dissonance the consumer ex-

[57] Ibid., p. 63.

perienced. One study examined the effect on the consumer of the number of alternatives and the relative attractiveness of the alternatives.[58] It was felt that the amount of dissonance was related to the number of alternatives offered. In order to evaluate this idea the researchers hypothesized that (1) the greater the number of relatively attractive alternatives, the more dissonance will be created after the choice decision; hence, the more pressure to reduce dissonance by reevaluation of chosen and rejected alternatives; and (2) the more equal the attractiveness of each dissimilar alternative and the greater the desirability of the alternatives, the more dissonance will be created after the choice decision; hence, the more pressure to reduce dissonance by reevaluation of the chosen and rejected alternatives. In other words, the individual would be motivated to reduce any dissonance by increasing the desirability of the chosen alternative and decreasing the desirability of the rejected alternatives.

The subjects of the experiment were assigned to one of four experimental conditions on a random basis. The experimental conditions are reproduced in Table 6-6.

Each subject was told to rate a set of sixteen products on a separate rating scale for each product. Through the use of these ratings the experimenter was able to select either a conflict situation or a preference situation. Following the ratings each subject was presented one of the four choice situations. The subjects understood that they would be given one of these products in return for a certain amount of laboratory work. Following their decision, each subject discussed the attributes of the other products that would be useful as possible advertising material. The subject was then asked to reevaluate all sixteen products using the same rating scale.

Attempts at dissonance reduction were measured by the change in the ratings of desirability for the selected product before and after

TABLE 6-6
Experimental Conditions[a]

	Conflict	Preference
Two alternatives	1. Both high in desirability*	2. One high and one low in desirability
Four alternatives	3. All high in desirability	4. One high and three low in desirability

* Desirability was determined from the first rating scale completed by the subject.

[a] Lee K. Anderson, James R. Taylor and Robert J. Holloway, "The Consumer and His Alternatives," *Journal of Marketing Research,* Vol. 3 (February 1966), p. 65.

[58] Lee K. Anderson, James R. Taylor, and Robert J. Holloway, "The Consumer and His Alternatives," *Journal of Marketing Research,* Vol. 3 (February 1966), pp. 62–68.

the choice decision was made. The experiment showed that the greater the number of choices, the greater the postdecision dissonance. Furthermore, attempt at dissonance reduction was greater in the conflict situation than in the preference situation.

This experiment pointed out the decision-making nature of the consumer in the marketplace. The experiment concluded that as the number of alternatives increased so did the magnitude of the dissonance, initiating dissonance reduction activities.

The possibility of segmenting cognitive dissonance is an interesting one. Many research studies have implicitly assumed that dissonance will occur whenever a decision is made between attractive alternatives. Another study has suggested that all customers may not be cognitively dissonant:[59] "Rather, the type of personality an individual brings to the dealership and the experience he has while purchasing his new car determine the extent of his dissatisfaction with the metallic object sitting in his driveway."[60] In this article, Gerald Bell examines the effects that self-confidence, persuadability, and the quality of service have on the level of dissonance a new car buyer experiences after the purchase. The objectives of this study were to (1) look for individual variations in dissonance among new car owners, (2) examine the specific causes of the development of dissonance, and (3) attempt to measure dissonance directly. Most of the earlier studies have measured dissonance indirectly; that is, observed attempts to reduce dissonance are assumed to imply that dissonance does in fact exist.

The research design consisted of interviewing customers who had just purchased a new Chevrolet from a specific dealer. Of the 289 new cars that were purchased, the buyers of 234 were interviewed. Each subject was personally interviewed from one to eight days after the purchase.

The attempt to measure cognitive dissonance directly was made by the asking of open-ended questions such as, "How do you feel about your new car? . . . To what extent do you wonder whether or not you made the right decision?"[61] In order to determine to what extent the subject could be persuaded, he was asked how much the salesman influenced his decision. Certain criteria such as price, payments, accessories, delivery, and service were used as an objective measure of persuadability. The salesman was also asked how easy it was to persuade the customer on the same items. A combined ranking of persuadability was developed using the evaluation of both the subject and the salesman. The study found that there was no relationship between persuadability and cognitive dissonance.

It was felt, however, that persuadability and cognitive dissonance would be a function of the individual's self-confidence. For instance,

---

[59] Gerald D. Bell, "The Automobile Buyer After the Purchase," *Journal of Marketing*, Vol. 31 (July 1967), pp. 12–16.

[60] Ibid., p. 16.

[61] Ibid., p. 14.

TABLE 6-7

Persuasibility and Dissonance for Those High on Self-confidence[a]

| | | Persuasibility (in percent) | | | |
		High	Medium	Low	Ns
Cognitive dissonance	High	56	31	13	36
	Medium	21	33	46	43
	Low	14	29	57	28
					107

$$X^2 = 17.23, P < .001$$

[a] Gerald D. Bell, "The Automobile Buyer After the Purchase," *Journal of Marketing,* Vol. 31 (July 1967), p. 14.

an individual who possessed a high degree of self-confidence but was easily persuaded by the salesman would experience dissonance. Tables 6-7 and 6-8 present the data for the customers with high and low self-confidence. Table 6-7 reveals that an individual who had high self-confidence but was easily persuaded experienced greater dissonance than an individual who had high self-confidence and was not easily persuaded. Table 6-8 shows the opposite case for individuals with low self-confidence. In other words, individuals with low self-confidence

TABLE 6-8

Persuasibility and Dissonance for Those Low on Self-confidence[a]

| | | Persuasibility (in percent) | | | |
		High	Medium	Low	Ns
Cognitive dissonance	High	45	24	31	42
	Medium	60	25	15	48
	Low	86	8	8	37
					127

$$X^2 = 54.05, P < .001$$

[a] Gerald D. Bell, "The Automobile Buyer After the Purchase," *Journal of Marketing,* Vol. 31 (July 1967), p. 15.

who were easily persuaded experienced less dissonance than individuals who had low self-confidence and resisted attempts to be easily persuaded.

It was also believed that dissonance would be a function of the service the customer received on his new automobile: "The potential cause of a customer's dissonance after the purchase is the quality of service he received."[62] Table 6-9 shows the relationship between dissonance and service.

Individuals who received good service experienced less dissonance than individuals who received poor service. Customers usually cite service as one reason for returning to a particular store or, in the case of automobiles, to a particular dealer. The findings of this study seem to add additional proof to this concept. Clearly, one could view service as an important variable affecting brand loyalty. Viewed in this light, the successful reduction of dissonance by the manufacturer or store is certainly worth any extra expense that may be incurred. Additionally, salesmen could be trained to detect the characteristics that induce dissonance and attempt to reduce dissonance while the final purchase decision is being made. Finally, this study helped to isolate some of the customer attributes that influence cognitive dissonance: "Two groups of customers stand out as deserving special attention in after-sale promotion. These are the buyers who were most easily persuaded and those who received the worst service."[63]

Although all the literature relating to cognitive dissonance and consumer behavior has not been reviewed here, some of the more sophisticated and lengthy experiments have been analyzed in this section. The majority of the experiments and surveys have concluded

TABLE 6-9

Quality of Service and Cognitive Dissonance[a]

| | | Quality of Service (in percent) | | | |
		High	Medium	Low	Ns
	High	14	28	58	78
Cognitive dissonance	Medium	22	41	37	91
	Low	63	25	12	65

$X^2 = 54.05$, $P < .001$

[a] Gerald D. Bell, "The Automobile Buyer After the Purchase," *Journal of Marketing,* Vol. 31 (July 1967), p. 15.

[62] Ibid., p. 15.
[63] Ibid., p. 16.

that consumers do experience dissonance during the postpurchase period.

One important point should be mentioned. At the present time no one has developed a method that will predict the situation or the type of individual who becomes cognitively dissonant. Another point is that the type of product, the individual, and the specific buying situation all interact to create a state of dissonance. Furthermore, any purchase decision that affects the individual's concept of himself takes on importance. Therefore, it is quite difficult to state unequivocally that low-priced purchases do not produce dissonance whereas high priced purchases do. For a specific individual a low-priced item that influences his self-concept may require a considerable amount of search and decision time, therefore increasing the possibility of dissonance.

The Impact of Consistency Theories on Consumer Behavior

We have delved rather deeply and dwelled at considerable length on this topic of cognitive consistency. Why? For several very important reasons.

1. It is a conceptually rich area, and it forms the real essence of a theory of cognitive psychology. Complex mental processes are the least understood of consumer activities and no really important strides in our understanding of consumer behavior are likely to occur without insight into these complex processes. Hopefully, the treatment of cognitive processes and cognitive consistency theories provided in Chapters 5 and 6 has generated an increased understanding of these activities even if such understanding is still "seen through a glass darkly."

2. Cognitive processes are increasingly being recognized as the seedbed from which other important behavioral or psychological phenomena grow. For example, motivation, always viewed as an important variable in consumer behavior, has its roots—at least from the point of view of cognitive theorists—in the concept of cognitive consistency. To illustrate, cognitive inconsistency, as we have seen, tends to create a tendency within the subject's psychological field to reduce inconsistency or imbalance. Thus, cognitive inconsistency in itself creates a motivated or aroused state and an explanation of motivation; that is, the reason that a person acts is in part that people act and behave so as to bring about balanced and symmetrical cognitive states. To elaborate even further, it must be pointed out, almost by way of preview, that almost all of the consumer behavior phenomena explored in this book have cognitive overtones and implications. The consumer is a user of social tools or symbols. He is a complex, reasoning, information-processing organism. In short, he is a cognitive animal. In every problem or situation he faces, he must contend with his own cognitive predilections. His values, attitudes, personality, role, group influences, culture, family, and so on are all products of his cognitive mechanisms. The consumer reconciles and reduces cognitive inconsistencies, under-

goes attitude changes, alters his role, restructures his own self-image and personality—all these things and more—by communication, information seeking and processing, and a host of other actions.

In general, cognitive consistency theories have contributed much to our understanding of consumer behavior. The theories are particularly relevant to problems of attitude formation and change, interpersonal attraction and dyadic relationships, personal perception, mass-marketing action, communication in groups, motivation and arousal, and other similar phenomena affecting consumers.

We shall turn our attention to these other concepts in subsequent portions of our overall analysis.

Questions for Study, Reflection, and Review

1 Discuss the possible conditions that may be satisfied by cognitive inconsistency.

2 Describe the consequences of the imbalanced states discussed in connection with Heider's balance theory.

3 Identify the concepts upon which Newcomb's A-B-X system is based.

4 Cite the corollaries derived from the congruity principle.

5 Discuss the significance of the relevant-irrelevant distinction between cognitive relationships in creating dissonance.

6 Describe some of the situations that might arouse dissonance in the consumer.

7 Discuss the effects of the importance of a decision, the strength of existing cognitions, and time on cognitive dissonance.

8 Identify the properties of the rejected alternative that result in increased dissonance in the consumer.

9 Cite the three major ways a consumer might reduce dissonance.

10 Discuss the relationship between information processing and perceptual distortion in postpurchase evaluation.

7

Motivation:
The Impetus of
Behavior

Introduction

From nearly the beginning of time, man has been a student of
motives and motivation. If the weather was bad and crops failed, or if
the game was scarce, men believed that the gods were angry and were
punishing their subjects for their lack of obedience. Men have always
attempted to understand their existence, often reasoning that the un-
examined life is not worth living. Thus it is with complex psychological phenomena like *motivation*—man wishes to understand it so that
he can best deal with it. Perhaps one of the foremost commonly understood characteristics of mankind is that behind each human action lies
a motive, and if we can understand motives we can understand behavior. There is more than a little truth to this reasoning.

As we have learned thus far, consumer behavior is selective, directed, and persistent. It is, in short, motivated behavior. But motivated by what? What is the mechanism of motivation? And much more
importantly, is the person to be understood in terms of the mechanism
or is the mechanism to be understood in terms of the person? Our
treatment will emphasize the latter approach.

Before proceeding further, however, let us pause and recall some
generalizations from several chapters back. First, a consumer, like all
human organisms, is a constantly active individual. As humans, consumers are in a near-constant state of arousal. The U.S. consumer is
not necessarily guided in his consumer behavior by an urge to reduce

tension. He appears to seek it. Therefore, motivation theories rooted in such concepts as drive reduction and physiological homeostatic processes are hardly adequate as explanations for consumer motivation and behavior. Recall also that in Chapter 4 our overall treatment of consumer behavior was labeled a *holocentric* model. The holocentric approach to consumer behavior posits that although some factor affecting behavior may appear dominant and may strongly affect certain individuals, that factor always operates in conjunction with all other factors present. Thus, we must constantly remind ourselves that motivation is not necessarily the only factor in consumer behavior. Other phenomena have an equally important impact.

In addition, we must review and remind ourselves of the problem of determinism discussed in Chapter 3. The determinist position states that all behavior is caused, that is, that all events are the inevitable result of antecedent conditions and that the human being, in acts of apparent choice, is the mechanical expression of his heredity and his past environment. There are several alternate theories of motivation that are determinist in origin. For example, *drive* theory and instinct theory are largely determinist concepts. However, recall additionally that the statement "All behavior is caused" can be restated as "All behavior has reasons." Humans are not simply agents of deterministic forces but instead are possessed of *free will,* meaning that they have choices; that they are at least partially free from the determining compulsion of heredity, environment, and circumstances. Such a point of view would, in an examination of motives and motivation, underscore the pulling notion of goals as opposed to the driving, compelling notion of drives and instincts. Such a view stresses the cognitive nature of human and consumer behavior; that is, it focuses upon the knowing, thinking, reasoning, information-processing capacity of the human organism. For that matter, the behaviorist tradition, which was presented and analyzed in Chapter 5, resists and even denies the concept of motivation in organisms because to accept it would admit the dissimilarity between man and machine.

Therefore, our treatment of motivation must be underscored with the earlier propositions. An active, aroused consumer still begs the fundamental question, What are the reasons for his arousal? The answer, grossly overstated, of course, is that he is largely motivated by his goals. But motivated toward what goal? In these terms, the consumer's behavior manifests a little of everything. Consumer behavior can be characterized as appeasing a stimulus hunger. On the other hand, we might emphasize a need for activity and thus explain consumer behavior as a desire to reach a pleasurable level of neuromuscular exercise. There are also other possible goals, perhaps a cognitive one whereby the consumer seeks knowledge and understanding of his environment and by so doing satisfies an exploratory tendency or the motive of curiosity. However, it is just as possible to assume that our consumer, like many human organisms, tends to manifest a desire for power or control and even a degree of self-assertion upon those aspects of the environment that respond in some way to his own activity and enterprise. But, alas! It would appear that we may be finding too many goals, and an immediate impulse may be to look for some device that would tell us which of all goals is predominant.

However, we shall resist that temptation for fear that we may take our reader too far before having laid sufficient groundwork for our analysis. We shall explore in considerable depth in this chapter the concept of motivation and how, within the constraints of a holocentric model, motivation is viewed as an important, though elusive, variable of consumer behavior.

The Language and Scope of Motivation

As individuals and as consumers we all know that there are things we want and that we take steps and actions to get them. Through our intuitive understanding of this process we say that a person is motivated in certain directions or toward specific goals. Thus the questions about the mainsprings of human action that motivational theory attempts to answer are at least as old as the generalized thinking of such Greeks as Plato, but the term *motive*, according to the *Oxford Universal Dictionary*, emerged at about the time of the Renaissance. It derives from the medieval Latin word *movere*, meaning "to move," and it is loosely defined as that which tends to move a person to a course of action.

MOTIVATION DEFINED

Motivation is thus concerned with the reasons that impel people to undertake certain actions. More precisely, a relevant and contemporary sociopsychological definition of motivation is that it is a state of the organism in which bodily energy is mobilized and directed in a selective fashion toward states of affairs often, though not necessarily, in the external environment called goals.[1]

It would therefore appear that motivation has at least two distinct dimensions:

1. It is a state of arousal or a tension system.
2. It is generally discriminate inasmuch as it gives both impetus and some direction to behavior. It is goal directing.

A word or two of explanation may be warranted here. Motives or drives are energizers but not a complete guide—an engine, so to speak, with a partial steering mechanism. In general terms, psychologically, we can distinguish two quite different effects of a motivated state. One is the *cue function*, which guides behavior; the other, less obvious but no less important, is the *arousal function*, which is a general drive

[1] Theodore M. Newcomb, Ralph H. Turner, and Phillip E. Converse, *Social Psychology* (New York: Holt, Rinehart & Winston, Inc., 1965), p. 22.

or motivated state.[2] *It must be emphatically pointed out that what is characteristically labeled and discussed as motivation is really the arousal function in the organism.* From a marketing and consumer behavior point of view, we are interested in both the cue function and the arousal function, though admittedly, like our theoretical counterparts in psychology, we appear to know less about the cue function. Nonetheless, our discussion and treatment of motivation proceeds as if there were little or no distinction between the cue and the arousal functions and as if each were an integral part of our concept of motivation.[3]

Suffice it then to say that motivation is an inner state that activates or moves people toward goals and that results in purposive means/ends behavior. The desire to be more attractive, have more friends, drive a luxury automobile, attend an elite Ivy college, and have a gargantuan wardrobe are all motives according to this definition. The goal (or goals) is the objective, reward, or condition toward which the action or behavior is directed and that will, temporarily at least, satisfy or reduce the striving. Motivation is thus a process or processes—something going on within the individual that moves him to action—and it is furthermore a function of rate, direction, and amount of pull toward a goal.[4] But even the goal, like the processes that underlie action toward it, is largely inferred.

OTHER DEFINITIONS

Although motivation is conceived of as the combination of forces that initiate, direct, and sustain behavior toward a goal, there are other concepts and terms related to motivation that need defining. For example, the literature of motivation is replete with such terms as *needs, drives, incentives,* and *goals.* Each of these concepts is defined here in turn.

NEEDS. Needs are usually treated under two broad categories: *biological needs* and *personal-social needs.* Biological needs are basic conditions (often chemical) that are necessary to the maintenance of life and the normal processes of health, growth, and reproduction. Personal-social needs, or *psychogenic needs,* as they are often called, can

[2] D. O. Hebb, "Drive and the Conceptual Nervous System," *Psychological Review,* Vol. 62 (1955), pp. 243–254.

[3] Recent work on the neurophysiology of the reticular formation of the brain stem suggests that this structure is the central locus of motivational states and that it is related to the functioning of the cortex and of the skeletal musculature. This relationship, which appears to involve facilitatory and inhibitory functions, has prompted some theorists to incorporate *arousal* as the motivation aspect of their cognitive theories. See Robert J. C. Harper et al., *The Cognitive Processes: Readings* (Englewood Cliffs, N.J.: Prentice-Hall, Inc., 1964), p. 17.

[4] Donald B. Lindsey, "Psychophysiology and Motivation," in *Nebraska Symposium on Motivation,* M. R. Jones, ed. (Lincoln, Neb.: University of Nebraska Press, 1957), pp. 44–105.

be less objectively described—as personal security, self-confidence, group status, prestige, aggression, and so on. Psychogenic needs are largely learned and secondary, and they are used to demonstrate motivation that is not necessarily in the direct service of physical needs.[5] It must be pointed out, however, that much behavior has real borderline characteristics; that is, both physiological and biological motives are bound closely to social behavior. Acts that basically satisfy such primary urges as hunger, thirst, and sexual desire take on important social and symbolic significance. And in a high-level, consumption-oriented society, almost all goods and services are sought as goal objects, not necessarily to serve the biological urges, drives, or motives of the consumer but rather to serve and fulfill his desire (motives) for psychogenic satisfactions.

DRIVES. Drives are generally defined as the internal stimuli or organic states that initiate activity and predispose the organism toward making differential responses that presumably aid in attaining satisfaction of needs but may well go beyond this.

GOALS OR INCENTIVES. Goals (we shall drop the term *incentive*) are the external stimuli toward which or away from which the animal orients itself in seeking satisfaction of its needs.

From these definitions, it should be understood that *drives, goals,* and *needs* are really only special aspects of motivation and are not to be construed as independent. These concepts necessarily overlap and they almost constantly interact. The separation of motivation into subunits such as drives, goals, and needs is admittedly arbitrary, and it is deluding, especially if we think of only the parts instead of the whole dynamic configuration.[6]

Thus, of course, the problem of motivation lies close to the heart of the general problem of understanding behavior. *Motivation* as used herein refers in a rather general sense to the energizing of behavior and especially to the sources of energy in a particular set of responses that keep them temporarily dominant over others and account for continuity and direction in behavior. *Drive* is regarded as a more specific conception about the way in which this motivation occurs. In a literal sense, however, motivation and drive are used interchangeably. Thus motivation is seen as a kind of human mainspring. It is a broad, almost generic, term that is applied to the reasons why people engage in certain actions. The reasons or motives, of course, are related to goals, but much remains to be explained as to how these goals come to be particularized through learning and socialization.

---

[5] Bernard Berelson and Gary A. Steiner, *Human Behavior: Shorter Edition* (New York: Harcourt Brace Jovanovich, Inc., 1967), pp. 159–161.

[6] See William N. Dember, "The New Look in Motivation," *American Scientist* (December 1965), pp. 409–427.

MOTIVATION AND MARKETING

Marketers have long been interested in the concept of motivation as an important determinant and variable in consumer behavior. Fifty years ago in a pioneering effort, Copeland analyzed and classified customers' buying motives.[7] From Copeland's early work, marketers' interest in motivation and motives took several directions. Essentially, however, this interest centered around such factors as *buying motives*, those reasons that impel consumers to buy goods. *Product motives*, those reasons that impel consumers to buy particular products or particular brands of products, and *patronage motives*, those reasons that impel consumers to shop at particular stores, were also explored and analyzed.

Other aspects of motives that concern marketers are such factors as *primary buying motives*, the reasons that impel consumers to be interested in a general class of goods, say, automobiles, as contrasted with *selective buying motives*, the reasons that impel a consumer to be interested in a particular style, make, or color of automobile.

Until most recently, marketers' attempts to study and analyze consumer motivation were chiefly concerned with listing and classifying motives. Copeland's tradition of categorizing motives as either emotional or rational was purely arbitrary and was predicated upon a meagre understanding of the behavioral and psychological dimensions of human conduct.

For example, Copeland's dichotomy, which is still widely stated in the literature and is the implicit basis for much advertising and promotion activity, views motives as falling into one of two distinct categories. For example, either:

(1) Rational motives . . . those which are aroused by appeals to reason. The group includes such motives as dependability in use, durability, and economy in purchase. Or

(2) Emotional buying motives . . . such as emulation, satisfaction of the appetite, pride in personal appearance, cleanliness, pleasure in recreation, securing home comfort and analogous motives. These motives were said to have their origin in human instincts and emotions and to represent impulse or unreasoning promptings to action.[8]

The fallacy of such arbitrary distinctions is today more readily apparent. A good purchased to enhance one's self-image or to give pleasure in recreation is a perfectly rational form of human behavior. Furthermore, the instinct theory of behavior and motivation has largely been refuted. Behavior and motivation are in the contemporary mode explained more in terms of goals that pull rather than as internal drives that push the subject to respond. Finally, goods as goal objects

[7] Melvin T. Copeland, *Principles of Merchandising* (New York: A. W. Shaw Company, 1924), pp. 155–167.

[8] Ibid., p. 162.

are hardly ever viewed as having only utilitarian or functional properties. Instead, goods are endowed or imbued with symbolic significance.
Levy has observed that:

> all commercial objects have a symbolic character and making a purchase
> involves an assessment—implicit or explicit—of this symbolism, to de-
> cide whether or not it fits. Energy (and money) will be given when the
> symbols are appropriate ones, and denied or given parsimoniously when
> they are not.[9]

Such a condition hardly makes the consumer an economic man. Nor
does he distinguish between his motives as either rational or emotional. Instead, all motives, in one sense, can be assessed only by an
examination of them on a buying motive continuum such as is shown
in Figure 7-1.

The true state of affairs is most likely that in the case of consumer
goods, the sociopsychological satisfactions derived from the product
nearly always exceed or transcend the satisfactions derived from the
raw, unadorned physical performance of the product.

It is interesting, though ironic, that marketers know much more
about motivation as a set of techniques than they do about motivational principles or theories. In various ways marketers have had
considerable success in structuring and implementing psychological
situations that led consumers to do what was hoped and even predicted
they would do.[10] However, with few exceptions, marketers are almost
never able to give a systematic account of why their efforts were
effective. Perhaps our current research and near-fetishistic interest in
consumer behavior will lead to these explanations. However, a caveat
is warranted. Because motives are usually inferred from behavior, there
is always the danger of circular reasoning, that is, of using a motive
as an explanation of the exact behavior from which it is inferred. For

FIGURE 7-1

The Buying Motive Continuum

Operational buying motives	Psychological buying motives
Satisfaction to be derived from physical performance of product	Satisfaction to be derived from consumer's social and psychological interpretation of the product and its performance

Source: Jon G. Udell, "A New Approach to Consumer Motivation," *Journal of Retailing*, Vol. 40 (Winter 1964–1965), p. 9.

[9] Sidney J. Levy, "Symbols for Sale," *Harvard Business Review*, Vol. 37 (July–August 1959), pp. 117–124, at p. 119.

[10] Jon G. Udell, "A New Approach to Consumer Motivation," *Journal of Retailing*, Vol. 40 (Winter 1964–1965), pp. 6–10.

example, if we see a consumer manifesting unusual search activity—prolonged shopping, reading consumer reports, asking the opinion of experts—we might infer that it is because of a cognitive need, that is, a need to know, to stir himself in the interest of personal goals and commitments or the desire to reduce dissonance or create balance. The observation of an active consumer is a *description* of behavior. The "why" of the activity is the *explanation*. Marketers today are necessarily becoming more interested in explanation than in description.

A SURVEY OF CONCEPTIONS OF MOTIVATION

Almost all of us have our private conceptions about "what makes people run" or "what makes customers tick." Such conceptions may even be necessary for getting along in our lives and in our work and for operating in the marketplace. We frequently ask such questions as "What's bugging him?" "What does so-and-so want?" "What would appeal to Marcia?" Our answers to such real or implied questions are almost always predicated upon some intuitive conceptualization about human motivation. And in the main our intuitive conceptualizations can usually be bracketed wthin one or two major categories.[11] Motivation is most often viewed as either (1) a set of innate characteristics or instincts arising from the constitution of the mind rather than acquired from experience, or (2) a set of learned social responses conditioned or acquired through a socialization process rooted in an extensive array of interpersonal situations. It must be quickly added that the issue of which of these two approaches is most scientifically correct is not as yet settled. However, instinct theories are no longer as fashionable as they once were in spite of a nearly perennial resurrection.

In the following section we shall examine several schools of thought regarding the conceptual basis of motivation. The field of motivation theory is, relatively speaking, so new that there is no single generally accepted theoretical framework for the analysis and treatment of the subject. Instead there are a number of competing conceptions borrowed from philosophy and biology. Our efforts are turned now to a discussion of these conceptions.[12] Our discussion throughout the later sections will necessarily build upon this present treatment.

INSTINCT THEORIES. As stated previously, the instinct theory of motivation holds that man, like lower animal forms, comes into the world possessed, or imprinted through the genes, with a series of in-

[11] Perry Bliss, *Marketing Management and the Behavioral Environment* (Englewood Cliffs, N.J.: Prentice-Hall, Inc., 1970), p. 55.

[12] For a more extensive review of these conceptions, the reader may wish to examine Edward J. Murray, *Motivation and Emotion* (Englewood Cliffs, N.J.: Prentice-Hall, Inc., 1964), pp. 1–9; or M. D. Vernon, *Human Motivation* (Cambridge, England: Cambridge University Press, 1969), Chapters 1, 3, and 6.

born instincts. Thus, our behavior and the motivation that arouses us to action are largely predetermined and beyond the control or will of the individual. This approach to motivation and behavior has its origins in classical philosophy and was given considerable impetus by the work of Charles Darwin. Darwin, of course, believed that instincts arise through a process of natural selection. Consequently, behavior and its motivation are seen as a long process of adaptation and accommodation by the organism to its environment. The instinct theory of motivation has continued, to a great extent, to hold its place in the thinking of many schools of psychology. Much effort by researchers in this area has been devoted to listing and classifying instincts. In 1908, McDougall's list was flight, repulsion, curiosity, pugnacity, self-abasement, self-assertion, parenthood, reproduction, hunger, gregariousness, acquisitiveness, and constructiveness.[13]

Many later psychologists have developed the instinct theory of motivation and behavior into what, for them, appeared to be an important explanatory concept in psychology.[14] Freud's theory has previously been reviewed, the gist of it being that man's sexual instincts motivate most of his behavior. Adler posited that man is motivated more by social instincts than by gross sexual urges.[15] Adler argued that man has an inborn social interest and a desire to relate to other people. Fromm has advanced the idea that man has a basic instinct for relatedness.[16] Horney has discussed the need or instinct of the child for security in relation to his parents, and Sullivan has suggested that man has an instinct for warm human relationships.[17]

Instinct theories of motivation are still prevalent, yet their influence on motivational thinking may be in the decline. The lists of "instincts" continue to grow at an alarming rate even though the predictive and analytical value of such theories is often questionable. Consumers may buy goods because of "acquisitive" instincts. They may buy goods in order to satisfy instincts for "aggressiveness," "status," or "dominance." Yet causal evidence suggests, as has already been mentioned, that specific purchases almost always involve some degree of learning or social influence. More sophisticated instinct theories, some of which will be discussed later, may shed some light on the question of why people buy.

---

[13] W. M. McDougall, *An Introduction to Social Psychology* (New York: Barnes & Noble, Inc., 1960, original copyright, 1908).

[14] For more information regarding these ideas, see Murray, op. cit., p. 86.

[15] Alfred Adler, *The Science of Living* (New York: Greenburg, publisher, 1929).

[16] Erich Fromm, *Man for Himself* (New York: Holt, Rinehart & Winston, Inc., 1947).

[17] Karen Horney, *The Neurotic Personality of Our Time* (New York: W. W. Norton & Company, Inc., 1937); and Harry Stack Sullivan, *Conceptions of Modern Psychiatry* (Washington, D.C.: White Psychiatric Foundation, 1947).

DRIVE THEORIES. If instinct theories are inclined to treat man as a lower animal, then drive theories reduce him to an even lower status —that of a machine or, at best, a biological machine. Still, drive theory is perhaps one of the most prominent concepts in motivation theory today. The concept was originated by Woodworth to describe the energy that impels an organism to action.[18] Drives are thus seen as a different mechanism than instincts or habits that tend to steer behavior in one direction or another, but there is a great deal of similarity between drive and instinct theories. The concept of drive refers to a tendency toward or away from specific goals and is an internal state usually resulting from some kind of biological disequilibrium. The drive theory of motivation is deeply rooted in the ideas of Cannon related to homeostasis.[19] You will recall from Chapter 6 that this concept is used to describe the steady states attained at any particular moment by the physiological processes at work in living organisms. The idea of a natural balancing tendency or an equilibrium seeking has been described earlier.

Thus psychological drives are one of the principal mechanisms used by the organism to return to both physiological and psychological equilibrium. The body, when cold, seeks warmth. When hungry, it seeks food. When cognitive dissonance or imbalance is present and disequilibrium ensues, equilibrium through cognitive balance or symmetry is sought. Hence, motivation has often come to be defined as the drive arising out of homeostatic imbalance or tension. Drive theory has had a profound impact on motivation studies, especially those relating to learning theory.

Lately a considerable amount of interest has centered upon the concept of external sources of motivation as opposed to the internal or homeostatic determinants. Such a situation considers the goal object as a product stimulus functioning in such a way as to reward learning and to induce behavior. Such a product stimulus "is a complex stimulus containing a perceived set of want satisfying attributes and a generally distinguishable symbolic character."[20] This product stimulus acts as a cue to reinforce or to bring about a motivated or aroused state. Such cues act as triggers or incentives to behavior. However, much of the difficulty in comprehending basic drives results from an inherent problem in perception. The individual's awareness of his motivation is not at the level of the basic, underlying drive but is of more specific wants: to buy a hat, to eat at Joe's Famous Restaurant, to own a Mercedes-Benz. As has been repeatedly emphasized in social situations—the main char-

---

[18] Robert S. Woodworth, *Dynamics of Behavior* (New York: Holt, Rinehart & Winston, Inc., 1961).

[19] Walter B. Cannon, *The Wisdom of the Body* (New York: W. W. Norton & Company, Inc., 1939).

[20] Thomas S. Robertson, *Consumer Behavior* (Glenview, Ill.: Scott, Foresman and Company, 1970), p. 2.

acterizing factor in consumer behavior—the motivating effect of the goal is often more profound than that of internal biological or physiological states. Motivation is thus aroused and brought into play by signs, cues, and other forms of suggestion, socialization, and learning.

HEDONISTIC THEORIES. In many ways, hedonistic theories are hardly a separate category of motivational theories. The basic idea of hedonism is that it is an instinct, and for that reason it might well be treated within our discussion of instinct theories. However, it is often treated as a distinct and separate category of motivational concepts. We shall continue that tradition.

Hedonism, in one broad sense, formed the basis of Smith's economic doctrine, especially to the extent that he argued that all men are motivated by self-interest in all their actions.[21] Bentham refined and elaborated on this idea by viewing man as a "hedonistic calculator" who weighs and measures the pleasures and pains of every contemplated undertaking.[22]

Hedonism leaves a great deal to be desired as a scientific theory. For example, it can be dangerously circular: "Why did you do that?" "Because I wanted to." Do we then state that the motive or motivation for that behavior was pleasure seeking and thus hedonistic? If a consumer seeks something, then it must be pleasurable and hence the motivation is hedonistic.

However, recent hedonic theories have largely abandoned the subjective reports of pleasure and pain and instead have substituted objective and measurable concepts of approach and avoidance.[23] From this perspective motivation consists of the learned anticipations and expectations of a goal as creating positive and/or negative emotional conditions. Thus, goal objects previously known to arouse pleasure are approached and, correspondingly, those that produce pain or displeasure are avoided. In this sense, all motives are learned. The affective arousal or basic condition is innate or inborn but the anticipation and the specific responses are acquired. Such a point of view shows promise for continuing research in consumer motivation and behavior.

COGNITIVE THEORIES. Cognitive theories of motivation are to a great extent attempts to bridge the gap between the innate theories of drive, instinct, and hedonism and the social theories of motivation. Man is viewed as a rational, thinking organism who has many

---

[21] Adam Smith, *An Inquiry into the Nature and Causes of the Wealth of Nations* (New York: Random House, Inc., 1937).

[22] Jeremy Bentham, *An Introduction to the Principles of Morals and Legislation, 1780* (Oxford, England: Clarendon Press, 1907).

[23] Major contributors to this thinking are Paul Thomas Young, *Emotion in Man and Animal* (New York: John Wiley & Sons, Inc., 1943); David C. McClelland et al., eds., *Studies in Motivation* (New York: Appleton-Century-Crofts, 1955); and Helen Peak, "Attitudes and Motivation," *Nebraska Symposium on Motivation, 1955*, M. R. Jones, ed. (Lincoln, Neb.: University of Nebraska Press), pp. 149–189.

conscious desires and who uses his physical and intellectual capacities to fulfill them. Human motivation is viewed as a decidedly human phenomenon. Humans are seen as organisms whose intellect places them in a special position and endows them with special capacity. This position and capacity lead to a desire to know, to systematize, to seek dominance and mastery of the environment and relationships to a social milieu. Motivation is viewed more in terms of the socially ac-quired goals that man has learned, though the cognitive view does not categorically deny the existence of certain innate drives or even instincts.

Cognitive theories of motivation seek a more concrete and specific set of answers regarding the motivational question. For example, they stress the interdependent relationships that exist among learning, performing, perceiving, attending, remembering, forgetting, thinking, creating, and feeling. They do not necessarily view behavior as some-thing that has to be put in motion. Instead, they recognize that behavior is continuously active, the main problem being the selection of specific alternatives and goal objects.

The specific goals that men as consumers seek are related to and rooted in their existential conditions. Thus choice and goals depend on a person's constructs—his ideas, values, knowledge, attitudes, and his images about the world and his relation to it. By changing the environment or the personal constructs of the individual, you change his existence and his perceptions and thus his reasons or motives for pur-chasing and consuming goods. The cognitive theorists, therefore, are likely to contend that what we call motives are really a particular kind of perceptual or cognitive event.[24] It would appear to be hardly neces-sary to repeat that the treatment throughout this book is decidedly cognitive in orientation.

THE TRADITIONALLY DOMINANT CONCEPTUAL THEME

Our review of the various conceptual schemes regarding the phenomenon of motivation has stressed at least one basic and dominant theme, namely, that motivation is one of the key factors that determine "why" and "how" a person will behave. Yet these questions in turn raise several more, and we shall dwell on these questions and the traditional and contemporary responses to them at this juncture. All major theories of motivation usually attempt to answer some por-tion of eight major questions. Needless to say, these questions form the very foundation upon which a theory of consumer behavior may be built. The major questions in their assumed order of importance are:[25]

[24] See William C. H. Prentice, "Some Cognitive Aspects of Motivation," *American Psychologist*, Vol. 16 (1961), pp. 503–511; and Mary Henle, "Some Effects of Motivational Processes on Cognition," *Psychological Review*, Vol. 62 (1955), pp. 423–452.

[25] These questions and the corresponding responses are based upon the work of J. McV. Hunt, "Motivation Inherent in Information Processing and Ac-tion," in *Motivation and Social Interaction*, O. J. Harvey, ed. (New York: The Ronald Press Company, 1963), pp. 35–39.

1. *The instigation question.* The instigation question concerns why organisms are active at all. Specifically, what instigates their activities and what stops them?
2. *The energization question.* The energization question is concerned with what factors control the vigor and intensity of activity.
3. *The direction-hedonic question.* This question is concerned with what controls the direction or valence of behavior and what will be the hedonic value of the situation.
4. *The cathexis question.* Here the question concerns what factors determine whether organisms become attached to certain objects, places, and persons and come to seek them rather than others.
5. and 6. *The response questions.* The first response question is concerned with the choice of response and the second is concerned with the choice of goals.
7. *The learning question.* This question focuses upon the factors underlying behavioral and conceptual change.
8. *The persistence question.* This final question relates to why organisms persist in responses that fail to achieve their goals and why they persist in seeking goals they do not achieve.

In the motivation area, questions may be more easily formulated than answers. Furthermore, it may be a simpler task to secure agreement on the questions than on the answers. Yet, there is a traditional body of responses that is offered as answer to or explanation for each of the previously posed questions.

First, for example, organisms are active because of both physiological and psychogenic needs that are either internal drives or external goals. These drives and goals impel action. When these conditions cease to operate, behavior stops or ceases temporarily until new drives or new goals manifest themselves.[26]

Second, the vigor and intensity of the motivation is both a perception and a learning phenomenon. Such factors as the intensity of the painful stimulation, the degree of homeostatic need, or the intensity of the emotional response are usually proffered as the traditional explanations. The vigor, the likelihood, and the persistence of response has characteristically been treated as a function of habits, goals, and drive.[27]

The third question is traditionally answered in terms of drive reduction. Organisms are presumed to seek and to approach situations that will reduce the level of drive and to withdraw from and to avoid situations that will increase the level of drive. However, tension reduc-

[26] George Katona, *The Powerful Consumer* (New York: McGraw-Hill Book Company, 1960), p. 132.

[27] C. N. Coxer and M. H. Appley, *Motivation: Theory and Research* (New York: John Wiley & Sons, Inc., 1964), pp. 814–821.

tion theories are gradually being challenged by tension management concepts. Some individuals are seen as having a stimulus hunger, an exploratory drive, and a need curiosity.[28]

The answer to the fourth question, relating to cathexis, has traditionally been related to drive reduction. The organism is presumed to develop emotional-affective attachments for those objects, places, and persons that are associated with drive reduction or lead to the anticipation of drive reduction. Conversely, for those who manifest stimulus hunger or exploratory drives and curiosity, those goal objects and product stimuli that satisfy these urges would be sought.

Fifth, the question of responses is basically a learning or associative phenomenon, and it is conceived as a function of the drive or need operative and the past experience of the organism with this drive. Each drive or internal motivated state would conceivably have a hierarchy of responses associated with it, and the one that is manifested is the one that has served sufficiently to reduce the drive in such situations in the past.

Sixth, the question of goals is much more idiosyncratic, and it relates to a host of sociopsychological factors. Recently, goals have been viewed as a function of such factors as life style, personality, role, and other existential considerations. Increasingly, goal selection and response is being viewed as an activity related to self-image or other self-concepts.[29]

Seventh, the basic explanation for behavioral change or learning in the overall conceptual scheme has been frustration. Frustration is the blocking of a motivated, goal-directed sequence of behavior. According to this concept, frustration frequently produces angry aggression and, conversely, anger is often traceable to frustration.[30] In a more general sense, frustration leads to learning and learning presumably leads to adaptive, accommodating, or coping behavior.

Finally, the answer to the persistence question is again viewed as a learning or association problem. Behavior often persists when it fails to bring about goal attainment because goals and their related motives are often only dimly envisaged or even subconscious, and they are, therefore, only partially understood and perceived. The human organism is constantly active and constantly changing, and there is little evidence to support the lay contention that he is a creature of habit or a victim of a Freudian "repetition compulsion."[31]

[28] See the work of H. Fowler, *Curiosity and Exploratory Behavior* (New York: Macmillan Publishing Co., Inc., 1965).

[29] Significant contributions to this thinking can be found in the work of Gordon W. Allport, *Pattern and Growth in Personality* (New York: Holt, Rinehart & Winston, Inc., 1961).

[30] This theory originated with a group of Yale psychologists; see John Dollard, Leonard W. Doob, Neal Miller, O. H. Mowrer, and Robert Sears, *Frustration and Aggression* (New Haven, Conn.: Yale University Press, 1939).

[31] Sigmund Freud, *Beyond the Pleasure Principle* (New York: Boni and Liveright, 1922).

The Emotions and Motivation

The consumer is not a machine or even a hedonistic calculator, and as he manifests motivated behavior in pursuit of goals he does so within the contexts of given emotional states; that is, he seeks some goals with a greater sense of anticipation than others. Some are joyfully sought. Once attained, a given goal may result in a feeling of acceptance, surprise, fear, sorrow, or even disgust. Thus, one researcher has proposed a theory of emotional mixture. He argues that there are eight basic emotional reactions.[32] Consequently, combinations of different emotions at different levels of intensity are used to explain the rather rich variety of emotional experience encountered in the usual approach-avoidance that characterizes consumption. For example, intense joy and mild fear or increased anxiety might account for the ambivalent feelings that result when we go on a big shopping spree.

Needless to say, consumers as human organisms are emotional creatures, and their behavior is subject to emotional influences.[33] Furthermore, emotional influences act in much the same way as motives, namely, as a process or concept related to energy mobilization. Also, it must be pointed out that emotions contain, as do motives, two essential dimensions: (1) an arousal function, and (2) a cue or differentiating function. Therefore, emotions tend to affect the motivated state in terms of its *arousal* or intensity and in terms of how the individual *organizes* his resources and energy in pursuit or avoidance of a goal. Such generalizations are predicated upon the notion that the principal role of emotions in human organisms is that they prepare the body for fight or flight.[34]

The impact of perception on motivation and emotion cannot be overlooked. Consider the following example:

1. *Perception*—the neutral reception of external stimuli. The ordering and interpretation of sensory stimulation. (A consumer sees a product displayed in an attractive surrounding in a downtown department store window.)
2. *Appraisal*—a judgment of the stimuli as good and beneficial or bad and undesirable. (The consumer judges the item to be something he has wanted—a goal object—and something to which he is thus further attracted.)
3. *Emotion*—a felt tendency toward stimuli judged as good and

---

[32] Robert Plutchik, *The Emotions: Facts, Theories, and a New Model* (New York: Random House, Inc., 1967).

[33] We shall not take time to debate the issue of how many emotions there are. Such an argument is fraught with all the futility that surrounds the attempts at listing and classifying motives.

[34] See Walter B. Cannon, "The James-Lange Theory of Emotion: A Critical Examination and an Alternative Theory," *American Journal of Psychology*, Vol. 39 (1927), pp. 106–124.

away from those judged as bad or undesirable. (The consumer approaches and looks more intently.)

4. *Expression*—a pattern of physiological changes organized toward approach or withdrawal that accompany the felt tendency. (The consumer's heart pounds faster, the galvanic skin responses increase, his eye movement or eye-blink-per-second increases.)

5. *Action*—approach or avoidance may occur if another emotion does not interfere. (The consumer may go inside and engage in further search and evaluation or pass on, fearing that the item is beyond his budget, and so on.)

The essential point here is that emotions are defined in a motivational sense.[35] Thus, our point of view throughout this treatment is that emotions are a special class of motives. However, emotions are aroused to a much greater extent by external and situational stimuli even though emotions may be both innate and learned. Therefore, an emotion is an externally aroused motive with important physiological accompaniments. The tendency to approach or withdraw is the directional aspect of a motive, and the bodily changes are viewed as preparations for the organism to carry out the behavior.

CURIOSITY AS A MOTIVE

There are quite a few emotional states or motives that appear to be endemic to the human condition; that is, they may actually be innate characteristics of humans.

There is a rather large body of evidence that supports the contention that curiosity acts as a motive in itself. Curiosity, it appears, induces purposive or goal directed behavior that leads either to satisfaction or to increased tensions or anxiety if frustrated. Thus, consumers who possess a heightened stimulus hunger and exploratory drives may simply be succumbing to a curiosity motive. It is rather well known that many consumers will go out of their way to introduce variability into otherwise constant and repetitive situations, even without much of an extrinsic reward.[36] Consumers, like human organisms generally, show intrinsic interest in puzzles, problems, and other contests. Furthermore, consumers show a generally marked tendency to resume interrupted mental and physical tasks related to shopping in order to bring them to completion.[37]

---

[35] The point of view and the example that preceded it are based upon the work of Magda B. Arnold, "Physiological Differentiation of Emotional States," *Psychological Review*, Vol. 52 (1945), pp. 35–48.

[36] This has been referred to previously as "the psychology of complication." See John A. Howard and Jagdish N. Sheth, *The Theory of Buyer Behavior* (New York: John Wiley & Sons, Inc., 1969), especially Chapter 3.

[37] This phenomenon is known by the psychological term *closure*. See Bluma Zeigarnik, "Über das Behalten von Erledigten und Unerledigten Handlungen," *Psychol. Forsch*, Vol. 9 (1927), pp. 1–85.

Marketers are generally not unaware of the importance of curiosity as a buying motive. For instance, one writer states that "Much of what passes for market segmentation is really an application of what might be called the 'variety' strategy."[38] The argument is that many consumers, in an attempt to satisfy their urge toward variety, do a considerable amount of brand searching.

FRUSTRATION AND CONFLICT

Frustration is an emotional state that arises when there is goal-directed motivated behavior and a barrier or conflict arises that impedes the attainment of the goal. Frustration is a difficult condition for most humans to manage. And when high levels of frustration exist, behavior often reverts to earlier and less adaptive modes. In short, at high levels of frustration the effectiveness and efficiency of one's behavior is likely to deteriorate markedly. The most systematic treatment of motivational frustration and conflict has been given by Lewin and his associates.[39] You will recall that Lewin described motivation as tensions set up by internal needs related to external environmental goals. According to Lewin, conflicts often occur between different need tension systems, especially when they are of approximately equal strength. Thus, several forms of conflict and the resulting behavior have been characterized as follows:

1. A conflict between positive valences, when two equally desirable objects or activities are perceived (approach-approach conflict). Such conditions, in the case of consumer behavior, may mean that the individual will attempt to obtain both goal objects, or if that is impossible, he may vacillate between both. Usually, however, one is seen as more desirable than the other and the consumer chooses it.

2. There may be a conflict between a positive and a negative valence, as when an object is seen as desirable and is approached but it is surrounded by negative factors and is therefore avoided (approach-avoidance conflict). This is perhaps the most characteristic of all consumer behavior. A product may be seen as desirable, but buying product A means foregoing product B, or buying A commits one to twelve easy (but undesirable) payments, or going into lovely store A means being waited upon by hideous salesperson B.

3. There may be a conflict between two negative valences, as when an individual cannot decide which of two evils to avoid (avoidance-avoidance conflict). Consumers sometimes find themselves faced with an avoidance-avoidance situation. The hot water tank leaks or bursts. It isn't a product of great symbolic significance. It means not getting some other more highly visible or useful appliance, and it means having to make a considerable outlay of money. Avoidance-

[38] William H. Reynolds, *Products and Markets* (New York: Meredith Corporation, 1969), pp. 137–154, at p. 138.

[39] Kurt Lewin, *A Dynamic Theory of Personality* (New York: McGraw-Hill Book Company, 1935).

avoidance conflict can lead to great amounts of vacillation, and it is often imbued with larger than normal amounts of frustration and conflict.

There can be many responses to frustration; for example, a *regression* to childish or earlier modes of behavior, indifferent *withdrawal*, or meaningful *information processing* and *problem solving*. Frustration itself is an emotionally arousing condition, *anger* is the usual intervening emotional state, and *aggression* is simply one of the many responses to anger.[40]

ANXIETY

Anxiety as a motivating condition was discussed much earlier in our treatment.[41] When consumers have goals and reasonable freedom of choice, it means that they have an opportunity to decide. Such choices often create a state of anxiety or emotional arousal. Fear and anxiety are similar phenomena; they both involve a palpitating heart and a mild feeling of dread. *Fear*, however, is a reaction to a specific threat, whereas *anxiety* is a reaction to more general threats.

Anxiety is often related to aspiration levels and self-perceptions. You might ask yourself what would make you anxious—disparagement of your intelligence, your honesty, your sexuality, your self-image? Anxiety over social disapproval is widespread, and indeed it acts as an important means of social control.

However, anxiety can organize and direct behavior as any other motive does. For example, consider the family who sees an advertisement for a new high-quality, low-priced acrylic carpet. They badly need a new carpet, and thus the advertisement raises their anxiety. But what effect does this anxiety have on their behavior? First of all, it facilitates *perception*—they see their floor as bare, hard, and cold. The anxiety facilitates *verbal behavior* and *symbolic processes*—they talk and think about purchasing a new carpet a great deal. The anxiety also increases *learning*—they search for and read literature about yarns, weaves, durability, and cleaning qualities. Finally, the anxiety strongly determines the *goals* of the individuals—they decide not to forego purchasing but instead to establish the carpet purchase as a number one priority.

Social Motivation and Consumer Behavior

Consumers are not isolated. They exist and behave within a network of interstimulation and interaction. And within this network they develop and acquire goals and motivation for their behavior. Thus, whether they be innate, learned, or both, social motives dominate a great part of the total range of consumer behavior. Almost the entire range of consumer behavior is affected by social relationships. We buy

[40] Murray, op. cit., p. 66.
[41] See Chapter 4.

goods not only to satisfy ourselves but to satisfy and impress our friends. We go shopping not only to seek information about goods but to spend a pleasant, socially oriented afternoon. The goods we seek as symbols are sought because they are esteemed by significant others. In general, consumers are motivated to seek the society of others and to attain social approval and acceptance, and to control and inhibit behavior that is disapproved by others. The universality of such behavior suggests the existence of innate or at least fundamentally based motivation. Such motivation includes the tendency to seek social contacts and interaction by living in the society of others, and it also includes the drive to obtain acceptance and approval, which itself appears to be desired as a means of legitimating and reinforcing our choices and actions. Our society and our culture thus become a matrix through which our motives become both fixated and generalized. These social motives are almost always entirely independent of physiological functions. They arise out of interaction with other people.

INTRINSIC VERSUS EXTRINSIC MOTIVATION

We have avoided, for about as long as is practical, the question of whether motives, instincts, drives, emotions, or other action tendencies are innate or learned, and thus socially acquired. In many ways, it is a moot argument and one that has waxed both long and hard in the psychological literature for many years. It would be pleasant to report that the issue has now been settled and to report the results, but such, unfortunately, is not the case. The argument continues unabated. Perhaps, at least at this juncture, we can elaborate on the basic nature of the argument. It is well known that almost any response can be learned and repeated on the basis of a reward that tends to reinforce the original act. In such situations the reward is *extrinsic* to the activity. In short, there is no inherent and necessary connection between the activity and the reward. The activity is undertaken in order to get the reward.[42] For example, consumers shop, compare, and evaluate because this behavior leads to better performance, that is, higher-quality goods, lower prices, and better terms. However, it has already been suggested that extensive shopping, comparing and evaluation, and other similar activities in consumer decision processes may be *intrinsically* rewarding. They may be engaged in for their own sake, for some inherent satisfaction or pleasure. Consequently, some motives are intrinsic. Perhaps novelty, curiosity, and stimulus hunger, as suggested by cognitive consistency and balance needs, are really intrinsic motives. The same behavior, as manifested by different consumers, might more aptly be attributed to some form of extrinsic motivation, that is, as a means to an end rather than an end in itself. Such a point of view is gaining widely in popularity and acceptance, and it has been found to be consistent with both instinct and hedonistic theories of motivation. Thus some evidence exists to support the innate or instinct theory of motivation. Yet in

[42] Murray, op. cit., p. 74.

sophisticated, high-level consumption-oriented societies the manifestation of innate and intrinsic motivations almost always takes on social
implications and significance.[43]

In the following paragraphs, we shall examine several socially
oriented motives that may be either intrinsically or extrinsically rewarding or both.

THE RANGE OF SOCIALLY MOTIVATED BEHAVIOR

One of the most comprehensive lists of socially motivated behavior
was generated in an investigation of personality characteristics by
Murray.[44] These he labeled *needs,* though they are more realistically
psychogenic motives or motivational tendencies. Murray did not necessarily argue that his needs were innate, though he would allow that
temperamental disposition may be involved. He further acknowledged
that his total list of needs or motives does not occur in everyone. The
full range of Murray's list is shown in Table 7-1.

Murray's list, although rather complete, is really more suggestive
than definitive. For example, it gives a rather sensitive description of
some of the motivational patterns of consumers. Consider, for example,
a consumer having a post-mortem session with a friend after a recent
shopping experience. He may attack a salesperson for having treated
him discourteously (aggression). He may state that he purchased
poorly because of his own inadequacy (abasement). He may assert that
in the future he is going to shop more diligently (counteraction). He
may even rationalize his behavior to his friend (defendance). He may
assert his intention never to shop at a particular store again (infavoid-
ance). His friend may reinforce and bolster his sentiments (nurtur-
ance) if he seems to need or want it badly (succorance). There is little
need to continue the illustration even though several more examples are
likely to come to mind. Many of the social motives that are likely to
play an important role in consumer behavior can be found in Murray's
list. Achievement, affiliation, aggression, deference, exhibition, order,
play, sex, and understanding are all well-recognized and important influences on consumer decision processes. We shall not discuss each of
these social motives. Several have already received limited attention.
We shall, however, examine in limited detail two of the more prominent and well-researched social motives—affiliation and achievement.

AFFILIATION. Affiliation is a well-known and reasonably well-researched social motive. It has profound importance and far-reaching
implications for the field of consumer behavior. Affiliation has been defined as concern with the establishment and maintenance of positive

---

[43] See Hubert Bonner, *Group Dynamics: Principles and Application* (New
York: Harper and Row, Publishers, 1956).

[44] Henry A. Murray, *An Exploration in Personality: A Clinical Experimental
Study of Fifty Men of College Age* (London: Oxford University Press, 1938),
pp. 80–83.

TABLE 7-1
H. A. Murray's List of Social Motives

Social motive	Brief definition
Abasement	To submit passively to external force. To accept injury, blame, criticism, punishment. To surrender. To become resigned to fate. To admit inferiority, error, wrongdoing, or defeat. To confess and atone. To blame, belittle, or mutilate the self. To seek and enjoy pain, punishment, illness, and misfortune.
Achievement	To accomplish something difficult. To master, manipulate, or organize physical objects, human beings, or ideas. To do this as rapidly and as independently as possible. To overcome obstacles and attain a high standard. To excel oneself. To rival and surpass others. To increase self-regard by the successful exercise of talent.
Affiliation	To draw near and enjoyably co-operate or reciprocate with an allied other (an other who resembles the subject or who likes the subject). To please and win affection of a cathected object. To adhere and remain loyal to a friend.
Aggression	To overcome opposition forcefully. To fight. To revenge an injury. To attack, injure, or kill another. To oppose forcefully or punish another.
Autonomy	To get free, shake off restraint, break out of confinement. To resist coercion and restriction. To avoid or quit activities prescribed by domineering authorities. To be independent and free to act according to impulse. To be unattached, irresponsible. To defy convention.
Counteraction	To master or make up for a failure by restriving. To obliterate a humiliation by resumed action. To overcome weaknesses, to repress fear. To efface a dishonor by action. To search for obstacles and difficulties to overcome. To maintain self-respect and price on a high level.
Defendance	To defend the self against assault, criticism, and blame. To conceal or justify a misdeed, failure, or humiliation. To vindicate the ego.

Source: Henry Murray, *An Exploration in Personality: A Clinical Experimental Study of Fifty Men of College Age* (London: Oxford University Press, 1938), pp. 80–83.

affectionate relations with other persons, with the desire to be liked and accepted.[45] Affiliation is usually thought to include a willingness to subordinate personal motivation to what is accepted by other group members. Fear, anxiety, and perhaps other aversive conditions probably underlie many social motives but most especially affiliation. Whether all such apparent motives can be reduced to this mechanism is, of

[45] See J. W. Atkinson and E. L. Walker, "The Affiliation Motive and Perceptual Sensitivity of Faces," *Journal of Abnormal and Social Psychology*, Vol. 53 (1956), pp. 38–41.

Social motive	Brief definition
Deference	To admire and support a superior. To praise, honor, or eulogize. To yield eagerly to the influence of an allied other. To emulate an exemplar. To conform to custom.
Dominance	To control one's human environment. To influence or direct the behavior of others by suggestion, seduction, persuasion, or command. To dissuade, restrain, or prohibit.
Exhibition	To make an impression. To be seen and heard. To excite, amaze, fascinate, entertain, shock, intrigue, amuse, or entice others.
Harmavoidance	To avoid pain, physical injury, illness, and death. To escape from a dangerous situation. To take precautionary measures.
Infavoidance	To avoid humiliation. To quit embarrassing situations or to avoid conditions which may lead to belittlement, the score, derision, or indifference of others. To refrain from action because of the fear of failure.
Nurturance	To give sympathy and gratify the needs of a helpless object: an infant or any object that is weak, disabled, tired, inexperienced, infirm, defeated, humiliated, lonely, dejected, sick, mentally confused. To assist an object in danger. To feed, help, support, console, protect, comfort, nurse, heal.
Order	To put things in order. To achieve cleanliness, arrangement, organization, balance, neatness, tidiness, and precision.
Play	To act for "fun" without further purpose. To like to laugh and make jokes. To seek enjoyable relaxation from stress. To participate in games, sports, dancing, drinking parties, cards.
Rejection	To separate oneself from a negatively cathected object. To exclude, abandon, expel, or remain indifferent to an inferior object. To snub or jilt an object.
Sentience	To seek and enjoy sensuous impressions.
Sex	To form and further an erotic relationship. To have sexual intercourse.
Succorance	To have one's needs gratified by the sympathetic aid of an allied object. To be nursed, supported, sustained, surrounded, protected, loved, advised, guided, indulged, forgiven, consoled. To remain close to a devoted protector. To always have a supporter.
Understanding	To ask or answer general questions. To be interested in theory. To speculate, formulate, analyze, and generalize.

course, impossible to judge at this time. Consumers with a strong bent for affiliation are likely to be more dependent on others and to seek a higher degree of social reinforcement for the legitimation of their behavior. They are not likely to want to shop alone but instead seek the companionship of a friend or relative during shopping expeditions. The affiliation tendency also suggests that such customers are likely to view the efforts of salespeople as more positive, especially if such salespersons project a warm and easy style and manner. The presence of anxiety suggests that salespeople may be sought and valued for their role in providing information, reinforcement, and other social comfort. The general role of social interaction among people with high affiliation motivation is that it provides an opportunity for both catharsis and distraction.[46]

ACHIEVEMENT. The achievement motive has been most extensively researched by McClelland and his associates.[47] Achievement motivation may be associated with a wide variety of goals—money, goods, status, power, dominance, and so forth, but in general the behavior adopted will be directed toward the attainment of some standard of excellence. Thus ambition is an important element in achievement motivation, but it is more likely that the standard is based more or less directly on the attainments and achievements of others or on general social standards. Persons found to have high achievement motivation have a strong continuing desire for achievement, especially of long-term goals, in a variety of situations and not merely an impulse to achieve a few, limited, short-term objectives.

Those who have high achievement motivation find satisfaction in striving and achieving for its own sake. The extrinsic rewards are not necessarily the only goals sought. Furthermore, those with high achievement motivation usually learn faster and make responses faster than those with low achievement motivation. In addition, those with high achievement motivation are often information seekers and utilizers. As opposed to those who are more affiliation motivated and are likely to use more personal sources of information—friends, relatives, and salespeople—the achievement-motivated individual is likely to use more nonpersonal and secondary sources of information for purposes of decision making. Achievement-motivated consumers are likely to possess a liking for taking moderate though not excessive risks and a confidence in the ability to succeed in such tasks. In addition, they manifest a desire for freedom and individual responsibility; they like choices and options. Finally, they obviously seek the attainment of individual success, which, in itself, is usually signaled by the acquisition and display of wealth. Such wealth, quite frequently, is in the form of goods and high levels of consumption activity. In general, achievement motivation is stronger in adults who have received a university education and are in professional occupations than in others.[48] This suggests that education as a socializing process tends to reinforce the achievement motive, which is normally thought to be inculcated in the individual as a

[46] See S. Schacter, *The Psychology of Affiliation: Experimental Studies of the Sources of Gregariousness* (Stanford, Calif.: Stanford University Press, 1959), especially pp. 121–122.

[47] David C. McClelland, J. W. Atkinson, R. A. Clark, and E. L. Lowell, *The Achievement Motive* (New York: Appleton-Century-Crofts, 1953).

[48] J. Verloff et al., "The Use of the Thematic Apperception Test to Assess Motivation in a Nationwide Interview Study," *Psychological Monogram*, Vol. 74, No. 12 (1960).

result of particular training and child-rearing practices found in the home.

MOTIVATION AND SELF-CONCEPTS

The literature abounds with lists of needs or motives. Some are brief and limited in range as, for example, Thomas's list, which includes only four motives or "wishes"—for security, for recognition, for response from others, and for new experience.[49] Some are longer and more detailed, such as Murray's list examined earlier. Some lists of motives are well documented and arrived at through painstaking empirical research. Others are speculative products of little more than armchair analysis—for example, such assertions as "People who like blue are trying to cool their fires." One writer, building upon such a reduced-form scheme, argues the fact that blue is regarded as a "soft" background color whereas red is a "hard" and imposing color. A highly motivated person, he suggests, is intent on playing an active role, on imposing his will upon the environment. Such a person likes a soft, unobtrusive, passive background. The person with low motivation is himself the quieter, softer, more passive element, and he favors a more imposing hard color.[50] Knapp points out that subdued and conservative dress characterizes North European Protestant cultures, where, as has been shown, the achievement motive seems to be stronger than it is in Catholic Mediterranean cultures, where dress is more colorful. However, throughout the world bright, vivid, even garish colors are currently more prominent, and middle-class dull gray is being supplanted by peacock greens, blues, yellows, reds, and oranges. The point is that the predictive value of such motivational schemes is extremely limited.

One final comment or two, however, about social motives and motivation would appear to be warranted. Whatever his total range of needs, motives, sentiments, and emotions, it would appear that everyone possesses what McDougall has termed the "self-regarding" sentiment. This is the organization of ideas, beliefs, emotions, and motivated behavior centered in the self.[51] Most people, certainly consumers, act in such a way as would seem likely to maintain their pride and enhance their self-esteem and the esteem of others. They act to protect themselves from contempt, disapproval, and frustration.

This self-regarding sentiment is closely related to the self-concept previously discussed—a concept that attempts to encompass the totality of the individual's own being; and along with this awareness of self there emerge certain self needs. These are needs that preempt an important part of the individual's time and energy. These self needs

[49] William I. Thomas, *The Unadjusted Girl* (Little, Brown and Company, 1923).

[50] R. H. Knapp, "Achievement and Aesthetic Preference," in *Motives in Fantasy Action and Society*, J. W. Atkinson, ed. (Princeton, N.J.: Van Nostrand Reinhold Company, 1958).

[51] W. McDougall, *The Energies of Men* (London: Methuen & Co., Ltd., 1932).

are an integrated totality, but they can be separated for analytical clarity into three major aspects:

1. The need for an accurate and acceptant self-image.
2. The need to verify this self-image through association.
3. The need to verify and legitimate the self-image through action.[52]

It has already been suggested that consumer behavior—the purchase, consumption, and utilization of goods as symbols—plays an important and instrumental role in each of these needs. These needs, along with basic physiological needs, constitute the basic needs of man. As needs they become goals that become, through socialization processes, the main motivating forces underlying much human behavior.

Toward a Theory of Consumer Motivation

We have gathered a rather monumental amount of raw material —ideas, concepts, theories—out of which we might now attempt to construct a limited theory of consumer behavior. Why limited? Because given the extraordinary nature of human beings—their sophistication, their complexity, their divergence from any major norm—all theories of human behavior, and consequently consumer behavior, must of necessity be limited. However, we can say a great deal and what we say can be important in terms of our major quest, namely, understanding. Consumer behavior is characterized by its organized, highly motivated, goal-directed nature. It possesses an overall purposiveness. The consumer is committed to a task, and his activities are dominated by this task. Consumer behavior, though often socially and emotionally motivated, is nonetheless directed by rational thought. By and large the accompanying sentiments and emotions are pleasurable, and although there is usually some anxiety it is normally easily managed. Thus consumer behavior as goal-directed activity is controlled by a conscious effort to achieve certain aims by means of specifically chosen courses of action. Consumer behavior is problem-solving behavior, and it is, therefore, characterized by large amounts of cognitive activity and information processing. Cognitive activity would include knowledge, perception, learning, and communication. Consumers are motivated to buy goods because goods as symbols are important to the individual's striving-becoming process. They facilitate the individual's need for self-identity, self-enhancement, and self-extension. Thus, consumer behavior is almost totally ego involved, not at all in the Freudian sense but as *ego* is often used as a synonym for *self-concept*. Much consumer behavior is a unifying or goal-directed kind of activity, the principal purpose of which is, in some sense, to coordinate inner needs and outer reality. Consumer behavior can be characterized in these terms:

[52] Snell and Gail Putney, *The Adjusted American* (New York: Harper and Row, Publishers, 1966), p. 27.

1. It is goal-directed behavior.
2. It is purposive and motivated.
3. The motives are more frequently goals that pull than drives that push.
4. Consumers have an enormous capacity for acquiring motives.
5. A goal once attained is no longer an important source of further motivated behavior.
6. Goals and their motives are not always operative at the conscious level, and even when they are they are often only dimly envisaged.
7. The striving to attain goods to fulfill goals is often a form of trial-and-error activity.
8. The consumer is both an animal and a social being. Along with the higher forms of life, he is possessed with other needs, as well as the classic needs of food, water, and sexual activity.

THE NEEDS-WANTS HIERARCHY

One scheme that offers some promise for understanding consumer motivation and behavior is the concept of a needs-wants hierarchy promulgated by Maslow.[53] Maslow contends that man has a general hierarchy of needs and that these needs become the principal motivation of behavior. These needs range from lower motives to higher ones, and they are thus arranged in a hierarchy that corresponds to the assumed evolutionary level of the motive. Maslow's hierarchy is as follows:

1. *Physiological motives.* These are the needs that must be fulfilled if the body is to survive. They include the need for oxygen, water, food, waste elimination, relief from pain, protection from the elements, and so on.
2. *Safety motives.* These are the need for security, protection, order, stability, and routine.
3. *Love motives.* These are the needs for affection and affiliation, for warm, satisfying, and fulfilling human interactions with family, friends, and other groups.
4. *Esteem motives.* These are the needs for self-respect, prestige, success, achievement, and self-validation.
5. *The self-actualization motive.* This is the need and desire for self-fulfillment—to become all that one is capable of becoming.

In many ways, this scheme represents simply another attempt to classify motives, but in actuality it does much more. For instance, Maslow argued that, with rare exception, lower needs must be fulfilled before the higher-level needs emerge. A hungry consumer is obsessed with and becomes a compulsive seeker of food. In a low-level subsist-

---

[53] Abraham H. Maslow, *Motivation and Personality* (New York: Harper and Row, Publishers, 1954), especially Chapter 5, pp. 80–107.

ence economy we probably wouldn't even need a theory of consumer motivation because all behavior would be motivated by the bodily needs. However, in a high-level consumption-oriented economy, the important insight stemming from a knowledge and understanding of a needs-wants hierarchy is that marketing contributes to the consumer's ability to help satisfy his total range of needs; that is, marketing is a means to the ends or goals sought by the consumer.

However, once man's basic physiological needs are supplied, other higher needs emerge and become prepotent. And when these in turn are satisfied, additional and again higher needs emerge, and so on. This is a significant concept relating to a needs-wants hierarchy, and it supports our earlier contention that consumers have an enormous capacity for acquiring needs and motives.

At each of the five needs-wants levels, notice the significance of goods. We buy food, clothing, and shelter to protect and nourish our bodies. However, instead of simple tissue gratification, we buy goods to satisfy particular tastes—sirloin steaks, redwood houses, and Pendleton jackets. We buy goods that stress safety—steel beams in the sidewalls of automobiles and belted glass tires that will get our loved ones home safely. We buy gifts for loved ones and we purchase items that will make us more appealing and more socially accepted. We buy insurance to protect (safety), but we also buy it because we love people and to love them is to want to protect them. Advertisements consistently stress both the social and the esteem motives for buying products. Finally, given the increased education, awareness, discernment, and income of the average American consumer, a considerable but varying degree of self-actualizing behavior may well have infected the mood and mode of much consumer purchasing activity.[54]

However, these motives should not be understood as exclusive or single determiners of behavior. Most consumer behavior is multimotivated—any specific act of purchase may be determined by several or all of Maslow's five basic motivators. Finally, it should be pointed out that some behavior is highly motivated and some behavior is very weakly motivated. Some behavior may not even be motivated at all—its underlying reasons are not necessarily motives in the sense in which we have been discussing motivation.

COMPETENCE AND EFFECTANCE MOTIVATION

One additional scheme of motivation appears to be useful for our analysis of consumer motivation and behavior. This conception is largely the work of Robert W. White, and it relates to what he calls competence and effectance motivation.[55] It considerably reinforces the

---

[54] For an extended view of self-actualization, see Abraham H. Maslow, *Toward a Psychology of Being* (New York: Van Nostrand Reinhold Company, 1968), pp. 189–215.

[55] Robert W. White, "Motivation Reconsidered: The Concept of Competence," *Psychological Review,* Vol. 66, No. 5 (1959), pp. 297–331.

generalizations that have previously been stated, namely, the consideration in its own right of those aspects of human behavior in which stimulation and contact with the environment seem to be welcomed, in which raised tension and even mild excitement seem to be cherished, and in which novelty and variety are apparently enjoyed for their own sake. Such considerations make dealing with the environment one of the most fundamental and cognition-involved elements underlying motivation. Such a proposition suggests that learning to deal effectively with one's environment is in itself an important motivation of behavior. The human organism's coping, adapting, and accommodating activities in relation to his environment are an attempt to attain what White calls *competence.* The activities that lead to competence are conceived to be motivated; and this motivation is designated as *effectance,* which is said to lead to a feeling of efficacy.

The urge toward competence is inferred most specifically from behavior that shows a lasting focus and that has the characteristics of *exploration* and *experimentation.* With this particular sort of activity, effectance motivation is being aroused, for it is characteristic of this activity that it is selective and directed and that it will be learned for the sole intrinsic reward of engaging in it. Thus, much of the behavior related to consumer decision processes, such as awareness, interest, evaluation, trial, and adoption, can be analyzed as a kind of competence behavior involving effectance motivation. Typically, such behavior involves continuous chains of events that include stimulation, cognition, action, effect on the environment, new stimulation, and so forth. Such actions are carried on with considerable persistence and with selective emphasis on the parts of the environment that provide changing and interesting feedback in connection with the effort expended.

CONSCIOUS VERSUS UNCONSCIOUS CHARACTER OF MOTIVES

Thus far we have spoken about motives as if they were something the organism was highly aware of or, at least, as if they could be readily identified by a market researcher or some other investigator. Such, however, is not always the case. Motives may be either conscious or unconscious. More often than not they exist and manifest their influence as a determinant of behavior at a level that is below the threshold of the average person's level of consciousness. Even when they exist at a higher level of consciousness, they are only dimly envisaged. There exists an overwhelming amount of evidence that suggests the crucial importance of unconscious motivation.[56] Thus, what are called basic motives or goals are more often unconscious or only dimly envisaged, internalized, goal-directed action tendencies. These motives, however, may be uncovered and brought to an understandable level of consciousness by well-qualified people with sufficient expertise and appropriate and suitable techniques.

[56] Maslow, op. cit., p. 101.

MOTIVATION AND DEFENSE MECHANISMS. Before a discussion of the methods for assessing motives is undertaken, some brief comments regarding defense mechanisms would appear warranted. As mentioned, motives may exist at either the conscious or the unconscious level. Some motives, however, are deemed so undesirable by the individual because they are either culturally or socially taboo, or because they are so ego- or self-threatening, that they are *repressed*. Thus an attempt to assess such motives would probably lead to the manifestation of some psychological defense mechanism like *repression*, that is, the pushing of conscious motives out of consciousness.

Consumers are especially inclined to engage in *rationalization*. For example, if asked, "Why did you buy that product?" they are likely to rationalize, substituting good, socially and culturally acceptable reasons for the real reasons. Other frequently used defense mechanisms are *projection*—attributing to others the unacceptable aspects of one's own personality ("Sally, my next door neighbor, is a spendthrift and can't resist buying everything she sees."), and *reaction formation*— behavior that is opposite to the repressed tendencies ("I hate to shop but I do it and I do it extensively because it's something my family expects, and to satisfy my own image of what a good housewife ought to do, I do it.").

It can be seen that behavior, attitudes, and motives are not always what they appear to be—not to the observer or even to the actor himself. Thus, motivation and the assessment of motivation and corresponding behavior are related but not always in a simple, direct, and conscious way.

THE ASSESSMENT OF MOTIVATION. As we have observed, it is difficult to assess motivation and motives with simple verbal reports, especially inasmuch as motivation is largely an unconscious phenomenon. A better measure is usually some kind of "projection test" that indicates motivation indirectly, without the subject's being aware of this.[57] One widely used test is the T.A.T. (Thematic Apperception Test). The T.A.T. consists of a series of pictures that relate more or less to a particular type of motivation. The test has been widely used for assessing individual differences in achievement and social motivation. The Rorschach test, a test devised for the analysis of personality calling for responses to ink blots and drawings, has also been used with some success to uncover unconscious motivation.

Psychoanalysis and depth interviewing have also been used to assess motivation but with limited and even dubious results, especially in relation to the question of consumer motivation and behavior.

More reliability is obtained by the use of validated and standardized objective testing instruments, for example, the Iowa Picture Interpretation Test, in which a set of four pictures is accompanied in

[57] M. D. Vernon, *Human Motivation* (London: Cambridge University Press, 1969), pp. 163–166.

each case by four statements about it. Individuals are required to rank the statements in order of their apparent relevance to the pictures. It is supposed that the rank order is determined by the individual's prevailing motivation. In the French Test of Insight a series of short sentences describing various types of motivated behavior is presented, and individuals are asked to explain or comment on these sentences. There is a great variety of questionnaires consisting of statements about motivated behavior. Here the subjects are asked to state whether or not they behave in these ways. Such tests often assess anxiety. As a general characteristic of motivation and personality, anxiety is frequently measured by means of the Taylor Manifest Anxiety Scale.

The responses to many of these tests depend to a great extent on verbal facility, and they can be made adequately only by persons who are reasonably well educated and who are able to invent and organize satisfactory stories and responses. Many of the tests do not measure specific motivation at all clearly or satisfactorily.

MOTIVATION RESEARCH. Immediately after World War II and continuing up into the early 1960s, many marketing research organizations promoted a kind of consumer research known as motivation research. Using many of the devices described in the previous section, these firms attempted to assess the unconscious "hidden persuader" motivations that underlie many consumer purchases. It was an exuberant, heady period for motivation researchers. The results of their studies were widely quoted. For example, consumers avoided prunes because they were wrinkled and reminded older consumers (who often did eat them for regularity) of death and old age. Milk was allegedly endowed with an aura of sinfulness and suggested many negative qualities associated with animal characteristics in relation to the utter perfection of mother's milk. One classic study found certain inhibitory tendencies in the purchase of instant coffee in the early 1950s. The housewife using instant coffee was characterized as being lazy, disliking cooking, and being a poor housewife in general.[58] Later, however, another researcher raised serious questions concerning poor classification, small sample size, and the use of leading questions.[59] Thus the application of these clinical and psychoanalytical techniques has come under rather serious critical attack.[60] Many of the attacks on motivation research revolve around the method used by the researchers and the researchers themselves. Although these methods have been fashioned out of clinical and psychoanalytical techniques, they are radically changed, both in con-

[58] Mason Haire, "Projective Techniques in Marketing Research," *Journal of Marketing,* Vol. 14 (April 1950), pp. 125–139.

[59] Conrad R. Hill, "Haire's Classic Instant Coffee Study—18 Years Later," *Journalism Quarterly,* Vol. 45 (August 1968), pp. 466–472.

[60] See Alfred Polnitz, "Motivation Research from a Research Viewpoint," *Public Opinion Quarterly,* Vol. 20 (Winter 1956–1957), pp. 663–673; and N. D. Rothwell, "Motivation Research Revised," *Journal of Marketing,* Vol. 19 (October 1955), pp. 150–154.

tent and in the intensity of their application, when applied to the business world and consumer behavior. The results of motivation research studies, although often interesting, are difficult to validate through replication. Too, the results are often useless in terms of management implications. Yet motivation research continues to have its adherents even though the number of firms specializing in such activities continues to decline.[61]

One of the greatest contributions of this type of consumer research is that it continues to underline the importance of *understanding the consumer*—not only his motives but everything about his behavior pattern. Motivation research, however, is not enough—there are too many unknowns and generalizations in motivation research for this concept to be able to give the correct answer to a marketing problem. Certainly more is involved. The question is What other factors are involved in consumer behavior besides motives and what must the marketer understand about these factors in order to allow him to make sound marketing decisions based upon predictions of the individual's behavior?

Some Ground Rules for a Theory of Consumer Motivation

We have ranged over a wide variety of material relating to motivation. As mentioned at the outset it is not a well-delineated, settled field in either social psychology or consumer behavior. Hopefully, however, our treatment has provided numerous important insights regarding motivation, especially motivation as it pertains to consumer behavior. We have as yet, admittedly, no clear-cut conception regarding motivation; that is, we have not yet discovered the human mainspring or what it is that specifically "makes consumers tick." Nor do I believe we ever will, especially in the sense that we may discover some deeply rooted "mechanism" responsible for all human and consumer acts, primarily because man and consumers are constantly striving and changing. Man is curious, he likes variety, he seeks competence in dealing with his environment, and he appears to desire to know and to possess a stimulus hunger for new experience and new situations. Consumers are a product of their choices and their choices stem from their environments and their existential circumstances. As these change so will the consumer and so will his requirements for fulfilling a needs-wants hierarchy. Thus the image of man, and perhaps man himself, is changing. As it does, so too must our theories of consumer motivation. A constantly changing, coping, groping, striving consumer suggests some ground rules from which our theories of consumer motivation

---

[61] See Dietz Leonhard, *The Human Equation in Marketing Research* (New York: American Management Association, 1967). Chapter 5 is especially interesting for those desiring to learn more about the use of projective techniques.

might too emerge.[62] Several of these propositions have previously been incorporated into our discussion.

1. The consumer is an integrated and organized whole. Consumer behavior and motivation are a part of the larger matrix of social, economic, and cultural behavior. We understand the mechanism of motivation not in terms of the mechanism per se but in terms of the holocentric nature of behavior.

2. Consumer motivation is not necessarily an end in itself but is a means to an end. Consumer behavior is instrumental behavior. The motives that pass through our unconsciousness are not in themselves as important as what they stand for, where they lead, and what they ultimately mean.

3. Consumer motivation is largely social in origin. We learn and acquire motives as a result of socialization processes, as a result of being in association with motives and attitudes, as a result of reinforcement from friends and significant others, and as a result of upbringing experiences in the family.

4. Consumers have an enormous capacity for acquiring motives and these numerous motives often manifest themselves in simultaneous clusters rather than as single-file entities. Thus, the purchase of most goods probably does not involve a single motive, but because of the complex symbolic significance of goods, they are purchased to satisfy multiple motivations.

5. Consumers are in a near-constant motivational state and such states are not easily differentiated from other states of the organism. Consumer motivation theory should assume that motivation is constant, never-ending, fluctuating, and complex.

6. Consumers are wanting animals. Their needs, in a strict physiological sense, are limited and in affluent societies easily fulfilled. However, wants are limited only by the boundaries of man's imagination. When one want is fulfilled, several more usually pop up to take its place.

7. An attempt to understand consumer motivation by listing atomistic and specific drives is theoretically unsound. Such lists erroneously assume that each drive is equally potent or important. Furthermore, the number of drives one chooses to list depends on the degree of specificity with which one chooses to analyze them.

8. In humans, motives are best understood in terms of goals that pull rather than drives that push. Fundamental goals remain rather constant though they do change over time.

9. Consumer behavior is human behavior. Thus motivation studies based upon animal data are not applicable. A white rat or a pigeon is not a human being, and to understand consumer motivation we had best study human organisms.

---

[62] Several of these propositions were suggested by Maslow, op. cit. See especially pp. 63–80.

10. Finally, we must recognize that behavior is a multivariable not a single-variable phenomenon. Motivation, although exceedingly important, is only one determinant of behavior. Cognition, perception, learning, memory, and other complex processes of the brain and central nervous system are also involved. Furthermore, all these things are unique to each organism. It is important, as has been mentioned, to recognize the impact of the situation. Consumer motivation rarely causes behavior except in relation to a given situation that involves life style, life cycles, role, and other social and group influences.

Questions for Study, Reflection, and Review

1 Describe Copeland's dichotomy of consumer buying motives and discuss its relationship to contemporary marketing endeavors.

2 Contrast the view of motivation as drive-push with that of goal-pull.

3 Discuss the nature of motivation as explained by instinct theories.

4 Explain the context within which motivation is viewed by cognitive theorists.

5 Discuss the relationship between the direction-hedonic question and the cathexis question from a drive theory viewpoint.

6 Identify the influences of social relationships upon consumer behavior.

7 Distinguish between consumer behavior that is extrinsically rewarding and that which is intrinsically rewarding.

8 Discuss the importance of the self-regarding sentiment and self needs in consumer motivation.

9 Describe Maslow's hierarchy of needs and its function as a motivator of consumer behavior.

10 Discuss the implications of the unconscious nature of motives for marketing research.

8

Perception

Introduction

Our treatment of consumer behavior will of necessity continue to be built upon the principles and concepts of a cognitive psychology. You will recall the discussion of cognitive psychology presented in Chapter 5. We stated at that time that cognitive psychology emphasizes the mental as opposed to the physical or physiological aspects of behavior. Such a psychology recognizes the roles of cognition, motivation, perception, learning, and communication as major determinants of behavior. Furthermore, it stresses social and environmental factors such as group membership, social interaction, and culture, which are instrumental in shaping tastes and molding behavior patterns and characteristics.

In our treatment to this juncture we have developed a brief, though important, cognitive theory of consumer behavior. This theory, in its most skeletal and succinct form states, "What and why a consumer does what he does is a function of what he knows." Put another way, "Consumer behavior is a function of consumer knowledge." It is an interesting minitheory and one that is conceptually quite rich. It offers the prospect for much analysis of behavior; it is an excellent framework for studying and analyzing consumers; and as a theory, it offers the prospect of further description, explanation, and even prediction. However, it is at this juncture only a minitheory in need of considerable refinement and elaboration. The theory or concept that

"Consumer behavior is a function of the consumer's knowledge" begs many questions. For example, "What is knowledge?" Here we are concerned with the questions "What do consumers know?" and "What do they think they know?" Thus we focus upon such things as values, knowledge, beliefs, attitudes, and opinions. We examine, furthermore, such concepts as images because, as has been implied, consumers form impressions of people, situations, ideas, and places. These impressions may be factual or they may be simply conjectural. Nonetheless, consumers behave in accordance with their impressions or images.

The brief cognitive theory of behavior, although somewhat meaningful, needs much additional refinement. For instance, it begs the question "Why are consumers stimulated or aroused 'to know' and why does this knowledge or these values or images propel or compel them to take action?" These, you will recognize, are *motivational* questions, treated at great length in the previous chapter. Another major question that will receive our attention presently is the question of *perception;* namely, how do people (consumers) organize, interpret, and order what they see? Perception is an exceedingly important variable in our cognitive theory of behavior. If behavior is a function of knowledge, we must ask, "How do we come to know?" "How do consumers generate single, unified meanings from sensory processes?" These are important questions of perception. Furthermore, our cognitive theory of behavior, which embraces the question of "how we come to know," is concerned with such additional phenomena as *learning, communication, attitude formation,* and *change,* plus a concern with many situational factors and processes, such as *group interaction, socialization, culture,* and others.

Understanding Perception and Perceptual Processes

Previously we stated that perception is an integral part of cognitive activity. It is now time to point out the real significance of and relationship between cognition and perception. *Cognition* is a broad, almost generic, term that means "to know" or "to be aware of." Perception is one of the principal psychological means by which we come to know. Goethe, the German philosopher and poet, is supposed to have said, "We see only what we know." Nowhere could one find a statement that more significantly relates the concepts of cognition and perception. Perception is a complex process by which people select, organize, and interpret sensory stimulation into a meaningful picture of the world.[1] We select, organize, and give meaning, however, on the basis of what we know—what we have previously witnessed or experienced. In short, our cognitions—our existing structure of knowledge, beliefs, attitudes, opinions, and images—act as a kind of behavioral matrix

---

[1] This is a rather traditional definition of perception. See Bernard Berelson and Gary A. Steiner, *Human Behavior: Shorter Edition* (New York: Harcourt Brace Jovanovich, Inc., 1967), p. 141. Other more elaborate definitions will subsequently be advanced.

Figure 8-1

The Relationship Between
Cognitive Structure and Perception

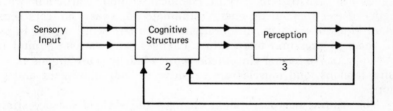

through which we filter our perceptions. Our perceptions and our perceptual processes, in turn, are the principal devices through which we acquire new knowledge or new concepts. Perception is the basic process by which we alter, change, and modify our existing value, belief, and knowledge systems. All this is illustrated very readily in Figure 8-1.

Cell 1 indicates that sensory input is received or experienced by the individual and is then channeled or fed to the central nervous system, where cognitive structures such as values, attitudes, beliefs, and images are stored. These cognitive structures enable the subject to interpret the nature of the sensation, organize it, and react to it in a meaningful way. This activity results in perception (Cell 3). Note now that the act of perception, having occurred, is fed back into the cognitive structure, and any subsequent sensory experience will be filtered and affected by this experience, which is now stored as a part of the cognitive structure. Some slight elaboration of this process might appear to be warranted. First of all, it is important to understand that the sensory information to which we are subjected—heat, light, noise, color, and so forth—does not correspond simply to the perception that it elicits or brings forth. Basically, of course, it does not because the sensory impulses do not act upon an empty organism. The individual is possessed with knowledge, previous experience, and prior awareness that are stored cognitive structures. Thus, the sensory input acts and interacts with these stored experiences and knowledge and what we experience or *perceive* is the result of that interaction. The consumer, therefore, does not always see or hear just what is there in the environment; instead he perceives on the basis of what he brought with him to the observing situation.

PERCEPTION AND SENSATION

As illustrated in Figure 8-1, sensory input or sensation is not the same as perception. Sensation is related to the immediate and direct apprehension of simple stimuli like color, loudness, shape, pitch, heat, and so on. However, for perception to occur, these stimuli or sensations must be given meaning through cognitive interpretation.

All of us are surrounded by various kinds and levels of physical energy that impinge upon our nervous system and our cognitive apparatus. What knowledge we have of the world comes through our sense organs, which read and respond to these energies. Our noses and tongues are sensitive to certain chemical stimuli. Particular wavelengths of electromagnetic energy stimulate our eyes. Our ears sense certain kinds of mechanical vibrations of the air. Sense organs in our skin react to pressure, temperature changes, and various stimuli related to pain. We have a kinesthetic sense whereby sense organs in our joints, tendons, and muscles are sensitive to body movement and position.

The central nervous system changes the various sensory stimulations that reach us through the environment into nervous impulses that are sent to the brain. The perceptual processes, however, do not reveal objects and events of the world. We see light and color, but there is no light or color in the electromagnetic waves that stimulate the eyes. The brain must organize and interpret nervous impulses from the eyes as light and color and impulses from the ear as sound. Collectively, the sense organs and the brain transform physical energy from environmental stimuli into information about the events that envelop us.[2] Thus, through the psychological process of perception, the patterns of energies become known as objects, events, people, and other meaningful aspects of the world.

SENSATION AND CONCEPT OF THRESHOLDS. For sensation to result in perception, there must be variety. Basically, sensation is a matter of energy change. When the environment is perfectly homogeneous, constant, stable, and, therefore, static, our ability to recognize sensation and to react to it through perceptual processes is exceedingly impaired. We are largely aware of our world and our environment to the extent that it changes. If subjects are denied normal amounts of sensory stimulation, the usual reaction is a marked deterioration in various mental capacities.[3] Contrariwise, when there is a great deal of sensory stimulation, the senses are simply inclined to ignore a great part of it. Thus, when there is a small amount of sensory stimulation, the senses have a rather keen ability to fine-tune and detect these very small intensities of stimulation, but when there is a large amount of sensory stimulation, the senses tend to ignore or filter away all but a relatively small part of the stimulation. The observation of this phenomenon led psychologists to work on what have become known as levels of absolute

[2] For a more extensive treatment of sensation and perception as a neurological and physiological process, see Clifford T. Morgan, "Some Structural Factors in Perception," in *Perception: An Approach to Personality*, Robert B. Blake and Glen V. Ramsey, eds. (New York: The Ronald Press Company, 1951), pp. 25–55.

[3] Woodburn Heron, "Cognitive and Physiological Effects of Perceptual Isolation," in Philip Solomon, et al., *Sensory Deprivation*, a symposium at the Harvard Medical School (Cambridge, Mass.: Harvard University Press, 1961), p. 142.

and differential thresholds. The absolute threshold is the minimum amount of energy that can be identified. For example, if you are placed in a dark room, what is the least amount of light energy you can detect? Or to conduct an even simpler experiment on yourself, turn on your TV set and vary the sound level. When you turn it up to the point where you can just detect the sound, that, roughly speaking, is your absolute threshold for sound. It ought to be pointed out that the absolute threshold of a sense becomes progressively lower, that is, sensitivity increases with disuse or rest. The longer a subject is in total darkness, the more sensitive vision becomes. Such a reaction is known as "sensory adaptation." [4]

It has also been found that it is possible for some stimuli to be physically perceived by the individual but still be too weak to create conscious awareness. Such a phenomenon is called subliminal perception because the stimulus is said to be below the threshold or "limen" of awareness. Subliminal perception was the focus of a great deal of marketing and consumer behavior controversy a few years ago, and we shall review the substance of that controversy in a subsequent section of this chapter.

Individuals have not only an absolute threshold but also what are called marginal or differential thresholds. A differential threshold is the minimum difference that can be detected between stimuli. Sometimes this concept is referred to as the *j.n.d.*, which stands for "just noticeable difference." This concept has been extensively researched and developed, and one of the principal researchers in this field has constructed what has come to be known as Weber's law. This law or generalization states that the size of the least detectable change depends upon the initial intensity of the stimulus. The stronger (brighter, louder, and so on) the initial stimulus, the greater the difference has to be. Some common sense illustrations will serve to demonstrate the nature of the j.n.d. If you turn your TV set very low at the outset, you will be able to discriminate rather small differences in the intensity of the sound as you turn it progressively louder. But if you turn it on at a rather high level of sound initially and turn it higher yet, it is doubtful that you will be able to detect the marginal difference in the new level of intensity. Try it!

Weber's law can be formulated symbolically in the following manner:

$$\frac{\Delta I}{I} = K$$

where

$\Delta I =$ the marginal or incremental increase in stimulus intensity that is noticeably different from the established intensity

[4] Selig Hecht and Simon Shlaer, "An Adaptometer for Measuring Human Dark Adaptation," *The Journal Optical Sociological American*, Vol. 28 (1938), pp. 269–275.

I = the intensity of the stimulus at the point where the increase takes place

K = a constant that varies according to the senses involved

The concept of marginal or differential thresholds has many implications for marketers and consumer behaviorists. When is a price change meaningful? Is a 99¢ price more meaningful than a $1.00 price? Is a price reduction from $5.00 to $4.50 as significant as a reduction from $500 to $450? They both amount to a 10 per cent reduction from the retail price. What size should newspaper ads and magazine ads be in order to capitalize most on consumers' differential thresholds? Why do some stores appear to be closer to some consumers than other stores that are actually a shorter physical distance away? We shall explore these and similar questions after having developed more fully some additional concepts relating to perception and perceptual processes.

THE SCOPE OF PERCEPTION

The scope of perception, now that we have dealt with some elementary definitions and concepts, is illustrated perhaps most meaningfully in Figure 8-2.

As stated earlier, perception falls somewhere between raw sensory sensation and the more cognitive term *concept*.[5] Perception is triggered

Figure 8-2

A Schematic Illustration of Perception

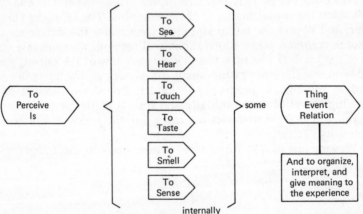

Source: Suggested by a paradigm used by Paul Thomas Young, *Motivation and Emotion: A Survey of the Determinants of Human and Animal Activity* (New York: John Wiley & Sons, Inc., 1961), pp. 298–299.

[5] For an excellent brief and general treatment of perception, see Perry Bliss, *Marketing Management and the Behavioral Environment* (Englewood Cliffs, N.J.: Prentice-Hall, Inc., 1970), pp. 68–79.

by sensory data or input. However, this input does not act on an empty organism; therefore, cognition and the thinking processes are involved in perceptual activity. The interactive and interstimulative aspects of psychological activities are once again present.

Earlier and more primitive treatments of perception almost always talked about a kind of distinct perceptual process referred to as *selective perception*. More contemporary and refined treatments of the topic point out that perception is always selective. Perception is selective by virtue of the nature and uniqueness of the individual organism. Selectivity can be demonstrated at birth in almost all species, though such selectivity varies among the various animal species. In man a rather gross selectivity at birth becomes increasingly refined and sophisticated with development and practice.

An important point is that selective perception is forced upon us by the nature of our human limitations. We cannot at one and the same time see all sights, hear all sounds, touch all objects that immediately surround us. When we walk into a major downtown department store there is a cacophony of sound, there is a stirring, rustling movement of people—myriad sights, colors, and movements confront us. Our senses are literally bombarded with sensory stimuli, most of which we totally and efficiently ignore. Were it not so, the world would appear to us all as a booming, buzzing confusion. Instead, however, we manage to filter out those stimuli and sensations that we deem unessential and inappropriate. We economize on the use of our perceptual processes by doing essentially three things.[6] First of all, we narrow the selectivity of attention to those things that we deem more essential and more related to the tasks in which we are engaged. To return to our department store example, suppose we have come in to see the new fall line of skiing accessories. A special on doubleknit suits or print shirts hardly registers in our consciousness. We perceive selectively. Second, we recode and simplify the abundance of sensory stimulation into a more ordered arrangement of information. Yes, the store is noisy and there is confusion and movement; but we recall from previous experience that as we move through the main floor, the crowds will thin, and that once we reach the sporting goods department we will be greeted by friendly faces and that more order and meaning will prevail. Memory and learning, therefore, preserve the necessary information and allow us to re-create specific information to the degree and extent desired.

Finally, because such an extensive amount of sensory stimulation strikes us and because it amounts to what might best be described as informational overload, we need a psychology of simplification, a means of eliminating much of the redundancy that surrounds us. We accomplish this via the use of both psychological and technological

[6] Jerome S. Bruner, "Social Psychology and Perception," in *Readings in Social Psychology*, E. E. Maccoby, T. M. Newman, and E. L. Hartley, eds. (New York: Holt, Rinehart & Winston, Inc., 1958), pp. 85–94.

aids. For example, we ignore, repress, and forget enormous amounts of specific information. Furthermore, we use technological aids such as pictures, graphs, tape recorders, and so forth to help us store and process information. All of these things help us to extract meaning from sensory stimulation, and that, in short, is what perception is all about.

Some can be more attentive to particular sensory experiences. By practice and diligence they learn to extract more meaning from the information that confronts them. The attention span and the degree of concentration that permit people to attune themselves to various experiences vary from individual to individual. The usual situation confronting most consumers is that they are surrounded by more sensory input than they are able to process efficiently, meaning that most consumers have not trained themselves to process the information at their disposal. Doing so would probably mean more satisfied and contented consumers.

PRINCIPLES OF PERCEPTION

It would follow from our previous comments that individuals not only select stimuli but also organize them into meaningful patterns and configurations. Even our simplest and most mundane experiences are organized, and invariably the perceived characteristics of any part are a function of the whole configuration to which it appears to belong. Perceptual principles of organization were first developed and explained by the Gestalt psychologist Max Wertheimer in his classic article written in 1922.[7] The fruits of his insight were contained in Gestalt principles of perceptual organization, the substance of which we shall now undertake to describe.

PRINCIPLE OF PRÄGNANZ. To quote Koffka, another of the well-known Gestalt psychologists, the principle of *prägnanz* states that "psychological organization will always be as good as the prevailing conditions allow."[8] *Good* is inferred to mean a configuration, pattern, or meaning that constitutes the simplest stable structure. The criteria for *prägnanz* embrace such properties as regularity, symmetry, simplicity, inclusiveness, continuity, and unification. *Prägnanz* is, therefore, the basic principle of perceptual organization that governs the segregation and division of the perceptual field into separate forms. Such separation of the elements of the psychological field will always be undertaken in a way that will create a minimum of psychological stress and confusion, thus resulting in maximum order and stability.

PRINCIPLE OF CLOSURE. The closure principle suggests that our perceptual experiences tend to be organized into whole or continuous figures. Even when the stimulus pattern is incomplete, the perceiver

---

[7] Max Wertheimer, *Untersuchen zu Lehre von des Gestalt*. I. *Psychological Forschenir 1922*, I, 47–58, II, 1923, 4, 301–350.

[8] Kurt Koffka, *The Principles of Gestalt Psychology* (New York: Harcourt Brace Jovanovich, Inc., 1935).

Figure 8-3

tends to fill in the missing elements. For example, in Figure 8-3 most viewers see a dog, not a collection of random blotches.

A more contemporary writer recognized this perceptual principle when he referred to "hot" versus "cool" personalities. Hot personalities project a large amount of sensory stimulation and develop their own images through excessive language and conversation. The "cool" personality, however, sends a reduced level of cues. Thus, we often read into the cool personality those characteristics we want to be there. We project a lot of our own ideas and images through closure into the "cool" personality.[9]

[9] Marshall McLuhan, *Understanding Media: The Extensions of Man* (New York: The New American Library, 1964), pp. 36–45.

PRINCIPLE OF INCLUSIVENESS. The principle of inclusiveness relates to the tendency of a unified whole to change the identity of a subwhole contained within it. Oftentimes, we must work on sensory stimulation to perceive something recognizable, especially if that something recognizable is submerged or included within a larger framework or configuration. We enter a large supermarket and are looking for a specific item. We may stand right in front of a gondola that holds the item we are seeking but be unable to find it among the many other items within which it is imbedded. We may look into a department store window and never perceive a particular item. The reason may be a poor differentiation between figure and ground. In order to be easily identified, figures must be well defined, at a definite location, solid, and in front of the ground. The ground (background) of the principle of inclusiveness utilizes changing figure and ground precepts. Do you alternately recognize two profiles and a rather elaborate goblet or vase in Figure 8-4?

PRINCIPLE OF CONTINUATION AND DIRECTION. This principle simply states that forms that have continuous and uninterrupted contours and dimensions are better configurations than figures, shapes, or spaces that have discontinuous contours. Space planners, window decorators, and layout experts for retail stores have long been aware of the Gestalt principle of continuation and direction. Consumers generally prefer a smooth and continuous flow of movement and experience rather than a disjointed or jerky transposition from one selling station, display, and so on to another.

PRINCIPLE OF PROXIMITY. We generally perceive items, events, or activities in close proximity as being related to one another. Furthermore, we often impute causality to an object or event if it is located in close proximity to another item or event. Thus, Store A located next to Store B is having a sale of a special line of merchandise. Customers

Figure 8-4

The Peter-Paul Goblet

are frequently known to enter Store B and say, "Store A is having a sale; why aren't you having a sale also?" If a specific item is to be featured as a special promotion, it usually behooves the manager to segregate that item from his other inventory. If not, all the items of that class located in the same area are likely to be perceived as being on sale also.

PRINCIPLE OF SIMILARITY. The principle of similarity is somewhat related to the principle of proximity. Similar objects, events, and situations tend to be perceived as similar, and in many instances the degree of differentiation is greatly modified. Hence, such comments as, "If you've seen one, you've seen them all." Downtown stores are not always likely to be perceived as greatly different. A specific suburban unit of the major downtown store is not perceived as greatly different from all the other suburban units. Store A's advertising, if too similar to Store B's, would result in the perception that Store A must be very much like Store B.

These Gestalt organizing principles have a profound impact on the way sensory stimulation is received, filtered from the environment, and used to create for us a meaningful picture of the world. Specifically which stimuli are selected depends upon these important factors: (1) the nature of the stimulus itself, (2) what the observer is prepared or cued to see, and (3) the nature of his needs, that is, the specific tasks that he is about.[10]

Perception and Information Processing

We have repeatedly characterized the human organism as a decision maker and an information processer. We shall look now briefly at the role of perception as it relates to information processing. When sensory data and stimulation impinge upon the organism—the human being, the consumer—they do so in the form of physical energy. This energy is a carrier of signals or messages, and it becomes sense data upon which the organism acts. Thus again, we find the organism or the consumer to be processing information, and this processing leads, in many instances, to behavioral change. The consumer's perceptual apparatus, therefore, has two major functions: (1) it is sensitive to certain types of physical energy or information, and (2) it is capable, when properly stimulated, of delivering and interpreting information or messages that modify the consumer's behavior.[11] Thus, a modern treatment of perception would define it as the process by which an organism receives or extracts certain information from the environment. Furthermore, contemporary treatments of perception recognize

[10] Ronald H. Forgus, *Perception* (New York: McGraw-Hill Book Company, 1966), pp. 104–131.

[11] William N. Dember, *The Psychology of Perception* (New York: Holt, Rinehart & Winston, Inc., 1960), p. 6.

the interrelationships that exist among several cognitive phenomena. For example, learning is defined as the process by which information is acquired through experience and becomes a part of the organism's storage of facts (cognitions). The results of learning facilitate the additional extraction of information because the stored facts (cognitive structure) become models against which cues are evaluated. Additionally, the most sophisticated of all cognitive processes, thinking, is an activity that is going on when the subject is engaged in problem solving that uses symbolic logic such as language and other models.[12] Much of our discussion regarding perception has focused upon its structural properties and the processes involved. Little, if anything, has yet been said about the functional properties of perception. Broadly speaking, perception has two major purposes. First and foremost, the purpose of perception is to keep the world about us a *stable* one—to give us a perspective or framework that does not change rapidly and that, therefore, is both stress and anxiety reducing. The second goal of perception is to achieve, for the individual, definiteness in what he perceives—to create meaning and pattern so that the world in which he finds himself is familiar and one in which he feels at home because he generally knows what to expect (what he expects does not differ very greatly from what he wants).[13]

We should reiterate here that the Gestalt principles that were discussed earlier operate in the efficient and effective interest of the individual because they facilitate the purposes of perception just stated. They do so by facilitating two concepts; namely, they emphasize the essential informational aspects of form and configuration. Second, they minimize errors through redundancy: oftentimes, transmission of essential information is assured by redundancy.

PERCEPTION AND DECISION MAKING

Not only is perception an important phenomenon of information processing, it is, as well, integrally related to decision making and decision processes. Several writers have pointed out that perceiving, because it involves inference, rests upon a decision-making process.[14] The essence of this argument is that any nervous system, given a set of cues or stimuli, must "decide" whether the thing is A or whether it is B, whether it is hot or cold, red or yellow, and so on. The organism interprets and organizes, but what is more important it decides *how* to

[12] Forgus, op. cit., p. 2.

[13] Ernest R. Hilgard, "The Role of Learning in Perception," in *Perception: An Approach to Personality*, Robert Blake and Glen Ramsey, eds. (New York: The Ronald Press Company, 1951), p. 119.

[14] Early proponents of this idea were E. Brunswick, *Systematic and Representative Design of Psychological Experiments* (Berkeley, Calif.: University of California Press, 1949); and W. P. Tanner and J. A. Swets, "A Decision Making Theory of Human Detection," *Psychological Review*, Vol. 61 (1954), pp. 401–409.

interpret and organize. Let us now examine the various stages in such a sequence of decision activities.

1. *Primitive categorization.* Primitive categorization is a kind of tentative or snap judgment. The environmental event is perceptually isolated, filtered, and reacted to but in a tentative and gross fashion.

2. *Cue search.* The event, object, or idea is now scrutinized more carefully and a larger number of cues and differentiating suggestions are sought and examined. One continues to scan the environment for additional data in order to find clues that permit a more precise delineation of the object.

3. *Confirmation check.* The object or event is about to be categorized. This is a near-final trial and check period. The subject begins now to consider reducing the effective input of stimulation and sense data. Openness to more or different sensory input begins to decline.

4. *Confirmation completion.* This is a closure stage of perception. All incongruent messages, information, and sensory input are now avoided, filtered out of the subject's perceptual decision processes. His "mind" is made up! And once this occurs, the threshold for recognizing cues contrary to this categorization increases enormously.[15]

Such a decision process no doubt is characteristic of most of our perceptual activities. This decision process itself is facilitated by several well-researched and well-documented perceptual phenomena; namely, *perceptual constancy, perceptual sets or readiness,* and *perceptual defense.* Each of these concepts will be briefly discussed.

PERCEPTUAL CONSTANCY. Perceptual constancy refers to the idea that once having perceived and categorized information about some thing, event, or relation, we continue to see that thing, event, or relation in much the same way as our original perception recorded it. For example, when we perceptually encode information about a specific product, say, a manual razor, we recognize razors as things that shave. Whether they are double-edged or single-edged and whether they have blades or bands and whether they have sharp edges on opposite sides or two sharp edges on the same side, they are still perceived as razors. Unless our vantage point changes too much, perceptual constancy implies that like objects are always viewed as like objects. New objects must differ radically from our categorized or encoded models or they will not be perceived as different. Thus although soaps and detergents are merchandised as "new" and "different," they usually are not perceived as different because they remain too much like the older products. Perceptual constancy thus negates a great part of many promotional and merchandising messages.

[15] See Jerome S. Bruner, "On Perceptual Readiness," *The Psychological Review,* Vol. 64 (1957), pp. 123–152.

PERCEPTUAL SETS. The Gestaltists refer to perceptual readiness as set or *eingestellt*. They argue that individuals are never randomly set (the meaning of *eingestellt*) but instead that they are always to some extent prepared for seeing, hearing, smelling, or tasting some particular thing or class of things. In short, perceiving takes place in an attuned organism. Individuals not only see, they look. They not only hear, they listen to. Thus, the readiness with which a stimulus input with given properties is coded or identified in terms of a category will depend upon the perceptual readiness or set of the individual. Perceptual sets, therefore, help consumers to perceive sensory input selectively. On the other hand, most retail firms attempt, by way of decor, color, atmosphere, music, light, motion, and so forth, to create a favorable buying mood, which is another way of looking at the concept of perceptual sets. Consumers can be cued; they can be given leading suggestions that conceivably will alter their actual perception of events, things, or relationships.

PERCEPTUAL DEFENSE. We mentioned earlier that all perception is selective. To the extent that it is, the individual can, to some extent at least, fail to perceive events or objects that appear to be threatening or not in the interest of tasks in which the subject is currently engaged. Perceptual defense may not necessarily be a failure to perceive but, what is more likely to be the case, is simply the result of *interference* with perception. Such interference is likely to result from such factors as attitudes, fears, anxieties, and other stresses that impede the individual's ability to tune in the incoming sensory stimulation. A customer who is snubbed by a haughty salesperson is likely to ignore the behavior or not to perceive it as deprecating. To a great extent, we see what we want to see. What meaning and what significance are attached to objects, events, and relations are often there because we ourselves put them there.

To summarize our treatment of perception to this juncture, we should state that in learning to perceive, we are learning the relations that exist between the properties of objects and events that we encounter, learning appropriate categories and category systems, and learning to predict and check what goes with what.[16]

Social Perception

Our main aim in this brief section will be to explore the ways and means by which we use the information immediately available in social situations in perceiving and interpreting these situations. Thus, our interest is in describing and analyzing what we know about how social information is received, or how social stimuli are interpreted, as well as how information is sent. Social perception is mainly concerned,

[16] Jerome Bruner and Leo Postman, "Perception, Cognition and Behavior," *Journal of Personality*, Vol. 18 (1949), pp. 14–31.

therefore, with what might best be called the psychology of perception as contrasted with the physiology or neurology of perception.

Almost all of us are endowed with the same perceptual apparatus. Each normal individual possesses a comparatively well-developed and sophisticated central nervous system. This central nervous system has intrinsic functions that are qualitatively much the same as everyone else's. However, from birth on, this central nervous system and its attendant perceptual apparatus are slightly modified by each stimulus distinction they make. Our experience is written in, or *programmed into,* our central nervous systems. Thus, the basic machinery of perception is very similar for all of us. Our sense organs are similar, if not identical; our sensory systems of the body function in a similar fashion; and it appears that our brains behave quite similarly in perceptual processes. Yet we perceive and understand complex behavior in highly unique and individualistic ways. So because our *structural* apparatus for perceiving events is very similar and yet so much variance exists from individual to individual in terms of what is actually perceived, the question remains: What is the basis for the variance or the differences that manifest themselves between individuals?[17] This topic emerged during the 1950s and was widely explored and researched by a group that referred to their efforts as the "New Look in Perception."[18] The approach employed was to investigate the psychological or behavioral determinants of perception. These behavioral determinants or experiential determinants (because they relate to experience) include such factors as need, social values, attitudes, personality, culture, and stress. Thus perception is a function of these factors as well as the stimulus factors. Such an approach again suggests that sensory stimulation does not act on an empty organism. Our treatment at this juncture then transcends the physical characteristics of the perceiving system, that is, the *structural* determinants of perception. Instead, we shall focus briefly upon some of the conditions that determine the individual's use of these structures in specific situations, and we shall refer to these conditions as *experiential* determinants. It must be pointed out that the two are inextricably interconnected. As previously mentioned, each experience modifies the reaction potentialities of the structure. In turn, the modified structures then set to define the next related situation in a characteristic way, and so on.[19] Such an approach underscores the determinants of individual differences in perceiving. As Murphy describes it,

[17] This idea is thought to have originated with William James. See *The Principles of Psychology* (New York: Henry Holt and Company, 1890), Vol. 2.

[18] Jerome S. Bruner, "Social Psychology and Perception," in *Readings in Social Psychology,* E. E. Maccoby, T. M. Newman, and E. L. Hartley, eds. (New York: Holt, Rinehart & Winston, Inc., 1958), pp. 85–94.

[19] Robert Blake, Glen V. Ramsey, and Louis J. Moran, "Perceptual Processes as Basic to an Understanding of Complex Behavior," in *Perception: An Approach to Personality,* Robert R. Blake and Glen V. Ramsey, eds. (New York: The Ronald Press Company, 1951), pp. 3–25. See especially pp. 9–10.

If we understand the differences in perceiving we shall go far in understanding the differences in the resulting behavior. The relation between the outer world and the individual is gravely misconstrued by the assumption that this world registers upon us all in about the same way, that the real differences between people are differences in what is *done* about this world.[20]

Such a statement suggests that consumer behavior is different not so much because there are differences in what consumers do—what stores they shop in, what goods they buy, or what advertising is read—but because experience, needs, values, personality, culture, and learning cause consumers to perceive—to order and interpret, to seek and extract information from their environment—differently.

We shall examine briefly several of these experiential factors or determinants of perception. A complete treatment of all the experiential factors at this juncture is beyond our scope. Several of these factors will be treated in subsequent chapters, not necessarily as determinants of perception but as determinants of consumer behavior in general. At this time our treatment will focus upon personality, motivation, and learning. Considerably more research has been devoted to these topics than others.

PERSONALITY AND PERCEPTION

Personality is a structural, organized complex of apparently diverse specifications, such as behavior, thoughts, impulses to action, and so on. These complexes have a common unity that may be phrased variously as a similar dynamic meaning, expression, function, or purpose.[21] We shall not now spend much time developing our definition or understanding of personality, but let us instead rely upon our basic intuitive understanding of personality as a basic, patterned complex of behavior, attitudes, or cognitive style, in order to view the relationship and interconnectedness of personality with perception. Personality is thus an organized pattern of all the characteristics of an individual.

Personality has been found to have an important influence on perception. Some personalities are characterized as perceiving *synthetically*, whereas others perceive *analytically*. As the names indicate, the person who adopts the first method tends to see the perceptual field as an integrated whole, whereas other personality types are more inclined to break up a perceptual field into its component parts or details.[22] Other personalities are likely to perceive events more objectively,

[20] Gardner Murphy, *Personality: A Bisocial Approach to Origins and Structure* (New York: Harper and Row, Publishers, 1957), p. 23.

[21] Abraham H. Maslow, *Motivation and Personality* (New York: Harper and Row, Publishers, 1954), p. 32.

[22] A. Gimelli and A. Cappallini, "The Influence of the Subject's Attitudes in Perception," *Acta Psychology*, (1958), pp. 12–14.

whereas still other personality types are inclined to be more subjective in their perception.[23]

Personality types are often categorized as risk seekers or risk avoiders. These types are known to process and use information differently and, therefore, to perceive undertakings, objects, events, and relationships differently.[24] The perceptual performance of introverts and extroverts has also been examined. It was found that extroverted individuals tended to show a higher degree of size constancy than did introverts, but this may be because the former respond more easily to synthetic instructions, the latter to analytic.[25]

Horney, who classifies individuals into three predominant orientations or personality types—those who move toward people (compliant), those who move against people (aggressive), and those who move away from people (detached)—reorganized the prevailing ideas about the impact of personality on perceptual processes.[26] Compliant individuals are thought to be ones who need people and who thus perceive in social relations the means for satisfying particular needs and for facilitating the attainment of social goals. Those with an aggressive orientation desire to excel, to achieve success, prestige, and admiration. Such personality types are likely to perceive social situations as means for confirming their own self-image, for bolstering their confidence in the use of social tools.

The detached orientation impels the individual to put emotional distance between himself and others. Social situations, shopping, all forms of social interaction are perceived as threatening experiences. These people are likely to be self-centered in their perceptual processes, eschewing the opportunity to share experiences or to be influenced.

Such findings, of course, are more suggestive than determinant. They suggest that such generalizations, especially in relationship to perception as a factor in consumer behavior, must be more fully researched and that studies predicated upon these suggested hypotheses must be more fully tested and examined.

MOTIVATION AND PERCEPTION

We have already noted that the individual perceiver is, at least in part, influenced by his motivated state. Objects and events perceived in a complex field, as well as the alacrity and specificity with which they are perceived, appear to be related to the observer's "interest" in perceiving them. His perceptual readiness or set, the degree to which he is

[23] O. Messmer, "Zur Psychologie des Desens bei Kendern and Erwachsen," *Arch. f. d. ges. Psychology* (1904), p. 190.

[24] See Chapter 7, especially the section on emotion.

[25] J. L. Singer, "Personal and Environmental Determinants of Perception in a Size Constancy Experiment," *Journal of Experimental Psychology*, Vol. 43 (1952), p. 420.

[26] Karen Horney, *Our Inner Conflict* (New York: W. W. Norton & Company, Inc., 1945).

aroused or attuned, will in turn affect the way he extracts information from the environment. Our motives and emotions play an important role in what and how we perceive, and a rather large amount of experimental work has been carried out to investigate the relationship between motivation and perception. Unfortunately these studies do not relate specifically to consumer behavior but to social behavior in general.

Hungry subjects have been observed to perceive food objects in ambiguous stimuli more readily than well-fed subjects.[27] Bruner and Goodman used two groups of subjects, one group consisting of ten-year-old poor children and the other group, ten-year-old rich children. The children in each group were required to adjust the size of a circle of light to apparent equality with various coins and cardboard disks. All children, it was found, tended to overestimate the size of coins up to a 25-cent piece, but the sizes of the cardboard disks were estimated correctly. The size of a 50-cent coin was not overestimated. Most significantly, poorer children overestimated size of the smaller coins to a larger extent than did the rich children.[28] The researchers thus concluded that the poorer children showed greater overestimation because they valued money more than the rich children did. Hence the need for money was shown to influence perception. Such studies suggest the fruitful possibilities for research in consumer behavior. For example, "How does perception among low-income recipients influence consumption or other dimensions of consumer behavior?" "What are the specific relationships that exist between consumer motivation and consumer perceptions?" However, our tentative knowledge suggests that it is not a simple matter of how the intensity of motivation or need affects behavior but the way in which a person or consumer *learns* to handle his needs. Such perceptual learning is an important bridge that attempts to connect the complex motivational processes with equally complex cognitive activities such as perception.

LEARNING AND PERCEPTION

Learning we defined earlier as the acquisition of new content for the individual's repertoire of habits. Hence learning is concerned with how events occurring in the individual's psychological field are incorporated into the organism. Hilgard has discussed the problem of learning in relation to perception in the following manner:

> The older question about the role of learning in perception had to do with the nativism-empiricism problem. To what extent is perception na-

---

[27] R. Levine, I. Chein, and G. Murphy, "The Relation of the Intensity of a Need to the Amount of Perceptual Distortion, a Preliminary Report," *Journal of Psychology,* Vol. 13 (1942), pp. 283–293.

[28] J. S. Bruner and C. C. Goodman, "Value and Need as Organizing Factors in Perception," *Journal of Abnormal and Social Psychology,* Vol. 42 (1947), pp. 33–44.

tively given by way of our inherited structures and capacities, and to what extent is it the result of our experience with the world of objects? But a new question is now being asked about the reciprocal relationship between learning and perception. This new and contemporary question is: To what extent is learning merely reorganized perception? We shall have to deal with both the older question and the contemporary one if we are to keep our thinking straight about both learning and perception.[29]

Much has been done to expand our understanding of the relationship between perception and learning through research of a concept known as *perceptual learning*. Perceptual learning refers to an increase in the ability to extract information from the environment, as a result of experience and practice with the stimulation coming from it.[30] Such learning is in the direction of getting better information and being better able to use the information for purposes of decision making and problem solving. It is a dynamic and active process in the sense that individuals explore and search and that this experience leads to more expertise.[31] Stimulation carries information. It is extraction of this information that characterizes perception, and it is the increasing ability to extract this information that characterizes perceptual learning and development.

Nature does not produce the consumer with knowledge and strategies ready-made for perceiving the complexities of all the information in the stimulation coming from the world, its furniture and events, and the man-made information bombarding him as well. These are acquired skills, and they are acquired basically through firsthand as well as vicarious experience. The purchasing agent in a manufacturing enterprise learns how to improve upon his buying performance. The housewife learns how to improve her buying performance in the marketplace.

Marketing activities are often designed to affect the consumer's capacity and ability to perceive. Hopefully, they are designed to enable the consumer to improve upon his perceptual processes. Advertisements, booklets, and hang-tags are usually designed to coach the consumer in what to look for by way of quality, durability, and value. Consumers learn by trial and error and by instruction that marbled red meats are usually more tender, that ripe cantaloupes have a distinctive flavorful smell. Vegetables, clothing, fabrics, and so forth all have characteristics and attributes, a knowledge of which can lead to a better perception of quality.

Thus, perceptual learning can and does lead to perceptual re-

[29] E. R. Hilgard, *Theories of Learning* (New York: Appleton-Century-Crofts, 1956), p. 95.

[30] Eleanor J. Gibson, *Principles of Perceptual Learning and Development* (New York: Appleton-Century-Crofts, 1967), pp. 3–4.

[31] J. J. Gibson, *The Sinus Considered a Perceptual System* (Boston: Houghton Mifflin Company, 1966).

organization. Such learning, much of which is undertaken in and facilitated by marketing activities, teaches consumers how to improve upon their perceptual capacities. Essentially, it teaches consumers (1) how to judge, (2) how to improve attendance to detail, and (3) how to make meaningful comparisons.

Finally, perceptual learning facilitates the consumer's perceptual processes relating to *sharpening* and *leveling*. Sharpening results from both redundancy and economical encoding, that is, categorizing the information into suitable chunks. Sharpening is a process of differentiation. Leveling, on the other hand, is a process of generalization and results when essential information about one object, event, or situation can be transferred or generalized to another object, event, or situation.

Interpersonal Perception

Social perception, which we have just discussed, emphasizes the psychology of perception, meaning that the emphasis is placed upon the behavioral determinants of perception rather than upon the physiological bases of perception or the treatment and analysis of the sense organs or receptors.[32] The psychology of perception, which characterizes both social perception and interpersonal perception, is chiefly concerned with the questions of what psychological processes affect perception and how psychological processes affect perception. Our treatment of social perception was largely directed to the question of "what" and our treatment of interpersonal perception will deal briefly with the "how." In total, however, the psychology of perception, including both social and interpersonal perception, is concerned with *explanation*.

Interpersonal perception is in many ways an extension of social perception, and it, too, emerged as an approach to understanding the complex processes of perceiving social objects and events. Interpersonal perception is a part of the "New Look in Perception," which originally emerged in the mid 1950s.

The term *interpersonal perception* is normally used when we mean the way individuals view and evaluate one another in direct interaction.[33] Tagiuri has pointed out that this is a process of considerable complexity that encompasses the interaction, the interstimulation, and the gross interrelationship of the perceiver, the person perceived, and the situation that serves as a backdrop for this perception.[34] Needless to say, interpersonal perception pervades much consumer behavior. Customer-salesperson interaction, opinion leader.and fashion diffusion, and peer group interaction are but a few of the situations in which inter-

---

[32] See D. W. Hamlyn, *The Psychology of Perception* (London: Routledge & Kegan Paul, 1957), pp. 1–11.

[33] E. P. Hollander, *Principles and Methods of Social Psychology* (London: Oxford University Press, 1967), pp. 194–203.

[34] R. Tagiuri, *Introduction to Person, Perception and Interpersonal Behavior* (Stanford, Calif.: Stanford University Press, 1958), pp. ix–xvii.

personal perceptual processes are at play. Furthermore, the principles of perception that we considered earlier in this chapter also apply to interpersonal perception. Tendencies toward *perceptual constancy, wholeness, imbeddedness,* and *closure* all play a part in this process. In addition, another perceptual principle, namely, *causality,* is known to play a leading role in interpersonal perceptual activities.

THE TRANSACTIONAL APPROACH

Interpersonal perception is built largely upon what has come to be known as the *transactional approach.*

The transactional approach stresses the reciprocity and inter-stimulation of the "transaction" between the perceiver and the perceived object.[35] The transactional approach emphasizes the importance of familiarity and value in the perception both of nonsocial objects and events and of people and groups. Thus our assumptions about the meaning of objects, events, and relationships affect our judgments about the actual characteristics of these perceived phenomena. If we think we are not going to like a product, the chances are good that we really will not like it. If our next-door neighbor tells us that a certain salesperson in a suburban store is a snob and/or a wise guy, the chances are very good that we will perceive the salesperson to be just that. Thus, the transactional approach suggests that the individual actually participates in the perceptual process in terms of assessments based upon past experience.

As mentioned earlier, interpersonal perception and the transactional approach place a heavy emphasis on *causality.* Heider contends that the perception of attributes of the other (O) controls the way the person (P) behaves toward O as well as what he expects from O.[36] Heider further contends that individuals tend to perceive persons as *origins,* that is, as causes and determinants of events and relationships.

Therefore changes in the environment are almost always perceived as caused by acts of persons in combination with other factors. For example, it is a well-recognized fact that Republicans are perceived as the cause of recessions and Democrats are perceived as the cause of wars. The tendency is, however, to ascribe changes entirely to persons. Changes in the environment, then, gain their meaning from the source to which they are attributed. If prices rise rapidly, the causes of this price rise are often attributed to persons or personified entities, for example, greedy merchandisers or avaricious producers. Heider's views have been extended by Pepitone, who says that "It is useful to assume that interpersonal relations consist of valued acts, valued positively or negatively depending on whether they are tension reducing or inducing, and the context of such acts. Of particular significance in the latter

[35] John W. McDavid and Herbert Harari, *Social Psychology* (New York: Harper and Row, Publishers, 1968), pp. 9, 12, 145, 173, 187.

[36] Fritz Heider, "Social Perception and Phenomenal Causality," *Psychological Review,* Vol. 6, No. 51 (1944), pp. 358–374.

category are the causal conditions which surround given acts."[37] He then identifies these three dimensions of causality:

Responsibility for the behavioral act, in the sense of the causal agent (O)

Intentionality of the agent, in regard to what he (O) seeks to achieve in motivational terms

Justifiability of the action, in the sense of what P thinks of O's action

Of the various features of interpersonal perception, the one that appears to be of extreme importance is the perceived *cause* for action. As a result, it is found that persons of higher status are seen to be the cause of their own actions more than those of lower status. Kind or benevolent action that appears to be motivated by an individual's desire rather than by a social demand is usually perceived more positively. Finally, if O is in a role obliging him to perform a distasteful action toward P, then O is normally excused if, as in the case of a role, the external cause of his behavior is apparent.

In the following few pages of this section, we shall review and explore briefly the scope of interpersonal perception and review several interpersonal perceptual devices that are utilized for understanding complex behavioral events.

THE IMPRESSION OF PEOPLE. Notably important to consumer behavior and marketing are the questions of how we perceive people and how impressions of people are formed. Marketing and especially retailing activities are largely people oriented. The way sales personnel are perceived can and does have an important impact on the success of the firm's merchandising programs. Models used in advertising and promotional campaigns are chosen largely in terms of their ability to project certain kinds of characteristics—warmth, friendliness, sociability, popularity, and so forth—because these models are then perceived by consumers as being the personification of the firm or product that they represent. As individuals, we try to make sense out of our experiences by integrating them into organized conceptual systems, sometimes through stereotyping. The term *stereotyping* describes overgeneralized and oversimplified conceptual categories in the perception of objects and events. We encode and simplify a great deal of information by the use of stereotypes, but the information is usually so simplified that meaning and understanding are impeded. The used-car salesman, the dumb housewife, the bumbling husband, and the absent-minded professor are all stereotypes that affect our perception generally of salesmen, housewives, husbands, and professors.

Another tendency toward blanket generalization about associated attributes of personality that affects our impressions or perceptions of

[37] A. Pepitone, "Attributions of Causality, Social Attitudes and Cognitive Matching Processes," in *Person, Perception and Interpersonal Behavior,* R. Tagiuri and L. Petriello, eds. (Stanford, Calif.: Stanford University Press, 1958), p. 259.

people is called *halo effect*. Halo effect is concerned with the tendency to blur one characteristic into another. For example, the display of a few desirable or valued characteristics may lead a perceiver to assume that a person generally displays favorable or liked attributes. A generally favorable impression of another person tends to spread into one's judgments of all that person's attributes. Conversely, however, an unfavorable impression may contaminate one's judgment about unknown characteristics of the person. Consequently, then, the halo effect in impression formation appears to be the most significant when (1) the perceiver has a minimum amount of information about the other person; (2) the perceiver's judgment of another concerns moral or ethical evaluation; or (3) the perceiver is unfamiliar with the traits or attributes he is judging in other people.[38]

The order in which a perceiver is exposed to particular characteristics of another person will determine his overall impression of another person.[39] First impressions have been found to be lasting ones. This dominance and durability of initial impressions is called the *primacy effect* in person perception. On the other hand, when a person is generally familiar with an issue, a person, or an object but later encounters an array of new information about that object, *recency effects* often occur. This means that the most recent information encountered tends to occupy a dominant position in interpersonal perception and, consequently, perceptual reorganization.

Interpersonal perception can thus be seen as an attempt to describe and understand how social and behavorial information is received and how such information is sent. It is a means by which we interpret complex behavior events.

LINE OF REGARD. The direction in which a person looks has been found to be a determinant in a behavioral event, and it can be a meaningful and rich source of information that affects our impression of people. We tend to react more favorably to people who look us directly in the eye. Hence, people whose line of regard is considered ambiguous are often referred to as shifty-eyed, and further inferences about their behavior, namely, their honesty and trustworthiness, are made.

Looking at someone is an observable action that can be engineered for experimental purposes. Gibson and Pick trained a woman to place her eyes precisely in any one of seven positions relative to an observer and to place her head in any one of these positions.[40] One of the eye

[38] P. M. Symods, "Notes on Rating," *Journal of Applied Psychology*, Vol. 7 (1925), pp. 188–195.

[39] See "Experimental Attempts to Minimize the Impact of First Impressions," and "Primacy and Recency in Impression Formation," in *The Order of Presentation in Persuasion*, C. I. Hovland et al., eds. (New Haven, Conn.: Yale University Press, 1957), pp. 181, 183, 374.

[40] James Gibson and Ann Pick, "Perception of Another Person's Looking Behavior," *American Journal of Psychology*, Vol. 76 (1963), pp. 386–394.

positions was fixation on the middle of the observer's forehead and one of the head positions was directly facing the observer. Each observer was then asked to state (for all the various positions, randomly varied) whether he was being looked at directly.

In spite of poor illumination, observers recorded very few errors. Their acuity in judging the looker's line of regard was at least equal to that in discriminating fine print on a visual acuity chart in an oculist's office. In summary, such line-of-regard activities as "peering," "glancing," "glowering," "contemplating," "looking wistfully," "letting the gaze wander," and so forth are activities that telegraph messages and that affect our interpersonal perceptions.

FACIAL EXPRESSION. Line of regard is quite similar to facial expression as a means of facilitating interpersonal perception. As a matter of fact, line of regard is usually judged in the context of facial expression. Facial form and expression are most often used as an index of what specific emotion is being manifested.

Schlosberg developed a theory that really only three dimensions are needed for describing all facial expressions: degrees of pleasantness versus unpleasantness, degrees of acceptance versus rejection, and degrees of arousal.[41] Of course, work has only begun on the social and personality conditions for sending facial expression information. Many questions remain. Why do people with diverse cultural backgrounds agree that some facial patterns show "determination"? Or why is Mickey Mouse (an international star) considered "cute"? Do such judgments reflect primitive facial expressions that under certain conditions do in fact "express emotions"? Research in the future will supply answers to these intriguing questions.

BODY LANGUAGE. The characteristic ways a person uses his line of regard, his facial expression, and his total gross bodily movements have recently come to be called *body language*. Body language expresses emotions and sends information. Thus, it enables us to form impressions of others' personalities. Such impressions are important, as everyone who interacts (and that is literally everyone) knows, because we use such signals, cues, or messages to predict a sender's future behavior and to determine our own behavior in response. Body language, or kinesis, as it is sometimes called, is based upon the behavioral patterns of nonverbal communication.[42] It should be pointed out that body language can actually contradict verbal communications. The essence of body language is that the body is the message and that through body movement and nuances in bodily manipulations—touch, nods, blinks, smiles, positions, and posture—we are communicating via a message

---

[41] Harold Schlosberg, *Psychological Review*, Vol. 61 (1954), pp. 81–88.

[42] Julius Fast, *Body Language* (New York: Simon & Schuster, Inc., 1970).

system. Body language is a subtle, silent language that communicates via perceptual principles of causality, similarity, and proximity in space and continuation.

Hall has stated that:

> Most Americans are only dimly aware of this silent language even though they use it every day. They are not conscious of the elaborate patterning of behavior which prescribes our handling of time, our spatial relationships, our attitudes toward work, play and learning. In addition to what we say with our verbal language we are constantly communicating our real feelings in our silent language—the language of behavior.[43]

Finally, before concluding this section we shall discuss the accuracy of interpersonal perception. It would appear, at least superficially, that effective interpersonal relationships might well depend in part on the ability of one person to understand accurately the behavior and experience of the other. Understanding is, of course, a function primarily of three factors: (1) the characteristics of the perceiver, (2) the characteristics of the perceived person, and (3) the situational context.

The perceiver may or may not have well-developed talents for judging or perceiving effectively in interpersonal situations. The well-trained perceiver will obviously perceive more and be better prepared to interpret correctly what he actually perceives. As we have already discovered, perceptual learning can lead to improved perceptual performance. It has been shown that individuals who generally accept themselves as they are and who possess accurate insight about their own personalities tend to judge and perceive others more accurately.[44]

Questions have been raised as to whether there are particular kinds of people who are unnecessarily "transparent" and thus are easily judged by others, as opposed to other kinds who might be relatively obscure and difficult to judge accurately. Evidence suggests that transparency or obscureness is probably related to the extremeness of particular characteristics. Certain kinds of attributes, such as friendliness, hostility, and so on, may become dominant even with relatively limited association with others. Consequently, individuals who show and project extreme amounts of such characteristics may be more readily judged and perceived accurately than people who show these characteristics only in moderate degree.[45]

Finally, with minimum elaboration suffice it to say that there is

[43] Edward T. Hall, *The Silent Language* (New York: Fawcett World Library, 1959), p. 10.

[44] R. D. Norman, "The Interrelationships Among Acceptance-Rejection, Self-Other Identity, Insight into Self and Realistic Perception of Others," *Journal of Social Psychology*, Vol. 37 (1953), pp. 205–235.

[45] B. O. Baker and Jeanne Block, "Accuracy of Interpersonal Prediction as a Function of Judge and Object Characteristics," *Journal of Abnormal and Social Psychology*, Vol. 54 (1957), pp. 37–43.

abundant evidence that the more one knows about the context in which he is attempting to judge or perceive another person, the more accurate and thus more meaningful will be his perception of that person.

Perception and Consumer Behavior

Intuitively there is little question but what perception is an important determinant of and influence on consumer behavior. Perception, it would appear, affects the entire gamut of consumer decision processes. Consumer problems are perceived problems. The search for information is largely a perceptual process involving sophisticated cognitive activities. Explored alternatives involve perceptual activities as do the actual choice decision and relative postpurchase activities. All the marketing information disseminated through marketing firms and agencies reaches the consumer through his complex sensory receptors as some form of sensory stimulation. Sensory stimulation, as we have learned, carries information in the form of messages, and consumer perception is that activity whereby such information is extracted from the environment, interpreted, and organized on the basis of known perceptual principles and utilized in the interests of consumer goals or motives.

Perception and perceptual processes pervade the entire range of marketing activities. Products are perceived differently. Brand loyalty is largely a function of how different market segments perceive different products. For example, many consumers are loyal to Listerine because it is perceived as strong and, therefore, effective in killing germs. Others may perceive the strong taste as offensive and, therefore, may be more loyal or receptive to a product like Lavoris, which has a sweet and more pleasant taste. Pricing is often an exercise in the psychology of perception. Thus, we have "psychology prices," that is, prices that are chosen because of their known impact on the consumer's perceptions.[46] For example, prices ending in 99 or 98 have usually been thought to be perceived differently than prices in even dollars. Store locations and promotional activities are no less concerned with perception than the other elements of the marketing mix. Yet although we believe that perception is an important part of consumer behavior and marketing, there have been few empirical studies that have attempted to relate perception to some aspects of consumer behavior. Furthermore, what studies have been done have not been replicated extensively.

In this final section of our treatment of perception, we shall review briefly several of the studies that treat perception as an important variable in consumer behavior. We shall conclude by examining a concept that at one time was considered as a major threat to consumers and a possible boon to advertisers—subliminal advertising. As we shall see, it proved to be neither.

---

[46] See A. Oxenfeldt, D. Miller, A. Schuman, and C. Winick, *Insight into Pricing* (Belmont, Calif.: Wadsworth Publishing Company, 1969), especially Chapter 4, "Perception and Pricing," pp. 66–102.

BRAND PREFERENCE AND PERCEPTION

Almost all of us are convinced that our perceptual power or capacity to discern differences in branded beverage products—especially beer—is greater than it actually is. In the selection of such products we can often be best characterized as "true believers!"; namely, our brand is best because it tastes best, and because it tastes best we can, therefore, recognize it from among other competing brands. Can we? The evidence suggests we cannot, especially if we are asked to judge and perceive differences in a "blind" or naked-bottle test, that is, when all identifying marks and labels have been removed. In just such a test, this hypothesis was tested: "Beer drinkers cannot distinguish among major brands of unlabeled beer either on an overall basis or on selected characteristics."[47] The test, conducted under careful design and control conditions, revealed that participants did not appear to be able to discern taste differences among the various beer brands, but apparently labels and their association (perceptual learning) did influence their evaluation. From the marketing point of view the significant generalization is that product distinctions arose primarily from the individual's receptiveness to the various firms' marketing efforts rather than through perceived physical product differences.

How QUALITY IS JUDGED. Perceiving is concerned with judging. We extract information from the environment and from products that are a part of that environment and, on the basis of this information in connection with our experience, our emotions, and our motivated state, we make judgments about products. For example, a product name is often an important cue as to the nature and worth of a product. Frigidaire is now just a brand name whose connotation no longer is as significant as it was during the early days of electrical household refrigeration when "frigid air" really connoted a desired and meaningful perception. It is well known that the typical automobile buyer does not do much more by way of prepurchase examination than to kick the tires, open and slam the door, and take a test drive. Of these limited factors, the way the doors open and close, especially the sound of the doors being closed, is known to be an important perceptual cue and one that is used for judging quality. Thus, touch, sound, sight, and taste are used in varying degrees to judge the quality of products.

One study considered the influence of faint smells upon the judgment of quality in women's hose.[48] A test set of hosiery consisted of four pairs of identical hose packed in identical boxes. One pair was left with the natural, slightly rancid scent that comes from the mixture of ester

[47] R. I. Allison and K. P. Uhl, "Influences of Beer Brand Identification on Taste Perception," *Journal of Marketing Research*, Vol. 1 (August 1964), pp. 36–39, at p. 36.

[48] Donald A. Laird, "How the Consumer Estimates Quality by Subconscious Sensory Impression—With Special References to the Role of Smell," *The Journal of Applied Psychology*, Vol. 16 (June 1932), pp. 241–246.

oil and sulfates used to lubricate the fibers to facilitate weaving and to create softness. A second pair of hose was given a very faint scent by the use of synthetic aromatic chemicals (the narcissus odor predominated in this scent). A third pair was given a complex fruity type of scent, and the fourth was given a sachet type of scent. The detailed structure and a description of how the study was conducted will not be undertaken here. However, the results showed two significant findings: (1) subconsciously perceived sensory impressions received through the olfactory apparatus were potent in determining the judgment of quality in silk hosiery, and (2) scents of one type were more influential in this judgment of quality than were scents of another type.

CONCEPTS AND PERCEPTION

Our general notions affect our perceptions. We established this relationship early in our discussion in this chapter. Bruner has claimed that "less redundancy is needed as we grow older."[49] The reasoning is that perception is based upon representation, on a constructed model of reality against which the input is tested.[50] As this model grows conceptually richer, the individual uses it to fill in details that are not given in stimulation. This writer disagrees to some extent with this position and this overly literal interpretation of perception. Perception is not a one-to-one process of matching to a representation in the head. It is instead a process of extracting the invariables in stimulus information. Decision making and problem solving are facilitated by the more effective extraction of this information rather than by less dependence upon it. Although our concepts increase in number, richness, and complexity as we mature, it does not necessarily follow that we perceive less because we conceive more. Such a condition would be maladaptive for extracting information about what is going on around us.[51] Still, however, the gross generalization that what we know affects what we see or perceive is still a meaningful one and it should be understood that what we know or think we know will condition what and how we perceive.

An interesting study in this regard concerned an attempt to match a product choice (automobiles) to self-images or self-concepts; that is, an attempt was made to relate empirically an automobile owner's perception of himself to his perception of his car.[52]

Twenty-five car owners were selected at random from four groups of all the new car purchasers in the universe.

The four groups were as follows:

[49] J. S. Bruner, R. R. Olver, P. M. Greenfield, et al., *Studies in Cognitive Growth* (New York: John Wiley & Sons, Inc., 1966), p. 23.

[50] This is the framework of analysis employed by J. Engel, D. Kollat, and R. Blackwell in *Consumer Behavior* (New York: Holt, Rinehart & Winston, Inc., 1968), p. 84.

[51] Gibson, op. cit., p. 449.

[52] A. Evans Birdwell, "Influence of Image Congruence on Consumer Choice," in *Reflections on Progress in Marketing*, L. George Smith, ed. (Chicago: American Marketing Association, 1964), pp. 290–303.

Group 1—owners of 1963 Cadillac, Lincoln, and Imperial.

Group 2—owners of 1963 Oldsmobile, Chrysler, Buick, and Pontiac.

Group 3—owners of 1963 Ford, Chevrolet, and Plymouth.

Group 4—owners of 1963 Volkswagen, Falcon, Renault, Rambler, Corvair, and Volvo.

Each of the groups was sampled systematically from a random starting point with the most recent purchaser until twenty-five interviews were completed. Using a semantic differential scale, the respondents were asked to judge themselves. The results of the study, as applied to the hypothesis that the experiment was designed to test, suggest that the hypothesis be accepted. In other words, an automobile owner's perception of his car is essentially congruent with his conception of himself. Given our earlier treatment of self-concepts and consumer behavior, we would intuitively, at least, expect to find these relationships prevailing.

It should be at least briefly mentioned that the most interesting innovation of psychological scaling or measurement in recent years has been the development of measurement procedures for characterizing people's perceptions and preferences as relationships to points in a *multidimensional* space. These methods, although sophisticated and usually involving computer programs for performing the many computations associated with their application, are beyond the scope of our treatment here. Nonetheless, such methods used in marketing research efforts are proving extremely useful in product-life-cycle analysis, market segmentation, vendor evaluation, and other decision areas in which customer preferences or perceptions are an important factor.[53]

SUBLIMINAL PERCEPTION: FACT OR FANCY

Recall from our earlier discussion that individuals have several thresholds for perceiving stimuli. First, they have a lower threshold, below which they perceive no stimuli. Second, they have a terminal threshold or upper threshold, above which no amount of increase can be discerned. Third, individuals have a difference threshold. The difference threshold is some incremental *just noticeable difference*—the least amount of sensed difference that can be discerned. An understanding of subliminal perception is related to an understanding of these different threshold concepts. For example, the difference in thresholds —lower, upper, and difference—varies considerably from individual to individual.

[53] For an expanded, in-depth treatment, see Paul E. Green and Donald S. Tull, *Research For Marketing Decisions* (Englewood Cliffs, N.J.: Prentice-Hall, Inc., 1970), pp. 212–250, especially Chapter 7, "Multidimensional Scaling of Perception and Preference." See also Jagdish N. Sheth, "The Multivariate Revolution in Marketing Research," *Journal of Marketing,* Vol. 35, No. 1 (January 1971), pp. 13–20.

Subliminal perception is perception that is below the *limen* or threshold of conscious recognition. It does not indicate how much or how far below the threshold the stimulus actually is. Subliminal perception implies, to the extent that perception is a determinant of behavior, that unconscious or subconscious or invisible perception would or could condition us or cause us to act in some manner of which we were unaware. The idea that consumers could be psychologically programmed to engage in acts the source or cause of which they were unaware was the spark of a great controversy during the 1950s. For some, even the controversy has not yet been fully decided. The impetus to this controversy was an experiment undertaken in a movie theater in New Jersey. By quickly and repeatedly flashing popcorn and Coca-Cola ads on the screen in such a manner that the viewers were unaware of their existence, nearly unbelievable results were said to have been obtained.

During a six-week period 45,699 people attending the theater were exposed to one of two subliminal messages: "Hungry? Eat popcorn," or "Drink Coca-Cola." Sales figures during the test period were compared with previous sales records. It was reported that popcorn sales increased 58 per cent and that Coca-Cola sales increased 18 per cent.[54] Critics have been extremely dubious about the merits of this experiment and, for that matter, about the merits of and/or possibilities for subliminal advertising generally. The experiment was grossly lacking in scientific controls. For instance, what was the nature of the movie being shown? What was the experience of other movie theaters in terms of popcorn and Coca-Cola sales? Why not have control days when the subliminal messages were not shown? What was the effect of the weather? In short, the absence of a control group violates one of the most basic principles of scientific experimentation.[55]

The prospect of subliminal perception and thus even subliminal advertising is both fact and fancy. It is a reasonably accepted scientific fact that perception without awareness can take place.[56] However, let us return now to our various concepts of thresholds. A subliminal message flashed upon a theater or television screen could conceivably be below the recognition threshold for all the people all of the time; it might be above the threshold for some of the people part of the time; or it might be above the threshold for all the people part of the time. Thus subliminal messages would not necessarily always be subliminal. For a large number they would be supraliminal, and to be effective evidence suggests that messages or stimuli must be very close to our threshold

---

[54] H. Brean, "What Hidden Sell Is All About," *Life* (March 31, 1958), pp. 104–114.

[55] J. V. McConnell, R. L. Cutler, and E. B. McNeil, "Subliminal Stimulation: An Overview," *American Psychologist*, Vol. 13 (1958), p. 229.

[56] J. K. Adams, "Laboratory Studies of Behavior Without Awareness," *Psychological Bulletin*, Vol. 54 (1957), pp. 383–405.

of recognition, that is, near or above our lower threshold.[57] What is ambiguous for one person can be and often is clearly visible for someone else. There are naturally many technical problems involved in keeping a given advertising message or stimulus subliminal, but even if the technical problems could be overcome the fact remains that any hopes for some silent, mysterious, and invisible selling technique via subliminal perception are still probably more fancy than fact. Have we not already learned that people perceive normal or supraliminal stimuli largely in terms of their own needs, motivations, values, and expectations? Is it not somewhat incredible to think that values, needs, aspirations, and motivations would be any less important in screening and extracting information from the environment or from sensory stimulation when this sensory stimulation is presented subliminally? Furthermore, the chances for distorting messages or information through misperception become extremely high when the stimuli are ambiguous, as would be the case in subliminal advertising. What is more, the further below the average lower threshold, the greater the likely probability of message distortion. Consider, too, the impact of competition. Consumers have the inherent capacity to be interested and aroused in terms of those factors that facilitate the task at hand. If many firms used subliminal advertising, wouldn't the effect be much the same as it is with advertising in general? We perceive selectively, and we perceive selectively whether the stimuli are supraliminal or subliminal. It does not appear likely, therefore, that we are about to be behaviorally engineered and made to respond like puppets to the desires and whims of Madison Avenue. Someone has suggested to avoid such a possibility that we all install a small subliminal flashing sign that we place on top of our TV screens that would say simply "Don't." Or why not have the Federal Communications Commission intermittently flash a subliminal message that would say, "Ignore all subliminal messages seen on this screen."

We move apace in our treatment of cognitive phenomena as they affect consumer behavior. We have learned in this chapter that our perceptions must usually strike a balance between rapidity and ease on one hand and accuracy on the other. Too much emphasis on rapidity and quickness and we overlook important events. We miss the finer details and the nuances of the messages contained in the sensory stimulation. On the other hand, if we over-attend and -atune, so much stimulation reaches our sense organs that we are likely to be inundated with messages, and such redundancy can retard perception to such an extent as to be ineffective. We have learned about the nature of perception and perceptual processes. Our interest has been focused upon certain perceptual principles that facilitate the extraction of meaningful

---

[57] J. Bruner and L. Postman, "Emotional Selectivity in Perception and Reaction," *Journal of Personality*, Vol. 16 (1947), pp. 69–77. See also R. Barthol and M. Goldstein, "Psychology and the Invisible Sell," *California Management Review*, Vol. 1, No. 2 (Winter 1959), pp. 29–35.

data from the consumer's environment. Our excursion led us to a brief encounter with another exceedingly relevant and important cognitive activity, perceptual learning. In the chapter that follows, our attention will be directed to a continued expansion of the role of learning generally and in consumer behavior and consumer decision processes.

Questions for Study, Reflection, and Review

1 Describe the relationship between cognition and perception.
2 Distinguish between the concept of sensation and that of perception.
3 Compare and contrast the perceptual principle of proximity with the principle of similarity.
4 Discuss the functional properties or purposes of perception.
5 Distinguish between perceptual constancy and perceptual defense.
6 Briefly discuss some of the experiential determinants of perception.
7 Discuss the relationship between perceptual learning and consumer problem-solving.
8 Explain the significance of the transactional approach in interpersonal perception.
9 Describe the halo effect and the conditions in which it is most apparent.
10 Briefly discuss subliminal perception and its implications for marketing.

9

Learning: Concepts and Processes

Introduction

The impact of learning on consumer behavior has been intuitively recognized from the inception of modern marketing practices. Yet, a significant understanding of learning concepts and processes and their intricate relationships to consumer behavior are just now being researched and tested. Much is now understood—a great deal remains as mystery and enigma. Consumers do learn; they adjust and modify their behavior and attitudes over time. These changes in behavior can often be attributed to learning. Mrs. Middle Majority decides to shop at the new supermarket that has just opened. She *learned* or became aware of its existence. She became interested (learned) in the new facility by reading its preopening advertisements in the local newspapers. Her present store, which she has patronized rather regularly for about three years, no longer seems as satisfying to shop in as it once was (another form of learning via experience). Her neighbor and close friend has instructed her that she knows this chain group well from having shopped in their stores when she lived in another community and that she liked their merchandise and service (affective learning). Mrs. M. M. shops at the store, forms several impressions of it (more learning), and decides for the time being at least that she will continue to shop at their facilities for at least a part of her family needs.

Learning permeates almost all human activity. Small wonder,

then, that it is so important a variable in and determinant of consumer behavior.

Almost without exception, consumer behavior is *adaptive behavior*. It is adaptive because the consumer is continually reappraising and re-evaluating his decision processes and his purchase strategies. It is, of necessity, adaptive because of the nature of consumers, that is, persons who are subjected to various and alternating motivations, whose goals, perceptions, aspirations, knowledge, images, and beliefs are undergoing rather constant and significant change. Consumer behavior is adaptive because of economic, psychological, social, and cultural reasons. Our incomes fluctuate, as do prices for goods and services. Our psychological fields are altered by changing motivations and perceptions. We grow older, our group affiliations and social class orientations are modified. Cultural factors such as age grading—moving from adolescence to adulthood—permit us to engage in certain acts of consumption that were previously legally or culturally denied. All of these changing dimensions of our existence force us to be adaptive creatures. But what forms of adaptive or accommodating behavior should we display? The answer, of course, is that we seek to display those adaptive mechanisms that we believe best enable us to attain our desired and perceived goals. In short, as problem-solving consumers, we engage in perceptual learning. *Perceptual learning is always a matter of learning more adaptive behavior patterns or habits.*[1] As a problem solver, the consumer is concerned with extracting as much meaningful information from his environment as possible and using this information to contribute to the attainment of his personal welfare and well-being. Consumer behavior, as we have already established, is problem-solving behavior. Problem-solving behavior is of necessity adaptive behavior, and adaptive behavior means learning new goals, learning about one's environment, and learning new modes of adjustment and response tendencies.

A considerable background for treating many of the concepts in this current chapter has already been laid down in previous chapters. For example, much of the controversy surrounding the cognitive versus the behaviorist tradition was dealt with in Chapters 4, 5, and 6. The reader might very well wish to review relevant sections of these chapters before proceeding. In this current chapter, we shall continue to build upon our cognitive theory of behavior, which has so thoroughly and meticulously been developed thus far. Our theory asserts in its most simple form that behavior is a function of cognitions or knowledge or that what a consumer does is a function of what he knows. We now add considerable complexity to this simple assertion. By way of elaboration we have added that behavior is not only a result of knowledge—it is not simply a result of what the consumer *knows* but also of what he *perceives* and believes and of the nature of his goals or

---

[1] For more on this topic, see Robert Ward Leeper, "The Main Concepts of Cognitive Learning," in *Learning: Theories,* Melvin H. Marx, ed. (New York: Macmillan Publishing Co., Inc., 1970), pp. 320–322.

motives. From the standpoint of our current interest our theory of consumer behavior must also account for what ways and means lead consumers to develop their cognitions or concepts; how consumers come to acquire motives; and how perceptual processes enable the consumer to order and interpret sensory inputs into meaningful and organized constructs. Finally, in terms of learning we are interested in the background factors and processes that produce these perceptual and/or motivational-cognitive representational processes.

We shall explore a range of alternative learning theories and processes. However, we shall continue our established cognitive tradition and emphasize a cognitive learning process that pictures the consumer as processing information by combining neural processes to form larger whole units. Cognitive learning theory, like our treatment of perception in Chapter 8, will be handled more from the point of view of its psychological than its physiological or neurological dimensions. The basic approach of a cognitive theory of learning is very much like what Neisser has described in his splendid book on cognitive psychology:

> The task of a psychologist trying to understand human cognition is analogous to that of a man trying to discover how a computer has been programmed. . . . Given this purpose, he will not care much whether his particular computer stores information in magnetic cores or in thin films; he wants to understand the program and not the "hardware." By the same token, it would not help the psychologist to know that memory is carried by RNA as opposed to some other medium. He wants to understand its utilization, not its incarnation. . . . Psychology, like economics, is a science concerned with the interdependence among certain events rather than with their physical nature.[2]

THE NATURE AND SCOPE OF LEARNING

As we observed in the introductory paragraphs, the nature and scope of learning are rather broad. Almost any change in behavior is sometimes conceived of as the manifestation of a learning process. Yet it is well known that not all behavior is the result of learning. It is also generally well known that we rapidly forget certain acquired insights and that the responses to a given situation are likely to vary widely over time. In short, consumers unlearn as well as learn; that is, they forget, and as a result of forgetting they seek new information and are likely to alter their responses. Furthermore, satisfactory modes of behavior are often abandoned in the interest of new drives or goals. Behavior patterns once thought to be rigid become extinct in the interests of new situations and new environmental demands. In this section, we shall attempt to delineate what is meant by learning, and we shall explore several alternative learning theories and examine in considerable detail the various elements of the learning process.

---

[2] Ulric Neisser, *Cognitive Psychology* (New York: Appleton-Century-Crofts, 1967), pp. 6–7.

LEARNING DEFINED

There are about as many definitions of learning as there are writers and theorists on the subject. Yet an examination of the concept reveals a great deal of agreement on what learning is and what it entails. One set of writers has most carefully defined learning as "the process by which an activity originates or is changed through reacting to an encountered situation, provided that the characteristics of the change cannot be explained on the basis of native response tendencies, maturation, or temporary states of the organism (e.g., fatigue, drugs, etc.)."[3] It is interesting to examine the content of this definition. First, observe that it states what learning is. To paraphrase, it suggests that learning brings about change in behavior that results from previous behavior in similar situations. It suggests that learning brings about a change in an individual's behavior that results from practice or experience. Thus, one would conclude that learning means all changes in behavior that result from previous behavior in similar situations.[4]

Observe also that Hilgard and Bower's definition states rather explicitly what learning is *not*. For example, learning is not physiological reflexes or instincts, nor can changes in response tendencies related to maturation (the unfolding and development of hereditary influences) be called learning. Finally, no changes in response tendencies or behavior relating to temporary states of the organism, such as fatigue, drugs, or any severe deprivation related to hunger or thirst, are considered the result of learning. These factors, admittedly, can affect learning, and in tests designed to measure the effects of learning they can distort results, primarily because of the difficulty of isolating these factors in learning situations.

LEVELS OF HUMAN RESPONSE TENDENCY

Our discussion of learning can be tied rather neatly to the various levels of adaptation employed by humans to cope with their environment. In coping with his environment, the individual may react positively $(+)$, negatively $(-)$, or neutrally (0); that is, the organism approaches, withdraws, or does nothing, depending upon the meaning that the object has for it.[5] What is to be emphasized at this juncture

[3] Ernest R. Hilgard and Gordon H. Bower, *Theories of Learning* (New York: Appleton-Century-Crofts, 1966), p. 2.

[4] Bernard Berelson and Gary A. Steiner, *Human Behavior: Shorter Edition* (New York: Harcourt Brace Jovanovich, Inc., 1967), p. 131. For a more detailed presentation, see Robert S. Woodworth and Harold Schlosberg, *Experimental Psychology* (New York: Holt, Rinehart & Winston, Inc., 1954), Chapters 18–22; also see James Deese, *The Psychology of Learning* (New York: McGraw-Hill Book Company, 1958).

[5] The basic ideas in this discussion follow closely those presented by Leslie A. White, "Four Stages in the Evolution of Minding," in *Evolution After Darwin*, Sol Tax, ed., Vol. 2 (Chicago: University of Chicago Press, 1960), pp. 239–253.

is that there are levels of response complexity and that these levels involve various degrees of learning and learning complexity.

The simplest type of reaction is the *simple reflex*. At this level of response the behavior of the organism is mechanically determined by the interaction of the intrinsic properties of both the organism and the stimulus. Because of the automatic and mechanical nature of reflexes, no learning is said to be involved.

The next response level is the *conditioned response*. Conditioned responses, as we shall soon discover, are brought about via a process of conditioning through reinforcement and simple association. Rather simple learning processes are involved at this level.

The next level of response complexity is designated as *sign behavior*. Sign behavior involves the use and manipulation of simple tools, and behavior becomes more clearly differentiated than in either simple reflex or conditioned response. Behavior differs in the sense that the response is still determined by the intrinsic properties of both the organism and the stimulus situations, but in sign behavior the organism plays the dominant role in that it is capable of formulating response alternatives and also has control over their execution.

Finally, the next level of behavior is called *symboling behavior,* and it is characteristic of man only. Symboling involves communication of meaning by symbols. The fact that man can learn things symbolically, through communication, distinguishes him most markedly from the rest of the animal world. He enjoys this capacity primarily because of his more sophisticated central nervous system and his unusual ability to reason and to learn the meaning of complex symbols. The principal idea is that the meaning of a symbol is derived from interaction of human beings and the resultant meaning is social in nature; that is, it is a shared meaning.

Because there are these various levels of human response tendencies, we must understand that we use our learning capacity to cope with encountered situations and that the kind of learning vehicle employed will depend in large part upon the nature of the encountered task. Man thus learns as a result of simple association and of the elementary and fundamental manipulation of tools and signs, and more importantly, he learns via complex cognitive processes involving symbols and reasoning, memory, thinking, and other forms of complex problem-solving.

The important point is this. Our definition and concept of learning applies to behavior that ranges all the way from the conditional response, through the use and acquisition of motor skills, to the solving of complex problems. In light of our cognitive orientation we assume further that learning is a correction or adaptation in response to information received about successes and failures. Hopefully, then, learning tends to make our behavior more efficient and more adaptive after a series of efforts than it was before. Generally, this does occur but there are, of course, exceptions.

LEARNING AS A PRODUCT AND A PROCESS

The term *learning* refers to both a process and a product. In discussing the levels of response tendencies in the previous section we frequently alluded to the processes involved in the transactions that take place between the individual and his environment. These transactions involve sensing, perceiving, feeling, symbolizing, remembering, abstracting, thinking, and reasoning.[6] Each of these involves complex cognitive processes. When we discuss learning, however, what we are often referring to is not so much the processes of learning as it is learning as a product of these complex processes. Learning as a mental activity is difficult to observe. As a matter of fact, it is usually impossible to observe as a process; what we witness instead is the product of learning, that is, changed or altered behavior or changed or altered response tendencies. Learning is invariably an inferred result when we see individuals engage in behavioral acts and subsequently come to modify their actions as a result of the experience gained. Learning does not have to result in observable actions, however. A broad conception of learning, such as is intended herein, would include such factors as the formation, modification, and breaking of habits; the acquiring of interests, attitudes, values, and images; the development of preferences and tastes; and the formation of bias and prejudices. Learning is a pervasive activity. In the normal individual it begins at birth and continues until death. It is involved continuously in the synthesis and application of cognitions in reasoning, thinking, building theories, and problem solving. Learning is the mechanism and thought process most actively involved in our deepest feelings and emotions, our self-concepts, and our total personalities.[7]

To the consumer, learning involves the process of acquiring the ability to respond adequately to a situation that may or may not have been encountered previously; it involves the favorable modification of response tendencies consequent to previous experience, particularly the building up of a new series of complexly coordinated decision rules and purchase strategies; the fixation of items and concepts in memory so that they can be recalled, recognized, and used for purposes of discrimination; in short, the process of acquiring insight into the purchase-shopping situation.

A TAXONOMY.OF TYPES AND THEMES OF LEARNING

There are many different ways to classify learning and learning theories. We shall explore briefly one such taxonomy, and later we shall reduce this classification to three more generally accepted classifications. In the final analysis all learning and all learning theories can be treated as falling within one or the other of two major categories: asso-

[6] Hugh V. Perkins, *Human Development and Learning* (Belmont, Calif.: Wadsworth Publishing Co., Inc., 1969), pp. 336–337.

[7] Ibid., p. 337.

ciative or cognitive learning. We shall begin by examining learning and learning theories within the broader context, and we shall ultimately move to the more reduced-form scheme.

Gagné has identified eight types of learning, each of which, according to his reasoning, requires a different set of conditions.[8] The conditions of learning are the events that must take place if a particular learning is to occur, such as drive, previous learning, and satisfaction, and conditions and events in the learning situation such as the nature of the task itself.

No attempt is made to elaborate on these various types of learning. They are listed here and discussed only briefly in order to illustrate something of the range and scope with which learning is viewed. With a little imagination these learning types can be fitted to the levels of human responses previously discussed.

Type 1: *Signal learning.* The individual learns to make a general diffuse response to a signal or a conditioned stimulus. This is the classical conditional response of Pavlov and the behaviorism of Watson.

Type 2: *Stimulus-response learning.* The learner acquires a precise response to a discriminated stimulus. What is learned is a connection or association (Thorndike) or a discriminated operant (Skinner), sometimes called an instrumental response.

Type 3: *Chaining.* What is acquired is a chain of two or more stimulus-response connections. The conditions for such learning have been described by Guthrie, Skinner, and others.

Type 4: *Verbal association.* Verbal association is the learning of chains that are verbal. Basically, the conditions resemble those for chained learning such as motor skills and habits. However, the presence of language in the human being makes this a special type because internal links may be selected from the individual's previously learned repertoire of language.

Type 5: *Multiple discrimination.* The individual learns to make n different identifying responses to n different stimuli, which may resemble each other in physical appearance to a greater or lesser degree.

Type 6: *Concept learning.* The learner acquires a capability of making a common response to a class of stimuli that may differ from each other widely in physical appearance. He is able to make a response that identifies an entire class of objects or events.

Type 7: *Principle learning.* In simplest terms a principle is a chain of two or more concepts. It functions to control behavior in the manner suggested by a verbalized rule of the form "if A, then B," where A and B are concepts.

Type 8: *Problem solving.* Problem solving is a kind of learning that requires the internal events usually called thinking. Two or more principles are combined to produce a new capability that leads to insight and higher order principles.

[8] Robert M. Gagné, *The Conditions of Learning* (New York: Holt, Rinehart & Winston, Inc., 1965), Chapter 2.

Notice that this classification scheme moves from the simplest to the most complex types of learning. As was suggested earlier, this expanded taxonomy can be readily collapsed into a more reduced-form scheme.

A TRIAD OF LEARNING THEORIES

Nearly all the contemporary literature of learning theory treats such theories as falling within one or the other of three categories: stimulus-response learning, operant conditioning or instrumental learning, and cognitive learning. We shall examine these three types of learning in considerable detail.

STIMULUS-RESPONSE LEARNING. Stimulus-response learning is most frequently understood in terms of classical conditioning exercises. The major proponents of S-R learning are such notable figures as Pavlov, Watson, and Guthrie.[9] The experiments of Ivan Pavlov, a Russian experimental psychologist interested in the digestive processes, pointed the way to the early S-R theories.[10] Pavlov became impressed with the modifiability of certain digestive reflexes in animals. He showed one way in which behavior can be modified—by conditioning. Conditioning is the process of achieving a response with a neutral stimulus that has been paired with a stimulus that "reflexly" produces a given response: "This and only this Pavlov averred was the basis of behavior flexibility and adaptability. But, it will be noted responses which have been thus conditioned were still reflexes, 'conditioned reflexes.' "[11]

This can be shown as follows:

$$S_a \longrightarrow R \longrightarrow S_b$$

$$S_a \longrightarrow R \qquad S_b \longrightarrow R$$

In this figure, response R can be brought about only by an unconditioned stimulus S_a. However, S_a may be closely associated with stimulus S_b. As a result of this association, conjunction, or "temporal contiguity," response R is associatively shifted from S_a to S_b. This classical view of S-R learning is often referred to as association or contiguity learning in the connectionist tradition, and it is usually depicted diagrammatically as follows:[12]

---

[9] For an elaborate breakdown and treatment of the various learning theories, see Winfred F. Hill, *Learning: A Survey of Psychology Interpretations* (San Francisco: Chandler Publishing Company, 1963). The material of this section relies heavily upon this work.

[10] Ivan P. Pavlov, *Conditioned Reflexes*, G. V. Anrep, trans. (London: Oxford University Press, 1927).

[11] O. Herbert Mowrer, *Learning Theory and Behavior* (New York: John Wiley & Sons, Inc., 1961), p. 14.

[12] Hill, op. cit., pp. 31–40.

$$\text{given together} \quad \begin{cases} S_1 \text{ given} \\ S_2 \text{ learned} \end{cases} \quad R$$

where S_1 is an unconditioned stimulus and S_2 is a conditioned stimulus. S-R learning is concerned only with objective behavior and like operant conditioning; such an approach denies the existence of such mental processes as perception, thinking, or reasoning. Learning occurs (if it really is learning) as a result of the contiguity and association between the stimulus and the conditioned response. The subjects are passive. They make no attempt to assess the nature of the situation or to examine alternate response modes. The subjects do not think; they simply behave or, at most, twitch.

S-R learning offers very little insight into consumers' learning processes. Consumer responses are seldom, if ever, conditioned reflexes, and it is quite unlikely that consumers can be effectively subjected to conditioning situations. The sophistication and complexity of consumer decision processes and the instrumental and symbolic nature of most consumer purchases place consumers beyond the influence of such simple and mechanistic approaches.

OPERANT CONDITIONING OR LEARNING. Operant conditioning or learning differs quite significantly from stimulus-response or classical conditioning. Whereas classical conditioning is characterized by stimulus substitution, instrumental conditioning is characterized by response substitution;[13] that is, unsuccessful responses tend to be replaced with responses that are reinforced. If the consumer is unsuccessful in reaching a desirable solution to a particular purchase situation he will probably modify that solution until a subsequent action is more satisfactory, hence reinforced.

Both S-R learning, which is often related to what is called respondent learning, and instrumental learning, which is called operant learning, are normally treated as an integral part of behaviorist psychology. Again, whereas the distinctive characteristic of respondent behavior is that it is a response to stimuli, the characteristic of operant behavior is that it operates on the environment. There is no particular stimulus that will consistently elicit an operant response. By the same token, the theory of respondent behavior presumes that the learner is always passive and that the responses he makes are always involuntary. The theory of operant learning assumes that subjects act voluntarily and that their behavior is goal directed. Specifically, the learner is said to be concerned with satisfying some need or perhaps with avoiding some unpleasant consequence. The subject is acting upon his environment, manipulating it, attempting to alter or modify it, rather than simply passively and involuntarily responding to it.

The theory of operant conditioning is still too much obsessed with

[13] For more on this topic, see J. Charles Jones, *Learning* (New York: Harcourt Brace Jovanovich, Inc., 1967), pp. 28–29.

behaviorist traditions, and it is by and large basically a rat psychology. The typical laboratory or clinical experiment used to dramatize operant conditioning is usually structured along the following lines.

A hungry rat is put in a box that contains a lever connected to an arrangement that delivers food pellets whenever the lever is pressed. The rat runs around restlessly until somehow he presses the bar. A food pellet follows (reinforcement), and he eats it. Soon he repeats the performance, and in a short time he is pressing the bar continuously. If the mechanism is now disconnected, the rate of bar pressing decreases and finally ceases, or almost ceases. Extinction has occurred, just as in classical conditioning. This process is also known as operant conditioning in that the response operates upon the environment.[14]

One of the striking features of operant learning is that when a response is followed by a reward or reinforcement the frequency or probability of the recurrence of that response increases. Now, isn't this a rather characteristic behavior phenomenon? When the consumer acts voluntarily, as he invariably does, he operates on the environment. His behavior, as we have mentioned so frequently, is goal and problem oriented. If a product satisfies him, his action is reinforced and the probability that he will again purchase the product is increased. Much of our everyday, routine behavior, certainly including consumer behavior, can be characterized as operant. It is trial and error, and from this trial-and-error behavior we develop heuristic decision rules. If our behavior is reinforced, we are likely to build up a given response tendency or habit. If, on the other hand, our behavior is punished or negatively rewarded, we continue to seek new responses, and we engage in alternate behavior until such time as our actions are more suitably rewarded.

Unfortunately, operant conditioning and learning has not been studied widely by consumer behaviorists and marketers in general. It is still the favorite clinical toy of the behaviorist psychologist and those bent on behavioral engineering.[15] Although it views subjects more as machines than human beings and basically denies or ignores most of the complex cognitive processes, these attitudes may be changing.

COGNITIVE LEARNING. So much has been said about cognitive processes so far that we will not describe cognitive learning at great length. First, recall that the basic difference between behaviorist psychology and cognitive psychology is, at one and the same time, the basic difference between theories of S-R learning or operant learning and theories of cognitive learning.

The behaviorists take their name from the fact that they are interested only in objective observable behavior. They deny or ignore the

---

[14] Berelson and Steiner, op. cit., p. 132.

[15] B. F. Skinner, as mentioned in an earlier chapter, is the principal contributor to operant conditioning theory. See *The Behavior of Organisms: An Experimental Analysis* (New York: Appleton-Century-Crofts, 1938).

conscious processes of perception, thinking, reasoning, remembering, and so forth and are militantly opposed to those aspects of any theory that involve assumptions about processes that cannot be observed. Behaviorist theories of learning consequently tend to be highly mechanistic and deterministic. Theories of cognitive learning, on the other hand, emphasize the high level and abstract nature of human beings and their ability and tendency to engage in symbolic processes and to use symbols and signs in problem solving. The behaviorist is inclined to ask, "What has the subject learned to do?" The cognitivist, on the other hand, would be inclined to ask, "How has the subject learned to perceive the situation?" The cognitivist is interested in examining a learning situation in terms of such factors as motivation, the perceived goals, the aspiration level, the overall nature of the situation, and the beliefs, values, and personality of the subject—in short, the entire range of the subject's psychological field. The cognitivist, as opposed to the behaviorist, contends that consumers do not respond simply to stimuli but instead act on beliefs, express attitudes, and strive toward goals. The cognitivist is thus concerned with this entire range of conscious experience and not just objective behavior.

Consumer behavior and learning can be characterized as ranging along a continuum from simple habit formation, operant conditioning, and multiple response learning to learning as the achievement of understanding. The complexity of consumer learning varies greatly from situation to situation. In consumer learning, habit formation or programmed decision-making involving associative learning and acquiring insight or understanding, as in the case of cognitive learning, and nonprogrammed problem-solving and concept formation ought to be looked upon as complementary. Neither is complete in itself as an explanation of learning and each helps to explain some of the features of learning that the other neglects or explains with great difficulty.[16] Cognitivists are well aware that a great part of consumer behavior is operant. Consumers engage in a great deal of trial-and-error behavior. However, they can and do readily modify their response tendencies. They do so when their insight and understanding (cognitions) lead them to a different view (perception) of the situation or when their goals and aspirations (motivation) change. Consumers cannot be locked into a ceaselessly repetitive stimulus-response behavior mode. Remember that consumers are information processors and that they use this information constantly to alter and modify their response tendencies.

BASIC ELEMENTS IN THE LEARNING PROCESS

Regardless of the type of learning theory involved—stimulus-response, operant conditioning, or cognitive learning—there are several elements that are thought to be basic to nearly all learning situa-

---

[16] E. R. Hilgard and R. C. Atkinson, *Introduction to Psychology* (New York: Harcourt Brace Jovanovich, Inc., 1967), p. 306.

tions. Furthermore, one of the identifying characteristics of all learning is association. Early theories of learning based upon association rested upon four "laws." These were the so-called laws of similarity, of contrast, of coexistence in space, and of succession in time. According to these laws of association one idea calls up another one because it is like another, unlike another, or close to another idea in time or space.[17] Subsequently, however, these four laws were reduced to a law of contiguity, according to which a basis for association was thought to be formed when two objects were thought about or perceived simultaneously or in close succession.

One of the oldest and most prominent laws of learning is the law of frequency. The law of frequency posits that the strength of an association depends directly on the frequency with which it has occurred. Another important law of learning is the law of effect. This law is related more closely to the concept of reinforcement than to the concept of association and states simply that:

> As long as an individual is being rewarded for what he is doing, he will learn these particular responses more thoroughly but he may not learn anything new by trial and error. This is partly because strengthening of the dominant response makes the occurrence of any new responses less likely and partly because its rewards if ample, will keep the drive at a low level.[18]

Although not universally held by all learning theorists, the idea of the law of effect is that learning does not take place without reinforcement. Other learning laws have been posited from time to time. For example, Guthrie advanced the notion of a law of vividness and a law of intensity.[19] These two laws supposedly cover the exception to the law of frequency by explaining that, other things being equal, of two associations with the same cue, one made the experience more vivid or was used under circumstances that included greater excitement. Guthrie's law of recency explains that of two associations that have equal practice, the more recent will prevail. Laws of learning have been found to have dubious validity. However, such statements continue to be explored as loose generalizations and guidelines for further research as well as for marketing practice.

From the investigation of these basic laws, the reader will discern that learning is either viewed as a function primarily of reinforcement (the law of effect) or of association (the law of frequency). We shall not explore the merits of this debate. Most modern theories emphasize varying degrees of both reinforcement and association although the

---

[17] Horace B. English, *Historical Roots of Learning Theory* (Garden City, N.Y.: Doubleday & Company, Inc., 1954), p. 6.

[18] N. E. Miller and J. Dollard, "Four Fundamentals of Learning," in *Theories of Motivation and Learning*, Richard C. Trevan and Robert C. Birney, eds. (Princeton, N.J.: Van Nostrand Reinhold Company, 1964), p. 58.

[19] E. R. Guthrie, *The Psychology of Learning*, rev. ed. (Gloucester, Mass.: Peter Smith, 1960; Harper & Brothers, © 1957), p. 80.

reinforcement theory has gained widely in popularity. We shall next explore briefly the basic elements that pervade nearly all learning processes.

DRIVE. Drive refers to an aroused or motivated state of the organism, one that goads the individual into action. Drives are usually the result of some stimulus, or what we will call later *cues*. The drive stimulus may be either internal or external. A consumer who responds to a counter display of a popular headache remedy, even though he doesn't have a headache, is responding to an external stimulus or cue. When hungry, individuals respond to internal stimuli in the form of stomach pains or contractions. Our own emotional states create drives or stimuli that prompt us to action. Drives are thus the basis of motivation and to understand the role of drive in consumer learning we ought perhaps to review the material in Chapter 7, which dealt at length with the motivational aspect of consumer behavior. Drives, like motives, are both primary and secondary in nature. Primary drives relate to the physiology of the individual in terms of such basic processes as hunger, thirst, sex, and so on. Secondary drives are learned drives and are usually associated with socialization processes. These secondary drives are related to such factors as social needs, safety needs, esteem needs, and self-actualization needs. All drives, whether primary or secondary, usually manifest themselves hierarchically;[20] that is, unfulfilled drives are prepotent and physiological drives usually take precedence over learned or secondary drives. Yet we are reminded once again that what we often consider drives are not really drives at all but appetites. We often eat not because we are hungry but because of the ritualized and symbolic nature of eating. We particularize our drive state by eating not just food but a particular kind of food—hamburgers, pizza, or sirloin steak. The primary characteristic about drive is that strong stimuli generally tend to increase our activity and the removal of strong stimuli decreases activity.

GOAL OBJECTS. The goal object, defined in the marketing context, is any new product or service that does or is expected to reduce or eliminate a need. From our earlier discussion of motivation, it will be recalled that drives or motives can be looked upon either as internal mechanisms that drive or push the subject to respond or as external goals or objects that pull the subject toward the attainment of goals. One writer has characterized the concept of a goal object as follows:

> A product that satisfies a physiological need . . . or a psychological need (such as prestige) thus becomes the reinforcement agent, or as it is often called a goal object.[21]

[20] See Clark L. Hull, *Essentials of Behavior* (New Haven, Conn.: Yale University Press, 1951), pp. 24–27.

[21] Gerald Zaltman, *Marketing: Contributions from the Behavioral Sciences* (New York: Harcourt Brace Jovanovich, Inc., 1965), p. 21.

It is with the attainment of the goal object that degrees of gratification of the initial needs will usually occur. The obvious implication is that the product or service purchased by the consumer for the purpose of reducing need had better live up to the expectations of the consumer if repeat sales are to be expected.

CUES. Cues are stimuli. In a marketing sense cues are the product characteristics and the characteristics of an innovation. Thus packages, prices, store design, and brand names are all cues. Cues as stimuli take the form of guiding suggestions. The importance of cues in the learning process may be shown in cases in which learning fails: "If the cues are too obscure . . . it is impossible to make a correct response with precision,"[22] the inference being that cues or product differentiations not only must be present but must actually be differentiating aspects of the product that are strong enough to elicit the wanted response (in this case, purchase of the given product).[23]

Cues, therefore, are the directing forces in consumer behavior. Cues determine the timing of a consumer's purchase, the place of his purchase, and the product or brand of product he will choose among alternatives. The importance of cues in the consumer learning process is far-reaching. Cues affect the response made in relation to these cues. Advertising and sales promotion almost always are concerned with projecting product and service cues to perceived market targets.[24] Thus these cues are motivating suggestions designed to arouse interest and lead, hopefully, to favorable response tendencies.

RESPONSE. A response is the organism's reaction to a cue or stimulus. Therefore, the act of purchase is a response to the original stimulus or drive and the purchase of a particular product is a response to cues that guide the purchase behavior. Responses are not always observable nor do they manifest themselves overtly. A given configuration of marketing cues such as pricing, purchasing, branding, color, style, and/or fashion influences may lead to directly observable behavior, that is, the purchase of the particular product. However, such cue configurations may lead also to the development of a favorable image of or predisposition toward the product, or previously held negative attitudes toward the product may be changed and the consumer may now have a positive or favorable attitude. Such reactions are characterized as response tendencies rather than simply as responses.

REINFORCEMENT OR REWARD. Reinforcement or reward tends to strengthen the bond or association between cues and response. Reinforcement takes place when the original drive is reduced, or in the case

[22] Miller and Dollard, op. cit., p. 48.

[23] Zaltman, op. cit., p. 21.

[24] See Richard N. Cardozo, "An Experimental Study of Customer Effort, Expectation, and Satisfaction," *Journal of Marketing Research* (August 1965), pp. 244–249.

of most goal-striving behavior, when sufficient satisfaction in the attainment of that goal is acquired. Applied to marketing, this suggests that the purchase response must be rewarded or reinforced to provide the increased probability that the response will again be elicited when the cue conditions once again present themselves.

The ideas of response and reinforcement are closely entwined; that is, the response depends to a large degree upon the reward of that response, and the ability to reinforce a response depends upon the elicitation of that response. A major problem for marketers is the attempt to elicit the first response so that it can be rewarded.

Reinforcement serves several purposes in learning. Most importantly, it serves to strengthen responses because it reduces drive, satisfies need, and builds up habit tendencies.[25] Furthermore, at the same time that reinforcement is resulting in observable changes in the external responses of the organism, it also functions to enforce unobservable changes in the response tendencies, internal states, and expectations of that organism.

Consumer behavior suggests two functions of reinforcement. The first is an information function that provides feedback on successful and unsuccessful responses. When the consumer acts, his sensory and cognitive mechanisms inform him of what he has done. If the action achieves its goal—if it is judged correct and satisfying—it is reinforced and, consequently, more likely to occur another time. If the action is judged to be incorrect or unsatisfying, it is more likely to be eliminated. Reinforcement also performs a motivational function that keeps the consumer learner at the task. A husband who extols the virtue of his wife's homemaking, her cooking, and her thrift in household budgeting is likely, via a secondary reinforcing process, to cause her to focus even more time and attention on these activities and thus become even more skillful and efficient in their execution. Secondary reinforcement involves the capacity to reinforce behavior with rewards not necessarily associated with stimuli that already have reinforcing qualities. For instance, in the example just related, the principal reward or reinforcement comes to the housewife in the form of lower-priced, higher-quality goods. However, a secondary reinforcer (praise) may cause the housewife to manifest the same behavior in relationship to different stimuli.

In a cognitive sense, the effect of rewards is that they produce incentive-anticipation habits by producing vivid perceptions of such rewards in relation to certain other features of the situation. It is not that "rewards stamp in and punishments stamp out," as Thorndike originally proposed, but that vivid perceptual processes tend to bring about altered and restructured cognitive mechanisms that reflect the specific properties that were perceived in the learning situation.[26]

[25] C. L. Hull, *A Behavior System* (New Haven, Conn.: Yale University Press, 1952).

[26] See E. L. Thorndike, *Selective Writings from a Connectionist's Psychology* (New York: Appleton-Century-Crofts, 1949); and Leeper, op. cit., p. 319.

RELATED PRODUCTS OF LEARNING

Having examined the basic elements in learning, let us look now at two related concepts of learning, *generalization* and *extinction*. It is these two learning phenomena that make our learning both economical and effective. These factors enable us to transfer what we have learned in one situation to another and enable us to forget or unlearn specific responses and response tendencies, resulting in the freedom and flexibility of the human organism.

GENERALIZATION. In many respects, the very essence of learning is related to the concept of generalization because it makes plausible the proposition that all behavior can be defined and modified on the basis of learning principles. For example, if each S-R bond were learned discretely then would it not be illogical to attribute the acquisition of complex repertoires to learning? If we were incapable of generalizing what was learned in one situation to another, just imagine how complex and cumbersome learning would be. Generalization, then, is the process whereby a novel stimulus elicits a response that had previously been learned to a different but similar stimulus.[27] Many theories of generalization have been advanced. However, the least controversial and, in many ways, one of the most satisfying explanations has been advanced by Braun, Bilodeau, and Baron.[28] They treat generalization simply as an empirical phenomenon that is manifested by the transfer of a training or learning situation. Their conceptualization entails an explanation no more profound than the following: a learned response to stimulus A will transfer to a previously neutral stimulus B under certain conditions such as similarity of the stimuli, similarity of the environmental cues, and instructional set. Others have viewed generalization as a breakdown in the ability of the organism or subject to *discriminate* between stimuli.[29] Thus, they see generalization not so much as a process but as the failure of a process. This is not, however, a widely held view. A much more prevalent view is that generalization is the result of the learning of a given response that takes place in relationship to a zone of stimuli. Those stimuli closest to the one (S_1) to which the response (L_1) was conditioned have the strongest tendency also to evoke R_1. Stimuli outside the zone cannot evoke R_1. The concept of the stimulus zone has been frequently referred to as a *generalization gradient*. In any case, generalization is an important learning concept and an

[27] J. F. Hall, *The Psychology of Learning* (Philadelphia: J. B. Lippincott Co., 1966).

[28] J. S. Braun, E. A. Bilodeau, and M. R. Baron, "Bidirectional Gradients in the Strength of a Generalized Voluntary Response to Stimuli in a Visual-Spatial Dimension," *Journal of Experimental Psychology*, Vol. 41 (1951), pp. 52–61.

[29] K. S. Lashley and M. Wade, "The Pavlovian Theory of Generalization," *Psychological Review*, Vol. 63 (1946), pp. 72–87.

important variable in consumer behavior. For example, the consumer, in the formation of brand or store images, will generalize from impressions that have a few brand or store cues. Such a process of generalization can work to the marketer's advantage. In other cases, the marketer may want to discourage generalization, in which case efforts are directed toward discriminate learning. Generalization is the organism's innate capacity to economize and organize his perceptions. However, just as organisms learn to economize their behavior by generalizing stimuli, they also learn to respond specifically to separate stimuli. This process is referred to as *discrimination* and technically it is defined as a condition or situation in which a previously generalized response is rewarded in the presence of one cue or stimulus and not rewarded in the presence of a second cue that was previously generalized. In such a case, the formally generalized response will become specific to the cue situation that leads to reward and drops out from the cue situation that does not.

The important points to be derived from the generalization concept are the implications of generalization gradients upon product substitution and product discrimination. To illustrate, let us revert to the cue-response-reinforcement concepts presented earlier. Expectations depend upon a pattern of cues; these cues in turn direct the response, and reinforcement strengthens the pattern of cues in the sense that this cue pattern will tend to elicit the same response in the future. This process of reinforcement, however, strengthens not only the tendency for that pattern of cues to elicit that response but also the tendency for similar patterns of cues to elicit the same response. Small changes in marketers' cue patterns from one product to another may be enough to cause changes in expectations and changed responses leading to the purchase of another brand. Therefore it would seem advisable for the seller to have a pattern of cues unlike that of his competitors so that the expectation associated with his product will not be generalized to include the brands of his competition. The seller wishes to maintain discrimination toward his product, discrimination being the consumer's preference for his product above all others. This discrimination will persist as long as the individual is rewarded in response to this brand's pattern of cues while he is not rewarded or rewarded less by the response to another brand.

EXTINCTION. Consumers are not automatons and they do not remain transfixed or locked in to a perpetual pattern of S-R reflexes. Instead they forget or unlearn or, put another way, they are constantly learning new habits that they add to their repertoire and response tendencies. Responses that are not reinforced tend to become extinct; that is, they are seldom or no longer manifested. Extinction, therefore, is explained most simply as the progressive decrement in response tendency under conditions of nonreinforcement. Response and response tendencies tend to persist even in the face of nonreinforcement. Such a condition is usually attributed to several factors.

1. The length and amount of prior enforcement.
2. The extent of the motive or goal sought; that is, the strength of the drive during extinction.
3. The amount of effort involved in performing the response.
4. The schedule with which reinforcement was administered during the learning period.[30]

Extinction is therefore closely related to reinforcement and the degree of satisfaction obtained by the subject in relation to reinforced responses. Responses do not necessarily have to be reinforced to remain active and dominant. As a matter of fact, animal studies support the contention that partial and intermittent reinforcement are more effective in preventing extinction than continuous reinforcement.[31] (See Figure 9-1.)

Responses once learned, however, do appear to manifest a tendency to persist and to resist the extinction mode. This has important implications for consumer behavior in several dimensions. Most importantly, it affects the consumer's resistance to attitude change, it

Figure 9-1

Cumulative Extinction Curves
After Partial and Continuous Reinforcement

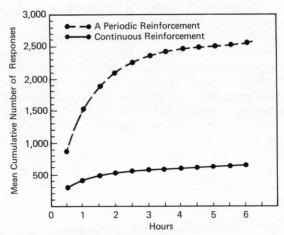

Source: W. O. Jenkins, H. McFann, and F. L. Clayton, "A Methodological Study of Extinction Following Aperiodic and Continuous Reinforcements," *Journal of Comparative Physiological Psychology,* Vol. 43 (1950), pp. 155–167.

[30] Marvin E. Shaw and Phillip R. Costanzo, *Theories of Social Psychology* (New York: McGraw-Hill Book Company, 1970), p. 37.

[31] See W. O. Jenkins and J. C. Stanley, "Partial Reinforcement: A Review and Critique," *Psychological Bulletin,* Vol. 47 (1950), pp. 193–234.

affects the consumer's extinctions of first impressions in person perception, and, finally, it affects the rate with which the consumer's entire cognitive and perceptual set can be restructured and reorganized. Nonetheless, consumers do forget and response tendencies tend to become extinct relatively rapidly. Learning and memory do decay over time and this decay or extinction of learning is usually shown as an exponential type of function.[32] Extinction in consumer learning is attributable to many factors. Consumers become satiated with stimuli; that is, standardized and repetitive cues tend to become in themselves rather boring. Second, responses, regardless sometimes of the extent and degree of reinforcement, tend to become less satisfying over time. Thus the restless, searching, and seeking nature of consumer behavior —the desire for variety and the nearly instinctive nature of some motives such as curiosity and exploration virtually assure a given amount of extinction in consumer learning experiences.

Concept Formation and Problem Solving as Learning Processes

Having established sufficient background, we can move now to a somewhat more complex treatment of learning processes and especially the learning processes that appear to be more directly related to consumers' learning activities. Concept formation and problem solving are cognitive learning processes. They are interrelated in the sense that consumers learn concepts and through the use of these concepts, they learn to solve problems. Concept learning is related to both generalization and discrimination. Without the capacity both to generalize and to discriminate, concept learning would be virtually impossible.

THE MEANING OF CONCEPT LEARNING

Concepts are formed when an individual perceives that two objects or qualities can be put in the same class.[33] This statement is a recognition that in any conceptual task, a given response will be correct for more than one stimulus. To a great extent what was said about discrimination learning and generalization in general applies to concept learning. Most significantly, stimulus coding is central to concept formation and identification. Once the subject starts responding to

---

[32] For more related to the concept of exponential decay of learning and its impact on promotional efforts, see Kristian S. Palda, *The Measurement of Cumulative Advertising Effects* (Englewood Cliffs, N.J.: Prentice-Hall, Inc., 1964).

[33] For a discussion of concept formation, see the following: Hugh V. Perkins, *Human Development and Learning* (Belmont, Calif.: Wadsworth Publishing, Inc., 1969), p. 405–407; Walter Kintsch, *Learning, Memory, and Conceptual Processes*, (New York: John Wiley & Sons, Inc., 1970), pp. 344–372; and Roger L. Dominowski, "Problem Solving and Concept Attainment," *Learning: Interactions,* Melvin H. Marx, ed. (New York: Macmillan Publishing Co., Inc., 1970), pp. 123–194.

the relevant stimulus dimension, the problem is moving toward solution. Concept formation may, therefore, be considered primarily as a problem of selecting the right stimulus dimension. To put all this in some sort of perspective, let us say that problem solving is a special kind of learning and that concept attainment and formation is a special form of problem solving.[34]

Concept formation is a fundamental learning process. It enables subjects, as in the case of consumers, to recognize or understand "sameness in difference." For example, a given pair of trousers is blue; another pair is also blue but a different shade. Both are trousers and both are blue. Consumers engage in considerable abstract thinking because of their ability to recognize and form concepts. Concept formation, as you would begin to sense, is closely related to perceptual processes, especially to the extent that subjects categorize information and fix in their minds conceptual models of quality, style, appropriate brands, acceptable stores, ideal sales personality types, and so on. All these processes relate to concept formation and utilization. Some theorists have argued that subjects vary in the way in which they categorize stimuli and thus form concepts. Some subjects are broad categorizers and others, narrow. These tendencies are said to be related to such factors as personality and cognitive style.[35] Subjects who are broad categorizers tend to assimilate or level stimuli and those who are narrow categorizers tend to sharpen or contrast stimuli. Such cognitive styles are most likely related to the ways in which the subjects process information.

One researcher has posited that wide or broad categorizers would be more likely to innovate and try new products than would narrow categorizers. Although his findings are not to be construed as determinate, sufficient support for his hypothesis suggests that terms of breadth of categorization and willingness to try new products are more than casually related in cognitive style.[36]

We begin learning concepts at a very early age and we continue to acquire concepts throughout our lifetime. Our concept attainment is facilitated by two important criteria: (1) common attributes and (2) sorting rules. The common attributes approach to concept formation involves assigning responses to standardized stimuli. Thus a concept is said to exist when the subject makes the same response to different stimuli having some attribute or combination of attributes in common. Such an approach to concept attainment is characterized by a multistage associative description.

The sorting rule approach states that when a subject learns a concept, he learns a decision rule for sorting stimuli into categories. Bruner,

[34] Dominowski, op. cit., p. 109.

[35] Riley W. Gardner, "Cognitive Styles in Categorizing," *Journal of Personality,* Vol. 22 (December 1953), pp. 214–233.

[36] Donald T. Popielarz, "An Exploration of Perceived Risk and Willingness to Buy New Products," *Journal of Marketing Research,* Vol. 4 (November 1967), pp. 368–372.

Goodnaw, and Austin have emphasized this approach.[37] The important point of this emphasis is that concept attainment is systematic, yet need not be based on common attributes. The sorting rule approach places a somewhat greater emphasis on transfer of the rule to new stimuli and includes a greater number of possible concepts.

CONCEPT LEARNING AND PROBLEM SOLVING

A very important point is that concept learning is integrally related to problem solving. Our concepts related to mathematics and language are the key tools or building blocks for solving many problems. As our concept attainment becomes greater and as our inventory and understanding of concepts increase, so too does our ability to solve problems.

We have repeatedly emphasized the problem-solving approach to consumer learning throughout this text. Such an approach emphasizes the role of understanding and insight in complex goal-striving behavior. Such an approach necessarily stresses the role of seeing through the problem, through what might be called implicit thinking, using high-level cognitive processes. The point is that although much consumer behavior is operant in nature and thus involves considerable trial-and-error experience, it still involves a considerable understanding of the relationships involved in the particular situation.

Recall that a problem exists when a goal is being sought and uncertainty exists as to the best way for reaching the goal. Consumer problems can be broadly categorized as falling into two main types: (1) insight problems and (2) search problems.

INSIGHT PROBLEMS. Insight problems were originally introduced by Gestalt psychologists and, as might by imagined, they are usually characterized in perceptual terms. Such problems would seem, however, to be an important class of consumer problem specifically because of their perceptual nature. An insight problem exists because of faulty or incorrect perception. The solution, therefore, requires changing one's perception of the situation. Such problems ordinarily involve manipulations of certain objects, concepts, or constructs in the environment or the psychological field of the consumer. All the relevant and necessary ingredients for the problem solution are available. All that is required is that the subject, via perceptual processes, see the proper relationship among the problem elements.

SEARCH PROBLEMS. Search problems are characterized by their ambiguous nature. The goal object sought or the various ways of attaining the goal are as yet unknown. Such factors constitute the problem solution. In search problems, the consumer must locate and evaluate one or more of a specified number of alternatives. Search problems

---

[37] J. S. Bruner, J. J. Goodnaw, and G. A. Austin, *A Study of Thinking* (New York: John Wiley & Sons, Inc., 1956).

are usually characterized by a large amount of both covert and overt search activities. Overt search activities would include visiting stores or trading centers and examining and evaluating goods directly. Covert search involves the vicarious examination and evaluation of goods via information processed by secondary information sources and neutral or independent primary sources such as friends, peers, neighbors, or other referents.

Both insight learning and problem solving are tasks that require the consumer-learner to apply some principle in selecting from among a number of possible responses those that will lead to a desired goal.[38] Problem solving requires the learner to identify important cues. In problem solving, understanding the nature of the task is of critical importance, and in the usual problem situation success in achieving a solution depends on the ability to use abstract concepts.

PROBLEM SOLVING AND KINDS OF THINKING

Our earlier definition of problem solving, although adequate, still leaves something to be desired. We often have to distinguish between problems that are presented or given and problems that are to be discovered or identified. In some situations, the problem is known and there is some specified procedure that, if followed, will result in a solution. At other times, however, the problem is undefined or unstructured and there may be no established way of attacking it. "Given a budget of $35.00, buy the necessary food requirements for a family of five" calls for different problem-solving behavior than "Give some reasonable explanation for the fact that you have never purchased an automatic washer and dryer." According to Guilford, problems like the first of these examples arouse *convergent thinking* processes.[39] Convergent thinking is such that we arrive at answers or solutions when we engage in evaluation through the use of known rules and information. Problems of the second type call for *divergent thinking*, that is, for thinking that is less determined by knowledge specifically related to the problem of established rules and procedures. In divergent thinking, there is no single or correct answer; instead, the solution may consist of a variety of explanations applicable to a universal solution.

Consumer behavior involves both convergent and divergent thinking. However, the consumer's emphasis on learning solutions to problems, rather than describing problems or seeking answers to problems, may result in the assumption that solutions exist for all problems; thus, if he wishes to become an efficient consumer (and so an efficient problem solver), his task is to learn solutions. Research also suggests, however, that our performance in problem solving that involves divergent thinking can be improved by training and experience.[40] Much more

---

[38] Jones, op. cit., p. 147.

[39] J. P. Guilford, "Three Faces of Intellect," *American Psychologist*, Vol. 14 (August 1959), pp. 469–479.

[40] I. Maltzman et al., "Experimental Studies in the Training of Originality," *Psychological Monographs*, Vol. 74 (1960), pp. 39–45.

creativity and originality in consumer behavior, as well as less dependence by the consumer on marketer-controlled sources of information, could be attained if consumers would avail themselves of the stimulation and experience that leads to more prevalent divergent thinking or creative problem-solving.

ALTERNATIVE WAYS OF VIEWING PROBLEM SOLVING

Problem-solving behavior, regardless of whether it involves divergent or convergent thinking, has usually been viewed as involving either (1) the learning of sets or what, earlier, we called concepts or (2) transfer of learning.

Most of us become more adept at solving problems as we become more experienced with a number of different problems. And instead of making our consumer choices on the basis of some simple principle such as "always choose the bigger package," we come over time to learn to operate on the basis of higher-order principles such as price per ounce, quality, attractiveness of product, and so forth—principles that are applicable to a variety of problems.[41] We become less stimulus bound, and we develop such rules of thumb as "Shift your choice if your first choice is unsuccessful," or "Discover the relevant stimulus dimension or gradient," that is, "determine whether it is appropriate to respond to size, color, position, rank, and so on."[42] Such an approach is characterized as *learning sets* or *concept learning*. The other approach to problem solving is referred to as *transfer of learning*.

Schulz argues that there are no problems except when transfer from previous learning is incomplete or negative.[43] His argument is that where there is insufficient transfer from previous experience, the individual does not know exactly how to respond. He has, therefore, encountered a problem. Where transfer is perfect, the person is not confronted with a problem. The subject simply makes the previously acquired response that the situation calls for. This approach is weak, however, in that it does not account for the acquisition of true insight or novel responses. What is significant is that we regard all problems as situations for which the individual's previous experience has not provided him with a ready response. It probably makes little difference which model (sets or transfers) guides our thinking about consumer learning; both are useful ways of thinking about problem solving.

VARIABLES AFFECTING PROBLEM SOLVING

Gagné has suggested that the independent variables in any problem-solving situation can be considered under two main headings: (1) conditions within the learner and (2) conditions in the problem

---

[41] R. M. Gagné, "Problem Solving," in *Categories of Human Learning*, A. W. Melton, ed. (New York: Academic Press, Inc., 1964), p. 311.

[42] Jones, op. cit., p. 163.

[43] R. W. Schulz, "Problem Solving Behavior and Transfer," *Harvard Educational Review*, Vol. 46 (Winter 1960), pp. 61–77.

situation.[44] We shall mention a few of the factors falling under each of these headings, primarily to emphasize the independent nature of learning from other behavioral situations and to demonstrate the full range and complexity of problem-solving–learning situations.

Conditions within the learner include such factors as motivation, intelligence, the effects of previous experience, and the presence or absence of problem-solving perceptual sets. It must be pointed out that these factors alone make for a high degree of idiosyncratic behavior in consumer learning. Thus different learners show wide variations in their ability to solve similar problems, and different subjects are, therefore, likely to manifest a wide range and divergent array of responses and response tendencies.

Conditions in the problem situation include the organization of the problem, the manner in which it is presented, and the direction and focus given the problem solver. No two consumers are likely to view any consumer-oriented problem in exactly the same way. Given individual differences, problems, no matter how similar, are almost invariably inclined to be perceived differently. What he knows about the problem (cognitions), how he views and interprets it (perceptions), and what he believes and feels about it (images) are likely to mean that for each person it is truly a unique problem.

As has been pointed out, success in problem solving is more likely if in representing the problem the problem solver uses symbolic processes, propositions, procedures, or images that are already familiar to him. It is probably also helpful if he can organize the task so that he has to recall only a minimum number of separate principles or items of information, because, as Gagné has commented, "The component principles . . . must in some sense be 'held in mind' all at once or be reactivated at will in close succession in problem solving."[45] This statement suggests the idea that consumer problem-solving is concerned with filling the gaps or doing what others have called "going beyond the information given."[46]

A Summary of Concepts Related to Problem Solving

Essentially, a person tries from infancy to construct for himself a meaningful and patterned inventory of concepts that will increase the correspondence between what he perceives in the environment around him and what this environment turns out to be when he acts within it to experience some consequences and to solve life's problems.

To facilitate his operation and behavior in this context, the subject

---

[44] Gagné, op. cit., pp. 162–164.

[45] Ibid., p. 162.

[46] F. C. Bartlett, *Thinking, An Experimental and Societal Study* (New York: Basic Books, 1958); and J. S. Bruner et al., "Going Beyond the Information Given," in *Contemporary Approaches to Cognition* (Cambridge, Mass.: Harvard University Press, 1957).

learns a series of concepts that give him a set of instrumental tools for enabling him to determine what is significant.[47] The following are a representative sample of these concepts.

1. *Concepts concerning the significance of objects.* The objects in the world around us have the meaning they do because we attribute to them certain characteristics, sizes, shapes, and properties. We learn to esteem goods not only as ends or for their functional qualities but as means or as social and economic symbols that are extensions of ourselves.

2. *Concepts concerning the significance of people.* We must learn to guess and understand the purposes of other people, and in the process we must realize that their purposes are just as real as any physical characteristic of objects. We learn concepts and make assumptions about the roles we play, the roles of significant others, their vocations, their status, and their social-class influences. All these concepts are likely to affect our decision processes.

3. *Concepts concerning the significance of sequential happenings.* Things and events keep moving and we learn to look for and interpret causal events. Christmas is usually followed by January sales events. A period of prolonged inflation means rising prices. A cold spring often means poor Easter sales and resultant markdowns. Weddings mean the necessity of buying gifts. Summer means planning for vacations and vacations, in turn, mean special wardrobes and other special-purpose items such as fishing or camping gear.

4. *Concepts concerning the significance of action.* All of us eventually learn, sometimes gradually, sometimes suddenly, what the probable significance of certain of our actions will be. Shopping, we learn, often leads to purchase. Purchase, of course, leads to satisfaction but it also often has dysfunctional effects. We spend time, energy, and money. Impulsive behavior, we learn, can lead to increased dissonance and the search for information can be dissonance reducing.

5. *Concepts concerning temporal and spatial significances.* We must learn the significance of different time and space measurements and the different values placed upon units of time and space. We must learn the significance of the "here and now" context of many of our decisions. We learn to forego and postpone, and we learn the satisfaction of immediate consumption.

6. *Concepts regarding the significance of values.* We always have alternatives. Whether aware of it or not, we weigh alternative courses of action in terms of the value significances they are likely to have for us. Inevitably we make the evaluation among various alternatives on the basis of the relative probability that each possible course of action will lead to the desired consequences or will produce the desired or valued goal object.

---

[47] Adapted from Hadley Cantril, "Transactional Inquiry Concerning Mind," in *Theories of the Mind,* Jordan Scher, ed. (Glencoe, Ill.: The Free Press, 1962), pp. 330–354.

Social Learning and Consumer Behavior

There are at least two contexts in which learning takes place. The first of these can be labeled simply the physical context. The physical context includes the material dimensions of the field of behavior. The other context in which learning takes place is the social context. The social context refers to the actual or implied presence and participation of others in the learning situation. Because, as we have emphasized so repeatedly, consumer behavior is social behavior, consumer learning must, of necessity, involve a great deal of social learning; that is, consumer learning, or at least a great part of it, must transpire within the social context.

Social context factors in consumer learning are numerous, but most frequently they are defined in terms of the roles of the others involved in the learning situation and the relationships and the degree of participation that exists between the consumer learner and the significant others. Both behaviorists and cognitivists recognize the important role of socialization and social influence in learning situations. In relation to operant learners, it has been observed that significant others tend to reinforce choices and thus modify response tendencies.[48] A consumer's behavior is gradually shaped by successive approximations that bring it to a level of maximum efficiency and social approval. Some degree of social facilitation or social participation is almost always involved in consumer learning.[49] This social participation manifests itself in two principal ways: (1) learning through the observation of the behavior and consequences of the behavior of others and (2) learning through the interactive and interdependent nature of rewards for the participants.

We shall examine first of all several models of learning that relate to (1) above, and then we shall treat briefly a few concepts and ideas that relate to (2).

TOLMAN'S PURPOSIVE BEHAVIORISM

An interesting link between objective behaviorism and the more subjective cognitivist approach to learning was forged by Edward Chance Tolman. This link has also become a rather important connection between physical and social learning. Tolman contended that individuals respond to many stimuli and that many of the cues that affect behavior are social in orientation.[50] He believed that individuals reacted not simply to stimuli but to beliefs, attitudes, and values and that behavior was goal striving and, hence, "purposive." One of the dis-

[48] B. F. Skinner, *Science and Human Behavior* (New York: Macmillan Publishing Co., Inc., 1953).

[49] See Jagdish Sheth, "How Adults Learn Brand Preference," *Journal of Advertising Research*, Vol. 8, No. 3 (September 1968) pp. 25–36.

[50] Edward Chance Tolman, *Purposive Behavior in Animals and Men* (New York: Appleton-Century-Crofts, 1932).

tinguishing characteristics of Tolman's theory was his concern with the effect of external social stimuli on behavior. Tolman emphasized the relation of behavior to goals and he underscored the role and importance of social goal-striving activity. Furthermore, Tolman was one of the first behaviorists to recognize the importance of cognitions. Cognitions, he reasoned, take the form, "If I do this, I will get that." He argued that individuals form many kinds of cognitions about the way the environment is structured, about things that go together, about what alternatives or paths lead to what goals. Tolman's theory also emphasized learning the location of goals—once an individual has learned where a given kind of reward is located, he can often get to that location by means other than those originally used. Tolman's psychology had important social and human orientations, even though as a cognitivist he experimented more with animals than with human subjects.

Tolman is largely remembered for his *sign-Gestalt-expectation* concept. This concept relates to the individual's expectation that the world is organized in certain ways, that certain behavior and social interaction leads to certain results and consequences. The inclusion of the word *sign* indicates that these expectations are mainly about stimuli that are signs of certain things, rather than simply physical responses. The word *gestalt* emphasizes that the signs must be considered in context, that is, that the whole pattern of stimulation is important. Tolman's work, in part at least, has been greatly responsible for several subsequent theories of social behavior and social learning.

MILLER AND DOLLARD'S MECHANISM OF IMITATION

Miller and Dollard have predicated a theory of social learning concerning imitation upon a Hullian type of learning model. Hullian models involve both association and reinforcement. The principal mechanisms of Hullian learning models are drive, cue, reinforcement, and reward, which have been previously discussed. The basic assumption of Miller and Dollard is that all forms of human behavior are learned: to comprehend complexity of behavior "one must know the psychological principles involved in its learning and the social conditions under which this learning took place."[51] Learning via imitation constitutes the basic principle of this approach, which suggests a formidable model for consumer behavior and learning. According to Miller and Dollard, most or all imitative behavior can be explained by three mechanisms: *same behavior, matched-dependent behavior,* and *copying.*

SAME BEHAVIOR. Same behavior occurs when two individuals respond to independent stimulation by the same cue after each has learned to make the appropriate response himself. Examples of this

---

[51] N. E. Miller and J. Dollard, *Social Learning and Imitation* (New Haven, Conn.: Yale University Press, 1941), p. 1.

process are numerous: for instance, two women waiting in line in a department store to gain access to a fitting room, or two subjects reading a copy of *Consumer Reports* because they are both searching for information. Same behavior may result from imitation but not necessarily.

MATCHED-DEPENDENT BEHAVIOR. This kind of behavior is often characteristic of two-party interactions in which one of the parties is older and more socially integrated and self-assertive. For example, a neighbor may *match* the behavior of and be *dependent* upon a friend or neighbor who is perceived as a key influence or an opinion leader. Consumer behavior is replete with stories of matched-dependent behavior. Fashion adoption, the emulation of fads, the diffusion of innovations such as color television in a given neighborhood, and so forth are all examples of matched-dependent behavior.

Matched-dependent behavior has been divided into four categories, which are here listed and described briefly.

1. *Common goal but differing responses.* In this case both imitator and leader seek the same general goal or objective but their responses are different. The drive to imitate will be aroused in an individual when he is confronted with another's response to a familiar and formerly pleasant cue situation to which his own response is blocked.

2. *Secondary reward.* In the case of secondary reward the imitator gains satisfaction (secondary reward) from hearing or seeing the response of another and he, therefore, matches that response.

3. *Testing.* In this situation the leader acts instrumentally by testing the viability of a given response for the imitator. If the leader's response is successful, the imitator will match it. The significance of this case is that the successful responses of the leader acquire cue value distinctiveness and encourage imitation.

4. *Secondary drives of imitation and rivalry.* Observing the rewarded responses of a leader generates a drive to imitate. In some cases, the follower is dependent upon the cues set up by the leader for the initiation of a response sequence. However, having learned the response sequence, he may seek to complete it with greater speed than the leader in order to be the first rewarded. This leads to the generalization that imitation, once established, will lead to rivalry between leader and imitator when the availability of rewards is limited.

COPYING. Copying is viewed as a more complex form of imitation than matched-dependent behavior. In both copying and matched-dependent behavior, the imitator relates his responses to cues derived from the responses of the model, but in copying, the subject responds to cues produced by his own responses as well as those of the model.

An excessive tendency either to copy or to imitate usually indicates that these drives may have components of anxiety, stress, and lack of identity or self-awareness. However, some amounts of imitation and copying are a normal pattern of behavior and can be attributed to socialization processes, even perhaps the "herd extinct."[52]

Bandura's Vicarious Process Theory of Imitation

Bandura, along with his associate, Walters, has generated an intriguing theory of imitation and social learning.[53] Their major proposition is that imitation is a form of associative learning. The basic concept involved is the contiguous relationship between the stimuli in the model's environment and his response to them. The object of the observer's learning is this contiguous relationship. Learning is facilitated simply by observation (hence the term *vicarious*) of the model's response, whether or not reinforcement results from it. Such an approach would appear characteristic of much consumer learning.

Bandura has described his theory as a mediational-stimulus-contiguity theory. According to this approach, "during the period of exposure modeling stimuli elicit in observing subjects configurations and sequences of sensory experiences which, on the basis of past associations, become centrally integrated and structured into perceptual responses."[54] Bandura contends that an individual's response to cues in a stimulus field leads to internalized imagined responses in the observer that can be retrieved when the observer is placed in a behavior field. Therefore a consumer, without being rewarded or without even having responded, has the capacity to integrate the cue connections in a model's (key influential or significant other) responses and thereby becomes able to imitate the model's response.

Bandura suggested that the exposure to models leads to three general effects in the observer. These are (1) *modeling effects,* (2) *inhibitory and disinhibitory effects,* and (3) *facilitation effects.*

MODELING EFFECTS

Modeling effects result when an observer acquires new response patterns through observing a model perform highly novel responses. Modeling effects are a kind of perceptual learning whereby the subject extracts information from the model's social environment. This information is used to alter perceptual structure and thus response tendencies.

---

[52] W. Trotter, *Instincts of the Herd in War and Peace* (New York: Macmillan Publishing Co., Inc., 1917).

[53] See A. Bandura, "Social Learning Through Imitation," *Nebraska Symposium on Motivation,* M. R. Jones, ed. (Lincoln, Neb.: University of Nebraska Press, 1962), pp. 211–269; and A. Bandura and R. H. Walters, *Social Learning and Personality Development* (New York: Holt, Rinehart & Winston, Inc., 1963).

[54] Bandura and Walters, op. cit., p. 10.

INHIBITORY AND DISINHIBITORY EFFECTS

Inhibitory effects implies that a subject modifies his behavior when observing a model engaged in activities containing aversive responses. Conversely, disinhibitory effects result when the subject observes a model engaging in either rewarded or unpunished socially unacceptable responses. These responses thus lead to increments in the same class of behavior or a general increase in socially disapproved behavior. Acts that are perceived as undesirable, aversive, or even repugnant generate inhibitory effects. Yet acts that at one time may have been viewed as socially undesirable (short dress lengths or bare breasts) may have a disinhibitory effect if a model manifests such behavior and it is rewarded or not punished.

FACILITATION EFFECTS

The facilitation effects of exposure to and association with models occur when the model's responses serve as discriminative stimuli for the observer. What this means is that the behavior of a model has a facilitative effect on similar behavior of the observer, specifically because it occasions consequent reinforcement and, hence, becomes distinctive as a cue. Facilitation effects remind us of the suggestible nature of consumers. The observation of given consumer behavior would serve to remind the subject that he, too, might engage in such activity. In many instances, novel responses are not involved; instead the response tendencies already are a part of the repertoire of the subject. Such behavior is characterized by much reminder advertising involving models and testimonials that admonish us to drink Cokes, smoke Marlboro cigarettes, and use Crest toothpaste or Listerine. We may already have done all these things, but the association and exposure may suggest to us the desirability of doing them again.

Bandura's theory of social learning via imitation involves a special kind of association, namely, vicarious association. His theories have important implications in terms of both motivation and learning. Motivation is involved to the extent that social cues that signal the emotional arousal of a model can lead to emotion-provoking properties in the observer. Bandura called this phenomenon *vicarious emotional arousal.*

This vicarious emotional arousal can lead to *vicarious classical conditioning* or learning if those stimuli that aroused emotional reactions in the model and the observer are associated with previously neutral stimuli. The consequence is that the neutral stimuli gain the power to elicit the emotional-social response in both the model and the observer.

Thus social learning is important to consumer behavior and consumer learning. Theories of social learning, especially imitation, have not been tested in the field of consumer behavior. However, their existence suggests a rich source of conceptual data that lends itself to further research and analysis in this area.

We have rather exhaustively examined a vast array of learning literature and theories. Our conclusions can be summarized rather briefly, yet the full implication of our conclusions has yet to be specified and examined, namely, that consumers learn adaptive behavior and that this adaptive behavior is an integral part of consumer behavior in general. Consumers are cognitive creatures and, unlike the rat in the maze, they do remain literally at times "buried in thought" as they proceed to seek goals, solve problems, learn concepts, and modify response tendencies. Consumer learning can seldom be characterized or explained at the reflex level. Consumer learning is often trial and error, but it is also purposeful and laden with cognitive implications. Consumers learn to discriminate among different drives or goals, and this learning makes their behavior highly specific. Consumers learn to seek certain goals rather than others when experiencing a certain drive. Consumers learn that a situation is equivalent to reward or punishment or that different alternatives lead to greater satisfactions than others. Consumers learn that actions lead to other actions and that certain learned responses can lead to the attainment of more distant physical, social, and psychological goals.

In the next chapter we shall examine another important cognitive determinant of consumer behavior, namely, the acquisition and measurement of attitudes.

Questions for Study, Reflection, and Review

1 Distinguish between the different levels of human response complexity and the nature of the learning involved in each.

2 Describe stimulus-response learning and discuss its applicability to consumer decision processes.

3 Discuss the significance of the environment in operant learning.

4 Distinguish between the cognitive approach to learning and the behaviorist approach.

5 Contrast the view of learning as a function of reinforcement with the view of learning as a function of association.

6 Identify the functions of reinforcement in consumer behavior.

7 Distinguish between the process of generalization and the process of discrimination.

8 Describe the process of concept formation and its relationship to learning.

9 Discuss the kinds of variables that affect consumer problem-solving.

10 Discuss the nature of the social context within which learning occurs.

10

Attitudes:
Structure, Function,
and Measurement

Introduction

The concept of attitudes is perhaps the most distinctive, important, and, therefore, indispensable concept in contemporary behavioral and social science. The importance and role of attitudes is stressed as a central feature in psychology, sociology, and related disciplines in business management and administration. Almost everyone, regardless of the nature of their occupation or industry, is concerned with the concept of attitudes. The politician and the political scientist are interested in attitudes regarding taxation, housing, urban renewal, and voter appeal. Managers are interested in employees' attitudes as they might affect morale and productivity. Managers are also interested from the marketing point of view in consumers' attitudes regarding the company's products and in competitors' attitudes as they reflect market and product intentions. Those responsible for law enforcement are concerned with the citizens' attitudes regarding crime and how these attitudes might affect subsequent behavior in the event of a riot or some form of civil disobedience. Attitudes are, therefore, deemed an important variable in as well as an indicator of behavior in nearly every walk of life: religious, governmental, judiciary, administrative, and commercial.

All those interested in describing, understanding, and predicting behavior are readily interested in gaining new insight into the importance, role, and measurement of attitudes. Consumer behaviorists are certainly no exception.

Attitudes play an important role in consumer behavior and marketing for many reasons, foremost of which is that attitudes are a special kind of cognition. We have earlier defined cognitions as bits of knowledge or information. Cognitions are what we know or what we believe. The concept of cognitions, therefore, includes knowledge, beliefs, values, opinions, images, and *attitudes*.[1] Throughout our treatment, a cognitive theory of behavior has been underlined. This theory, in its most succinct and compact form, states that what a person knows affects his behavior. This statement suggests that behavior is a function of cognition or knowledge. Now, if attitudes are a special set of cognitions, then it would follow that behavior is a function of attitudes. To a great extent this is a widely adopted and pervasive theory of social behavior and, considering the attention and emphasis placed upon attitudes by marketers and consumer psychologists, it is no less an important theory of consumer behavior. Like all theories, it has its shortcomings and much research and testing remains to be done. Nonetheless, attitude is strongly regarded by many to be an important variable and determinant of consumer behavior.[2] Unfortunately, too many view attitudes in a reductive-functional sense as the all-important variable or determinant of behavior. Our treatment will be less restrictive.

Few would deny that attitudes are one of the major influences on behavior. In many ways attitudes are the distillation of one's experiences. A common understanding regarding behavior is that we incorporate experience or perceptual knowledge as feedback into our cognitive structure or psychological field, and this information or knowledge becomes structured and integrated to form cognitions or attitudes. Hence, as a result of experience we learn, and from learning we form attitudes that condition or predispose our reactions to similar stimuli in a subsequent situation.

Hopefully, the reader is now well prepared to treat the subject of attitude at this juncture because considerable groundwork has purposely been laid in previous chapters. Attitudes are formed in the interest of one's goals and objectives, and therefore our discussion of motivation and motivational processes has been a prelude to our treatment of attitudes. Attitudes are wrought out of the informational processing activities of consumers, and therefore one's understanding of perception ought to lead one to a better understanding of attitude and attitude formation. Finally, attitudes are a learned construct; they

---

[1] The reader is urged at this time to recall and perhaps to reread the material presented in Chapter 5.

[2] The reader is reminded once again that attitudes play a central role in nearly all the major models of consumer behavior. See Chapter 4 for a review and discussion of several of these models.

are not inborn, and therefore an appreciation of learning and the various approaches to learning facilitates one's understanding of attitudes.

In this chapter we shall examine in considerable comprehensive detail the construct of attitude. Our major focus will center around the nature, scope, and role of attitudes in influencing behavior. Furthermore, we shall explore the functional significance of attitudes as well as their structural qualities. Most importantly, however, our treatment will focus upon the relationship between attitudes and behavior, because in many respects this is the crux of the issue. Our treatment will conclude with a survey of approaches and methods of attitude measurement and will look briefly at some newer approaches and points of view regarding the general concept of attitude and its viability as a determinant and predictor of behavior.

The Nature and Meaning of Attitudes

Almost everyone has a relatively good intuitive understanding of what attitudes are. We are often asked, "How do you feel about product X?" or "How do you feel about the four-day week? or door-to-door solicitation? or night hours in retail stores?" We understand from these questions that our attitudes are being sought. The inquiries are intended to reveal for assessment our mental set or our proclivity to respond in a certain way when a given situation or object is presented to us. Attitudes, then, are most commonly thought of as dispositions to act.

There are about as many definitions of attitudes as there are writers and theorists on the subject. Let us look at a selected number of definitions.

> Attitudes are predispositions to behave in specific ways to specific stimuli.[3]

> Attitudes refer to the stands the individual upholds and cherishes about objects, issues, persons, groups, or institutions.[4]

> Attitudes are learned predispositions to respond to an object or class of objects in a consistently favorable or unfavorable way.[5]

> Attitudes are learned predispositions to respond. Attitudes . . . are learned and relatively enduring organizations of beliefs about an object or situation disposing a person toward some favored response.[6]

---

[3] Irving Crespi, *Attitude Research*, Marketing Research Technique Series No. 7 (Chicago: American Marketing Association, 1965).

[4] Carolyn W. Sherif, Muzafer Sherif, and Roger Nebergall, *Attitude and Attitude Change* (Philadelphia: W. B. Saunders Company, 1965), p. 4.

[5] Gordon W. Allport, "Attitudes," in *A Handbook of Social Psychology*, C. A. Murchinson, ed. (Worchester, Mass.: Clark University Press, 1935), pp. 798–844.

[6] Milton Rokeach, *Beliefs, Attitudes, and Values* (San Francisco: Jossey-Bass, 1968), p. 112.

It is not our intention to exhaust the reader by presenting him with an overly long list of definitions. These have been presented for several reasons. First, they are generally illustrative of the way attitudes are typically and commonly defined. Second, they reveal to some extent something about the general nature of attitudes in terms of both their structural properties and their functional attributes.

In many discussions of attitudes, it is fashionable to present a long list of definitions; the author then concludes by discarding these and supplying his own. We shall resist this temptation primarily because, of the definitions offered above, almost any one is sufficient for defining attitudes.

Several relevant and salient attributes of attitudes can be deduced from the definitions given. Attitudes always suggest a relationship between the person and objects or situations.[7] Attitudes are formed in relationship to identifiable referents. Several definitions point out that attitudes are learned; they are not innate; we do not come into the world possessing attitudes. Attitudes tend to be value specific, that is, they express values as they relate to specific objects, ideas, or concepts. To illustrate the interdependency between values and attitudes, consider the situation in which an individual might value social recognition and as a result hold a specific attitude toward clothing style. Our attitudes are not temporary or briefly transient states. Instead, they are relatively enduring, patterned predispositions. Attitudes do change but usually not very rapidly. As enduring predispositions, they form a kind of psychological regulatory function.

Attitudes are inferred constructs; that is, we cannot "see" or "touch" attitudes. Instead, researchers infer attitudes from behavior or from stated preferences or intentions.[8]

Finally, one very important characteristic of attitudes is that the relationship between the person and the object or situation that gives impetus to the arousal or development of an attitude is not neutral but has perceptual-motivational and affective properties. We shall explore this condition more fully later. However, the meaning is rather clear. Attitudes are positive or negative perceptual states that affect the way we extract information from the environment. Attitudes are motivation in that they affect the goals and rewards for which people strive; they predispose us to act. Furthermore, attitudes possess affective qualities. They dispose us to like or dislike, to seek or forego, to evaluate as favorable or unfavorable, desirable or undesirable. Thus attitudes have properties that define what is *expected* and what is *desired*. Because attitudes are enduring, they reflect a kind of perceptual constancy that

---

[7] Several of these attributes were suggested to the author by the following work: Carolyn W. and Muzafer Sherif, *Attitude, Ego-Involvement, and Change* (New York: John Wiley & Sons, Inc., 1967), pp. 112–113.

[8] There is a technical difference between concepts and constructs. Concepts are usually defined as a generalized notion. Constructs, on the other hand, are complex images or ideas resulting from a synthesis made in the mind. These technical differences are seldom observed in the literature, however.

we discussed earlier under the concept of *sets*.[9] Attitudes are organizations of beliefs and sentiments, and such organization stresses the idea that attitudes do not exist in nonintegrated isolation so much as they cluster together in patterned hierarchies. Because attitudes implicitly refer to *response,* a motivational aspect is inferred.

We would point out again, as we did in Chapter 5, that attitudes and values, although interrelated, are usually treated as being distinctive. Individuals usually hold many more attitudes than values. A given consumer, it was earlier suggested, has tens of thousands of beliefs, hundreds of attitudes, but perhaps as few as a dozen values. Opinions are normally characterized as being verbalized attitudes.

ATTITUDES AND CONSUMER BEHAVIOR

Our more formal and explicit treatment of attitude to this juncture ought to underscore and reinforce our earlier proposition that attitudes are an important variable in consumer behavior. To the extent that attitudes are perceptual-motivational and affective states influencing behavior and responses, we need to know with clarity and precision how attitudes are formed and changed, what are the component or structural features of attitudes, what are their functional role and importance, and, above all, how they are measured. Evidence continues to be generated that supports the contention that a knowledge of attitudes can be used to predict behavior. Achenbaum, for example, has shown a direct relationship between attitudes and product usage. His studies contend that:

1. The more favorable the attitude, the higher the incidence of product usage.
2. The less favorable the attitude, the lower the incidence of usage.
3. The more unfavorable people are toward a product, the more likely they are to stop using it.
4. The attitudes of people who have never tried a product tend to be distributed around the mean in the shape of a normal distribution.[10]

More and more marketers and consumer psychologists are researching the relationships between attitudes, purchase intentions, brand switching, store loyalty, product acceptance, and self-concepts. The studies are too numerous to list in detail, but examples of such studies are indicative of the interest in and scope of the influence of attitudes on consumer behavior.

[9] Asch considers that attitudes are enduring sets formed by past experience. See Solomon E. Asch, *Social Psychology* (Englewood Cliffs, N.J.: Prentice-Hall, Inc., 1952), p. 585. Also, Edwin P. Hollander, *Principles and Methods of Social Psychology* (New York: Oxford University Press, 1967), p. 115.

[10] Alvin A. Achenbaum, "Knowledge Is a Thing Called Measurement," in *Attitude Research at Sea,* Lee Adler and Irving Crespi, eds. (Chicago: American Marketing Association, 1966), pp. 111–126.

Assael and Day have found attitudes to be effective in explaining variance in market shares among brands.[11]

Jacobsen and Kossoff have explored the relationship between consumers' self-percept (a kind of patterned set of attitudes) and consumer attitudes toward small cars.[12]

Roman has researched the implications of consumers' attitudes toward objects as opposed to their attitudes toward situations.[13]

Mullen has investigated the relevance of the congruity principle as applied to television commercials.[14]

Other researchers have explored the more theoretical implications of attitudes as well as their implications for consumer behavior.[15] Some marketing-oriented researchers have concentrated their efforts on questions of methodology and measurement.[16]

Yet in spite of the demonstrated interest and the extensive research, the construct of attitudes is still not well understood, nor is there unanimous agreement concerning the nature and role of this construct as either an influencer or a predictor of consumer behavior. As our treatment continues, the many causes of this disagreement will become more apparent.

THE STRUCTURAL IMPLICATIONS OF ATTITUDES

Attitudes refer to consistencies or regularities in an individual's thought, feelings, and predispositions to act in a certain manner toward values, objects, or situations. As was mentioned earlier, attitudes are inferred constructs. They cannot be observed or pointed to but are instead complex configurations or ideas resulting from a configuration of the mind. Because they are abstract and cannot be "pointed at" or observed, some writers and psychologists deny their existence and

[11] Henry Assael and George Day, "Attitude and Awareness as Predictors of Market Share," *Journal of Advertising Research,* Vol. 8 (December 1968), pp. 3–10.

[12] Eugene J. Jacobsen and Jerome Kossoff, "Self Percept and Consumer Attitude Toward Small Cars," *Journal of Applied Psychology,* Vol. 47 (August 1963), pp. 242–245.

[13] Hope S. Roman, "Semantic Generalization in Formation of Consumer Attitudes," *Journal of Marketing Research,* Vol. 6 (August 1969), pp. 369–373.

[14] James J. Mullen, "The Congruity Principle and Television Commercials," *Journal of Broadcasting,* Vol. 7 (Winter 1962–1963), pp. 35–42.

[15] G. David Hughes, *Attitude Measurement for Marketing Strategies* (Glenview, Ill.: Scott, Foresman and Company, 1971); also, George S. Day, *Buyer Attitudes and Brand Choice Behavior* (New York: The Free Press, 1970).

[16] William D. Barclay, "The Semantic Differential as an Index of Brand Attitude," *Journal of Advertising Research,* Vol. 4 (March 1964), pp. 30–33; Jon G. Udell, "Can Attitude Measurement Predict Consumer Behavior," *Journal of Marketing,* Vol. 24 (1965), pp. 46–50; and Jagdish Sheth, "Canonical Analysis of Attitude-Behavior Relationship," unpublished paper presented at the TIMS XVIII International Meeting, Washington, D.C., March 21–24, 1971.

influence.[17] One writer has argued that there is no scientific basis for the concept.[18] He sees *attitude* as a mere logical or omnibus term that is devoid of any generic features. He contends that individual attitude studies may be measuring something, but it is not at all established that they are all measuring the same thing.

Blumer's views, however, are not widely regarded. Most schools of psychology and sociology place considerable emphasis on the role of attitudes in behavior. The field of consumer behavior appears overwhelmingly convinced of the conceptual richness of attitudes and attitude research as a means of generating insight into a host of consumer and related marketing problems.

A summary examination of most definitions of attitude reveals readily that the construct consists of several elements. Let us examine several of these alternative views regarding attitude in terms of their structural features or components.

THE ROSENBERG VIEW. Rosenberg has formulated a conception of attitudes that has been widely adopted, and a great part of the research on attitudes has been predicated upon his structural analysis of attitudes. Today, with minor exceptions, attitudes are viewed as possessing three components. Attention to these different aspects of attitudes goes back at least to McDougal and persists in contemporary work.[19] The three components of attitude as delineated by Rosenberg are (1) a cognitive component, (2) an affective component, and (3) a behavior component.[20]

The cognitive component is made up of knowledge, beliefs, values, and images about the object situation, and these are usually elicited by verbal responses. The affective component or response is sometimes inferred from measures of such physiological variations as pupil dilation, eye blink, blood pressure, galvanic responses, or other factors.[21] However, the affective component is more typically inferred from verbal statements of how much like or dislike one feels toward the object of the attitude. In much the same sense, how the individual says he will act (the behavior response or component) toward a given situation is

---

[17] This is especially so in the case of behaviorist psychologists.

[18] See Herbert Blumer, "Attitudes and the Social Act," *Social Problems* (October 1955), pp. 60–61.

[19] W. McDougal, *An Introduction to Social Psychology* (London: Methuen & Co., Ltd., 1908).

[20] Milton J. Rosenberg, "An Analysis of Affective-Cognitive Consistency," in *Attitude Organization and Change*, M. J. Rosenberg, Carl I. Hovland, et al., eds., (New Haven, Conn.: Yale University Press, 1960).

[21] For examples of such research and measurement approaches, see P. D. Bricker and A. Chapanis, "Do Incorrectly Perceived Tachistoscopic Stimuli Convey Some Information?" *Psychological Review*, Vol. 60 (1953), pp. 181–188; and M. Weiner and P. H. Schiller, "Subliminal Perception or Perception of Partial Cues," *Journal of Abnormal and Social Psychology*, Vol. 61 (1960), pp. 124–137.

Figure 10-1

Schematic Conception of Attitudes

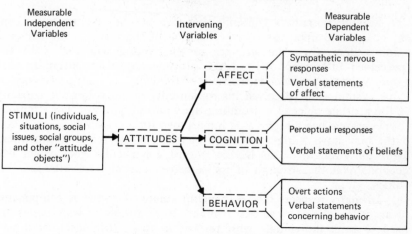

Source: Milton J. Rosenberg, Carl I. Hovland, et al., *Attitude Organization and Change* (New Haven: Yale University Press, 1960), p. 3.

often measured against how he does respond when directly confronted with the situation. The affective component is also often inferred from what the person says he will do in the particular situation. A schematic illustration of Rosenberg's view is presented in Figure 10-1.

The essence of Rosenberg's theory is that by altering attitude we can conceivably bring about three kinds of responses. For example, a persuasive message can lead to more knowledge or altered beliefs, it can change our feelings toward the object, or it may modify our behavior or our response tendencies.

Rosenberg's model placed a heavy emphasis on consistency between the cognitive and the affective elements of attitudes. Therefore, his model has some important implications for attitude change. His principal argument is that the nature and strength of the feelings toward an attitude object are correlated with the beliefs associated with the attitude object.

Another important idea in Rosenberg's theory is contained in the notion of affective-cognitive consistency. If a state of consistency exists between the affective and the cognitive components in regard to an object or situation, then the subject is said to have an attitude toward that value. From this general statement Rosenberg derived the following basic propositions.

When the affective and cognitive components of an attitude are mutually consistent the attitude is in a stable state; when the affective and cognitive components are mutually inconsistent (to a degree that exceeds the individual's present tolerance for such inconsistency) the attitude is in an unstable state and will undergo spontaneous reorganizing activity until such activity eventuates in either (1) the attainment of affective-cognitive consistency or (2) the placing of an "irreconcilable" inconsistency beyond the range of effectiveness.[22]

Finally, Rosenberg contends that if a person's feeling toward an object is based upon the relative position of the value in the personal value system, then the strength of the feeling will vary with the "perceived instrumentality" of the attitude object for attaining that value. Value importance is the rank of the value in one's preference or value system, and perceived instrumentality is the subjective capacity of the attitude object for attaining the value in question. For example, if appearance has a high value importance for a consumer, then a new outfit may have a high perceived instrumentality for that consumer. Thus the strength of his feeling toward a particular goal object will depend upon the strength of its perceived capacity for attaining his values.

In many respects the relationship among the various components of an attitude is so close that it makes little difference which ones are used to rank individuals with respect to their attitudes toward particular objects or situations. In experimental research, one component of a belief is difficult, if not impossible, to isolate and to manipulate independently from a second component. Thus an attitude is often viewed simply as an organization of interrelated beliefs around a common object, with certain aspects of the object being at the focus of attention for some persons and other aspects for other persons. The attitude, therefore, has cognitive and affective properties by virtue of the fact that the several beliefs comprising it have cognitive and affective properties that interact and reinforce one another. Space will not permit an exhaustive treatment of all the ramifications of Rosenberg's model or, for that matter, other component or structural models of attitudes.

DEFLEUR AND WESTIE. Defleur and Westie do not necessarily counter the argument of Rosenberg and others regarding the three-component nature of attitudes in terms of cognitive-affective-behavioral responses. Instead, they posit simply that attitudes are made up of two major conceptions. The first are what they call *probability conceptions* and the second are *latent process conceptions.*[23]

Probability conceptions refer to the fact that attitudes are viewed as predispositions to act and that these predispositions can be evaluated in terms of probabilities. For example, earlier it was stated that the more favorable the attitude the higher the incidence of product usage. This statement reflects the probability conception of an attitude. In effect, it states that given a favorable attitude toward a brand there is a reasonably high probability that a consumer might purchase the

[22] Milton J. Rosenberg, op. cit., p. 22.

[23] Melvin Defleur and Frank Westie, "Attitude as a Scientific Concept," *Social Forces* (October 1963), pp. 20–23.

brand. Many of our brand loyalty and brand-switching models have been predicated upon this assumption. Probability conceptions acknowledge that favorable attitudes toward an object generate a positive probability for that product's acceptance and usage.

Latent process conceptions acknowledge that there is, however, much more to an attitude than the behavioral response and some subsequent probability. It is an implicit argument that holds that attitudes are complex mental and cognitive phenomena. The response is governed by abstract cognitive-motivation-perceptual activities that act as intervening or mediational variables between the stimulus and the observable, measurable response.

KRECH, CRUTCHFIELD, AND BALACHEY. Krech, Crutchfield, and Balachey also hold the view that attitudes possess the three major cognitive, affective, and behavior components.[24] Furthermore, the interdependent and organized nature of each of these components is acknowledged. The total attitude structure is seen as a unified and enduring system with all attitude components integrated and related to other corresponding attitude components. Thus attitudes form patterned clusters and these patterned clusters in turn are organized into systems. However, Krech, Crutchfield, and Balachey have added two additional dimensions, *valence* and *multiplexity,* to the structural components of attitudes. Valence refers to the degree of favorability or unfavorability, positiveness or negativeness relating to the individual's beliefs, feelings, or response tendencies. Usually, the more intense or extreme the valence of an attitude, the more difficult it is to modify or restructure.

Multiplexity pertains to a measure of the number and variety of elements that make up an attitude component and refers to the complexity of the information possessed by the individual regarding the object of the attitude. Attitudes that are complex, deeply ingrained in beliefs and value systems, and integrated as a part of complex attitudinal clusters and systems have a high degree of multiplexity. On the other hand, simple sentiments not deeply ingrained or endowed with much symbolic significance or infused with large amounts of ego involvement are low in multiplexity. It would follow that attitudes high in multiplexity are ordinarily more difficult to change.

FUNCTIONAL IMPORTANCE OF ATTITUDES

Although much insight is to be gained through the exploration of the structural approach to attitude formation and change, there is nonetheless a rather large number of researchers who prefer an alternative approach. Their reasoning is that, although structural considerations are important, the real meaning and significance of

---

[24] The behavior component of attitude is also referred to as conative, meaning motivational. Some writers refer to this component as the response or response tendency component.

attitudes is to be discovered at the functional level. To understand the reasons why people hold the attitudes they do and to understand the purposes that attitudes serve for them is the real crux of the problem. Briefly, then, in this section we shall explore three different functional approaches to attitude formation and change. Two of these—namely, the Katz approach and the Smith, Bruner, and White approach—are quite similar, and because of the more general acceptance of the Katz scheme, it will be more fully emphasized. To conclude the section we will briefly examine Sarnoff's psychoanalytic approach to attitudes.

KATZ'S FUNCTIONAL APPROACH. Katz argues rather convincingly that knowledge of the functions that support and bolster an attitude can affect the strategy for modifying that attitude, determine the reasons why it is currently held, and provide suggestions why it has changed in the past. In his words:

> Stated simply, the functional approach is the attempt to understand the reasons people hold the attitudes they do. The reasons, however, are at the level of psychological motivations and not of the accidents of external events and circumstances. Unless we know the psychological need which is met by holding of an attitude we are in a poor position to predict when and how it will change.[25]

Katz lists four functions that attitudes serve. Each of these functions will be listed and some brief explanation provided. In several cases, these functions suggest definite consumer behavioral implications.

1. *The instrumental, adjustive, or utilitarian function.* Essentially, the utilitarian or adjustive function refers to the favorable responses the individual receives from his associates and friends when he manifests favorable, socialized, and acceptable attitudes. Such a function recognizes the adaptive nature of the individual and his willingness in many instances to be shaped by group processes. The utilitarian or adjustive function underscores the tendency toward what we described earlier as much approach-avoidance behavior on the part of individuals. As a result of reality-based experiences connected with success and failure related to objects in the environment—food, clothing, automobiles, houses, accessories, and so forth—some of the objects are associated with successful achievement of positive values, goals, and symbols and others with avoidance of desired objects. As a result of his adjustment to a world of reality, the individual learns some enduring responses called attitudes. His behavior is thus shaped by its consequences.

2. *The ego-defensive function.* Attitudes are formed and shaped by the desire of the individual to protect himself from acknowledging his deficiencies. Thus, much behavior is presumed to stem from at-

---

[25] Daniel Katz, "The Functional Approach to the Study of Attitudes," *Public Opinion Quarterly*, Vol. 24 (1960), p. 170.

titudes that are held to protect the delicate sensitivities of the ego. Such a functional basis of attitudes has its origin in Freudian psychoanalysis. We shall not elaborate here but shall treat this functional basis of attitude in the concluding portions of this section.

3. *The value-expressive function.* Through this function the individual attempts and achieves self-expression in terms of those values that he most cherishes. Thus, attitudes that are rooted in the value-expressive function are those that attempt to project the values and the commitments of the individual into the open, to make them known to society. They differ from the ego-defensive function in that they relate to the larger, more psychologically healthful concept of self. Thus, value-expressive attitudes are self-expressive, self-extending, and self-enhancing. So although the ego-defensive attitudes have the function of obscuring a person's true nature from himself, other attitudes, especially those in the value-expressive category, have the function of giving positive expression to an individual's central values and self-concept. Value-expressive attitudes generate pleasure and satisfaction to the individual from the expression of opinions that reflect his cherished beliefs and his self-concept.

4. *The knowledge function or object appraisal.* According to Katz, people seek a degree of predictability, consistency, and stability in their perception of and interaction with the world. Knowledge—knowing and understanding—represents the cognitive component of attitude that helps to provide coherence and focus for experience. Katz argues that people seek knowledge to give meaning to what would otherwise be an unorganized and chaotic universe. This argument reinforces much of what we have stated before in terms of our cognitive theory of consumer behavior, namely, that consumers are information seekers. They wish to know. It also appears to square well with our treatment of motivation, a part of which stated that much motivated behavior is prompted by a desire for knowledge stimulated by curiosity or by a desire for competence or effectance, that is, a desire to deal satisfactorily with one's environment-oriented problems.

The reader should recognize that such a treatment and understanding of the functional roles of attitudes immediately leads to an understanding of the difficulty of changing certain attitudes and of the conditions that must be created in order to bring about significant and lasting changes in attitudes. For example, utilitarian attitudes are often changed when it is discovered that holding and expressing such attitudes no longer leads to reinforced or rewarded responses. Changing ego-defensive attitudes is perhaps the most challenging, if not the most difficult. As one writer has suggested, marketers do not so much want to change ego-defensive attitudes as to assiduously avoid behavior or communications that trigger them.[26] Marketers can use value-expressive attitudes by stressing the symbolic nature and role of goods and the

[26] Thomas S. Robertson, *Consumer Behavior* (Glenview, Ill.: Scott, Foresman, and Company, 1970), p. 61.

TABLE 10-1

Determinants of Attitude Formation, Arousal, and Change in Relation to Type of Function

Function	Origin and dynamics	Arousal conditions	Change conditions
Adjustment	Utility of attitudinal object in need satisfaction. Maximizing external rewards and minimizing punishments	1. Activation of needs 2. Salience of cues associated with need satisfaction	1. Need deprivation 2. Creation of new needs and new levels of aspiration 3. Shifting rewards and punishments 4. Emphasis on new and better paths for need satisfaction
Ego Defense	Protecting against internal conflicts and external dangers	1. Posing of threats 2. Appeals to hatred and repressed impulses 3. Rise in frustrations 4. Use of authoritarian suggestion	1. Removal of threats 2. Catharsis 3. Development of self-insight
Value Expression	Maintaining self-identity; enhancing favorable self-image; self-expression and self-determination	1. Salience of cues associated with values 2. Appeals to individuals to reassert self-image 3. Ambiguities which threaten self-concept	1. Some degree of dissatisfaction with self 2. Greater appropriateness of new attitude for the self 3. Control of all environmental supports to undermine old values
Knowledge	Need for understanding, for meaningful cognitive organization, for consistency and clarity	1. Reinstatement of cues associated with old problem or of old problem itself	1. Ambiguity created by new information or change in environment 2. More meaningful information about problems

Source: Daniel Katz, "The Functional Approach to the Study of Attitudes," *Public Opinion Quarterly,* Vol. 24 (Summer 1960), pp. 163–204.

way goods relate to such value-expressive activities as self-enhancement and self-extension. Goods, as has been repeatedly emphasized, are a direct means of expressing value-oriented needs.

Finally, knowledge-oriented attitudes may be changed by the provision of new information or by the restructuring of the individual's perception of a given situation. To a great extent, the advertising-communication processes of marketers are directed to this end.

The many implications of Katz's approach are summarized in Table 10-1, which shows the functions and the origin and dynamics of attitudes, the arousal conditions, and the necessary conditions for change.

SMITH, BRUNER, AND WHITE. We shall not dwell long on the Smith, Bruner, and White approach. Both they and Katz list four functions (see Table 10-2) that an attitude may serve.

Although the two sets do overlap considerably, there are some respects in which their similarity breaks down. We shall do little more here than to list the functions contained in the Smith, Bruner, and White approach and discuss the implications of each. One major distinction between the two approaches does, however, appear most significant and, therefore, warrants mention. Katz's scheme emphasizes the utilitarian function of the object of the attitude. On the other hand, Smith, Bruner, and White emphasize the utilitarian function of the attitude per se. Furthermore, Katz emphasizes all needs that an object might serve. Conversely, Smith, Bruner, and White focus rather selectively on the social functions served by attitudes.[27]

1. *Social adjustment.* The social adjustment function closely parallels the adjustment or utilitarian function reported by Katz. Smith, Bruner, and White underscore two major kinds of social adjustment. The first relates to needs for autonomy or

TABLE 10-2
The Functions of Attitudes

Katz	Smith, Bruner, and White
1. Instrumental, adjustive utilitarian	Social adjustment
2. Ego defensive	Externalization
3. Knowledge	Object appraisal
4. Value-expressive	Quality of expressiveness

Source: Charles A. Kiesler, Barry E. Collins, and Norman Miller, *Attitude Change* (New York: John Wiley & Sons, Inc., 1969), p. 304.

[27] M. B. Smith, J. S. Bruner, and R. W. White, *Opinions and Personality* (New York: John Wiley & Sons, Inc., 1956).

independence and the second relates to needs for holding opinions contrary to those of others.

2. *Externalization.* Externalization suggests that a person forms attitudes and behavior in relation to an external event in a way that is colored by unresolved inner problems. Thus attitudes toward such objects and situations are in reality those that correspond in some way to the attitudes that are taken toward the inner conflict.

3. *Object appraisal.* This function of attitudes is more like Katz's utilitarian function. Smith, Bruner, and White contend that the possessing of an attitude provides a way of judging and sizing up objects and events in the environment from the point of view of one's major interest and on-going concern. Objects and situations are thus perceived and classified in terms of their value in seeking and attaining goals.

4. *Quality of expressiveness.* Smith, Bruner, and White, contrary to Katz, reject the notion of an expressive need. They contend that the expressive aspects of an attitude do not serve a function for the rest of the personality. From their perspective, attitudes are consistent with the information sought and processed by the individual. Their expressive nature of attitudes underscores the basic fact that a person's attitudes simply reflect the deeper and obscured patterns of his life.

All functional theories pose at least this minimum question: What would one do if asked to change a person's attitudes? Remember that the functional theories suggest that one cannot accomplish this task unless he knows what function the attitude in question serves. This, in itself, is a considerable obstacle because it becomes readily apparent that this is another individual difference theory. The point is that the same attitudes can serve different functions for different people. Unless one knows specifically what function a given attitude serves for a particular person, efforts toward changing attitudes, especially through mass communication techniques, are likely to lead to serious mistakes at worst and mixed results at best.

SARNOFF'S PSYCHOANALYTICAL THEORY OF ATTITUDES. Sarnoff's theory is predicated upon the contention that attitudes are held to serve the function of defending the ego against both internal and external threats.[28] Thus, where *ego-defensive* attitudes for Katz and *externalization* for Smith, Bruner, and White are only one of the major reasons for holding attitudes, the defense of the ego becomes the *only* reason for holding attitudes according to Sarnoff. As would be imagined his theory is popular with the psychoanalytical school of psychology but is not widely endorsed by the cognitive psychologists. It is reported

[28] I. Sarnoff, "Psychoanalytic Theory and Social Attitudes," *Public Opinion Quarterly*, Vol. 24 (1960), pp. 251–279.

here only briefly in order to acknowledge a more comprehensive treatment of ego-defensive reasons for holding attitudes and to emphasize that many attitudes are related to ego-defensive needs that, in many instances, are only dimly envisaged or operate at the subconscious level of psychological experience.

Sarnoff's theory is built around four basic concepts. The dynamics of his theory invoke the basic discrepancies and congruities that emerge between attitudes and motives and the reactive and defensive behaviors used to resolve the various forms of motive attitude discrepancy. We shall briefly explain and describe the structure of this theory.

1. *Motives.* According to Sarnoff, motives are internally operative, tension-producing stimuli that provoke the individual to act in such a way as to reduce the consciously experienced tension generated by them.
2. *Conflict.* Conflict arises whenever two or more motives are activated at the same time and their coalescence generates a state of tension.
3. *Ego defense.* Ego defense consists of the combination of perceptual and motor skills that facilitate the individual's drive to maximize the reduction of the tension of his motives within the constraint of his environment.
4. *Attitude.* Attitudes are defined more or less conventionally as a predisposition to react favorably or unfavorably toward a class of objects.

From this structure the following dynamic relationships emerge. Attitudes are inferred from overt responses; that is, we witness the response and attribute an attitude to the response. Overt responses are made in order to reduce motive-generated tensions. Thus attitudes are a kind of emergent product of the tension-reducing responses made in relationship to objects or situations. Individuals' attitudes toward objects and situations are determined and structured by the nature of the role those objects have come to play in facilitating responses that reduce the tension of particular motives and that facilitate the resolution of conflicts among motives.

Sarnoff's is an interesting conceptualization. Notice that it holds that attitudes serve an adjustment function that is at the same time utilitarian. However, the principal adjustive need is the need to defend or protect the ego.

Sarnoff's theory is a congruence theory in that attitudes and motives may be in a state of either consonance or discrepancy. He postulates a tendency toward congruence seeking on the part of the individual. When motives and attitudes are discrepant or out of congruence, the individual, according to Sarnoff, is aware of neither the underlying motive nor the goals of his own response. This, of course, is a conceivable and often likely case in many instances of consumer behavior. According to this theory, then, attitudes are formed to serve ego defense and, as such, attitudes would serve the purpose of facilitating denial, repression, projection, rationalization, and reaction formation.

Sarnoff's theory does shed much light on the role of ego-defense mechanisms and their relationship to attitude formation and change. His theory supports the contention that when one arouses the defenses of an individual, that person usually responds by mobilizing his ego defenses and this, of course, lessens the probability of attitude change, which is the real goal being sought. This contention is in harmony with the findings of Janis and Feshbach, who report that although strong-threat appeals increase the anxiety of the subject, he is much more inclined to display attitude and behavior changes as a result of low-threat appeals.[29]

Attitudes and Behavior

It is time now to analyze critically our most fundamental assumption, namely, that attitudes affect behavior. Not surprisingly, there are many who question this basic and fundamental proposition. Do our attitudes affect our behavior? There is a considerable amount of research to support such a contention. Yet, on the other hand, there is much evidence to suggest that the flow of influence may be the other way around, and there is even some research that questions the connection between attitude and behavior in general. We shall explore the ramifications of this controversy in considerable detail throughout this section.

THE FLOW OF INFLUENCE

Normally we view behavior as the dependent variable and attitudes as the independent variables in simple models of consumer behavior. We affect the dependent variable by changing the independent variable attitudes. Thus, in studies of brand preference, brand attitudes are usually treated as the independent variable.[30] Brand preference as indicated by purchase is the dependent variable and, therefore, the flow of influence diagrammatically would appear as follows:

Attitudes ⟶ Behavior

Yet it is rather well known that the flow of influence can very well be just the opposite. Namely,

Behavior ⟶ Attitudes

Our behavior does affect our attitudes. How else would one explain such activities as learning, socialization, and perception? Furthermore,

[29] I. L. Janis and S. Feshbach, "Effects of Fear Arousing Communications," *Journal of Abnormal Psychology*, Vol. 47 (1950), pp. 78–92.

[30] Studies treating the relationship between attitudes and behavior are relatively old in marketing. For an example of an early study, see Seymour Banks, "The Relationship Between Preference and Purchase of Brands," *Journal of Marketing*, Vol. 15 (October 1950), pp. 145–157.

it is well known that marketers often attempt to influence the behavior of their customers directly by admonishing them to "visit the store," "buy now," "take the car out for a drive," and "try this free sample." Marketers, recognizing that behavior can and does lead to attitude change, do not wait until their customers acquire attitudes or beliefs requiring them to act. Instead marketers work on the now firmly established psychological principle that attitudes change following a commitment to behavior that may be discrepant with original beliefs.[31] The explanation for such behavior is that cognitive reorganization via learning follows an induced change in affect.[32]

Still, however, the normal and persistent view is that attitudes influence behavior rather than the other way around, although evidence continues to mount that challenges the value and predictive ability of such an assertion. One of the now classic studies that was first presented to cast aspersions on the relationship between attitudes and behavior was that of LaPiere. This study deals with the apparent inconsistency created when motel or restaurant proprietors actually served a Chinese couple even though they said they would not do so when asked by letter.[33] Space will not permit a detailed analysis of this study. Yet it has been used by nearly all sides in the attitude-behavior, consistency-inconsistency argument.

ATTITUDE CONSISTENCY

Must we be totally consistent in our behavior? Must we maintain a direct one-to-one relationship between attitudes and behavior? There are those who would insist upon such rigidity. Yet there are too many forces working against such a condition. It is not at all unusual to discover that even though a significantly large number of customers state that they prefer a given brand, they often buy another brand in an actual purchase situation. To explain such behavior is not very difficult. For example, perhaps the store was out of the preferred brand. Another brand may have been on special sale for that particular day. Another brand may have been displayed more attractively and conveniently. The purchaser may have been requested by another family member to try the other brand. Or perhaps out of curiosity and in the interest of variety the other brand was selected. A degree of inconsistency is a normal part of one's humanity. We are not intellectual slaves programmed forever to endless repetitive patterns of behavior. Thus consistency between attitudes and behavior is dependent upon several factors, some of which we shall now explain.

[31] For more on this idea, see Phillip Zimbardo and Ebbe B. Ebbesen, *Influencing Attitudes and Changing Behavior* (Reading, Mass.: Addison-Wesley Publishing Co., Inc., 1970), especially Chapter 5, pp. 63–94.

[32] Milton J. Rosenberg, "An Analysis of Affective-Cognitive Consistency," in *Attitude Organization and Change*, Milton J. Rosenberg, Carl I. Hovland, et al., eds. (New Haven, Conn.: Yale University Press, 1960), p. 24.

[33] R. T. LaPiere, "Attitudes vs. Action," *Social Forces*, Vol. 13 (1934), pp. 230–237.

SALIENCY. Consumers have literally thousands of attitudes pertaining, in turn, to thousands of objects and situations. Not all attitudes are of equal relevance or salience to an individual. There are literally hundreds of brands of products and, in most instances, differences between brands are virtually nonexistent. Is it any wonder, then, that consumers are not totally brand loyal or that there should exist some inconsistency between attitudes as brand preferences and the actual brands purchased? Many of the consumer's attitudes toward brands are not necessarily strong indicators of his purchase behavior because these attitudes are simply not salient for him. They are not considered relative or central enough in terms of his current needs, goals, or enterprises to be important indicators of behavior. The Reynolds Tobacco Company would certainly like to think that people would "walk a mile for a Camel," but for most such an attitude would simply not be salient and such behavior would be considered a little foolish.

Finally, inconsistency between attitude and behavior relating to salience can be explained in terms of the inconsequential nature of some attitudes. Attitudes about salt, catsup, or garden fertilizer are bound to differ markedly in terms of salience for most consumers, as opposed to the salience of attitudes regarding dress clothing, household furniture, automobiles, or housing. Attributes relevant to purchasing vary widely from the first category of products to the second. It has been shown that when we are repeatedly exposed to information on television about a brand or a product, our purchase responses may be altered without a change in our underlying attitudes "by shifting the relative salience of attributes suggested to us by advertising as we organize our perception of brands and products."[34]

CENTRALITY AND COMMITMENT. The degree of consistency between attitudes and behavior is also viewed as a function of the attitude's centrality and the degree of commitment the subject has toward the attitude and the attitude object.[35] To elaborate, the persistence, the saliency, and the overall strength of the attitude would be determinants of attitude-behavior consistency. Thus, persistence, saliency, and strength are generally functions of the centrality of the given attitude in the overall attitude cluster and the attitude system, and the degree to which the attitude is germane to the individual's self-concept. Strong, professed personal commitments are likely to generate rather consistent patterns of behavior. As was stated much earlier, man appears to learn to love the things for which he suffers. And, in turn, those things for which he develops a deep sense of personal commitment are most

[34] Herbert E. Krugman, "The Impact of Television Advertising: Learning Without Involvement," *Public Opinion Quarterly,* Vol. 29 (Fall 1965), p. 353.

[35] Thomas M. Ostrom and Harry S. Upshaw, "Psychological Perspective and Attitude Change," in *Psychological Foundations of Attitudes,* Anthony G. Greenwald, Timothy C. Brock, and Thomas M. Ostrom, eds. (New York: Academic Press, Inc., 1968), p. 217–241.

likely to endure. Attitudes stemming from such commitments are likely to prove good indicators of future behavior.

We mentioned earlier that attitudes that are a central part of an overall and more complex attitude-value-belief hierarchy are most difficult to change, and it follows that such attitudes can also be considered a rather good and consistent guide to subsequent behavior.[36] Attitudes that are simple and not highly integrated are also likely to be perceived as inconsequential and not a good index for determining behavior.

Somewhat related to the concept of centrality and commitment is the concept of *social anchoring*. The impact of socialization and group processes on attitude formation and change is well known. Attitude and behavior consistency, in turn, can be viewed as a function of social anchoring. Social anchoring is concerned with the extent to which our personal attitudes about objects and events are widely held or "anchored" within the overall value and belief systems of the groups to which we belong. Obviously, if a given set of attitudes is well anchored, then behavior, especially to the extent that it is subject to the scrutiny of the group, is likely to manifest considerable consistency with the professed attitudes.

PRIVATE ATTITUDES VERSUS PUBLIC COMMITMENT. Life seems to demand a little hypocrisy from all of us. For example, our behavior is not always consistent with our attitudes because extenuating circumstances compel us to act publicly in some ways when our training, norms, or attitudes would dictate otherwise. Thus, we say to a salesman that we like his product when we actually do not. We may buy a product to please a friend or some member of the family when actually we would have preferred something else. We respond to interviewers' questions in ways that we perceive will be pleasant to the interviewer. Our friends ask us our opinions or attitudes and we tell them what we think they want to know rather than the unvarnished truth.

Also, we must remember that attitudes and behavior are not always consistent because many attitudes are not well formulated. The unconscious nature of many attitudes suggests that what we think are our attitudes may not be our true attitudes at all.[37]

ATTITUDES TOWARD OBJECTS VERSUS ATTITUDES TOWARD SITUATIONS. One of the more complex explanations advanced to explain attitude-behavior discrepancy is that of Rokeach. He contends that behavior is always a function of at least two attitudes, that is, an attitude toward the object and the attitude toward the situation.[38] His thesis, which is rather widely held, is that an attitude may be focused on either

[36] See Krech, Crutchfield and Ballachey, op. cit., pp. 246ff.

[37] M. Brewster Smith, *Social Psychology and Human Values* (Chicago: Aldine Publishing Company, 1969). See Chapter 6, "Attitude Change," pp. 93–96.

[38] Milton Rokeach, *Beliefs, Attitudes, and Values* (San Francisco: Jossey-Bass, Inc., Publishers, 1968), pp. 133–156.

an object or a situation and that behavior is always a function of at least these two types of attitudes. These assumptions, he argues, have two noteworthy implications. In his words:

> First, a given attitude-toward-object, whenever activated, need not always be behaviorally manifested or expressed in the same way or to the same degree. Its expression will vary adaptively as the attitude activated by the situation varies, with attitude-toward-situation facilitating or inhibiting the expression of the attitude-toward-object and vice versa.[39]

This is an interesting thesis and may explain a great part of the inconsistency that exists between attitudes and behavior, for example, when a person indicates that he has a favorable attitude toward Brand X, say, a Cadillac automobile, but he does not buy a Cadillac. Why? Perhaps it is because his attitudes toward the object are discrepant with his attitudes toward the situation. Attitudes toward the situation might include the high cost of ownership or the reactions of his friends toward the idea of his driving such a high-priced, high-status vehicle. For behavior to follow consistently from attitudes, the attitudes toward the object and toward the situation must be in a relatively high state of congruence. Crane has shown that behavioral changes can be brought about by the changing of the consumer's perception of how a product is categorized or classified.[40] For example, Metrecal sold more widely and successfully as a food product in supermarkets than as a pharmaceutical product in drugstores. Geritol is now promoted as a general health item (one of the nice things you do for yourself) rather than as a geriatric product. Thus marketers attempt to create favorable attitudes toward products. Snowmobiles take one out to adventure. Motorcycles have sold more briskly since the image of those who ride motorcycles and the circumstances or situations under which motorcycles are ridden have been more extensively promoted.

In a holistic sense, then, it is helpful to conceive of any particular attitude object as the *figure* and the situation as the *ground*. Just how a person will behave and how consistently his behavior will follow from his attitudes will depend, on the one hand, on particular beliefs or attitudes activated by the attitude object and, on the other hand, by the attitudes aroused and brought into play by the attitudes activated by the situation.

What all this suggests is that behavior involves estimating certain *situational hurdles*.[41] We may hurdle a given situation and behave in one manner on a given occasion. But given another occasion of different complexity or magnitude we may choose not to hurdle that situation, and therefore our behavior may appear to be inconsistent.

[39] Ibid., p. 135.

[40] Edgar Crane, *Marketing Communications* (New York: John Wiley & Sons, Inc., 1965), pp. 35–68.

[41] D. T. Campbell, "Social Attitudes and Other Acquired Behavioral Dispositions," in *Psychology: A Study of a Science*, S. Koch, ed., Vol. 6 (New York: McGraw-Hill Book Company, 1963), pp. 94–172.

LEARNING ATTITUDES VERSUS LEARNING RESPONSES. We shall conclude our treatment of attitude-behavior consistency by examining one final argument. Doob has presented the interesting proposition that attitudes are learned predispositions to respond, that is, that attitudes are learned mediating responses.[42] Thus, we learn attitudes—the appropriate predisposition toward any given object. However, Doob argues further that once we learn an attitude we must also learn what response to make to it. He argues that there is no innate relationship between attitude and behavior. Two people may very well learn to hold the same attitude toward a given stimulus, but they may still learn to make different responses to this same learned attitude. Thus two people may have the same attitude toward Listerine. They both hate it! One, however, uses it twice a day. The other never uses it, preferring instead the better-tasting product, Lavoris.

What we have learned thus far is that there is no one-to-one consistent relationship between attitudes and behavior. This holds because of the complex nature of attitudes and the complex and sophisticated nature of behavior. Our attitudinal response to stimuli is threefold: cognitive, affective, and behavioral. In addition, our attitudes possess dimensions of valence and multiplexity. We have attitudes toward objects and attitudes toward situations. Questions of salience, centrality, and commitment are involved. Given the multidimensionality of attitudes, it is small wonder that questions of attitude-behavior consistency arise.

How Attitudes Are Acquired and Changed

Throughout this entire book, the discussion has related implicitly to the topic of how attitudes are acquired and how attitudes change. The earlier chapters on cognition and the material on motivation, perception, and learning have all dealt both directly and indirectly with attitudes. The chapters that follow this one will also deal to some extent with the issue of attitude formation and change. Chapter 11 will deal explicitly with the topic, "The Process and Role of Communication in Attitude and Behavioral Change." However, at this point we wish to deal concretely with some of the problems and processes involved in acquiring and forming attitudes.

ATTITUDE FORMATION AND ATTITUDE CHANGE

An overwhelming proportion of the literature on attitudes deals with attitude change rather than attitude formation.

In a common sense way it is often thought that the process of attitude formation is the same as that of attitude change. Others have viewed the two processes somewhat differently, positing that attitude formation involves creating some sort of positive or negative valence

---

[42] L. W. Doob, "The Behavior of Attitudes," *Psychological Review*, Vol. 54 (1947), pp. 135–156.

whereas previously there was only a neutral valence. Attitude change is construed as a process whereby the attitude is changed from one valence (positive) to another valence (negative) or vice versa. Some argue that both attitude change and formation involve a conditioning or an operant conditioning process.[43] The more eclectic and utilitarian researchers would argue that both processes are present in formation and change. Such will be the point of view presented in this section.

Attitude change is usually considered a change in predisposition.[44] The change, furthermore, is either a change in the organization or the structure of beliefs or a change in the content of one or more of the beliefs or belief clusters entering into the attitude organization. Thus, at least according to Rokeach, attitude change is the change brought about in predisposition or the state of the organism that when activated by a stimulus causes the person to respond selectively, affectively, or preferentially to the stimulus.[45] Attitude formation is the creation of a predisposition where none previously existed. It is a moot point as to whether the processes for inducing attitude formation are significantly different from those related to inducing attitude change. We shall not pursue further what may be a needless distinction.

ATTITUDE DYNAMICS. What we are concerned with, of course, is attitude dynamics, that is, the changes that take place in attitudes and belief systems and how these changes can be induced, understood, and predicted. Our usual impression regarding attitude as an influencer of behavior is that by changing the cognitive component of the attitude we will in turn affect the affective component, which will lead to change in the behavioral component of the attitude. Thus, the flow of influence looks something like this:[46]

Stimulus Communication	→	Cognitive or Belief Component	→	Affective Component— Like versus Dislike	→

	Behavioral Component Position Action Tendency	→	Purchase, Trial, Examination, More Search, etc.

Marketers and advertisers, however, quite often attempt to influence or stimulate the affective component directly; that is, they minimize the use of cognitive appeals and instead attempt to create a strong feeling about the product. Conditions often change, however, which, in turn, means changes in the strategy for inducing attitude

[43] Charles A. Kiesler, Barry Collins, and Norman Miller, *Attitude Change* (New York: John Wiley & Sons, Inc., 1969), p. 345.

[44] Rokeach, op. cit., p. 135.

[45] Ibid., p. 135.

[46] Such schematics or models are usually referred to as process models of attitude formation and change.

formation and change. For example, the demand for more product information especially in regard to safety and pollution factors has recently led Ford Motors to switch from appeals oriented toward "long, low, and luxurious" (affective appeals) to safety, engineering, steering, braking, and so forth (cognitive components).

However, it must be remembered that we are dealing with a multifaceted problem. Attitudes are formed and changed not only in relationship to products as objects but also in relation to situations. Therefore, there are at least four possible determinants involved in attitude dynamics: (1) interaction between attitude-toward-object and attitude-toward-situation, (2) a change in only the attitude-toward-object, (3) a change in only the attitude-toward-situation, or (4) a change in both attitude-toward-object and attitude-toward-situation.

The brief, schematic, flow-of-influence or process model presented is a two-process model of attitude dynamics. It suggests that when attitudes are either formed or changed, the process involves either one or both of two sequences. The first sequence concerns the modification of the cognitive or belief component. Through interaction or direct encounter with the object or its surrogate through communication, a person acquires one or more beliefs that link or connect the object to some source of like or dislike. The second sequence involves the modification of the affective component. Through learning, reinforcement, or information processing the subject acquires an affective disposition toward an object.[47]

THE SOURCE OF ATTITUDE FORMATION AND CHANGE

Essentially, there are three major sources from which subjects acquire all attitudes.[48] These sources and a brief description of each follows.

1. *Direct contact with objects.* As perceiving, observing, and witnessing subjects we come into contact and association with countless new objects each day. The consumer shops, compares, evaluates, tries on, feels, and otherwise examines both directly and vicariously all the objects that come into his range of view. Through this direct contact one learns to judge, evaluate, and choose. Thus, attitudes are formed and changed as a result of this experience.

2. *Social interaction with those holding attitudes.* As was mentioned previously, our feelings and beliefs and our likes and dislikes, as well as our actual behavior are affected by the attitudes, beliefs, and norms of our friends and other members of our reference group affiliations. We acquire and take on the dispositions of those around us. If we like a salesman, we are likely to be more inclined to accept his influence. If we identify

[47] This two-sequence model of attitude dynamics can be reviewed more extensively in Rosenberg and Hovland, op. cit., pp. 51–54.

[48] Hollander, op. cit., pp. 127–129.

strongly with significant others, our attitudes and behavior are likely to reflect their values and beliefs.

3. *Upbringing experiences within the family.* Almost all of our significant values and beliefs and, to some extent, our attitudes are a function of our upbringing experiences within the family. Certainly, most basic personality features of the individual are familybound and determined, and to the sense and degree that attitudes stem in large part from personality considerations the role and the influence of the family on attitude formation and change cannot be underestimated.

Attitudes are formed and changed largely by *association* and *learning*. However, the functional orientation toward attitude formation and change would remind us that attitudes are self-serving and that therefore they are both formed and changed as a part of our overall *need-satisfaction* and goal-striving behavior. There are numerous schools of thought or theories as to how specifically attitudes are formed and changed. We have already examined some of these in this chapter and the others we have largely examined in previous chapters. For example, Table 10-3 depicts the major theories about and approaches to attitude change and formation.

Our basic orientation throughout has emphasized the cognitive

TABLE 10-3

Theories of Attitude Formation and Change

A. *S-R Behaviorist Theories*	
1. Classical Conditioning	Chapter 9—Learning
2. Operant Learning	Chapter 9—Learning
B. *Cognitive Theories*	
1. Cognitive Learning	Chapter 9—Learning
2. Perceptual Learning	Chapter 9—Learning
C. *Consistency Theories*	
1. Heider's P-O-X	Chapter 6—Cognitive Consistency
2. Newcomb's A-B-X	Chapter 6—Cognitive Consistency
D. *Dissonance Theory*	
Festinger's Cognitive	
Dissonance	Chapter 6—Cognitive Consistency
E. *Functional Theories*	
Katz	Chapter 10—Attitudes
Smith, Bruner, and White	Chapter 10—Attitudes
Sarnoff	Chapter 10—Attitudes
Kelman	Chapter 10—Attitudes
F. *Communication Theories*	
1. Transactional Models	Chapter 11—Communication
2. Others	

and social learning significance of attitude formation and change. Social learning emphasizes the role of information that is perceived through modeling, direct and indirect reinforcement, and persuasive communications. The social learning approach, which is decidedly cognitive in orientation inasmuch as it is derived from a learning theory orientation, assumes a given rationality in man as an information-processing organism who can be aroused and motivated to attend to communications and incorporate them into a repertoire of responses when such learning is self-serving. The instrument of attitude formation and change is thus a structured communication. The agent of change is the knowledge or insight gained, which leads to improved behavior. All this assumes, of course, that man is a social animal who needs other people to act as a basis for self-knowledge, to determine appropriate responses to environmental demands and situations, and to facilitate and regulate his behavior through the operation of group norms and other dynamic group processes.[49]

As all this suggests, the very expression of attitudes depends upon the social setting. It further suggests that apparent changes in attitudes occur when an individual perceives shifts in his own situation in terms of what is construed and evaluated as approved and appropriate.

KELMAN'S APPROACH. This viewpoint has been incorporated into a theory that deals largely with the process of attitude formation and change. Kelman's theory clearly implies that knowledge of *how* an attitude was acquired is the key to knowing how to change or restructure the attitude. Kelman[50] discusses three processes by which attitudes are acquired:

> *Compliance.* Compliance occurs when an individual accepts influence because he hopes to achieve a favorable reaction from another person or group. The behavior is induced and it, therefore, is not likely to be lasting. As the influence of the group or the communication changes, the attitudes involved or induced are likely to change also.
>
> *Identification.* Identification occurs when an individual accepts influence because he wishes to establish or maintain a self-defining relationship with another person or group. Through identification, behavior is emulated: the subject apes the manner and behavior of some significant-other. Attitudes that arise through identification are affected by the strength of character, self-concept, and autonomy of the subject. The responses are often viewed as more relevant than their content.
>
> *Internalization.* Internalization occurs when an individual accepts influence because of the content of the induced behavior. In short, the ideas and action of the behavior and attitudes are in themselves intrinsically rewarding.

[49] Actually, such an approach is built upon two major schools of attitude change: the communication school (exemplified by Carl Hovland and his associates at Yale University) and the group dynamics school (exemplified by Kurt Lewin and the Center for Group Dynamics at the University of Michigan). See Zimbardo and Ebbeson, op. cit., p. 16.

[50] H. C. Kelman, "Three Processes of Social Influence," *Public Opinion Quarterly*, Vol. 25 (1961), pp. 57–78.

Kelman suggests that much persuasive communication can be analyzed in terms of his process model of attitude formation and change. For instance, there exists a large amount of compliance communication in which the communicator is made to appear as though he possessed the means of control. Identification communications are structured in such a way that the communicator has a high degree of perceived attractiveness. Internalization communications are constructed in such a way as to endow the communicator with high credibility. Table 10-4 summarizes considerable information concerning the distinctions between the three processes.

TABLE 10-4

Summary of the Distinctions Between the Three Processes

	Compliance	Identification	Internalization
ANTECEDENTS			
1. Basis for the *importance of the induction*	Concern with social effect of behavior	Concern with social anchorage of behavior	Concern with value congruence of behavior
2. Source of *power of the influencing agent*	Means control	Attractiveness	Credibility
3. Manner of achieving *prepotency of the induced response*	Limitation of choice behavior	Delineation of role requirements	Reorganization of means-ends framework
CONSEQUENTS			
1. Conditions of performance of induced response	Surveillance by influencing agent	Salience of relationship to agent	Relevance of values to issues
2. Conditions of change and extinction of induced response	Changed perception of conditions for social rewards	Changed perception of conditions for satisfying self-defining relationships	Changed perception of conditions for value maximization
3. Type of behavior system in which induced response is embedded	External demands of a specific setting	Expectations defining a specific role	Person's value system

Source: H. C. Kelman, "Three Processes of Social Influence," *Public Opinion Quarterly,* Vol. 25 (1961), p. 67.

Kelman's theory recognizes implicitly a great part of what has been considered thus far, namely, that attitudes vary in strength and valence, that they are rooted in social interaction processes that entail learning, and that the same attitude can be expressed for a variety of reasons.[51]

Measuring Attitudes—Approaches and Problems

In keeping with the more scientific and mathematical approach, methods for measuring attitudes are increasingly being sought and developed. Much of the reasoning behind this activity stems from the dictum that if there is something to anything, there is enough to measure. If, therefore, attitudes are to be a central construct in the social and behavioral sciences and in consumer behavior, then our constructs must be measurable and thus lend themselves to the usual mathematical and statistical analysis. The entire range of methods for measuring and scaling attitudes is broad and comprehensive. A complete treatment of this range is beyond the scope of our present treatment. However, we will attempt to survey briefly this range of methods, describe each method briefly, and conclude the section with a few caveats regarding the shortcomings and pitfalls of our present methodology.

ATTITUDE MEASUREMENT TECHNIQUES

There are basically five general categories of attitude measurement techniques that researchers might employ. These are as follows:

1. Self report measures.
2. Inferences from on-going behavior.
3. Inferences from partially structured stimuli.
4. Performance of objective task.
5. Inferences from physiological reactions.[52]

SELF-REPORT MEASURES

There are numerous self-report measures, most of which stem from the work of Allport and Hartman.[53] This work began a new tradition in attitude measurement because, instead of asking the traditional question, they asked the subject which of the opinions presented best characterized his attitude.

[51] For one of the better comprehensive treatments of these processes, see Arthur R. Cohen, *Attitude Change and Social Influences* (New York: Basic Books, 1964), especially Chapter 8, pp. 121–129.

[52] S. W. Cook and C. A. Selltiz, "A Multiple Indicator Approach to Attitude Measurement," *Psychological Bulletin*, Vol. 62 (1964), pp. 36–55.

[53] F. H. Allport and D. A. Hartman, "The Measurement and Motivation of Atypical Opinion in a Certain Group," *American Political Science Review*, Vol. 19, No. 4 (1925), pp. 735–760.

THURSTONE'S EQUAL-APPEARING INTERVAL SCALE. Building upon Allport and Hartman's work, Thurstone built his scale upon a procedure that involves scaling the attitude statements along an attitude continuum.[54] The statements are printed on cards and the judges are asked to sort the statements into eleven piles. The left-most pile represents the most unfavorable statements and the right-most pile represents the most favorable statements. The judges are required to make the interval between the piles equal—hence, the name *equal-appearing intervals*. The subject is then asked to check all the opinion statements with which he agrees.

METHOD OF SUMMATED RATINGS. Likert's method, which is called the method of summated ratings, permits the researcher to score attitudes directly from the attitudinal responses without recourse to a panel of judges.[55] Such a short-cut method has gained widespread popularity. The subject being tested by the Likert method is asked to indicate the degree of his agreement with or approval of all items on a five-point scale. For each attitude item in the scale, five response categories are provided. These are "strongly approve," "approve," "undecided," "disapprove," "strongly disapprove." The Likert scale requires an item analysis to show that all items measure the same attitude.

THE SEMANTIC DIFFERENTIAL. The semantic differential as developed by Osgood, Suci, and Tannenbaum has previously been discussed.[56] This method calls for a direct evaluation of the attitude object and does not, therefore, depend upon opinion statements. The semantic differential consists of a series of bipolar adjectives such as "fair-unfair," "competent-incompetent," "pleasant-unpleasant." Each pair of adjectives is separated by seven intervals and the subjects are asked to indicate where, along the continuum between the two pairs of adjectives, the attitude object lies.

There are several other self-report measures for scaling attitudes. Scalogram analysis and the unfolding technique of Coombs have not been discussed.[57] However, a more comprehensive treatment on a how-to-do-it basis can be found in most standard reference works.[58]

[54] L. L. Thurstone, ed., *The Measurement of Social Attitudes* (Chicago: University of Chicago Press, 1929), pp. 129–134.

[55] R. A. Likert, "A Technique for the Measurement of Attitudes," *Archives of Psychology*, No. 140 (1932), pp. 1–55.

[56] C. E. Osgood, G. J. Suci, and P. H. Tannenbaum, *The Measurement of Meaning* (Urbana, Ill.: University of Illinois Press, 1957).

[57] L. Guttman, "The Basis for Scalogram Analysis," in *Measurement and Prediction*, S. A. Stauffer et al., eds. (Princeton, N.J.: Princeton University Press, 1950), pp. 46–59; and C. A. Coombs, *A Theory of Data* (New York: John Wiley & Sons, Inc., 1964).

[58] W. A. Scott, "Attitude Measurement," in *Handbook of Social Psychology*, G. Lindzey and E. Aronson, eds., rev. ed. (Reading, Mass.: Addison-Wesley Publishing Co., Inc., 1968).

INFERENCES FROM ON-GOING BEHAVIOR

Inferences concerning attitudes are frequently made from on-going behavior. For example, in-store analysis of customer shopping behavior, traffic patterns, and time spent examining displays are examples of how direct observation is sometimes used to infer attitudes. Other examples of direct observation are panel studies and pantry analysis. Sometimes subjects are asked to play a role or to choose, from among several personality types, those whom they would most like to have waiting on them as salespeople in a retail store.

Most consumer behavior studies include little direct observation of behavior, yet some caution is in order. Too often, perhaps, the attitudes inferred from customer behavior are those put there by the observer or researcher.

INFERENCES FROM PARTIALLY STRUCTURED STIMULI

The tools used to draw inferences from partially structured stimuli are often referred to as projective techniques. Recall that the subject is not to state his actions directly but instead is ostensibly to describe a scene, a character, or the behavior of a third person. Such reporting is hopefully more objective and thus more revealing than first-person interviews or direct observation.[59] However, as previously discussed, projective techniques have several pitfalls.

PERFORMANCE OF OBJECTIVE TASKS

Attitudes are often inferred from the subject's performance of objective tasks. The assumption is that performance may be influenced by attitude. The customer may be given a budget and asked to shop for the family's grocery needs for the week. Customers are sometimes asked to list their favorite brands or stores. Such methods assume that subjects are able to remember information consistent with attitudes longer than other information.[60] Such approaches, although perhaps useful, are subject to serious flaws, most noticeable of which are interpretation and the tendency for subjects to rationalize their performance.

INFERENCES FROM PHYSIOLOGICAL REACTIONS

Galvanic skin responses have been related to verbal measures of attitude, and eye movement has been treated as a variable in discerning customers' attitudes about products and shelf placements.[61] More

[59] For a comprehensive review of projective techniques, see J. Zubin, L. O. Eron, and F. Schumer, *An Experimental Approach to Projective Techniques* (New York: John Wiley & Sons, Inc., 1965).

[60] E. E. Jones and R. Kohler, "The Effects of Plausibility on the Learning of Controversial Statements," *Journal of Abnormal and Social Psychology*, Vol. 57 (1958), pp. 315–320.

[61] R. E. Rankin and D. T. Campbell, "Galvanic Skin Response to Negro and White Experimentors," *Journal of Abnormal and Social Psychology*, Vol. 51 (1955), pp. 30–33.

gross measures of customers' physiological reactions to stimuli such as advertising have been studied by what is called conjugatively programmed analysis.[62] However, these methods are still largely experimental and are not widely used in research on consumer attitudes.

PROBLEMS OF ATTITUDE MEASUREMENT

There are several problems of attitude measurement that are simply methodological problems. These problems relate to the statistical questions of *reliability* and *validity*. Reliability refers to consistency; that is, if a given method is employed, does that method consistently produce results? Numerous tests are available for evaluating the reliability of a given measurement.[63] Validity refers to the degree to which a technique measures what it is designed to measure.[64] Validity presents an especially difficult and recurring problem in attitude scaling for consumer behavior. Recall that we still have considerable disagreement as to just what attitudes are. Our ability to measure something is directly related to our ability to define that something and separate it from everything else. It is generally known that even though various researchers are measuring what they call "attitudes," they are not all necessarily measuring the same thing.

Remember also that it is generally agreed that an attitude as a response and a disposition to stimuli has more than one component. Usually at least two components (cognitive-affective) are considered and, oftentimes, three components (cognitive-affective-behavioral) are considered. Yet most of the methods for measuring and scaling attitudes are self-report measures. In short, they are pencil-and-paper tests and the usual thing that is measured—often the only thing—is the affective component. Thus the subject's degree of like or dislike is assumed to be tantamount to his "attitude," and his "attitude" is presumed then to be an indicator of his behavior. Such an assumption has already been rather seriously criticized in a previous section. Until more definitive understandings of attitudes are delineated, our measuring devices are likely to continue to leave something to be desired.

Finally, we must contend with some other problems relating to attitude measurement. For example, people and their attitudes are not always the same from one time period to another. Subjects are changeable and capable of learning new responses and new attitudes. People are also often reluctant to express their opinions and attitudes regarding deep-seated, personal feelings and thus we encounter the problem of *private attitudes* versus *public opinion*. Subjects often report answers and express attitudes that they feel the researcher wishes to hear. An-

[62] Peter E. Nathan and Wallace H. Wallace, "An Operant Behavioral Measure of T.V. Commercial Effectiveness," *Journal of Advertising Research*, Vol. 5 (December 1965), pp. 13–20.

[63] E. E. Ghiselli, *Theory of Psychological Measurement* (New York: McGraw-Hill Book Company, 1964).

[64] L. J. Cronbach and P. E. Meehl, "Construct Validity in Psychological Tests," *Psychological Bulletin*, Vol. 52 (1955), pp. 281–302.

other problem with which attitude research and measurement must contend is the problem that people do not always know specifically what their attitudes are. This is true for several reasons. First of all, most situations are so complex and involve so many different value positions that they lead to a great deal of ambiguity and confusion. Second, attitudes, like values, are dimly envisaged. People are not always sure just where they stand on a given complex issue. Can we expect consumers to know with calculator precision just how much they like or dislike a particular product or to have a well-ordered set of priorities for all their needs or perceived goal objects? Not likely.

New Directions in Attitude Research

Before concluding this chapter we shall look briefly into what many consider to be new approaches or new directions in attitude research. Much of this new research stems from the dissatisfactions that have persisted to plague on-going attempts to research attitudes scientifically and to assess their importance as determinants of behavior. In the forefront of these dissatisfactions looms the question of what attitudes really are. The disagreement over this question led one writer to specify five dimensions that stem from this disagreement.[65] First there is the disagreement about the psychological locus of attitudes. Are they mental and neural states; motivational, cognitive, or perceptual sets; or simply collections of responses? A second dimension of disagreement relates to whether attitude should be defined as a response or as readiness to respond. A third concern is the degree to which attitudes are organized. A fourth dimension of disagreement among definitions concerns the extent to which attitudes are learned through previous experience, and, finally, the fifth dimension concerns the extent to which attitudes play a dynamic motivational function.

We have examined the issues involved in the various dimensions of this controversy throughout our treatment. However, before concluding, let us briefly examine the nature of the most contemporary research underway in the area of attitudes.

One of the foremost authorities in attitude research has now conceded that the traditional approaches to attitude research have not led to much prediction between attitudes and behavior. In his words:

> viewing the attitude-behavior relationship within the framework of a multi-attitude object–multimethod approach, it becomes clear that the most important determinants of behavior may be other variables than an individual's beliefs about, attitude toward, or general behavioral intentions toward, a given object. Indeed this approach clearly indicates that behavior toward an object may be implicitly determined by situational or individual difference variables, rather than any variable associated with

[65] W. J. McGuire, "Nature of Attitudes and Attitude Change," in *Handbook of Social Psychology*, G. Lindzey and E. Aronson, eds. (Reading, Mass.: Addison-Wesley Publishing Co., Inc., 1968).

the stimulus object per se. *In other words, this approach points out that behavior toward a given object is a function of many variables, of which attitude toward the object is only one.*[66]

Thus we are reminded once again of the dangers of reductive-functional schemes. Fishbein, like others, is now inclined to collapse the concept of attitude and treat behavior in a larger scheme as a function of attitudes that are composed of cognitions or beliefs and behavioral intentions or connotations. This view is in keeping with that of another well-known contemporary researcher, Rokeach, who contends that an understanding of man's beliefs, attitudes, and values will not come about unless we are willing to distinguish these concepts from one another. His further contention is that values, beliefs, and attitudes are all organized together to form a functionally integrated cognitive system. A change in any part of the system will affect other parts and will culminate in behavioral change. Rokeach and others have come to argue that beliefs are as central to behavior as are attitudes and that, therefore, our focus must shift from that of mere attitude research to the more expanded view that encompasses value and belief systems.[67] One prominent researcher, Sheth, has adopted this point of view, and his studies and efforts are now predicated upon the notion that a restrictive subelement of cognitive structure (called the evaluative beliefs) about the brand may be more appropriate because it is a determinant of attitude.[68] Sheth's conceptual model is reproduced in Figure 10-2. Behavior (*B*) refers to buying behavior with respect to a brand in a product class. Behavioral intention (*BI*) is the verbal expression of intent or commitment to buy that brand in some future time interval. Affect (*A*) relates to like or dislike of the brand. Evaluative beliefs (*EB*) refer to a set of evaluations of the brand on its characteristics that are intimately related to the goals of the consumer. (*TB*) or total beliefs represent awareness and comprehension of the brand. Social factors (*SO*) imply external pressure from social sources such as family, friends, and so forth. Finally, (*PS*) and (*NS*) respectively refer to situational factors impinging upon the purchase of the brand that the buyer can anticipate and situational factors that did not occur at the time of purchase and could not be anticipated beforehand by the consumer.[69]

In a recently constructed model built upon this scheme highly

[66] Martin Fishbein, "Attitude and Prediction of Behavior," in *Attitude Theory and Measurement*, Martin Fishbein, ed. (New York: John Wiley & Sons, Inc., 1967), p. 491. Italics provided by the author.

[67] Rokeach, *Beliefs, Attitudes, and Values*, op. cit., ix and pp. 1–22 and 23–62.

[68] Jagdish N. Sheth, "Attitude as a Function of Evaluative Beliefs," unpublished paper presented at the AMA Consumer Workshop, August 22–23, 1969.

[69] Jagdish N. Sheth, "Canonical Analysis of Attitude-Behavior Relationships," unpublished paper presented at TIMS XVIII International Meeting, Washington, D.C., March 21–24, 1971.

Figure 10-2

A Conceptual Model of
Attitude-Behavior Relationship

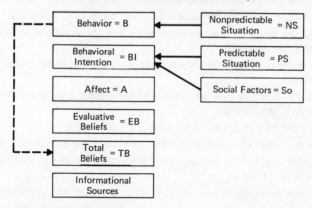

Source: Jagdish N. Sheth, "Canonical Analysis of Attitude-Behavior Relationships," unpublished paper presented at TIMS XVIII International Meeting, Washington, D.C., March 21–24, 1971.

significant canonical relationships were found that indicate strong relationships. However, the task of defining and isolating the variances relative to social factors, predictable situation, and nonpredictable situation must be carefully attended to. Without their careful observation and inclusion, the question of attitude as a predictor of subsequent behavior will, as Sheth suggests, remain a controversy.

The new directions in attitude research are conceptually very rich models and offer opportunities for generating fruitful research findings. It is too early to predict just what results are likely to be discovered. We may very well learn that because we couldn't satisfactorily deal with attitudes, we abandoned that topic to pursue an equally elusive and ambiguous one, namely, beliefs.

Throughout this chapter we have treated rather comprehensively the construct of attitudes. The meaning and nature of attitudes was discussed, as was the role of attitudes in consumer behavior. Our analysis was both structural and functional, and a large portion of our effort dealt with the relationship between attitudes and behavior. This discussion led us readily to a treatment and review of the question of how attitudes are acquired and changed. Finally, our treatment concluded with two relevant sections, one on the important topic of attitude measurement and its attendant problems, and the final section, which took us to the horizon for a brief look at some of the newer issues involved in attitude research. We shall continue the examination of attitudes in the next chapter by exploring the role of communication as a vehicle for facilitating the formation and change of attitude.

Questions for Study, Reflection, and Review

1 Discuss the nature of attitudes as perceptual-motivational states.

2 Distinguish between the three structural components of attitudes.

3 Describe the functions that attitudes serve and the resultant implications for behavior according to Katz.

4 Explain the implications for attitude change of the functional theory approach to attitudes.

5 Discuss the basic contention upon which Sarnoff's psychoanalytical theory of attitude is predicated.

6 Describe the flow of influence between attitudes and behavior.

7 Discuss the effect of social anchoring upon attitude-behavior consistency.

8 Explain the relationship between attitudes toward situations and attitudes toward objects.

9 Identify the three major sources from which attitudes are acquired.

10 Cite some of the statistical problems encountered in attitude measurement.

Part III

Facilitating Process Variables

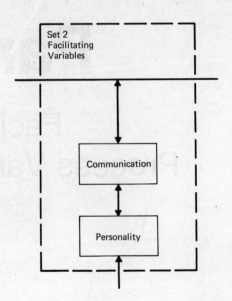

Set 2
Facilitating
Variables

Communication

Personality

11

The Process and Role of Communication in Attitude and Behavioral Change

Introduction

In the previous chapter, it was reasonably well established that underlying attitudes predispose behavior in a situation and that the situation itself also conditions behavior. We were not so bold as to state that behavior is caused by attitudes. As a matter of fact, as pointed out, attitudes are often caused by behavior. Furthermore, to the extent that attitudes influence behavior, they do so mostly indirectly and usually in conjunction with other variables and determinants.

Attitudes, nonetheless, continue to be viewed as a key influencer or variable in consumer behavior. And the myriad ways in which attitudes are formed and changed continue to preoccupy the research and theoretical interests of many consumer behavioralists. In the consideration of the dynamics of attitude change, one very important factor that was not extensively discussed in the last chapter was the processing of information through cognitive interaction. The usual interpretation given to information processing by the consumer is that such activity leads to the formation of new attitudes or the alteration of existing attitudes as a result of reorganization of the psychological field. A schematic illustration of the flow of influence from such a point of view can be demonstrated as follows:

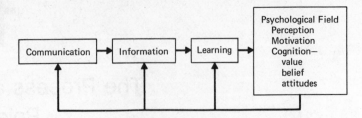

Information is a term used to cover any type of message (sign, content, or affective) transmissable from sender to receiver. The act of transmitting such messages is communication. Thus, in an affluent, commercial, and consumption-oriented world, a large number of the messages that reach the consumer's senses do so as a result of persuasive communication. Thus communication is intended to affect a consumer's learning and to alter his response repertoire, in turn altering his overall psychological field. The psychological field is composed of perceptions, cognitions, and motivations that condition the consumer or predispose him to certain behavior. Communicated information is intended to be extracted from the environment and to be used to order and interpret the events that surround him. Communicated information is intended to provide sense data or knowledge (cognition) that in turn is said to affect our values, attitudes, and beliefs. Finally, of course, communicated information, especially to the extent that it is persuasive communication, is designed to alter the consumer's response tendencies or his motivations. Effective persuasive communications are those that increase arousal, generate greater attention to or willingness to attend, and create a more positive state of conviction regarding some object or situation. Therefore, in this chapter, we shall examine the role of communication in change of attitude as well as other behavioral change.[1] Communication as a process implies a systematic series of actions directed to some end. Our examination will focus both upon the series of activities involved in communications and upon the ends or the objectives sought. In addition, our discussion will attempt to outline the consequences of communication upon overall consumer behavior. To this extent we will be concerned with the role of communication in overall consumer behavior and to some extent with the role or the entire characteristic pattern of behavior imposed upon the consumer in particular and upon marketing in general as a result of communication strategy and influences.[2]

[1] For an interesting look at communications and advertising interactions, see Donald L. Kanter, "Communication Theory and Advertising Decisions," *Journal of Advertising Research,* Vol. 10, No. 6 (December 1970), pp. 3–8.

[2] Portions of this chapter appeared in an earlier publication of the author. See *The Psychology of Consumer Behavior* (Englewood Cliffs, N.J.: Prentice-Hall, Inc., 1969). The material has been reorganized, updated, and revised for this publication.

Information-Processing Models of Communication

In an early and influential work, Allport listed four conditions for the formation of an attitude: the *integration* of numerous specific responses within an organized structure; the *differentiation* of more specific action patterns; the *trauma* that stems from the compulsive organization of the mental or psychological field following an intense emotional experience; and *emulation*, the adoption of attitudes by the imitation of parents, teachers, or press.[3] Such an approach to attitude formation and change is now recognized as overly descriptive and not sufficiently explanatory. However, each of these suggested conditions does tend to emphasize the different aspects of attitudinal learning and they each underscore the informational basis on which attitudes are acquired.

Campbell has examined attitudes as a special case of acquired behavioral dispositions and in so doing has focused on the problem of informational bases and processes.[4] He has suggested six ways of acquiring information upon which behavioral dispositions are based: blind trial and error, general perception, perception of others' responses, perceptions of the outcomes of others' explorations, verbal instructions relevant to behavior, and verbal instructions about objects' characteristics. Such a list of activities is highly suggestive of consumer decision processes and how consumer dispositions are created. Furthermore, Campbell's processes readily underscore the importance of the informational basis of attitude and other behavioral dispositions.

The informational basis of attitude and behavioral disposition change is most consistent with the cognitive view of consumer behavior outlined earlier; that is, it recognizes the information-processing nature of consumers, who when confronted with new information attempt to absorb and deal with it as effectively as possible and hence to alter their behavior accordingly. McGuire, using an information-processing approach to attitudes and behavioral change, has argued that there is a sequential series of steps or activities, each probabilistically tied to the preceding one, through which the individual must pass if he is to be effectively persuaded.[5] To some extent this is a process model of communication involving a kind of Markov chain predicated upon a hierarchy of effects or a ladder of persuasion. The high frequencies would occur in the low-conviction stage with the intermediate stages

[3] G. W. Allport, "Attitudes," in *A Handbook of Social Psychology*, C. Murchinson, ed. (Worchester, Mass.: Clark University Press, 1935), pp. 810–812.

[4] D. T. Campbell, "Social Attitudes and Other Acquired Behavioral Dispositions," in *Psychology: A Study of Science*, S. Koch, ed., Vol. 6, *Investigations of Man as Socius: Their Place in Psychology and the Social Sciences* (New York: McGraw-Hill Book Company, 1963), pp. 107–111.

[5] William J. McGuire, "An Information-Processing Model of Advertising Effectiveness," a paper presented at the Symposium of Behavioral and Management Science in Marketing, Center for Continuing Education, The University of Chicago, July 1969.

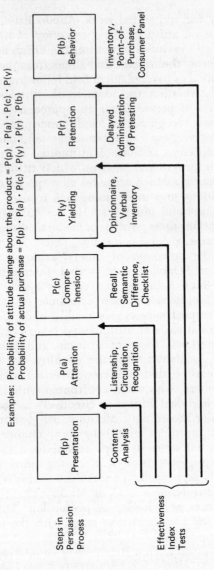

Figure 11-1

Indexes of Advertising Effectiveness Related to the Behavioral Steps in Being Persuaded

Examples: Probability of attitude change about the product = $P(p) \cdot P(a) \cdot P(c) \cdot P(y)$
Probability of actual purchase = $P(p) \cdot P(a) \cdot P(c) \cdot P(y) \cdot P(r) \cdot P(b)$

Steps in Persuasion Process					
P(p) Presentation	P(a) Attention	P(c) Comprehension	P(y) Yielding	P(r) Retention	P(b) Behavior

Effectiveness Index Tests:
Content Analysis
Listenship, Circulation, Recognition
Recall, Semantic Difference, Checklist
Opinionnaire, Verbal inventory
Delayed Administration of Pretesting
Inventory, Point-of-Purchase, Consumer Panel

Source: William J. McGuire, "An Information-Processing Model of Advertising Effectiveness," a paper presented at the Symposium of Behavioral and Management Science in Marketing, Center for Continuing Education, The University of Chicago, July, 1969.

ranging themselves in a normal pattern of distribution or logical gradation.

As shown in Figure 11-1, a message intended to affect and persuade a consumer may never reach him or be *presented*. Even if presented, the consumer may not *attend* to the message. Although the message may be attended to, it may not be *comprehended*. The probability of persuasion then rests on whether or not the consumer will yield to what he has understood and, if he does, whether he will manifest this new behavioral inclination. In the event that these five steps are taken, the final question arises as to whether the consumer will actually *behave* according to this inclination. Thus persuasive communication can be seen in a new light—not as a simple process of inoculation or cause and effect but as a highly complex process of multidimensional variables in which interaction is likely to affect behavior only probabilistically and indirectly in concordance with other factors. The steps and sequence of activities shown in Figure 11-1 can be considered the dependent variables of the information-processing approach. The independent variables can be thought of as the communication factors in operation.[6] We shall examine in considerable detail both the dependent and the independent variables involved in this process in the subsequent sections of this chapter.

The Communication Process

Consumer behavior is almost always the result of some form of communication. Communication is so pervasive and so much a part of our lives that we take it as readily for granted as breathing. Communication, therefore, is the determinant of much of behavior—the receiving of stimuli and the formation of mental and physical responses are a part of the living state of the organism. Our opinions, thought both public and private, attitudes, moods, predispositions, and cognitions are the products of myriad communications—some direct and loud, others subtle, subdued, and indirect.

Because communication is so important in all walks of life, all branches of the social sciences, and more recently many of the business administration theorists are becoming increasingly concerned with it and are studying and adding to the general fund of knowledge about it.[7] Our orientation is that of the student in a professional school of business administration. We wish to know, for pragmatic purposes, how communication functions as well as how it is structured. The advancement of science itself depends in considerable measure upon communication. Science, at least in one sense of the term, is the set of symbols that scientists use to communicate their knowledge to other scientists. And the advancement of science in marketing depends in

[6] This approach is followed in Thomas S. Robertson, *Consumer Behavior* (Glenview, Ill.: Scott, Foresman, and Company, 1970), pp. 46–48.

[7] See John Parry, *The Psychology of Human Communication* (New York: American Elsevier Publishing Co., Inc., 1968).

large part upon our ability to understand the consumer and to link him more closely to our decision processes—in short, we need to understand the communication process better and to incorporate the consumer into our communication network. In order for man, and the systems and institutions that he creates, to survive and function adequately in an ever-changing world, the state of the organism and the state of the environment must be able to mold and direct the organism's behavior. The adaptation process or the act of accommodation is facilitated through communication in terms of messages, signs, and language.

Virtually all directive language has an implicit future-oriented element.[8] By using this future-oriented element of language, communicators and persuaders attempt to transmit a sense of hope, fear, expectation, or anticipation regarding the consequences of currently urged action. Astute advertisers make extensive and frequent use of such directive language. These advertising tactics are often referred to as the "promise" in advertising.[9] Most advertising refers to such promises as "looking younger," "feeling better," "no more worries about . . ." Notice the "promise" and the use of the directive forms *how* and *can* in advertising. Ogilvy argues that the most powerful words used in advertising are *FREE* and *NEW*. Other words and phrases that he attests are effective are *ANNOUNCING, NOW, HOW TO, SUDDENLY, IT'S HERE, IMPORTANT, JUST ARRIVED, AMAZING,* and *SENSATIONAL.* As we shall subsequently learn, the use of persuasive language is big business.

Words are signs that conveniently replace the objects or ideas they represent. It would be misleading, as we will learn later, to imply that this representational character of words distinguishes them sharply from all other stimuli to which we respond. Listeners respond to spoken words in the same way they respond to other energies that impinge upon their receptor organs.

At the same time, stimuli do not present themselves in random, unorganized ways. It is an important psychological problem to discover the conditions under which stimuli are responded to as stable configurations. This is a basic problem related to verbal behavior and communication, because without such organization we can achieve no agreement as to the objects our words represent. For example, as we have not yet presented a formal definition of the word *communication,* there is likely to be considerable variance between what the writer has in mind and what is conjured up in the mind of the reader. Words have only an arbitrary significance—they signify only what we have learned they signify.[10] The fact that we say *store* instead of *retail oper-*

[8] S. I. Hayakawa, *Language in Thought and Action,* 2nd ed. (New York: Harcourt Brace Jovanovich, Inc., 1964).

[9] David Ogilvy, *Confessions of an Advertising Man* (New York: Dell Publishing Company, 1963).

[10] For a more comprehensive treatment of these ideas, see George Miller, *Language and Communication* (New York: McGraw-Hill Book Company, 1951).

ating unit is a matter of social coincidence and convenience. Verbal signs that are organized into linguistic systems are usually called verbal symbols. In order that we learn to respond correctly to certain words, it is usually necessary for another organism to intervene and reward us each time we respond correctly.

Once a given group or system has adopted a set of symbols, which we call vocabulary, and rules for combining them, which we call grammar, the conventions are no longer quite so arbitrary. What we have then by way of communication processes and systems is a set of mutually agreed upon concepts.

DEFINITIONS

Let us see how, through usage and consensus, this word *communication* has taken on arbitrary significance. Several definitions and their authoritative sources are as follows:

> Communication: The transmission of information, ideas, emotions, skills, etc. by the use of symbols—words, pictures, figures, graphs, etc.[11]

> Communication: The process of transmitting meaning between individuals.[12]

> Communications: The study of who says what to whom in what settings, by which channels and with what purposes and what effects. It deals with messages designed to influence human behavior, the media that carry such messages, and the markets that respond to such messages.[13]

> Communication: In essence, it implies the sharing of thoughts, feelings or apperceptive perception.[14]

There is, as there obviously should be, a high degree of similarity or commonness among these various definitions. As a matter of fact, the word *communication* comes from the Latin *communis*, which means "common." Therefore, when we communicate with someone we are trying to establish a "commonness" with him. We have just concluded, hopefully, an act of communication whereby you are convinced that the essence of communication is to get the sender and the receiver tuned in, so to speak, on the same wavelength for the purpose of exchanging information and perhaps even, under certain circumstances, for the purpose of altering beliefs or behavior.

[11] Bernard Berelson and Gary A. Steiner, *Human Behavior: An Inventory of Scientific Findings* (New York: Harcourt Brace Jovanovich, Inc., 1964), p. 527.

[12] Charles Wright, *Mass Communications* (New York: Random House, Inc., 1959), p. 11.

[13] Edgar Crane, *Marketing Communication* (New York: John Wiley & Sons, Inc., 1965), p. 10.

[14] Wilbur Schramm, "How Communication Works," in *The Process and Effects of Mass Communication*, Wilbur Schramm, ed. (Urbana, Ill.: University of Illinois Press, 1955), p. 3.

If you concur and find the conclusions regarding communication both as a word and as a symbol logically consistent and satisfactory, we have accomplished at least two things. First, we have communicated and, second, we have demonstrated the arbitrary significance of words. We now can see that words signify only what we have learned they signify. We could, if necessary, become arbitrary to the point where we would settle for only one of the definitions to the exclusion of the others. Inasmuch as they are all similar in meaning, it appears unnecessary to do so.

KINDS OF COMMUNICATION

Communication as an act or process can be divided into two major kinds. The first is referred to as mass communication and the second as personal or face-to-face communication.

Mass communication receives its name in the main from the kinds of media that are employed for the purpose of disseminating information. Mass communication, in other words, employs the mass media—newspapers, magazines, books, films, radio, and television. The characteristics of the mass media are suggested by the terms themselves: *massiveness*, or ability to communicate from a single source to large numbers of people, and what has been called *mediativeness*, or ability to communicate through a mechanical device such as print or a TV screen, creating an impersonal relationship between communicator and audience.[15]

Another distinguishing characteristic of mass communication is that it is directed toward a relatively large, heterogeneous, and anonymous audience; messages are transmitted publicly, often timed to reach most audience members simultaneously, and are transient in character. Furthermore, the communicator tends to be, or to operate within, a complex organization that may involve great expense.[16]

In contrast to mass communication, personal or face-to-face communication is defined as communication in which sender and receiver interact on a face-to-face or personal basis. Personal conversation, therefore, on either a face-to-face basis or via telephone, is communication. However, it is not massive and not necessarily mechanically mediated.

Generally speaking, mass communication evokes images of television, radio, motion pictures, and newspapers. But these technical instruments should not be mistaken for the process with which we are concerned. A nationwide telecast of a new product to thousands of consumers in their homes is mass communication. A closed-circuit showing of this product to a sales group in a test market city is not.

In short, communication is the process of transmitting meaning between individuals, and mass communication is a special kind of communication involving distinctive operating conditions, primary among

[15] Berelson and Steiner, op. cit., p. 528.
[16] Wright, op. cit., pp. 12–13.

which are the nature of the audience, the communication experience, and the communicator.[17]

Marketing firms are of necessity interested in both mass communication and personal communication. As a matter of fact, given the increased complexity and sophistication of marketing activities and the widespread spatial and temporal separation of marketers and consumers, mass communication has become one of the principal means of communication and promotion. Broadly speaking, mass communication activities are generally subsumed in the marketing organization under the heading "advertising and promotion," whereas personal communication of an external nature is subsumed under "personal selling or sales management."

EFFICIENT COMMUNICATION

In human societies the communication process is efficient to the degree that rational judgments are facilitated. This statement in no way implies that we have unlimited rationality or omniscience but rather that we have a bounded rationality that implements value goals and facilitates the decision-making process. In democratic societies rational choices depend on enlightenment, which in turn depends upon information and communication, and especially upon the equal attention toward communication of leaders, experts, and rank and file.

We are concerned with communication as a tool or means of developing improved marketing strategies in order that we may better serve our existing and potential markets and thus enhance our chances of making higher profits and using our resources more fully. Inasmuch as some marketing communications attain these ends, they are efficient. Much marketing communication, however, for numerous reasons, including both ignorance and greed, is anything but efficient.

One can distinguish between consequences and the aims behind the activity. Thus marketing communication may strive for all the noble and well-meaning objectives listed in the previous paragraph, yet the consequences of the activity may fall short of the stated objectives. Clearly, objectives and consequences need not be identical. Merton terms consequences that are intended *manifest functions* and those that are unintended *latent functions*.[18] It is certainly true that in marketing communication, as in other areas, not every consequence of an activity has positive value for the social system in which it occurs or for the groups or individuals involved. Consequences that are undesirable from the point of view of the welfare of the society or its members are called *dysfunctions*. Any single act may have both functional and dysfunctional effects. Therefore efficient marketing communications would be concerned with bringing about the manifest functions or objectives of the communication system and eliminating or minimizing the dysfunctions of that system.

[17] Ibid., p. 13.

[18] Robert K. Merton, *Social Theory and Social Structure*, rev. ed. (Glencoe, Ill.: The Free Press, 1957), Chapter 1, "Manifest and Latent Functions."

THE PROCESS

Earlier it was stated that a process is a systematic series of actions directed to some end. Naturally, the communication process is concerned with the transmission of information or apperceptive perception. A convenient way to break down the communication process and to look at the individual series of actions is to answer the following questions:

Who?
Says what?
In which channel?
To whom?
With what effects?[19]

The scientific study of communication tends to concentrate upon one or another of these questions. In reality, the field of communication is rather well specialized on the basis of this breakdown. Scholars who study the "who," the communicator, look into the factors that initiate and guide the act of communication. This aspect of communication is called control analysis. Other areas of specialization within the field of communication include content analysis, media analysis, audience analysis, and effect analysis. From the standpoint of the socioeconomic system, communication has at least three manifest functions: (1) the surveillance of the environment; (2) the correlation of the parts of society in responding to the environment; and (3) the transmission of the social heritage from one generation to the next.[20]

Inasmuch as marketing communication is a part of our total socioeconomic system, the manifest functions of marketing communication must at least be compatible with and contribute to the overall attainment of these objectives.

THE IDEALIZED COMMUNICATION SYSTEM

The communication process as a series of systematic actions is directed to the end that information is passed from one place to another. Whenever communication occurs, we say that the component parts involved in the transfer of information constitute a communication system. Every communication must have a *source* and a *destination* for the information that is transferred, and these must be distinct in time and space. Between the source and the destination there must be some connecting link that spans the intervening time and space; this link is called the *communication channel*. In order that the information can pass over the channel, it is necessary to operate on it in such a way that it is suitable for transmission; the component that per-

[19] Harold D. Lasswell, "The Structure and Function of Communication in Society," in *Mass Communications*, Wilbur Schramm, ed. (Urbana, Ill.: University of Illinois Press, 1960), pp. 117–130.

[20] Ibid., pp. 128–129.

Figure 11-2

Communication Components

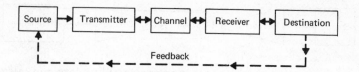

forms this operation is a *transmitter*. At the *destination* there must be a *receiver* that converts the transmitted information into its original form. These five components—source, channel, transmitter, receiver, and destination—make up the model communication system shown diagrammatically in Figure 11-2.

This communication model can be simplified, however, where source and transmitter or destination and receiver are the same. The simplified version is shown in Figure 11-3.

In terms of basic components, it can be seen that communication requires three elements—the source, the message or signal, and the destination or receiver. The source may be an individual or a spokesman for a small group or a multiunit organization. The message may be visual or audible, face-to-face or mediative. The receiver or destination, like the source, may be an individual, a group, a crowd, or a mob.

The communication process begins with the *encoding* of the message by the sender. This involves putting the information or feelings he wants shared into a transmittable form. The *code* is a pattern of energies that can travel over the connecting link. In other words, a code is simply an agreement on symbols between the two major parties of a communication act, that is, source and destination.

The receiver's behavior at his end of the channel is just the opposite of that of the source. His responsibility is to *decode* or reconstruct the message into a more useful and intelligible form. Diagrammatically, the process just described can be seen in Figure 11-4.[21]

One can observe that both structural and functional aspects are present in the diagrammed system. And like any system it can be no

Figure 11-3

A Communication Model

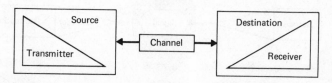

[21] Figure 11-4, as well as the rest of this section, owes much to the article by Wilbur Schramm entitled "How Communication Works," op. cit., pp. 3–26.

Figure 11-4

The Communication Process

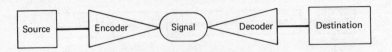

stronger than its weakest link. It is important to understand, also, that once encoded and sent, the message is quite free from its sender and that what it does is beyond the power of the sender to change.

A message is much more likely to succeed if it fits the patterns of understanding, attitudes, values, and goals that a receiver has, or at least if it starts with this pattern and tries only to reshape it or alter it slightly. Earlier we defined this process as *canalizing*, which, again, means that the sender provides a channel to direct the already existing motives to the receiver. This is what is meant when advertising people speak of starting where the audience is.

Once again, Schramm has provided us with an effective diagram for illustrating this phenomenon.[22] (See Figure 11-5.)

The area of intersection between the two fields of experience must be of some consequence in order for the two parties to communicate effectively. Those familiar with set theory will readily grasp the idea that if there is no intersection between the two sets or fields of experience communication will, at best, be difficult and at worst impossible. Those without an understanding of set theory should have no difficulty grasping the idea intuitively. The greater the area of intersection between the two sets of experiences, the greater the probability of effective communication. The source then, because he is the one who initiates the communication process, should attempt to encode in such a way as to make it easy for the receiver to tune in the message, to relate it to parts of his experience that are like those of the source.

Figure 11-5

Communication and Field of Experience

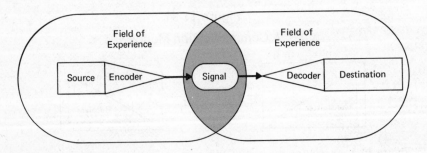

[22] Schramm, op. cit., p. 6.

REDUNDANCY. An important concept involved in communication is that of redundancy. The encoder and transmitter has a choice at all times between sending more information in a given time or transmitting less and repeating more in the hope of being better understood. Communication and learning are often facilitated by the transmission of less information at a given time and more frequent repetition. Thus, understanding may grow as a result of a building-up process—that is, first learning simple ideas on which more sophisticated ideas can be structured—and the well-known psychological principle that repetition facilitates learning. The astute student will have recognized that this text uses both of these ideas in its treatment of concepts and in its organization.

FEEDBACK. Another well-known communication concept is that of feedback. It was stressed earlier that both sender and receiver, if two-way communication is to be established, must play dual or reversed roles. Senders, if our system is to be an open one, must be receivers and vice versa. This concept is known as feedback. Feedback is an effort to recover a part of the output of a system in order to correct, modify, or control the total system. Marketing firms may often be more interested in establishing a communications system, the purpose of which is to feed back information, than in the transmission of information. Remember that a marketing message may consist of the firm's product, its distribution system, and its promotional activities. The transmission of messages composed of these elements is likely to be very ineffective if predicated on faulty perception regarding where the audience is. It is feedback that allows us to sharpen our focus and zero in on our marketing targets.

An example of the value of the feedback mechanism may illustrate our point more fully. Some communication systems may be developed for the manifest purpose of receiving feedback, for example, a suggestion box. Management's goal is to receive information so that it can evaluate its organization and personnel policies.

SIGNALS. Signals are messages that are made up of signs. A sign stands for something in experience. The word *store* is a sign that stands for our generalized experience with stores. The word would be meaningless to a person who knew nothing about the world of commerce and who came from a noncommercial culture. We learn the word as a result of association. A sign will not call forth all the responses that the object itself will call forth. For example, in Brown County, Indiana, there is a replica of an old-fashioned general store filled with fixtures and artifacts of a bygone era. Throughout the store is diffused the odor of old wood, worn leather, stick candy, sassafras bark, and spices. The store, as a sign, conjures up delightful memories, aromas, and associations. But the sign (Brown County store) always represents the object (the reality) at a reduced level of cues. By this is meant simply that the sign will not call forth all the responses that the object itself will call forth. This is a price we must pay for portability in language.

Our signal system is a kind of shorthand that enables us to categorize, locate, and store objects. As the sender transmits signals, he is receiving signals almost simultaneously, both from the person to whom he is sending and from the external environment. As he receives these signals he must interpret them and decide what portion of these signals he wishes to incorporate in his own transmission or how his transmission ought to be altered in light of these signals. When the signals are received, they come in the form of signs. If you know the sign, you generally know that there are certain responses associated with it. These are called *mediatory responses* because they mediate what happens to the message in your nervous system. Therefore these responses are the meaning the sign has for you. The mediatory responses have an effect on how you react to the sign. Specifically, just what you decode will depend on your choice of the responses available in the situation, connected with the meaning the responses have for you.

LEARNING. The process by which the sounds of a language and its signs come to acquire meaning is a part of the learning process. Communication obviously is intended to develop a commonness of feelings, agreement, mutual understanding, sharing of ambitions, and attitudes. Learning theory is, to a considerable extent, concerned with how these conditions come about. It is as difficult, however, for psychologists to agree about learning as it is for a group of theologians to agree on a definition of sin. Association theory or stimulus-response theory breaks behavior down into elements, studies the elements independently, and attempts to discover laws governing the combination of elements. It is rather typical for the association or stimulus-response theorists to emphasize the importance of learning as an explanation of behavior and to talk of the stimulus-response connections that a person acquires during the course of his life.

Cognitive or field theory, as we learned earlier, is both a protest against and a substitute for association theory. The cognitive theorists do not build the action pattern out of its component parts. Instead, they feel the parts have significance only in relationship to the whole. The cognitive theorists, it will be recalled, tend to emphasize the structure or configuration of the organism at the time an act is performed.

It is not necessary or tremendously important that we settle the dispute between the stimulus-response and the cognitive schools of learning. From our point of view the differences are not of paramount importance. Instead, it is sufficient to determine that learning occurs when insight is obtained and changes in behavior or attitude sets are manifested and that communication is the principal means by which we attempt to bring about learning, whether it be viewed from the simple stimulus-response approach or the somewhat more sophisticated, but less tidy, cognitive or Gestalt view. Most assuredly, we need much more knowledge and greater understanding of both communication and learning, as well as greater understanding concerning their interaction.

COMMUNICATION EFFECTS

Because of the uncertainty surrounding the interaction between learning theory and communication, it is difficult to talk either convincingly or conclusively about "the effect" of communication. As we shall see in the next section, communication has many effects or roles, and the measurement of any of these, deterministically, is subject to considerable difficulty. However, the difficulty of measuring or evaluating communication effects does not, in and of itself, abate the urgent desire of many to undertake such activity or make them less interested in its accomplishment. Nagging questions arise concerning the effect of mass communications on society as well as on consumer behavior. Do advertising and sales promotion lead to waste and inefficiency? Can consumers be misled or influenced to the point of being caused to buy unneeded or shoddy goods? Does cigarette advertising influence more young people to adopt the smoking habit than otherwise would? Only within the context of a carefully structured scientific framework can such topics be handled dispassionately.

There are two highly relevant causes that fuel the fantasies regarding communication effectiveness. The first is the extreme shortage of scientific evidence on media effects, and the second is the tone of economic and social urgency that often surrounds the questions about effects.[23]

Lazarsfeld and Merton have identified four sources of public concern about mass media.

1. Many people are alarmed by the ubiquity of the mass media and their power to do good or evil.
2. Conceivably economic interest groups may use the mass media to insure public conformity to the social and economic status quo.
3. Critics argue that the mass media, in accommodating large audiences, may cause a deterioration of aesthetic tastes and popular cultural standards.
4. In many instances, it is believed that mass media have nullified social gains for which reformers have worked for decades.[24]

It is not our task at this juncture either to support or to refute these arguments. Instead, it is sufficient to point out that communications, and especially marketing communications, are highly suspect in terms of their effect in persuading consumers to a particular point of view or frame of mind.

[23] Wright, op. cit., p. 90.

[24] See Paul Lazarsfeld and Robert Merton, "Mass Communication, Popular Taste and Organized Social Action," in *The Communication of Ideas*, L. Bryson, ed. (New York: Harper and Row, Publishers, 1948), pp. 95–118.

The effect of communication is largely concerned with the relationship of learning and communication. It is sufficient, for at least this stage in our understanding of communication, to conclude that communication has a positive effect, at least from the sender's point of view, if the receiver acts favorably to his message or request. Instead of establishing a simple and predictable relationship between communication messages and responses or effects, it is easier to describe what might be called the conditions that must be fulfilled if the message is to arouse the intended response.

1. The message must be so designed and delivered as to gain attention of the intended destination. It must be available.
2. The message must employ signs which refer to experience common to both source and destination, in order to "get the meaning across."
3. The message must arouse personality needs in the destination and suggest some way to meet those needs. We take action because of needs and toward goals.
4. The message must suggest a way to meet those needs which is appropriate to the group situation in which the destination finds himself at the time when he is moved to make the desired response.[25]

Given these conditions, communication is likely to have some kind of effect. Communication effects, as pointed out by Schramm, result from a number of forces, of which the communicator can really control only one. This is the *message*. The other three are situation, the personality state of the receiver, and group relations and standards.[26]

We will turn our attention in the following sections to a more exhaustive treatment of communication effects, or what the writer prefers to call the role of communications.

UNDERSTANDING COMMUNICATION'S ROLE

Our knowledge about the effects of communication has been fairly adequately, if not precisely, outlined by Berelson in the statement that "some kinds of *communications* on some kinds of *issues*, brought to the attention of some kinds of *people* under some kinds of *conditions*, have some kinds of *effects*."[27] This is not, operationally speaking, much of a valid conclusion or a predictive tool for marketers or communications researchers. And the task of both of these groups has been, of late, an increasing and more scientific attack upon the general problem of analyzing the role of communications, both in the more general social context and in the expanding world of commerce. Twenty-five years after Berelson's statement concerning the "role" of communication, we are still engaged in research studies and speculation regarding the ex-

[25] Schramm, op. cit., p. 13.
[26] Ibid., p. 17.
[27] Bernard Berelson, "Communications and Public Opinion," in *Communications in Modern Society*, Wilbur Schramm, ed. (Urbana, Ill.: University of Illinois Press, 1948), p. 172.

panding role of communication. And despite the added intensity and the sophistication of our research studies and methodology, we can today assert little more, and with little more assurance, accuracy, and predictive value, than did Berelson.

Consequently, the discussion that follows must necessarily be of such a nature and couched in such qualifications as to be tentative rather than assertive. Our analysis necessarily leads to suggestive prescriptions, which, however, must lack conclusiveness. In keeping with our skepticism regarding direct cause-effect relationships, we arrive at the point where the "hypodermic effect" is refuted in favor of a situational, functional, or what Klapper calls *phenomenistic* approach, which he defines as "a shift away from the tendency to regard mass communication as a sufficient cause of audience effects, toward a view of the media as influences, working amid other influences, in a total situation."[28] This viewpoint, if not entirely the same as our framework for cognitive behavior developed earlier, is at least similar to and consistent with it. This view regards the role of communication as the observation of existing conditions or changes, followed by an inquiry into the factors along with communications that produced these conditions or, as was stated earlier, the range of the characteristic set of behavior patterns produced by the communication process. The communication process is thus viewed as a set of influences, working in conjunction with other influences, in a total system or situation. Klapper thus defines the phenomenistic attitude regarding communication effects as a situation in which "attempts to assess a stimulus which was presumed to work alone have given way to an assessment of the role of that stimulus in a total observed phenomenon."[29]

This approach appears to make possible certain generalizations regarding communication as a process and the role of this process. These generalizations are by no means verified to the point where they would warrant the label *law*, and scarcely *principle*. Instead, at least until more conclusive evidence is gathered, they might more nearly be called *testable hypotheses*. Some, of course, have progressed further in terms of the usual tests of validity and therefore might possess a greater operational usefulness. Others, however, represent only vague impressions and are highly conjectural and of doubtful operational validity. Again, let it be pointed out that the usefulness of the generalizations will vary depending on the purposes to which they are put. As guideposts for acquiring a greater understanding regarding the process and role of communications, they are of inestimable value. Likewise, as a basis for incorporating our understanding of communication into an overall framework of marketing strategy and theory, they would appear as at least the bare framework for such an undertaking. The generalizations that have emerged as a result of the phenomenistic

[28] Joseph T. Klapper, *The Effects of Mass Communications* (Glencoe, Ill.: The Free Press, 1960), p. 5.

[29] Ibid., p. 5.

study of the communication process as reported by Klapper are as follows:[30]

1. Mass communication ordinarily does not serve as a necessary and sufficient cause of audience effects, but rather functions among and through a nexus of mediating factors and influences.
2. These mediating factors are such that they typically under mass communications are a contributory agent, but not the sole cause, in a process of reinforcing the existing conditions.
3. On such occasions as mass communication does function in the service of change, one of two conditions is likely to exist. Either:
   a. the mediating factors will be found to be direct; or,
   b. the mediating factors, which normally favor reinforcement, will be found to be themselves impelling toward change.
4. There are certain residual situations in which mass communication seems to produce direct effects, or directly and of itself to serve certain psycho-physical functions.
5. The efficacy of mass communication, either as a contributory agent or as an agent of direct effect, is affected by various aspects of the media and communications themselves or of the communication situation (including for example, aspects of textual organization, the nature of the source and medium, the existing climate of public opinion, and the like).

The lay person commonly believes that communication has a considerably more direct and profound effect on the receiver than these generalizations assume.

In order that we may proceed to examine the range in the characteristic set of behavior patterns produced by the communication process, as outlined by Klapper's generalizations, the reader is urged to reread and examine them. We shall then proceed to investigate more fully this set of behavior patterns, first within a general communication framework, and later within a more behavioristic consumer framework as it relates to the marketing strategy development of the firm.

It is a widely held lay opinion (and also true) that the aim of most communication is to persuade. Persuasion is the act of attempting to bring about some known reaction. But what are the ranges of reactions that communication as a persuasive force attempts to bring about? The remainder of this chapter is largely concerned with this problem. Persuasive communication attempts to win people over to particular courses of action. But what about the range of behavior that falls in the category of "particular courses of action"? What are the alternatives available to the receiver of the communication message? Are these alternatives acceptable to the communication source and transmitter in light of his (or their) goals and objectives? In short, in discussing the role of the communication process we are necessarily concerned with the effects of communication, the previous qualifications and generalizations notwithstanding. We have tentatively discov-

---

[30] Ibid., pp. 8–9.

ered that instead of direct cause-effect relationships, there are only mediating effects, depending on other related phenomena. We shall continue our discussion of effects within this context and attempt now to assess (1) the possible range of effects within (2) the context of the other related phenomena.

ALTERNATE VIEWS OF PERSUASIVE COMMUNICATION

Our discussion thus far leads us to the point of a flat assertion: *Communication does not directly affect consumer behavior but may positively or negatively affect behavior given the presence or absence of certain mediating factors and their interaction.* Nowhere is this assertion shown to be more valid than in the two-step theory of flow of communication. As the name implies, *two-step* means that communication and resulting behavior or attitudinal changes are the function not of one factor but of two or more. The developers of the two-step flow theory contend that influences stemming from the mass media first reach opinion leaders, or what might be called key influentials, who in turn pass on what they read and hear to those of their everyday associates for whom they are influential.[31]

The concept of the audience as a large homogeneous mass of disconnected individuals hooked up in direct cause-and-effect linkage with the media, but not to each other, cannot be readily reconciled with the two-step-flow-of-communication model, which implies complex networks of interconnected individuals through which mass communications are channeled.[32] The theory further provides several additional concepts or ideas worthy of exploration in our effort to structure the relationship between communication and consumer behavior. First of all, we now must recognize the role of personal influence in the overall decision processes of consumers. Second, it would appear that some people are likely to play a more important role as key influentials than others in the transmission of information and as persuaders in certain kinds of consumer behavior.[33] And, third, how do mass communications affect the decision processes, and thus behavior, of this select group of opinion leaders or influentials? An exhaustive treatment of these questions is naturally beyond the scope of this book, but we will explore at least the fundamental dimensions of these questions as we proceed to a more thorough examination of the role of personal influence in consumer decision-making.

Figure 11-6 shows three alternate models of communication. The

[31] Paul F. Lazarsfeld, Bernard Berelson, and Hazel Gaudet, *The People's Choice,* 2nd ed. (New York: Columbia University Press, 1948).

[32] See Elihu Katz, "The Two-Step Flow of Communication: An Up-to-Date Report on an Hypothesis," *Public Opinion Quarterly,* Vol. 21 (1957), pp. 61–78.

[33] For a look at how such opinion leaders or key influentials are identified, see Laurence G. Corey, "People Who Claim to Be Opinion Leaders: Identifying Their Characteristics by Self-Report," *Journal of Marketing,* Vol. 35 (October 1971), pp. 48–53.

Figure 11-6
Alternate Views of Persuasive Communication

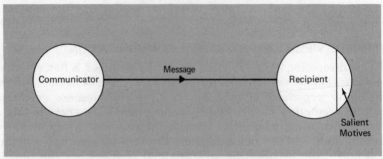

A. Traditional Advertising-Propaganda Model

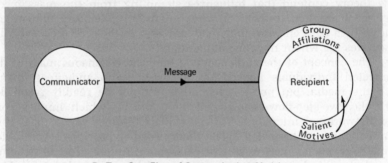

B. Two-Step Flow of Communications Model

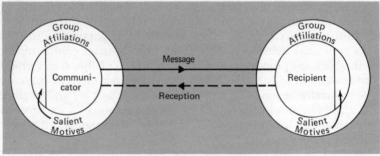

C. Transactional Model of Communication

Source: Edwin P. Hollander, *Principles and Methods of Social Psychology* (London, England: Oxford University Press, 1967), p. 153.

models are progressive in that they show the development and progression of the research and thinking regarding communication's effect. In Model A, the "hypodermic effect" of communication is underlined, whereby the audience is innoculated by the message and the expectation is that the recipient acts upon the message when his salient motives are aroused. In Model B, the two-step flow of communication is emphasized. This model suggests that the message is originally screened and filtered by the recipient's group affiliations before it affects the salient motives. In Model C, the message is received and interpreted by the recipient within the context of his own group affiliations and motives and, most importantly, of the recipient's perceptions of the motives and group affiliations of the communicator. This latter view has come to be known as the transactional model of communication. The transactional model places great emphasis on the interaction of the motives and social identities of both communicator and recipient. It eschews the idea that the recipient of the communication is passively receptive to the message. The transactional view instead contends that the recipient may be, and often is, actively resistant to communication messages. Furthermore, the transactional model contends that acceptance of the communication as a basis for attitude or behavioral change involves a *transaction* between the communicator and the recipient, producing influence effects of sufficient magnitude only where there is a fair exchange.

Bauer, the originator of the transactional view, puts it this way:

> communication and the flow of influence in general must be regarded as a transaction . . . in the sense of an exchange of values between two or more parties; each gives in order to get. The argument for using the transactional model . . . is that it opens the door more fully to exploring the intention and behavior of members of the audience and encourages inquiry into the influence of the audience on the communicator by specifically treating the process as a two-way passage.[34]

Thus it would follow from the transactional model that persuasive communication is limited by the perceptual and cognitive processes of consumers. All communication is, therefore, filtered through the existing value, belief, and attitudinal systems. And as previously pointed out, information via communication will generate attitudinal or behavioral change only to the extent that it is perceived as having instrumental value. This instrumental value implies that communication must be perceived as meaningful and facilitating in terms of uncertainty reduction or in terms of providing content that is viewed as containing new knowledge.

Perhaps the most significant feature of the transactional model and the two-step model of communication is that both emphasize the role of personal influence and the fact that people trust and listen to their friends.

Mass communication by its very impersonal nature is subject to considerable suspicion. The mass media are much more purposeful in their intent—that is, they have a definite axe to grind—whereas per-

---

[34] R. A. Bauer, "The Obstinate Audience: The Influence Process from the Point of View of Social Communication," *American Psychologist*, Vol. 19 (1964), p. 327.

sonal influence is somewhat less purposeful or more subtle in its approach to influencing or altering opinions, behavior, or position.

Research has shown that the strength and flow of personal influence depends to a considerable extent on the individual's role and status within the group.[35] Therefore, in attempting to analyze something of the relationship between consumer behavior and marketing communications we must be aware of and deal with the problem of personal influence as both a causal and a mediating factor. People talk with, seek advice from, or allow themselves to be influenced by other people. Usually the other people are those who are very much like themselves, having the same or closely allied interests, backgrounds, or life styles. Just who is likely to become a key influential, or why, is not thoroughly understood, but one's degree of influence seems somehow related to three factors.

1. Personification of certain values (who one is).
2. Competence (what one knows).
3. Strategic social location (whom one knows).[36]

These factors strongly suggest that a high degree of social interest is therefore involved in the process of decision making as it is affected by personal influence; that is, group norms, reference groups, class, and status are phenomena that affect the communication process and have a determining influence on the overall effects of communication, including personal influence on the consumer behavior decision processes.

THE REALISTIC OR TRANSACTIONAL POINT OF VIEW

In developing a communication strategy the marketer must be attuned to a particular point of view regarding the nature and behavior characteristics of his audience. There are at least two viewpoints regarding the audience. One is egotistical and the other is realistic.[37] The shortsighted, egotistical point of view regards the audience as a relatively inert and undifferentiated mass that can be persuaded in something like a direct cause-and-effect manner via the mass media. This point of view is egotistical because it attributes great powers to the communicator and regards the audience as a swayable mass. In short, the two-step model and the transactional model of communication are not considered. The realistic point of view, given our knowledge of human behavior and influences on behavior, offers greater promise for the more effective use of communication inasmuch as the audience is viewed as a body of interacting individuals who may respond to a communication in a variety of ways depending on their individual predis-

[35] Ibid., pp. 62–64.
[36] Ibid.
[37] The ideas in this section are developed from Donald F. Cox, "Clues for Advertising Strategists, II," *Harvard Business Review,* Vol. 39 (November–December 1961), pp. 160–182.

positions. The realistic or transactional point of view enforces the notion that although the communicator, the communication, and the medium play important roles in the communication process, it is the cognitive set of the audience, in the final analysis, that determines *if* and *to what extent* it (the audience) will be influenced. Remember from our earlier discussion that cognitions are attitudes, values, predispositions, opinions, and so forth that tend to make our perceptions meaningful. Therefore, in order for the audience to be influenced in the desired manner by a communication, several conditions must be met:

1. The message must reach the sense organs of the people to be influenced. (*Perception* must occur.)
2. If perception occurs, the message must be compatible with and accepted as a part of the person's beliefs, opinions, and knowledge. (A high state of *congruence* must be present.)
3. To induce favorable behavior by communication, this action must be seen by the person as a path to some goal that he has. (*Canalizing* or matching means to ends must be accomplished.)
4. To induce a given action, it is necessary that the consumer's behavior be under the control or influence of appropriate motivation, attitudes, and opinions relating to the purchase decision. (*Cognitions* must operate to provide behavior insights.)

It is obvious from viewing the conditions necessary for influence to occur that the consumer becomes a gatekeeper or decision maker regarding the communication process and its effects. The consumer *decides* what messages to receive by deciding what kinds of communication messages or media he will expose himself to. He also decides what messages to *perceive* and what messages to *retain* on the basis of certain sociopsychological factors. These sociopsychological factors are basically the consumer's *predispositions, which are in the nature of anticipatory reactions or conditions of readiness brought about by social phenomena such as group norms, attitudes, and culture.*

A large amount of marketing communication must function either to reinforce existing attitudes and behavior or to accelerate or stimulate the behavior sequences of consumers who are already *predisposed* to act in a given manner. As was emphasized in the previous section, communication is not in itself a *direct* cause of audience effects but works with and through various mediating factors such as audience *predispositions* and *personal influence,* which themselves are subject to mediating factors such as group norms, attitudes and opinions, and culture. It therefore appears logical to conclude that the major function of marketing communication is to select consumers or target markets that are already predisposed to buy certain products and present them with appeals that encourage and facilitate cognitive learning and thus the desired responses.

Thus in developing communication strategy the marketer is advised to keep in mind that he should begin his effort by looking at de-

fined market segments, because based upon the behavioral and attitudinal characteristics of the defined segment, he then knows what should
be the objective of the communication, for example, to influence a particular component of attitude or perhaps to change a characteristic of
behavior. In this way, also, the marketer can define the goal of the
message source. Knowing the characteristics of the individuals in the
market segment, the marketer has a great deal of information that
should prove useful in the encoding proesss. Furthermore, because the
marketer has knowledge of the personal characteristics of the segment
members, the process of selecting the specific channels of communication becomes, at once, more rational and objective.

THE RANGE OF POSSIBLE COMMUNICATION EFFECTS

Communication as a persuasive tool is most often used to affect
the learning process. Earlier we discussed learning and concluded that
the term, used very broadly, means the acquisition of skills and understanding and involves a process of perceptual and cognitive reorganization. In measuring the effects of learning, we discover that such effects
can lead to very minor attitudinal changes or to completely reversed
opinions and insights leading to observable and manifest behavior characteristics—conversion. We might just as well be discussing the possible range of effects for communication, and actually we are because,
as has been repeatedly demonstrated, the communicator is using his
knowledge, at least as he understands it, of the learning process in
order to accomplish his communication goals. Once again it must be
repeated that communication is the *means* of implementing the learning process. Communication, therefore, can be instrumental in accom-
plishing three levels of characteristic behavior results: (1) minor attitude change and reinforcement, (2) creation of opinion on new issues,
and (3) conversion—significant changes in thought and behavior.

REINFORCEMENT AND MINOR CHANGE. There is an overwhelming
amount of evidence, both from the researcher's laboratory and from
the world of commerce, that strongly suggests that communication is
far more effective as an agent of reinforcement than as an agent for
change or conversion. As a matter of fact, in light of the direction of
changes in relation to communication as mentioned earlier, Klapper
has stated that "it would appear to be no exaggeration to say that the
efficacy of mass communications in influencing existing opinions and
attitudes is inversely correlated with the degree of change."[38]

Our task here can only be to survey briefly the three levels of
change or, as we have called them before, the range in the characteristic set of behavior patterns produced by the communication process
and to look within each of these categories at some of the phenomena
responsible for both the type and the intensity of the communication

[38] Klapper, op. cit., p. 15.

response. Our treatment will be hardly more than a survey and a description.

The human mind is hardly a blank slate upon which messages are indelibly inscribed by the communication process. As a matter of fact, we are at any one moment the product of countless communication messages, plus a host of other mediating factors including heredity, intelligence, life style, group norms, and culture. Therefore the idea that we receive messages of any kind with an "open mind" is a rather absurd suggestion. On the other hand we may be somewhat open to the *reception* of messages, even if we are not necessarily open to the *perception* of messages. In fact, we generally "see" only what we "know" or have been conditioned to see.

A man's perception is fashioned by his existence. Thus, the communication process is affected by the psychological phenomenon described in earlier chapters as perception, and perception together with its influence as a mediating factor of communication is in turn affected by a group of phenomena known as *selective perception, selective exposure,* and *selective retention.* Consequently, our predispositions, which are brought about by a multitude of factors, cause us to expose ourselves selectively to the messages that are compatible with those predispositions. We subject ourselves to the messages and appeals that we want to hear, resulting, to a considerable degree, in a constant reinforcing of our predispositions. Normally, over time we tend to become more rigid in our behavior patterns instead of more flexible.

Not only do we selectively expose ourselves to the media, messages, and appeals that support our predispositions, but we perceive what we want to perceive. Media messages and appeals that are in conflict with our norms of behavior and our predispositions are converted, in the event of exposure, to positions more nearly compatible with our own. We tend to see, hear, and believe only those things that we wish to see, hear, and believe. Finally, our predispositions induce us to retain only what is congruent or compatible with our life style. This is known as *selective retention.* Ideas, concepts, messages, and appeals to which we have been subjected are rapidly forgotten if they do not tend to reinforce our existing attitudes and predispositions.

Thus we see that our predispositions give rise to selective exposure, selective perception, and selective retention. These phenomena have the tendency, in turn, to *reinforce* our existing opinions, norms, or predispositions. Therefore, one of the more probable effects of communication is that of reinforcement or the inducement of minor attitudinal changes.[39]

Our attitudes and predispositions do not spring forth full blown, however, and remain forever fixed. Man is a learning animal and he does change over time. The reasons that man's attitudes or predisposi-

[39] For well-documented examples of and research into these phenomena, see Bernard Berelson and Hazel Gaudet, *The People's Choice* (New York: Columbia University Press, 1948).

tions change over time are far from obvious and are not yet completely understood. Only a most succinct treatment of a few of the factors mediating the change in predispositions is possible here. Predispositions, as we have said, grow out of one's existence. We live, think, act, and behave in a group or societal situation. We are further disposed to do these things within a milieu in which others live, think, act, and behave in a fashion similar to our own or in a fashion to which we aspire. Consequently, our attitudes, opinions, and predispositions are to a considerable extent those that come to us via the selective processes just discussed and that reflect the attitudes, opinions, and predispositions of the groups to which we belong. Thus, the group tends to act as a filter that aids the selective process. The group tends to aid reinforcement of existing predispositions in a number of ways.[40] It makes possible selective exposure to sympathetic communication; that is, two individuals in group interaction discussing commonly held views are likely to reinforce their own respective positions. Argument and discussion most often tend to bring our own attitudes and prejudices into sharper focus.

Sometimes, given the nature of our own personality, its strength or weakness, its dominance or submissiveness, we discover that we take our cues regarding predispositions and attitudes from *opinion leaders* or that we ourselves may be opinion leaders on certain issues or in a particular sphere of issues. The opinion leader is generally a most representative member of the same group as the followers, but he is likely to be more exposed to communication, and perhaps even more articulate in his dissemination of the group norms or attitudes. The opinion leader is most often a force for reinforcement and minor change, as opposed to conversion. The opinion leader, like any leader, is one who follows the same path of action as the group but is a little further advanced than his followers. The point is this: conversion is not often the aim of the opinion leader nor the result of his actions. To be an opinion leader, one must first be a member of the group and hold the basic attitudes and predispositions of the group. An individual with attitudes and opinions contrary to the group norm is not likely to become either a member of that group or an opinion leader.

Individuals are subject to influence and change of attitudes as a result of communication persuasion depending to a considerable extent upon how important they perceive the issue to be. Issues that are essential to their self-images or the perpetuation of their life styles are often referred to as ego-involved attitudes. Such attitudes are extremely difficult to change. Therefore communications aimed at converting ego-involved attitudes are quite likely to fail. Conversely, communications designed to bolster or reinforce ego-involved attitudes have a high probability of success.

[40] Elihu Katz and Paul F. Lazarsfeld, *Personal Influence: The Part Played by People in the Flow of Mass Communication* (Glencoe, Ill.: The Free Press, 1955).

THE CREATION OF OPINION. Individuals generally have neither open nor closed minds. They have not made up their minds about all things for all time. New issues are constantly arising out of the dynamic forces of the world of society and commerce. One practitioner of the blackest side of communication, Joseph Goebbels, Hitler's minister of propaganda, stated that "Whoever says the first word to the world is always right."[41]

Many persons today, though with far less sinister motivation, both believe and practice this communication dictum. The basis for this position is that mass communications can play an important role in fostering and developing attitudes and opinions concerning issues on which individuals have no opinions or attitudes. However, one must be cautious in pursuing this line of reasoning too far. In an age of mass communication miracles in which whirling satellites make instantaneous communication from the local to the international scene not only possible but actually operational, the number of truly "new" issues that are likely to confront an individual is apt to be quite small. So-called new issues will tend to have decided areas of similarity to issues that have already been considered and toward which we have built up a reservoir of attitudes and predispositions.

However, when issues arise toward which the individual or group has no particular feeling one way or the other, communication is believed to be widely efficient in creating opinion or in developing what we have called predispositions. Under these circumstances communication is likely to have more of the so-called hypodermic effect, whereby the communication receiver or the audience is inoculated with a message that supposedly predisposes it favorably toward the given position of the message source.[42] When a subject has no firmly held opinions, communication is likely to play an instrumental role in the formation of opinions on an issue. When opinions have already been formed, the mediating factors listed earlier—the selective processes, group norms, and opinion leaders—are likely to filter and greatly affect the communication messages directed toward receivers, and thus a communication contrary to the predispositions of the individual and the group is likely to be rejected outright. When the message is compatible with the predispositions of individual and group, it will tend to reinforce the existing predispositions. On new issues or on issues on which the individual and the members of his group have not taken positions or on which they have arrived at a state of relative indifference, communication, because it is not hampered or mediated by the selective processes or group predispositions, is allowed to get through to the receiver un-

---

[41] Leonard Doob, "Goebbels' Principles of Propaganda," *Public Opinion Quarterly*, Vol. 14 (1950), p. 435.

[42] Irving L. Janis and M. Herz, "The Influence of Preparatory Communication in Subsequent Reactions to Failure," summarized in Carl I. Hovland, Irving L. Janis and Harold H. Kelly, *Communication and Persuasion* (New Haven, Conn.: Yale University Press, 1953), pp. 114–116.

contaminated, and he is likely to formulate opinions at least partially on the basis of the communications.

CONVERSION: THE ABOUT-FACE IN COMMUNICATION. Conversion is not well understood. This phenomenon lies at the very heart of the individual's behavior mechanisms. Communication is seldom, if ever, solely responsible for conversion; instead, much like reinforcement though in a somewhat introverted fashion, it requires extra communication factors working in a mediating fashion to bring about the desired effect. However, in the case of conversion as opposed to reinforcement, the extra communication factors appear to be less active or to work in an imperfect manner. For example, the selective processes may actually sensitize an individual to change. A person who is upward mobile, whose reference groups are rapidly changing, and whose group norms are therefore fuzzy and not well defined may be alerted to change or conversion by communication. Individuals already impelled toward change would, conceivably, selectively expose themselves to the communications that offer a fresh insight or point of view or that are congruent with their new outlook.[43]

Group norms may become, at least for certain issues, considerably less important and thus less effective in the conversion processes. An individual may find his personal aspirations no longer closely tied to his existing group memberships, and he may therefore be more inclined to go it alone on particular issues. Also not to be overlooked is the fact that not every issue germane to the individual is germane to the group or groups to which he belongs. Certainly, for issues on which the group has taken no stand, the individual remains somewhat naked in his defense against the communication messages to which he is subjected.

The role of personal influence and opinion leaders can be highly effective in the whole range of influence of mass communications and will be dealt with at considerable length later. However, it has been shown that personal influence tends to exercise a more direct and important effect toward change than does mass communication when both such influences are present.[44]

As a matter of fact, it has been rather conclusively shown that conversion—real change in attitude and behavior—is most often the product of personal influence and face-to-face communication and is reinforced by the mass communication media; that is, it is the product of a two-step flow or double-barreled communication effect.[45] The gist of this hypothesis is that the mass media reach the opinion leaders and the opinion leaders reach the masses.

[43] Bernard Berelson, Paul F. Lazarsfeld, and William N. McPhee, *Voting: A Study of Opinion Formation in a Presidential Campaign* (Chicago: University of Chicago Press, 1954).

[44] Katz and Lazarsfeld, op. cit., pp. 253–258.

[45] Katz, op. cit., pp. 61–78.

As was previously discussed, some individuals appear by dint of personality to be more persuasive than others, and their persuasiveness appears to be related more to their own self-image or self-esteem than to their actual intelligence. The degree of persuasiveness appears also to be topic free; that is, regardless of the topic or issue, the highly persuasive personality remains the highly persuasive personality.[46]

There are many stratagems for facilitating conversions. Boring from within, the idea of planting an idea within a group or individual and letting him convince others within his reference group of the merits and advantages of a given issue or cause, can be an effective means of facilitating conversion. The stratagems of the camel's head in the tent, the red herring, and Fabianism are all longer-run methods for bringing about conversion.

THE COMMUNICATION SITUATION

It was stated earlier in this chapter that the communication process is viewed as a set of influences working in conjunction with other influences in a total situation. Our task is not yet completed, however, inasmuch as we have not dealt explicitly with another set of interacting variables affecting the persuasiveness of communicating, namely, the communication itself and its aspects. The situations in which communications occur have been found to be related to the effectiveness of persuasion or the degree of effectiveness in bringing about reinforcement, attitude change, or conversion. However, certain aspects of the communication situation have been categorized and partial explanations of their persuasiveness documented. The communications situation consists of (1) the source of the communication, (2) the medium through which it is transmitted, and (3) the content of the communication itself.[47]

Earlier we viewed the communication process in terms of:

Who?
Says What?
In Which Channel?
To Whom?
With What Effect?[48]

Now our task here is to examine briefly how effects are brought about by the "Who," or source, speaking through a particular channel or medium and giving a particular message that "Says What."[49]

---

[46] Carl I. Hovland, Irving L. Janis, and Harold H. Kelly, *Communication and Persuasion* (New Haven, Conn.: Yale University Press, 1953), p. 175.

[47] Klapper, op. cit., pp. 98–99.

[48] Lasswell, op. cit., p. 117.

[49] For an up-to-date and comprehensive treatment of this topic, see Thomas S. Robertson, *Innovative Behavior and Communication* (New York: Holt, Rinehart & Winston, Inc., 1971), especially Chapter 6, pp. 136–168.

SOURCE EFFECT. The audience is most likely to have opinions and predispositions regarding the source of the communication, and this audience image of the source will probably affect the communication's persuasive intensity. Sources viewed as authoritative, trustworthy, reliable, and so on are likely to be viewed favorably and in turn favorably dispose the audience toward their messages, even though the qualifications of the source are not in the area of its message dissemination—for example, an actor who becomes active in politics. Normally, however, highly specialized sources appear to be more effective for similarly specialized audiences than are more general sources for specialized audiences.

MEDIA EFFECTS. The media or channels of communication can themselves be an effective force for bringing about desired results in the range or characteristic set of behavior patterns produced by the communication process. Many people are somewhat in awe of the mass media, and messages carried over such media are likely to have a persuasive effect on certain listeners or viewers. The fact that a known personality endorses a particular issue creates certain positive communication effects. The additional fact that this personality endorses the issue on network television may, other things being equal, only add to the persuasiveness of his given message. The different media or channels of communication are in turn affected by the selective processes of both individual and group, depending on a host of psychological, sociological, and other factors including life style and the relative position in the family life cycle. People with more education generally tend to watch less television and a different mix of programs than their less-educated counterparts. Commuters tend to listen to more radio than those who do not commute. Generally speaking, as we noted earlier, personal appeal or face-to-face contact is more effective as a persuasive tool than various forms of mass communication, including print, radio, and television.

Conclusive evidence attesting to the persuasive ability of the various mass media has yet to be brought forth. Suffice it to say that each of the media possesses certain qualities and characteristics that, depending on the nature and characteristics of the audience, the goals and objectives of the communicator, and the structure of the message itself, have a given probability of persuasive success.

MESSAGE EFFECTS. The actual content and the structuring of the message itself are known to have an effect on the persuasiveness of communication. Messages that are clearly stated, simple in construction, and unambiguous have a better chance of clearly conveying the attitudes and wishes of the sender or source and thus a greater likelihood of bringing about the desired communication objectives. The highly educated receiver is likely to be suspect of one-sided messages, and therefore he is likely to receive and act more favorably upon two-sided messages. On the other hand, the less-educated receiver will probably be less responsive to the two-sided messages, perhaps because they confuse him. People can, perhaps, be presented with too many facts that can be interpreted in too many ways and offer too many choices. On the other hand it would seem safe to conclude that the middle-class majority probably prefer a choice between something and something rather than something and nothing in the messages they receive.

Pointed communications appear to be more successful than indirect messages. For example, communications that convey facts, draw conclusions, and suggest courses of action are likely to be more effective than those that present only facts and allow the audience members to draw their own conclusions. The reason again can probably be found in the selection process and the fact that certain audience members need to be told what they are supposed to see, hear, or read and, specifically, what the things they have seen, heard, or read imply in terms of attitudes, opinions, or behavior.

Fear appeals have been shown to be less effective in persuading the audience to certain prescribed attitudes and behavior than appeals that are tempered with reason and more calmly emphasize a given threat. Attempts to motivate or to alter attitudes predicated upon fear appeals have been shown to be more effective for those consumers who have not perceived themselves as part of the market for the recommended product or brand.[50] Wheatley has attempted to verify this generalization but with limited results.[51] Most likely, fear appeals that are alleged to be more effective are more effective because they are not *perceived* as fear appeals and are therefore not so anxiety inducing.

Repetition that does not harangue and annoy the receiver has been found to be an effective means of increasing the persuasiveness of communication.[52] Such results are said to stem from the increased awareness and retention that stems from repetition. Generally speaking, the probability of purchasing an advertised brand increases with the frequency of exposure to communication messages.[53] However, there does exist a point of diminishing returns. Stewart found this point at fifteen exposures and Light found increases in awareness to stabilize after four exposures.[54] The value of repetition in communication, no doubt, results from its reinforcing tendency. A thing heard or seen re-

[50] Michel L. Ray and William L. Wilkie, "Fear: The Potential of an Appeal Neglected by Marketing," *Journal of Marketing*, Vol. 34 (January 1970), p. 59.

[51] John J. Wheatley, "Marketing and the Use of Fear-or-Anxiety-Arousing Appeals," *Journal of Marketing*, Vol. 35, No. 2 (April 1971), pp. 62–64.

[52] "Frequency in Broadcast Advertising: 1," *Media/Scope* (February 1962); see also "Frequency in Print Advertising: 1," *Media/Scope* (April 1962).

[53] "More Exposure Means More Effectiveness," NBC *Research Bulletin*, 1960.

[54] J. B. Stewart, "Repetitive Advertising in Newspapers: A Study of Two New Products," (Boston: Harvard Business School, 1964); and M. Laurence Light, "An Experimental Study of the Effects of Repeated Persuasive Communications upon Awareness and Attitudes," unpublished dissertation, The Ohio State University, 1967.

peatedly is more likely to become both (1) more familiar and (2) more believable.

It is something of a surprise to one's intuitive understanding of communication and persuasion to learn that attitudes are changed more in the direction of a communication if distraction occurs during that communication.[55] A study by Freedman and Sears has demonstrated that both distraction alone and forewarning alone are important variables in attitude change via communication.[56] The exact psychological processes that make attitude change more positive when distraction is used are not known. Some studies point out that distraction often limits counter arguments.[57] Others have focused upon the tendency of distraction to shift attention to the personality of the communicator and this suggests the well-known source effect in communication.

Finally, in terms of looking at the role of distraction in terms of message effects, some investigation has been given over to what kinds of distraction are most effective in changing attitudes via communication. In a study by Zimbardo, Ebbesen, and Fraser, the presence of a sexual distractor (slides of female nudes) made the message more potent in terms of generated change in attitudes.[58] The use of female models in a sexist way in commercial advertising is widespread. The Zimbardo, Ebbesen, and Fraser study would suggest a positive benefit to such usage. However, the role of distraction and the use of sexual distractors in generating increased change in attitudes through communication is not yet fully validated. Considerable study and research remains to be undertaken.

Communication is an interpersonal event and it would, therefore, seem apparent that whether and to what degree a communication is effective will depend upon the way in which the sender and the message are perceived. The attributes that the receiver evaluates, before evaluating the message, center around the attractiveness of the sender, his group affiliations, and his credibility. These findings have important implications for the marketing firm from the standpoint of both personal selling and advertising.

Insurance salesmen are usually projected as attractive, well-groomed, mature, conservative people, as men of position, stature, and

---

[55] This hypothesis was first advanced by L. Festinger and N. Maccobby, "On Resistance to Persuasive Communications," *The Journal of Abnormal and Social Psychology,* Vol. 68 (1964), pp. 359–366.

[56] J. L. Freedman and D. O. Sears, "Warning, Distraction and Resistance to Influence," *Journal of Personnel and Social Psychology,* Vol. 1 (1965), pp. 262–266.

[57] W. J. McGuire and D. Papageorgis, "Effectiveness of Forewarning in Developing Resistance to Persuasion," *Public Opinion Quarterly,* Vol. 26 (1962), pp. 24–34.

[58] P. G. Zimbardo, E. B. Ebbesen, and S. C. Fraser, "Emotional Persuasion: Arousal State as a Distractor," unpublished manuscript (Stanford University, 1968).

integrity—in short, as people you can put your trust in because they have your best interests at heart. Firms that promote via mass communication often attempt to make their promotional campaigns and appeals more acceptable by promoting the company and its institutional values as well as the individual products.

Another dimension of this concept, which we called earlier the source effect, is the sleeper effect. Studies have shown that compared with immediate attitude change, there is, over an interval of some weeks, a *decrease* in the amount of agreement with the trustworthy source and an *increase* in the amount of agreement with the less trustworthy or the untrustworthy source.[59] This phenomenon is explained by the assumption that with the passage of time the identity of the communicator becomes less relevant than the content of the actual message.[60] Put more simply, it means that with the lapse of time attitudes regarding "who said it" become less important than attitudes regarding "what was said."

At the outset, receivers who are initially disposed to accept the message because of the trustworthiness of the communicator generally show a decreasing acceptance of the message as this awareness of the trustworthy communicator decreases over time. The role of consumer attitudes and their effect and influence on consumer behavior are, as yet, more suggested than demonstrated. The attitudes of receivers toward the senders of messages really amount to something of an independent judgment by the audience as to whether they will be more or less influenced. This concept of source effect and the related concept of sleeper effect were more thoroughly analyzed in terms of their marketing relatedness by Levitt in a simulated study at the Harvard Graduate School of Business.[61] The simulated study of source effect and sleeper effect led Levitt to posit a series of questions and answers pertaining to these phenomena and industrial selling. A summary of relevant findings and conclusions are as follows:[62]

1. "Does corporate or institutional advertising by industrial product companies pay?"

   Yes! Advertising can be an effective means of creating a favorable corporate image (bundle of attitudes) and increasing a given company's ability to make sales. The strong presumption regarding advertising is that mere visibility of a company's message is in some way helpful and reassuring, provided that

[59] Carl I. Hovland, A. A. Lumsdaine, and Fred P. Sheffield, *Experiments in Mass Communication* (Princeton, N.J.: Princeton University Press, 1949).

[60] See Gary I. Schulman and Chrysould Worrall, "Salience Patterns, Source Credibility and the Sleeper Effect," *Public Opinion Quarterly*, Vol. 34 (Fall 1970), pp. 371–382.

[61] Theodore Levitt, "Communications and Industrial Selling," *Journal of Marketing*, Vol. 30 (April 1967), pp. 15–21. By permission of the American Marketing Association.

[62] Ibid., pp. 16–17.

the impressions that are created are not negative. Generally speaking, the better a company's reputation, the better its chances of (a) getting a favorable first hearing for a new product among customer prospects and (b) getting early adoption of that product.

2. "Do well-known companies' salesmen have an edge over the salesmen of other companies?"

Yes! And customers generally seem to have a different set of expectations and reactions (attitudes) to the better-known companies' salesmen. In short, customers expect more of them. However, there is some indication that some buyers or prospects actually attempt to help the lesser-known company's salesmen.

3. "Is it better to advertise more or to select and train salesmen better?"

There is what Levitt calls a presentation effect surrounding the well-done sales presentation. The smaller company may benefit more from a really effective sales presentation than from its advertising. However, the larger and more prestigious company loses the advantage of its reputation *if* its direct sales presentation is clearly inferior to that of an unknown or a little-known company. The general conclusion would be that the less-known and prestigious company, in terms of its communication mix, can do an exceedingly effective job for itself through a more careful selection and training of salesmen.

4. "Is there a sleeper effect in industrial selling?"

Yes! The research indicates that there exists in industrial purchasing a phenomenon that communication researchers call the sleeper effect. The favorable influence of a company's generalized good reputation does indeed erode away over time. Erosion appears to occur specifically when there is no intervening reinforcement or reinstatement of the identity of the source. The sleeper effect, it would appear, thus tends to hurt the well-known company relatively more and the lesser known company relatively less.

Throughout the last two chapters we have had a look at attitudes. This chapter has focused upon the process and role of communication as a vehicle for attitudinal and behavioral change. The essential point of view has been maintained, namely, that consumers are problem solvers and that their problem-solving efforts are facilitated as a result of information processing. *Information* is a term that covers any type of message that can be transmitted from a sender to a receiver. The transmission of this information involves the process of communication. Communication is not necessarily direct or one-to-one but rather affects attitudes and behavior indirectly. Communication is an influencer of behavior working amid other influences, such as the cognitive phenomenon already discussed, and other factors yet to be discussed, such as personality, social influences, culture, and so forth. In the next chapter we shall explore the concept of personality as a variable in consumer behavior.

Questions for Study, Reflection, and Review

1 Explain the probabilistic nature of McGuire's process model of communication.

2 Describe the basic characteristics of mass communications.

3 How does the area of intersection between fields of experience affect the communication between two parties?

4 What is the significance of signals and signs in the communication process?

5 Compare the hypodermic approach to the role of communication with the phenomenistic approach.

6 Discuss the nature of the two-step flow of communication.

7 Describe the transactional model of communication in terms of the interaction between communicator and recipient.

8 Describe the process by which selective exposure, selective perception, and selective retention tend to reinforce our existing opinions and beliefs.

9 Explain the nature of a conversion in communication and the conditions under which it is facilitated.

10 Discuss the phenomenon called "sleeper effect" and its implication for marketing and advertising.

12

Assessing the Impact
of Personality

Introduction

Throughout the discussion thus far we have attempted to develop
and examine a series of concepts and constructs that appear to be
causative factors in consumer behavior. Traditional treatments of consumer behavior are for the most part reductive and functional; that
is behavior is assumed to be caused (the functional element) by
some single or isolated determinant or variable (the reductive element). The literature of marketing and consumer behavior is replete
with studies focusing upon the impact of some independent variable
—motivation, perception, attitudes, and so forth—on some isolated
dependent variable such as purchase or nonpurchase, brand usage,
heavy or light use, and so on. Earlier we eschewed this reductive-
functionalist orientation in favor of a holocentric model of consumer
behavior. This holocentric approach emphasizes the wholeness or the
Gestalt aspects of behavior. This point of view is that behavior is seldom, if ever, caused or determined by a single variable but instead
that behavior is a multivariable phenomenon. One variable may in a
given situation assume paramount or central (hence the *centric* suffix
to our adjective) importance, but it does so in a transactional or situational sense, with many other variables present and exerting some influence. Thus, although our own discussion has necessarily moved
from one variable to another, it has done so by stressing the interactional nature of behavior within the holocentric concept. All too fre-

quently, consumer behavioralists are inclined to focus upon the mechanisms of behavior (attitudes, values, perceptions, and so on) rather than upon the actual person who is behaving. To some extent, at least, this situation is remedied when the independent variable in question is that of personality. In its broadest and most intuitive sense, personality is a distinct *person*-related variable. The word *personality* has as its basic root the word *person*, which comes from the Latin word *person-alis*, which means "personal" or "relating to person." Thus when the psychologist or the consumer behavioralist interested in consumer behavior focuses upon the construct of personality, the emphasis is on the person as a whole, as an organized system—not as a series of distinct functions or mechanisms but as a total functioning, integrated being. The researcher would recognize, of course, that the personality is made up of both structure and functions and that personality is a composite of various subordinate processes, such as motivation, emotion, cognition, perception, and roles, but that these are organized into a larger system.

Personality is an often-used variable in studies of consumer behavior. Almost every facet of purchasing behavior and consumption has been examined within the context of personality—media choice, store choice and preference, innovation, market segmentation, packaging, product and brand choice, heavy versus light use, opinion leadership, attitude change, perception, and virtually every other conceivable variable have been linked to personality. The predictive results of personality as a variable in consumer behavior have not been empirically proved. Yet theorists continue to engage in research efforts designed to show the statistical significance of personality in some aspect of purchase and/or consumption.

Throughout this chapter, we shall examine the concept of personality. Our initial effort will focus upon the basic concept. After examining and describing the various characteristics of personality, we shall move toward a more comprehensive attempt to circumscribe the construct by examining the many ways by which personality as a sociopsychological variable is determined. Most centrally, however, our major concern within the chapter will be to examine the evidence that has resulted from the empirical research efforts aimed at relating personality to specific instances of consumer behavior. The chapter will conclude with an examination of the relevance of personality as a consumer behavior variable. As we shall see, there is much to suggest that some new direction should be taken in our continuing efforts to predict behavior on the basis of personality characteristics.

What Is Personality?

Personality, at least in the popular sense, is a reasonably familiar term to most everyone. People are characterized as having or not having personality. The truth is, of course, that everyone has "personality" or "a personality" but some people's personalities are perceived as being more pleasant than others' and it is often the amount of like or dislike that causes us to characterize people's personalities as good or bad, desirable or undesirable. Personality, in the lay sense, is often equated with charisma or charm. However, when the social psychologist or the consumer behavioralist talks about personality he is discussing what he feels are observable traits and characteristics of people. Because they are observable they are measurable by psychographic or other psychometric measures.

There are numerous definitions of personality. Let us examine some of them, not so much to observe the many variances but instead to observe the many similarities that persist from one definition to another.

Hilgard has defined personality as "the configuration of individual characteristics and ways of behavior which determine an individual's unique adjustment to his environment."[1] Bonner defines personality as "the organized needs and abilities of an individual, or the characteristic manner in which he satisfies his needs and actualizes his potential."[2] Hebb has defined personality as "the characteristics that determine the general pattern of behavior in a higher animal, especially as it makes the individual distinctive in relations with others."[3]

Thus the definitions quoted have a high degree of similarity. However, these quoted definitions by no means suggest the great range and diversity that does exist—a range and diversity that prompted Hall and Lindzey, in attempting to deal with the myriad approaches that exist in the literature, ultimately to contend that "personality is defined by the particular concepts which are part of the theory of personality employed by the observer."[4]

Several comments would appear to be warranted. First, notice that of the three definitions first quoted, each tends to define personality largely from the standpoint of personal behavioral characteristics. Second, these personal behavioral characteristics are viewed as being organized, related, and patterned. Third, these patterned characteristics are said to be self-serving; that is, they facilitate the attainment of the needs and goals of the individual.

These, then, are several of the features of personality. For our purposes a simple, distilled definition of personality will suffice. We shall treat personality as *the sum total of an individual's patterned characteristics that make him unique.*

Personality, it must be noted, is another sociopsychological con-

---

[1] Ernest R. Hilgard, *Introduction to Psychology* (New York: Harcourt Brace Jovanovich, Inc., 1967),.p. 21.

[2] Hubert Bonner, *Psychology of Personality* (New York: The Ronald Press Company, 1961), p. 37.

[3] D. O. Hebb, *A Textbook of Psychology* (Philadelphia: W. B. Saunders Company, 1966), p. 9.

[4] Calvin S. Hall and Gardner Lindzey, *Theories of Personality*, 2nd ed. (New York: John Wiley & Sons, Inc., 1967).

struct much like attitudes, cognitions, or motivation. It is an inferred entity. We cannot "see" an attitude; neither can we "see" personality. *Personality* is a label that is used to characterize a person's repertoire of response tendencies. It is generally felt that personality consists, at least in part, of the individual's attitudes, motives, response traits, and so on, all of which are highly interdependent. Although personality cannot be directly observed, we nonetheless learn about personality by inference. Personality is not observable, but the effects of personality on behavior are.

Characteristics of Personality

It is perhaps easier to describe personality than it is to define it. Invariably our definitions of personality turn out to be descriptions. Personality is a complex construct possessing both structural and functional features. Keep in mind that when personality is characterized as having structural and functional features it does not mean that we can actually look at personality or its components in any physical sense. Instead, for analytical purposes we examine personality "as if" it possessed these features.

STRUCTURAL DIMENSIONS OF PERSONALITY

Earlier our definitions suggested that personality consisted of organized characteristics. These structures collectively make up the total configuration that we call personality. Moore and Anderson have suggested that there are at least six parts to a fully functioning human personality. These are (1) a data tape, (2) an agent, (3) a patient, (4) a reciprocal perspective, (5) an umpire, and (6) a feeling-emotion system.[5] Without undue elaboration, the data-tape aspect emphasizes that subjects who make decisions, seek goals, and cope with their environment must be able to take information in, process it, and have some output. They must also be able to recognize and differentiate things in their environment. The data-tape concept implies rather sophisticated central processing mechanisms.

The agent aspect of personality suggests that subjects must possess an ability to execute an action, or do something. This ability must be combined with some ability to evaluate the results of action. The patient aspect of personality suggests that subjects not only initiate action but that they, in turn, are the recipients of action. A patient is one to whom something is done. Each human must be able to take both perspectives. Reciprocal perspective suggests that subjects must be able to see themselves as others see them. It considers the fact that others have agent and patient roles and that they are looking at the subjects while the subjects are looking at them. The concept of

---

[5] Omar Khayyam Moore and Alan Ross Anderson, "The Structure of Personality," in *Motivation and Social Interaction: Cognitive Determinants*, O. J. Harvey, ed. (New York: The Ronald Press Company, 1963), pp. 167–186.

reciprocal perspective underscores the transactional nature of personality.

The umpire aspect of personality suggests that subjects judge and evaluate. Like an umpire, the subject takes a detached standpoint from which he decides whether rules or practices have or have not been broken. Finally, the feeling-emotion aspect of personality suggests that all the activities just described are continually checked against the system of human emotions and that the subjects evaluate and choose on the basis of what they like.

This particular structural model of human personality has not been extensively analyzed. However, it is interesting in terms of its rather novel analysis and especially in terms of how well it appears to parallel much of our own treatment of consumer behavior and decision-making.

Maddi has characterized personality in terms of a structural analysis by discussing what he calls the core and the periphery of personality.[6] The core of personality relates to those attributes, traits, or characteristics that delineate the things that are common to all people. These core features disclose the inherent attributes of man and they do not change much in the course of everyday living. As core aspects of personality, they constitute the central and essential factors that exert a continuous and pervasive influence upon behavior. However, Maddi argues that there is another feature or dimension of personality and that this dimension is much more concrete and closer to behavior than can be readily observed. The attributes in this dimension are generally learned, rather than inherent, and have a circumscribing influence on behavior. These attributes, called the *periphery of personality*, are basically those that are used to explain the differences among people.

Most theories of personality, as we shall later discover, have both core and peripheral statements. Core statements usually underscore the basic concepts relating to the direction, function, and purpose of behavior. Peripheral statements, on the other hand, circumscribe and highlight the characteristics concerning the concrete styles of life that differ from person to person. Concrete peripheral characteristics are the basic building blocks of personality construction. They constitute the most homogeneous explanatory elements the theorist believes possible. As we shall subsequently learn, peripheral characteristics are most usually defined in terms of personality *traits*.

FUNCTIONAL ASPECTS OF PERSONALITY

Most of the definitions of personality contain both implicit and explicit references to functional characteristics. For instance, such phrases as "makes for inward unity" and "organized patterns of characteristics which make for consistent behavior" are examples of func-

[6] Salvatore R. Maddi, *Personality Theories: A Comparative Analysis* (Homewood, Ill.: The Dorsey Press, 1968), especially pp. 13–15.

tional aspects. Personality has several functional qualities. Those that we shall discuss briefly include consistency, accommodation or plasticity, and unity and integration.

CONSISTENCY. Functional aspects of a system refer to the processes or activities engaged in by that system. Every given personality can be viewed in terms of its consistent patterns. Without a measure of consistency we could literally not think of personality because people would be changing so much that they could not be characterized in terms of personality. Consistency in personality is observed in several ways. The most important, of course, consists of observation of what is called the *external* level of personality and of attitude scales or projective tests that attempt to discern the internal levels of personality.[7] External levels of personality relate to expressive feelings and manifest themselves in styles of action. They express certain underlying qualities of personality. In Chapter 5 we referred to such expressive movements as *cognitive style*. Cognitive styles, you will recall, are ways of thinking and perceiving that characterize a person independently of the content of the act. Cognitive style, broadly conceived, relates to expressive movements such as motor acts as well as unique cognitive processes like perception and thinking. Internal levels of personality include such nonobservable factors as attitudes, values, interest, and acquired motives in the subject's psychological field. Consistency is a basic characteristic of personality. People tend to manifest consistency at both levels of personality. However, it must be quickly pointed out that the consistent aspect of personality does not make for robot- or automaton-like behavior. Some people are more consistent than others. Some manifest low, and others high, degrees of consistency. But almost all people are less than 100 per cent consistent in their personalities. This lack of consistency is no doubt a desirable feature. Because of it people are able to accommodate and adjust to new demands. The flexibility and plasticity of human behavior can be attributed in part to a lack of total consistency in personality.

ACCOMMODATION AND PLASTICITY. Although personality is often viewed as a way of construing the world, including the perception of self in relation to the world, it is also a device that enables us to accommodate ourselves to a dynamic environment.[8] Accommodation and plasticity reflect the cognitive-information processing-learning aspects of behavior. Although there are consistent and stable aspects of personality, there is at the same time, in most subjects, a continuing

[7] See Edwin P. Hollander, *Principles and Methods of Social Psychology* (London: Oxford University Press, 1967), pp. 275–279.

[8] This view has been expressed by George Kelly, *A Theory of Personality: The Psychology of Personal Constructs*, Norton Library ed. (New York: W. W. Norton & Company, Inc., 1963). See also E. L. Kelly, "Consistency of the Adult Personality," *American Psychologist*, Vol. 10 (1955), pp. 659–681.

tendency toward change and accommodation as a result of changing environmental conditions. Change occurs and the subject accommodates to it. When a consumer encounters a dramatic new situation or identity through marriage, more education, travel, or increased or decreased income, his outlook and response tendencies may be altered. Consumers are constantly creating new goals, evaluating new alternatives, processing and evaluating new information. The impact of this cognitive behavior results in degrees of both consistency and flexibility. As Rogers maintains, human growth requires constant reorganization; it is this reorganization of the levels of personality, both external and internal, that results in a relatively high degree of plasticity in the human organism; and it is this plasticity that makes possible accommodation and, ultimately, survival.[9]

INTEGRATION. Finally, as a functional activity or process of personality, we must speak of integration. Integration refers to the fact that the various aspects of personality are organized and integrated into some kind of patterned whole. Goldstein has suggested that the normal personality is integrated and that sufficient lack of integration is equivalent to pathology.[10] Integration thus suggests a harmonious, if not totally congruent, organization of personality. Personality is characterized as a dynamic construct that seeks harmony and integration and that directs activity in self-congruent ways. The normal development and growth of personality suggests integration—progression from one lower or primitive stage to more advanced stages of personality development. Thus most theorists of personality view human development as a progression toward more sophisticated structure and the increasing integration of motivational, emotional, and cognitive processes.[11]

OTHER FEATURES OF PERSONALITY. Only a few examples of the numerous ways to characterize the structural and functional features of personality have been offered. However, two additional properties of personality that must be touched upon briefly are the concepts of *motivation* and *control*.

Without exception, all personality theories posit certain behavioral tendencies and responses that relate to both the motivation and the control properties of the organism. For example, qualities such as consistency, accommodation and plasticity, and integration in effect relate to other inferred qualities of pesronality such as control. Personality is often considered the executive or decision-making center of the individual. Self-control is an example of this idea. Personality is

[9] Carl A. Rogers, *On Becoming a Person* (Boston: Houghton Mifflin Company, 1961).

[10] See K. Goldstein, *The Organism* (Boston: Beacon Press, 1963).

[11] Gordon W. Allport, *Becoming: Basic Considerations for a Psychology of Personality* (New Haven, Conn.: Yale University Press, 1955).

viewed as the inhibiting feature of the human organism that tells us when to proceed and when to withdraw. Personality is responsible for controlling and managing the selective inhibition of impulses. In other instances, personality is not only given the responsibility for selectively inhibiting impulses but is also charged with the responsibility of transforming impulses previously directed toward one goal to those directed toward another goal. Thus a desire to purchase a new car is channeled instead into the act of depositing one's money in the local savings bank.

More important than control as an aspect of personality is that of motivation. Recall if you will from our earlier treatment of motivation in Chapter 7 that theories of motivation are invariably theories of personality and vice versa. For example, Maddi has classified all theories of personality into three major classes or schools.[12] Each of these schools posits a set of generalizations regarding the nature of motivation. To illustrate, Maddi argues that all personality theories or models are (1) conflict models, (2) fulfillment models, or (3) consistency models. Conflict models include such theories as those of Freud, Murray, Sullivan, and Rank. Fulfillment models include such theories as those of Adler, White, Fromm, Rogers, and Maslow. Consistency models include such theories as those of Kelly, Festinger, McClelland, and others. You will recall many of these names from our earlier treatment of motivation. Each of these classifications or schools posits a central personality core tendency that relates to motivation. For example, the conflict school agrees that behavior is caused by man's conflict with the environment. Essentially, the motivation for behavior is to maximize instinctual gratification while minimizing punishment and guilt. The fulfillment school argues that behavior is caused or motivated by such factors as man's striving for superiority or perfection, his pushing toward actualization of inherent potentialities, or his functioning in a manner expressive of the self. Finally, the consistency school suggests that behavior is caused or motivated by man's attempts to predict and control the events he experiences, to minimize large discrepancies between expectation and occurrence, to eliminate cognitive dissonance, or to maintain the level of activity to which he is accustomed.

Thus, in exploring and assessing the impact of personality on consumer behavior, we must be apprised of the structural and functional features of personality, as well as the additional roles attributed to personality in terms of its motivational and control features.

APPROACHES TO PERSONALITY DETERMINATION

We come now to the question, "How is personality determined?" Like most questions in social psychology and consumer behavior, there are several answers. To examine this question we had best look at what constitutes a psychological event. By examining the nature of a

[12] Maddi, op. cit., pp. 481–502.

psychological event, we come in turn to an appreciation of the various frames of reference in which personality determination is explored.[13]

A psychological event is comprised of a stimulus, an organism, and a response, often shown as S-O-R. Stimuli are usually defined in terms of the reactions they induce. Responses include both specific actions like searching or buying and the more difficult aspects of behavior subsumed under styles of action. The organism consists of the person and the combined set of mediating structures and processes. This description and characterization of a psychological event gives us an interesting and meaningful way of exploring the question, "How is personality determined?" Some theories focus upon personality essentially in terms of responses. These are usually referred to as the trait or typological approaches. Others focus upon the stimulus side of the psychological event and the physical stimuli and learning as the central mechanisms that lead to response repertoires and personality. Finally, some theorists focus upon the mediating processes and structures of the organism and infer that these processes are the principal means by which personality is shaped and acquired. This latter approach is sometimes referred to as a phenomenological approach.[14]

TRAIT APPROACHES TO PERSONALITY. The trait approach to personality determination, as has been said, emphasizes the *response* aspect of personality. Given recurring stimuli and certain mediating structures and processes, a person's personality is characterized by the traits or attributes that are persistently generated as responses. For example, the California Personality Inventory attempts to profile personalities by graphing such traits as dominance, sociability, self-acceptance, responsibility, socialization, self-control, tolerance, achievement, and so forth.[15] In the trait approach to personality we identify, through factor analysis and other techniques, the most important characteristics in human personality and attempt to analyze their organization. Traits have been analyzed in terms of their impact on role dispositions (ascendance, dominance, social initiative, and independence) and in terms of their sociometric dispositions (acceptance of others, sociability, friendliness, and sympathy). Finally, traits have been treated in

---

[13] This analysis and framework follows the work of Richard S. Lazarus, *Personality and Adjustment* (Englewood Cliffs, N.J.: Prentice-Hall, Inc., 1963), pp. 53–63.

[14] Phenomenology is a school of philosophy and psychology that emphasizes the subjective or apperceptive nature of stimuli. For example, a product has physical, concrete, and objective properties. Products are stimulus objects. However, the physical, concrete, and objective properties constitute what is called the distal stimulus. In addition to these properties, products are viewed subjectively: they have images and perceived subjective qualities. The perceived subjective qualities of a product are referred to as the proximal stimulus. Phenomenology would also emphasize the subjective perceived "phenomena" qualities and characteristics of a psychological event.

[15] Not all the traits included in the CPI have been listed here; this is only a representative listing.

terms of expressive dispositions (competitiveness, aggressiveness, self-consciousness, and exhibitionism).[16] Traits are considered to be attributes of the individual and not of the situation. If traits are response characteristics, we can assume that similar stimuli will always elicit a given trait. If the traits, however, are situation-bound, not only must we know the stimulus that will generate a given response or trait, but we must know the characteristics of the situation as well. An overwhelming amount of the work on personality analysis and determination is based upon trait measurement and evaluation. Such tests as the Gordon Personal Profile, the Edwards Personal Preference Schedule, and the Thurstone Temperament Schedule, as well as the California Personality Inventory, are measurement tools that are designed to determine and measure personality traits.

THE TYPE APPROACH TO PERSONALITY. All of us characterize personality on the basis of both traits and types. Our friends are described as kind, generous, and warm. Enemies are seen as suspicious, greedy, malevolent, and evil. We also tend to type our acquaintances as cortical or emotional (thinking and responding to reason or responding and behaving emotionally), introverted or extroverted, autonomous or dependent. Such tendencies toward type-casting have existed for thousands of years. Hippocrates, in the fifth century B.C., characterized all men's personalities as falling into four classifications based upon the influence of the body fluids or "humors": yellow bile, black bile, phlegm, and blood. Yellow bile in too great concentration led to a choleric or irascible temperament, black bile to melancholy and depression, phlegm to sluggish apathy, and blood to a cheerful, active, full-functioning personality.

The best-known and most frequently employed contemporaneous typology is that of Carl Jung.[17] Jung's typology includes two classifications: introverts and extroverts. Introverts are people who are preoccupied with themselves and their own subjective world, whereas extroverts are people who are oriented primarily toward others and the external world.

Karen Horney has classified personalities into three categories or types: those who move toward people (compliant), those who move against people (aggressive), and those who move away from people (detached).[18]

David Reisman has typed what is often called social character, which smells mighty like personality, into three categories or types: (1) tradition-directed people who behave largely in accordance with

[16] The orientations of these traits have been taken from D. Krech, R. S. Crutchfield, and E. L. Ballachey, *Individual in Society* (New York: McGraw-Hill Book Company, 1962), Chapter 4, especially p. 106.

[17] Carl Jung, *Modern Man in Search of a Soul* (New York: Harcourt Brace Jovanovich, Inc., 1933).

[18] Karen Horney, *Our Inner Conflict* (New York: W. W. Norton & Company, Inc., 1945).

tradition (they are slow to change, depend on elders and kin relationships, and have low social mobility); (2) innerdirected people who have a highly developed internalized set of values that act as a sort of built-in gyroscope that guides and directs behavior; and (3) otherdirected people who almost literally take their marching orders or cues from those around them.[19]

There are many other procedures for classifying personality. It should be pointed out that personality *types* most often are a composite of given personality *traits*. By the manifest pattern of traits we type a personality. Both the trait and the type approaches to personality have certain disadvantages. Both approaches are most useful when the relevant behavior pattern or response is absolutely consistent. Such traits and types are useful for prediction only insofar as they manifest themselves in all or most situations. For instance, if a customer is a risk avoider in only certain circumstances, then we can predict his behavior only if we know what those circumstances are.

This limit on prediction really underscores the shortcoming of the trait and type approaches to personality; namely, that they both largely ignore the dynamic interplay between a person and his environment. Traits and types are usually so excessively broad that a given classification applies to a person only to a limited degree. The identification of someone as an introvert can tell you, perhaps, a great deal about that person's consumer behavior. But the category is so wide and the range of behavior subsumed under the category so broad that to predict behavior because the consumer has been typed an introvert would be virtually impossible. As we shall learn, personalities are not static structures that can be typed from consistent and habitual responses. They are instead dynamic and adaptive structures in constant transaction with the environment.

STIMULUS THEORIES OF PERSONALITY DEVELOPMENT. We shall not dwell long on the stimulus theories of personality development. The essential point is that personality is a set of structures and processes acquired as a result of learning. Learning has been covered extensively in Chapter 9 and therefore most of the essential generalizations have been made. Personality is shaped as a result of learning. Learning may be simple and direct, as in the case of simple classical conditioning involving association, or it may be operative and instrumental, as when behavior is affected by its consequences. To some extent personality is seen as literally "shaped up" as a result of learning experiences. Finally, learning, and thus personality development, is seen as a complex cognitive process involving reasoning, problem solving, and goal striving— and emphasizing complex information-processing, involving motivation and perceptual processes. From our point of view the important thing to consider is that personality development and determination

[19] David Reisman, *The Lonely Crowd* (New York: Doubleday Anchor Books, 1953), pp. 32–34.

are a function of the stimuli to which the organism is subjected. Broadly conceived, then, personality is not a bundle of native response tendencies but a bundle of predispositions that are acquired as a result of existence and a socializing process and that have a sociocultural basis. This idea suggests a transactional basis of personality; that is, personality is seen as an "open system involving a mutual transaction between the person and his environment."[20]

PHENOMENISTIC APPROACHES TO PERSONALITY DEVELOPMENT. Without undue elaboration, the phenomenological approach to personality development is this: personality emerges in terms of how a subject subjectively interprets his world. This approach rests upon the concept of private apperception. We all have our own private view of the world. Because of our uniqueness as individuals we selectively attune ourselves and attend to our environment. Lewin referred to this private apperception as *life space* and Rogers referred to it as *phenomenal field*.[21] Both of these terms relate to the subjective experience of the individual in terms of what he perceives, what he feels, and what he thinks he needs. Phenomenologists are often referred to as self theorists who are concerned with what they call self-concepts, that is, the individual's notion of who he is in relation to his environment. Self-concepts are at least first cousins to personality, and there are those who make no distinction between these concepts. According to self theorists this portion of personality and the psychological field, or the self-concept, determine all behavior.

The self theorists and the phenomenologists argue for the influence of the organism in determining personality and behavior. The basic psychological datum for them is not a stimulus and response but the organism, who individually and uniquely perceives and reacts to subjective stimuli and who conciously and cognitively reacts and responds in accordance with his needs and perceived goals.

Does the mystery deepen? It should! Personality is a complex, not really well-understood, well-defined, or well-delineated concept. The language and terminology of personality theory are obscure and ambiguous. One theorist talks about *personality* and another talks about *cognitive style* and yet another talks about *self-concept*. Is there a difference? Are they really one and the same thing? It is a matter of fact that our understanding of this elusive construct will improve little until we refine our approach and reach some agreement on these questions. A schematic diagram of personality is presented in Figure 12-1. This is not a "picture" of personality but an illustration drawn, to shed

[20] Gordon W. Allport, "The Open System in Personality Theory," *Journal of Abnormal and Social Psychology*, Vol. 61 (1960), pp. 301–311.

[21] Kurt Lewin, *Principles of Topological Psychology* (New York: McGraw-Hill Book Company, 1936); and Carl Rogers, *Client Centered Therapy: Its Current Practice, Implications, and Theory* (Boston: Houghton Mifflin Company, 1951).

Figure 12-1

A Schematic Illustration of Personality

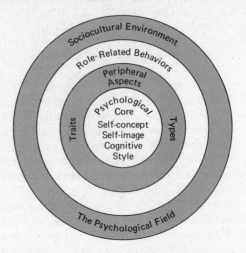

some light on what might be viewed as some structural components of personality and their interrelationships.

Notice that at the center of personality lies the psychological core of the individual, containing the subject's most internalized feelings and his most central concepts of self. As a matter of fact, the psychological core consists essentially of the individual's perception of his self.[22] The self-concept consists of all aspects of personality that create inward unity. According to Allport, it has the function of synthesizing inner needs and outer realities.[23] The self-concept is an integral part of and grows out of the *self-image*, the person's conceptualization of what he is like. As one writer notes, "The individual perceives himself as figure in the figure and ground pattern."[24] The figure aspect of personality includes essentially the psychological core, but it also includes the peripheral aspects of personality, plus the role-related behavior that subjects are compelled to adopt or that they voluntarily adopt in pursuit of their everyday interests. The *cognitive style* is the unique mode or fashion of expression manifested by the individual as a result of an insightful cognitive map.[25] Such a cognitive map is composed of

[22] Margret Boden, "McDougall Revisited," *Journal of Personnel*, Vol. 33 (1965), pp. 1–19.

[23] Allport, op. cit., pp. 40–41.

[24] Gardner Murphy, *Personality: A Bisocial Approach to Origins and Structure* (New York: Harper and Row, Publishers, 1947), p. 766.

[25] Cognitive style has been defined earlier in this chapter and in Chapter 5. Cognitive styles are essentially ways of thinking and perceiving that characterize a person independently of the content of the act. See Lazarus, op. cit., p. 39, for an example of distinct cognitive styles.

values, attitudes, beliefs, and images, and it plots a course, so to speak, by which much psychological movement is guided and cognitive progress achieved.

Personality must also be characterized in terms of its peripheral aspects; that is, traits and types are response sets or manifestations of personality, as is role-related behavior. For that matter, personality is largely an integration of all roles that have been played or assumed by the individual. Recall that a role is a kind of scenario prescribing certain actions and a script prescribing the lines to be spoken and the behavior to be manifested.[26] Roles, as shown in Figure 12-1, are conditioned and bounded by the sociocultural environment, and they are therefore units of a social system, whereas personality is defined as a pattern or set of enduring traits and motives linked to a human organism. Roles and personality, however, as suggested in Figure 12-1, have a determinative effect on one another.

Finally, personality in all its dimensions is affected and conditioned by the total sociocultural environment. This subjective, naïvely perceived environment constitutes the individual's essential *psychological field,* which consists of the person's needs and the potentialities of action available to him. There is much in the sociocultural environment to which the individual does not attend and that is not a part of his psychological field. The psychological field, in effect, is that bundle of specific psychological forces affecting that individual and in operation at that moment. The schematic illustration of Figure 12-1 suggests a dynamic, functioning personality. Personality is a determinant of behavior to the extent that behavior is a result of inner psychological core needs and wants. Outer realities in turn shape and affect the inner psychological core. This depiction is truly fully suggestive of the transactional nature of personality structure and function.

The Cognitive Approach to Personality

The cognitive approach to personality is essentially like the cognitive approach to human behavior generally; that is, it focuses upon the mediating and intervening processes of the organism such as cognition, motivation, perception, and learning. It posits that there is a conceptual nervous center or central processing unit that facilitates the problem-solving—goal-striving activities of the subject via complex information and symbol-processing activities. These activities relate to a collection of psychological phenomena such as bodily sense, self-identity, ego enhancement, ego extension, rational decision-making, and self-image projection and protection.

This approach to human behavior generally has been implemented extensively in our studies of and attempts at understanding

[26] For a more complete treatment of role theory, see Roger Braun, *Social Psychology* (New York: The Free Press, 1965), especially Chapter 4, "Roles and Stereotypes," pp. 152–197.

personality. It focuses upon and emphasizes the stable components of the individual's psychological field that mediate and intervene between experience and action.[27] Such an approach focuses upon the isolation of certain psychological dispositions. Once these dispositions or potential response sets are isolated, they are then measured and evaluated in terms of their impact upon given aspects of behavior. In this section we shall examine several of the dispositions that have been rather widely explored.[28] Some of them, though certainly not all, have been the basis for studies that have explored the relationship between personality and consumer behavior. However, several of the dispositions have yet to be researched in terms of their impact on specific or general acts of consumer purchasing and consumption. We shall begin by examining the authoritarian disposition.

AUTHORITARIANISM

The authoritarian personality is characterized as being both dominant and submissive. He is dominant to those whom he perceives as weaker and submissive to those whom he perceives as more dominant than himself. Thus the subject's perception of the situation constitutes an important determinant of his interaction patterns. Furthermore, the authoritarian personality is characterized as being more rigid in his perception than others and also less inclined to be intolerant of ambiguity.[29] What is more, the authoritarian personality is characteristic of people who tend to wall off their ideas or to think in logic-tight compartments. Such a personality disposition has obvious implications for sociopsychological behavior, but its impact has not been assessed in terms of consumer behavior. Yet such a disposition suggests several research areas for consumer behavior, for example, the use of clerk service versus self-service merchandising, the use of various communication media, the role of testimonials and the choice of models for testimonials, and the strength and character of specific advertising appeals. However, as we shall see later, almost every one of the personality dispositions suggests a similar number as well as kind of research possibility.

DOGMATISM

Another researcher has extended the concept of authoritarianism to what he calls *dogmatism*.[30] *Dogmatism* is defined as "close-mindedness." The dogmatic person has a set of rigid and tightly held beliefs

[27] Hollander, op. cit., p. 292.

[28] This section follows closely the material in Hollander, op. cit., pp. 292–304.

[29] T. W. Adorno, Else Frenkel-Brunswick, D. J. Levinson, and R. N. Stanford, *The Authoritarian Personality* (New York: Harper and Row, Publishers, 1950).

[30] Milton Rokeach, *The Open and Closed Mind* (New York: Basic Books, 1960). See also his "The Nature and Meaning of Dogmatism," *Psychological Review*, Vol. 61 (1954), pp. 194–205.

that are usually derived from authority. The most interesting aspect of dogmatism is the way it manifests itself as rigidity in the subject's psychological field and impedes the acceptance of information that is contrary to the individual's system of beliefs. The dogmatic individual says, "Don't argue with me, my mind is made up," or "Don't confuse me with the facts, my mind is made up." The dogmatic person tends to have a closed belief system. Dogmatic consumers, of course, do not process the information that is made available to them. They would be inclined always to buy the same goods. They would certainly be less receptive to and less inclined to believe the appeals of most advertisements, especially, of course, if the advertisements were contrary to their own beliefs and convictions. However, it was shown in one study that highly dogmatic persons agreed more with persons of high status than with those of low status. Those who are low in dogmatism tend to agree more with the low-status source of communication.[31] Would this not suggest that the source effect discussed in Chapter 11 would play a critical role in communicating to highly dogmatic receivers?

ACHIEVEMENT MOTIVATION

In Chapter 7, we briefly discussed the concept of achievement motivation. An achievement-motivated personality is characterized as having an unusual desire to achieve and to strive for the symbols and perquisites of success.[32] Achievement motivation is created by shaping or instrumental learning whereby the small child is given a kind of conditional love: "Yes, we will love you and reward you but you must perform." High achievers take moderate risks and they avoid excessive risks. As we shall see later, risk taking or seeking as a personality disposition appears to be distinct from achievement motivation. The high achiever seeks greater amounts of opportunity for success and appears to be a person who performs better on tasks involving his own individual initiative.[33] This suggests something about how the achievement-motivated consumer might be likely to initiate and manifest certain decision processes; that is, he is a person of high energy who seeks information from objective sources; he is autonomous in his behavior and not dependent on the influence of peers or other group members. However, these statements are only suggestive and they are inferred from the other characteristics that appear related to achievement motivation as a personality disposition.

[31] R. N. Vidulich and I. P. Kaiman, "The Effects of Information Source Status and Dogmatism upon Conformity Behavior," *Journal of Abnormal and Social Psychology*, Vol. 63 (1961), pp. 639–642.

[32] D. C. McClelland, J. W. Atkinson, R. W. Clark, and E. L. Lowell, *The Achievement Motive* (New York: Appleton-Century-Crofts, 1953).

[33] J. W. Atkinson and W. R. Reitman, "Performance as a Function of Motive Strength and Expectancy of Goal Attainment," *Journal of Abnormal and Social Psychology*, Vol. 53 (1956), pp. 361–366.

RISK TAKING

It has been found that there is a decision-making style that characterizes people's choices. For example, Wallach and Kogan have discovered that persons who are cautious in one kind of a choice situation tend to feel a subjective probability of failure in a variety of tasks.[34] Some persons thus can be characterized in terms of personality dispositions as risk seekers and others as risk avoiders. Risk avoiders would tend not to buy new products as readily as risk seekers. The risk seeker is likely to be more impulsive, to be an early adopter rather than a late adopter, and to be more receptive to new products and other marketing innovations.

INTERNAL-EXTERNAL CONTROL

Persons are also characterized in terms of how they believe events are managed or controlled. Some subjects act as if rewards follow from their own behavior, whereas others believe that rewards are controlled by forces outside themselves. Thus internal control persons are those who believe that their actions are instrumental in managing their affairs. External control subjects feel more inclined to accept the notion that conditions are controlled by "fate" or other persons.[35] Internals are usually found to be more independent and resistant to influence attempts, but they have also been found to take longer in making decisions.[36] Whether one is an internal or an external is thought to have some impact upon expectations concerning sources of reinforcement and upon the individual's response time in different kinds of tasks.

LEVELERS AND SHARPENERS

Another way of viewing personality dispositions is in terms of levelers and sharpeners, or what is sometimes referred to as category width. Thus some persons appear to be more inclined in their perceptual judgments and symbolic manipulations to overlook similarities and accentuate differences. These persons are characterized as sharpeners. On the other hand, levelers have a greater tendency to overlook differences and stress similarities. Broad categorizers or levelers appear to have a tendency to risk negative instances in an effort to include a maximum of positive instances (Type I error). Narrow categorizers or sharpeners exclude positive instances by restricting their

---

[34] N. Kogan and M. A. Wallach, *Risk Taking: A Study in Cognition and Personality* (New York: Holt, Rinehart & Winston, Inc., 1964).

[35] Julian Rotter, "Generalized Expectancies for Internal vs. External Control of Reinforcement and Decision Time," *Journal of Personal Social Psychology*, Vol. 2 (1965), pp. 598–604.

[36] D. P. Craune and S. Liverant, "Conformity Under Varying Conditions of Personal Commitment," *Journal of Abnormal and Social Psychology*, Vol. 66 (1963), pp. 547–555.

category ranges in order to minimize the number of negative instances (Type II error).[37] These two dispositions are thought to reveal much about the individuals' perception of the world and about how this perception is related to receptiveness to social influence and other dimensions of social and, perhaps, consumer behavior.

MANIFEST ANXIETY

We have explored in a limited sense in Chapter 7 the role of anxiety in motivation and therefore indirectly in personality. Anxiety is a mild state of dread and tension usually measured by what is called the Manifest Anxiety Scale (MAS). Anxiety as a predisposition affects such behavioral phenomena as motivation, perception, and learning.[38] It therefore affects subjects' attention span and their ability to attend to information and communication. Most importantly, the degree of anxiety manifested in the individual is an index of the degree to which the subject inclines toward emotionality in coping with the environment. More anxious consumers are likely to be receptive to emotional appeals but not to those that are heavily oriented toward fear and threat. Anxious consumers are low in self-confidence and buy larger amounts of deodorants and cosmetics than less anxious ones. Anxious subjects are usually found to have a higher drive level than less anxious ones.

SOCIAL APPROVAL

Another often-displayed characteristic of personality is the extent to which some subjects seek to project themselves in a favorable light. So often is this true that the tendency or disposition is called the approval motive.[39] Some subjects appear to have a high distinct need for social approval and are likely to conform to the judgments of others. Those who score high in their need for social approval are likely to be positively affected by situational cues as to the appropriate response in social and, presumably, commercial situations. Peer-group influence, salespeople, and significant others are likely to play an instrumental role in the consumer decision processes of those who seek and appear to need a great deal of social reinforcement and approval.

PERSUADABILITY

Another major personality disposition of critical importance to consumer behavioralists is that of *persuadability*. Persuadability relates to the degree to which individual difference in responsiveness to communications manifests itself as a variable factor throughout a popu-

---

[37] T. F. Pettigrew, "The Measurement and Correlate of Category Width as a Cognitive Variable," *Journal of Personnel*, Vol. 26 (1958), pp. 532–544.

[38] Work with this concept has been undertaken by Janet A. Taylor, "Drive Theory and Manifest Anxiety," *Psychological Bulletin*, Vol. 53 (1956), pp. 303–320.

[39] D. P. Crowne and David Marlowe, *The Approval Motive: Studies in Evaluative Dependence* (New York: John Wiley & Sons, Inc., 1964).

lation.[40] Persuadability is related to personality differences as well as to sex difference. For instance, on the average, females are found to be more persuadable than males. Persuadability has also been related to situational factors and to such psychological factors as confidence, social dominance, and self-image. As we learned in Chapter 11, persuadability is also related to the character of the communication, its source, the message, and the medium.

However, even if some subjects are more readily persuaded than others, it still remains the task of the communicator and those attempting to influence behavior to discover what appeals are most successful. Then, too, it must be remembered that a high degree of persuadability does not assure immediate success. Many are trying to persuade. Your message must be received and attended to more favorably than are the others, and your message must be viewed as having a higher degree of needed and desired information useful in terms of the subject's problem-solving activities.

Throughout the past several pages we have explored the many dimensions of personality structure and functions. Our most recent concern was with certain personality dispositions and their consequent impact upon behavior and cognitive psychological processes. It should be pointed out that much of the work quoted is highly exploratory and that the actual impact of such personality dispositions as were discussed is more suggested than empirically verified. However, these dispositions have been discussed for two major reasons. First, they expose the reader to a vast amount of research and literature relating to various personality dispositions that may have significance as variables in and determinants of behavior. Second, the findings already made, though tentative, strongly suggest the need for more empirical research in the testing and relating of these variables to more concrete instances of actual consumer behavior. We can hope that later work will verify the extent, if any, to which these concepts are relevant.

Next we shall examine a rather wide range of studies that have actually attempted to assess the impact of personality on consumer behavior. As we shall learn, the findings of these studies are more remarkable for their ambiguity than for any clear, positive statement of causal relationships.

Personality and Consumer Behavior: The Research Evidence

Prior to the gathering of the great welter of research evidence, there was a widely held notion that personality and personality characteristics were an important determinant of consumer behavior. The

[40] I. L. Janis and C. I. Hovland, "An Overview of Persuasibility Research," in *Personality and Persuasibility*, C. I. Hovland and I. L. Janis, eds. (New Haven, Conn.: Yale University Press, 1959), pp. 1–26.

popular, though unempirical work of the motivation researchers suggested that personality characteristics and differences were largely responsible for much of the different demand characteristics that were found among different target customers or market segments. The immensely popular and highly readable work of Pierre Martineau reinforced the lay notions pertaining to the critical role of personality as a determinant of consumer behavior, and yet when more sophisticated and more scientifically oriented studies were undertaken the results were not only disappointing but were, in addition, confounding.

For example, on the basis of Martineau's ideas, the automobile companies ceased selling cars and instead sold personalities. Martineau had suggested that there were three basic personality types underlying the demand characteristics of car buyers: (1) conservatives, (2) moderates or sociables, and (3) attention getters.[41] Martineau not only offered personality as the main variable in auto buying but suggested further that personality was an important factor in most product and brand choice as well as store choice. Personality, according to Martineau, was a critical if not the central variable in marketing planning and strategy. Personality attributes to match those of the buyer were, thus, literally programmed into the entire product development and merchandising activity of the automobile companies.

In what has become a landmark study, in the late 1950s Evans put forth the assumption that automobile buyers have discernible and different personality characteristics and that these differences are statistically significant in terms of their impact on the brand of automobile purchased.[42] Space and other considerations will deter us from making an overly detailed attempt to describe the studies relating to personality as a consumer behavioral determinant. However, Evans attempted to test the ability of psychological and objective methods to discriminate between owners of the two largest-selling automobiles, Ford and Chevrolet. The test was based essentially on the paper-and-pencil test known as the Edwards Personal Preference Schedule, consisting of sets of paired statements in which each sentence in a pair describes a personality need. From each pair the respondent selects the statement he feels best portrays himself. Evans used 110 sets of paired comparisons. The results were conclusive and disappointing: personality needs as measured in his study are of little value in predicting whether an individual will buy a Ford or a Chevrolet.

In a similar study, designed again to test the validity of the assertion that successful marketing occurs "when the personality of the product is matched with the personality of the consumer," Westfall attempted further to discover the impact of product personality on the

---

[41] Pierre Martineau, *Motivation in Advertising* (New York: McGraw-Hill Book Company, 1957).

[42] Franklin B. Evans, "Psychological and Objective Factors in the Prediction of Brand Choice," *Journal of Business*, Vol. 32 (October 1959), pp. 340–369.

consumer and how this impact or influence works.[43] Using the Thurstone Temperament Schedule, Westfall arrived at the following conclusions:

1. Compact and standard car owners *do not seem to differ* to any marked degree.
2. Personality characteristics or traits such as active, impulsive, stable, and sociable *appear to have* the greatest value as predictors of type of car owned.
3. Owners found low in the traits mentioned in 2 above are found to be *less likely* buyers of convertible cars than the average individuals.
4. All the conclusions must be taken *with caution* because of the limitations of sample size, method of selection, and application of probability techniques to quota sample data.[44]

Thus the results suggest that personality differences were found between the owners of convertibles and the owners of regular automobiles, but, again, no appreciable differences were found between Ford and Chevrolet owners on the basis of personality.

Personality and a wide range of products and product uses have also been explored. Tucker and Painter, using the Gordon Personal Profile and a test group consisting of college business students, demonstrated some connection between personality and product usage.[45] Thirteen of a possible thirty-six such relations were significant at the .05 level or above. In a somewhat similar study, Koponen, using the Edwards Personal Preference Schedule administered to five thousand members of the J. Walter Thompson consumer panel, concluded that no more than about 10 per cent of the purchase data were significantly related to personality factors. The phase of the moon might just as well be statistically significant.

As suggested earlier, the literature and the studies related to personality and consumer behavior continue to grow. Cohen, using a framework for analysis based upon Karen Horney's paradigm of personality types—namely, compliant, detached, and aggressive—found little statistical significance between products purchased and personality type.[46] Some products, as might be intuitively expected, do appear to express either compliant, aggressive, or detached responses to life. However, the significance of these findings for marketing planning is at best nebulous.

[43] James F. Engel, "Motivation Research—Magic or Mendel," *Michigan Business Review*, Vol. 13 (March 1961), pp. 28–32; and Ralph Westfall, "Psychological Factors in Predicting Product Choice," *Journal of Marketing*, Vol. 26 (April 1962), pp. 34–40.

[44] The italics were supplied by this author to emphasize the rather cautious and tenuous nature of the findings.

[45] W. T. Tucker and John Painter, "Personality and Product Use," *Journal of Applied Psychology*, Vol. 45 (October 1961), pp. 325–329.

[46] Joel B. Cohen, "An Interpersonal Orientation to the Study of Consumer Behavior," *Journal of Marketing Research*, Vol. 4 (Chicago: American Marketing Association, August 1967), pp. 270–278.

Kassarjian attempted to isolate and specify the relationship between social character (which is implicitly related to personality types), such as inner-directedness and outer-directedness, and preferences for mass communications.[47] In a study design notable for ingenuity and effort, the results were nonetheless disappointing to the extent that differential exposure to the mass media and differential preferences for media content were not on the whole significant. Social character as a surrogate for personality types and as a meaningful variable in communication and persuasion processes has not yet been shown conclusively.

Personality as a consumer behavior variable has been explored in connection with a host of dependent variables: attitudes toward commercial banks as opposed to savings-and-loan institutions and attitudes toward private brands and toward such anxiety-arousing practices as cigarette smoking and cigarette brand choice.[48] The results again leave much to be desired. At the same time, the methodology used to discover the impact of personality has become much more sophisticated.[49] Multivariate analysis and economic analysis add only a slight measure of statistical significance to most studies.[50]

THE LESSONS OF A FAILURE

As the review in the previous section suggests, we have not shown with a high degree of statistical significance or accuracy the value of using personality as a major or critical variable in consumer behavior. In spite of the evidence, many continue to persist in this elusive search for positive relationships. And well they should. Our research is designed to give us feedback and insight. We learn a great deal from our failures. In this instance, specifically, we are told by our results to stop insisting that positive relationships of sufficient magnitude exist where apparently they do not. Yet, again, our intuitions keep leading us back to explore these relationships. If positive relationships cannot be shown, why not? Why have we been unable to nail down the relationship between personality and consumer behavior? Several possible explanations are suggested.

[47] Harold H. Kassarjian, "Social Character and Differential Preference for Mass Communication," *Journal of Marketing Research*, Vol. 2 (May 1956), pp. 146–153.

[48] H. J. Claycamp, "Characteristics of Owners of Thrift Deposits in Commercial Banks and Savings and Loan Associations," *Journal of Marketing Research*, Vol. 2 (1965), pp. 163–170; J. G. Myers, "Determinants of Private Brand Attitude," *Journal of Marketing Research*, Vol. 4 (1967), pp. 73–81; and Joseph N. Fry, "Personality Variables and Cigarette Brand Choice," *Journal of Marketing Research*, Vol. 8 (August 1971), pp. 298–304.

[49] Robert B. Brody and Scott M. Cunningham, "Personality Variables and the Consumer Decision Process," *Journal of Marketing Research*, Vol. 5 (February 1968), pp. 50–57.

[50] David L. Sparks and W. T. Tucker, "A Multivariate Analysis of Personality and Product Use," *Journal of Marketing Research*, Vol. 8 (February 1971), pp. 67–70.

TOO MUCH REDUCTIONISM. The slavish attempts to attribute too much significance to personality are yet another example of the tendency to overwork and overdramatize the reductive-functional approach to consumer behavior. Consumer behavior is not the product of a single determinant. Consumer characteristics and/or response tendencies cannot be reduced to a single common denominator—personality. Nor is personality the single derivative of the human behavior equation. Sparks and Tucker acknowledge the low statistical significance of research in this area.

> The most obvious explanation for these findings lies in the notion that it is the person in some gestalt in which the entire personality and the entire situation form a particular configuration, who acts, not the individual personality trait . . . this view includes the possibility that the most useful approach to the subject is to measure individual personality characteristics and synthesize the molar personality from such measures.[51]

Kassarjian, in a delightfully informative review article, states that "personality researchers in consumer behavior much too often ignore the many interrelated influences in the consumer decision process, ranging from price and packaging to availability, advertising, group influences, learned responses, and preferences of family members."[52] He might well have added a host of other related factors, such as motivation, cognition, learning, and the entire range of interpersonal factors, such as socialization, life style, social class, and culture.

Too often, the shortcoming of reductive-functional analysis is that we look at events needing explanation as if they were a system of deterministic happenings rather than a heap or collection of events. We *assume* that there is some set of systematic interrelations among the events we watch and we *assume* we can pick out the parts for explanation.[53] Furthermore, our reductive-functional syndrome insists that we pursue things as far as possible, and in our zest to do so we so overreduce as to lose sight of the human subject we have under investigation.

INADEQUATE RESEARCH DESIGN AND METHODOLOGY. Most of the research design and the methodology used in the study of personality in relationship to consumer behavior have been borrowed from the fields of experimental and clinical psychology. We have virtually no personality tests that relate specifically to consumer behavior. Furthermore, many of the studies that purport to relate personality to consumer behavior are undertaken by researchers who use their captive student

---

[51] Ibid., p. 70.

[52] Harold H. Kassarjian, "Personality and Consumer Behavior—A Review," *Journal of Marketing Research*, Vol. 8 (November 1971), pp. 409–418.

[53] This idea is more fully elaborated by Reinhard Bendix, "The Pitfalls of Personality Reductionism: Compliant Behavior and Individual Personality," *American Journal of Sociology*, Vol. 58 (1952), pp. 292–303.

audiences as subjects. The results are then generalized to consumers. Regarding the question of research design and methodology, one authority contends that:

> Careful examination reveals that in most cases, no *a priori* thought is directed to *how,* or especially *why* personality should or should not be related to that aspect of consumer behavior being studied. Moreover, the few studies which do report statistically significant findings usually do so on the basis of post-hoc "picking and choosing" out of large data arrays.[54]

Most of this argument has been summarized nicely by Kassarjian, who concludes the following:

1. If unequivocal results are to emerge, consumer behavior researchers must develop their own definitions and design their own instruments to measure the personality variables that go into the purchase decision rather than using tools designed as part of a medical model to measure mental schizophrenia or mental stability.
2. Studies must not be conducted on the basis of a shotgun approach with no specific hypothesis or theoretical justification.
3. Finally, to expect the influence of personality variables to account for a large portion of the variance of consumer behavior is most certainly expecting too much.[55]

This last statement is at least a tacit acknowledgement of the overemphasis on reductive-functionalist approaches. It also suggests something additionally unique and untoward regarding personality as a major variable in consumer behavior.

PERSONALITY: A FACILITATING VARIABLE. Many of our findings lead us to this conclusion: personality might best be viewed not as a major determinant of or variable in consumer behavior but instead as a facilitating process variable or what is sometimes called a "moderator variable."[56] What this suggests is that market planning, including such strategic considerations as product development, promotion and communication, pricing, and even channel decisions, can be more meaningfully undertaken if consumer analysis first proceeds upon the basis of more objective behavioral criteria. For example, purchase rate, heavy versus light use, economic factors such as income, or social factors such as social class or life style might be viewed as the more significant factors contributing to consumer behavior differences. Personality might be found upon later analysis to contribute significant differences and therefore insight into more specific dimensions of the behavioral act.

Personality as a facilitating process variable is a human condition that is known to affect our cognitions, our motivations, our perceptions

---

[54] Jacob Jacoby, "Personality and Innovation Proneness," *Journal of Marketing Research*, Vol. 8 (May 1971), p. 244.

[55] Kassarjian, "Personality and Consumer Behavior—A Review," op. cit.

[56] Fry, op. cit., p. 298.

—in short, in an interactive and interstimulating fashion, personality is seen as both cause and effect. It may cause or determine behavior. What is more likely, our personalities are the products of our experiences. Personality may be, to some extent, an important variable relating to consumer behavior—for some people, for some products, at some times, in some situations. Personality traits and personality characteristics probably do predispose us to given acts in situations of apparent choice. Personality is a kind of matrix or filter through which all of our behavioral possibilities are likely to be examined. A personality gives us a cognitive style and a self-image but it does not imprint us with a finite pattern of behavior or response tendencies. In the holocentric sense, personality may contribute as much as 20 or 50 per cent of the variance of consumer behavior but, little or large, personality is only one variable and in most cases it is likely that it is a facilitating variable. It facilitates the way consumers seek, extract, receive, and process information and use it in their consumer decision processes. Personality may at times be a central process variable, but when it is, it reacts in conjunction with the presence of many other factors.

The chapter was begun with a description and an analysis of what is normally considered an important behavioral determinant—personality. Our treatment considered both the structural and the functional aspects of personality, and considerable attention was devoted to personality dispositions as meaningful and significant variables in consumer behavior. The research results of studies that have attempted to assess the impact of personality on consumer behavior have not been very satisfactory. In short, determinate relationships are not normally shown. This failure of research suggests that personality should not necessarily be viewed as a reductive-functional determinant of consumer behavior, that research designs and methodology have to be improved, and that personality ought to be construed and treated as a facilitating process variable rather than as a single, determinist, critical variable.

Personality may yet be shown to be an important and critical variable in consumer behavior. However, further research that attempts to show this relationship should be based upon at least these assumptions:[57]

1. Consumer behavior consists of acts but our unit of analysis must be the total composite act. The total act of the personality must be considered. A simple stimulus-response couplet is not sufficient to account for complex consumer decision processes.
2. Personality is formed in relation to and in conjunction with the total situation of the consumer. Therefore, we must consider in our studies of personality not only such core characteristics as cognitive style, self-image, and self-concept but the other related characteristics, including traits, types, and dis-

[57] These generalizations are based upon the work of Bruner, op. cit., pp. 36–40.

positions, plus role-related factors and the subject's total psychological field.

3. Personality is characterized by consistency but not total rigidity. Personality imposes predispositions but not instinctive and rigid reactions. It does not mean freedom from change.

4. Personality is self-serving in the interest of goal-striving and goal-directed behavior. To a considerable extent, personality is the product of and is therefore derived from the direction of acts toward goals set up in advance.

5. Finally, personality is not a mechanical expression of energy dispositions. Rather, it is a bundle of organized potentialities striving to actualize themselves.

In Part IV, we shall examine the socialization process, of which we have spoken so often. Hopefully, our appreciation for these concluding generalizations regarding personality will be sufficiently reinforced by Part IV.

Questions for Study, Reflection, and Review

1 Describe the approach to personality based on a structural analysis of core and periphery.

2 Explain the need for consistency at both the external and the internal levels of personality.

3 What is the relationship between the functional aspect of accommodation and information processing?

4 Describe personality with respect to the three major schools and their generalizations regarding motivation.

5 Distinguish between the trait approaches to personality and the type approaches.

6 What is the disadvantage common to both trait and type approaches to personality?

7 What is the basis upon which the phenomenological approach to personality development is predicated?

8 Compare the personality concept of authoritarianism with that of dogmatism.

9 Distinguish between internal and external control and their implications for decision making.

10 What are some of the problems encountered in attempts to determine the relationship between personality and consumer behavior?

Part IV

Interpersonal Variables of Behavior

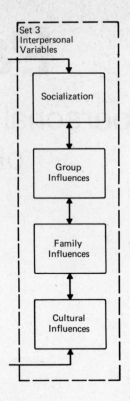

Set 3
Interpersonal
Variables

Socialization

Group
Influences

Family
Influences

Cultural
Influences

13

Socialization
Processes:
The Role of
Social Interaction

Introduction

Throughout our discussion and treatment of consumer behavior we have implicitly dealt with the issue of socialization and the role of social interaction. It is time now, however, to underscore and treat ex-explicitly this important variable and determinant of consumer behavior. Socialization, which is the product of social interaction, is a pervasive feature of everyday life. We are all literally taught the ways of society. As primarily social creatures we observe, perceive, and learn the norms, folkways, values, beliefs, and attitudes of those around us. Consequently, our personalities and our behavioral predispositions reflect the influence of these shaping and upbringing influences. From the cradle to the grave, we are but a link in a vast network of social interaction processes whereby a complicated and sophisticated pattern of actions and sentiments are subtly incorporated into our individual response repertoires. It is for these reasons and others that will be elaborated that we are interested in individual consumers in society. Such a statement acknowledges that we cannot meaningfully isolate the consumer and study him as a distinct, nonsocial entity but that we must instead study and analyze the consumer as the central character in a larger framework of social relationships. Such a point of view recognizes the importance of interaction as an influencer and molder of behavioral characteristics. Furthermore, it recognizes that "our very ability to experience, to decide, and to control our own behavior through our decisions is dependent in many subtle and involuntary ways upon our relationship and interactions with our fellows."[1]

In effect, what is meant by this statement is that many of what have been called intrapersonal determinants of consumer behavior—the psychological processes unique to each individual, such as cognition, perception, learning, and motivation—are still nonetheless affected by socialization processes. Our cognitions are affected by social interaction as are our motives, our perceptions, and our capacity and tendency to modify our behavior as a result of experience. Furthermore, what we have called facilitating and moderator variables—namely, communication and personality—are themselves largely the product of social influence and, most importantly, symbolic and interaction processes. Thus, given our previous tendency to examine consumer behavior from the standpoint of its sociopsychological determinants, it should be no surprise that we turn our attention now more concertedly to the social dimensions of consumer behavior. It is to be continually reemphasized that there is not, on the one hand, a kind of "psychology of consumer behavior" and, on the other hand, a kind of "sociology of consumer behavior" but that instead psychological processes are constantly affected by sociological considerations and vice versa. Hence, the social psychology of consumer behavior is emphasized.

Consumers learn adaptive behavior. Most of their activities in the marketplace, we have learned, are related to a kind of coping behavior that is both conforming and idiosyncratic; that is, we must not overemphasize the impact of socialization. Although consumers are taught the ways of society, it should not be misunderstood that all consumers march to the same drumbeat. Social norms, practices, customs, and folkways are constantly being modified. Although society influences the individual, the individual in turn, in an exchange and transactional fashion, is also influencing society. Even the most conformist social structure has its share of deviates: those who turn away and seek new goals and new modes and methods of expression. Consumers are no exception. Thus, although socialization processes do tend to create common modes, similar attitudes, and convergent behavioral dispositions, they do not create at the same time a society of mindless automatons all seeking and striving for the same goals and all manifesting a homogeneous blend of identical characteristics. Consumers particularize their behavior. They learn to express themselves in their own unique and individuating manner. Through sociopsychological processes consumers manifest patterns of both consistency and inconsistency in their response tendencies.

In this chapter, we shall explore in considerable detail the impact of socialization and the role of social interaction on consumer behavior. In the usual fashion, our treatment will begin with a description and

[1] A. P. Hare, E. F. Borgatta, and R. F. Bales, eds., *Small Groups*, rev. ed. (New York: Alfred A. Knopf, Inc., 1965), p. 192.

analysis of socialization and the socialization processes. From this beginning, we shall proceed to explore the question of consumer behavior from the vantage point of systems analysis and thus treat consumers as behavioral systems of action. The major focus of the chapter will center upon the issue of personal influence, that is, a direct encounter of two or more people that results in behavior or attitude change in the participants. The treatment of socialization and personal influence will largely center around the concept of social exchange theory. The chapter will conclude with an in-depth examination of several contemporary social exchange theories.

This chapter, although important in itself, is also important inasmuch as it is the essential prologue to the remaining chapters in Part IV. As the reader proceeds, he will recognize that socialization is a dynamic process that pervades group processes, social class, family influences, life style, and culture, which are the essence of the remaining chapters of Part IV.

Socialization and Socialization Processes

Socialization and the socialization process have to do with the activities and methods by which people influence one another through mutual interchange of thoughts, feelings, and actions. In many ways the process of socialization involves the association of a value with every act of behavior, every belief, and every sentiment. In so many words, we are taught to value and esteem particular actions. Such reinforcement leads to the repeating of such actions; thus through this process of social learning we are taught the ways of our society in relationship to our own need-fulfillment activities.

Socialization is typically viewed as the process by which the culture patterns of a society become the habitual response patterns of the members of that society.[2] Socialization is also viewed as the sequence of total social learning experiences that result in the integration of the individual into a society.[3] Thus socialization, as can be seen, is defined at times as the process by which individuals acquire their culture. It is culture that binds many of man's meaningless acts into purposeful and meaningful patterns of behavior. Out of culture there emerge whole patterns of perceptions, role taking, and norm giving that affect consumer behavior. Socialization is therefore the process by which what exists outside the individual is internalized and incorporated into his own cognitive structure and processes. Socialization is not restricted to behavior in which a conscious effort is made to teach others particular things or in which a conscious effort is made to learn particular things. Via the socialization and interaction process individuals may learn

[2] John T. Doby, *Introduction to Social Psychology* (New York: Appleton-Century-Crofts, 1966), pp. 200–201.

[3] John W. McDavid and Herbert Harari, *Social Psychology* (New York: Harper and Row, Publishers, 1968), p. 89.

things that no one ever intended them to learn. Therefore, many important attitudes, beliefs, sentiments, and dispositions are "caught, not taught."[4]

THE SOCIALIZATION PROCESS

The socialization process can best be described as a learning process involving social interaction. The socialization process is thus thought of as an interactional process in which a person's behavior is modified to conform with the expectations and norms held by the members of the groups to which he belongs. It is rather commonly held today that the socialization process does not cease with a certain age or maturity but that it continues throughout life. Socialization becomes an important factor in influencing and shaping behavior when a person, say, a consumer, occupies a new role or a new position, as when a young girl is married or when she has her first child or buys her first home. Socialization processes then shape, influence, and sometimes even mildly dictate norms of behavior that are associated with these particular roles. By what earlier was called social learning or perceptual learning she extracts information from the environment and uses this information in the interest of her current enterprise. Her perceptual and social learning are affected by the network of social interaction and socializing experiences in which she is embedded. Thus socialization and socialization processes are influencing and shaping factors, and as such they are important determinants of consumer behavior. As individuals interact with each other in various settings, both formal and informal, they transmit and exchange large amounts of information in the form of values, attitudes, and sentiments. By way of this interaction, social and perceptual learning occurs that affects major as well as minor purchasing decisions. The influence and impact of socialization are not, as we have seen, always deliberate or even conscious; yet the type of social influence that emanates from social interaction and leads to social learning is an important dimension of consumer behavior.

FACTORS AFFECTING SOCIALIZATION. An entire cataloguing and discussion of all those factors affecting socialization are beyond the scope of this chapter. Several of these factors, because of their extreme importance, will be treated more fully in subsequent chapters.

The family. Surely the family must rank as a more important influencer and shaper of personality, attitudes, values, and behavioral dispositions than any other known institution. Most of our attitudes, habits, and appetites are acquired within the family setting. Consumption patterns, likes and dislikes, attitudes regarding the role of goods, spending versus saving syndromes are largely inculcated within this important primary group.

[4] Glen M. Vernon, *Human Interaction* (New York: The Ronald Press Company, 1965), p. 171.

The community. The community and the immediate environment surrounding the individual and his family are important shapers and influencers of behavior. The values, attitudes, norms, and sentiments of one growing up in the Amish community outside Nappanee, Indiana, will vary markedly from the values, attitudes, norms, and sentiments of the person growing up in the more modern and contemporary suburbs around Indianapolis.

The groups. The groups to which one belongs or to which one aspires to belong become important influencers of attitudes, values, and norms. Groups include many kinds of institutionalized arrangements for interaction, both formal and informal. Members of the local or national Consumer Protection Agencies are likely to view marketing activities differently than, say, the members of the local Retail Merchants' Association.

Culture. The more or less consistent patterns of thought and action that pervade a given society are referred to as culture. Culture creates modal patterns of behavior and underlying regulatory beliefs, values, and norms. Culture is thus an important factor in socialization because it plays such an important and central role in training the new members of a society in that society's ways of life. The North American culture emphasizes goods acquisition and ownership as a means of enhancing the esteem of the individual. Other cultures are decidedly less materialistic in their orientation.

The mass media. Finally, we must emphasize the role of the mass media as an integral part of the socialization process. Never have so many been exposed to such a vast amount of information disseminated so rapidly. Such rapid information dissemination is leading to the rapid homogenization of values, norms, attitudes, and tastes on a near-global scale. It will be some time, if ever, before local, regional, national, and international tastes all converge in some common denominator, but, by the same token, no longer is it possible for people to wall themselves off against the inroads and impact of new modes of expression, changing values, and human dispositions.

As an example of the impact of the mass medium television on socialization, consider the case of the American adolescent. The average American preschooler spends 64 per cent of his time watching television. By the age of fourteen, this child will have seen 18,000 murders on TV, by the age of seventeen, some 350,000 commercials. In the course of his life, the TV will have consumed ten years of his time. Television, to some extent, has replaced both parent and teacher as the primary socializer of children. The American preschool child, during his critical preschool years, spends more time watching TV than he would in the classroom during four years of college.

Although there are no doubt other factors that affect the socialization process—that is, social influences that help to form attitudes, values, and sentiments, and thus influence and shape society's members—those that have just been discussed are perhaps the most impor-

Figure 13-1

An Illustration of Socialization's Impact upon Behavior

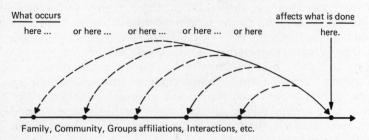

What occurs here ...   or here ...   or here ...   or here ...   or here   affects what is done here.

Family, Community, Groups affiliations, Interactions, etc.

tant.[5] Socialization therefore implies a rather continuous molding, shaping, influencing, and determining of our behavioral dispositions, that is, our attitudes, values, beliefs, and sentiments. Diagrammatically, the impact of socialization on behavior is illustrated in Figure 13-1.

What Figure 13-1 depicts, of course, is the cumulative impact of socialization. It is important to emphasize again that socialization should not be thought of as molding a person to a standard behavioral pattern. Individuals are subjected to different combinations of socialization processes and they do react differently and idiosyncratically to them. Consequently, socialization processes can and do produce distinctive differences among persons as well as similarities.[6]

TRADITIONAL VERSUS MODERN APPROACHES TO SOCIALIZATION

Our approach to understanding and analyzing the socialization process and its impact upon behavior has gone through a series of successive stages or orientations. The most characteristic of these stages and the emphasis applied to each are as follows.

THE CREATURE MAN APPROACH. The creature man approach interprets the observation of man and his behavior in terms of the conflict between man's needs and nature and the demands and pressures of the social environment. Man is viewed essentially as a biological organism endowed at birth with a set of innate drives and motives, and the role of socialization is to convert the creature man into an acceptable social organism. The Freudian approach to socialization was aimed principally at the objective of eliminating "childish naughtiness" in the individual in order that he might comport himself in accordance with the

[5] For a slightly different approach and listing, see William W. Lambert and Wallace E. Lambert, *Social Psychology* (Englewood Cliffs, N.J.: Prentice-Hall, Inc., 1964), pp. 10–11.

[6] Paul F. Secord and Carl W. Backman, *Social Psychology* (New York: McGraw-Hill Book Company, 1964), pp. 526.

social norms of the grown person. Thus socialization in accordance with the creature man concept and Freudian psychology was seen essentially as an educational process of modifying the person's original nature.[7]

THE CULTURE MAN APPROACH. In contrast to the creature man approach, the culture man approach sees the human organism as a kind of empty vessel capable of learning, whose character and nature and behavior are to be understood in terms of what he learns. Such a point of view places a heavy emphasis upon man's capacity to learn a nearly infinite variety of social roles and it is sometimes criticized as the "over-socialized conception of man."[8] Within such an orientation, the socialization process is seen as the accommodation of behavior to the requirements of various roles (expected patterns of behavior) appropriate in the given society to various status situations (positions in the social framework or structure).

THE SYMBOLIC MAN APPROACH. Both the creature man and the culture man approaches are what might be called stable man views; that is they conceive of the human organism as having a rather permanent nature, whether it is inborn or learned, that provides the major source for the motivation and orientation in adult behavior. The symbolic man approach, on the other hand, views man as an actor rather than a being. Such an approach treats man's acts as symbolic in character rather than primarily physical and, most importantly, views interaction as the basic social and psychological process from which personalities and all behavioral dispositions and sentiments emerge. The symbolic man approach thus emphasizes the symbolic-interactional approach to socialization. When interaction mediated by gestures is transmitted into communication in terms of significant symbols, a reconstruction of biological into social individuality is inevitable. The meaning of a gesture is found in the response of another to what would normally be the completion of the act of which the gesture is a part. When interaction is mediated by significant symbols, a world of universal meanings opens to all parties in the act. The symbol can call out a specific response not only to the one to whom it is communicated but to anyone who understands it. The symbol evokes in the person producing it the same meaning he conveys to others.[9] Thus symbols involve the sharing of meaning in which individuals take the perspective of the

[7] Anna Freud, *Psychoanalysis for Teachers and Parents,* trans. Barbara Law, (Boston: Beacon Press, 1935), pp. 57–58.

[8] Dennis Wrong, "The Over-socialized Conception of Man," *American Sociological Review,* Vol. 26 (April 1961), pp. 185–193.

[9] The person who more than anyone else brought the symbolic-interactional theory of socialization into coherent form was George Herbert Mead. See *Mind, Self, and Society,* Charles W. Morris, ed. (Chicago: University of Chicago Press, 1934).

other. Symbolic interaction is the foremost and most significant contemporary point of view regarding socialization. The symbolic interactionist point of view emphasizes the role of symbols, signs, signals, and messages in contemporary social behavior. It furthermore emphasizes that the basic social process that makes all other social phenomena possible is the interaction of men, the everyday intercourse between two or more human beings.[10] Such a point of view seems highly relevant to our analysis of consumer behavior. It acknowledges the symbolic nature of much of consumer behavior, and it emphasizes the role and impact of interaction on consumer decision processes and the influence of socialization processes on consumer's perceptions, motivations, cognitions, and learning.[11] Socialization is a process that facilitates the consumer's attempts at reality testing, that is, his attempts to perceive and judge the impact of his behavior on the reactions of his fellows. Socialization facilitates the acquisition of adaptive and accommodative modes of behavior by generating social cues that are perceived as indices and measures of what is appropriate and what is not. In terms of the consumer's problem-solving orientation, socialization suggests that consumers exist as parts of integrated social systems and that such systems themselves are composed of goal-oriented tasks and exist mainly in terms of the attempt to achieve goals. Such systems are integrated by the decision-making process, which selects and structures the tasks in terms of their goal-achieving capacity. Integration is measured by the degree of goal achievement: by indicators of effectiveness and efficiency such as lower cost, reduced search time, decreased anxiety through the lowering of perceived risk, and so forth.

Finally, as Shibutani has suggested, socialization is the process responsible for the person's perspective, the ordered view of one's world, the matrix through which one perceives his environment.[12] In short, perspective is a kind of outline scheme that, running ahead of experience, defines and guides it. All consumer behavior is affected by that particular consumer's perspective. The consumer's view of himself, the way he defines his own unique situation, whether he sees himself as rich or poor, black or white, innovator or laggard, aggressive or conforming, venturesome or shy—all are largely affected and conditioned by the socializing experiences to which he has been subjected. Furthermore, any change in perspective—becoming a parent for the first time, sending a son to college or marrying off the only daughter, or suffering

[10] See C. K. Warriner, *The Emergence of Society* (Homewood, Ill.: The Dorsey Press, 1970), pp. 97–104.

[11] The impact of symbols and symbolic aspects of consumer behavior have been treated throughout this work. The reader would benefit from exposure to such work as Sidney J. Levy, "Symbols for Sale," *Harvard Business Review*, Vol. 37 (July–August 1959), pp. 117–124.

[12] Tamotsu Shibutani, "Reference Groups as Perspective," *The American Journal of Sociology*, Vol. 60 (May 1955), pp. 562–569. See also Tamotsu Shibutani, *Society and Personality: An Interactionist Approach to Social Psychology* (Englewood Cliffs, N.J.: Prentice-Hall, Inc. 1961).

the failure of well-laid plans—leads one to notice things previously overlooked, to see new alternatives juxtaposed to new or old problems, or generally to see the familiar world in a new light.

A Systems Approach to Socialization Processes

Given our interest in the consumer as an individual in society, we come to a rather prominent contemporary point of view regarding influence situations, namely, the systems point of view. The basic tenet of this point of view is that everything is connected to everything else. A systems point of view is a holistic concept resting upon the assumption that systems are complex and organized wholes, an assemblage or combination of things or parts forming a complex or unitary whole. Systems are seen as collections of entities or things (animate or inanimate) that receive certain inputs and are constrained to act concertedly upon them to produce certain outputs with the objective of harmonizing some function of inputs to outputs. A more abbreviated statement regarding systems is that a system is a set of interacting variables.[13] The socialization process, as we have said, is the impact upon the individual that results from learning through interaction with his social environment. Therefore, within a given social system, the socialization process involves an interdependent and interrelated set of social training practices. From the standpoint of consumer behavior in particular and all other behavior in general, family structure and kinship systems; religious beliefs and practices; educational, legal, and political systems; and standards of social desirability are all mutually interdependent. All the devices of social conditioning and control, including child-rearing practices, motivation for achievement, the values and attitudes relating to the ownership of goods and consumption, work together *systematically* to facilitate the assimilation of the individual into the society, maximizing the congruence between his behavior and that of the other members of his society. Thus the systems point of view has as its primary focus neither the individual nor the group as such but the *social system* and its action. The action, of course, results from the interaction of one or many persons in relation with other units, such as artifacts, attitudes, sentiments, and other expressive movements.

THE SOCIAL SYSTEM

The social system is the basic framework that affects the process of socialization. The social system is composed of components (people, ideas, values, institutions, subcultures) of varying manipulative powers

---

[13] For a complete treatment of systems, see R. A. Johnson, F. E. Kast, and J. E. Rosenzweig, *The Theory and Management of Systems* (New York: McGraw-Hill Book Company, 1967).

in regular, nonrandom patterns of action with one another.[14] This action and interaction involves the sending and receiving of energy/information among components of the system. The system is simultaneously involved in the sending and receiving of energy/information within its environment, including other systems. Its patterns of action within and with its environment constitute modal norms providing it with a distinctive identity. Its power units seek positive feedback implementing their directing of system action and resist negative feedback impeding this action. Change that is perceived by the system as providing positive feedback is permitted and encouraged, whereas change that is perceived as providing negative feedback is resisted through action patterns of expulsion, confinement, or conversion. Change that succeeds in creating negative feedback produces varying degrees of system disintegration.

The cybernetic concept of feedback means anything that influences a system's current action. Whatever keeps a system going as it has been going or enhances its action in its present direction is positive feedback. Those things that tend to stop, slow down, or deter a system from its present course are negative feedback.

Systems are therefore structural patterns of senders and receivers. Thus any social organization or system that is to change through learning, innovation, and interaction must contain certain feedback mechanisms, a certain variety of information, and certain kinds of input, channel storage, and decision-making facilities.[15]

In addition to the structural pattern of senders and receivers, systems are also content patterns of what is sent and received. System components, therefore, are the items of energy/information, especially people, involved as either structural patterns or content patterns.

SOCIAL SYSTEMS AND CONSUMER BEHAVIOR

Consumer behavior is certainly subjected to a great amount of socialization. Consumers are linked to the network of social interaction processes—existing as both structural and content components in social systems. They both send and receive large amounts of energy/information, and as a result of feedback and learning their attitudes and values are modified and changed over time. Such change in one component of the social system (the consumer or an aggregate of consumers) in turn creates change in other components of the system over time. For example, consider the current controversy regarding the deteriorating environment. A few, recognizing the dangers of increased pollution through rampant and unchecked consumption, may bring about changes in many spheres of influence, such as government, eco-

---

[14] This section on social systems rests heavily on the work of Joseph H. Monane, *A Sociology of Human Systems* (New York: Appleton-Century-Crofts, 1967); see especially Chapters 1 and 2.

[15] See Mervyn L. Cadwallader, "The Cybernetic Analysis of Change in Complex Social Organizations," *American Journal of Sociology*, Vol. 65, No. 2 (1959), pp. 154–157.

nomics, and political and legal institutions. Such changes may ultimately result in a reevaluation of and a complete change in behavior and attitudes regarding the merits of an overly consumption-oriented philosophy.

Such a systems point of view must acknowledge, as Parsons has emphasized, that society is not a neatly articulated system in full control of its own internal processes and mechanisms, but that instead it consists of a loosely federated group of systems and subsystems of many different sorts, each with its own internal system problems and each with its own crucial degrees of freedom.[16] These subsystems stand in relationships of interdependence and interpenetration with one another. The result is that almost any pattern of actions has consequences for many different sorts of system referents. Figure 13-2 illustrates diagrammatically some of the relationships that exist between the consumer and his other system referents.

Looking at the entire range of systems encompassed in the general theory of consumer behavior and action, we might well conclude that there is an order or hierarchy among them. In the central sense, the organic system is the biological and human organism, the consumer. This organism is influenced and controlled by the psychological system of needs and wants. Such a system has as its basic mechanisms of influence such factors as cognition, motivation, perception, and learning. Psychological systems are influenced and controlled by social systems, having as their basic mechanisms of influence such factors as family influences, child-rearing practices, roles, life styles, and social class influences. Finally, social systems are influenced by cultural systems. Cultural systems have as their basic mechanisms of influence such factors as customs, norms, and folkways. Culture constitutes the basic

Figure 13-2

A Hierarchy of Controlling Systems

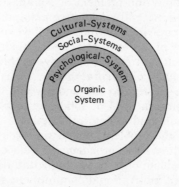

[16] See Edward C. Devereux, Jr., "Parsons' Sociological Theory," in *The Social Theories of Talcott Parsons*, Max Black, ed. (Englewood Cliffs, N.J.: Prentice-Hall, Inc., 1961), pp. 1–64.

boundary conditions by which consumer values, or for that matter, all values, wants, desires, and aspirations are more or less conventionalized and directed.

Such a view of consumer behavior can be elaborated even further. For example, the consumer as a distinct personality is pictured as receiving as output from the organic system such facilities as motivational energy, perceptual capacity, performance or response capacity, and a sort of integrative facility rooted in the mechanisms of learning. In return, the personality generates outputs with respect to the organic system in the form of motive force conceived as a sort of feedback process in which motivational energy contributed by the organic system is controlled by the psychological system and brought to bear upon instrumental processes. Thus the personality system (the consumer) contributes a directional component and an attitudinal set that functions to focus perception and guide the consumer's goal-seeking activities. The interrelationships of all systems (organic, psychological, social, and cultural) occur along essentially similar lines. Each is regarded as an analytically separate order of systems partially independent but partially interpenetrating the others in such a way that all participate jointly in the determination of concrete action systems.

The consumer as the central feature of a behavioral system is faced with some basic functional problems. These are now seen as four in number, two having to do with the relations of the behavioral social system to the external environment and the other two with conditions internal to the system itself. The reader will find in these problems some degree of familiarity.

First, there are the instrumental problems incident to *goal attainment*. These are seen as including the solution to what might be called the consumer behavior dilemma. This dilemma relates to a means/end scheme and the coordination of activities in such a way that the behavioral system moves toward whatever goals it has set for itself.

Second, there are problems of *adaptation* to the external situation. Adaptation is not merely the problem of coming to terms with the environment; it includes basically the active manipulation of the environment to the end of acquiring facilities that have a generalized value as a means for a variety of system goals. Decision strategies and learning are all regarded as relevant for the adaptive problem.

Third is the problem of *integration;* the focus here is upon the relations of units in the system to one another and the problem of establishing and maintaining a level of solidarity or cohesion among them adequate to permit the total system to function.

Finally there is the problem, which we discussed much earlier in our treatment, called *tension management*. Tension management, simply defined, is the problem of maintaining within the behavioral system or consumer a level of motivational commitment sufficient for required role performances.

To this juncture we have explored something of the basic nature of total socialization processes, and we have treated these phenomena within a behavioral or social systems context. Such an overview seemed essential to the basic notion that socialization as an influence process in consumer behavior exists or manifests itself as a network of interdependent, interrelated, and interactive variables or components. In the remaining sections of this chapter, we shall explore the role of personal influence in consumer behavior and finally examine influence and other socializing processes within the context of social exchange theory.

Socialization and Personal Influence

Solutions to consumer problems may all be viewed as an array of information cues perceptible to the consumer.[17] For most solutions the array can include information such as price, color, style, size, taste, and feel. Consumers become aware of this information via opinions of salesmen, mass media advertising, and interaction with experts, groups, and friends. It is thus this *personal influence* that contributes significantly to the consumer's learning process through interaction. Consumers learn adaptive behavior, but much of that adaptive behavior stems from interaction with other people. Consumers emulate others. Mrs. Jones next door is Mrs. Smith's closest neighborhood friend. They interact frequently and visit in each other's home at least once a week. Mrs. Jones redecorates her kitchen and installs a new stain-resistant, soft floor covering in her kitchen. Because of their close association and interaction there is a good possibility that Mrs. Smith is now more receptive to soft floor covering in her kitchen than previously. We all emulate and indulge ourselves in vicarious learning situations. We ape, to some extent, the manners, dress, and consumption patterns of those we admire and esteem. Much of the socialization that takes place as a result of personal influence comes about as a result of instrumental learning. We often generate responses to others on whom we ourselves are dependent for favorable responses. In the vernacular, we call this fishing for compliments. For example, if you manifest a little anxiety about a new outfit or garment, you may seek some reaction from your friend regarding it by commenting favorably on the outfit he is wearing. This social situation, which involves operant conditioning, is known as *interpersonal response conditioning*.[18] Not only do we emulate and copy the consumption patterns and other habits of those we know well and actually interact with on a day-to-day basis, but we also learn and emulate from a process known as *anticipatory socialization*;[19] that is, we actually tend to adopt the attitudinal and

---

[17] See Donald F. Cox, "The Measurement of Information Value: A Study in Consumer Decision Making," *Emerging Concepts in Marketing*, proceedings of the Winter Conference of the American Marketing Association, William S. Decker, ed. (Pittsburgh, Pa.: American Marketing Association, 1962), p. 413.

[18] John T. Doby, *Introduction to Social Psychology* (New York: Appleton-Century-Crofts, 1966), p. 236.

[19] Robert K. Merton, *Social Theory and Social Structure*, rev. ed. (New York: The Free Press, 1957), p. 265.

behavioral characteristics of groups to which we ourselves do not yet actually belong. People who have a constantly rising set of expectations and aspirations are particularly susceptible to this phenomenon. Adolescents emulate teen-agers; college freshmen may emulate upperclassmen; the management trainee emulates the junior executive; all these are examples of anticipatory socialization.

THE NATURE AND SCOPE OF PERSONAL INFLUENCE

Socialization—that is, learning via interaction—implies a range of possible situations, such as learning and adaptation within the confines of the group, the family, the community, and the culture. We shall, however, eschew the treatment of these subjects, at least for the present, in order that we may deal with a more explicit case of socialization, namely, that of personal influence. According to Merton, personal influence occurs during a direct encounter of two or more people resulting in behavior or attitude change in the participants.[20] Such a definition, however, leaves many unanswered questions. For example, why do people find it both desirable and meaningful to interact? What is the basis of the bonds that link actors together? What is the structural basis of personal interaction? We shall dwell at length on a response to the first question in the latter part of this chapter. Suffice it to say at this juncture that in face-to-face interaction one person shows specific behavior in the presence of another. Such behavior leads to reciprocal behavior. Each therefore can create products for the other in the form of rewards that are satisfying and reinforcing. The value of the reward will, however, depend upon the unique requirements of the various participants. Furthermore, these rewards are also balanced by the costs of the interaction in terms of the values given in return or foregone. This general contribution toward an understanding of personal influence based upon social exchange is based upon the work of Homans and Thibaut and Kelley.[21] We shall deal more extensively with these theories in the concluding sections of this chapter.

THE NATURE OF INFLUENCE BONDS. If personal influence is to be viewed as a form of socialization and social organization, the participants must be bound together into some unit larger than themselves. Analysis of such binding forces reveals at least five types of social bonds.[22]

Ascription. Owing to the social position two persons happen to occupy, and quite independent of any individual characteristics, these persons may be linked by a role relationship. The typical personal in-

---

[20] Ibid.

[21] See George C. Homans, "Social Behavior as Exchange," *American Journal of Sociology,* Vol. 63 (1958), pp. 597–606; and J. W. Thibaut and H. H. Kelley, *The Social Psychology of Groups* (New York: John Wiley & Sons, Inc., 1959).

[22] George J. McCall and J. L. Simmons, *Identities and Interactions* (New York: The Free Press, 1966), pp. 170–175.

fluence relationships that stem from ascription are those based upon blood relationships or kinship.

Commitment. Commitment is a bonded-influence relationship that occurs when one party has pledged the semiexclusive use of the other party as a source of certain specified behaviors, role supports, and other rewards. Commitments are a strategy for increasing and ensuring the dependability of a source of exchange rewards.[23]

Attachment. Specific persons and their behavior get built into the contents of role identities and become crucial to the legitimation and enactment of these identities. This building of specific others into the very content of role identities is what we mean by becoming attached to particular others.

Investment. Investment represents the expenditure of scarce resources like money, time, and life chances in establishing and maintaining a relationship. Such a condition acknowledges that one cannot throw away these "investments" without realizing substantial returns. Hence, the justification for many continuing personal influence relationships.

Reward dependability. Finally, as a major reason for the continuation of many of our personal influence bonds, our recurring needs for role and image support, and of course the other commodities of social exchange, suggest that we are disposed to seek dependably recurring sources of them.

Thus, these five bonds are perhaps the most important forces serving to bind two persons together, making it likely that they will continue to interact on a personal basis in the future.[24]

THE DIRECTION AND MAGNITUDE OF INFLUENCE

The foregoing discussion served to tell us something about the nature of the bonds in a personal influence situation, but it told us little or nothing about the direction and magnitude of the influence situation. Although each personal influence dyad must be examined in relation to the situational factors, the mediating factors, and the various interrelationships between these factors before specific conclusions can be drawn and discerned, some general observations at least can be noted.[25]

Personal influence is largely a function of what might be called role identities or, better still, perceived self-concepts. This self-concept

[23] Howard S. Becker, "Notes on the Concept of Commitment," *American Journal of Sociology,* Vol. 66 (1960), pp. 32–40.

[24] See George J. McCall, "The Social Organization of Relationships," in George J. McCall, et al., *Social Relationships* (Chicago: Aldine Publishing Company, 1970), p. 7–8.

[25] For a specific study listing and discussing these factors, see Sidney P. Feldman and Merlin C. Spencer, "The Effect of Personal Influence in the Selection of Consumer Services," in *Marketing and Economics Development,* Peter Bennett, ed. (Chicago: American Marketing Association, 1965), pp. 440–452.

is a conception of oneself as occupying a number of social positions or behavioral roles. It is further assumed that no one is acquainted with the entire set of social or behavioral roles or self-concepts of another and that for reasons of economy and security the individual reveals somewhat different aspects or subsets of these different positions or self-concepts to different others. These different revealed subsets of identities or self-concepts we shall call *persona* from the Latin word meaning "mask."[26] With this brief prelude, we may define the character of a personal influence relation as the fit between the personas that the members of a relationship present to one another.

Thus to grasp the magnitude and direction of a personal influence relationship one must first examine each of the pair of self-concepts or role identities that are included in the structure of the relationship along the following lines.

AFFECT STRUCTURE. The affect structure of a relationship must be approached in terms of the question, "Which member (if either) likes the other more than he is liked?" Affect structure basically reflects the bonds of attachment and rewards dependability.

POWER STRUCTURE. Both members of a personal influence situation are seen as having some power over the other. The power structure, however, is seen in terms of power differentiation. According to Waller's "principle of least interest" he who is least dependent on the other for resources maintains a power differential over the other.[27] Power would thus reflect differences in the bonds of investment, attachment, and commitment.

AUTHORITY STRUCTURE. Authority, as distinguished from power, is the right rather than the ability to exact compliance and is typically ceded in exchange for the assumption of responsibility. In personal influence relationships the authority structure depends on which member (if either) is accorded the right of asking the other to comply. This structure is determined clearly by ascription.

In general most studies of personal influence have revealed a rather close correspondence among these three structures; that is, a person who ranks high (or low) in one of these dimensions tends to rank high (or low) in the others. In any event, personal influence as a persuasive factor in behavior and attitude change is strongly affected by the consideration of affect, power, and authority. And these factors are highly relevant in a study or an assessment of the impact and magnitude of a personal influence situation.

[26] These ideas are from McCall, op. cit., p. 11.

[27] For more on this concept, see Willard Waller, *The Family: A Dynamic Interpretation* (New York: Holt, Rinehart & Winston, Inc., 1938); and Richard M. Emerson, "Power-Dependence Relations," *American Sociological Review*, Vol. 27 (1962), pp. 31–41.

PERSONAL INFLUENCE AND CONSUMER BEHAVIOR

Consumer behavior is affected and determined by personal influence to the extent that each person in the behavior dyad can create products for the other in the form of rewards that are satisfying and reinforcing. These rewards, as we have seen, are balanced by the costs of the interaction in terms of the values given in return or foregone. Such is the nature of personal influence interaction within the framework of social exchange theory.

Bauer has commented upon the notion that perhaps people engage in two different kinds of personal influence interactions, the psychosocial game and the problem-solving game.[28] In the psychosocial game, the person participates and interacts to gain social acceptance and reward. In the problem-solving game, the individual uses information gained from his interaction and participation with other people as a reference point in defining his environment and in decision making. Given the nature of much consumer behavior, this may be a needlessly fine distinction. Consumers engage in face-to-face interaction with others within a behavioral context both because they seek social approval and reinforcement of their actions and because their behavior is of necessity goal oriented and constrained by the necessity of making choices from among alternatives, that is, decision making. Consumer behavior cannot be neatly separated into one category of behavior, which we label as problem solving or instrumental, or another category labeled as social exchange or psychological fun and games. Consumer behavior, like most forms of social behavior, is both.

Robert F. Bales, a sociologist, recognized these two interrelated dimensions of behavior when he constructed his objective method of interaction process analysis.[29] His system, although too elaborate and detailed to repeat here, briefly consists of twelve interaction categories into which all conceivable types of behavior that can be assigned meaning are placed by an observer. Six of the categories are for social-emotional behavior that is positive or negative in nature.[30] The system of interaction process analysis, as it is formally called, is designed to give an objective account of quantitative and qualitative characteristics of the dynamics of interaction in a personal influence context.

Personal influence affects consumer behavior through a dynamic referred to by Festinger as *social comparison processes*. The social

---

[28] Raymond A. Bauer, "Source Effect and Persuasibility: A New Look," in *Risk Taking and Information Handling in Consumer Behavior,* Donald F. Cox, ed. (Cambridge, Mass.: Harvard University, 1967), pp. 559–578.

[29] Robert F. Bales, *Interaction Process Analysis* (Reading, Mass.: Addison-Wesley Publishing Co., Inc., 1950).

[30] For an example and illustration of this process applied to consumer behavior, see David M. Gardner, "Can Bales' Interaction Process Analysis Be Used to Explore Consumer Behavior?" in *Consumer Behavior,* R. J. Holloway, R. A. Mittelstaedt, and M. Venkatesan, eds. (Boston: Houghton Mifflin Company, 1971), pp. 258–266.

comparison process, like the theory of social exchange, recognizes both the psychosocial and the problem-solving aspects of personal influence and interaction. Festinger contends quite logically that individuals tend to seek to evaluate their opinions and their demonstrated behaviors. When objective nonsocial means for such evaluations are available, people will use them. To the extent that such nonsocial and objective means are unavailable, individuals will turn to others for advice and information. Hence, the reasons for using others for gaining perspective and engaging in what we called earlier reality testing are even more explicit.

Personal influence is not just something to which consumers are subjected. It is something that almost everybody seeks. Because consumers both seek social approval and are faced with the necessity of making decisions, interaction within the confines of a personal influence situation is deemed not only necessary but desirable.

OPINION LEADERS AND KEY INFLUENTIALS

One of the most extensively researched phenomena or concepts relating to personal influence is that of the role of opinion leaders or key influentials.[31] In any influence dyad or larger influence situation the ones most influential are designated as opinion leaders or key influentials.

The role of key influentials has been studied extensively by both marketers and social scientists. Katz and Lazarsfeld characterized influentials in terms of status and gregariousness, whereas Rogers's influentials manifested three basic traits: social participation, social status, and cosmopolitanism.[32] Key influentials are often the early adopters of new products and new fashions, they are usually more knowledgeable than the other members of the influence situation, and they can generally be expected to have greater exposure to the relevant mass media but not to mass media in general.[33]

There has been a raging controversy as to whether opinion leaders are situation-bound or topic-free. One position holds that influence and opinion leadership is situation-bound;[34] that is, an opinion leader is a

---

[31] *Opinion leader* is the term most commonly used in the literature but *key influential* appears to be more descriptive and broader and thus more significant.

[32] Elihu Katz and Paul Lazarsfeld, *Personal Influence* (Glencoe, Ill.: The Free Press, 1955); and Everett M. Rogers, *Diffusion of Innovations* (Glencoe, Ill.: The Free Press, 1962).

[33] Thomas S. Robertson, "The Effect of the Informal Group upon Member Innovated Behavior," in *Marketing and the New Science of Planning*, Robert L. King, ed. (Chicago: American Marketing Association, 1968), pp. 334–340; also, Charles W. King, "The Innovator in the Fashion Adoption Process," in *Reflections on Progress in Marketing*, L. George Smith, ed. (Chicago: American Marketing Association, 1964), pp. 325–326; and John O. Sommers, *The Identity of the Women's Clothing Fashion Transmitter*, unpublished Ph. D. dissertation, Purdue University (1968).

[34] Katz and Lazarsfeld, op. cit., p. 334.

leader only in relation to a particular situation. This position, however, is challenged by those who argue that influence and opinion leadership is topic-free or that a generalized opinion leader seems to exist and that overlap is greatest between similar product categories.[35] More evidence will have to be generated, however, before this controversy is resolved.

To the extent that marketers wish to understand consumer behavior, they correspondingly wish to understand personal influence and the role of opinion leaders and key influentials. To the extent that key influentials are capable of influencing and shaping the behavior of other consumers, marketers are interested in identifying them and reaching them effectively. As we have noted, the characteristics and traits of influentials are generally well known, and, to this extent at least, these persons can be reasonably well identified. However, it is not easy to separate the influentials from the noninfluentials and reach them effectively via the mass media. This dilemma has prompted one authority to comment:

> Personal influence may be more effective than persuasive mass communication but at present mass communication seems the most effective means of stimulating personal influence.[36]

What Klapper is acknowledging is the near impossibility and high cost associated with (1) identifying influentials and (2) developing specialized messages to be disseminated over specialized media to reach them. He is furthermore acknowledging the presence and influence of what we called in Chapter 11 the two-step flow of communication. Recall that the two-step hypothesis asserts that messages reach the influentials through the mass media and that the influentials in turn reach the other members of society. Surely, however, the mass media must have some impact on the masses and not just on opinion leaders and influentials. This writer argues that it does so in the manner suggested by Figure 13-3.

What Figure 13-3 depicts is simply this. Although the influential may be presumed to be influenced by the mass media and the significant others by the influentials, the significant others are also wired in to the network of mass media, and the media messages tend to act as secondary reinforcers of the messages and opinions of the key influentials. Communication and influence are facilitated by both the mass media and the key influentials.

Robertson has argued that for marketers to develop effective marketing strategies based upon our knowledge of personal influence situa-

---

[35] Charles W. King and John O. Sommers, "Overlap of Opinion Leadership Across Consumer Product Categories," working paper, Krannert Graduate School of Industrial Administration, Purdue University, 1968.

[36] Joseph T. Klapper, *The Effects of Mass Communication* (Glencoe, Ill.: The Free Press, 1960), p. 72.

Figure 13-3

The Role of the Mass Media, Influentials, and Significant Others

The Flow of Communication and Influence

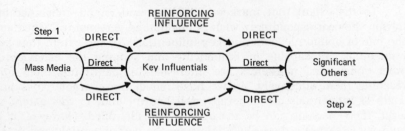

tions they must (1) simulate personal influence, (2) stimulate personal influence, and (3) monitor personal influence.[37]

By simulating personal influence the marketer stresses the kinds of people who buy the product, reinforcing and broadening where possible the existing image and stereotype of users. Testimonials, perceptional phenomena such as figure and ground, direction and continuity, and other devices can be used to create the aura that the product is widely used and accepted in "in" situations and by desirable and esteemed models.

The marketer can stimulate personal influence by getting customers to talk about his product. Products advertised with a large amount of plot value, such as the Alka-Seltzer campaign in 1972 ("Try it, you'll like it" and "I can't believe I ate the whole thing"), have a large amount of conversational impact and value. Advertising designed to encourage new purchasers to tell their friends or giving rebates to customers who give the names of friends they believe will buy are examples of stimulating personal influence.

Monitoring personal influence involves auditing and evaluating specific customer reaction to products and messages. If reactions are poor or nonexistent, a reevaluation of both product and messages may be warranted. When reactions are monitored, new uses for old products are often discovered, or features or attributes of the product not previously appreciated may be pointed out by customer usage. Such reactions can lead to the development and use of new appeals and, of course, an extension of the product's life and profitability cycles.

Alternate Theories of Social Exchange

Throughout our treatment thus far we have implied that socialization and socialization processes are dependent upon the concept of social exchange. For example, socialization leads to adaptive behavior

[37] Thomas S. Robertson, *Consumer Behavior* (Glenview, Ill.: Scott, Foresman and Company, 1970), p. 93–96.

that results from learning and interaction. However, the subject is not imprinted like wax with the norms, customs, attitudes, and values of society, but in the transactional or exchange sense, the subject both acts and is acted upon. Consumer behavior can affect the larger matrix of behavior out of which it emerges, but at the same time the larger social and cultural matrix of behavior also structures, alters, and conditions consumer behavior. Our treatment of socialization within the systems framework of analysis was intended to illustrate the dynamic play or interdependent and interactive nature of socialization. Finally, our discussion of personal influence in consumer behavior explicitly recognized the exchange basis of interaction, namely, that persons interact for a purpose to fulfill needs and to generate reinforcing responses related to their own actions. The role of key influentials and opinion leaders can largely be explained in terms of social attraction. Key influentials and opinion leaders are those persons whose characteristics best approximate the information seeker's perception of the composite reference group or individual with whom he aspires to associate and interact. So once again, interaction and exchange suggests that socialization and personal influence occur because people seek to achieve social and psychological rewards at relatively low cost. Social exchange becomes a kind of psychological glue that cements individuals into the units we know as social relationships. Because of the conceptual fertility of exchange theories, we shall conclude our chapter by examining more fully several of the more prominent social exchange theories. These have not been widely used, if at all, to explore consumer behavior phenomena. For that matter, with the exception of a limited amount of work on dyadic interaction, social exchange theories and personal influence have not been widely explored in relation to consumer behavior.[38] For this reason, as the various approaches are discussed some effort will be made to suggest their applicability to consumer behavior, and, where convenient for illustrative purposes, the models will be presented as if they had been applied to consumer behavior situations.[39]

Homans' Theory of Elementary Social Behavior

Homans developed his theory with the intent of explaining the elementary face-to-face social interchange that occurs between two persons. He limited the behavior that he considered explicable through his analysis by the following criteria:

1. It must be social; thus when a person acts, he must be directly reacted to positively or negatively by another.

[38] See Franklin B. Evans, "Selling as a Dyadic Relationship—A New Approach," *American Behavioral Scientist*, Vol. 6 (May 1963), pp. 76–79.

[39] Such "as if" approaches are well established in scientific analysis. See Hans Vaihinger, *The Philosophy of "As If": A System of the Theoretical, Practical, and Religious Fictions of Mankind* (New York: Harcourt Brace Jovanovich, Inc., 1925).

2. When a person acts, he must be rewarded or punished by the person toward whom his action is directed and not by a third party.
3. The behavior must be actual and not merely a norm or societal expectation of appropriate behavior.[40]

Homans defined elementary social behavior as occurring in two-party interactions involving the direct and immediate exchange of rewards and punishments between the participants in the interaction. The basic unit of his analysis is the two-person dyad, diagrammed as follows: A⇌B where A's behavior (reward or punishment) affects B's behavior (reward or punishment) and where B's behavior in turn affects A.

Based upon his analysis, Homans generated five propositions regarding human behavior. We shall list first his proposition and then supply our own elaboration of how such a proposition could apply to consumers. The reader will recognize immediately that the terminology employed and the basic ideas involved are those of Skinnerian or instrumental learning and conditioning.

1. *Stimulus Generalization.* "If in the past the occurrence of a particular stimulus situation has been the occasion on which a person's activity has been rewarded, then the more likely he is to emit the activity, or some similar activity now" (p. 53).

Consider the following example: Consumer A has at some time in the past emitted a help-requesting activity directed at Person B (another consumer), and this activity occasioned Person B's emission of positive helping activity toward Consumer A. Consumer A responded to Person B's help-giving activity by emitting help-requesting activities toward B. At present Person C is emitting help-requesting activities directed at Person B and resembling the help-requesting activities of Consumer A in the past. Because in the past interaction Person B's help-giving activity had been reinforced by Consumer A, he is, according to proposition 1, likely to perform help-giving activities toward C in order to experience C's rewarding positive sentiment activity.

2. *Reinforcement Frequency.* "The more often within a given period of time a person's activity rewards the activity of another, the more often the other will emit the activity" (p. 54).

Quite succinctly this means that the more often a customer thanks a salesperson for his help, the more often the salesperson will give help to the customer. Or turn it around. The more frequently a salesperson rewards a customer for his patronage, the more often the customer will patronize that salesperson.

---

[40] George C. Homans, *Social Behavior: Its Elementary Forms* (New York: Harcourt Brace Jovanovich, Inc., 1961). The page numbers following each proposition refer to this work.

3. *Magnitude of Reinforcement.* "The more valuable to a person a unit of activity another gives him, the more often another will emit activity rewarded by the activity of the other" (p. 55).

The greater the person's need for help, the more valuable help becomes and the more reward and gratitude he will give when it is received. Thus a store or a salesperson who provides generous assistance and help when it is truly needed will be gratefully rewarded.

4. *Reactive Inhibition and Satiation.* "The more often a person has in the recent past received a rewarding activity from another, the less valuable any further unit of that activity becomes to him" (p. 55).

Isn't this an interesting note! For what it says is this: as a merchant or marketer, if you continue to please and do it too frequently, you will be likely to reach a point of diminishing marginal return with your customers. They will become satiated with the rewards you can deliver and in the interest of maintaining variety and satisfying curiosity they will shop elsewhere. Isn't this, therefore, the major reason why we have large numbers of low store- and brand-loyal customers?

5. *The Rule of Distributive Justice.* "A person in an exchange relation with another will expect that the rewards of each person be proportioned to his costs—the greater the rewards, the greater the costs— and that the net rewards or profits of each man be proportioned to his investments—the greater the investments, the greater the profit" (p. 75).

Thus, when the desired proportion between rewards and costs or investments and profits does not occur from social exchange, the rule of distributive justice is violated. For example, consider a personal influence situation. Person A largely follows the consumption patterns and dictates of Person B. They are close neighbors, they interact almost daily, and their husbands share the same occupation. Person B is usually flattered by this behavior (rewards) but on occasion irritated because Person A copies every new thing that Person B buys (costs). These two have developed a rather strong attraction for each other over time (investment) and on balance the arrangement is a successful (profitable) one. However, if Person B buys new furniture for the living room and if Person A copies this behavior too closely, the costs to B are likely to exceed the rewards or profits and the influence relationship is likely to be seriously strained.

Homans's elementary theory of social behavior is thus a stimulating and challenging one and it offers some insight for the continued and further analysis of influence and interaction situations. To the extent that consumer behavior is social behavior, the relevance of Homans's propositions seems assured. His theory recognizes that consumers take many of their cues from the significant others with whom they interact and that, in an operant sense, consumer behavior is shaped by its consequences.

A THEORY OF INTERACTION OUTCOMES

The theory of interaction outcomes as developed by Thibaut and Kelley was proposed to explain the manner in which two or more persons in an interactive relationship are dependent on one another for the attainment of positive outcomes.[41] The basic premise of their theory is that a socially significant interaction will be repeated only if the participants in that interaction are reinforced as a function of having participated. Their theory, like that of Homans, posits that a social interaction must yield positive outcomes if it is to be continued. Rewards stemming from social interaction may be material (object gain) or psychological (gain in status, power, affection, and so on).

Thibaut and Kelley's basic unit of interaction is the dyad. And the major analytical technique used is the *outcome matrix*. The outcome matrix is formed of all the behaviors that two individuals might jointly perform. Thibaut and Kelley's basic model is concerned primarily with the determinants of reward and cost, and they acknowledge that rewards and costs are the product of several factors.

EXOGENOUS DETERMINANTS. Rewards and costs that do not directly ensue from social interaction and that are in fact determined by factors outside the interaction are termed *exogenous*. Such exogenous determinants may include the individual needs and abilities of the participants, the similarities or differences in their attitudes and values, and the situational context of their interpersonal contact with one another. A word of further explanation about some of these exogenous variables might conceivably offer some insight into personal influence and interaction regarding consumer behavior.

Abilities. Persons who are preferred or chosen by others as dyadic partners often have abilities that the nonchosen do not have. They therefore possess a greater potentiality for rewarding the others in an interaction.

Similarities. Individuals with similar attitudes and orientations are more prone to select one another as friends, mates, or partners. Therefore, preinteraction similarities between participants in a dyad should facilitate the attainment of positive outcomes by both members.

Proximity. If one considers the similarity of the two members of a dyad, those dyads in which the members are in physically close proximity to each other should be more long-lasting and should yield a greater opportunity for positive outcome than the dyads in which members are spatially separated.

Complementarity. In a complementary relationship each person can perform activities for the other that the other cannot perform for himself.

Thus, these exogenous determinants of rewards and costs function as boundary conditions or givens in any interactive relationship. How-

---

[41] Thibaut and Kelley, op. cit.

ever, the maximum rewards and minimum costs that are potentially available to individuals in an interactive situation are achieved only when certain endogenous factors to the relationship are operative.

ENDOGENOUS DETERMINANTS. The endogenous factors that determine reward-cost payoffs are those factors that arise during and as a consequence of the interaction process itself. Endogenous determinants are largely of two types: (1) those related to the *production of behavior* and (2) those related to the *perception of behavior*.

The basic factors affecting the production of behavior are *strangeness* and *accessibility* or *cultural norms*. Strangeness relates to the early stage of most relationships that is characterized by stereotypic politeness and other forms of stereotyped behavior. Accessibility or the degree and intensity of initial interaction is usually limited, and this situation is normally attributed to cultural norms that dictate the degree of intimacy between two individuals in a casual social contact.

The *perception of behavior* involves the factors that influence one's evaluation and appraisal of another's responses with some thought for the forecasts he might make of future outcomes.

The perception of behavior is dependent upon the *availability of cues*. From these, certain inferences are made about the likely behavior repertoires of the subject. Perception of behavior is also related to the *primary effect;* that is, in most cases, recency of information seems to be a potent determinant of one's perceptions. Furthermore, the *organization of perceptions*—that is, the order of presentation of salient elements, the consistency of information, the manner in which another person presents himself—will determine the way one organizes his perceptions of that person. Finally, the state of the observer (his needs, emotions, cognitions, motivations, and so on) at the point of initial contact with another will in part color and affect his perceptions of that other and the possible outcomes that might ensue from a continued interaction with him.

One very interesting dimension of dyadic interaction in Thibaut and Kelley's treatment is *power*. Their theory holds that each person in a dyadic interaction has at least the possibility of exercising power over the other. This power is usually manifested by one individual's capability of controlling the reward-cost positions of the other individual; that is, power is a function of A's ability to affect the quality of outcomes attained by B."[42] Thibaut and Kelley discuss two types of power: *fate control* and *behavior control*.

Fate Control. If A can alter B's outcomes by varying his own behavior, he has fate control over B. In consumer behavior and an influence situation through interaction, this would mean that Consumer A can alter B's rewards or punishments (either real economic or psychological status, satisfaction, and so on) by varying his own behavior.

[42] Ibid., p. 101.

Behavior Control. If A can make it desirable for B to vary his behavior by varying his own behavior, he has behavior control over B.

There are consequences of power to both the dyad and the individual. In the case of the dyad, the general proposition is that the greater the correspondence and extent of power held by both members, the greater the cohesiveness of that dyad. The greater the power the members have over each other, the greater the convergence and hence similarity in values and attitudes.

The possession of power or control in the dyadic situation yields a series of benefits to the high power person: (1) he gains better reward-cost payoff positions; (2) he has better control of the dyad and the resulting behavior sequences; and (3) he has at least the potential of inculcating the other member of the dyad with his set of values and attitudes.

Thus Thibaut and Kelley's theory offers a rich conceptual framework for consumer behavior analysis, and although these implications are not always stated explicitly as such, the treatment of the conceptual material readily allows interpretations of these implications. Personal selling, personal influence, and many other socialized activities that lead to learning and behavioral modification through interaction would readily lend themselves to such an analytical framework.

A Functional Theory of Authority Interactions

A most interesting analysis of authority relationships has emerged from the work of Adams and Romney.[43] Their theory is interesting from the viewpoint of consumer behavior because they contend that authority can be characterized as the behavioral control that one person has over another. Before proceeding to examine the determinants of authority interactions, perhaps we should look first at Adams and Romney's basic assumptions.

Their first contention is that authority relationships are asymmetrical. By this they mean that one person in the relationship has greater power over the other person than that other person has over him (this is the usual case in a personal influence situation regarding consumer behavior). Second, the authority relationships are *stable;* that is, the same person is in the superordinate position across most of the interactions in which two people engage. (This assumption is challenged by researchers in opinion leadership who argue that opinion leaders are situationally determined. However, it squares well with the idea of those who advocate a topic-free key influential or opinion leader as one who is simply a supernormative member of society.) Finally, contrary to conventional wisdom, authority is not just institutionalized by society and society's definition of roles. It arises, instead,

[43] J. S. Adams and A. K. Romney, "The Determinants of Authority Interaction," *Decisions, Values, and Groups,* N. F. Washburne, ed., Vol. 2 (New York: Pergamon Press, Inc., 1962), pp. 227–256.

in any social interaction regardless of society's legitimation. Authority, therefore, is not viewed as formal power to act but as a functional and operational power and status that emerge from all kinds of social interaction.

The theory of authority interactions is quite similar to both Homans's theory of elementary social behavior and Thibaut and Kelley's theory of interaction outcomes. All are conceptually an application of Skinnerian principles to interaction situations. Because of this similarity and the possibility of some repetition, we shall only briefly examine the various determinants of authority interactions.

REINFORCING STIMULUS VARIABLES

Reinforcing stimuli increase the probability of the occurrence of a previous response. For example, B's giving advice and information to A and A's thanking B in return are both reinforcing stimuli. As such they increase the probability that on some future occasion A will emit the same response and initiate the same behavior sequence and that B will follow through by continuing the sequence, culminating in his own reinforcement. Thus A's control or authority over B in this particular sequence of behavior is partially a function of previous reinforcing contingencies in similar situations.

DEPRIVATION AND AVERSIVE STIMULUS VARIABLES

In an authority relation, there is usually an inverse correspondence between A's initial state of deprivation and A's response and B's reinforcement. This suggests that A's response must specify the conditions that are the inverse of his deprivation state and that B must present these conditions in order for A to be reinforced. In effect, then, the deprivation of A controls the response that he makes in the presence of B.

DISCRIMINATIVE STIMULUS VARIABLES

Discriminative stimulus variables are of two types: (1) the stimulus characteristics of B, and (2) the situational stimuli, excluding B. In the case of (1) it is obvious that without the presence of another person, A could not exercise any authority and hence his initial response could not be reinforced.

In the case of (2), situational variables that constitute discrimination stimuli for A's initial response can be conceptualized in terms of the physical or social context when a given authority sequence is initiated.

Thus authority interactions attempt to deal with the question of behavioral control (authority) given certain power and status relationships. It is a fundamental and paramount question in almost every case involving social interaction, and it is indeed a question of considerable interest to consumer behavioralists and marketers. Our knowledge of the power and influence relationships in personal and social interaction in consumer behavior is both sketchy and skimpy. However, as we have seen, there is a much vaster and conceptually much richer literature on this general subject in the field of social psychology. Although admittedly we cannot borrow indiscriminately from other disciplines, surely we must not overlook the important contributions of social psychology to the question of how socialization, personal influence, and other forms of group interaction modify and restructure our behavior and predispositions via social and perceptual learning. To a great extent, such has been our task throughout this chapter. Now that this groundwork has been laid, we shall proceed in the following chapter to explore the impact of the group, and such group-related phenomena as social class, on various aspects of consumer behavior.

Questions for Study, Reflection, and Review

1 Explain the relationship between perceptual or social learning and the socialization process.

2 What are the major influencing factors in the socialization process?

3 Distinguish between the creature man approach to socialization and the culture man approach.

4 Describe the symbolic man approach to socialization and its implications for consumer behavior.

5 What are the basic functional problems faced by the consumer?

6 Briefly discuss the role of personal influence in the socialization process and in consumer behavior.

7 Distinguish between the psychosocial game in personal influence interactions and the problem-solving game.

8 Discuss the role of opinion leaders and key influentials in personal influence situations.

9 What is the basic premise upon which social exchange theories of interaction are constructed?

10 Discuss Homans's theory of elementary social behavior with respect to magnitude and frequency of reinforcement and the implications for marketing.

14

Group
Influence
and Social
Class

Introduction

In this chapter we shall continue our inquiry into the nature and scope of interpersonal variables or determinants of consumer behavior. Actually, our work in the preceding chapter was, for all practical purposes, a prologue to the treatment of group influence and social class, the central concern of this chapter and for the work to be undertaken in the succeeding chapters of this section, which will deal with family influence in consumer decision-making and the cultural implications of consumption.

Group influence and social class are, of course, extensions of the concept of personal influence introduced and discussed in Chapter 13. Again, the significance of social influence considerations in relation to consumer behavior is that we are concerned with the impact and extent of such factors as socialization, imitation, interpersonal perception, and social learning as they emerge from social interaction processes. In other words, consumers learn adaptive behavior, and a large amount of this learning stems from socialization processes whereby, via emulation and imitation, individual consumers, in their larger social settings and as a result of interaction with others in group surroundings, accommodate themselves to the perceived roles and norms of the group.

Thus, groups are instrumental in casting the individual consumer in a series of roles. The groups to which consumers belong, or aspire to belong, will have standards of behavior or norms to which the individual either must conform or submit to group censure. Group activity plays some role in both instrumental and cue-producing responses in social learning situations, but, most importantly, group activities, reference group concepts, group norms, and social class concepts and roles are directly concerned with consumer behavior because of their cue-producing effects. The activities of one's groups often dictate within a rather narrow range the instrumental response choice of the individual. For that matter, there are few persons whose purchase decisions and consumption behavior are not to some degree affected by group activity. The influence that groups exert on our total individual actions and psychological states gives them a place of unparalleled importance in our study of consumer behavior and consumer decision processes. This importance has been underscored by Sherif and Cantril in the statement that "Once an individual identifies himself with a group and its collective actions, his behavior is, in a major way, determined by the direction of the group's action.[1]

To the extent that such a generalization is true, a knowledge of group influence is essential to an understanding of consumer behavior. Furthermore, it must be recognized that groups are not so much the focus of our inquiry as they are the place where that inquiry takes place. This thought has been stated most aptly by Homans. He contends:

> groups are not what we study but where we often study it. . . . If you will look at the behavior that students of small groups actually investigate, you will find it has the following characteristics. First, at least two men are in face to face contact, each behaving toward the other in ways that reward or punish him and therefore influence his behavior. Second, the rewards or punishments that each gets from the behavior of the other are direct and immediate rather than indirect and deferred. And third, the behavior of the two men is determined in part by something besides their conformity to institutional rules or roles.[2]

Thus we emphasize once again that our major concern is largely with the role and impact of interaction and the corresponding effect of socialization on consumer behavior. Our major concern in this chapter is to explain and analyze the psychological consequences of an individual's participation in and identification with various groups or social classes, that is, to explain why some people anxiously adapt their reactions to what is expected of them or readily conform to group or class standards of behavior, whereas others view groups as opportunities to seek influence roles, to lead and persuade rather than follow, to set standards and norms rather than follow them. Our inquiry into the

---

[1] M. Sherif and H. Cantril, *The Psychology of Ego Involvements* (New York: John Wiley & Sons, Inc., 1947), p. 290.

[2] George C. Homans, "Small Groups," in *The Behavioral Sciences Today*, B. Berelson, ed. (New York: Basic Books, 1963), p. 165.

psychological consequences of participation in groups will necessarily focus upon both the dimensions of external restraint and the relational systems. The strength of external restraints is the degree to which behavior is required to conform to the demands and expectations of other persons. The strength of the relational system is the degree of involvement in social or cathectic relationships with other persons. Consumer behavior as influenced by group association is affected by both the factors of external restraints and the nature of the relational or interactive system of which the consumer is a part.

We shall continue our basic cognitive orientation by conceiving of social groups as a set of organized forces acting upon the individual member. The cognitive tradition would suggest that the individual's perception of these forces and his representation of them in his own conceptual life space or psychological field will determine and affect his behavior in groups.

Thus we turn now to an examination of how consumer behavior is affected by group considerations. Our basic interest in this chapter will be to chart the impact of groups on the overall socialization and learning process of the individual consumer. We shall look first at the role of small primary groups and then turn our attention to the impact of a larger secondary group, social class, on the consumer and consumer-related activities.

THE NATURE AND PERSISTENCE OF GROUPS

There is so much of our behavior that is conformist in character that most of the time we fail to realize that we are conforming. As a student, look about the classroom in which you may be seated. Isn't it strange that the attire worn by most of the group is practically a uniform of the day? Now it is true that dress standards vary from time to time and slightly from person to person, but there is also a great tendency for the widespread adoption of given fads and fashions among students. Students are not alone in their conformist behavior. Look at the businessman as he sits around the lunch table with his associates. The uniform of the day here is a business suit, dress shirt, and tie. They are eating lightly or pretending to in order to maintain the acceptable image of the time—youthful slenderness. Or picture the housewife at home in the suburbs. Suburban houses are very similar in terms of design, decor, and furnishings. Housewives engage in routines that are strikingly similar—a little gardening, PTA meetings, shopping at the supermarket, coffee klatches, an occasional trip to the city.

Attitudes, opinions, expressive movements, and value orientations all seem pretty much to coincide among the various groups just mentioned. For example, there is a great similarity of sentiments and behavior among students, businessmen, and suburban housewives. Why? Because behavior and sentiments are in large measure the product of our group memberships. From our earliest infancy until death or loss of perceptual contact with the world, our character, our personality, our general behavior pattern, our dress, speech, and mannerisms are shaped by the forces exerted upon us in the groups in which we have membership and thus interactions.

Groups, therefore, are a pervasive force in our psychological field. They exist fundamentally to aid individuals in attaining goals that would otherwise be unattainable. Groups are said to represent an organization of effort beyond a mere aggregation of individuals. As Blumer has said:

> A human society is composed of diverse kinds of . . . groups. To a major extent our total collective life is made up of the actions and acts of such groups. These groups are oriented in different directions because of special interests.[3]

It is inevitable that the groups to which we belong exert a significant influence on our total behavior. The spectrum extends from the fads and hobbies we pick up to the deepest traits of character and personality.[4]

WHY GROUPS PERSIST. Group emergence and development were caused by the purposes that groups serve; that is, groups emerge and develop because of their instrumental and utilitarian value to mankind. Perhaps initially the group was the primary means of defense and survival. However, as man evolved and as his behavior became more sophisticated, the function of the group likewise took on a more sophisticated role. Thus, the persistence and ubiquitous nature of the group has come to be explained in this fashion:

1. Man is biologically interdependent or social, but he is not equipped with biologically built-in behavior patterns.
2. Being biologically social, man's survival depends upon his interaction with those who can help him meet his needs.
3. Man's interaction skills depend in turn upon the processes of perception and learning and the quality of the perceptual materials available for learning and problem solving.
4. Both norms and roles develop out of efforts to solve problems through social interaction. The particular norms and roles that evolve are the ones that the more powerful members of the group perceive as best assuring their goal aspirations or definitions.[5]

Groups persist, therefore, because they provide man with numerous yardsticks for measuring and testing his behavior. And, most

[3] Herbert Blumer, "Public Opinion and Public Opinion Polling," *American Sociological Review*, Vol. 13 (1948), pp. 542–554.

[4] For a more comprehensive treatment of the subject of groups and group influence, see the following: Elton T. Reeves, *The Dynamics of Group Behavior* (American Management Association, Inc., 1970); and Michael S. Olmsted, *The Small Group* (New York: Random House, Inc., 1959).

[5] Adapted from John T. Doby, *Introduction to Social Psychology* (New York: Appleton-Century-Crofts, 1966), pp. 251–252.

importantly, groups generate a measure of economic, social, and psychological pleasure or benefit for their individual members. Such a statement is in keeping with the exchange theory of interaction introduced in Chapter 13 that states that individuals are attracted to social interaction processes because they expect to receive satisfactory rewards at low costs as a result of their interaction with others.[6]

GROUP NORMS AND ROLES. Two of the more interesting and dynamic aspects of groups are the concepts of group norms and roles. Group norms are the basic rules of the game and indicate what is considered normal behavior. These basic rules or norms constitute the behavioral expectancies of the participating members of the group and are defined by several properties that have been called constitutive properties:

1. The constitutive expectancies provide a set of boundary conditions within which each member must make decision choices regardless of personal likes and dislikes, plans, and consequences for himself and others. The choices are independent of the number of members, patterns of moves, or territory of behavior.
2. Each member assumes a norm of reciprocity with respect to the alternatives which are binding on each other.
3. The members assume that whatever they expect of each other is perceived and interpreted in the same way.[7]

Such a way of viewing norms and social interaction within groups suggests that group interaction is a kind of social game constituted by the mutual expectations of the participants. If there are no mutual expectations, then there are in effect no rules or norms and the interaction will be unstable and disorganized. Therefore, group norms as expectations regarding the appropriate behavior of group members within a given group activity are an important property of group interaction. In addition to norms, group configurations and interactions also affect our roles. We have discussed roles before and concluded that roles are prescribed actions and behavior patterns. Roles are sets of norms. In essence, roles are the different behaviors that we display in connection with the given social position we occupy. Thus there is an expected behavior pattern or role associated with a consumer advocate, and there is a role attributed to the college professor or the student or the suburban housewife. All of us have a multiplicity of roles that we must fill

[6] For more on this topic, see H. H. Kelley, J. W. Thibaut, Roland Radloff, and David Mundy, "The Development of Cooperation in the Minimal Social Situation," *Psychological Monograph,* Vol. 76, No. 19 (1962).

[7] See Aaron V. Circaurel, *Method and Measurement in Sociology* (New York: The Free Press, A Division of the Macmillan Company, 1964), p. 204. Circaurel credits Harold Garfinkel with this conception, taken from a paper by Garfinkel on "A Conception of and Experiments with 'Trust' as a Condition of Stable Concerted Action," read at the annual meetings of the American Sociological Association, Washington, D.C., 1957.

in the course of our daily lives. The group dynamicist has a very refined set of meanings that he uses to define the concept of role.[8] A *position* is a structural aspect of the group's organization; an *enacted* role is the actual stabilized pattern of behavior displayed by an occupant of a position; a *perceived* role is the stabilized perception of a group member's behavior, as perceived either by himself or by others within the group; a *prescribed* role is a set of expectations as to the behavior that ought to be displayed by a group member according to the norms and goals of the group; and a *predicted* role is a set of probabilistic expectations about the behavior a group member will show in a particular position within the group configuration.

Thus in our inquiry and discussion of group influence and social class we shall come to learn that group norms and roles, as variously defined, have a profound and significant impact upon consumer behavior.

THE CONCEPT OF GROUP. We have talked at great length about groups, yet to this juncture we have not yet formally defined the concept. Perhaps it is time that we do so. Almost every one of us has some intuitive understanding as to what constitutes a group. The real distinguishing characteristic of a group, as opposed to a crowd or any other random collection of people, is continuing interaction. Thus a group is defined as two or more persons in interaction under these basic conditions: (1) the relations among the members are *interdependent;* that is, each member's behavior involves some role relationship with the others; and (2) the members or participants share a common set of norms or standards that regulate their mutual or reciprocal behavior.[9] This definition and description of a group is generally and widely accepted by most authorities. Newcomb, for example, has commented that "the distinctive thing about a group is that its members share norms about something."[10] The sociologist Olmsted has stated that a group is "a plurality of individuals who are in contact with one another, who take one another into account, and who are aware of some significant commonality."[11] Sharing norms and interlocking roles thus presupposes more than transitory relationships of interaction and communication. In normal usage what we ordinarily call groups might best be called functional groups. Such a designation implies that the members are mutually involved in on-going social interaction aimed at achieving some common goal. There are other kinds of groups that might best be called groupings. Such collections or groupings are of

[8] See John W. McDavid and Herbert Harari, *Social Psychology: Individuals, Groups, Societies* (New York: Harper and Row, Publishers, 1968), pp. 268–269.

[9] Doby, op. cit., p. 248.

[10] T. M. Newcomb, "Social Psychological Theory: Integrating Individual and Social Approaches," in *Social Psychology at the Crossroads,* J. Rohrer and M. Sherif, eds. (New York: Harper and Row, Publishers, 1951), pp. 31–49.

[11] Olmsted, op. cit., p. 21.

two types: categories and aggregates. A category is made up of people who possess a common characteristic that can be used to describe them. Consumers constitute a category. An aggregate is a special category composed of individuals who share a time-space relationship but do not have a common goal, unless circumstances should create one.[12] For example, an aggregate of consumers riding a given subway to downtown Boston is not a group in the functional sense. Finally, it should be added that social classes are kinds of quasi groups because, without being groups in the strict literal sense, social classes are recruiting fields for groups and their members do have certain characteristic modes of behavior in common, including both norms and roles.

KINDS OF GROUPS. The distinction between functional groups, categories, and aggregates is only the first step toward the ordering and classification of human collectives. For our major purpose—that is, the analysis of groups in terms of their impact upon consumer behavior—we are primarily interested in functional groups. As explained earlier, functional groups are those whose members are mutually involved in on-going social interaction aimed at achieving a common goal. Functional groups, however, are of two major kinds: primary and secondary.

Primary functional groups are those characterized by intimate face-to-face association and cooperation. Though they are primary in several senses, the most basic is that they are fundamental in forming the social character, behavioral expectations, and values of the individual and that they give him his earliest and fullest experience of social unity. One authority on primary groups has stated that they are "the result of intimate association psychologically"; and the result of this association "is a certain fusion of individualities in a common whole, so that one's very self, for many purposes at least, is the common life and purpose of the group."[13] The individual in the primary group thus feels a strong allegiance to common standards of service and behavior.

Primary groups are important determinants of consumer behavior. The most important spheres of this intimate face-to-face interaction and association are the family, the play groups of children, and the neighborhood or community groups of adults. Within the interaction dynamics of these group configurations a large part of our sentiments and behavior is acquired via socialization. The primary groups to which we belong supply many of our economic, social, and psychological needs.

Secondary groups, on the other hand, are by contrast more impersonal, larger, and characterized by contractual relations among their members. Secondary groups are characterized more by the fact that

[12] Edwin P. Hollander, *Principles and Methods of Social Psychology* (London: Oxford University Press, 1967), pp. 345.

[13] Charles Horton Cooley, *Social Organization* (New York: Charles Scribner's Sons, 1929), pp. 23–24.

membership is viewed to be desirable in terms of the utilitarian value performed by the association. Identification with secondary groups is not an end in itself but rather a means by which other ends may be achieved. Most work groups are secondary groups. So too are such groups as formal organizations, lodges, fraternities, churches, and professional affiliations. And although membership in such groups also carries with it behavioral expectations in the form of shared norms and roles, the psychological impact of membership in such secondary groups is not usually considered either as pervasive or as profound as that of primary group membership.

Finally, we should mention at this juncture another very important group concept called *reference group*. Group membership, whether it be primary or secondary, is important as a determinant of individual behavior only to the extent that the particular individual is, psychologically speaking, wired in and committed to the values, goals, norms, and roles of the group. The fact that different consumers have varying psychological affiliations to groups would mean, in turn, that there are differences in the degree to which the individual is affected by the group's norms and goals. The average consumer, for example, belongs to many different groups, both primary and secondary, but not all these groups hold the same importance and meaning for the individual. Thus the individual consumer may have one or several reference groups that are the most frequently used as bench marks for evaluating his judgments, as sources for information, or as general referents. Hence, a reference group is a group conceived of as having some relevance for the individual's opinions, evaluations, aspirations, and so forth.[14] Reference groups are the actual or imagined sets of people one uses as a model, usually those whose approval one wants. A reference group may be the people one lives and interacts with closely (for example, family or friends) or one's professional or political associates, the circle one aspires to, and so on. Consumers might normally be expected to have different reference groups for different needs. In the broadest sense, a reference group can even be an individual. Thus the impact of opinion leaders and key influentials is an extension of the reference group concept. The important characteristic of reference groups is that the concept ties together the psychological and behavioral impact of any group to which an individual refers when considering his own attitudes and behavior. We shall treat reference groups more extensively in a later section of this chapter.

Structural and Functional Properties of Groups

Having now laid a basic groundwork by establishing the role of groups in the socialization process of individuals and by treating some of the problems relating to the taxonomy of groups, let us proceed to examine the structural and functional properties of group configura-

---

[14] See Herbert Hyman, "Reflections on Reference Groups," *Public Opinion Quarterly,* Vol. 24 (Fall 1960), pp. 383–396.

tions. We shall look first at some structural characteristics of groups and then proceed to examine in fuller detail some of the functional consequences of group membership and interaction.

GROUP STRUCTURE

In all groups the roles and status of the members become to some extent different and unique but integrated into a system that is called group structure. The group structure, in turn, affects the behavior and functioning of the group and the satisfactions that the individuals derive from the group association. Thus, whatever it is that motivates people to come together to achieve perceived goals, these people take on organizational properties that create certain relationships among them. In more specific terms, group structure suggests that the members divide certain functions, establish communication links, become more sensitive to the expectations and aspirations of each other, and take on a sense of group identity. This further suggests that group members acquire a psychological relevance to one another that influences and conditions the interactions that occur among them.

GROUP STRUCTURE AND COMMUNICATION. The previous point can be aptly demonstrated. For example, group structure affects interaction to the extent that communication is either impeded or facilitated.

Studies of small-group behavior have given us considerable insight into the nature of the communication process. Festinger and Thibaut have investigated the effects of interpersonal communication on attitudes and opinions. They discovered that belonging to a given group tends to induce changes in opinions and attitudes to produce conformity. They reasoned on the basis of their investigation that the amount of shift toward uniformity that may be accomplished is a function of the attractiveness of the group in question for its members.[15]

Leavitt has demonstrated that the structure or form of the interactional connections of a group influences the communication of the participating individuals in a diverse manner. He structured four experimental patterns: circle, chain, Y, and wheel. These patterns are shown in Figure 14-1.

Leavitt tested twenty groups of five men each in these four patterns of communication. The experimental task involved passing messages back and forth with the objective of solving a problem that no one man could solve alone. His principal discoveries centered around the following proposition: Major behavior differences can be attributed to communication patterns, and these affect deviations in accuracy, the satisfaction of the group members with their work, and differences in organization.[16]

[15] Leon Festinger and John Thibaut, "Inter-personal Communication in Small Groups," *Journal of Abnormal Psychology,* Vol. 46 (1951), pp. 92–99.
[16] Harold J. Leavitt, "Some Effects of Certain Communication Patterns on Group Performance," *Journal of Abnormal and Social Psychology,* Vol. 46 (1951), pp. 38–50.

Figure 14-1

Experimental Patterns of Communication

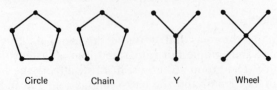

Circle	Chain	Y	Wheel

Source: Harold J. Leavitt, "Some Effects of Certain Communication Patterns on Group Performance," *Journal of Abnormal and Social Psychology,* Vol. 46 (1951), p. 42.

For example, in the circle pattern, where there was no leader, there was little adequate organization. In the wheel group, on the other hand, there very quickly developed an organization and an effective leader soon emerged. Furthermore, the positions occupied by the individuals in the communication chain influenced their positions during the time they occupied the positions. One of the most characteristic aspects of this study was that of *centrality;* that is, those at the center of the structure were affected more thoroughly than those at the periphery of the communication chains. Apparently, when a member's position is low in centrality relative to other persons in the communication network, the removed member will tend to take a follower position and be dependent upon the leader. This may partially explain the leadership-followership phenomenon.

Another significant factor relating group behavior to communication is that of group norms. Inasmuch as communication involves sharing meaning, communication is virtually impossible without some mutual understanding of group norms.

> People can interact without any common body of norms, but they cannot communicate in the sense of sharing meaning through this interaction. . . . Communication, in this sense (i.e., the sharing of common experiences) presupposes frames of reference (norms) which are shared by the communicating persons, so that similar meanings are shared by them.[17]

Effective communication is thus closely linked to both the structure and the function of group associations.

OTHER ASPECTS OF GROUP STRUCTURE. The structure and organization, and thus functioning, of a group association are also affected by other considerations. For example, communication and interaction are affected by *group size.* As groups grow in size they grow arithmetically, but the network of interaction and communication among the members grows geometrically. Thus, the larger the group, the more

[17] Theodore M. Newcomb, *Social Psychology* (New York: Holt, Rinehart & Winston, Inc., 1950), pp. 267–268.

complex the interaction and communication task becomes. Group cohesiveness is also a structural factor that affects group functioning and behavior. *Cohesiveness* is a term that is used to describe a group property in the nature of solidarity and unity and has been defined as the "total field of forces which act on members to remain in the group."[18] Cohesiveness is thus related to commitment. More cohesive groups are those to which the members have a strong sense of commitment and identification. Consequently, cohesive groups are alleged to be better coordinated and to have a greater sense of the "we" feeling than noncohesive groups. Cohesiveness is at least in part a function of the attractiveness of the group. Furthermore, attractiveness is said to arise primarily from the satisfactions a group provides, achieving what it is in the member's interest to have it achieve.[19]

Finally, we might summarize our treatment of the structural properties of groups and the impact of these properties on group performance and behavior by examining a listing by Hemphill. He has designated fifteen structural properties affecting group performance and individual behavior. They are

1. *Size* of the group.
2. *Viscidity* or the degree to which the group functions as a unit.
3. *Homogeneity* of group members with respect to socially relevant characteristics such as age, sex, background.
4. *Flexibility* of a group's activities in terms of informal procedures rather than adherence to established procedures.
5. *Stability* of a group with respect to frequency of major changes over time.
6. *Permeability* of a group regarding ready access to membership.
7. *Polarization* of a group in terms of its orientation and functioning toward a single goal.
8. *Autonomy* of a group with respect to its functioning independently of other groups.
9. *Intimacy* of group members in regard to mutual acquaintance, a familiarity with details of one another's lives.
10. *Control* or the degree to which a group regulates the behavior of individuals, while they are functioning as group members.
11. *Participation* of group members in applying time and effort to the group's activities.
12. *Potency* or importance of the group for its members.
13. *Hedonic tone* in terms of the degree to which group membership is accompanied by a general feeling of pleasantness or unpleasantness.
14. *Position* of group members with respect to an ordering of status in a hierarchy.
15. *Dependence* of group members upon the group.[20]

[18] D. C. Cartwright and A. Zander, eds., *Group Dynamics: Research and Theory*, 2nd ed. (Evanston, Ill.: Row, Peterson and Company, 1960).

[19] Ibid.

[20] J. K. Hemphill, "The Measurement of Group Dimension," *Journal of Psychology*, Vol. 29 (1950), pp. 325–342; and J. K. Hemphill, *Group Dimen-*

GROUP FUNCTIONS

The basic function of groups is to satisfy the needs and aspirations of the constituent members.[21] Through membership in various groups the individual strives for need fulfillment. The group may protect the individual from threats as basic as extinction, or it may be the ladder for achievement of certain social goals that necessitate cooperative effort. The group, therefore, becomes a means to the ends of its members. And as the group comes into being and its members interact, there is an emergent group ideology that regulates their attitudes and behavior. It is a well-known fact that a person will work for the group and its goals only if he believes that its achievement will satisfy his own wants.[22]

As long ago as 1920, F. H. Allport had begun to examine the impact of the group on individual behavior. One of his earliest generalizations was that the group was a means of energizing individuals and that the individual used the group as a means of attaining personal and social goals. He called this function of groups *social facilitation.*[23]

The group functions in terms of two important aspects for the individual. First of all, it designates or denotes his *status*, and second, it assigns or delegates his *role*. Members of a group generally exercise two important kinds of behavior with respect to both role and status. Behavior that is directed toward fulfilling the dictates of a given role is called operative behavior; behavior directed toward perceiving or enhancing one's status or position in the power structure is called positional behavior. For example, the role of a housewife in a family group may well be that of the designated purchasing agent of that group. Her purchasing behavior in carrying out this role is, therefore, operative behavior. On the other hand, in order to enhance her position in the status hierarchy of the family, the housewife may go to extra lengths to perform her role responsibilities as household purchasing agent. This amounts to positional behavior. Early in the history of instant coffee it was discovered that many housewives would not purchase this item because of a fear of being thought lazy and not having the best interests of their family at heart—a form of positional behavior related to perceived role and status.

In the broadest sense, groups, then, function fundamentally to

sions: A Manual For Their Measurement (Columbus, Ohio: Ohio State University, Ohio Studies in Personnel, Monogram #87, Bureau of Business Research, 1956).

[21] K. D. Benne and P. Sheats, "Functional Roles of Group Members," *Journal of Social Issues,* Vol. 4 (April 1948), pp. 41–49.

[22] S. E. Asch, "Effects of Group Pressure on the Modification and Distortion of Judgments," in *Readings in Social Psychology,* E. E. Maccoby, T. M. Newcomb, and E. L. Hartley, eds. (New York: Holt, Rinehart & Winston, Inc., 1958).

[23] F. H. Allport, *Journal of Experimental Psychology,* Vol. 3 (1920), pp. 159–182.

help individuals attain goals that would be unattainable otherwise. More specifically the major functions of groups are as follows:

1. They serve to establish a sense of personal worth and social identity. We take a measure of ourselves and our overall worth in terms of the feedback supplied by our group associations. If we are valued and esteemed by others, it follows usually that we value and esteem ourselves.

2. Groups tend to strengthen and reinforce the self-concept. The self-concept is in many ways our personality. It is a constellation of attitudes and beliefs that we conceptualize regarding our "selfs." Groups tend to shape and determine our concepts of self.[24] To the extent that our judgments are validated by the group and our actions and sentiments emulated, our concept of self in turn is strengthened and reinforced.

3. Groups serve to facilitate the need for social interaction, approval, and reinforcement. And they provide a medium for communication. We have emphasized so often that consumers are not isolated. They are instead, to varying degrees, gregarious social creatures who seek and appear to need the interaction and communion of their fellowman. Groups are used, therefore, as a source and a means of *reality testing*.

THE PSCYHOLOGICAL EFFECTS OF GROUPS. Although groups function to affect the economic, social, and psychological behavior of individuals, it is the psychological functions that are important in terms of consumer behavior. Thus, the very concept of groupness has important psychological consequences for consumers and, of course, marketers. For example, our cognitive theory of consumer behavior states in a rudimentary sense that consumer behavior is a function of cognitions. Cognitions, we have learned, are bits of knowledge or, more broadly conceived, knowledge, attitudes, beliefs, images, and so forth. An important function of group membership and interaction, therefore, is that such membership is an important vehicle for affecting the psychological mechanisms of its members. Most importantly, cognitions and cognitive activities are influenced and affected by group membership. For example, group membership and interaction affect the following:

1. *The individual's motivation.* Consumer motivations and aspirations are to some extent affected by the motivations and aspirations of the groups to which the consumer belongs or the reference groups with which he identifies. Motivations, you will recall, pertain to the reasons that impel us to engage in certain actions or activities. Thus to understand motivation we must appreciate the impact of the group in forming our motives and predispositions. This impact, of course, is related to the

[24] Erving Goffman, *The Presentation of Self in Everyday Life* (New York: Doubleday & Company, Inc., 1959).

role of socialization and social learning and stems in part from one's tendency to imitate and emulate the behavior of significant others. *Significant others* are those who really matter in shaping one's basic motivations and behavior patterns.[25]

2. *Individuals' attitudes and behavior.* All groups constitute a social system that has the capacity to affect or influence members' *activities, interactions,* and *sentiments.* Activities refer to movements that people do to or with nonhuman objects. Interaction refers to things people do together. And sentiments essentially refer to feelings and attitudes about things or events. It follows that:

Interaction between persons leads to sentiments of liking, which express themselves in new activities, and these in turn mean further interaction. . . . The more frequently persons interact with one another, the stronger their sentiments of friendship for one another are apt to be. . . . The more frequently persons interact with one another, the more alike in some respects both their activities and sentiments tend to become.[26]

In more concise language the implication is that interaction leads to liking and common sentiments or attitudes. Common attitudes thus lead to common or shared behavior.

3. *The individual's perception.* Group membership and interaction also affect the individual's perception. Perception relates to the ways in which stimuli are organized and interpreted. It is how we give and impart meaning to what surrounds us and pertains to the information that we extract from our environment and how and to what ends we use this information. We have already shown how the structuring and functioning of the group affect communication. Group functioning and interaction affect a whole range of perceptional or perception-related activities. To a great extent, group membership affects our perceptual sets and works in the interest of selective perception. Our group memberships and interactions can lead to (1) distortion of perception, (2) distortion of judgment, and (3) distortion of action and behavior.[27]

Thus, we can learn something about consumer behavior and consumer decision processes by understanding *group dynamics,* that is, the processes and their consequences occurring within groups. With this in mind, it is clear that a reciprocal sequence of mutually interdependent activities is involved. By joining groups, individuals often

[25] See Ralph H. Turner, "Role-Taking, Role Standpoint, and Reference Group Behavior," *American Journal of Sociology,* Vol. 61 (January 1956), p. 328.

[26] George C. Homans, *The Human Group* (New York: Harcourt Brace Jovanovich, Inc., 1950), pp. 119–120, 133.

[27] Asch, op. cit., pp. 6–7.

are attracted by the group's activity, then play a role in it that rewards them with others' approval. It is in this sense that motivations, attitudes, and perceptions become intertwined over time.[28]

The Concept of Reference Groups and Marketing

A general knowledge of groups and group theory can and does help one to understand more fully the impact of group membership and interaction on consumer behavior and consumer decision processes. However, there are many kinds of groups: they vary in size and complexity, and they have varying degrees of psychological impact upon the behavior of the consumer. For these reasons, we turn our attention now to a kind of group that we have briefly mentioned but have not explored, the *reference group*.

In the 1930s, in connection with a study of the social origins of attitude development and attitude change, Newcomb formulated a distinction between *membership groups* and *reference groups*.[29] A membership group is one to which an individual belongs formally, either in name or in body; that is, one may become a nominal member of a group simply by listing his name among the membership or just by being physically present among other members of the group. Such nominal association, however, does not necessarily imply any intense or genuine psychological participation in the group as an organized system. In contrast to this condition, Newcomb proposed that the term *reference group* be used to describe groups in which an individual is genuinely a *psychological participant* so that he is committed to the group's purpose, occupies a particular role within its structure, and adheres to its regulative norms. Reference groups are thus those that have the power and capacity to influence an individual's behavior. A reference group may be a group in which the individual does hold membership, or it may be a group to which an individual aspires to belong. But the important and distinctive feature of a reference group is that it is a group or an individual whose perspectives and attitudinal posture are assumed by others. Stated another way, a reference group is a group association with whose ideology, style, and norms an individual identifies; that is, such a group influences the behavior of individuals even though they are not members of that particular group. Reference groups can be extremely important in influencing consumer behavior.

Reference groups affect individuals' sources of information; they affect consumer motivation, perception, attitudes, and purchase behavior. For example, one researcher discovered that:

---

[28] R. S. Wyer, "Effects of Incentive to Perform Well, Group Attraction, and Group Acceptance on Conformity in a Judgmental Task," *Journal of Personnel and Social Psychology,* Vol. 4 (1966), pp. 21–26.

[29] Theodore M. Newcomb, *Personality and Social Change* (New York: Holt, Rinehart & Winston, Inc., 1943).

The sources of information most frequently consulted by durable goods buyers were friends and relatives . . . more than 50 percent of buyers turned for advice to acquaintances and in most instances also looked at durable goods owned by them. Even more striking is the finding that a third of durable goods buyers bought a brand or model that they had seen at someone else's home, often the house of relatives.[30]

HOW REFERENCE GROUPS AFFECT BEHAVIOR

We know that reference groups are thus groups that possess special kinds of psychological attributes and significance for the individual. First, they are groups that afford comparison points in making self-appraisals and self-judgments. Second, they are groups whose frame of reference is adopted for conduct. Third, reference groups are those to which the individual aspires.[31] In short, reference groups are those against which an individual evaluates his own attitudes, status, and behavior.

Bourne has argued that reference groups influence individual behavior in two ways.[32] First, he states that reference groups influence one's *aspiration* levels. Groups against which an individual evaluates his own attitudes, status, and behavior are thus capable of causing one to be less than satisfied with his own attainments, possessions, attitudes, or expressive movements. Such a reaction may tend to affect the individual's motivation to attain more, to reevaluate his attitudes, and to alter behavior in the direction of the reference group level. Second, reference groups influence *kinds* of behavior. Bourne suggests that reference groups establish approved patterns of using one's wealth, of displaying one's symbols such as designing and furnishing the home, of choosing and wearing apparel, or of other practices relating to the development of characteristic patterns of living.

Reference groups influence behavior because, from the standpoint of the individual, they are perceived as having power. This power implies that reference groups can and do establish taboos and apply sanctions. To this end reference groups potentially can produce conformity and contentment. In the exchange sense, reference groups may dispense both psychological rewards and psychological punishments.

THE BASIS OF REFERENCE-GROUP POWER. Reference groups are capable of influencing consumer behavior to the extent that they are perceived to have power. Reference groups influence aspiration levels through this power, as well as the kinds of instrumental and symbolic

[30] Eva Mueller, "The Sample Survey," in *Consumer Behavior,* Vol. 1, *The Dynamics of Consumer Reaction,* Lincoln H. Clark, ed. (New York: New York University Press, 1954), p. 45.

[31] Elizabeth Bott, "The Concept of Class as a Reference Group," *Human Relations,* Vol. 7, No. 3 (1954), p. 265.

[32] Francis S. Bourne, "Group Influence in Marketing and Public Relations," in *Some Applications of Behavioural Research,* Rensis Likert and Samuel P. Hayes, Jr., eds. (Paris: UNESCO, 1957), pp. 208–224.

behavior engaged in. Let us briefly mention four types of power as delineated by French and Raven and acknowledge some of the effects of each.

1. *Reward Power.* Reward power is based upon one person's perception of other's ability to mediate or influence rewards for him.
2. *Coercive Power.* To the extent that reference groups can reward, they can also coerce. Reference groups have the capacity to force compliance with their norms and standards. The strength of these power sources and hence their degree of influence depends upon (a) the magnitude of the rewards or punishments involved and (b) the perceived likelihood of their occurrence should one elect a given course of action.
3. *Referent Power.* It would go without saying that reference groups have referent power. Referent power suggests that one comes to like so well the "others" who significantly reward him that he psychologically identifies with the rewarder.
4. *Expert Power.* Expert power is derived from "others" holding scarce or valuable knowledge that is highly prized. The opinion leader or key influential in fashion or the use of new products or services may possess power to influence those in need of such knowledge.[33]

Again referring back to the Thibaut-Kelley and Homans transaction and exchange theories of behavior, we can readily see that these forms of power may be translated into notions of rewards and costs.

REFERENCE GROUPS AND ATTITUDE CHANGES. One of the early contentions of social psychology has been that attitude and behavior change are largely a function of communication in group-oriented situations. In a now classic study, Lewin demonstrated that consumers were much more apt to modify their attitudes and behavior regarding nontypical meat dishes (heart, kidney, tongue, and so on) via group discussions about these items, their preparation, and nutritional value, than they were when such information was presented to them in the form of a lecture presentation.[34]

Lewin, as a matter of fact, was quite emphatic in pointing up the process by which the group brings the individual to a more ready acceptance of new conditions and requirements via attitude change. An extension of Lewin's ideas about the impact of groups upon individuals in rendering change and thus perceiving new alternatives more favorably can be found in Cartwright's principles drawn from group dynamics. Such generalizations sum up a number of points growing out of the group dynamics framework. Namely:

[33] J. R. B. French, Jr., and B. H. Raven, "The Bases of Social Power," in *Studies in Social Power,* Dorwin Cartwright, ed. (Ann Arbor, Mich.: University of Michigan Press, 1959), pp 118–149.

[34] Kurt Lewin, "Group Decision and Social Change," in *Readings in Social Psychology,* 3rd ed., Eleanor E. Maccoby, Theodore M. Newcomb, and Eugene L. Hartley, eds. (New York: Holt, Rinehart & Winston, Inc., 1958), pp. 197–211.

The more attractive the group to its members, the greater is the influence that the group can exert on its members.

In attempts to change attitudes, values, or behavior, the more relevant they are to the basis of attraction to the group, the greater will be the influence that the group can exert upon them.

Efforts to change individuals or some parts of the groups which, if successful, would have the result of making them deviate from the norms of the group will encounter strong resistance.[35]

Such generalizations tend to stress the impact of the reference group concepts in terms of the "we" feeling associated with such psychological interaction and identification.

REFERENCE GROUPS AND CONFORMITY. Another long-held contention of social psychology is that identification and interaction with reference groups tend to generate conformity by the members to the overall group norms. This proposition was tested in the early 1950s. The experimental task was ostensibly labeled as an experiment in visual perception. Seven- to nine-man groups of male college students were asked to state publicly one after another which of three lines on various cards matched a standard line on another card. Except for one "naïve" or critical subject, all other members in a given group were preinstructed confederate subjects. The confederate subjects were instructed to be unanimous in their pronouncement of an inaccurate judgment, which they delivered in an impersonal and detached manner. When the judgments of the confederate subjects were unanimously incorrect, about 37 percent of the 123 naïve subjects erred by compromising or yielding to the group's incorrect judgment.[36]

In something of a parallel study, Venkatesan attempted to test two major hypotheses:

1. In a consumer decision-making situation where no objective standards are present, individuals who are exposed to a group norm will tend to conform to that group norm.
2. In a consumer decision-making situation where no objective standards are present, individuals who are exposed to a group norm, and are induced to comply, will show less tendency to conform to the group judgment.[37]

The findings of Venkatesan's study were that both hypotheses were accepted. Such findings tend to underscore the notion that consumers do accept information provided by their peer or reference groups. Even

[35] Dorwin Cartwright, "Achieving Change in People: Some Applications of Group Dynamics Theory," *Human Relations*, Vol. 4 (1951), pp. 381–393.

[36] Solomon E. Asch, "Studies of Independence and Submission to Group Pressure; I. A Minority of One Against a Unanimous Majority," *Psychological Monograph*, Vol. 70, No. 9 (1956).

[37] M. Venkatesan, "Experimental Study of Consumer Behavior, Conformity and Independence," *Journal of Marketing Research*, Vol. 3 (Chicago: American Marketing Association, November 1966), pp. 384–387.

more significantly, the reference or peer group's norms direct the attention of its members to new styles or a new product. However, Venkatesan's study also tends to support the notion that attempts to force compliance in behavior in a buying situation can be perceived as restricting the buyer's choices and consequently his freedom and independence. Such efforts are likely to lead to a form of behavior and rejection known as *reactance*.[38] Reactance is a motivational state that impels the individual to resist further reductions in his set of free behaviors. Reactance is thus a kind of boomerang reaction to too obvious pressures to bring about conformity or compliance in behavior.

Others in marketing research studies have demonstrated, to varying degrees, the impact of reference-group influence on aspects of consumer behavior and attitudes. For example, Stafford concluded that:

1. Informal groups had a definite influence on their members toward conformity behavior with respect to brands preferred.
2. In more cohesive reference groups, the probability is much higher that the members will prefer the same brand as the group leader, and therefore the value of cohesiveness is that it provides an agreeable environment in which informal leaders can effectively operate.
3. Leaders influence group members two ways. First, the higher the degree of brand loyalty exhibited by a group leader, the more likely are the other members to prefer the same brand. Second, the greater the degree of leader brand loyalty, the higher the percentage of the group also becoming brand loyal.[39]

REFERENCE GROUPS AND MARKETING: A SUMMARY OF FINDINGS. The formation, structuring, and functioning of groups have many important implications for marketing. Consumer purchase behavior may be a highly individualistic process; on the other hand, there is much to indicate that it is a socially oriented process on which group norms, reference groups, roles, and status have an important bearing.

The groups that one belongs to or that affect one's decision making—that is, reference groups—affect consumer decision processes in at least two important ways.[40] First of all, reference groups affect the aspiration levels of individuals. They may influence members, or individuals who simply relate to the reference groups, to provide aspiration guides for certain kinds of goods. Second, reference groups are influential in initiating kinds of reactions or behavior in individuals related to taboos, sanctions, and so forth. In short, the norms of the reference group may become guidelines that constrain an individual's

[38] J. W. Brehm, "A Theory of Psychological Reactance," unpublished paper (Durham, N.C.: Duke University, 1965).

[39] James E. Stafford, "Effects of Group Influence on Consumer Behavior," *Journal of Marketing Research*, Vol. 3 (Chicago: American Marketing Association, February 1966), pp. 68–75.

[40] Bourne, "Group Influences in Marketing and Public Relations," op. cit., pp. 217–224.

market behavior. Marketers simply cannot afford to overlook the importance of the influence exerted on the individual by the groups with which he is associated. The possibility for group influence on consumer decision processes is illustrated graphically in Figure 14-2.

According to the classification of Figure 14-2, the purchase of a particular item is likely to be susceptible to reference-group influence in three different ways. Reference group influence may operate with respect to brand or type but not with respect to product (brand +, product −), as for example in the upper left cell; or it may operate both with respect to brand and product (brand +, product +), as for example in the upper right cell; and so forth.

It would appear that the preceding kind of reference-group analysis would have strong implications for marketing and especially for marketing communication. At least two of the more important implications have been suggested by Bourne.

Figure 14-2

Product and Brands of Consumer Goods May Be Classified by Extent to Which Reference Groups Influence Their Purchase

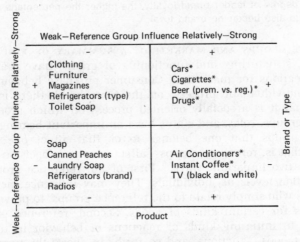

* The classification of all products marked with an asterisk is based on actual experimental evidence. Other products in this table are classified speculatively on the basis of generalizations derived from the sum of research in this area and confirmed by the judgment of seminar participants.

Source: Francis S. Bourne, "Group Influences in Marketing and Public Relations," in *Some Applications of Behavioral Research,* Rensis Likert and Samuel P. Hayes, Jr., eds. (Paris, France: UNESCO, 1961). Reprinted by permission of Charles Y. Glock, Director, Survey Research Center, University of California.

1. Where neither product nor brand appear to be associated strongly with reference group influence, advertising should emphasize the product's attributes, intrinsic qualities, price, and advantages over competing products.
2. Where reference group influence is operative, the advertiser should stress the kinds of people who buy the product, reinforcing and broadening where possible the existing stereotype of users. The strategy of the advertiser should involve learning what the stereotypes are and what specific reference groups enter into the picture, so that appeals can be tailored to each main group reached by the different media employed.[41]

In summary, the basic decisions marketers must make in connection with reference-group theory center around the following ideas:

1. *Reference-group relevance.* The marketer must decide if reference-group concepts are applicable to a given situation.
2. *Reference-group identification.* The marketer must identify the particular relevant reference group and its members.
3. *Reference-group identification and effective communication.* Having identified the nature and relevant characteristics of the reference group in a given situation, the marketer must then develop a program of effective communication with the groups or individuals he desires to influence.

Other studies have suggested that group formation and behavior can affect the process of innovation and especially the diffusion process for new products.[42] The relationship between gatekeeper and opinion leader can be an important determinant of certain kinds of consumer purchase decisions. For example, in the American household the male head is usually given the role of deciding what brand of coffee should be purchased even though the wife is the official family purchasing agent. The small children of the household, on the other hand, are the key decision-makers or opinion leaders regarding choices of cereals or other breakfast foods. Consequently, innovations or new product offerings in coffee or breakfast foods must meet with the approval of these opinion leaders or gatekeepers before their success can be assured.

Other studies have suggested that social class can be an important factor in the adoption and rate of adoption of certain innovations.[43] Research in this important area has revealed that the amount of contact between the innovation and the potential acceptors is extremely

[41] Ibid., p. 222. Reprinted by permission of Charles Y. Glock, Director, Survey Research Center, University of California.

[42] Thomas S. Robertson, "The Process of Innovation and the Diffusion of Innovation," *Journal of Marketing,* Vol. 31 (January 1967), pp. 14–19. See also Everett M. Rogers, *Diffusion of Innovations* (New York: The Free Press, 1962).

[43] Saxon Graham, "Class and Conservatism in the Adoption of Innovations," *Human Relations,* Vol. 9, No. 1 (1956), pp. 91–100.

critical in determining the degree of acceptance. It has been found that as each innovation is unique, each is compatible in different degrees with the culture (behavior) of a given group. No single class or group has been found to be conservative in reacting to innovations. Instead, the upper classes are found to be conservative in some cases, the lower class in others, and sometimes both are conservative.

The Concept of Social Class

The concept of *social class,* which is a special kind of group affiliation, has received considerable attention from researchers who seek clearer implications of the concept in terms of specific marketing problems. For many who harbor deep personal feelings of egalitarianism, the idea that a class system exists is psychologically most unpalatable. However, even though we like to attempt to deny the existence of a class society in America, it has been recognized widely that a class hierarchy is a characteristic of any society, be it the People's Republic of China, England, the university, the community, the business organization, or if you are a student living on campus, your living group.

Warner, in his early studies of social class in the United States, observed that:

> those who interact in the social system of a community evaluate the participation of those around them . . . and members of the community are explicitly or implicitly aware of the ranking and translate their evaluation of such social participation into social class rating.[44]

Although social class "typing" is an admitted part of social behavior and part of the invidious comparison process, we have to define what a social class is. There are various definitions. Social classes in an elementary sense are status categories within larger social groupings. One researcher, taking a psychological point of view, contended that social classes are psychosocial groupings of the population of persons whose socioeconomic positions are objectively similar, in the main, and whose politicoeconomic interests tend to coincide.[45]

For marketing purposes such an approach to defining and delineating social classes would appear to have considerable merit.

DETERMINING SOCIAL CLASSES

Several approaches have been used for the purpose of determining social classes. Warner, whose work in social class theories has approached classic proportions, determines one's class standing by using what he labeled an index of status characteristics (ISC). This index

[44] W. L. Warner and P. S. Lunt, *The Social Life of a Modern Community,* Vol. 1, Yankee City Series (New Haven, Conn.: Yale University Press, 1941).

[45] R. Centros, "The American Class Structure: A Psychological Analysis," in *Readings in Social Psychology,* rev. ed., C. E. Swanson, et al., eds. (New York: Holt, Rinehart & Winston, Inc., 1952), 299–311.

consists of four determinants: (1) occupation, (2) source of income, (3) residential area, and (4) type of dwelling. Of course, other criteria have been used to identify social classes. Several such criteria are power, authority, ownership of property, income, consumption patterns and life style, occupation, public service, religious status and affiliation, ethnic status, role, and, of course, education.[46] Usually, however, social stratification is based upon some sort of index comprised of such variables as the occupation of the head of the household, education, and the place of residence. Occupation is often given more weight than other attributes. An index, however, is merely a measure of another variable—from occupation, for example, one infers social standing. One currently popular method of social stratification employs weighted factors of education, property values, and occupation. A respondent who is not a property owner is classified according to the amount of rent paid. These factors are weighted differently, based upon age and property ownership. Thus four equations must be used: one each for property owners under fifty and over fifty and for renters under and over fifty. Such an approach produces a social class score for each family, and these scores can be arrayed into a single distribution. With this distribution it is then possible to establish as many social class groups as desired and to place any given percentage of the total sample within each group.[47]

SOCIAL CLASS IN THE UNITED STATES

On the basis of his studies, Warner concluded that there are six social classes in the United States. These social classes, some characteristics of each class, and the percentage of each class in terms of the total population (based on 1960 data) are shown in Table 14-1.

TABLE 14-1
Warner's Social Class Breakdown

Social class	Membership	Population percentage
upper-upper	aristocracy	0.5
lower-upper	new rich	1.5
upper-middle	professionals and managers	10.0
lower-middle	white-collar workers	33.0
upper-lower	blue-collar workers	40.0
lower-lower	unskilled laborers	15.0

Source: W. L. Warner et al., *Social Class in America* (New York: Harper and Row, Publishers, 1960).

[46] See Bernard Berelson and Gary Steiner, *Human Behavior: An Inventory of Scientific Findings* (New York: Harcourt Brace Jovanovich, Inc., 1964), p. 454.
[47] James M. Carmen, *The Application of Social Class in Market Segmentation* (Berkeley, Calif.: IBER Special Publications, University of California, 1965)

Many communities, however, because of newness, high mobility, and other factors, do not lend themselves well to Warner's classification. Upper-upper-class families are either nonexistent or so few as to be difficult to identify. Therefore, the most frequently employed social class ranking today consists of a fivefold classification rather than Warner's sixfold classification. Table 14-2 shows a fivefold classification scheme adopted by several researchers.

This scheme, as can be seen from the researchers whose work in social class is documented, has become a highly popular method for social stratification, especially in marketing studies.

Upper-class persons consist of the upper levels of intellectual, professional, and managerial personnel. Upper-middle-class persons possess similar characteristics but they have lower incomes or less wealth than their upper-class counterparts, live in generally less desirable neighborhoods, and have occupations with slightly lower status. People in the upper and upper-middle classes generally have discriminating tastes and manifest considerable variety in their overall life styles, consumption habits, and general behavioral characteristics.

The middle-class person is usually upward mobile in terms of both his economic and his psychological characteristics. Such persons are often seen as practical, with a functional and pragmatic point of view. They are usually operatives rather than professionals. However, they tend to have a strong work ethic and believe in the dictum that work

TABLE 14-2
Social Class Distribution Percentages

Level	Definition	McCann*	Warner†	Matthews & Slocum‡	Rich & Jain§
I	upper	3.0%	0.9%	10.5%	4.2%
II	upper-middle	12.0	7.3	20.6	23.6
III	middle	29.5	28.7	27.5	37.2
IV	lower-middle	34.1	43.4	35.3	13.6
V	lower	21.4	19.7	6.1	21.4

Source: James H. Myers, Roger R. Stanton, and Arne F. Haug, "Correlates of Buying Behavior," *Journal of Marketing,* Vol. 35 (October 1971), p. 9.

* C. B. McCann, "Women and Department Store Newspaper Advertising," *Social Research,* Vol. 24 (1957), pp. 45–46.

† L. W. Warner, *Social Class in America* (New York: Harper and Row, Publishers, 1960), pp. 123–126.

‡ H. L. Mathews and J. W. Slocum, Jr., "Social Class and Commercial Bank Credit Card Usage," *Journal of Marketing,* Vol. 33 (January 1969), pp. 71–78.

§ S. U. Rich and S. C. Jain, "Social Class and Life Style as Predictors of Shopping Behavior," *Journal of Marketing Research,* Vol. 5 (February 1968), pp. 41–49.

leads one to the enjoyment of consumption and leisure. They value goods for both their utilitarian and their symbolic significance. Basically they extol the "good life" and appreciate the value of recreation and the necessity for striving to get ahead. They will often defer gratification in the interest of other values such as security or thrift.

The lower class and the lower-middle class would have relatively high average propensities to consume. However, consumption expenditures, especially for those persons whose incomes approach the poverty level, are for basic necessities: food, clothing, and shelter. They dream the middle-class dream, which for them is a good job, which means a good income, a nice home, and a nice car. Lower-class persons tend to stress the necessity for immediate gratification—probably because their basic needs seem so pressing. Lower-middle-class persons usually have blue-collar jobs and relatively low skills. Lower-class persons, if they are employed at all, are domestics, field hands or migrant workers, car washers, janitors—occupations requiring little skill and virtually no education and have little or no status.

RELATIONSHIP BETWEEN SOCIAL CLASS AND GROUP BEHAVIOR

There is a direct and distinct relationship between social class and group behavior. For instance, social class influences the groups we enter or to which we become psychologically committed. This means that class membership may suggest something about the nature of the person's attitudes and his behavioral dispositions. Class points to a hierarchical ordering of roles along the scale of a group's values. Class also conveys the notion of differences among men in the extent to which they possess things valued by the group: wealth, wisdom, and especially goods. Class invariably connotes more or fewer possessions, more or less power or prestige. Thus, class-linked differences in patterns of living—in occupation, aspirations, possessions, prestige, values, self-perceptions, and so on—set the stage for socialization in differing patterns of conduct and conviction.[48] Through class or social stratification, our reference-group patterns are determined. Through such a process, the person becomes *socialized;* that is, he is inculcated with the norms and roles of his groups. Thus interaction and social learning are affected by our *class* as well as our *group* affiliations. As one authority has put it, class is "seldom the exclusive factor in [life's] choices, but it is also seldom absent."[49] Some scholars argue that attitudes, values, and behavioral predispositions are caused by social class differences. Others more cautiously assert simply that such differences in attitudes and behavior are associated with class. In any case, let us look at some of the behavioral matters in which the social classes in contemporary America differ.

[48] Everett K. Wilson, *Sociology: Rules, Roles and Relationships* (Homewood, Ill.: The Dorsey Press, 1966), p. 181, 184.

[49] Edward A. Shils, "Class," in *Encyclopedia Britannica*, Vol. 5 (1960), p. 768.

SOCIAL CLASS AND BEHAVIORAL CONSIDERATIONS

Social class is of concern to us as marketers or consumer behavioralists to the extent that social class is a determinant of consumer behavior; that is, to the extent that there are behavioral differences associated with social class, we should attempt to identify these differences and thus assess their importance in terms of marketing planning and strategy.

Many of the behavioral characteristics of persons belonging to different social classes have been identified and reported in the relevant literature.[50] We shall summarize only briefly here some of those major characteristics.

VALUES. The value and belief systems of persons in different social classes are different. These values and beliefs affect aspirations and motivations and the entire pattern of social and economic striving.

ATTITUDES. Attitudes, which are themselves a kind of value, differ among persons in different social classes. As relatively enduring psychological sentiments of liking and disliking, attitudes are predispositions to behavior.

PERCEPTIONS. The way sensory stimulation is ordered and interpreted varies among persons from different social classes. One's view of the world is altered by class considerations. Priorities in living, working, spending, and consuming are affected by one's perception of the social, economic, and psychological world in which he lives. Furthermore, one's self-perception is affected by membership in a particular social class.

COGNITIVE STYLE. The characteristic manner of expression, the degree to which information is valued, sought, and used, the information sources used, and the network of primary and reference-group affiliations are affected by social class standing.

OTHER DIFFERENCES. Other behavioral differences often associated with social class include such factors as personality, life style, social relations, social interactions, morality, and life chances. The important thing, of course, is that it is normally assumed that all these factors eventually convert themselves into real differences in observable behavior.

[50] See, for example, Berelson and Steiner, *Human Behavior: An Inventory of Scientific Findings,* op. cit., pp. 476–490; Wilson, *Sociology: Rules, Roles and Relationships,* op. cit., pp. 200–206; and Sidney J. Levy, "Social Class and Consumer Behavior," in *On Knowing the Consumer,* Joseph W. Newman, ed. (New York: John Wiley & Sons, Inc., 1966), pp. 146–160.

IMPACT OF SOCIAL CLASS AND CONSUMPTION

Differing living patterns and life styles connected with class are revealed in many ways. The way a person spends his money often indicates both what his heart feels and what his head and cognitive system dictate. A consumer's budget may well disclose conceptions of need and of customary behavior, offering a clue to his style of living, his interpersonal attitudes, and his deep-rooted value orientations. "The budget of an individual or family," says Warner, "is in part a symbol system, or a set of collective representations that expresses the social value of a person's membership in a group life."[51]

Some consumers feel that money must be translated into socially approved behavior and possessions, and they in turn must be translated into intimate participation with and acceptance by members of a superior class. The "right" furniture, car, and clothes, the proper behavior—all are symbols that can ultimately be translated into social and group-sanctioned behavior.[52]

Social class is thus found to have an important bearing on the consumer's entire range of consumption expenditures. For that matter, according to Martineau social class is an important indicator of store choice.[53] People in the higher classes seek out and shop higher-class merchandising establishments. For that matter, each class attempts to match its class, attitude, and value orientation with stores that they perceive to project similar characteristics. Social class is also an important factor in marketing communication. Class determines what is read, listened to, and watched, and thus advertising becomes affected by class considerations. Furthermore, class membership and identification affect such economic and marketing activities as who saves and who spends, as well as behavior related to credit and various forms of credit use. When some indexes of social class go so far as to include the appraisal and ranking of the family's living-room furnishings, then the relationship between consumption and social class is no longer subtle.[54] A study of consumer budgets by social class suggests the necessary preoccupation of the lower class with matters of the body and hedonic products and the concern of the middle class with the furniture of life: house, cars, clothing, and education. The upper-class budget reflects concern for aesthetics: books, magazine subscriptions, country-club membership, travel, and sporting and recreational equipment—

[51] W. Lloyd Warner, ed., *Yankee City,* abridged one-volume edition (New Haven, Conn.: Yale University Press, 1963), p. 93.

[52] H. Laurence Ross, *Perspectives on the Social Order* (New York: McGraw-Hill Book Company, 1968), p. 420.

[53] Pierre Martineau, "Social Classes and Spending Behavior," *Journal of Marketing,* Vol. 23 (October 1958), pp. 121–130.

[54] For a review of measures of class standing, see Joseph A. Kohl, *The American Class Structure* (New York: Holt, Rinehart & Winston, Inc., 1957), pp. 32–47.

the goods interpreted as the necessary cost of a taut and stressful life oriented toward peak achievement.

Thus the evidence indicates that class conditions the groups people enter or aspire to enter and that, beyond this, class is linked with a set of beliefs or subjective psychological states that alter people's plans and expectations.[55] To know the class structure is to know, then, something about the objective probability of differing group memberships, about the subjective states (motivations, perceptions, cognitions) of persons identified with different classes, and about different life styles and the differing transmission of culture to the members of the group.

Social Class as a Determinant of Consumer Behavior

The empirical evidence stemming from research into the relationship between social class and consumer behavior is nebulous if not contradictory. There has long been at least an intuitive agreement that social class offers insight into certain aspects of consumer behavior. Increasingly, however, as empiricism replaces intuition, the connection between social class and consumer behavior becomes more controversial. Many early writers were adamant about the clear superiority of the social class concept over income as a predictor of spending and consumption habits. Martineau was one whose efforts were instrumental in popularizing the social class concept in relation to consumer behavior. He alleged that social class explained a richer variety of consumer behavior than simply income alone.[56] Another marketer recently exclaimed: "Whatever validity income classification ever had was due to a rough and now disappearing correlation with occupational status."[57] In spite of the enthusiasm of these and many other persons, however, there are those who oppose the use of social class as a determinant of consumer behavior. For example, in a controlled study in the Los Angeles area, three researchers recently concluded that with few exceptions social class is basically inferior to income as a correlate of buying behavior for packaged convenience goods.[58] In another study, based upon the attitudes and behavior of Cleveland shoppers, it was concluded that social class as a predictor of consumer behavior has limited usefulness because of recent changes in income, education, leisure time, movement to suburbia, and other factors.[59]

[55] See Herbert M. Hyman, "The Value Systems of Different Classes: A Social Psychological Contribution to the Analysis of Stratification," in *Class, Status and Power: A Reader in Social Stratification*, Reinhard Bendix and Seymour Martin Lipset, eds. (New York: The Free Press, 1958), pp. 426–442.

[56] Martineau, op. cit.

[57] Chester R. Wasson, "Is It Time to Quit Thinking About Income Classes?" *Journal of Marketing*, Vol. 33 (April 1969), p. 54.

[58] James H. Myers, Roger R. Stanton, and Arne F. Haug, "Correlates of Buying Behavior: Social Class vs. Income," *Journal of Marketing*, Vol. 35 (October 1971), pp. 8–15.

[59] Stuart U. Rich and Subhash C. Jain, "Social Class and Life Cycle as Predictors of Shopping Behavior," *Journal of Marketing Research*, Vol. 5

In a series of studies Mathews and Slocum at first contended that social class was a basic determinant of credit card use.[60] Thus, they argued that members of different social classes exhibit different credit card uses. Their basic contention, along with several others, was that the lower classes tend to use their credit cards for installment financing to a greater extent than the upper classes. This factor, they argued, stems largely from the lower classes' inability to cope with deferred gratification or "impulse renunciation."[61]

Middle-class persons presumably feel that they should save money, postpone purchases, and thus renounce a number of gratifications. The study concluded that upper-class persons, therefore, use credit cards as a convenience device or a form of ready money that facilitates record and budget keeping, whereas lower-class persons use credit cards as a means of attaining and using installment credit. However, in a second article based upon some additional data, Mathews and Slocum contended that neither segmentation variable appears to be superior to the other.[62] They further assert that the widely held assumption that social class is a more important determinant of consumer buying than income has to be critically reevaluated. Thus, although writers like Rainwater, Coleman, and Handel have found social class to be a significant factor in determining consumer behavior, others question this concept.[63]

However, Coleman has noted that either income or social class, when used alone, is often misleading and of little predictive value in the analysis of many product markets.[64] He found, for example, that the basic market for compact cars was not simply among low-income families or among lower-middle-class or blue-collar workers. He found, instead, that there was an active market for compacts among certain

---

(Chicago: American Marketing Assn., February 1968), pp. 41–49. For another supporting view regarding this contention, see Kurt Mayer, "Diminishing Class Differentials in the United States," *KYKLOS*, Vol. 12 (1959), Fasc. 4, pp. 615–626.

[60] H. Lee Mathews and John W. Slocum, "Social Class and Commercial Bank Credit Card Usage," *Journal of Marketing*, Vol. 33 (January 1969), pp. 71–78.

[61] See Murray S. Straus, "Deferred Gratification, Social Class, and the Achievement Syndrome," *American Sociological Review*, Vol. 27 (June 1962), pp. 325–335.

[62] John W. Slocum, Jr., and H. Lee Mathews, "Social Class and Income as Indicators of Consumer Credit Behavior," *Journal of Marketing*, Vol. 34 (April 1970), pp. 69–74. The interested reader may wish to follow this controversy further by examining William W. Curtis, "Social Class or Income," *Journal of Marketing*, Vol. 36 (January 1972), pp. 67–68; and H. Lee Mathews and John W. Slocum, "A Rejoinder to 'Social Class or Income?'" *Journal of Marketing*, Vol. 36 (January 1972), pp. 69–70.

[63] Lee Rainwater, Richard Coleman, and Gerald Handel, *Workingman's Wife* (New York: MacFadden-Bartell Corporation, 1962).

[64] Richard P. Coleman, "The Significance of Social Stratification in Selling," in *Marketing: A Maturing Discipline*, Martin L. Bell, ed. (Chicago: American Marketing Association, Winter 1960), pp. 171–184.

segments of each social class. Coleman, therefore, used family income as it related to the average income of the family's social class to divide each of Warner's social classes into overprivileged, underprivileged, and average groups. It was his argument that this concept of family income relative to the social class is of more value in the analysis of certain product markets.

Another researcher has recently suggested that *relative occupational class income* is a meaningful predictor of buyer behavior, especially in the marketing of automobiles.[65] This concept of relative occupational class income means that total family income relative to the family's occupational class is considered. It is an extension of the relative income hypothesis, which holds that the proportion of a consumer's income spent for consumption depends not on the family's absolute income but instead on how the family's income compares to the incomes of other families within the community.

Both the Coleman and the Peters hypotheses, related to the concept of social class, indicate researchers' continuing interest in and fascination with this concept. If social class is not a good predictor of consumer behavior, this deficiency most likely stems from the fact that social class is a complex and difficult variable. It is too often arbitrarily defined, taking into consideration education, income, and neighborhood, as well as occupation, depending upon the whims of the researcher. To improve the predictability of social class as a variable in consumer behavior, we must first of all improve our understanding of the phenomenon of social class and then insist on some rigor and consistency in its use.

This much seems certain. First, there are social classes in U.S. society. Second, there are behavioral differences among the various social classes. Third, these behavioral differences manifest themselves in purchasing behavior and consumption patterns. Fourth and finally, these purchasing and consumption patterns operate as prestige symbols and signs that tend to define class membership. These assertions lend credence to the words of Joseph A. Kahl, who states, "If a large group of families are approximately equal to each other, and clearly differentiated from other families we call them a social class."[66] Clearly, then, social classes must surely be a beginning point in terms of product differentiation and market segmentation for the development and implementation of special marketing programs using differential product, promotional, pricing, and place strategies in accordance with the special needs or demand characteristics of the particular social class.

In the next chapter we shall continue our inquiry into the role of interpersonal variables affecting consumer behavior by examining the

---

[65] William H. Peters, "Relative Occupational Class Income: A Significant Variable in the Marketing of Automobiles," *Journal of Marketing,* Vol. 34 (April 1970), pp. 74–77.

[66] Kohl, *The American Class Structure,* op. cit., p. 22.

interpersonal influence and socialization consequences of the *family*, the concept of *life style*, and the impact of life cycle on purchase and consumption patterns.

Questions for Study, Reflection, and Review

1   Explain the persistence of groups and their significance in terms of a social exchange theory of interaction.

2   Distinguish between the two major kinds of functional groups.

3   Discuss the influence that group structure has upon the communication process.

4   What are the major functions of these groups?

5   Distinguish between a membership group and a reference group.

6   Briefly discuss the types of power possessed by reference groups with respect to an exchange theory of behavior.

7   Describe the role of reference groups in generating conformity among group members.

8   Discuss the concept of social class and some of the factors used in determining various class groups.

9   What is the relationship between social class and group behavior?

10   Discuss the impact of social class upon consumption patterns.

15

Family Influence on Consumer Behavior: Life-Style and Life-Cycle Concepts

Introduction

The impact of the family upon consumer behavior has not been totally assessed. Certainly the idea that the family as an integrated behavioral unit would affect consumption patterns and consumer decision processes is at least intuitively understood. Yet the complex and sophisticated interrelationships that exist in the family structure and influence consumer behavior have not been extensively investigated. Many of the conclusions and generalizations that have been drawn are, in many cases, as much conjecture as fact. So many important questions relating to family influence on consumer behavior remain to be answered. For instance, What are the relationships between social class standing and family decision-making? Who is the family purchasing agent and why? How do the relative role structures within the family unit affect consumer decision processes? What are the relative role structures within the major contemporary nuclear family structure of the United States? What changes are taking place in family structure and function, and how do these changes affect marketing strategy? Will the family remain a viable and important interpersonal social institution? What forces are auguring change in Western family traditions? Should marketers attempt to promote certain products to families, or to individual members within family units? Should marketers, in the light of changing institutional practices—marriage, divorce, cohabitation without benefit of marriage, and so forth—discard the concept of family as a consumption unit and focus more upon the concept of *household*? The list of questions is endless and is dramatic evidence of the role and importance of family-oriented concepts in consumer behavior.

The task of this chapter will be to explore many of the more relevant questions relating to the concept of *family* as a consumption and behavioral unit that affects consumer decision processes.

Our treatment will continue along the line of inquiry established at the outset in Part IV. Our concern, of course, is with the family as an influencer of individual behavior. The family plays an important mediating or editing function in individual behavior. For example, the family unit is the major socializing institution of society. Within the framework of the family organization we, as individuals, experience our major and most significant interaction processes. The degree of social learning—the acquisition of values, tastes, attitudes, and behavioral dispositions—that takes place within the family is unparalleled in relation to other socializing institutions.

The family unit is, for most individuals, the most significant primary group. For others, the family is an important reference group and constitutes an important source of information and the acquisition of behavioral and social norms. The social class of the individual is in large part determined by his family membership. In short, then, the family is a major determinant, an important independent variable in a large part of consumer behavior. At the very least, the family is an important filter through which, via socialization, our early attitudes and values about goods, achievement, acquisition, approval, and consumption are mediated and formed.

In this chapter, we shall examine the many fascinating dimensions of family influence upon consumer behavior. In addition, this chapter appears to be the appropriate juncture at which to look at two important family-related concepts, namely, life style and life cycle as variables in or determinants of consumer behavior.

WHAT ARE FAMILIES?

Before proceeding further with our discussion, we must first define what amount to some conceptual differences regarding families. In the United States and Canada, we are inclined to think of husband, wife, and offspring as the basic family unit. In other parts of the world, the family may be conceived of as all blood relatives or kin who are both living and dead. In still other places the concept of family is likely to take on other cultural, economic, and social meanings. As emphasized in the introductory comments, the major significance of family as a variable affecting behavior is that family is an important source of interaction. Family interaction is interaction between individuals who manifest these kinds of distinct characteristics:

1. They are related by birth, marriage, or adoption.
2. They consider themselves (define themselves) as constituting a family

group, and as being subject to family norm-role definitions of their group, whatever they may be.
3. They engage in interaction sufficient to support this family definition.[1]

Family interaction usually, though certainly not always, occurs among individuals who share a common living facility. Normally three types of interaction are subsumed under the more inclusive family label: (1) husband-wife relationships, (2) parent-child relationships, and (3) sibling relationships. Most of us, especially those who are married, consider that we have at least two "families" and sometimes three. First, there is our own family (husband-wife-siblings). Then there are the husband's family and the wife's family. Just exactly who is included when one uses the label *family* varies from one group to another, and within one group different types of families can be identified. For example, Berelson and Steiner define the following kinds of families:

Nuclear (core) or conjugal family = husband and wife and children if any.

Extended or consanguine family = husband and wife and their children plus one or more other persons related to these by biological descent.

Family of Orientation = family into which the individual is born.

Family of Procreation = family established by marriage ceremony.[2]

In the United States, with a population slightly in excess of 200,000,000, there are almost 49,000,000 families. The U.S. Department of Commerce defines a number of basic marketing and living units as follows:

A *household* (58,845,000)—A household consists of all the persons who occupy a living unit.

A *family* (48,921,000)—A family consists of two or more persons living in the same household who are related to each other by blood, marriage, or adoption; all persons living in one household who are related to each other are regarded as one family.

A *subfamily* (1,283,000)—A subfamily is a married couple with or without children, or one parent with one or more children under 18 years living in a housing unit and related to the head of the household or his wife.[3]

You will observe that *families* are defined by the Bureau of the Census as two or more persons who are related by blood, marriage, or

---

[1] Glen M. Vernon, *Human Interaction: An Introduction to Sociology* (New York: The Ronald Press Company, 1965), p. 327.

[2] Bernard Berelson and Gary Steiner, *Human Behavior: An Inventory of Scientific Findings* (New York: Harcourt Brace Jovanovich, Inc., 1964), p. 297.

[3] Bureau of the Census, U.S. Department of Commerce, *Census of Population: 1960*, Vol. 1, *Characteristics of the Population* (Washington, D.C.: United States Government Printing Office, 1961), pp. LV–LVIII.

adoption and who live together. In contrast, a *household* is determined by where people live without regard to their relationships. It should be pointed out that households, too, are important determinants of consumption expenditures and total consumer behavior. And given the many remarkable and dramatic social changes that are taking place, the household may become a more important influencer of consumer behavior and a more economically and socially important factor in consumption than the family.[4] As yet, however, the family as a sociological and behavioral unit is still viewed as a more important influencer of behavior than is the household. Blood ties that result in continuous and dynamic interaction and in the socialization of the young are all firmly entrenched family-related activities. The point of significance is that there are differences in the roles or functions of families as opposed to households. A household denotes where one lives, but it does not say a great deal about the relationships or interactions among those living there. On the other hand, the concept of family is directly related to relationships and interactions. The family historically and contemporarily has many functions, including reproduction, socialization, social placement, and affection.[5] The family also has been viewed as having the functional responsibility of status placement, emotional maintenance, and social and sexual control.[6] We shall return again to the functional role of the family unit in a later section of this chapter.

THE IMPACT OF CHANGE IN FAMILY STRUCTURE

The social psychologist, the consumer behavioralist, and others look upon the family as a major reference group, perhaps even as the foremost primary group of one's existence and as an important shaper and influencer of individual behavior. Yet the family is a dynamic cultural institution. It changes over time, and as it changes its norm-role expectancy changes as well. The family of today, to the extent it can be characterized, is a far different social and economic configuration than was, say, the family of the early 1800s or the family of rural America in the early 1900s. Perhaps a brief look at the history of family development and at the various theories offered to explain and predict change in family organization will increase our understanding of the role and impact of the family unit in terms of consumer decision processes.

[4] For more related to this argument, see Ingrid C. Kildegaard, "A Household Is Not a Family," *Journal of Advertising Research,* Vol. 7 (June 1967), pp. 44–46.

[5] Alvin W. Gauldner, *Modern Sociology* (New York: Harcourt Brace Jovanovich, Inc., 1963), p. 504–507.

[6] Ely Chinay, *Society: An Introduction to Sociology* (New York: Random House, Inc., 1963), pp. 103–121. Also see Everett K. Wilson, *Sociology: Rules, Roles and Relationships* (Homewood, Ill.: The Dorsey Press, 1966), pp. 410–418.

PATRIARCHAL FAMILIES. The patriarchal family is in many ways the most stereotyped family image. Characteristic of American families before the Industrial Revolution were such features as male household head dominance. Decisions were centralized in the male head and the family's welfare was placed far above the welfare of the individual. Offspring were viewed as resources whose efforts were supposed to increase overall family welfare. Children grew up expecting to remain in the geographical area in which they were born and maintaining a loyalty to their family of orientation.[7]

COMPANIONSHIP FAMILIES. Companionship families began to emerge after the sweeping social and economic change wrought by the Industrial Revolution era. Companionship families ordinarily stressed more individual initiative, self-control and independence and some autonomy in individual decision-making. Whereas in the patriarchal family most goods were owned in common, the individual ownership of goods became more widespread within the companionship family. The economic autonomy that resulted from factory work by individuals as opposed to work on the family farm led to greater individual discretion and freedom as to what to buy, what to wear, and what to use. This era of beginning mass production saw also the beginning of mass marketing and consumption. Members of companionship families seemed to have a sense of moral obligation to go out, compete, and subdue both persons and things.

COLLEAGUE FAMILIES. The new bureaucratic structures of contemporary man are said to have led to the development of a new kind of family unit, namely, the colleague family. Such a family is bent upon doing what is considered proper and upon being flexible. Members of the colleague family look upon one another as specialists who have different talents, interests, and functions, many of which are complementary to each other. Such role specialization is not usually viewed as threatening. Instead, it promotes and enriches the common family well-being. Children within colleague families are trained and shaped to be "nice guys"—affable, unthreatening, responsible, competent, and adaptive. Members of colleague families are permitted, even encouraged, to express their individuality through goods and consumption so long as one member's well-being is not enhanced at the overexpense of other family members.

This progression of changes in family types appears to be real enough, yet it should be clearly emphasized that it is a broad social change that treats abstract family concepts, not a process that has penetrated every family.

[7] See E. Earl Baughman and George Schlager Welsh, *Personality: A Behavioral Science* (Englewood Cliffs, N.J.: Prentice-Hall, Inc., 1962), p. 211–213.

THEORIES OF FAMILY STRUCTURE AND FAMILY CHANGE

There are relatively few theories of family structure and family change. Most analyses of family units treat the family either as a causal agent bringing about change in a larger society or, more frequently, as a passive agent adapting to changes in other aspects of the social structure. The family is, it must be remembered, an adjunct of culture. As such, the family is subjected to all the forces of social, economic, political, and historical development. Our understanding of the role and impact of family operation on consumer decision processes may increase with an increased knowledge of family structure and family change. Three theories are briefly explored in the following pages.

A CYCLICAL THEORY. Zimmerman's cyclical theory of family structure and change is based upon data from the society of the ancient Greeks to modern civilization.[8] Throughout history, he argues, there have been three recurring family types—the trustee family, the domestic family, and the atomistic family. Change has occurred in sweeping historical cycles. As each society emerges out of the primordial darkness, its institutions are relatively undifferentiated and the trustee family prevails. The trustee family completely subordinates individuals to its needs, and gradually outside power develops to restrict its abuses. The domestic family, associated with society's greatest achievements, is an intermediate type in which familism and individualism are in balance. However, the forces of change, once set in motion, continue, and the atomistic family form evolves. The insatiable demands of rampant individualism lead to societal decay, and the society gives way to another turn of the wheel in which the trustee family is likely to be found.

The pessimist would be inclined to state that given the trend of today's society and family orientation, we may soon return to a more conservative, trustee type of family.

A PROGRESSIVIST THEORY. The progressivist theory is based upon data from colonial times to the present and deals essentially with the concept of family in a Western civilization context.[9] Ogburn asserts that technological developments are the prime causes of social change and features the family as passively adjusting to outside changes. Changes in nonmaterial culture lag behind changes in material culture, however, producing at least temporary social disorganization. Many functions, according to Ogburn—economic, protective, religious, recre-

[8] Carle C. Zimmerman, *Family and Civilization* (New York: Harper and Row, Publishers, 1947).

[9] William F. Ogburn, *Technology and the Changing Family* (Boston: Houghton Mifflin Company, 1955).

ational, educational, and status—formerly performed by the family have been at least partly removed from the home. He associates rising divorce rates and other forms of family pathology with the loss of functions. The two remaining functions central to family activity— affection and personality—are more important than they used to be.

A STRUCTURE-FUNCTION THEORY. The structure-function theory focuses on the integration of the family system with the occupational system.[10] Talcott Parsons is concerned primarily with the isolated nuclear family system, in which there are no effective larger kinship groups and in which normative prescriptions encourage the minimizing of ties with the parental generation. Marriage is the structural keystone of the system, and because the marital unit is not incorporated into a larger kin group, marriage is based upon romantic love. The segregation of roles permits only one member, the husband, to be a free participant in the occupational system. Such a situation requires that the nuclear family be both geographically and socially mobile. This theory was advanced during the 1950s to explain our small, relatively unstable family system as being well adapted to the requirements of an industrial society.

THE FAMILY IN TRANSITION

The American family is certainly in a stage of transition today. The structure-function theory of Parsons failed in many ways to anticipate that the family would most likely adapt and accommodate to human needs as opposed to technological ones. The nuclear-atomistic family today is a diffuse and amorphous configuration. U.S. society is characterized by a range of family types from patriarchal to companionship to colleague family structures. The advent of the feminist or women's liberation movement, the sexual revolution, and the changing value orientation of youth culture and radical culture subsystems are resulting in vast and profound change and experimentation with communal living and collective family configurations. Other couples are viewing the marriage-family configuration as a contractual arrangement between equal partners whose role responsibilities and expectations are in some cases specifically articulated in written contractual agreements.[11] Much of this change would lead some to conclude that the family is a dying institution. However, *the* family is an institution, by which is meant a recognized and accepted way of doing things. It is to be distinguished from *a* family, which is a group. The

[10] Parsons's most comprehensive work on the family is one written with Robert F. Bales, *Family, Socialization and Interaction Process* (Glencoe, Ill.: The Free Press, 1955). The summation of his views, on which the present discussion rests, is found in Talcott Parsons, "The Social Structure of the Family," in *The Family: Its Function and Destiny*, Ruth N. Anshen, ed. (New York: Harper and Row, Publishers, 1959), pp. 241–274.

[11] For a review of these contemporary developments, see "The Marriage Experiments," *Life* (April 28, 1972), pp. 51–76.

family is a set of norms, roles, and expectations pertaining to the family group. The family as a social institution is in a state of transition. But then again it probably always was. It is changing to the extent that the larger cultural and social world of which it is a part is changing.[12] The family is changing in response to changes in economic, cultural, social, technological, and human needs. It is a changing, but not necessarily a dying, institution.[13] We, as consumer behavior analysts, must seek to understand the changing role structure, value system, and norms that emerge from family units. For example, our traditional thinking about family influence relationship via family interaction has been that the children are influenced and shaped in an instrumental and cognitive sense by the attitudes, values, roles, and perceptions of the parent. Thinking along these lines has conformed to the notion that as the twig is bent so grows the tree. A more enlightened view, however, would recognize something of the interdependence of family members and would acknowledge that influence, in a transaction sense, flows both ways. Parents and offspring learn from each other. Mead, in an insightful analysis, traces the development of culture and family organization along three lines: *postfigurative*, in which children learn primarily from their forebears; *cofigurative*, in which both children and adults learn from their peers; and *prefigurative*, in which adults and parents learn from the children. She contends that we are now entering a new period in which the young are taking on new authority and playing new roles as norm makers and norm givers.[14]

THE BEHAVIORAL IMPACT OF FAMILY INTERACTION

Let us look now at some of the distinguishing behavioral characteristics of family interaction. The important point is that regardless of the family orientation, its particular role structure, its manifest norms, its style or characteristics—whether the family orientation is strong or weak, whether it is parent dominated or child dominated—the important consideration is that living within the context of a family conditions and influences the behavior, sentiments, and predispositions of the individual members.

COGNITIVE ORIENTATION. The family affects the cognitive structure and thus the style of its individual members.[15] Cognitions are knowledge or awareness, and specific cognitions include values, at-

[12] W. F. Ogburn, "Why the Family Is Changing," *Sociologus*, Vol. 4, new series (1954), pp. 160–170.

[13] Burrington Moore, Jr., *Political Power and Social Theory* (Cambridge, Mass.: Harvard University Press, 1958). See also Chapter 13, "The Family," in *Perspectives on the Social Order*, H. Laurence Ross, ed. (New York: McGraw-Hill Book Company, 1968), pp. 346–368.

[14] Margaret Mead, *Culture and Commitment: A Study of the Generation Gap* (Garden City, N.Y.: Natural History Press, Doubleday & Company, Inc., 1970).

[15] Vernon, op. cit., p. 328.

titudes, and images. Individual family members' conceptions and level of awareness are affected by family orientations. The concept of goods, wealth, acquisition, achievement, cooperation, and so forth are all cognitions that, if not totally family acquired, are family influenced. Ideas and attitudes about saving versus consumption, immediate need gratification versus gratification renunciation and postponement, and the adoption and use of the appropriate symbol systems are largely inculcated through family interaction.

NORM-ROLE RELATIONS. Family interaction also teaches and influences the individual in terms of societal norms—rules and expectations as to what is appropriate behavior and how one should conduct himself in the best interest of society and the family.[16] The family is also an important training ground for acquiring one's concepts of roles. Boys are usually shaped to conform to masculine, male-oriented roles that emphasize competition and aggression. Girls are taught to be feminine and cooperative and learn such skills as sewing and cooking. Goods as symbols are often used by parents to mold and shape sex-role behavior.

THE FAMILY AS REFERENCE GROUP. For most individuals the family is an important reference group involved especially in the development of self-definitions. Who we actually are, our concept and image of self, and our sense of dignity and self worth are often rooted in our family orientation. Our family's social class standing, style of life, residence, wealth, and inventory of goods are a kind of social anchor that is in many ways a surrogate, but real, yardstick of who we are. To this extent the whole concept of individual personality is largely related to family interaction and behavior.

THE FAMILY AS SOCIALIZING AGENT. Finally, the family serves as an important editing and mediating function for information that is conveyed to its members. A major function of the family is culture transmission.[17] What is read, spoken, and conveyed is many times controlled by family authority. What is eaten, worn, driven, or displayed is also related to family authority or emerges out of the life style and family orientation of a given family. The family conditions and complements the individual's total educational process; it stipulates, at least loosely, the rules and norms regarding recreation, husband-wife roles, acceptable deviance patterns, and acceptable characteristics in the role models of various family members. Thus, the family has an impact on the individual's motivations and his percep-

[16] Conrad M. Arensberg, "The American Family in the Perspective of Other Cultures," *The Nation's Children*, Eli Ginzberg, ed., Vol. 1 (New York: Columbia University Press, 1960), pp. 50–71, 74–75.

[17] Talcott Parsons and Winston White, "The Link Between Character and Society," in *Culture and Social Character*, Seymour M. Lipset and Leo Lowenthal, eds. (Glencoe, Ill.: The Free Press, 1961).

tions, attitudes, and general cognitions. The family influences and affects the individual's learning processes and structures and, in part, his communication channels and networks. The total personality of the individual is conditioned by family membership to the extent that family membership signifies group interaction that results in socialization. As we shall shortly determine, all these factors have most important implications for consumer behavior and consumer decision processes.

The Family and Consumer Behavior

Our treatment to this point has been concerned with developing a general frame of reference and sufficient background in order that we might discover what relationships or influences, if any, exist between the family and consumer behavior. To this juncture our analysis has been general; that is, we have posited that the family acts as an important mediating influence on individual behavior. Through the social learning of the family interaction and other forms of socialization, individual attitudes, perceptions, tastes, dispositions, and actual overt behavior are affected.[18] We shall attempt to relate more specifically in the following pages the more explicit influences and relationships that exist between family-oriented interaction and consumer behavior.

CONSUMER DECISION PROCESSES

It must be remembered that consumer behavior is not per se a discrete and distinctive act but is instead a series of sequential and often reiterative actions. Consumer behavior is thus the composite of all the activities related to the consumption and use of goods and in its minimum dimensions includes the following activities:

1. Awareness.
2. Search.
3. Evaluation.
4. Decision.
5. Postdecision consideration.

From this point we must assert quickly that the role of the family or some individual family member is often over- or under-estimated because of a too common tendency to regard consumer behavior as a distinct act. For example, the husband may very well decide, or appear to be deciding, what brand or make of automobile to purchase. Yet the teen-age son may have been an early agitator for Dad to make the decision to trade. Thus the son created the awareness by pointing out the shoddiness of the old car or by emphasizing its inadequate pollution control devices, and so on. Furthermore, although the father may

[18] For an excellent, highly detailed treatment of this process, see William F. Kenkel, *The Family in Perspective* (New York: Appleton-Century-Crofts, 1966), especially Chapter 11, "The Function of Socialization," pp. 228–268.

make the final decision about make and/or model, the mother and the daughter may have played instrumental roles in choosing the color, the accessories, and the interior decor. And, it may be the mother who, after the decision and the commitment are made, creates the dissonance when she reports that because of the new car expenditure this year's vacation will have to be foregone.

For many years the housewife was construed in the marketing literature as the family purchasing agent. In many respects she is Her role often dictates that she do the family shopping and marketing. But such a view is shortsighted if it presumes that because the housewife *buys* she also is the one who *decides*. Such is not necessarily the case. All family members are *consumers*, some are *buyers*, and some are *influencers*. Small children may actually dictate the brands of cereal or other products consumed in the home. They do not buy the products but they play an important role in the buying process. The mother or father may act as a gatekeeper, permitting only parent-approved products to be purchased and consumed. Thus individual influence within the context of a family behavioral unit will vary considerably with the nature of the product, the size of the expenditure, and the extent to which it relates to a particular role specialization. Kenkel, for example, suggests that two basic kinds of behavior are exhibited in small groups such as the family: (1) task- or goal-oriented behavior and (2) social, emotional, or expressive behavior.[19] Both forms of behavior are evidenced by all family members, yet in the U.S. culture, role specialization suggests that men usually engage in task-oriented behavior and women in social-emotional behavior. Such reasoning would suggest that men would be more concerned with the functional aspects of products—cost, efficiency, durability, maintenance, and so forth—whereas women would be more concerned with aesthetic product attributes such as style, color, design, appearance, and suitability as an expressive symbol befitting the family's status and life style. As we shall learn, the stereotyped role specialization normally attributed to men and women is weakening.

FAMILY ROLE STRUCTURE AND DECISION MAKING. The idea that family role structure would influence family decision-making is worthy of exploration. You will recall from earlier discussions of role that the concept refers to a behavior pattern as a functional part of a social position.[20] The term *role* is used to designate the obligations or behavioral patterns necessary to validate a particular status. Role signifies and acknowledges the social context that affects an individual's action. It has been suggested that the term *role* has at least three

[19] William Kenkel, "Family Interaction in Decision Making on Spending," in *Household Decision Making*, Nelson N. Foote, ed. (New York: New York University Press, 1961), pp. 140–164.

[20] John T. Doby, *Introduction to Social Psychology* (New York: Appleton-Century-Crofts, 1966), pp. 10–11.

different definitions. For example, *enacted role* is the actual overt behavior displayed by an individual in a particular position within a social organization. *Perceived role* is the perception of behavior associated with a particular position in a social organization. *Prescribed role* is defined as the set of expectations held by the other members of a group of the behavior to be displayed by an individual in a particular position in the group.[21] The concept of prescribed role is paramount in family role structure and decision-making to the extent that it relates sex role standards—those attributes and behavior patterns that the members of a culture prescribe as appropriately masculine or feminine. For example, men within the family structure are supposed to be the "head of the household" or to "wear the pants in the family." They are expected to do most of the yard work, to look after the auto, to shovel the walks in the winter, to clean the furnace, and to do any and all heavy lifting. Women are prescribed to do the housework, most marketing (shopping), sewing, mending and repair, cooking, and interior decorating and to look after the children's needs, attend PTA meetings, and so forth. Yet these stereotypes vary from situation to situation. For example, Dalrymple has reported that joint decision-making is most pronounced among white American families. Husband dominance is most pronounced among Japanese-American families, and wife dominance is most pronounced among black American families.[22] Thus family role structure, or the effect of the behavior and expectations of the various family members on the total consumer decision process, will vary from family to family depending upon such factors as social class, social mobility, life cycle, and the presence of children.

Family role structure may assume a number of distinct patterns and characteristics. For example, one researcher classifies the organization of family activities and decision-making in terms of *complementary, independent,* and *joint* organization. In *complementary organization* the decisions of husband and wife are different and separate but fitted together to form a whole.[23] Each pursues his own bundle of goods and satisfactions but with the thought of gaining or creating maximum family utility. Too much imbalance favoring either party would tend to violate the law of distributive justice.[24] In *independent organization,*

[21] John W. McDavid and Herbert Harari, *Social Psychology* (New York: Harper and Row, Publishers, 1968), pp. 268–269.

[22] Douglas J. Dalrymple, Thomas S. Robertson, and Michael Y. Yoshima, "Consumption Behavior Across Ethnic Categories," working paper, Graduate School of Business, Indiana University, 1969.

[23] Elizabeth Bott, *Family and Social Network* (London: Tavistock Publications, 1971), pp. 52–53.

[24] For a more elaborate model of family structure and decisions, see Richard W. Pollay, "A Model of Family Decision Making," *British Journal of Marketing* (Autumn 1968), pp. 206–216. The concept of distributive justice stems from the transaction–social-exchange model of interaction. Such concepts were discussed in Chapter 13. Briefly, distributive justice relates to the equal or near-equal distribution of utilities (satisfactions or rewards) according

decisions are carried out separately by husband and wife without reference to each other, insofar as this is possible. Such family decision-making usually results when a clear division of role responsibilities is made, when both husband and wife are working and each makes his own income, or when the wife is given a sufficient allowance to support such autonomous behavior. Furthermore, such a role arrangement is a high risk and often a conflict type of family role structure. Finally, in *joint organization* decisions are carried out by husband and wife together, or the same activity or set of decisions is carried out by either party at different times. Hence, the degree of role specialization in family decision-making is minimized.

Family role structure has also been categorized as (1) *autonomic,* when decisions are made about equally by husband and wife, (2) *husband dominant,* (3) *wife dominant,* and (4) *syncratic,* when decision making is democratized and thus decisions are made jointly by husband and wife.[25] Thus marketing strategies must very often consider the family role structure in terms of such variables as promotion planning (media and appeals) and channel selection. For that matter, there are few marketing planning variables that should not be reviewed and considered in terms of their relationship to family role structure.[26] Such relationships may be concerned with the general pattern of decision making or more specifically with unique products or even brands.

Finally, it should be noted that the general role structure within the American nuclear family amounts to what might be considered a relative power structure. The nuclear-atomistic family of contemporary America stresses the autonomy and the individuality of each family member. Even the small children are often treated permissively, given generous allowances, and permitted to buy goods on their own and to sit as near equals in the family decision-making councils. Yet some generalizations or theories have been advanced to explain who has power or dominance within the family and why. For example, the *relative contributions* theory suggests that role structures are affected by the relative resources (income, earnings, wealth) contributed by the various nuclear family members. Because the male usually does the most earning and is the major household provider, he is usually perceived as the major or dominant member of the household. Another theory, the *comparative resources* theory, suggests that male heads of households or families whose earnings are high and who therefore have high prestige and status have more in-the-home decision-making au-

to a priority structure so that each person who is a party to the exchange and interaction perceives the distribution to be mutually agreeable and fair.

[25] Murray A. Straus, "Conjugal Power Structure and Adolescent Personality," *Marriage and Family Living,* Vol. 24, No. 1 (February 1962), pp. 17–25.

[26] See Donald H. Granbois, "The Role of Communication in the Family Decision Making Process," in *Proceedings of the American Marketing Association,* Stephen A. Greyser, ed. (Chicago: American Marketing Association, 1963), pp. 44–57.

thority than husbands whose wives work. In such cases, the high-income-earning husband is perceived as better equipped to manage the intricate and demanding task of major household decision-making.[27] Finally, another theory, the *least-interested-partner* theory, contends that it is not the value of the resource contributed by each partner but the value of these resources outside the marriage.[28] For example, the greater the difference between the value to the wife of the resources contributed by her husband and the value to the wife of the resources she might earn outside the marriage, the greater the influence of the husband in family decision-making.

It is difficult to weigh and judge the relative merits of these various theories of power and role structure within the modern nuclear-atomistic family. Families in total are likely to manifest considerable variation in power and role structure. The *least-interested-partner* theory is perhaps more explanatory than either the relative contributions or the comparative resources theory and it alone would seem to manifest sufficient characteristics to accommodate to the changing role structure of the individual family members over the life cycle of the family. Furthermore, as we shall see directly, family role structure is also affected by such factors as social class, mobility, life cycle, and the presence of children.

SOCIAL CLASS. Family role structure and its impact upon family decision-making are affected and conditioned by social class considerations. At the lower social class levels the wife usually has more decision-making responsibilities than wives at the upper-class levels.[29] However, the reality is not quite as simple as that. For example, joint involvement in decision making is more prevalent at the middle social class levels. Thus a curvilinear relationship exists between a family's social class and the degree of democratized or joint decision-making. Joint decision-making is most usual and prevalent in the middle class and least usual and prevalent in the lower and upper classes.

The middle-class life-style appears to generate an increasing amount of communication and interaction.[30] The "family" and the "home" become the center of existence, and family well-being becomes an important overall individual consideration. Middle-class Americans usually show concern with the home and family as the setting for the most important living experiences and interpersonal relations and they

[27] Robert O. Blood, Jr., and Donald M. Wolfe, *Husbands and Wives: The Dynamics of Married Living* (New York: The Free Press, 1960), pp. 12–13, 30–33.

[28] David M. Heer, "The Measurement and Bases of Family Power: An Overview," *Marriage and Family Living*, Vol. 25 (1963), p. 139.

[29] Elizabeth H. Wolgast, "Do Husbands or Wives Make the Purchasing Decisions?" *Journal of Marketing*, Vol. 22 (October 1958), pp. 151–158.

[30] Mira Komarovsky, "Class Differences in Family Decision Making on Expenditures," *Consumer Behavior: Household Decision Making* (New York: New York University Press, 1961), pp. 255–265.

desire to make this setting and environment as attractive, comfortable, and aesthetically pleasing as possible. To this end, joint involvement and total family participation are sought.

LIFE STYLE. The characteristic patterns of living manifested by various families will also influence and affect family role structure and decision-making. For example, the usual case is that the wife shares more in family decision-making if she is employed outside the home and thus has an independent source of income.[31] Such a condition is compatible with the relative contributions theory discussed earlier, and it suggests that the wife broadens her credentials for household participation in decision making both cognitively and economically; that is, she knows more and she commands some share of the resources. Families who manifest upward social mobility as well as geographic mobility tend to manifest more intrafamily communication and joint sharing of decision making.

Moving tends to throw spouses together and creates a need for mutual dependence and shared responsibility.[32]

LIFE CYCLE. Finally, some research indicates that joint decision-making tends to decrease over the life cycle.[33] The reasoning is that over time an increasing familiarity with the other spouse's needs and tastes and the resultant tendency for the development of larger amounts of role specialization lead to a decrease in joint involvement in family decision-making.[34] The increasing stability and resulting lack of tension and anxiety manifesting itself in the family over time is said to be a further reason for the decline of shared communication and joint family decision-making.

FAMILY VERSUS INDIVIDUAL INFLUENCE

There is some evidence to suggest that too much may be made of family role structure and its impact on family decision-making. The family as a behavioral unit and as a consuming unit is an entity in one sense—a kind of small group mind. As such it filters information, provides a network of communication and social influence, affects attitudes, creates motives, and alters perception. Its role in this regard must be understood. However, much of the research on family has been concerned more with individual decision-makers within the family than with the family as a mediating and editing influence upon individual members. Thus the literature on family role structure is overwhelming and characterized by many diverse theories about the structure of marital roles in family decision-making. Researchers often make oversimplified assumptions about the structure of husband-wife

---

[31] Ibid.

[32] Ibid., p. 258.

[33] Granbois, op. cit., pp. 44–57.

[34] Wolgast, op. cit., pp. 151–158.

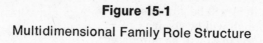

Figure 15-1

Multidimensional Family Role Structure

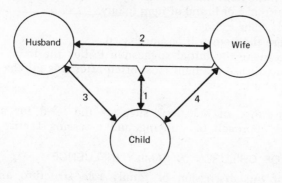

roles in consumer decisions. Especially questionable is the tendency to seek responses about role responsibilities from only one spouse. The sufficiency of these responses is highly suspect. Much evidence is beginning to accumulate that suggests perhaps a less differentiated role structure than that which is often presented in the literature.[35] Thus a multidimensional family role structure is probably the more genuine case in family decision-making. Such a multidimensional family role structure is shown in Figure 15-1.

Figure 15-1 shows something of the interactive role structure of a family unit. The numbers represent a possible sequence of interdependence and interaction and the diagram represents the interlocking set of relationships that characterize the nuclear family. In each case, one can consider some aspect of the relationship that varies either as an independent or as a dependent variable in the consumer decision process. For example, in Number 1, the husband and wife as parents influence and affect the consumption pattern and decisions of the children of the household. As the children become more mature, they in turn affect parental decisions regarding consumption. In Number 2 we see the interaction between husband and wife. In Number 3 we see the interaction between the male head of the family and the offspring. This interaction, too, is interdependent for many decisions and for many steps in the consumer decision process. In Number 4 the same interaction is shown between the female head of the household and the children. Thus the question of who makes the important family decisions is a difficult one. Implicit in the question is the assumption that people can accurately remember and report how decisions were made. Too often they cannot. There is a wide range of questions that marketers must research in regard to role structure and family decisions. For example, "Who decided?" entails who decided:

[35] Harry L. Davis, "Dimensions of Marital Roles in Consumer Decision Making," *Journal of Marketing Research*, Vol. 7 (May 1970), pp. 168–177.

1. What item will be purchased.
2. How much will be spent.
3. When the item will be purchased.
4. What make or brand of item to buy.
5. What color to buy.
6. Where the item will be purchased.
7. Who made the initial suggestion to buy the item.
8. Who will use the item most often after it is purchased.
9. And so on.

Such a range of questions suggests the need for a multitrait-multimethod approach to studying and assessing family influence.[36]

THE ROLE OF CHILDREN IN FAMILY INFLUENCE

Most of our discussion of family role structure and decision-making has centered upon the husband-wife dyad, yet children, as would be expected, have an important influence role in the Western nuclear-atomistic family. Several factors are causing marketers and researchers to look at more closely and define more carefully the role of adolescents and teen-agers in family decision-making relating to consumer behavior. First of all, as we saw in Chapter 1, the size of this market is growing rapidly. It is growing in terms of numbers and of economic impact. Second, children within the family behavioral unit obviously influence the family's decision-making. They not only buy goods in their own interests but they influence and condition the interests of parents. Third, it is reasonably well assumed that habits, attitudes, motives—the entire range of sociopsychological factors that are inculcated and acquired during youth—will affect these same factors in the youth as adult. In short, training in consumption begins early. One writer, with tongue somewhat in cheek, characterizes youth indoctrination as follows:

> Many of their earliest memories involve television. As toddlers they were handed over to the Box and were propagandized by merchandisers who, speaking directly to them, encouraged them to believe in their own importance and in the importance of Something Else (Something New, Improved) and in the obligation to acquire status through possessions.[37]

From youth indoctrination stems youth influence. Youth have become an important market segment for many goods. Over 60 per cent of all tape recorders, over 30 per cent of all radios, and over 80 per cent of all transceivers are owned by children under twelve years old.

---

[36] Harry L. Davis, "Measurement of Husband-Wife Influence in Consumer Purchase Decisions," *Journal of Marketing Research,* Vol. 7 (August 1971), pp. 305–312.

[37] Roger Price, *The Great Roob Revolution* (New York: Random House, Inc., 1970), p. 88.

Teen-agers account for 81 per cent of all record sales, 55 per cent of all soft drink sales, and 53 per cent of all movie ticket sales. What is more, young people do not necessarily have to have their own money. To *want* is sufficient to have! The nuclear-atomistic family value system is such that affection, loving, caring, and concern are often demonstrated by the giving of things. Parents often seem to want their children to have the "things of the good life," and the "ideal-parent role" is one that is characterized by a good deal of permissiveness, often meaning giving in to the demand, "I want _____!"[38]

The influencing role of the child in family decision-making is not totally understood. One research effort focused upon this relationship in terms of the following hypotheses:

(1) The more assertive the child, the more likely the mother to furnish the child's requested brand of breakfast cereal.
(2) The more child-centered the mother, the more likely she will purchase the child's favorite brand of breakfast cereal.[39]

Both hypotheses were rejected by the researchers. Most likely the influence of the child is more subtle than either of these hypotheses would suggest. Influence is unquestionably related to the age of the child and more specifically to the perceived role of the parent figure. Child centeredness, it is quite likely, would entail a perceived role of "mother or father knows best" and such a role could mean that the parent might acknowledge the child's influence by allowing him to choose *a brand* from a parent-approved list of possibilities. As we have learned before, influence is seldom one-way. Parents are often gatekeepers, but the choice and influence of children are still recognized as vital and dynamic parts of family decision-making.

There are many issues regarding the influence of children in family decision-making that relate to the larger question of the consumer behavior of children. In an exploratory study, McNeal raises these questions.

1. Does the child really want to enter the role of a consumer? Why?
2. Does the child seek emancipation from parental control in the consumer role?
3. How does the child view the acquisition process?
4. Does he find the buying act stimulating regardless of what he buys, or are there varying feelings depending on whether the purchases are for him or his parents?
5. Does he want to share the consumer role of his parents?

[38] William F. Kenkel, "Husband-Wife Interaction in Decision Making and Decision Choices," *The Journal of Social Psychology,* Vol. 54 (August 1961), pp. 255–262.

[39] Lewis A. Berey and Richard W. Pollay, "The Influencing Role of the Child in Family Decision Making," *Journal of Marketing Research,* Vol. 5 (February 1968), pp. 70–71.

6. What opinions does he have about the goods that his parents buy for him?
7. Is he aware of the varying social value of some goods?
8. What material goods are most significant to him?
9. What would he buy if there were no limitations? Why?
10. Does he concern himself with the purchases of others?
11. How do his peers influence his behavior in the consumer role?
12. Where does he enjoy shopping most? Why?
13. Is he aware of business ownership and the motivation for it?
14. Does he know where goods in a store originate?
15. Is he aware of the functions performed in a typical store?
16. Does he have any general opinions of businessmen?
17. How does he view the relationship between himself and business?
18. Is he aware of advertisements?[40]

Obviously, only some of these questions are relevant to the issue of family role structure and the influence of children in family decision-making. Yet we also obviously need to understand a great deal more about the total consumer behavior of children. Children's role perceptions, their attitudes, their needs, their motivations, their cognitions, and their total social interaction processes most assuredly lead in at least two directions: (1) they are the raw material out of which later adult patterns of behavior will emerge; (2) they are currently the influencing materials that condition child roles within the total present family role structure.

Children and teen-agers are many-sided buyers and influencers. They are highly innovative, communicative, and thus influential.[41] They are future family builders, and therefore marketers must look at at least two things in terms of their behavior. First, marketers must incorporate them into their planning regarding market segmentation and product differentiation and thus serve the growing needs of these consumers during the 1970s. And, second, marketers must look beyond the 1970s to the 1980s, to the development of future family consumers—when the children and teen-agers of this present period become the important acquisitive family builders of the future.

In these previous sections we have examined the impact of family structure in consumer behavior, looked at the behavioral impact of the family on consumer decision processes, and, more specifically, examined the relationship between the family and consumer behavior in terms of family role structure and family decision-making. In the remaining sections of this chapter we shall look at two additional variables of consumer behavior, both of which have family implications, namely, the concepts of *life style* and *life cycle*.

[40] James U. McNeal, "An Exploratory Study of the Consumer Behavior of Children," in *Dimensions of Consumer Behavior*, James U. McNeal, ed. (New York: Appleton-Century-Crofts, 1969), pp. 256–257.

[41] "Do Ad Men Understand Teenagers?" *Printers' Ink*, Vol. 272 (July 29, 1960), pp. 21–23, 26.

Life-Style Concepts and Consumer Behavior

Individual and family life-styles have been recognized by some as important determinants of or variables in consumer behavior. As the term implies, individuals and/or families manifest particular and often unique methods of doing, living, appearing, and consuming, and these patterns of attitudes, behavioral dispositions, and expressive movements are referred to as *life style*. Much earlier, in Chapter 5, we discussed *cognitive style* as an integral part and a basic precondition of one's life style. Life style as a consumer behavior variable suggests that how people spend their time, what they are interested in, what they consider important in their immediate surroundings, what they believe, where they stand on important issues, and where they live all together act to influence and affect such factors as what goods they consume, what brands they prefer, whether they are heavy or light users of a product or a service, what stores they patronize, what services they seek, and so forth.

A CLOSER LOOK AT LIFE STYLE

One of the better definitions of life style has been offered by Lazer. He contends:

> Life style is a systems [holistic] concept. It refers to the distinctive or characteristic mode of living, in its aggregative and broadest sense, of a whole society or segment thereof. It is concerned with those unique ingredients or qualities which describe the style of life of some culture or group, and distinguish it from others. It embodies the patterns that develop and emerge from the dynamics of living in a society.[42]

Life style is the patterned result of such forces as culture, values, resources, symbols, license, and sanctions. The goods that people buy, the symbol systems they use, and the ways in which they consume goods reflect a society's life style. In short, life style is the orientation to self, others, and society that each individual develops and follows.[43] Such an orientation reflects a value or cognitive orientation. Thus the individual's value or cognitive orientation reflects his basic inclinations and generalized orientation. They are the elements that shape the preference system one develops to guide himself in the formulation of goals and in the exercise of choice. Thus the sequential decisions of consumer decision processes are not random but are meaningfully related to each other because the consumer's preference system rests upon a limited number of distinct values that give meaning and direc-

[42] William Lazer, "Life-Style Concepts and Marketing," in *Toward Scientific Marketing*, Stephen A. Greyser, ed. (Chicago: American Marketing Association, 1964), pp. 130–139, at p. 130.

[43] Eli Ginzberg et al., *Life Styles of Educated Women* (New York: Columbia University Press, 1966), p. 145.

tion to his life and influence his choices among confronted alternatives. We have alluded to many of the values or cognitions that form the basis of a value or cognitive orientation: the desire for leisure; the "good life" syndrome; the meaningfulness and importance of work; the symbolic nature of goods; abundance; the urge to compete and cooperate; the desire to belong, to fit, to conform; the urge to possess, to use, to participate; the desire to deal effectively with one's environment, to be of one's time, to acquire status, and to play one's "proper role."

Life style, therefore, is a conceptualization of one's patterned attitudes, interests, and opinions, and it is presumed that these patterned attitudes, interests, and opinions constitute one's life style and that such a life style would affect one's pattern of purchased and consumed goods and services. For example, because the professor would probably have attitudes, interests, and opinions different from those of the businessman, his behavior regarding the purchase and consumption of goods could conceivably be better understood and predicted from an assessment of his value or cognitive orientation, that is, from an assessment of the professor's attitudes, interests, and opinions.[44]

LIFE STYLE AND SOCIAL CLASS

Life style is not totally unrelated to our earlier-discussed concept of social class. For example, the individual's or family's life style, to the extent that it reflects the value orientation of a particular social class standing, is similar to social class as a predictor and influencer of behavior. Yet life styles do vary among individuals and families who occupy the same social class standing. Again, contrast the life style and the emerging patterns of consumption of two families in essentially the same social class. Each family head is about the same age, approximately forty and has two children, a boy and a girl, ages twelve and sixteen, respectively. They live in the same neighborhood, have approximately the same income, and manifest some similar characteristics. Yet because of basic differences in their total bundle of attitudes, interests, and opinions, family A is highly consumption oriented; they spend, go, and consume. Family B, on the other hand, is fiscally much more conservative. They are savings oriented; they forego large amounts of consumption activity; they eschew materialism for a more aesthetically oriented and frugal existence. Family A eats out often; family B seldom eats out. Family A vacations at Disneyland and other resort places. Family B goes camping with relatively primitive equipment. Family A is fashion and style conscious and buys new products; family B is relatively unconcerned with fashion and style, preferring instead to seek items that are functional rather than stylish.

Social class in some instances may be a good indicator of consumer behavior to the extent that it does signify certain kinds of gross

---

[44] See James N. Porter, Jr., "Consumption Patterns of Professors and Businessmen: A Pilot Study of Conspicuous Consumption and Status," *Sociological Inquiry*, Vol. 37, No. 2 (1965), pp. 255–265.

value orientations. For example, Paterson suggests that the working-class family's orientation affects marketing behavior to this extent:

1. Working class families are oriented in a limited experience world and this causes them to restrict their consumption of goods and services to a narrower range of items. They tend to be less exploratory and more concerned with immediate gratification.

2. Working class families avoid spending for items that are not regarded as respectable or in keeping with their working-class orientation.

3. Working class families strive only for a "common man" level of recognition. They are concerned with goods as symbols but they are careful that the symbols are working class symbols. They stress the functional implications of goods perhaps more than their symbolic value.

4. Working class families seek the security of the known. They are brand loyal and seek well-known, popular, and acceptable brands.

5. They shop stores where they are known and they place great emphasis on personal relationships.

6. They seek to avoid shopping experiences in which they would be subjected to status-grading or being "put down" by either sales clerks or higher class customers.[45]

Such a value orientation can be contrasted with middle-class values, and the contrast can be used as a meaningful predictor of shopping and purchase behavior.[46] Yet more subtle differences in life style are also likely to be masked and lost in the overall social class configuration. For this reason, life style, based as it is on discernible patterns of attitudes, interests, and opinions, may be a more meaningful indicator of behavior.

LIFE-STYLE RESEARCH

The basic approach to life-style research has been based upon what is called AIO inventories. AIO refers to attitudes, interests, and opinions. The basic inventory is made up of three hundred statements developed from previous research.[47] These three hundred activity, interest, and opinion statements measure such activities as membership

[45] James M. Paterson, "Marketing and the Working Class Family," in *Blue Collar World: Studies of the American Worker*, Arthur B. Shostak and William Gomberg, eds. (Englewood Cliffs, N.J.: Prentice-Hall, Inc., 1965), pp. 76–80.

[46] See Conrad M. Arensberg, "The American Family in the Perspective of Other Cultures," in *The Nations' Children*, Eli Ginzberg, ed., Vol. 1 (New York: Columbia University Press, 1960), pp. 50–71, 74–75. See especially the section entitled, "The Middle Class Ideal."

[47] The study by Tigert et al. reported in the following pages was based upon panel data maintained by Market Facts, Inc. Each panel matches the total United States population demographically and was controlled on the basis of income, education, family size, and geographic dispersion.

in clubs and community organizations, hobbies, travel, shopping, work, and entertainment. The basic kinds of interests and opinions that are represented in the three hundred AIO statements are interest in the home, the family, and the community and opinions on such topics as economics, fashion, politics, business, advertising, and mass media. Each of the three hundred AIO statements is rated by a respondent on

TABLE 15-1

The Carry-Out Fried Chicken User Profile

Percentage of Non- and Heavy Users Who Generally or Definitely Agree with Each AIO Question

Life style (AIO) questions	Never use (N = 201)	Use once/ month or more (N = 138)
THE SWINGING PARTY-GOER		
I like parties where there is lots of music and talk	31%*	49%
I like to think I am a bit of a swinger	17	37
I do more things socially than do most of my friends	16	31
I like to do things that are bright, gay, and exciting	38	48
NOT A HOMEBODY IN A RUT		
I am a homebody	66	50
Our days seem to follow a definite routine such as eating meals at a regular time, etc.	72	55
I would like to have a maid to do the housework	25	42
OPTIMISTIC MOBILES		
My greatest achievements are still ahead of me	34	55
Five years from now, the family income will probably be a lot higher than it is now	37	69
I will probably have more money to spend next year than I have now	38	62
We will probably move once in the next five years	22	40
FASHION AND PERSONAL APPEARANCE CONSCIOUS		
I often try the latest hairdo styles when they change	10	27
I would like to be a fashion model	15	30+
Women wear too much makeup these days	53	39
I like to feel attractive to men	36	55
I like the natural color of my hair	67	41

Read: * 31 per cent of those respondents who never purchase at carry-out fried chicken restaurants generally or definitely agreed they like parties where there is lots of music and talk.

+ Percent who moderately, generally, and definitely agreed rather than just generally or definitely agreed.

a six-point agreement scale. In some studies, the respondents are asked to respond to the AIO questions only on a yes-no basis.

Life-style research has proceeded generally on the assumptions (1) that people live according to established behavior and attitude patterns that can be identified and measured and (2) that these life styles or patterns of living are related to behavior of more direct economic

Life style (AIO) questions	Never use (N = 201)	Use once/ month or more (N = 138)
CREDIT, BORROWING, AND INVESTMENT		
I buy many things with a credit card or charge card	30%	45%
In the past year, we have borrowed money from a bank or finance company	28	41+
I like to pay cash for everything I buy	65	48
Investing in the stock market is too risky for most families	56	44
I find myself checking the prices in the grocery store even for small items	75	57
INFLUENTIAL, NEW BRAND BUYER, INFORMATON SEEKER		
I often try new brands before my friends and neighbors do	46	70
I sometimes influence what my friends buy	23	33
My neighbors usually give me pretty good advice on what brands to buy in the grocery store	41	65
I like to be considered a leader	17	31
CONVENIENCE FOODS, CASUAL SHOPPING		
I *never* go shopping in shorts or slacks	48	25‡
A good mother will not serve her family TV dinners	31	21
I depend on canned food at least one meal a day	41	58
I use Metrecal or other diet foods at least one meal a day	23	35
SIGNS OF MIDDLE-CLASS AMERICA		
I buy many things at Sears Roebuck or Montgomery Ward	47	67+
Every family should have a dog	39	57
I thoroughly enjoy conversations about sports	16	26
I like bowling	29	45
I would rather live in or near a big city than in or near a small town	31	52

Read: ‡ Definitely agreed only.

Source: Douglas J. Tigert, Richard Lathrope, and Michael Bleeg, "The Fast Food Franchise: Psychographic and Demographic Segmentation Analysis," *Journal of Retailing,* Vol. 47, No. 1 (Spring 1971), pp. 86–87.

importance, such as product purchase and media exposure and that knowledge of such patterns or life styles, in combination with other variables, can be of economic value in marketing management.[48]

Two examples of such research efforts are briefly discussed. Tigert and his associates developed a psychographic life-style profile of the heavy users of RECFC (Ready to Eat, Carry-Out Fried Chicken).[49] Their study was based upon:

1. Three hundred questions covering the daily activities, the interests, and the opinions (AIOs) of the respondents (scored on a six-point scale from "definitely disagree" to "definitely agree").
2. One hundred and fifty questions on product use.
3. Readership questions on most of the major national magazines.

Table 15-1 shows the profile of the RECFC user and it also illustrates the questions used to determine the psychographic or life-style profile of a given consumer group. Demographically, the heavy users of RECFC are young homemakers, and a substantial number hold outside jobs. Psychographically, the heavy users of RECFC exhibit a zest for life. They are optimistic, happy-go-lucky, pro credit, active, influential, and ready to take risks. They shop in casual clothes at places like Sears and Wards and they use TV dinners, canned foods, and other easy-to-prepare items. Actually, two major profiles exist. One is of the younger housewife who works and swings and the other segment was composed of older mothers with children.

In another study based upon the same research approach and methodology, Plummer developed a psychometric or life-style profile of the commercial-bank credit-card user.[50] The profile of the male who is a heavy user of credit cards manifests these characteristics. He is a busy young businessman who is focusing upon upward job mobility. He is concerned with individuality and achievement. He is highly trained and well educated. He is symbol conscious and, therefore, aware of appearance and strives to maintain an appearance congruent with his work and social position. He perceives the use of a credit card as a convenience. He is contemporary rather than traditional in his basic attitudes. Finally, he is something of a joiner and belongs to several organizations, and he reads as a source of both information and entertainment.

The female who is a heavy user of charge cards manifests these psychometric characteristics. She, too, leads an active, upper-socio-

[48] For a look at such an effort, see Clark L. Wilson, "Homemaker Living Patterns and Marketplace Behavior—A Psychometric Approach," in *New Ideas for Successful Marketing*, John S. Wright and Jac L. Goldstrucker, eds. (Chicago: American Marketing Association, 1966), pp. 305–336.

[49] Douglas J. Tigert, Richard Lathrope, and Michael Bleeg, "The Fast Food Franchise: Psychographic and Demographic Segmentation Analysis," *Journal of Retailing*, Vol. 47, No. 1 (Spring 1971), pp. 81–90.

[50] Joseph T. Plummer, "Life Style Patterns and Commercial Bank Credit Card Usage," *Journal of Marketing*, Vol. 35 (April 1971), pp. 35–41.

economic style of life, belongs to social organizations, and is concerned with her appearance. She is, in many ways, the archetypical suburban housewife. She perceives her role as housewife as one of managing and purchasing as opposed to the traditional role of cleaning, cooking, and caring for children. She is liberal and liberated in her attitudes and orientations. Like her male counterpart, the female charge-card user is a risk seeker rather than a risk avoider, so that she is innovative and somewhat experimental, that is, willing to try new things.

Thus, life style adds another rich dimension to consumer behavior research, and the development of life-style profiles based upon consumers' AIOs holds considerable promise for the development of a more meaningful and sophisticated segmentation analysis.

GEOGRAPHIC MOBILITY AND LIFE STYLE

Before concluding this section on life-style profiles, let us look briefly at another rather distinctive life-style profile, geographic mobility. It is rather well understood and assumed that place of residence affects life style and social class and in turn would influence consumer decision processes. Yet it is only quite recently that *changing* one's place of residence has been given much attention as a variable in consumer behavior. Those who move account for about 20 per cent of the nation's population. Each year nearly two thirds of those who move make local or intracounty moves, one-sixth go to different counties in the same state, and one sixth go to other states. Most research on consumer mobility is concerned with at least intercounty movement, that is, moves from one county to another that involve distances of at least fifty miles.

Studies of geographic mobility have been concerned with postulating theories about why people move and with the problems (socioeconomic and psychological) that arise among the mobile sections of the population.[51] Our interest, of course, is in the significance of geographic mobility in consumer behavior. The most fundamental question about this relationship is whether geographic mobility acts as a stimulant to consumer behavior. And if so, why and how? The research evidence thus far suggests an affirmative answer to the major question. Those who move may be said to be a rather distinct and definable market segment and their consumer behavior in relation to their mobility characteristics is the result of three rather distinct or unique kinds of pressures:

1. The need to revise household inventories of durables and non-durables to conform to new living quarters and to new retail availabilities.

2. The need to conform to a different set of regional norms in attitudes and behavior.

[51] Alan R. Andreason, "Geographic Mobility and Market Segmentation," *Journal of Marketing Research*, Vol. 3 (November 1966), pp. 341–348; Arnold M. Rose and Leon Warshay, "The Adjustment of Migrants to Cities," *Social Forces*, Vol. 36 (October 1957), pp. 72–76; and Peter Rossi, *Why Families Move* (Glencoe, Ill.: The Free Press, 1955).

3. The need to adjust inventories, attitudes, and behavior to different income, occupational, or social class levels (or aspirations) attained in the move.[52]

Finally, it should be added that moving often acts as a trigger to the replacing of many dated or obsolescent items, or moving may act as a perceptual cue that signals that it is time to implement purchase plans already considered.

One researcher has developed a kind of life-style profile of the mobile family.[53] For example, mobile families have a past history of geographic mobility. They have higher than average levels of education and income, and they have an upward-rising level of status aspirations. The mobile family averages one long-distance move about every three years, a mobility rate nearly five times the national average. Mobile couples have been married about eleven years, and two thirds of them have children under five years of age. Only about 10 per cent of the wives work outside the home for pay. Half the mobile families are two-car families, over 80 per cent occupy single-family dwellings, and 55 per cent own their own residences. The mobile market thus is characterized by families who are willing to move, have high aspirations, and are youthful. Such families exhibit homogeneous socioeconomic and life-cycle profiles.

MOBILES AND CONSUMER BEHAVIOR

Geographic mobiles—the families who make frequent and long-distance moves across country—manifest some particular and unique demographic and psychographic characteristics, and these characteristics, in turn, identify these families as unique market segments possessing unique demand characteristics. In short, geographic mobiles have some peculiar and unique consumer behavior characteristics. For example, moving necessitates a rethinking of many of the routinized, habitualized forms of shopping. Shopping patterns and habits have to be rebuilt following a long-distance move. Brands that were readily obtainable and familiar in the old location may not be available in the new community. The conventional sources of information—friends, reference groups, news media, retail stores—are now different, and new sources of information must be sought and evaluated.

Research indicates that geographic mobiles rebuild their shopping-purchase processes in terms of four major elements.

1. *Information Sources.* Mobiles use personal information more than any other source in rebuilding shopping patterns. Such a finding suggests and underscores the importance of reference groups, personal influence, and the two-step flow of communication.

[52] Ibid., p. 345.

[53] James E. Bell, "Mobiles—A Neglected Market Segment," *Journal of Marketing*, Vol. 33 (April 1969), pp. 37–44.

2. *Decision Responsibility.* Decisions as to where to shop, what to buy, etc., are shared by both husband and wife. Wives shoulder the responsibility for decisions relating to supermarkets, dry cleaning establishments, and physicians and dentists. Husbands basically make the decisions regarding family bank, insurance firms, and men's clothing stores.

3. *Time Required to Reestablish Shopping Patterns.* Sources of supply and buying habits are quickly reestablished. The mean time span varies from about 1.0 week for selecting a new supermarket to 9.2 weeks for a dentist. Shopping patterns are more quickly reestablished for convenience goods than for shopping and specialty goods. The mobile consumer is thus "available" to a given retail store for only a relatively brief time. After that, patronage is reasonably well established. However, some experimentation, store and brand switching will continue as new information is received and as experience accumulates and is evaluated.

4. *The Number of Suppliers Contacted.* Mobiles contact or actually shop in no more than three or four stores of each type before settling down to one or two favorites. Mobiles exhibit a strong tendency to carry both store and brand loyalty from one community to another and they most frequently visit and shop those stores where they hold national charge plates and purchase familiar brands.[54]

Thus the mounting research evidence suggests that the geographic mobile is an important market segment and that his consumer behavior may warrant a special kind of marketing program or strategy. Such a generalization suggests that marketing firms continue in their efforts to delineate and characterize this particular consumer group and give added consideration as to how this market should be serviced. A number of specific tactical decisions have to be made regarding how and when mobile families should be contacted and whether a particular family member should be the sole target of contact and appeal. The mobile family is thus a special case of the more general need to analyze and understand family considerations in consumer behavior and consumer decision processes.

The Life-Cycle Concept and Consumer Behavior

As we have just seen, life style relates to the patterned ways of characterizing attitudes, behavioral dispositions, and expressive movements of either individuals or families. Or as we stated previously, life style is the orientation to self, to others, and to society that each person develops and follows. *Life cycle,* on the other hand, is concerned with how attitudes, behavioral dispositions, and expressive movements change over time. Such behavioral changes are often caused by role changes, and role changes, in turn, are caused by changes in maturity, experience, and so forth. For example, life cycle is a phenomenon with

[54] Ibid., pp. 40–41.

which all persons must deal. As individuals we are born into a state of dependency and infanthood. We progress through a series of stages in the life cycle:[55]

1. Infanthood.
2. Childhood.
3. Adolescence.
4. Teen-ager.
5. Young adulthood.
6. Middle age.
7. Old age.

Our experiences as we progress through these stages shape our cognitions and ultimately our behavior. Often the culture age-grades the individual. Children are not expected to smoke cigarettes or drink alcoholic beverages. Behavior is supposed to conform to or fit one's particular stage in the cycle. The implication of the life cycle is that our behavior is affected by certain age-related conditions, namely, roles, norms, expectations, and so forth.[56]

Consumer behavior is affected by the individual's position on the life-cycle scale, and we have correspondingly acknowledged the relationship between consumer behavior and the life cycle by discussing throughout various parts of this text certain perceived market targets or segments and corresponding consumer behavior phenomena. Thus we have acknowledged the special demand characteristics of children as consumers, teen-agers, young mobiles, and senior citizens.

However, at this juncture the intent is to relate the life-cycle concept to that of the family.[57] Overall family behavior as it relates to consumption and consumer decision processes does change over the family's life cycle. Why? Because the value orientation, needs, attitudes, perceptions, and motivations that affect and influence family consumption change over time. Family role structure and, hence, family decision-making change over time, that is, as a family is formed via marriage, as children are added, as the children grow and mature, as

[55] This classification is general and is that of the author. For a description of life-cycle activities and influences, see Talcott Parsons, *Social Structure and Personality* (New York: Macmillan Publishing Co., Inc., 1964), especially Part II, "Stages in the Life Cycle," pp. 129–254.

[56] For the economic and financial implications of this generalization, see M. H. David, *Family Composition and Consumption* (Amsterdam: North Holland Publishing Company, 1962); and Richard F. Kosobud and James N. Morgan, *Consumption Behavior of Individual Families over Two or Three Years* (Ann Arbor, Mich.: Monograph No. 36, Survey Research Center, Institute for Social Research, University of Michigan, 1964).

[57] See John B. Lansing and Leslie Kish, "Family Life Cycle as an Independent Variable," *American Sociological Review* (October 1957), pp. 512–519; and Rose Laub Coser, ed., *Life Cycle and Achievement in America* (New York: Harper and Row, Publishers, 1969).

the children leave, when one of the marriage partners dies, and so on. The nature of family consumption and decision-making reflects this cyclical progression of activities or stages.

FAMILY LIFE-CYCLE

In the United States it is generally acknowledged that most households pass through an orderly progression of stages:

1. The bachelor stage; young, single people.
2. Newly married couples; young, no children.
3. The full nest I and II; young married couples with dependent children:
   a. youngest child under six.
   b. youngest child over six.
4. The full nest III; older married couples with dependent children.
5. The empty nest; older married couples with no children living with them.
   a. head in labor force.
   b. head retired.
6. The solitary survivors; older single people:
   a. in labor force.
   b. retired.[58]

It is relatively easy to visualize the life-cycle concept and its various stages as a rich source of consumer information and to appreciate the value of the life-cycle concept as an independent variable in consumer behavior research.

For example, newly married couples are highly involved in capital and asset formation. More than likely, they are concerned with the purchase of household furnishings, small appliances, and accessories. Before children arrive, they are more likely to be entertainment and recreation oriented—more inclined to be on the go and thus concerned with style and fashion in clothes as well as decorating. Children alter this orientation somewhat. Now a major concern is with the nursery, more space—a house perhaps rather than an apartment. The need for savings and insurance arises. The wife, who may have been working, may now decide to stay home and hence family income declines. Thus family needs, which arise out of the various problems that emerge at the different stages of the life cycle, change over time. Income, expenditures on durable goods, assets and debts, and subjective feelings about financial position differ at different life-cycle stages.[59] In many ways the young to middle-aged couples with and without children are

[58] William D. Wells and George Gubar, "Life Cycle Concept in Marketing Research," *Journal of Marketing Research*, Vol. 3 (November 1966), pp. 355–363.

[59] John B. Lansing and James N. Morgan, "Consumer Finances over the Life Cycle," in *Consumer Behavior*, Lincoln H. Clark, ed., Vol. 2 (New York: New York University Press, 1955).

TABLE 15-2

An Overview of the Life Cycle

Bachelor stage; young single people not living at home	Newly married couples; young, no children	Full nest I; youngest child under six	Full nest II; youngest child six or over six	Full nest III; older married couples with dependent children
Few financial burdens	Better off financially than they will be in near future	Home purchasing at peak	Financial position better	Financial position still better
Fashion opinion leaders	Highest purchase rate and highest average purchase of durables	Liquid assets low	Some wives work	More wives work
Recreation oriented		Dissatisfied with financial position and amount of money saved	Less influenced by advertising	Some children get jobs
Buy: Basic kitchen equipment, basic furniture, cars, equipment for the mating game, vacations.	Buy: Cars, refrigerators, stoves, sensible and durable furniture, vacations.	Interested in new products	Buy larger sized packages, multiple-unit deals	Hard to influence with advertising
		Like advertised products	Buy: Many foods, cleaning materials, bicycles, music lessons, pianos.	High average purchase of durables
		Buy: Washers, dryers, TV, baby food, chest rubs and cough medicine, vitamins, dolls, wagons, sleds, skates.		Buy: New, more tasteful furniture, auto travel, non-necessary appliances, boats, dental services, magazines.

Empty nest I; older married couples, no children living with them, head in labor force	Empty nest II; older married couples, no children living at home, head retired	Solitary survivor, in labor force	Solitary survivor, retired
Home ownership at peak Most satisfied with financial position and money saved Interested in travel, recreation, self-education Make gifts and contributions Not interested in new products Buy: Vacations, luxuries, home improvements.	Drastic cut in income Keep home Buy: Medical appliances, medical care, products which aid health, sleep, and digestion.	Income still good but likely to sell home.	Same medical and product needs as other retired group; drastic cut in income Special need for attention, affection, and security.

Source: William D. Wells and George Gubar, "Life Cycle Concept in Marketing Research," *Journal of Marketing Research*, Vol. 3 (November 1966), p. 362.

concerned with building up the proper inventory of goods in aggregating an appropriate and adequate bundle or package of symbols. These symbols relate to cars, homes, furniture, clothing, vacation and recreation items such as boats, vacation cabins, campers, and so on. The older family, especially after children are gone, may begin to look at travel, a trip abroad, trading up in assets or moving out of the "family home" into an apartment, and shifting resources from physical goods to more near-liquid assets in anticipation of retirement. Younger couples, in buying furniture, are likely to look for functional pieces, modestly priced and modern or contemporary in style. Older couples are more concerned with quality and fine construction and are more interested in Early American, or some other distinctive period style.[60]

Thus we must conclude with this generalization. The life-cycle concept is an important variable in consumer behavior and an exceedingly important concept in relationship to family considerations regarding consumer decisions. We have traced only sketchily the relationship between life cycle and family-oriented consumer behavior. However, Table 15-2 summarizes and captures a great part of this relationship. The future will probably find marketing researchers and others interested in consumer behavior and consumer decision processes using this important concept to an increasing degree.

In this chapter we have covered considerable territory. We have been basically concerned with the impact of interpersonal relationships within the context of family interaction, on consumer behavior, and we have explored the nature of family interaction and the changes in family role structure. Our concern has centered around the family as a basic behavioral and consumption unit. To augment our understanding of family influence on consumer decision processes, we have explored at some length two additional family-related phenomena, namely, life style and life cycle. In the concluding chapter of this section, our attention is turned to *the major socializing influence of man—culture*.

Questions for Study, Reflection, and Review

1 What constitutes a family and how is it differentiated from a household?

2 Describe the history of family development and the changes in family structure.

3 What are some of the factors responsible for generating change in the family as an institution?

4 Discuss the significance of the family as a socializing agent.

5 Describe the relationship between various family role structures and decision making.

6 What is the role of children in family decision-making?

---

[60] Social Research, Inc., "Furniture Buying and Life Stages," in *Understanding Consumer Behavior*, Martin M. Grossack, ed. (Boston: The Christopher Publishing House, 1964).

7 Discuss the concept of life style as a consumer behavior variable.

8 Compare social class and life style as meaningful indicators of consumer value orientation.

9 Briefly discuss the concept of geographic mobility and its implications for consumer behavior.

10 Describe the family life-cycle and its influence upon consumption patterns and consumer decision processes.

16

The Cultural-Social
Matrix of
Consumer Behavior

Introduction

We come now to the final chapter of Part IV, which has been concerned mainly with what are called *interpersonal variables of behavior*. These interpersonal variables might very well have been labeled the *cultural-social aspects of consumer behavior* because this is essentially the concern of these variables. Tradition and general usage dictate that we treat cultural implications separately from such other variables as socialization, group influences, family influences, life style, and life cycle. Yet the reader will soon recognize that it is culture that is really significant throughout most interpersonal and interactive situations. As a matter of fact, one's culture and the impact of culture are significantly important throughout the whole spectrum of human and consumer behavior. For example, culture, as will be shown later, dictates and not only influences consumer behavior in terms of what we have called interpersonal variables but influences as well such uniquely psychological and intrapersonal variables as cognitive organization and function, motivation, perception, learning, and attitudes. Furthermore, who would deny the impact of culture on such facilitating process variables as communication and information processing and the development and manifestation of personality. Culture is most significantly, then, a filter through which our behavior is largely influenced and determined. It is culture, to a great extent, that is responsible for our individual differences as well as for our many similarities. People who

454

are close knit, who interact frequently, who belong to similar groups, who share common motivations, who view and read similar communications are in effect sharing a common culture. The American child who is nurtured on television and socialized within the normal atomistic-nuclear family and who learns and plays in the average suburban elementary and secondary school acquires a far different set of images and symbols regarding goods and consumption than does, say, a black child reared and socialized in the ghetto or a Chinese child in a state nursery or a Jewish child in an Israeli kibbutz. That I write these words on paper, with pencil, in a room outfitted as a study, and use certain phrases and expressions to convey meaning is the result of my culture. That you read them in your home or classroom or library as printed words in a text, that you may be examined about their meaning and content, that we are able to share in this process while separated in some instances over great geographical distances—all this, too, is largely the result of our common culture. Thus, our understanding of symbolic interaction processes—the basic stuff of Chapters 13, 14, and 15—has emphasized that man collectively develops a complex and intricate system of symbols with which he labels the aspects of the universe to which he becomes sensitized. Further, we have learned that he then patterns his behavior according to the plans of action he has learned to associate with those labels.

Culture is the most integral aspect of all behavior. For example, throughout this work the emphasis has been largely on a cognitive theory of behavior, and the cognitive theory of behavior espoused in this effort is that behavior is a function of knowledge or, more correctly, cognitions—bits of knowledge, ideas, attitudes, values, opinions, or images. But from where do we acquire those cognitions? From many sources—from socializing, from group interaction, from introspection, *but* largely from our culture and the enculturation process. We are taught the ways, the norms, the customs, the values of our society. Our behavior is largely the manifestation of a system of values. But these values are the products of a given culture. Culture is group knowledge, and, as we have learned, the group indoctrinates its new members in the rules and norms and ways of the group. Our family behavior and interaction is principally devoted to enculturating family members. Our children are taught to mind Mommy and Daddy, to love their country, to respect God, to brush their teeth (preferably with Crest), to protect the environment (by not littering), to drink plenty of milk, to eat their vegetables, and to do and like whatever else the cultural norms, customs, and folkways dictate at a particular time. Culture is the principal socializing agent, and therefore people in groups are carriers of culture.

Our culture is interrelated with our personalities. In one sense culture is the expression of personality. In another sense, personality is the individual expression of culture. Broadly, culture provides the rules that define the roles that in turn create the relationships that constitute the group. Culture generates behavior that is a patterned whole. It is the result of learned behavior, and it consists of rules (norms) and values that are shared by members of a society. Surely, then, such an important concept deserves an equally important treatment. In this chapter we shall finish our treatment of consumer behavior variables by examining the cultural-social influence on consumer behavior. We shall explore the concept of culture and then treat all consumer behavior variables within the framework of the cultural-social matrix. Most importantly, we shall also explore the significance of cultural-social processes and the many sociopsychological ones already discussed. In addition, we shall attempt to describe the American core culture system, explore and treat some new directions in cultural trends and developments, and look briefly at some significant subculture and counterculture movements. Finally, an assessment of the cultural implications for marketing and consumer behavior will be undertaken.

The Many Aspects of Culture

From our introduction it ought to be clear that culture is not a simple concept. Nor is it always readily understood. Culture is a rather diffuse and sometimes ambiguous concept. To appreciate more fully the nature of culture and *how* and *why* culture affects consumer behavior, we must first understand several of the facets of culture. Probably we should not have to point out that the word *culture* has many meanings. We refer sometimes to some people as being cultured, the implication being that some other people are not. Playing the piano, reading *Faust*, and mastering the intricacies of chess do not make one a more cultured person than another. Culture does not apply only to those who earn $50,000 per year, vacation in Trinidad, and drive a Mercedes. Everyone is cultured in one sense of the word. Our culture consists of our nonbiological heritage. It is the body of customs, laws, norms, and folkways with which we are socialized and taught the ways of our society. Culture is ubiquitous and nearly all-pervasive. It affects nearly all dimensions of our lives—the way we sleep, eat, work, play, love, shop, and consume are all in some measure a function of culture.

CULTURE DEFINED

There are a great many definitions of *culture*. We will catalogue several of these definitions at this juncture. Our list, however, will not be exhaustive. Instead, we shall discuss several different definitions of culture merely to reflect their different orientation to the subject.

Probably one of the most widely quoted and acceptable of all definitions of culture is that of Linton. He defines culture as

the configuration of learned behavior and results of behavior whose component elements are shared and transmitted by the members of a particular society.[1]

[1] Ralph Linton, *The Cultural Background of Personality* (New York: Appleton-Century-Crofts, Inc., 1945), p. 32.

Linton's definition emphasizes several points. First, it suggests that culture is a dynamic rather than a static concept. Second, it posits that culture is not only the sum of accumulated traditions but, even more than that, that it is concerned with the transmission and communication of ideas, values, artifacts, and ways of doing things. Third and finally, the Linton definition underscores the organic nature of culture, its vibrancy and aliveness, its togetherness and mutually shared characteristics.

Kroeber and Parsons have defined culture as the

transmitted and created content and patterns of values, ideas, and other symbolic-meaningful systems as factors in the shaping of human behavior and the artifacts produced through behavior.[2]

Notice how this definition emphasizes the patterned or ordered system of symbols that become the objects and the orientation of action for members of a given society. Observe, too, that such a definition places, at least implicitly, a great deal of importance on both the internalized components of the personalities of individual actors and the institutionalized patterns of social systems.

Finally, we shall quote one more definition, primarily because it describes and is so well oriented to our special and specific purpose—consumer behavior analysis. Ullman defines culture as

a system of solutions to unlearned problems as well as learned problems and their solutions, all of which are acquired by members of a recognizable group and shared by them.[3]

From the standpoint of consumer behavior and its emphasis on problem solving and decision making, the last definition appears highly relevant. Such a definition suggests that culture is an accumulation of a given society's heuristically discovered solutions to problems—an acquired inventory of conventional wisdom and cognitions; hence traditions, attitudes, and images regarding proper responses to recurring individual and societal problems that are transmitted and incorporated into the response repertoires of individuals. Culture thus affects consumer behavior because culture influences and dictates, in many instances, what is proper and acceptable in terms of consumer behavior and the whole range of consumer decision-making processes. Finally then, in a pertinent but limited sense, we shall employ the term *culture* to mean essentially *learned behavioral dispositions passed from one generation to another.*

CHARACTERISTICS OF CULTURE

Perhaps now, before proceeding further, we ought to characterize culture in a little greater detail. Essentially, this detail grows out of the more acceptable definitions of culture, and such characterization tends

[2] A. L. Kroeber and Talcott Parsons, "The Concept of Culture and of Social System," *American Sociological Review,* Vol. 23 (October 1958), p. 583.

[3] Albert D. Ullman, *Sociocultural Foundations of Personality* (Boston: Houghton Mifflin Company, 1965), p. 181.

to describe and explain in greater depth the full range and significance of culture.

1. *Culture is a guide to action.* Culture, to a great extent, represents a set of programmed solutions to individual and societal problems. One's culture dictates that it is appropriate (only in some circles) to doff one's hat on meeting a lady, to shake hands upon being introduced (if one is male and is being introduced to another male), to say "thank you" when given a courtesy. Culture also dictates that one not eat with his fingers in a public restaurant, belch, or pick his nose.

2. *Culture includes standards or norms for judging behavior.* These programmed solutions that we have called culture often become standards or norms by which we judge and evaluate behavior.

3. *Culture is a set of learned responses.* We learn through enculturation and the many forms of socialization—church, school, family, and home—a whole repertoire of response patterns, and it is these response patterns basically that constitute the stuff of culture.

4. *Learned responses are value laden.* Culture teaches us what to extol and what to esteem. It inculcates to some extent a sense of the imperative *ought,* namely, that one ought to do so and so or like such and such and that such conformity will lead to the greater good of society. For example, "All ought to obey the law" and "We ought to buy and consume goods" are two nearly equally important imperative *ought's* in U.S. culture.

5. *Culture facilitates problem solving.* Culture is an entire mélange of problem-solving facilitators. What this means simply is that culture consists of a set of routinized instrumental behavioral responses. It enables or facilitates what amounts to the adapting, accommodating, coping process of the individual in relation to his demanding environment.

6. *Other characteristics.* Finally, culture is man-made. No other living creature is thought to have what we consider culture.

Thus, culture is learned and it is learned through interaction. Culture is the common property of the group and it is cumulative. We build upon our existing knowledge and we pass on our knowledge from age to age. This means, then, that culture is constantly changing—sometimes the change is slow and imperceptible; other times the culture changes rapidly and markedly. Culture, because it contains learned behavioral predispositions, affects our motivations and perceptions. Not unimportantly, culture often includes emotional or nonrational elements that must be reckoned with in accounting for behavior.[4]

CULTURAL CLASSIFICATION

There are many ways of classifying and analyzing the cultural elements of behavior. Linton has classified the culture of people in terms of three dimensions: (1) *material,* that is, the products of indus-

---

[4] For a more detailed list of cultural characteristics, see Glen M. Vernon, *Human Interaction: An Introduction to Society* (New York: The Ronald Press Company, 1965), especially Chapter 6, pp. 85–90.

try; (2) *kinetic,* that is, overt behavior; and (3) *psychological,* that is, the knowledge, attitudes, and values shared by the members of society.[5] It would go without saying that our interest as consumer behavioralists is centered more in the kinetic and psychological than in the material, which is more related to anthropology than to social psychology.

Our focus, it will be remembered, is from the standpoint of solutions or distinctive modal patterns of behavior and the underlying regulatory beliefs, norms, and premises of a given society. Another way of classifying culture is in terms of such dimensions as (1) the distributive, (2) the organizational, and (3) the normative.[6]

THE DISTRIBUTIVE. The distributive dimension of culture is largely predicated upon demographic characteristics. You will recall in Chapter 1 we characterized the American market in terms of income, age, education levels, occupation, and geographical location.

THE ORGANIZATIONAL. The organizational dimension looks at culture from the standpoint of participation patterns within the culture and of the structure, power, and influence of such social and cultural institutions as the family, the church, the school, and the business organization. Social class structure and the power structure of cities and communities are the concern of the organization dimension of culture.

THE NORMATIVE. The normative dimension relates to values and norms and is more concerned with political, religious, social, and economic values and philosophies and their impact on what might best be termed the psychological aspect of culture, that is, the knowledge, values, and attitudes that are espoused and shared by the members of a given society.

Throughout various sections of this treatment we have explored, in some detail each of these various dimensions of culture. However, in this current chapter our interest and concern rest primarily with the normative dimensions.

CULTURE IN TRANSITION

Culture is not static. It does change over time, and to the extent that it does change it usually means that the *knowledge* or cognitions on which behavior is predicated change. For example, culture is sometimes conceived of as transmitted knowledge.[7] But this statement raises

[5] Ralph Linton, *The Cultural Background of Personality* (New York: Appleton-Century-Crofts, 1945).

[6] This classification and approach was suggested in the work of Thomas S. Robertson, *Consumer Behavior* (Glenview, Ill.: Scott, Foresman and Company, 1970), pp. 99–102.

[7] This point of view is espoused by Everett K. Wilson in *Sociology: Rules, Roles and Relationships* (Homewood, Ill.: The Dorsey Press, 1966), see p. 51.

the question, "What is knowledge?" Knowledge is many things and we shall make no effort to define the concept fully, but among the many things that knowledge is, it is certainly a system of values, norms, customs, beliefs, attitudes, and images. Therefore, when culture changes or is in a state of transition, as all open cultures almost certainly are, then it is usually because values, norms, and so forth are in a state of change as well. Culture changes for many reasons, but the foremost of these is probably technology. Cultural change is almost always the product of the invasion of new ideas. These ideas emerge or are introduced as a result of voluntary or forced interaction, and the resulting effect is that the culture is touched by new concepts, new ideas, methodology or technology and that the underlying structure of values and norms upon which the culture rests are modified. When this happens the culture—that is, the system of solutions for solving and coping with society's problems—is changed and modified.

VALUES. We talked much earlier about values but we should perhaps underscore their significance again in terms of their importance to cultural considerations regarding consumer behavior. Value orientations underlie all forms of human behavior, and consumer behavior is no exception. Kluckhohn has stated, in a manner sympathetic to our own earlier contention, that values are individually or commonly shared conceptions of the desirable, that is, what I and/or others feel we justifiably want—what it is felt proper to want.[8] To this end values are aspects of personality based upon the way a person feels about something. Values are motivations in form to the extent that they dictate to us what we ought or ought not to do, hence the term *imperative ought* used earlier. However, values involve other things besides "ought to" or "correctness." As Pepper says, "In the broadest sense anything good or bad is a value."[9] Hence, "good" or "bad" becomes "desirable" or "undesirable," or even better in terms of language previously used, "approach evoking" or "avoidance evoking." Values have positive or negative tone or direction and in the absence of such a valence, there is indifference.

NORMS. Norms flow out of and originate in values but there is a difference between norms and values. Norms are generally accepted, sanctioned prescriptions for or prohibitions against others' behavior, beliefs, or feelings.[10] Values are held by individuals. Norms must be shared prescriptions and apply to others. Norms always include sanc-

[8] See Clyde Kluckhohn et al., "Values and Value Orientations in the Theory of Action," in *Toward a General Theory of Action*, Talcott Parsons and Edward A. Shils, eds. (Cambridge, Mass.: Harvard University Press, 1951), pp. 388–433.

[9] Stephen C. Pepper, *The Sources of Value* (Berkeley, Calif.: University of California Press, 1958), p. 87.

[10] Richard T. Morris, "A Typology of Norms," *American Sociological Review*, Vol. 21 (October 1956), pp. 610–613.

tions; values never do. Hence, norms refer to aspects of culture that can be conceptualized and transmitted from one person to another. Norms are rules (solutions) for guiding the conduct of individuals and society. But we can note with Spiro that norms do not direct our behavior unless we are aware of them and have developed feelings about them, that is, unless we have internalized them as values.[11]

Cultural norms are divided into two categories: *folkways and mores.*[12] Norms are folkways when the behavior they dictate, if violated, is not considered vital to the welfare of the group and when effective means for enforcing such behavior is not fully operational. Norms are mores when the behavior they dictate is vital to the welfare of the group and when effective means for assuring such behavior have been established. Many of our habits and customs are related to cultural folkways and mores.

CULTURE AND CONFLICTING VALUE SYSTEMS. If culture determines behavior through an underlying system of values and norms, we must certainly understand that most cultures are endowed with conflicting values and value systems. It would go without saying that in a culture as diverse in its origin and so complex and rapidly changing as the culture of the United States certain inconsistencies and antitheses would certainly appear. Some of these antithetical elements in the cultural values of the United States have been pointed out by Lynd.

> Individualism, "the survival of the fittest," is the law of nature and the secret of American greatness; and restrictions on individual freedom are unAmerican and kill initiative.
>
> BUT: No shrewd person tries to get ahead nowadays by just working hard, and nobody gets rich nowadays by pinching nickels.
>
> It is important to know the right people. If you want to make money, you have to look and act like money. Anyway, you only live once.
>
> Education is a fine thing.
>
> BUT: It is the practical man who gets things done.[13]

From conflicts in cultural values emerge *new* values. And these new values become the basic predicates upon which new and different cultural norms, customs, and folkways are established. Kotler has speculated about the nature of such a dialectical process by providing a list of American cultural values that he believes are in the process of adapting to new positions.[14] To the extent that they are emergent

[11] See Melford E. Spiro, "Culture and Personality: The Natural History of a False Dichotomy," *Psychiatry,* Vol. 14 (February 1951), pp. 190–192.

[12] This division was established almost seventy years ago by William Graham Sumner; see his *Folkways* (Boston: Ginn and Company, 1906).

[13] Robert Lynd, *Knowledge for What?* (Princeton, N.J.: Princeton University Press, 1939), p. 138.

[14] Philip Kotler, *Marketing Management* (Englewood Cliffs, N.J.: Prentice-Hall, Inc., 1967), pp. 37–38.

values and in a state of transition, it would follow logically that they are furthermore the source of some conflict and confusion in our cultural-behavioral framework. His list of changing cultural values is as follows:

1. Self-reliance .... government reliance.
2. "Hard work" as a
   goal in itself .... the "easy" life.
3. Religious convictions .... secular convictions.
4. Husband-dominated home .... wife-dominated home.
5. Parent-centered home .... child-centered home.
6. Respect for individual .... dislike of individual
   differences.
7. Postponed gratification .... immediate gratification.
8. Saving .... spending.
9. Sexual chastity .... sexual freedom.
10. Parental values .... peer group values.
11. Independence .... security.

As we shall learn in a subsequent section of this chapter, there is a great deal of change taking place within the total culture of the United States. However, the presence of *cultural assimilation* and *structural pluralism* in the United States has always complicated the understanding and analysis of U.S. culture. Cultural assimilation suggests that the major segments of United States society share a common core culture and its underlying basic value system. Structural pluralism, on the other hand, suggests that major groups or subcultures also retain a strong sense of group identity that means embracing some cultural values that are *counter* to the mainstream culture.

CULTURAL BORROWING. Cultural borrowing raises a very interesting point. Given the vast number of different subcultures and ethnic groups in the United States, there does exist a considerable amount of what might be called cultural borrowing. The average American diet today includes pizza, egg rolls, bagels, French pastry, German sausage, and cheeses and wines from around the world. We adorn ourselves and our homes with the trinkets and artifacts of many foreign lands.

Linton has dramatized this concept of cultural borrowing so very effectively that some of his comments warrant space in our treatment. His comments certainly elucidate the point about cultural diversity. The average American upon arising and eating

places upon his head a molded piece of felt invented by the nomads of Eastern Asia and if it looks like rain, puts on outer shoes of rubber, discovered by the ancient Mexicans, and takes an umbrella, invented in India. He then sprints for the train—the train not the sprinting being an English invention. At the station he pauses for a moment to buy a newspaper, paying for it with coins invented in ancient Lydia. Once on board he settles back to inhale the fumes of a cigarette invented in Mexico, or a cigar invented in Brazil. . . . As he scans the latest editorial pointing out the dire results to our institutions of accepting foreign ideas, he will not fail to thank a Hebrew God in an Indo-European language that he is one-hundred percent (decimal system invented by the Greeks) American (from Americus Vespucius, Italian geographer).[15]

CULTURAL BORROWING VERSUS CULTURAL UNIVERSALS. There is most decidedly a great deal of cultural borrowing within the United States among its many diverse subcultures and ethnic groups, and among the United States and the many other countries of the world. This cultural borrowing is enhanced and facilitated by mass communication, by governmental and social interaction, and by educational exchange programs. Some go so far as to argue that there is occurring a massive homogenization of world culture.[16] In many foreign lands ancient customs and traditions have disappeared under the onslaught of instant communication, rapid transportation, and mass production. Millions of words and pictures flash around the globe in minutes; American products find their way to the most distant corners of the earth.

To some extent, such a view is fostered by the notion that there exist *cultural universals*. Cultural universals are values and norms that appear to permeate all cultures. For example, it has been reported that all cultures react positively toward bright, light colors and negatively toward blacks and grays. In religious matters all cultures have terms equivalent to our heaven and hell, and heaven is perceived as a better place than hell. Most cultures, it has been found, agree that hate is a bad concept, yet some exception is found among the Greeks. War is universally disliked but apparently is tolerated in most cultures on justifiable grounds.[17] The existence of such universals reflects the fact that there are certain things a group must do if it is to maintain its existence as a group. These things are sometimes referred to as functional requisites. For a group to exist there usually must be interaction, and this interaction is often symbolic. There is usually the need for communication, for protection, defense, and perpetuation. Such functional requisites are expressed in such cultural rites as courtship, dancing, fighting, eating, procreating, feasting, rites of emergence and death, greeting, gift giving, and goods production and distribution.[18] *However, one is likely to make a tragic error of judgment if, on the*

---

[15] Ralph Linton, "One Hundred Percent American," *The American Mercury*, Vol. 40 (April 1939), p. 158.

[16] One authority holding this view is Dr. Charles E. Osgood. See "It's the Same the World Over," *Parade* (February 27, 1972), p. 22.

[17] Ibid.

[18] See George P. Murdock, "The Common Denominators of Culture," in *The Science of Man in the World Crisis*, Ralph Linton, ed. (New York: Columbia University Press, 1943).

basis of a few limited and so-called cultural universals, he assumes that all cultures are basically alike.

As more and more U.S. firms turn their attention to foreign markets and international operations and to fine-tuning their own domestic marketing strategies to nuances in subcultures, the necessity for understanding cross-cultural differences increases.[19]

Quite frequently, the major differences between domestic and foreign marketing or business boil down to the fundamental differences between the United States and the foreign businessman, or the United States businessman and the foreign consumer. The biggest error that U.S. marketers in foreign countries commit is to assume that only the place is different and that the customs, norms, and values of the people are the same all over. Dichter has put together an impressive list of cultural differences that should guide the American businessman in his conduct of affairs in foreign countries. Among these differences, he notes:

Frenchmen have an aversion to brushing their teeth.

Germans change shirts only about once a week.

French women are more concerned with quality than fashion.

Natives often prefer non-local products.

Over attention to the body in terms of cleanliness, scented soaps, perfumes, etc., is considered immoral in many Catholic countries abroad.

French women bathe with laundry soap instead of toilet soap.[20]

Such findings suggest that the cultural anthropologist can be of enormous help to businessmen and marketers in enabling them to understand better the buying behavior of consumers in a particular cultural environment.

The Cultural-Social Matrix of Behavior

Throughout this text the focus has been upon what has been called a holocentric orientation rather than a reductive-functional one. In effect, our concern repeatedly has been to point out the wholeness of consumer behavior rather than its separate parts. Consumers are seldom impelled or simply motivated to buy goods; consumers do not change their behavior simply because they have learned about a new product; nor do they shop at a particular store because that is where all the better people shop or because it is where their friends shop. Consumer behavior is seldom the single result of anything, whether it be attitudes, communication, personality, social class, or the impact of

---

[19] For an illustration of cross-cultural studies, see S. Watson Dunn, "The Case Study Approach in Cross Cultural Research," *Journal of Marketing Research*, Vol. 3 (February 1966), pp. 26–31.

[20] Ernest Dichter, "The World Customer," *Harvard Business Review*, Vol. 40 (July–August 1962), pp. 113–122.

culture. To reduce behavior to a single variable or two is the essence of *reductionism.* On the contrary, consumer behavior is the result of a host of complex interacting and interdependent variables. Some one of these variables may, at a given time, be more important than others and thus be more *central* to the analysis of that person's or group's behavior, but even so that variable, which may be accounting for, at most, 20 to 30 per cent of the variance in total behavior, is operating within the framework of a whole host of additional variables or factors. Such again is the essence of *holocentrism.*

A MATRIX OF CONSUMER BEHAVIOR

Figure 16-1 illustrates more graphically the ideas contained in the preceding paragraph. This figure, the "Cultural-Social Matrix of Behavior," is intended to illustrate more completely the interrelated nature of consumer behavior by underscoring its holocentric features. For example, the matrix is composed of rows and columns. You will observe that the columns consist essentially of cultural-social variables, labeled accordingly "Distributive," "Organizational," and "Normative"—the major classifications of cultural variables discussed earlier. The rows

Figure 16-1

Cultural-Social Matrix of Consumer Behavior

	Distributive				Organizational				Normative		
	AGE	INCOME	GEOGRAPHIC LOCATION	LIFE CYCLE	OCCUPATION	LIFE STYLE	SOCIAL CLASS	EDUCATION	VALUES	NORMS	CUSTOMS
Cognitions, Images, Attitudes											
Motivation											
Perception											
Learning											
Communication											
• Information Processing											
• Problem Solving											
• Decision Making											
Personality											
Socializing											

consist largely of sociopsychological variables, the ones that we have dealt with at such great length in Chapters 5 through 12. Such a matrix indicates at a glance that any specific act of consumer behavior is the result of a combination of factors. For example, if the researcher were concerned with the role of motivation in relationship to a particular purchase, he might well wish to move along the row labeled "Motivation" and examine this variable in terms of the cultural-social variables listed on the column headings. Motivation is thus likely to be affected by such factors as the age of the user-consumer, income, geographical location, occupation, life style, social class, and so forth. Conversely, in considering the cultural-social aspects of behavior or some dimension of it, say, "Social Class," the researcher or decision maker may wish to consider such factors as are listed as headings for the rows: "Attitudes," "Motivation," "Perception," "Learning," "Communication," and so on.

The cultural-social matrix of consumer behavior presented in Figure 16-1 does dramatize the holocentric nature of behavior and, in addition, such a matrix provides a convenient framework for directing one's attention to the necessity of considering all possible relevant factors when he is considering consumer behavior.

The Relationship Between Cultural-Social and Sociopsychological Processes

Our preceding discussion has related essentially to what has been thus far an unasked question or at least one that has only been implied: What is the relationship between the cultural-social processes discussed in Chapters 13 through 16 of this text and the sociopsychological processes discussed in Chapters 5 through 12?[21] There are several apparent answers to this important question.

First, the sociopsychological processes are often dependent on the occurrence of larger cultural-social events. Such sociopsychological activities do not occur unless some other larger event is in progress or has already occurred. For example, sexual mores that lead to the changes in fashion, such as the "nude look" that makes bareness the expression of our times, are the outcome of major cultural-social processes related to science and technology (contraceptives), which in turn lead to changing values regarding sexual freedom and liberation.[22] This view regarding the relationships between sociopsychological processes and cultural-social ones leads some to believe that social psychology has little to offer on larger questions. Attitude change, for example, is simply the inevitable result or by-product of the great, lum-

---

[21] For a comprehensive treatment of this question the reader might like to explore William W. Lambert and Wallace E. Lambert, *Social Psychology* (Englewood Cliffs, N.J.: Prentice-Hall, Inc., 1964), especially pp. 106–108.

[22] See "Modern Living," in *Time Magazine,* Vol. 99 (June 26, 1972), pp. 76–78.

bering cultural process. Attitudes are then simply a squeak made by the social machine.

Another approach to the question is to consider that massive cultural-social changes are the summation of sociopsychological events and that values or other cultural processes change because of changing attitudes and social perceptions of individuals and groups. Much consumer behavior, as well as sociopsychological inquiry in general, is predicated upon this set of beliefs, beliefs that economic development is a matter of changing people and changing directions, that politics is often the complex interaction of persons and attitudes, and that innovation and even revolution are new social perceptions or new attitudes that have emerged from a relatively small number of human activists on the normally passive social scene.

Finally, a third answer is suggested by our question, and that is that sociopsychological processes are causally important as events that tend to *mediate* or *integrate* the broad events and processes that occur in society and culture, and that this relationship and causality is two-directional, interactive, and therefore interdependent. Such a generalization does not state simply that there is always a relationship between sociopsychological processes and cultural-social ones, but it does recognize that sociopsychological processes are often related to, caused by, or captured by cultural-social phenomena.

Figure 16-2 provides a rather simple, anecdotal example of our final generalization.

Figure 16-2 suggests the kinds of interaction discussed earlier. Various levels of up-down or down-up combinations may be developed, and the results and hypotheses may actually be put to the test by a systematic collection of information. A kind of chicken-or-egg question surrounds such efforts at causal analyses. Nonetheless, we must attempt to trace the nature of such relationships. Furthermore, this interpretation, with all its circularity, may well symbolize the circularity of a good many of the causal sequences in the relations between sociopsychological processes and those of the broader culture and society. Our aim in studying consumer behavior, as well as in social psychology and all of the behavioral sciences, is to study the facts of social and economic life with systematic diligence and with the greatest possible rigor.

Figure 16-2
Cultural-Social and Social-Psychological Processes

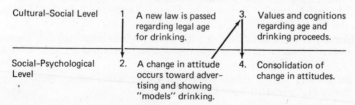

| Cultural–Social Level | 1 | A new law is passed regarding legal age for drinking. | 3. | Values and cognitions regarding age and drinking proceeds. |

| Social-Psychological Level | 2. | A change in attitude occurs toward advertising and showing "models" drinking. | 4. | Consolidation of change in attitudes. |

CULTURAL RELEVANCE

For every consumer problem, for every decision process, for each and every consumer or market segment, it *may not* be necessary to consider cultural-social phenomena. Such cultural-social variables, in some instances, may simply not be relevant.[23] Yet marketers should not be blinded by their ignorance regarding cultural considerations. It has been pointed out that cultural anthropology can contribute three important dimensions to market planning and consumer behavioral analysis:

1. Specific knowledge.
2. Awareness of themes of a culture.
3. Sensitivity to taboos.[24]

However, it has also been suggested that "cultural values typically come in dead last in the parade of exhortations about economic variables, social class, buyer psyches, and so on. This attitude probably stems from a common misconception regarding the relevance of culture to marketing."[25] The most appropriate admonishment to marketers would, therefore, appear to be that they "should endeavor to develop the capacity to understand organized cultural systems which are fundamental components of a holistic behavioral approach to marketing."[26]

CULTURE AND PREDICTION OF CONSUMER BEHAVIOR

One final comment or two would appear to be warranted at this juncture. First of all, the principal claim that can be made for the culture concept as an aid to analysis in consumer behavior is that it helps us enormously toward predicting that behavior. One of the factors limiting the success of such predictions thus far has been the naïve and intellectually gross assumption of a minutely homogeneous "human nature." In the framework of this assumption all human behavior proceeds from the same assumption: all human beings are motivated by the same needs and goals. Those who have the cultural point of view are more likely to look beneath the surface and bring the culturally determined premises to bear upon their analysis.[27] Thus knowledge of a culture makes it possible to predict a good many of the actions

[23] See Maneck S. Wadia, "The Concept of Culture," *Journal of Retailing*, Vol. 41 (Spring 1965), pp. 21–29, 55.

[24] Charles Winick, "Anthropology's Contributions to Marketing," *Journal of Marketing*, Vol. 25 (July 1961), p. 53.

[25] Montrose Sommers and Jerome Kernan, "Why Products Flourish Here, Fizzle There," *Columbia Journal of World Business*, Vol. 2 (March–April 1967), pp. 89–97, at p. 89.

[26] J. Allison Barnhill, "Marketing and Cultural Anthropology: A Conceptual Relationship," *University of Washington Business Review*, Vol. 27 (August 1967), pp. 73–84, at p. 74.

[27] See an elaboration of these points in Clyde Kluckhohn, *Mirror for Man* (New York: McGraw-Hill Book Company, 1949).

of the persons who share that culture. Because behavior is somewhat orderly, one familiar with the culture of a group can, to a certain extent, predict its future behavior. The same is true at the personality level. If one knows the culture of the group or of the individual (personality), he can anticipate both the behavior of others and their anticipation of his own behavior. Thus we attempt to study and understand the culture of a group in order that we can better understand its behavior. Understanding, it is hoped, will lead to an increased capacity for prediction. As consumer behavior analysts, we observe and describe consumer behavior, but our next job as scientists is to attempt to explain it. Our consuming interest is always with us: Why do the members of a given culture, subculture, or marketing segment behave in uniform and predictable ways?[28]

One cannot predict the future consumer behavior of an individual or a group with much success by studying only its biological or psychological inheritance. Consumer behavior and other forms of social behavior can, however, be better understood if one directs his attention to the culture of the group. Familiarity with the American culture, as we shall subsequently see, permits one to predict many things about the purchase and consumption behavior of individuals as well as particular market segments or subcultures.

American Core Culture Features

Earlier it was stated that U.S. culture or society can best be characterized as involving *cultural assimilation* and *structural pluralism*. *Cultural assimilation* suggests that there exists a large bundle of basic values and beliefs upon which a kind of middle-majority or centrist culture rests. Conversely, *structural pluralism* suggests that there are factions or subcultures, ethnic and minority groups, that embrace values and beliefs that are deviant from those of the middle-majority core culture. Hence, the term *counterculture* is popularly used today to describe or label the values, beliefs, and behavior of these groups.

We often generalize about American culture or the American society as if it were a cohesive, integrated, and homogeneous unit. In actuality, of course, it is not. When we are talking about American culture, we are talking about a particular group of people. When we talk about American culture, we are talking about the accumulated solutions, the plans of action, and the institutionalized customs and means of coping with existence used by this group. Of course, we are also talking about the underlying scheme and hierarchy of values upon

[28] The phrase "uniform and predictable" should not be interpreted as meaning "homogeneous." It means instead that given stimulus Y, the majority of the members of any subculture or market segment X will respond in a similar fashion Z, in which Z is taken to be a range of responses that could be plotted along a J curve. See Floyd Allport, "The J-Curve Hypothesis of Conforming Behavior," *Journal of Social Psychology*, Vol. 5 (1934), pp. 141–183.

which these solutions and plans of action are based. The concept of *society* is used in relating a body of solutions or plans of action to a particular group of people. Interaction involves members of a society's mutually influencing each other, partly on the basis of the value orientations they share, and partly on the basis of their own individual perceptions of the sequence of behavior in which they are involved.

In order to understand the core culture of American society we must first understand and come to appreciate the values upon which this core culture rests. But what are the essential features of the American core culture? Lipset isolated six categories to help identify the relevant values. To this researcher, core culture patterns can be distinguished by the degree to which people (1) are either egalitarian or elitist; (2) are prone to lay stress on accomplishment or on inherited attributes; (3) expect material or nonmaterial rewards; (4) evaluate individuals or products in terms of objective norms or subjective standards; (5) focus upon the distinctiveness of the parts (intensiveness) rather than the general characteristics of the whole (extensiveness); and (6) are oriented toward personal rather than group gain.[29] Without undue elaboration, suffice it to say that in the core culture, middle-majority Americans for the most part share the attributes described by the first term of the paired groups listed. Naturally, there is some diversity in terms of the extent to which values are shared by any group. To this extent the cohesiveness and degree of homogeneity of the group will vary. Yet despite the gaps and gulfs there are prevailing themes, motifs, or underlying value orientations that thread their way through the core of a culture. The underlying assumption is that the ideas of every epoch in history are related, usually with one dominant concept setting the key tone for the others.[30] In *Patterns of Culture,* Benedict tried to isolate such basic cultural configurations, summarizing them in such words as *Dionysian* (for the Kwakiutl) and *Appollonian* (for the Pueblo Indians).[31] Many writers have rather aptly characterized, from time to time, the American core culture. Gorer has interpreted the American core character in terms of rebellion against the European father image, and he contends that Americans, for this reason, extol egalitarianism and abhor authority.[32] Riesman looked to uncover the value design of Americans in *The Lonely Crowd.*[33] And many others, too numerous to mention, have attempted to discover

[29] See Seymour M. Lipset, "A Changing American Character," in *Culture and Social Character,* Seymour M. Lipset and Leo Lowenthal, eds. (New York: Doubleday & Company, Inc., 1971), pp. 136–171.

[30] J. B. Bury, *The Idea of Progress* (New York: Dover Publications, Inc., 1955).

[31] Ruth Benedict, *Patterns of Culture* (New York: New American Library, Mentor Books, 1953); first published in 1934.

[32] Geoffrey Gorer, *The American People* (New York: W. W. Norton & Company, Inc., 1964).

[33] David Riesman, Nathan Glaser, and Revel Denny, *The Lonely Crowd* (New Haven, Conn.: Yale University Press, 1950).

the cultural mainspring that tends, in their minds, to make middle-majority America tick.

There are unquestionably a number of core culture values that collectively tend to characterize and condition the behavior of middle-majority Americans. These values affect all Americans of all regions, national origins, races, classes, and both sexes. However, the extent to which they influence behavior or the extent to which middle-majority core culture society is a significant reference group for other subcultures will vary. However, the core culture characteristics that are about to be discussed are drawn primarily from classes of the middle levels of income and status. It is from this sector of the population that most change agents and the most potent value orientations are drawn. To the extent that these values reflect middle-majority core culture, it should be recognized also that they represent the values of the mass consumer. The center is where the mass consumer, or Mr. Middle Majority, resides. The great majority of American consumers are un-young, unpoor, and unblack. They are middle-aged, middle class, and middle-minded.

By no means definitive, the following attributes, attitudes, and values have, however, been deemed an integral part of the American core culture value orientation.[34]

TWOFOLD JUDGMENTS. Twofold judgments are the rule in American life: moral-immoral, legal-illegal, right-wrong, success-failure, clean-dirty, practical-impractical. The existence of such a method of dividing human activities into opposites is largely attributed to the necessity for Americans to compromise to solve problems. It also facilitates behavior in terms of an approach-avoidance kind of reaction to all situations, persons, or products. However, it means too that Americans too often behave in terms of their emotional reaction to things—a condition that leads to a kind of intellectual primitivism that requires no more intelligence than that possessed by a dog. A dog can easily say, "I like it," or "I don't like it."

WORK AND PLAY. To most Americans, the Puritan or Protestant ethic dictates that work is what one should and must do regularly, grimly, and purposefully. Man is judged by his work and it is what he must do to deserve his leisure and play. Work is serious adult business that enables one to get ahead and make a contribution. Work is viewed as a means of attaining whatever one desires—and it is better (a cultural value) if one has a great achievement motivation. Play is different. It is fun, an outlet from work, without serious purpose except to make us more efficient (happier, more relaxed, and longer-lasting)

[34] This list is, of course, not intended to be exhaustive, but it does focus upon the main core culture values of middle-majority Americans. It is adapted in part from Conrad M. Arensberg and Arthur H. Nichoff, *Introducing Social Change: A Manual for Americans Overseas* (Chicago: Aldine Publishing Company, 1964), pp. 153–183.

working machines. Play is related to our leisure, but the average American attitude toward leisure is that it ought to be active leisure. An idle mind is still the devil's workshop, and although Americans spend about one out of six dollars of disposable income for leisure activities, such leisure dollars are spent to buy goods to help us "fill" our leisure time in an active, participatory way.

EFFORT AND OPTIMISM. Americans are usually optimistic about the future and they are optimistic because they are convinced that through good old "Yankee ingenuity" all problems can be solved. Americans are doers and believe that when confronted with a problem one should do something, even if it is wrong. When there is an obstacle one should do something about it. Effort pays off with success. This thinking is based upon the value orientation that the universe is mechanistic, man is its master, and man is perfectible.[35] American core culture value also extols the future. Tomorrow things will be better. Tomorrow I will have more. Tomorrow I will be smarter, better looking, more desirable. Such a value orientation generates a constantly rising level of expectations regarding the future.

MAN AND NATURE. American core culture has traditionally extolled the virtues of man over nature. Nature is man's garden and his role is to till and harvest—maybe even to plunder and exploit. Raw materials in nature are there to be extracted and turned into goods. And accordingly, such extraction and plundering have gone largely unchecked. Nature should not interfere with man's progress and his material well-being. Thus, American core culture values suggest a conquering attitude toward nature. Rivers are to be dammed, forests cut and harvested, wild life decimated, and green spaces paved over with concrete —why? Because this is progress and progress is stimulated by change. Progress is usually related to growth, and growth means bigger, and bigger is automatically equated with better.

RELIGIOUS MORALITY. All things are touched with the religious attributes of being good or bad. This is part of the core culture American's tendency to indulge himself in either/or decisions. Things are either good or bad, moral or immoral. Work, as depicted in the Puritan ethic, is "good," it is virtuous, and a good worker is rewarded by being successful—which means he may come to own a large inventory of goods as symbols of his virtue and dutifulness to God. Men are judged as "good" if they work hard and are good "providers," that is, if they generate the appropriate symbol system for their families. Goods are judged, too, in terms of their religious and moral values. Whether discussing the conduct of foreign affairs, bringing up children, or any other action, it is generally agreed that core culture Americans tend to

[35] Cora Dubois, "The Dominant Value Profile in American Culture," *American Anthropologist,* Vol. 57, No. 6 (1955), pp. 1233–1234.

moralize. Our tendency to moralize leads to a large amount of *ethnocentrism;* that is, no god is as virtuous as our god, no religion as pious as our own, no government as democratic, no economic or political system as capable of generating distributive justice. In a smaller sense, Americans imbued with core culture value orientations become unduly myopic in the sense that what is theirs is almost invariably perceived as better, in a moral sense as well as all others, than what is yours. Religious morality dictates appropriate standards for purchase and consumption in such matters as food, clothing, housing, entertainment, and other services.

EQUALITY AND HUMANITARIANISM. Americans make a cult of the "average man." Inequality in achievement, merit, and worth is wrong, bad, or unfair, and the conventional folk value is to help the underdog. The average American is shocked and repelled by any ostentatious display of wealth or circumstances and many Americans will push to remedy such situations. Yet in a list of core culture values, hypocrisy should perhaps be included because most Americans are a bit two-faced when it comes to racial equality. Many approach the question of racial differences from a castelike standpoint—blacks and whites ought to be separate but equal. However, this is the basic exception to the core culture American's attitudes regarding equality and humanitarianism. The additional exception is one related to the sexes. More recently, however, the American's obsession with egalitarianism has moved in the direction of "women's liberation," and more women are now being considered for positions and roles from which they have historically been barred. The American concern with equality in human relations has generated a desire for casual and informal living—an unpretentious social style. Manners are simple and direct and the behavior of one person to another, regardless of status, rank, or role, is usually outwardly unpatronizing. Our concern for equality is humanitarian in that core culture Americans normally extol the virtues of equal opportunity. In the race of life all should start from the same starting line, but any contrived efforts to assure that all finish at the same point would violate the cultural norm of fair competition and individuality. American humanitarianism is often manifested in the form of outright generosity. Americans are essentially great unselfish givers and respond liberally to calls for help.

MATERIALISM. Finally, the great, overwhelming value that lies at the very heart of the American core culture value system is materialism. Middle majority Americans want "more." Anyone who would understand our culture must of necessity understand the role and the value that is placed upon goods and consumption. Americans have assigned a high priority, almost a "right," to material well-being and comfort. This material well-being and comfort is often interpreted by some Americans as cleanliness—which as we all know is next to godliness. We wash more, use more toothpaste, mouthwash, deodorant, sprays, powder, soap, and detergent per capita than any other country in the world.

In the United States achievement and success are primarily measured in terms of material goods, both because they are abundant and because they are indicative of how much money an individual earns. The average American buys mountains of prestige articles that have high visibility: expensive clothing and furniture, fine cars, fancy houses and assorted paraphernalia; power mowers, television sets, stereo sets, dishwashers, disposal units, and now automatic garbage compactors that help to rid the household of the "throwaway items" so prevalent in our society. The middle majority American has discovered in himself a great talent for consuming, a talent that would justify the sublimation of his personality into one overriding need—the need for self-gratification. Consuming more and more has become an end in itself.

THE OTHER-DIRECTED

The previous listing may constitute an incomplete categorization of American core culture values. Not all Americans march to the same drumbeat. There are large numbers of people characterized as belonging to the youth culture, the minority groups, the third-world peoples, and other counterculture groups and subcultures that do not embrace the total complex of American core culture values. As a matter of fact, these groups largely stand aside, alienated from core culture values and therefore rejecting middle-majority American behavior.[36] What is more, there are forces that are constantly at work that tend to change core culture values and, hence, the attitudes and behavior of middle-majority Americans. One writer has attributed the changes that are taking place in American core culture values to the rapidly accelerated rate of change in our technological society and has characterized the condition as future shock.[37] Future shock is the result of living in an affluent society characterized by overchoice, overstimulation, technophobia, and modularism. Perhaps overchoice is the most relevant of these conditions from our point of view. Overchoice is defined as the point at which the advantages of diversity are canceled by the complexity of the buyer's decision-making process. In a condition of overchoice, all decisions become harder to make. With the increased number of products available, a decision concerning only one aspect of the product requires still more data. The increased pull of life, even in more trivial matters, necessitates more information. Yet it is time- and energy-consuming to seek and process information. Rather than seek one's own values and base one's behavior and attitudes on a dis-

[36] The word *alienated* was chosen most deliberately to label the variance between core culture and counterculture values and behavior. It is a word frequently chosen by counterculture people to describe their own condition. See, for example, Steven Kelman, *Push Comes to Shove* (Boston: Houghton Mifflin Company, 1970), especially Chapter 3, "The Alienated," pp. 77–101.

[37] Alvin Toffler, *Future Shock* (New York: Random House, Inc., 1970).

covered value system, it is easier to join a subculture. Subcultures offer respite from overchoice. They offer a way of organizing all products, ideas, and values—not a single commodity but a whole style, a set of guidelines that help the individual reduce the increasing complexity of choice to a more manageable size. Thus by making a single decision, that is to join or identify with a particular subculture, the individual is actually making many decisions that become routinized or programmed by the one choice. Thus the tendency for an increasing number of subcultures to emerge in the United States is creating centrifugal forces that are pulling American institutions apart, causing a rejection of American core culture values and throwing the pieces outward from the center.[38] America may be losing its stable middle majority with its authority to dictate the cultural norms that underlie behavior.[39]

Another writer, Reich, contends that America is undergoing a revolution in terms of its cultural values, caused by the new generation and based, of course, upon a new set of value orientations. The new generation is composed mostly of youths but includes minorities and some radicals and even "reformed" core culture Americans. His contention is that their values constitute a consistent philosophy that is both necessary and inevitable and that in time this philosophy will not only prevail in the youth culture but will engulf all people in America.[40] Reich has developed what amounts, in effect, to a cognitive theory of behavior. He suggests that a person's basic values or beliefs constitute his "consciousness" or awareness. Observe that *cognizant* has a similar meaning, "to be aware." Reich suggests that our awareness or consciousness, which is predicated upon an underlying scheme of values, makes up our entire perception of reality and that a given consciousness level creates a set of boundary conditions that affect or determine our entire range of behavior. He argues further that we have moved and/or are moving through some different levels of "consciousness" and that it is these conflicting levels of consciousness that are causing the major cultural upheavals within the United States. Our first level of national consciousness was what Reich calls *Consciousness I*. Consciousness I is the traditional outlook of the American farmer, small businessman, and worker who are striving to get ahead. In Consciousness I, competition and rugged individualism are extolled. Competition is the law of man and nature; life is a harsh pursuit of individual self-interest. The American imperative under Consciousness I is to work hard and acquire and enjoy material success, which is determined by character, morality, hard work, and denial. Consciousness I is predi-

[38] For an extended view, see Yōnosuki Nagai, "The United States Is Disintegrating," an article written in the Japanese language that appeared in the September 1970 issue of *Chuo Koron*.

[39] This contention is explored more fully by Richard M. Scammon and Ben J. Wattenberg, *The Real Majority* (New York: Coward-McCann, Inc., 1970), especially pp. 72–85.

[40] Charles A. Reich, *The Greening of America* (New York: Random House, Inc., 1970).

cated upon the notion of scarcity. So in order to survive, let alone prosper, you must get more than somebody else because there cannot be abundance for all. The religion of Consciousness I was and is the Puritan ethic. Consciousness I, you will observe further, is strikingly possessed of many of the American core culture values discussed earlier.

CONSCIOUSNESS II. Consciousness II relates to another level of awareness and to this end it locks one into a system of values and attitudes that colors perception and ultimately largely determines behavior. Consciousness II is in many ways tied to the bundle of core culture values discussed previously. The central ideology of Consciousness II is technology—the combination of man and environment by technique. To this end, science, technology, organization, and planning receive prime priority in the overall scheme of values. The major theme of Consciousness II behavior is that society will function best if it is planned, organized, rationalized, and administered. Consciousness II bred the era of the organization man—the man who plans, organizes, motivates, and controls everything. Consciousness II mentality runs to a slavish belief in the evaluation of ability and accomplishment to the end that the race of success is always won by the able, the competent, and the credentialed. Merit and success are demonstrated by one's rank in the organization or by the degrees one has earned. Consciousness II thinking extols an elitist society. Furthermore, Consciousness II is a symbol-oriented society wherein one must have the proper inventory of symbol systems—houses, cars, vacation cottages, boats, clothes, and miscellaneous paraphernalia.

CONSCIOUSNESS III. Finally, we come to what Reich calls *Consciousness III*, a level of awareness and a set of values, cognitions, attitudes, and perceptions that are essentially those of the new generation. The essence of Consciousness III is liberation or freedom and lack of cultural constraint—freedom to search, to explore, and to redefine one's essence, or what one is, in terms of one's existence. It is the freedom or awareness that comes from the rejection, rather than the automatic acceptance, of the imperatives of society and the false consciousness that society imposes. Consciousness III awareness contends that the major activities of the individual must directly satisfy his own creative and emotional impulses—must always be more than means to an end.[41] Those cultures that provide for this consideration possess genuine culture; but those cultures in which the individual does not satisfy his creative and emotional impulses are spurious. The U.S. culture, especially in terms of Consciousness I and Consciousness II, is spurious, at least from the standpoint of Reich, because it sacrifices the individual's emotional needs to the technological machine

---

[41] This point is made most dramatically by Edward Sapir, "Culture, Genuine and Spurious," *American Journal of Sociology*, Vol. 29 (1924), pp. 401–429.

and/or to the organization, or the system of groping and getting that is materialism. Consciousness III is largely a rejection of Consciousness I and Consciousness II value orientations. The values of Consciousness III are largely emergent. First of all, it rejects the notion that all change is progress and that all progress is technological. Second, it rejects much of the philosophy of materialism, believing instead that goods are important as means, but not as ends in themselves. It rejects the notion of subjugation of self to the organization or system. Life is viewed as an excursion with many options, each or many of which are to be explored or tried on, so to speak, in the interest of the fuller development of oneself and one's potentialities. In short, Consciousness III is a rejection of the neon colors and the plastic artificial look of the affluent society—it is the rejection of middle-majority core culture values and the set of symbols that accompany it.

SUBCULTURES AS COUNTERCULTURES

Consciousness III as the awareness level that affects behavior is largely the property and philosophy of a relatively few subcultures today. But, as Reich contends, it may lead to "the greening of america," a complete reevaluation and wholesale overhaul of America's value system. If it does and to the extent that it does, it will have a profound impact upon all of our economic, social, political, and marketing institutions. Even if Consciousness III thinking never transcends the youth culture of the new generation, Consciousness III people are already of such significant numbers that they constitute a meaningful and viable market segment that needs understanding and analysis. There is invariably some transference of cultural values and behavior among the various subcultures of a total society. *Subculture* means the manner of behaving peculiar to a group that is part of some larger group.[42] In terms of strategy design and the development of marketing programs, a knowledge and understanding of culture and subculture configurations is a *sine qua non*. Subcultures, representing definable target groups for specific products and logical units for the segmenting of larger markets, are the relevant units of analysis for market research.[43] The possibility of increasing the firm's effectiveness by product differentiation and/or market segmentation is being explored increasingly by business organizations. To this end, they have to understand those differences in value orientations, nationality, race, age, and other factors that tend to separate a total society into a series of smaller subcultures. We have looked in terms of other concepts—for example, family and life style—at some elements of youth culture behavior; and we have discussed youth culture values and attitudes to some extent in Chapters 2 and 3. Therefore, we shall not dwell upon this topic long.

[42] Bernard Berelson and Gary Steiner, *Human Behavior: An Inventory of Scientific Findings* (New York: Harcourt Brace Jovanovich, Inc., 1964), p. 645.

[43] Gerald Zaltman, *Marketing: Contributions from the Behavioral Sciences* (New York: Harcourt Brace Jovanovich, Inc., 1965), p. 8.

But we will in the next several pages explore briefly a couple of the more relevant subcultures, primarily because their value systems are largely or to some significant degree at variance with or counter to the American core culture value system.

YOUTH CULTURE. One writer has commented most aptly regarding youth culture values. He states:

> The young often talk as though they have given up all achievement-oriented goals and all money produced objects for the realization of an inner life and a real concern with sensual immediacies.[44]

In actuality, of course, they have not. Many of the basic values of the youth culture are not totally out of kilter with American core culture values. Youth, by and large, still appreciate the value of goods. They have not nor are they likely to forego the consumption of goods for a life of simplicity and austerity. They recognize the inherent as well as the apparent convenience of things. Although they might become obsessed with a back-to-nature urge, by doing so they swell the demand for hiking shoes, rucksacks, pack frames, and assorted camping equipment. To the end that they are concerned with the environment, they may limit their use of the automobile, but they substitute instead a demand for ten-speed racing and touring bicycles that sell for well over one hundred dollars—to the point where there is a national shortage of such equipment in retail stores. The youth culture life-style is packed with an elaborate assortment of goods and services. The more apparent fact is that the methods of expression and the new living arrangements of the young are different. They seek a new bundle of symbol systems. These developments and tendencies have to be monitored in terms of their own significance as well as in terms of their cross-cultural significance to other subcultures, core cultures, or market segments. Contrary in many respects to Charles Reich's assertions, the young do not represent the coming of age. The impact of youth culture values will continue throughout the decade of the 1970s. Among the many developments that will warrant careful auditing by business decision-makers are the following:

1. *Resistance to the rationality of restraint now for later gratification and emphasis on expressivity.* Youth manifests a kind of "now" logic. Their dictum is often "do it now," or "dare to struggle," "dare to win," "indulge today." In many ways youth culture is both epicurean and hedonistic. They often act impulsively, if not precipitously. They forego normal routine and ritual. One eats when hungry, buys an item that satisfies sensual needs at the time they are manifested. Youth culture is in many ways based upon the value of self-indulgence and self-gratification.

[44] William Lazer, John E. Smallwood, et al., "Consumer Environments and Life Styles of the Seventies," *MSU Business Topics,* Vol. 20, No. 2 (Spring 1972), pp. 5–17, at p. 6.

2. *Resentment of achievement drives and symbols.* Youth culture demonstrates a great amount of inverse snobbishness. In the language of Mies van der Rohe, from the standpoint of youth "Less is more." The young reject many of the normal routes to achievement, the long, slow, slavish addiction to discipline and conformity. They reject many establishment values or the values of the organization. Yet, as mentioned earlier, they are rediscovering "goods" and "achievement," and they are reinterpreting and redefining them in terms of their own values and life style. They act as if they are underconsuming by wearing old clothes, living in run down "pads," and driving reconverted van-type automobiles, but in actuality they spend large sums for hi-fi component equipment, have gargantuan record collections, and spend inordinate sums for travel or rock concerts.

3. *Reduction of object accumulation.* Youth culture consumers are rather utilitarian in their approach to accumulating goods. They realize rather well that "What a man owns, owns him." Consequently, youth culture consumers are not very interested in accumulating large, conspicuous assortments or inventories of goods. They truly believe that people should not be burdened or bound by possessions.

4. *Counterculture opinion leaders.* Perhaps the most important fact about the youth culture is that their standards of taste, values, attitudes, and behavior are inoculating the major core culture. And their tastes, values, and attitudes must be reckoned with. It is to a great extent the youth culture, plus blacks and radical groups in other minorities, who are most concerned with such movements as consumerism, the eradication of racial inequality, and the recognition of their social responsibilities by business organizations. To this end, then, youth culture must be monitored in terms of its impact upon the larger cultural fabric of our society.[45]

BLACK CULTURE. To the extent that the culture of black society suffers from the culture of white society or from the centrist tendencies of America's core culture, blacks are likely to manifest differences in taste, motivations, perceptions, and attitudes regarding goods and consumption patterns. In many ways our thesis is that differences in cultural norms and values among different subcultures lead to differences in tastes and preferences for goods. To some extent this is a valid generalization. However, the problem in relation to black culture is somewhat different. Blacks, by virtue of their physical characteristics, are easily identifiable and thus separable from the mainstream core culture, which is essentially WASP (White, Anglo-Saxon, Protestant). The majority of blacks manifest easily recognizable differences, such as language (dialect) and primary residence (ghetto). Yet the black

[45] Ibid., p. 7.

is wired into many of the same socializing networks of communication as his white core culture counterpart, that is, radio, television, movies, magazines, and newspapers.[46] As a result, blacks are committed to many of the core culture values of middle-majority America but at the same time are denied the opportunity to secure the goods and the package of symbols extolled by the core culture because of social, political, and economic discrimination.

Thus the basic dilemma of blacks, according to Bauer, Cunningham, and Wortzel, is whether to accept middle-class values and hence to strive for the goods that largely confer middle-class status or to give up and live without either goods or status.[47] Such a dilemma has spawned several reactions: (1) a posture of waiting and patience, (2) the mildly aggressive behavior—largely nonviolent but bordering on civil disobedience—that implicitly says, "We want in," "We want more jobs, better education, more opportunity, and more goods," and (3) the posture of black radicals and militants, which in effect says, "Take your system and its values and cram it! We'll create an alternative system that will effect a better income distribution for black people."

There are some differences in the consumption-purchase patterns of blacks and whites. However, many of these differences result from a combination of societal restraints as well as cultural traditions. For example, blacks tend to underspend in relation to whites of equal income in four major areas: (1) housing, (2) automobile transportation, (3) food, and (4) medical care. The reasons for this discrepancy again are more related to social and economic discrimination than to cultural tradition.[48]

On the other hand, the same societal and cultural forces mainly lead blacks to spend proportionately more than their white income counterparts on (1) clothing, (2) furniture, and (3) alcoholic beverages.[49]

Blacks usually impute a greater symbolic significance to some goods than do whites. For example, blacks are exceedingly quality conscious and manifest a high preference for quality in most goods. Blacks, both men and women, are highly fashion conscious and tend to display considerable anxiety in their purchase behavior. The explanation is probably related to the fact that goods are perceived by them as ego extending and ego enhancing, and in their urge to seek identity and create a more positive sense of self, they want to be very sure that they are making the right choice. The simple psychological answer is that a higher degree of perceived risk surrounds blacks' consumer decision

---

[46] Harold H. Kassarjian, "The Negro and American Advertising, 1946–1965," *Journal of Marketing Research,* Vol. 6 (February 1969), pp. 29–39.

[47] Raymond A. Bauer, Scott Cunningham, and Laurence H. Wortzel, "The Marketing Dilemma of Negros," *Journal of Marketing,* Vol. 29 (July 1965), pp. 1–6.

[48] Ibid.

[49] Ibid.

processes. One study in relation to the question of insistence on quality showed that blacks tended to buy higher-priced automobiles, higher-priced models regardless of make, and automobiles with more cylinders than white families with comparable incomes.[50]

Value orientations are also likely to lead to differences in attitudes, perceptions, and motivations. Bullock has shown how motivations and other psychological phenomena are affected by different situations. He states that:

> Although human needs are basically the same for all people everywhere, these drives tend to become plated with the compulsions, checks, and guidance systems of different cultures. It is this cultural overlay that forms the foundation for all motivational differences between groups.[51]

Bullock's research and findings concerning black purchase and consumption behavior bear stating. They tend to support several of our own generalizations. Bullock has demonstrated that:

1. Many Blacks are striving for group identification with American society as a whole.
2. The Black has a conflicting self-image, in which he is forced to love and hate himself simultaneously.
3. Blacks wish to be individually distinct in their own right.
4. Blacks are subject to insecurity, masculine-feminine role confusion, and economic anxieties.[52]

OTHER SUBCULTURES. There are many other subcultures worthy of an exploration that space prohibits at this juncture. There are age subcultures; ethnic subcultures such as those of the Chicanos and the Native Americans, whose values and attitudes do differ somewhat from the middle majority American core culture; and ecological or geographical subcultures based upon differences in life style because of different places of residence, that is, the North versus the South or the East versus the West. There are subcultures based upon occupation, income, and other factors. Each of these categories within each of these subculture classifications offers an important market opportunity and therefore, potentially at least, holds out the promise of becoming an important market segment or target of special market programs in terms of either the firm's goods or service mix, its communication mix, or its distribution mix. This is to say that these various subcultures or market segments may respond more readily to (1) products or services especially tailored to meet their specific needs, (2) personal selling or

[50] Fred C. Akers, "Negro and White Automobile-Buying Behavior: New Evidence," *Journal of Marketing Research*, Vol. 5 (August 1968), pp. 283–290.

[51] Henry A. Bullock, "Consumer Motivations in Black and White," *Harvard Business Review*, Vol. 39, Part I (May–June 1961), pp. 89–104; Part II (July–August 1961), pp. 110–124.

[52] Ibid., pp. 93–97.

promotion that incorporates their special cultural needs into effective appeals and message design, or (3) retail stores, branches, or direct selling outlets that will reach these particular and unique market targets.

CULTURAL DIFFERENCES AND MARKETING STRATEGY. Marketing strategy, it has been argued from the outset of this work, ought to be predicated upon the firm's understanding of its customers. But we have learned also through the pages of this text that consumer behavior is not just the simple act of purchase. It is instead a complex bundle or sequence of actions and activities that are affected by economic constraints as well as cultural-social processes working as mediators upon a host of sociopsychological processes. (The reader is urged once again to examine Figure 16-1.) Now, imagine, if you will, a kind of three-dimensional configuration such as is illustrated in Figure 16-3. We see that the firm's total marketing strategy—its price, promotion, product, and channel elements—is likely to be affected by cultural-social processes as well as sociopsychological ones. For example, the firm's product is perceived as a bundle of expectations. Both perceptions and expectations are, however, likely to be influenced by many factors—age, income, geographical location, occupation, social class, education, group norms, and cultural belief systems. Furthermore, perceptions and expectations are likely to be products of other psychological cognitions, attitudes, or images. They will be affected by such phenomena as learning, motivation, communication processes and activities, personality factors regarding the individual, and the whole host of cognitive processes that relate to information seeking, storage, retrieval, and processing.

Thus we come to realize that the development of marketing strategy as well as the understanding of consumer decision processes is no mean task.

Figure 16-3

The Relationship Between Cultural-Social Processes,
Social-Psychological Processes, and Marketing Strategy:
An Interactive Configuration

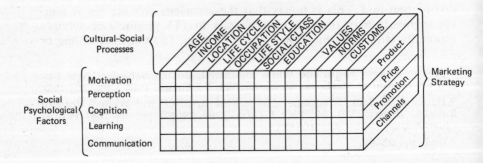

In this chapter and other chapters of Part IV, we have come to grips with a very elusive dimension of consumer behavior. We have now, hopefully, a better understanding and conceptualization of the whole range of interpersonal variables affecting consumer behavior—those relating to socialization, group influence, social class, family role structure, life cycle, and life style. And finally, the role and impact of culture upon consumer behavior has been explored. In the next section of this book, our concern will center upon a discussion and analysis of consumer decision processes.

Questions for Study, Reflection, and Review

1 Briefly define culture and identify some of its major characteristics.

2 What are the dimensions used in the classification of the cultural elements of behavior?

3 Discuss the dynamic nature of culture and the influences that generate change.

4 Distinguish between the two categories of cultural norms: folkways, and mores.

5 Discuss the significance of the discovery of cultural universals and its impact upon foreign marketing endeavors.

6 What is the relationship between sociopsychological processes and cultural-social processes?

7 Briefly comment on the predictive value of culture regarding consumer behavior.

8 Identify and discuss some of the major core culture characteristics of middle-majority Americans.

9 Explain the concept of subculture and its implications for marketers.

10 Discuss the value orientation exhibited by the youth culture and how it differs from core culture values.

Questions for Study, Reflection, and Review.

Part V

Aspects of Consumer Decision Processes

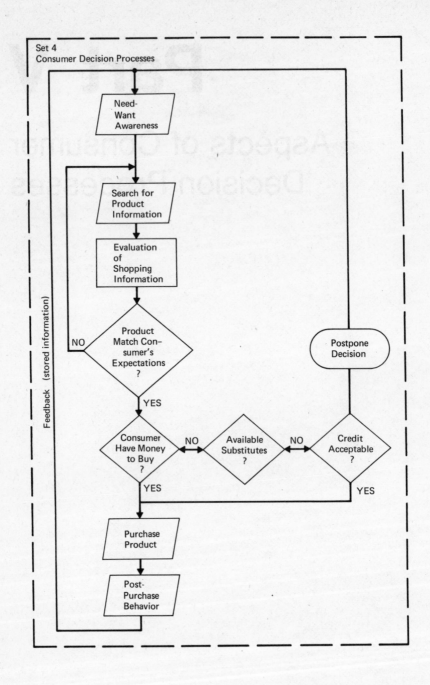

Set 4
Consumer Decision Processes

17

Consumer Decision Processes: Scope and Implication

Introduction

Throughout the preceding chapters we have analyzed and discussed various aspects of consumer behavior in great detail. In this chapter and in the chapter to follow our attention is diverted to a discussion of consumer decision processes. To set the stage for the ideas that are about to be presented let us first indulge in a recapitulation of some ideas first mentioned in Chapter 4. At that juncture, consumer behavior was defined as "the physical and mental activities and the resultant actions of those who purchase and/or consume economic goods." Consumer behavior is thus seen as a host of complex activities and actions, some physical and some mental. At an earlier point, we also acknowledged that our perspective encompassed a broader view than the simple and direct objective observation that characterizes the strict behaviorist tradition. Consequently, our treatment has focused in considerable detail on a wide range of mental processes such as cognition, perception, motivation, and learning, and we have repeatedly emphasized the social and cultural impact upon consumer behavior.

The title of this chapter, "Consumer Decision Processes: Scope and Implication," suggests that one way of analyzing consumer behavior is to consider it as a distinct kind of decision process or set of related problem-solving activities. Thus, consumer behavior can be conceived of as a bundle of responses to various marketing and other stimuli. Much of what we have talked about and discussed as consumer behavior is in actuality the mental processes that affect consumer behavior. However, consumer behavior is not a single act or a unique kind of singular response. It cannot be adequately treated as a part of a simple stimulus-response mechanism. To repeat, consumer behavior is a collection of complex activities and actions, some of which are physical and thus objective and observable, and some of which are mental, ideational and subjective and therefore not observable.

It might be well to consider once again the holocentric model presented in Chapter 4. You will observe that what we propose to treat in this Chapter is the area labeled Set 4 in Figure 17-1. It should be further pointed out that consumer decision processes, again as depicted in the model, are affected by Set 1, the intrapersonal variables or such factors as cognition, motivation, perception, learning, and attitudes; Set 2, facilitating variables such as personality and communication; and Set 3, interpersonal variables such as socialization, group influences, family influences, and cultural influences. The consumer is seen as a kind of central processing unit or decision maker.

One way of viewing consumer behavior is to consider it as a decision process. Such a point of view posits that consumer behavior is problem-solving behavior. Consumers go to the market to seek solutions for problems and to fulfill the demands and dictates of their need-wants hierarchy. Such a position holds, therefore, that consumer behavior and the related and emergent set of decision processes is an exercise in problem-solving and, hence, goal-striving behavior. Consumers, then, in many ways take on the general characteristics of all problem solvers or decision makers; consumer behavior is thus seen as a sequential-reiterative series of activities linked to a multistage decision process under conditions of uncertainty. It shall be our task in this and the following chapter to explore the ramifications and implications of this point of view.

Consumer behavior, therefore, is simply another label for consumer decision processes.[1] Decision processes and decision making imply that consumers seek goals and solutions to problems. This assertion further implies that consumers must recognize or become aware of problems, search and seek information, process and evaluate information, discover and evaluate alternatives, explore the consequences of certain behavior, decide, and eventually reflect and consider the consequences of their actions within a postpurchase time frame. Stated another way, all this suggests that consumer decision processes involve a search for significant structure within the problem environment,

---

[1] This particular point of view is not always acknowledged in the literature. Consumer decision processes are often treated, at least implicitly, as if they were something separate and distinct from consumer behavior itself. However, at least one writer whose work and contributions this author has greatly esteemed has explicitly acknowledged that *consumer behavior* and *consumer decision processes* are synonymous terms. See Francesco M. Nicosia, *Consumer Decision Processes* (Englewood Cliffs, N.J.: Prentice-Hall, Inc., 1966), pp. 8–12.

Figure 17-1

A Holocentric Model of Consumer Behavior

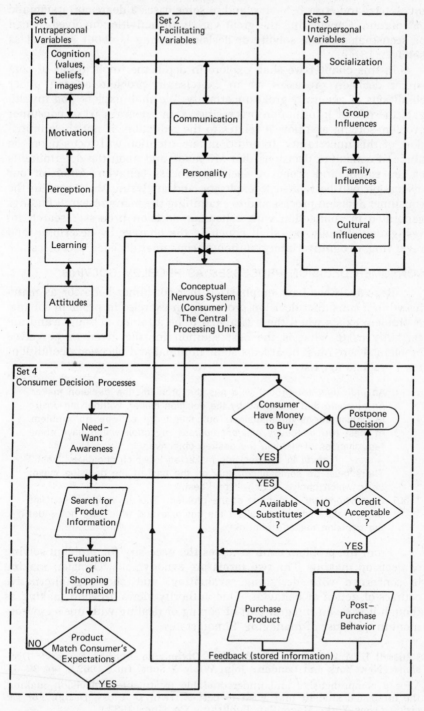

489

much trial-and-error behavior, and in some cases a degree of systematic calculation. Considering the great variety of activities involved, it can be seen that problem solving or decision making is about as broad as behavior itself.

In this chapter we shall explore in depth the implications of consumer decision processes as an exercise in problem solving under conditions of generally great uncertainty. We shall explore and investigate the role of information processing as an integral part of consumer problem-solving and how it relates to the reduction, if not the elimination, of this uncertainty. In addition, our attention will focus upon the kinds of consumer decisions that are made and upon the determinants of the extent and scope of decision process behavior. Much of our discussion will be related to exploring and analyzing the stages in the consumer decision process and to examining the many research findings generated in connection with consumer decision process research investigation. Finally, we shall conclude the chapter by describing and reviewing a cognitive interpretation of consumer decision processes.

CONSUMER DECISION PROCESSES AS PROBLEM SOLVING

Repeatedly we have emphasized that consumer behavior as manifested in a consumer decision process is an exercise in problem solving. A problem exists when there is a goal to be attained or sought and uncertainty as to what is the best solution for the given or perceived problem. There must be at least some minimal and necessary conditions for a problem to exist.

1. An *individual* (or group) who has the problem: the decision maker.
2. An *outcome* that is desired by the decision maker. Without the desire to obtain an as-yet-unattained outcome there can be no problem.
3. At least *two unequally efficient courses of action* which have some real chances of yielding the desired objective.
4. *A state of doubt* in the decision maker as to which choice is "best." There must be some uncertainty on the part of the decision maker as to which choice is or will be "best."
5. *An environment or context* of the problem. The environment consists of all factors which can affect the outcome and which are not under the decision maker's control.[2]

From the problem context arises the necessity for problem solving or decision making. The two terms are synonymous. Decision making is concerned with designing, evaluating, and choosing alternative courses of action or behavior.[3] One authority views decision making as though it were an integral part of coping or dealing with one's environment in the sense of managing. Simon states:

[2] Russell L. Ackoff, *Scientific Method: Optimizing Applied Research Decisions* (New York and London: John Wiley & Sons, Inc., 1962), pp. 30–31.

[3] For a comprehensive and understandable treatment of decision making, the interested student may wish to peruse Irwin D. Bross, *Design For Decision* (New York: Macmillan Publishing Co., Inc., 1953).

In treating decision making as synonymous with managing, I shall be referring not merely to the final act of choice among alternatives, but rather to the whole process of decision. Decision making comprises three principal phases: finding occasions for making decisions; finding possible courses of action; and choosing among courses of action.[4]

These activities described by Simon correspond closely to the stages of problem solving first described by John Dewey:

1. A difficulty is felt.
2. The difficulty is located and defined.
3. Possible solutions are suggested.
4. Consequences are considered.
5. A solution is accepted.[5]

Thus consumer behavior as problem-solving activity involves a sequential and reiterative series of activities that is designed to produce a decision or a solution to a perceived problem. Consumer decision processes involve at least these minimum activities. It should be acknowledged that decision process stages 1 through 4 and 2 through 4 in particular need not follow in the sequence presented. Conceivably these stages can take place simultaneously in some instances, and in other circumstances a time sequence may exist but not necessarily in the order presented.

1. Problem recognition.
2. Search activity.
3. Evaluation of information.
4. Commitment—go or no-go.
5. Postpurchase considerations.

We shall explore and discuss each of these activities in much greater detail in a later section of this chapter. Suffice it to say at this point that consumer problem-solving is designed to produce *solutions* to consumer problems. But what is a decision or a solution? A decision or a solution is an effective response or course of action that provides a desired result to a currently perceived behavioral state of the organism. Two important points must be emphasized in connection with this statement. First of all, problem solving is related to the perceptual state of the consumer. Problem recognition itself results from cognitive-perceptual activities; that is, a problem arises only when the consumer *perceives* a variance between some actual state of affairs and a desired state of affairs. Furthermore, even though the problem-solving activity of individuals is not thoroughly understood, it can be and is normally viewed as an information-processing system.

[4] Herbert A. Simon, *The New Science of Management Decision* (New York: Harper and Row, Publishers, 1960), p. 1.

[5] John Dewey, *How We Think* (Boston: D. C. Heath & Company, 1910), Chapter 8.

INFORMATION PROCESSING AND DECISION MAKING
—THE PERCEPTUAL ORIENTATION

Perception itself, as we learned earlier, is basically concerned with how information is extracted from the environment and used in the interest of the individual's instrumental or problem-solving–coping activities. The consumer's information-processing–perceptual system engages in essentially three distinct kinds of activity: storing, transforming, and recalling. *Storing* amounts to ingesting information, facts, figures, concepts, ideas, and images for future use. *Transforming* involves certain mental operations that make the raw data or raw information more amenable to decision-making purposes. *Recalling* is concerned with bringing up the right information in the right form for the problem or decision at hand. Thus it can be seen that consumer problem-solving is strongly involved with the cognitive processes and most specifically with perception and information processing. Another way of putting this would be to say that the problem is interpreted and dealt with in light of the individual consumer–decision-maker's perception. It is his values, his cognitions, and his perceptions that give life and meaning to the problem.

It has been pointed out that not only is perception an important phenomenon of information processing, it is, as well, integrally related to decision making and decision processes. The essence of this argument is that any individual, given a set of cues or stimulus inputs, must decide whether the thing is A or not A, whether it is hot or cold, desirable or not desirable. The individual interprets and organizes, and what is more important, the individual decides *how* to interpret and how to organize. The processes of perception are themselves very much akin to the processes related to consumer choice behavior. Recall from Chapter 8 that perceptual processes can be viewed as a series of stages in a sequence of decision activities and that such a series consists of the following:

1. *Primitive categorization.* Primitive categorization is a kind of tentative resolution or snap judgment. The environmental event is perceptually isolated, filtered, and reacted to, but all in a tentative and gross fashion.
2. *Cue search.* The event, object, or idea is now scrutinized more carefully and a larger number of cues and differentiating suggestions are sought and examined. The subject continues to scan the environment for additional data in order to find clues that permit a more precise delineation of the object.
3. *Confirmation check.* The object or event is about to be categorized. This is a near-final trial-and-check period. The subject begins now to consider reducing the effective input of stimulation and sense data. Openness to more or different sensory input begins to decline.
4. *Confirmation completion.* This is a closure stage of perception.

All incongruent messages, information, and sensory input are now avoided, screened, or filtered out of the perceptual decision processes. Our "minds" are made up! And once this occurs, the threshold for recognizing cues contrary to this categorization increases greatly.[6]

Such a decision process no doubt is characteristic of much of our perceptual activity. When sensory data and stimulation impinge upon the organism—the human being, the consumer—they do so in the form of physical energy. This energy is a carrier of signs and messages, and it becomes sense data upon which the organism acts. Thus the consumer is processing information, and this processing leads, in many instances, to behavioral change. The consumer's perceptual apparatus, therefore, has two major functions: (1) it is sensitive to certain types of physical energy or information, and (2) it is capable, when properly stimulated, of delivering and interpreting information or messages that modify the consumer's behavior.[7]

The perceptual–information-processing orientation toward consumer decision processes has been treated extensively by Cox.[8] He contends that a product is perceived as an array of cues. This array includes information such as price, color, scent, friends' opinions, taste, feel, salesmen's opinions, and so on. The essence, then, of consumer behavior in choice situations is to use cues or information from the array as the basis for making judgments about the product. The argument is proposed that consumers are selective (perceptive) in their use of information about a product and tend to base their evaluation primarily on high-value information or cues. Cox further contends that consumer decision-makers assign value to information or cues in two different and independent dimensions—predictive value and confidence value. Predictive value is seen as a measure of the probability with which a cue seems associated with (that is, predicts) a specific product attribute. As an example, consider that a buyer knows that a stereo amplifier contains high-quality internal components; then it would follow that there is a high probability that the amplifier is of good quality. Confidence value is seen as a measure of how certain the consumer is that the cue is what he thinks it is. Again consider an audiophile and a housewife who knows little about stereo equipment, both of whom are trying to form independent judgments of the quality of a stereo amplifier. Both might share the belief that the internal components represent a high predictive value; that is, if they know for certain that the components are good, they would also feel that in all

[6] See Jerome S. Bruner, "On Perceptual Readiness," *The Psychological Review*, 1957, pp. 123–152.

[7] William N. Dember, *The Psychology of Perception* (New York: Holt, Rinehart & Winston, Inc., 1960), p. 6.

[8] Donald F. Cox, "The Measurement of Information Value: A Study in Consumer Decision Making," in *Emerging Concepts in Marketing*, William S. Decker, ed. (Chicago: American Marketing Association, 1963), pp. 413–421.

probability the amplifier itself is good. In addition, however, the audiophile presumably could tell with a high degree of confidence whether or not the components are of good quality. Thus, for the more expert and practiced buyer, the audiophile, the components have both a high predictive cue value and a high confidence cue value. The less experienced buyer, the housewife, is unable to discriminate with confidence between good and bad components. Decisions are often made, then, on the consumer's perception of certain predictive cue values and the basing of certain confidence levels on these cues. Much low-value information, when measured by the predictive value, is overused because its confidence level is high. For example, the consumer who estimates the quality of a stereo amplifier on the basis of wattage alone (100 watts would automatically be presumed better than 60 watts) or on the basis of external appearance—color, design, or some other nonfunctional feature of the equipment—rather than on the basis of its internal components, is basing his evaluation on low-predictive-value information. Thus it is sadly apparent that many consumers are poor decision-makers primarily because of inadequately trained perceptual processes—in short, they seek and process information poorly and misinterpret many cues. Thus they often perceive that a noiseless mixer is powerless, that the sound of a car door closing is indicative of quality, or that a detergent packaged in a violently colored box is harsh, whereas dishwashing detergents that are light pink, blue, or white or are packaged in pleasing colors are mild.[9]

All this suggests that the traditional picture of the rational, objective consumer decision-maker is vastly overdrawn. The consumer is hardly a roving, prowling computer calculator, ever sensitive to the sound of a falling price and alert to the day's best buy.

When faced with two or more choices in relation to a given problem, the consumer is largely oriented toward making a subjective and, to a degree, impartial evaluation of the alternatives. Much consumer behavior takes the form of collecting information about the alternatives, evaluating the information in relation to himself (this alone makes consumer decision-making largely a subjective affair), and establishing a preference order among the alternatives. However, establishing a preference order does not immediately result in a decision. The consumer probably continues to seek new information and to reevaluate old information.[10] When the required level of confidence is reached, the consumer makes a decision. It is a well-recognized fact that the closer together in attractiveness the alternatives are, the more important the decision, and the more variable the information about the alternatives, the higher is the confidence that the person will require before he

---

[9] Ibid., p. 417.

[10] For an extended treatment of this view, see Leon Festinger, *Conflict, Decision and Dissonance* (Stanford, Calif.: Stanford University Press, 1964), pp. 152–158.

makes his decision. The real essence, then, and the matter of greatest time consumption in consumer decision-making is the time and effort related to the process of seeking and evaluating information.

A GENERAL PROBLEM-SOLVING MODEL

Much of our discussion to this juncture can be summarized in an examination of the general problem-solving model shown in the schematic illustration in Figure 17-2.

This general operational model of problem solving is highly suggestive of the sequential and reiterative sequence of activities pursued by consumers in their search for solutions to consumption problems. The model itself is considered to be a communication system with inputs from the environment (E) and from the soma or subject (S).[11] The latter are concerned with behavioral information regarding the individual's own psychological field, that is, his motivational and emotional condition. The direction of flow of information is indicated by the arrows, sometimes in one-way connections and sometimes in two-way connections. Observe that the model's operation rests upon the long rectangle at the base of the model. Four kinds of content are represented, and they are segregated only for illustrative purposes. The arrows extending from memory to any other operations indicate the effects that memory storage, resulting from past experience and hence learning, has upon all those events. Arrows extending in the direction of memory storage indicate some degree of search in memory storage for pertinent information; also, in the cases of cognition and perception, such arrows indicate the commitment of new or modified information to storage. Some of the transmission from memory storage to the central activities (cognition and perception) is through evaluation, which may be said to have some filtering function. Some of the transmission is direct, bypassing the evaluation, as in the case of suspended judgment.

The operation of evaluation is also quite generally distributed, for there is testing of information at any step of the way. Some kind of evaluation occurs at the filtering stage, determining the selective action of the filtering mechanism. The operation of evaluation is not shown as affecting memory storage.

Input II and Input III are included to take care of the individual's active search for information in the environment, as shown by the arrow going up toward the input station, and also to take care of any new input as the operation of cognitions continues. Filtering action for the new input is indicated, but in this connection arrows to and from memory storage and evaluation, as for Input I, should be imagined.

The exit stations indicate possible points of cessation of events in

[11] The description of the model follows J. P. Guilford, *The Nature of Human Intelligence* (New York: McGraw-Hill Book Company, 1967). See especially Chapter 14, pp. 312–344.

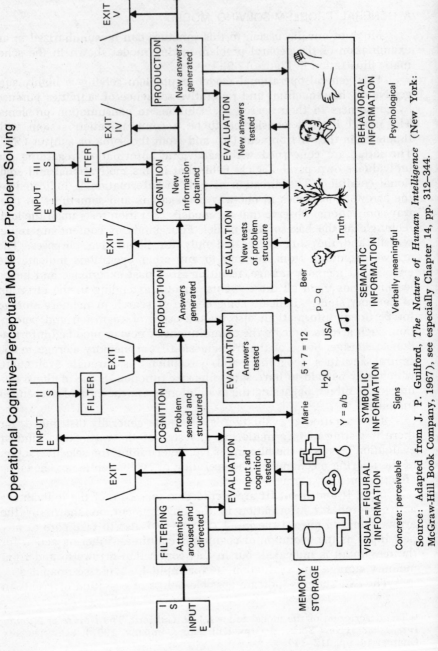

Figure 17-2

Operational Cognitive-Perceptual Model for Problem Solving

Source: Adapted from J. P. Guilford, *The Nature of Human Intelligence* (New York: McGraw-Hill Book Company, 1967), see especially Chapter 14, pp. 312–344.

problem solving. The first exit may be due to a recognition that the problem is not important or that it is impossible to solve, or it may mean the postponement of problem-solving activity for the time being, possibly with an intention to renew the activity and with a condition of incubation occurring in the interim. Exit III might mean that a satisfactory solution has been reached.

Quite importantly, one feature of the model is the liberal allowance for looping phenomena, with the involvement of feedback information. For example, with each cognitive phase and each production phase, there is a loop from cognition to memory, to evaluation, and back to cognition. This activity can be repeated many times and gives rise to our use of the descriptive phrase *sequential and reiterative* in describing consumer decision processes. These looping phenomena permit some flexibility with respect to the order or sequence of events.

The model thus tends to describe and explain the sequence and series of events involved in the cognitive production related to general problem-solving activities. It is an easy and simple matter to generalize the model to consumer decision processes.

After we next briefly examine the kinds or range of consumer decisions and explore and treat the determinants that affect the extent of consumers' decision process behavior, we shall return to treat further the stage of consumer decision processes that fits nicely into the model we have just explored.

KINDS OF CONSUMER DECISIONS

Our treatment thus far has been concerned with emphasizing the consumer-decision-process approach to consumer behavior. Such an approach stresses the view that the consumer moves through a series of sequential and reiterative stages or procedures in reaching or not reaching a decision regarding some aspect of consumption. The decision process approach that is outlined here consists of five major activities or steps including (1) problem recognition, (2) search activity, (3) information evaluation, (4) decision or commitment, and (5) postpurchase evaluation or reconsideration.[12]

Quite naturally, the extent of the efforts devoted to each of these activities will vary considerably from individual to individual, depending upon such factors as the way the problem is perceived, the degree of importance of the problem situation, ego involvement, symbolic consequences of the issue, and so forth. We shall discuss these factors and others momentarily.

However, at this juncture it can be stated that there are qualitative differences in the kinds of decisions that consumers make and that different kinds of decisions will call forth different degrees of effort and

[12] This formulation is similar to others in the field of consumer behavior, and it is also similar to the general decision processes formulated by social psychologists. See, for example, Robert M. Gagné, "Problem Solving and Thinking," *Annual Review of Psychology*, P. R. Farnsworth and Q. McNemar, eds. (Palo Alto, Calif.: Annual Reviews, 1959), pp. 147–172.

variations in the extent of the decision process behavior manifested by consumers. For example, some decisions require an abbreviated decision process. The psychological movement, so to speak, between problem recognition and purchase commitment is swift and deliberate, little or no external information search or information processing by way of systematic calculation is undertaken, and the purchase situation itself is characterized by an absence of perceived risk, anxiety, and dissonance of either a prepurchase or postpurchase variety. On the other hand, however, there are purchase and decision situations that are quite the opposite, and there are, of course, a wide range of decision situations stretching from those involving utter simplicity to those characterized by extreme complication.

Broadly conceived, it can be stated that consumers make two contrasting types of decisions—programmed and non-programmed.[13]

PROGRAMMED DECISIONS. The term *programmed* implies that a predetermined procedure for routinely handling a decision-purchase situation has been evolved. Decisions are programmed to the extent that they are repetitive and routine, to the extent that a definite procedure has been worked out for handling them so they do not have to be treated anew each time they occur. The general assumption regarding programmed decisions is that if a particular problem occurs often enough, a routine procedure will be worked out for solving it. Needless to say, a great portion of our consumer behavior and our consumer decisions are programmed decisions. Consumers, in the interest of using time and other resources efficiently, find a solution to a particular marketing problem and then often stay with that solution as long as it continues to contribute what they perceive to be an adequate margin of satisfaction. Most consumers engage in a surprisingly large amount of habitual and therefore routinized behavior. To say, however, that consumers are creatures of habit or to construe that programmed decision processes result in a kind of stimulus-response bond that locks consumers into a continuously repetitive pattern of purchase activity is to ignore the consumer's capacity for learning, his tendency toward satiation and boredom, and his nearly constant quest for variety and effectance motivation, that is, his desire to deal effectively with his changing environment.

NONPROGRAMMED DECISIONS. Nonprogrammed decisions are non-routinized decisions. Decisions are nonprogrammed to the extent that they are novel, unstructured, and usually consequential (either economically or psychologically). There is no cut-and-dried method for handling the problem because it may not have occurred before, or because its precise nature and structure are elusive or complex, or be-

---

[13] These categories and the definitions stemming therefrom have been adapted from Herbert Simon, op. cit.

cause it may be so important that the decision maker feels that it deserves a custom-tailored treatment. Such is particularly the case in what is often called extended problem-solving activity. Such activity is likely to bring forth a large number of cognitive processes because the consumer is largely open-minded about the problem. It is a non-programmed decision because he may not have made similar decisions of this type before. At this juncture, the consumer is receptive to information; he is groping and searching and learning. He is testing and feeling himself out regarding product and service attributes. And he is matching these attributes or images with his own self-images and life-style. For many nonprogrammed decisions, especially those involving extended problem-solving behavior, the consumer is looking for detailed and complete information about products or services and he is likely to respond favorably to the firm that provides such information.

As has been mentioned, programmed and nonprogrammed decisions represent only the two extremes of decisions considered by consumers. Figure 17-3 suggests some additional variety as to the kinds of decisions confronted by the consumer-buyer.

Figure 17-3 suggests that the category of nonprogrammed decisions includes in itself a range of decision process considerations. Basically our delineation of the nonprogrammed decision situation dealt mainly with what is best described as external problem-solving. Such problem solving involves a great deal of information processing. And the basic difference between extended and limited problem-solving is involved with the issue of how much information is sought, processed, and evaluated. The extent of information processing, however, is a function of many other factors of both an economic and a behavioral nature, that is, the degree of perceived risk surrounding the purchase, the size and magnitude of the expenditure, the psychological and social importance of the product, and the extent to which imagery and symbolism are involved in the purchase situation.

Extemporaneous or impulse purchase situations involve an un-

Figure 17-3

Kinds of Consumer Decisions

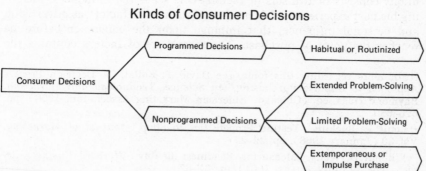

usual kind of cognitive-decision process.[14] The entire consumer decision process is a kind of explosive, rapid, and telescoped procedure in the case of impulse purchases. By definition, impulse purchases involve little or no deliberation and virtually no external search activity. What information is processed is largely stored information, or whatever information is projected by the particular perceived pattern of cue configurations surrounding the purchase-decision situation, namely, point-of-purchase display material, a specific advertising message or appeal, or personal salesmen's comments. What is apparent from our overall discussion of the kinds of consumer decisions is that not all purchase situations necessarily involve all five stages of the decision-making process and that some consumer decisions involve a much greater degree of emphasis upon some particular stage of the decision process than others.

WHAT DETERMINES THE EXTENT OF DECISION PROCESS BEHAVIOR?

As has been mentioned, the extent of the consumer decision process manifested by a particular consumer will be a function of many variables or determinants, some of which are integral to the consumer himself, some of which are integral to the nature of the product, and some of which are integral to the situation and to the environment. For example, one researcher has contended that:

1. The consumer will shop more extensively where the cost of shopping is low.
2. The consumer will shop more extensively when she initially knows little about the product that she is buying and the stores that sell it.
3. The consumer will shop more extensively when the value of the product is high.[15]

It has further been suggested that consumer-decision-process behavior, especially as it relates to search and information processing, is a function of the consumer's awareness.[16] However, we are reminded that awareness is a perceptual phenomenon with varying threshold levels. Nonetheless, the consumer's awareness and hence his readiness to buy consists of two sets of factors. One set is the influences, including his past experiences, felt needs and such other factors as advertising and personal influence, that impinge upon the consumer before he reaches the point of purchase. The second set of factors contains the

---

[14] For more regarding this topic, see David T. Kollat, "A Decision Process Approach to Impulse Purchasing," in *Science, Technology and Marketing,* Raymond Haas, ed. (Chicago: American Marketing Association, 1966), pp. 626–639.

[15] Louis P. Bucklin, "Testing Propensities to Shop," *Journal of Marketing,* Vol. 30 (January 1966), pp. 22–27.

[16] William D. Wells, "Measuring Readiness to Buy," *Harvard Business Review,* Vol. 39 (July–August 1961), pp. 81–87.

conditions that affect the consumer after he has reached the point of purchase, including such things as size, location, the attractiveness of the display, shelf-space allotment, retailer influence, and so forth.

It does appear that one of the single most important features that distinguishes programmed or routinized decisions, or those involving limited problem-solving, from extended problem-solving is the degree and extent to which information is sought, processed, and evaluated. And this activity is a function of how much perceived risk or anxiety surrounds the particular purchase.[17] This risk may be financial, physical, social, or psychological or, for that matter, some composite of all. In any case, extended problem-solving related to nonprogrammed decision processes is often manifested as a way of reducing, if not totally eliminating, this perceived risk.

We shall examine a number of relevant findings regarding what determines the extent of decision process behavior. As has been stated these determinants relate to (1) product characteristics, (2) situational variables, (3) consumer characteristics, and (4) environmental conditions.[18]

PRODUCT CHARACTERISTICS. There is a marked tendency toward extended problem-solving decision processes when:

1. The product is high in price relative to the consumer's income.
2. Given alternatives possess both desirable and undesirable attributes or features.
3. The purchase decision will commit the consumer for an extended period of time. This applies to items that the consumer is likely to purchase on an infrequent basis and that have relatively long and useful functional life, for example, major appliances, household furniture, housing, and other consumer capital goods items.[19]

---

[17] We shall treat the concept of perceived risk much more extensively in Chapter 18. The concept has been developed and treated by Raymond Bauer, "Consumer Behavior as Risk Taking," in *Dynamic Marketing for a Changing World*, Robert S. Hancock, ed. (Chicago: American Marketing Association, 1960), pp. 389–398.

[18] Much of this material is taken from the work of Donald H. Granbois. See his unpublished review article entitled "Research Approaches to Decision Making in the Family" (Bloomington, Ind.: Indiana University Graduate School of Business, 1964), pp. 22–25.

[19] Some of these findings are based upon conclusions and generalizations from other sources. For example, see George Katona and Eva Mueller, "A Study of Purchase Decisions in Consumer Behavior," in *Consumer Behavior*, Lincoln Clark, ed. (New York: New York University Press, 1954), pp. 30–87. Also see Wroe Alderson and Robert Sessions, "Basic Research Report on Consumer Behavior," in *Quantitative Techniques in Marketing Analysis*, Ronald E. Frank, Alfred E. Kuehn, and William F. Massey, eds. (Homewood, Ill.: Richard D. Irwin, Inc.), pp. 129–145.

SITUATIONAL VARIABLES. There is a greater likelihood that consumers will manifest more extended decision-process behavior if:

1. The buyer is a novice buyer with little or no relevant experience bearing on the purchase situation.
2. The product is new and, therefore, unfamiliar to the buyer. In short, he has little knowledge of the product.
3. Formerly acquired experience is no longer relevant because of changed purchase requirements or because the information gained from the experience has become obsolete.
4. Past experience or information has subsequently proved to be inadequate, irrelevant, or unsatisfactory.
5. The purchase is perceived to be psychologically and socially important because of social and/or cultural visibility, that is, if the purchase must fulfill certain proscribed social and/or cultural requirements, such as housing to meet given social class requirements or clothing to match particular role expectations.

CONSUMER CHARACTERISTICS. There is a greater tendency for decision process behavior to be extended rather than limited or habitual provided the consumer possesses these characteristics:

1. The consumer has a college education.
2. The consumer is basically a middle-income person.
3. The consumer is under thirty-five years of age.
4. The consumer perceives no urgency or immediate pressing need for the product.
5. The consumer has a white-collar occupation.
6. The consumer perceives shopping as somewhat enjoyable rather than strictly burdensome.[20]

ENVIRONMENTAL CONDITIONS. Consumer decision processes are more likely to be extended in scope and involve a greater degree of information processing when:

1. There is disagreement and dissonance among family members as to what constitutes an appropriate solution to the consumption problem.
2. There is a difference between the customer's intended behavior and that which his regular or normal reference group would perceive as appropriate behavior.
3. The consumer's feelings and expectations about the future are clouded or uncertain, for example, when environmental cues suggest the threat of war, recession, or some new impending technology that would bear upon the efficacy of the impending decision.

[20] The consumer characteristics are mostly from Katona and Mueller, op. cit., p. 80.

The consumer decision process approach thus stresses the importance of consumer behavior as a sequential and reiterative series of activities. Consumer behavior is treated and reacted to, given this perspective, as a process rather than as a discrete act, and from the marketer's point of view this process takes on a significance that actually transcends the significance of the decision itself. Thus the question of what goods are bought or not bought is important, but even more important is the series of questions pertaining to such issues as how consumers recognize problems; what is involved in creating interest and awareness; what information consumers seek; what alternatives they evaluate; how much actual search consumers manifest; and what the consumer does and how he reacts after a decision has been made. Hence, a realistic measurement of marketing effectiveness must be related to its impact on the consumer's total range of decision processes. It would thus be helpful to think of a situation in which marketing is likened to a force that, if successful, moves people up a series of steps toward purchase.

Measurements of the effectiveness of marketing should provide measurements of changes at all levels on these steps, not just at the levels of the development of product or feature awareness and the stimulation of actual purchase. In the following section we shall explore these ideas and elaborate further on the concept of consumer decision processes as a progression of activity.

Stages of Consumer Decision Processes

The consumer's decision process has been described thus far as a sequential and reiterative series of psychological and physical activities ranging from problem recognition, search, evaluation, and decision to postpurchase considerations. It has already been suggested that these stages are not necessarily unidirectional or linear. It is well known that it is possible for a person to become aware (problem recognition) of something in a store, buy it without much search (if any at all), and then enjoy it tremendously. Evaluation may even follow the decision to purchase some items. In general, the reiterative nature of the decision process suggests that people can go backward and forward in their decision processes and, for that matter, even skip around. For example, problem recognition may lead to search activity and such search activity may generate insight that would warrant a reformulation of the problem. The fact that the given consumer is in one stage is neither sufficient nor a necessary condition for moving to another.[21] Once the consumer recognizes a problem, it does not inexorably follow that he launches himself into search and information-processing activity that leads automatically to purchase, consumption, and postpurchase evaluation and consideration.

[21] Philip Kotler, *Marketing Management: Analysis, Planning and Control*, 2nd ed. (Englewood Cliffs, N.J.: Prentice-Hall, Inc., 1972), p. 630.

At least one of the common features of consumer decision-making is that separate stages of thinking are linked together over time. The potential buyer supposedly passes through these stages in a loose but specified order as he approaches a decision regarding some act of consumption, that is, brand or product choice, store choice, and so on. Lavidge and Steiner's cognitive-affective-conative sequence of psychological states is at least one explicit statement of the sequence idea.[22] These researchers viewed consumer behavior as a series of steps.

1. At the bottom of the steps or hierarchy stand potential customers who are *completely unaware of the existence* of the product or service in question.
2. Next are those *who are aware of the product's existence* but not necessarily interested in purchasing.
3. Further along are those *who know what the product has to offer.*
4. Even closer to purchasing are those *who like the product.*
5. Next are those who have developed favorable attitudes to the point of *preferring* the product or service in question over all others.
6. Even closer to purchasing are those consumers who couple preference with a desire to buy and a *conviction* that the purchase would be wise.
7. Finally, of course, is the step that translates this attitude, including its preference valences and conviction, into an actual commitment—purchase.

This series of actions and the resultant psychological states suggest that consumer decision processes are affected by three important kinds of psychological activity.

1. *Cognitive activity.* Cognitive activity relates to a knowledge and awareness dimension of consumer behavior. It implies that behavior is a function of knowledge, values, ideas, attitudes, and images and that to facilitate and affect consumer decision processes marketers must provide information or knowledge that facilitates and triggers awareness and knowledge.
2. *Affective activity.* Affective activity relates to the emotional states of the individual. Affective activity suggests that consumers must be taught to like or to manifest a preference for one commodity or one brand over another. This in turn suggests that if the consumer's decision process is to be influenced much information of an affective sort must be disseminated. Hence, it implies also that underlying consumer decision processes is a learning curve and that consumers learn, via information processing and communication, to recognize, prefer, and sometimes even insist on a given brand or product.
3. *Conative activity.* Conative activity relates to the striving state

[22] Robert J. Lavidge and Gary Steiner, "A Model for Predictive Measurements of Advertising Effectiveness," *Journal of Marketing*, Vol. 25, No. 6 (October 1961), pp. 59–62.

or the motivational state of the individual and stresses the tendency of consumers to treat objects—that is, goods and services—as positive or negative goals. Conative activity thus stresses the goal-striving and problem-solving nature of consumer behavior. Conative or motivational activity persuades the consumer to buy particular brands or commodities or to shop at specific stores. It pertains, in short, to the reasons that consumers are impelled to buy goods.

The Lavidge-Steiner hypothesis of a hierarchy of effects offers in a clear and concise manner the viewpoints that have been widely held in the marketing literature for many years. Attention, interest, desire, and action; awareness, acceptance, preference, intention to buy, and provocation of sale; awareness, comprehension, conviction and action— these are but a few of the internal psychological processes a typical consumer is supposed to experience from the perception of an advertisement, the confrontation of a personal salesman, or some other internalized problem recognition process.[23] Figure 17-4 shows four concep-

FIGURE 17-4

Conceptions of Consumer Decision Processes

	CONCEPTIONS			
Psychological activities	Problem-solving model	"AIDA" model[a]	Hierarchy of effects model[b]	Innovation-adoption model[c]
Cognitive activity	Problem recognition	Attention	Awareness Knowledge	Awareness
Affective activity	Search evaluation	Interest Desire	Liking Preference	Interest Evaluation
Conative (motivational) activity	Decision Postpurchase behavior	Action	Conviction Purchase	Trial Adoption

Sources: [a] E. K. Strong, *The Psychology of Selling* (New York: McGraw-Hill Book Company, 1925), p. 9.

[b] Robert J. Lavidge and Gary Steiner, "A Model for Predictive Measurements of Advertising Effectiveness," *Journal of Marketing*, Vol. 25, No. 6 (October 1961), pp. 59–62.

[c] Everett M. Rogers, *Diffusion of Innovations* (New York: The Free Press, 1962), pp. 79–86.

[23] C. H. Sandage and Vernon Fryburger, *Advertising Theory and Practice*, 6th ed. (Homewood, Ill.: Richard D. Irwin, Inc., 1963), p. 240; Harry D. Wolfe, James K. Brown, and G. Clark Thompson, *Measuring Advertising Results* (New York: National Industrial Conference Board 7, 1962); and Russell H. Coley, *Defining Advertising Goals for Measured Advertising Results* (New York: Association of National Advertisers, 1961), p. 55.

tions of consumers' decision processes. The first column shows the stages in the consumer decision process treated throughout this chapter. The AIDA model, the hierarchy of effects model, and the innovation-adoption model all show the consumer passing through various psychological and physical stages of activity. The minor differences that exist among the various models are more semantic than real. The most important aspect of the entire configuration is that it suggests that the various sequences are subject to a persuasive process and that this total process is comprised of cognitive, affective, and conative or motivational dimensions.

CONSUMER DECISION PROCESSES AND PERSUASION

To know something about the stages of the consumer decision process is to know also that individual marketers can conceivably affect this process by persuasion or other influences. The interesting question that arises is "What happens when someone or some firm attempts to influence the decision process and, hence, the behavior of another person?" The answer within a psychological context has been at least partially provided by Cartwright. He contends that:

> To influence behavior, a chain of processes must be initiated within the person. These processes are complex and interrelated, but in broad terms they may be characterized as (i) creating a particular cognitive structure, (ii) creating a particular motivational structure, and (iii) creating a particular behavioral (action) structure. In other words behavior (and decision processes) is determined by the beliefs, opinions, and "facts" a person possesses; by the needs, goals, and values he has; and by the momentary control held over his behavior by given features of his cognitive and motivational structure. To influence behavior . . . requires the ability to influence these determinants in a particular way.[24]

The reader will observe how closely Cartwright's conception matches our own cognitive theory of consumer behavior. He goes on to stipulate four specific steps that must be taken to influence a decision process.

1. Dissemination of information must reach the cognitive mechanism (sense organs) of the persons who are to be influenced.
2. Having reached the cognitive mechanisms or sense organs, the information must be perceived as compatible with the person's existing cognitive structure and belief system.
3. To induce action by transmitting and projecting information, the suggested action must be perceived by the person as a path or alternative to some goal that he has.
4. To induce a given action or to alter a given decision process an appropriate cognitive and motivational system must gain control or prepotence over the person's behavior at a given point in time.

[24] Dorwin Cartwright, "Some Principles of Mass Persuasion," *Human Relations*, Vol. 2 (1949), pp. 253–267, at p. 255.

The concept of a hierarchy effect or the fact that there is a series of stages, or progression of activities, inherent in consumer decision processes is generally well accepted. Such a concept implicitly and to some extent explicitly assumes that each succeeding stage implies a higher probability that the person will purchase the product. For example, one study reported that, of the actions of twenty-eight hundred persons toward a particular brand, 69 per cent of those regarding it as acceptable bought it and 9 per cent of those reporting only an awareness of the brand bought it.[25]

It must not be construed, however, that the hierarchy-of-effects hypothesis, which stresses a progressive series of steps or stages in consumer decision processes, is meant to be a totally deterministic explanation of consumer behavior. The concept simply suggests that as the consumer moves from one stage to another there is an increased likelihood or *probability* that he will ultimately purchase the product. Much can and does happen between the point of problem recognition or awareness and the actual decision on which specific product will be purchased, *if* any is purchased at all. Some have shown much skepticism and even hostility to the hierarchy-of-effects proposition. Palda has argued somewhat convincingly that, in addition to many unresolved problems related to the research upon which the hierarchy-of-effects model rests, there are other substantial weaknesses surrounding the idea. In effect he contends that there is no logical necessity for awareness of a brand to precede its purchase. He argues also that purchasers of a particular brand may be better rememberers than nonrepeat purchasers. The most telling of his criticisms relates to a problem that we have already explored in much detail in our earlier treatment of attitudes, namely, that there is not a strong correlation between a consumer's attitude toward a product and his actual purchase of that product.[26] In this regard we must agree with Palda that attitude may thus be viewed either as a mechanism or disposition that guides behavior or as a mode that gives behavior its meaning.

The hierarchy-of-effects proposition regarding a progression of stages in the consumer's decision process, however, continues to be a useful and rich device for guiding consumer research studies. The hierarchy-of-effects concept posits four variables that are themselves operational statements regarding the stages of decision making. Awareness is a product's or brand's prominence or salience. Attitude is an evaluative relationship of preference and desire. Intention to purchase is the extent of commitment to a future action, self-prediction of anticipated behavior, or, more simply, a plan. Based upon this conceptualization, O'Brien recently tested three hypotheses that relate to a hierarchy-

[25] Charles K. Raymond, "Must Advertising Communicate to See?" *Harvard Business Review*, Vol. 43 (September–October 1965), pp. 148–161.

[26] Kristian S. Palda, "The Hypotheses of a Hierarchy of Effects: A Partial Explanation," *Journal of Marketing Research*, Vol. 3 (February 1966), pp. 13–24.

of-effects model. Once again you will notice that his problem formulation falls within our cognitive tradition.

1. Awareness influences attitude over time and the relationship is expected to be positive.
2. Attitude influences over time and is positively associated with intention to purchase.
3. Intention influences over time and is positively associated with actual purchase.[27]

Using panel data collected in the Columbia University project on buyer behavior, O'Brien concluded that within the sequence of cognitive, affective, and conative psychological states over time, results basically support the hierarchy predictions. Awareness was found causally prior to attitude, intention, and purchase; and attitude and intention were each causally prior to purchase. However, an indeterminate relationship was found between attitude and intention.

Thus it appears that the concept of stages in the consumer decision process and even a limited hierarchy-of-effects notion will continue to hold sway in the minds of many marketers regarding consumer behavior. It is a useful and meaningful notion and, as we suggested earlier, its usefulness and richness for research purposes are, somewhat at least, responsible for its continued longevity. We shall conclude this section by reviewing briefly some aspects of the consumer decision processes and their implications.

A REVIEW OF CONSUMER DECISION PROCESSES

We have yet to explore some of the more significant aspects of consumer decision processes. Thus far we have established that consumer behavior consists of a series of sequential and reiterative activities that facilitate the consumer's need to make decisions or solve problems. We have expanded on the decision-making aspect of consumer behavior and stressed the role of information processing as a vital part of this process. Also, we have explored the range and the implications that stem from the fact that consumers make different kinds of decisions and that these different kinds of decisions call forth variations in the pattern of consumer decision processes. It is time now to explore the steps in the consumer decision process in greater detail. Recall that the steps in the consumer decision process are as follows:

1. Problem recognition.
2. Search activities.
3. Information processing and evaluation.
4. Decision.
5. Postpurchase evaluation.

We shall explore each of these activities in some detail.

[27] Terrence O'Brien, "Stages of Consumer Decision Making," *Journal of Marketing Research,* Vol. 8 (August 1971), pp. 283–289.

PROBLEM RECOGNITION. Problem recognition is largely, at least in a behavioral sense, a perceptual phenomenon. A problem is *perceived* when there is a goal to be attained and uncertainty exists as to the best way or the better way of attaining the goal. Consumer problems exist or rise to cognitive threshold levels when a consumer *recognizes* (becomes aware of) a difference of sufficient magnitude between what is *perceived* as the desired state of affairs and what is *perceived* as the actual state of affairs. The result is some incongruity or dissonance that triggers the onset of a state of motivated behavior. The motivation may be a kind of deficiency motivation or the motivation may be related to almost any kind of goal-seeking or striving activity. In any event, problem recognition means that the consumer manifests some felt need even though it may be only dimly envisaged. A tensional state or some disturbance in the consumer's psychological field thus develops, and there arise motives or reasons that impel the consumer to respond. A whole set of mental reactions and attitudinal sets develop that we call cognitive processes.[28]

It is important to understand that for a problem to exist there must be more than one alternative. If there is no inherent act of choice there can be no problem, only a worry.

SOURCES OF CONSUMER PROBLEMS. To live is to encounter consumer problems. As the consumer strives to fulfill the demands of his needs-wants hierarchy he encounters problems. Most consumer problems arise as a result of the following conditions:

Assortment inadequacies. Assortment inadequacies implies that the consumer witnesses a deficiency in his stock of goods. Existing goods are consumed or literally used up. In order to maintain one's existence, to continue the activity of the household, to continue the use of the automobile, and so on, goods must be restocked and replenished. Hence many consumer problems are perceived to be much like that of Old Mother Hubbard—the cupboard is bare and hence the need for additional goods is perceived.

New information. Consumer problems are also perceived when new information is injected into the consumer's psychological field. Perception itself has been described in terms of how information is extracted from the environment and used in the interest of the consumer's tasks at hand. New information creates cognitions and states of awareness. These cognitions sensitize consumers to products and services that are seen as solutions to consumer problems. Not only does new information result in problem recognition but so does different information or existing information presented in a different light.

Expanded desires. Man is often described as the wanting animal. Consumers generally have a constantly rising level of aspirations and expectations. Out of these rising levels of aspirations comes the desire

[28] See Rom J. Markin, *The Psychology of Consumer Behavior* (Englewood Cliffs, N.J.: Prentice-Hall, Inc., 1969), p. 20.

for new goods, and hence new problems are triggered that demand new or modified solutions. Our roles, images, and life styles change over time, and to the extent that they do new consumer problems are generated.

Expanded means. A generally rising standard of living or state of affluence means also an expanded package of desired goods and services. Thus the consumer's awareness as to what constitutes an appropriate package or system of symbols is to some extent a function of his means. If income is rising or expected to rise, there is a strong likelihood that consumption expenses will rise also.

Problem recognition, once it occurs, generates certain consequences. For one, problem recognition signals the onset of both physical and mental activity. This suggests a second consequence, namely, that once brought up or rising above the individual's threshold level, problems require treatment. It does not follow that every problem leads to a solution but problems are treated. Some information is processed or some mental and physical activity is engaged in as a result of the perception of the problem. Finally, in many instances, problem recognition will require difficult comparisons of complex variables. Often such activity is not enjoyed. It can and does lead to dissonance states and feelings of frustration and anxiety, and is so psychologically burdensome to some individuals that they shun their decision-making responsibilities.

SEARCH FOR INFORMATION. Search activity is undertaken by consumers to provide information on the number of available solutions to a perceived problem, the relative merits of the various alternatives, and the consequences of selecting the various alternatives. Consumers themselves implicitly and intuitively understand the nature of a cognitive theory of behavior. They "know" that their behavior is to some extent a function of what they "know," and they understand further that knowledge can lead to better decisions. Hence, in many purchase situations when the problem has been recognized, the consumer begins to seek information. Sometimes the consumer does nothing more than recall his experience from previous purchase situations. Sometimes he does nothing more than to evaluate the experience of a friend or another family member. In other instances the problem may be of sufficient magnitude or surrounded by sufficient complexity, importance, or risk to warrant an extended search process. In every decision process the consumer must somehow manage to answer the question, "How much search?" This involves balancing the factors of information seeking. Essentially, these factors are costs and benefits and in some way, either objectively or subjectively, the consumer will engage in search activity to the extent that the marginal value of search cost equals the marginal benefit of search activity.

The two criteria used as a basis for classifying consumer products are (1) the degree to which the consumer is aware of the exact nature of the product before he starts on his search effort and (2) the satisfaction received from searching for and comparing products weighed against the time and effort required for this task. For example, in considering the ratio of cost of search to gain from search, Holton has posited that if the ratio for a certain good is low it is a convenience good; if the ratio is high, it is a shopping good.[29]

FACTORS AFFECTING SEARCH. Essentially the extent of the consumer's search process depends upon the rapport that he establishes with each purchase situation, and this rapport is subjectively determined by the consumer himself. Once again we find ourselves dealing with the selective and subjective aspects of perception. If the consumer perceives the purchase situation as important to his personal situation, then there is likely to be an increased amount of search activity. Other factors, too, are likely to affect and influence the extent of search behavior.

Experience. The consumer's experience or previous learning that has transfer value may affect the extent of search activity. Novice consumers or purchase situations that are new and different are likely to generate increased amounts of search. Older, more experienced shoppers may be able to reduce search effort and still generate satisfactory performance levels.

Availability of information without search. Much information is literally stored in the cognitive structure of consumers, and this reservoir of knowledge may be used to shorten what might otherwise be a necessarily long and extended search process. Some information presents itself more readily than other information. Consumer advisory services, store shopping services, information prepared and catalogued by shelter magazines, and other information sources often eliminate the necessity for the consumer to seek and ferret out information on his own.

Satisfaction derived from search. It has been well established that different consumers have different cognitive styles. For instance, a given personality type may show a marked tendency to seek more information simply because a search and/or shopping expedition is perceived by these individuals as a pleasurable activity. Conversely, other personality types may derive little or no pleasure from information seeking and may actually avoid such activity. *Levelers* may perceive nearly all information as possessing nearly the same value or utility, whereas *sharpeners* may perceive great differences in the value and utility of information.

Perceived consequences of search. The extent to which search activity is undertaken is related to its subjectively perceived conse-

---

[29] See Richard H. Holton, "The Distinction Between Convenience Goods, Shopping Goods and Specialty Goods," *Journal of Marketing,* Vol. 22 (July 1958), pp. 55–56. See also Louis P. Bucklin, "Retail Strategy and the Classification of Consumer Goods," *Journal of Marketing,* Vol. 27 (January 1963), pp. 50–55; and Bucklin, "Testing Propensities to Shop," op. cit.

quences. If the consequences of not searching are serious, then search will be undertaken. On the other hand, if the consequences of not searching are negligible, then search effort will be reduced or foregone. In many instances, the consequences of searching or not searching are related to the value of the product. Studies by Katona and Mueller, and Alderson and Sessions have indicated that consumer search efforts involving shopping, as measured by the number of interstore comparisons, are not very extensive under any circumstances.[30] Udell has substantiated this contention by showing that in the case of small appliances, consumers do not go from store to store to gather information and to compare products and prices. Instead, he contends, they prefer to do much of this shopping in the comfort of the home by using out-of-store sources of information, especially past experience with products and brands, discussion with friends, and printed advertising.[31] Finally, one researcher declares that search effort for food and small household items is related to the quantity purchased and is measured by the price paid. He finds that families reporting heavy buying in a product class also tend to pay less for a given container size than those reporting light purchases. He infers support for the general hypothesis that the amount of search for lower prices is a function of the expected gain relative to the cost.[32]

Consumer information sources. Consumers use various information sources including their own personal experience and that of friends, family, and other reference groups, as well as published sources, such as business periodicals, newspapers, magazines, and other media.

Personal contact with friends, relatives, or neighbors, or professional contacts with medical journals, specialized farm papers, or colleagues, are very frequently mentioned sources of information.[33] The use of nonneutral business sources such as advertising, publicity, sales promotion, and personal selling varies among product classes.

In choosing new food and household products, buyers mention radio advertising, newspaper advertising, magazines, and salespersons in that order of frequency.[34] In choosing new fashion items such as clothing, hairdo styles, makeup techniques, and cosmetics, buyers mention exposure to magazines more frequently than salespersons.[35] Buyers of major household appliances most frequently mention shopping

[30] Katona and Mueller, op. cit.; Alderson and Sessions, op. cit.

[31] Jon G. Udell, "Prepurchase Behavior of Buyers of Small Appliances," *Journal of Marketing,* Vol. 30 (October 1966), pp. 50–52.

[32] James U. Farley, "Brand Loyalty and the Economics of Information," *Journal of Business,* Vol. 37, No. 4 (October 1964), pp. 9–14.

[33] For a comprehensive and detailed review of consumer decision processes, see Frederick E. May, "Buying Behavior: Some Research Findings," *Journal of Business,* Vol. 38 (October 1965), pp. 379–396. Many of the generalizations included in this section are borrowed from this source.

[34] Elihu Katz and Paul F. Lazarsfeld, *Personal Influence* (Glencoe, Ill.: The Free Press, 1955), p. 172.

[35] Ibid., p. 174.

among stores, advertisements and circulars, magazines, and newspaper articles in that order. Reports of listing agencies and mail order catalogues are mentioned rarely.[36] Finally, buyers of new major appliances mention shopping among stores infrequently, and those who do consult reading material frequently mention buying guides.[37]

Information sources play a diversity of roles in consumer decision processes. Some sources are more important in terms of the consumer's first knowledge or awareness; others serve to create interest or facilitate information gathering; other sources enhance the consumer's capacity to evaluate the alternatives; and other sources are responsible for producing a trial or first-use response.[38] To be remembered is the fact that the importance of the source is fundamentally related to the consumer's own subjective evaluation of that source. However, the sources sought and the information evaluated are a function of such factors as the type of product, the type of information desired, the product's life expectancy, and, again, the consumer's previous experience.[39]

EVALUATION OF INFORMATION. The evaluation of information is a group of activities that are undertaken to determine and compare alternative solutions to market-related problems. Evaluation brings the consumer right up to the point of making a decision on a given course of action. There are several important phases of evaluation activity. First of all, information must be catalogued and systematized. Second, at this juncture the consumer must establish his decision criteria. Third, the major alternatives to be considered are established. And finally, the decision processes have boiled down to comparing these alternatives. In conjunction with the evaluation of information, Mason's analysis confirms that the use of mass media sources is higher at the awareness stage than any other information source, except for peer source use by influentials. Use of mass media sources is lower than all other sources in the final adoption stage.[40] Most importantly, however, all sources of information are used to some extent as the general consumer moves through an adoption process or uses a decision process approach to market problem-solving. The range of information cues that must be evaluated by a consumer is indeed broad; for example, the alternatives

[36] Katona and Mueller, op. cit.

[37] W. E. Bell, "Consumer Innovators: A Unique Market For Newness," in *Toward Scientific Marketing*, S. A. Greyser, ed. (Boston: 1963), pp. 85–95, proceedings of the Winter Conference of the American Marketing Association.

[38] May, op. cit., pp. 385–386.

[39] See N. Havas and H. M. Smith, *Customers' Shopping Patterns in Retail Food Stores* (AMS 400) (Washington, D.C.: U.S. Department of Agriculture, Agricultural Marketing Service, Marketing Development Research Division, August 1960).

[40] R. G. Mason, "The Use of Information Sources in the Process of Adoption," *Rural Sociology*, Vol. 29, No. 1 (March 1964), pp. 40–52.

involving a consumer decision have at least these minimum dimensions:[41]

Product	Store	Method of purchase
Brand	Location	Mode of travel
Manufacturer	Type, quality of	In store, mail, or
Price level	service	telephone
Product	Assortment mix	Time of day
performance	Layout	Single versus multiple
Product use	Personal treatment	purchase
		Cash, charge, layaway

THE PURCHASE DECISION. To make a decision is simply to choose a course of action from among those available. There are many ramifications to decision making. Defining the problem itself is an act of decision. We decide to seek a solution to problem A versus problem B and therein is an act of choice. Decision making is thus concerned with defining the problem, defining expectations, developing alternative solutions, and deciding what to do with the decision after it has been reached. The final act of choice—the ultimate decision—may be to purchase a product; it may be not to purchase the product; or it may be to launch oneself into a reiterative process involving a reformation of the problem, search evaluation, and so forth. There are many pitfalls related to consumer decisions. First, consumers may sometimes find the right answer to the wrong problem. Second, consumers may make a decision at the wrong time. And third, consumers may make decisions that do not really result in solutions. In the latter case, decisions that are designed to reduce tensional states but do not are clearly poor decisions. The decision actually to buy in most instances usually follows very closely the customer's tentative decision to buy. In one study, respondents were asked when they had tentatively decided to buy the product that they had just bought, even though they had not been sure of such things as the model, brand, and price. There were 83 per cent who bought within one month, 50 per cent within one week, and 22 per cent on the same day they made their tentative purchase decisions.[42]

Buying decisions are typically explained as a learning process, with differing amounts of exploratory search effort depending on the degree of risk and uncertainty about product and other decision attributes. In his study of frozen orange juice purchase sequences, Kuehn

[41] From an illustrative table by G. Glen Walters and Gordon W. Paul in *Consumer Behavior: An Integrated Framework* (Homewood, Ill.: Richard D. Irwin, Inc., 1970), p. 210.

[42] James C. Byrnes, "Consumer Intentions to Buy," *Journal of Advertising Research,* Vol. 4 (September 1964), pp. 49–51. For more related information on this topic, see William D. Wells, "Measuring Readiness to Buy," *Harvard Business Review,* Vol. 39 (July–August 1961), pp. 81–87.

found the following behavior, which appears to be similar to that observed in the process of habit formation and memory decay.[43]

1. The probability of a consumer's buying the same brand on two consecutive purchases of frozen orange juice decreases exponentially with an increase in the time between those purchases.
2. Consumers buying frozen orange juice with the greatest frequency have the highest probability of continuing to buy the same brand.
3. The probability of a consumer's buying a particular brand on the fifth trial in a purchase sequence decreases exponentially with the recency of the last purchase of that brand.
4. Finally, Kuehn describes the act of decision as a kind of incomplete learning, incomplete extinction model. This means that consumers will generally not develop such strong brand loyalties (or buying habits) as to ensure either the complete rejection or the complete acceptance of a given brand.

To conclude our discussion of the consumer's decision processes, it should be added that according to one study the average shopper purchases about 50.5 per cent of all his products on an unplanned basis.[44] This surely does imply that the consumer decision process, at least for a large number of goods and on a large number of occasions, must be at best a rapid and tenuous processing of immediate cue configurations and information. Of course, much of this begs the question as to what is an unplanned purchase. Kollat explains the large reporting of unplanned purchases as the customer's inability or unwillingness to commit the time and cognitive resources to make "measured purchase intentions" equal to "actual purchase intentions." The real issue, however, is whether unplanned purchases are really unplanned, and from the standpoint of the customer the answer is probably yes. A great many, perhaps even as much as 50 per cent, are actually unplanned to the extent that they are neither specifically nor generally perceived as buying intentions until triggered by some in-store shopping cue.

Consumer decision processes, whether for impulse or unplanned convenience items or for major durable goods purchases, are much the same.[45] They involve problem recognition, search, information

[43] Alfred A. Kuehn, "Consumer Brand Choice—A Learning Process," in *Quantitative Techniques in Marketing Analysis*, Ronald Frank, Alfred A. Kuehn, and William F. Massey, eds. (Homewood, Ill.: Richard D. Irwin, Inc., 1962), pp. 390–397.

[44] David T. Kollat, "A Decision Process Approach to Impulse Purchasing," in *Science, Technology, and Marketing*, Raymond Haas, ed. (Chicago: American Marketing Association, 1966), pp. 626–639.

[45] See Robert W. Pratt, Jr., "Understanding the Decision Process for Consumer Durable Goods: An Example of the Longitudinal Approach," in *Marketing and Economic Development*, Peter Bennet, ed. (1965), pp. 244–260.

processing, decision, and postpurchase consideration. The only difference is in the emphasis that the individual customer places on the various stages in the decision process, and this emphasis will vary with the subjective preferences of each customer.

POSTPURCHASE CONSIDERATION. The consumer's purchase tactics are not complete when a purchase has been made. Next the consumer will evaluate and reconsider the effect and impact of that decision. This activity is referred to as *postpurchase consideration*, or the consumer's estimate of the results of his purchasing activities. It, too, is simply another type of decision that must be made by the consumer, but it is an estimate or a kind of subjective audit, because the consumer cannot be positive that his evaluation and decision have been correct.

Postpurchase consideration can be accomplished either formally or informally, and it, too, is another kind of cognitive-perceptual phenomenon because postpurchase consideration is always the result of *new information*. Essentially, the new information is the experience gained as a result of the purchase and is used as feedback into the cognitive mechanism to shape our subsequent perceptions and to mold our behavior.

Often the consumer begins to have doubts about a purchase even before it is made, but even more doubt may occur after the purchase decision or commitment is made. The factors in the following list are important generators of doubt and uncertainty, and it is mainly these that trigger sufficient levels of anxiety and ultimately lead to postpurchase consideration activities.

1. The product purchased does not measure up. Consumers often expect too much from products. This is sometimes especially true of products that are purchased for their imagery or symbolic significance. Some products actually fail to fulfill even their functional or utilitarian claims. Such results are likely to precipitate postpurchase consideration and large amounts of dissonance.
2. There are many other desirable alternatives. When a choice is made for one desirable commodity, it usually means that other desirable alternatives have had to be foregone. This often leads to second-guessing.
3. The consumer's attitude may change. The new experience of having purchased and owning a given commodity constitutes a sufficient learning experience. Such an experience may create a change in attitude that may mean that we now *know* something that we did not know before, or that our degree of *like* or *dislike* for a given commodity may have changed, or, finally, that what was earlier a strong behavioral action tendency is now weakened as a result of our learning experience.

A great part of consumer postpurchase consideration behavior can be analyzed and explained in terms of the theory of cognitive dissonance.[46] The important point to consider now, however, is that consumers do perceive information differently. They may perceive information one way during the predecision stage and yet another way in the postdecision stage. Furthermore, another point to consider is that a natural outcome of the consumer's postpurchase consideration or dissonance is some change in the consumer because his experience has been broadened. This may or may not lead to a change in his purchase tactics and his decision processes. Normally, at least one of three major reactions to a consumer purchase decision may be anticipated:

1. Consumer satisfied.
2. Consumer partially satisfied.
3. Consumer dissatisfied.

Even satisfied consumers are likely to manifest a degree of postpurchase consideration. However, heightened or accelerated levels of postpurchase evaluation activities, especially those involving increased levels of anxiety and dissonance, are more likely to be incurred in conditions 2 and 3, namely, when consumers are only partially satisfied or when they are essentially dissatisfied.

A General Model of Consumer Decision Processes

It would seem appropriate to conclude our discussion with an examination of a general model of consumer decision processes. Such models are useful to both students and researchers. They provide a useful framework for research efforts, and they also yield tentative hypotheses about marketing strategy applications. The particular model illustrated has a cognitive-perceptual orientation, and it posits that the decision process is conditioned on the value of a set of perceptual cues.[47] It is in effect, then, an information-processing model. Much of the underlying rationale of the model rests with the notion that persons perceive the external world in terms of cue patterns or configurations, in holistic rather than reductive terms of separate cues. And, if perceptual structure is such that many products are characterized by a certain configuration of cues, then a simple conditional model using only a small set of cues may be invoked a large proportion of the time. Consistency of cues is defined in terms of expectations. Those cue inputs that are expected and are coded into normal configurations are seen as *consistent*. Those that are unexpected, and hence coded differently, are seen as inconsistent. It would follow then that inconsistent configurations would call up more complex subprocesses. The progression of perceptual activities is, thus, a two-step process: cue consistency is assessed and then the relative subprocesses are invoked. If, on the

---

[46] We dealt at great length with this concept in Chapter 7. A rereading of this material would be a useful aid to the student at this juncture.

[47] James R. Bettman, "The Structure of Consumer Choice Processes," *Journal of Marketing Research*, Vol. 8 (November 1971), pp. 465–471.

other hand, cues are consistent, then habitual, simple decision rules are followed. Because such consistent cue combinations occur rather frequently (we see what we know), the simple rules will account for a good portion of the total number of decisions. The model rests upon a general scheme of cognitive motivation theory:

> It is suggested that individuals develop general adaptation levels concerning the amount of incongruity they expect in their environments. The GIAL [general incongruity adaptation level] would represent an optimum incongruity level within an organism. It is proposed that as incongruity falls below the optimum, cognitive action will produce more input (e.g., exploration, novelty seeking, etc.). As incongruity increases beyond the optimum, cognitive action will attempt to reduce or simplify input (as in dissonance reduction).[48]

The schematic flow chart for the general model is shown in Figure 17-5, and the originator's comments and descriptions of the model's operation follow:

ASPECTS OF THE GENERAL MODEL

> *Block 2: Incongruity level as a goal.* The goal of the decision maker is to attain his incongruity adaptation level through choice of behavior. An incongruity adaptation level specific to a decision area (IAL) is considered here, rather than a generalized level.
> *Blocks 3 through 5: The cue manipulation process.* The inferences discussed earlier bear on this portion of the scheme. In Block 4, it is further assumed that use of a dominant decision mode tends to reduce incongruity. Continued use of a simple decision rule may lead to a level below the IAL—boredom will set in. This is seen later in Block 7.
> *Block 6: Process dynamics.* Block 6 represents learning, which was not considered in the consumer models above. However, speculations about processes conditional upon cue configurations lead one to infer that a dynamic process is at work, with nodes becoming combined into learned cue configurations which invoke subprocesses.
> It is hypothesized that the more problem-solving processes are used, the more expected and hence more consistent are the associated sets of cues. At a level peculiar to the individual, these cues are learned as consistent, and the decision net collapses into a process conditional on that learned cue configuration. The process is no longer a problem-solving process, but is now a simple standard decision rule. This learning process would lead to a switch of decision processes from Block 5 to Block 4. As an example of this process, consider Figures 2 and 3. Figure 2's abstract decision process has five cues. After this decision process has been used several times, suppose Cues 2 and 4 were combined into a learned configuration. Then the process would collapse to the conditional process shown in Figure 3.
> The idea of a monitor process which controls the collapsing of

[48] Michael Driver and Siegfried Streufert, "The General Incongruity Adaptation Level (GIAL) Hypothesis—An Analysis and Integration of Cognitive Approaches to Motivation," Institute Paper No. 114, Krannert School of Industrial Administration, Purdue University, 1964, p. 59.

Figure 17-5

A General Choice and Consumer Decision Process Model

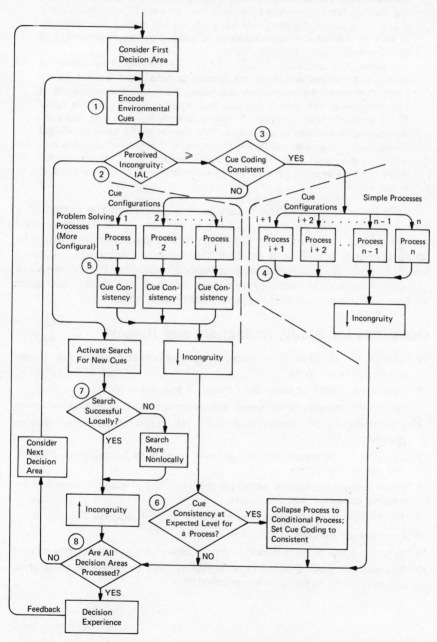

Source: James R. Bettman, "The Structure of Consumer Choice Processes," *Journal of Marketing Research,* Vol. 8 (November 1971), p. 469.

decision process graphs has been implemented with varying specificity by other researchers. However, growth of decision nets has not been considered in the general scheme, although some information processing models have considered decision net growth. This is definitely a shortcoming, since decision nets obviously do not spring into existence in all their complexity. More research is needed on the development of decision nets. . . .

Block 7: Exploratory behavior or novelty seeking. This aspect of decision processes embraces the consumer who "just wanted to try something new." As incongruity decreases from Block 4, eventually it may become so low (below the IAL) that boredom sets in. At this point, Block 2 would lead to Block 7, and a search for new and more incongruous alternatives would begin. This search would be local at first —that is, for consumer decisions, for example, it might be for a different brand of the same type. However, if this search were not successful, more nonlocal search, such as for a new, exciting, or unfamiliar product might ensue.[49]

We have introduced the reader in this chapter to the notion of a consumer's decision processes. Consumer decision processes have been treated within the context of consumer problem-solving and information-processing, which is a continuation of our established cognitive orientation. In the following chapter, which concludes Part V, we shall examine consumer decision processes in terms of risk taking and other aspects of information seeking and information processing.

Questions for Study, Reflection, and Review

1 Discuss the significance of perception and information processing in consumer decision-making.

2 Describe the general operational model of problem solving.

3 Distinguish between programmed and nonprogrammed consumer decisions.

4 Briefly discuss the factors determining the extent of consumer decision process behavior.

5 Describe the consumer decision process as affected by cognitive, affective, and conative activities.

6 Discuss the probabilistic nature of the hierarchy-of-effects proposition regarding consumer decision stages.

7 Briefly discuss the stages in the consumer decision process.

8 Describe the sources of consumer problems.

9 What are some of the factors that affect a consumer's search for information?

10 Describe the general model of consumer decision processes in terms of its perceptual-information processing orientation.

---

[49] Bettman, op. cit., p. 468.

18

Information Processing and Consumer Risk-Taking

Introduction

The proposal that consumer behavior involves risk taking was first put forth by Raymond A. Bauer, who was concerned with communications research and information handling.[1] He believed the communication process is a two-way street and that the audience plays at least as important a role as does the communicator in determining communication effectiveness. Bauer gained additional insight through his association with Robert O. Schlaifer, also of the Harvard Business School, who shared his concern with decision making under conditions of uncertainty. Bauer's paper, "Consumer Behavior as Risk Taking," crystallized many ideas that had been forming and set a theme for future research to be undertaken.

In late 1959 and early 1960, Cox conducted a long series of intensive interviews with two housewives.[2] The interview data revealed specific patterns of using information to handle uncertainty in decision making.

[1] Raymond A. Bauer, "Consumer Behavior as Risk Taking," *Proceedings of the 43rd Conference of the American Marketing Association*, Robert S. Hancock, ed., 1960, p. 389.

[2] Adapted from Donald F. Cox, "Introduction," *Risk Taking and Information Handling in Consumer Behavior*, Donald F. Cox, ed. (Boston: Division of Research, Graduate School of Business Administration, Harvard University, 1967), pp. 1–19.

Consumer behavior as risk taking is founded upon three basic axioms:

1. Consumer behavior is not a random process, but is oriented toward identifying and attaining buying goals.
2. Consumer decision-making activity is a type of problem-solving behavior. The consumer attempts to identify performance and psychological buying goals, to find the differences between these goals and the existing states of nature, and to match these goals with the products that provide a degree of perceived risk that is acceptable to the consumer.
3. The consumer may acquire, transmit, and process information in the problem-solving activity of identifying and satisfying buying goals. The value of this information is a function of its ability to modify the uncertainty encountered by the consumer.

This chapter is primarily concerned with the consumer's perceived risk in a purchase situation and the information-handling processes used by the consumer to alter the perceived risk.

A secondary concern is to examine the interaction of consumer characteristics with the information characteristics of acquisition, transmission, and processing. In sum, we will examine how and why different consumers handle different types of information under varying conditions of perceived risks.

Much of the research done in fields related to perceived risk and information handling will also be examined. The research studies are selected to acquaint the reader with the concepts of perceived risk. By drawing from several disciplines, we will tie together many of the bits and pieces of consumer behavior to provide a better understanding of consumer behavior as risk taking.

The Concept of Perceived Risk

A definition of *perceived risk* will be at best nebulous. There are several reasons for the lack of understanding of exactly what it is. First, even the researchers in this field define it somewhat differently. Bauer centers his idea of perceived risk around the idea that any action that a consumer takes will produce consequences that cannot be anticipated with anything approaching certainty and some of which are likely to be unpleasant.[3] Thus, Bauer argues, perceived risk permeates consumer behavior. This concept of perceived risk seems to have been highly influenced by Festinger's work, *A Theory of Cognitive Dissonance.* Festinger is primarily concerned with the ways in which people reduce perceived risk after decisions are made; Bauer extends this to prepurchase activity.

Cox feels each consumer has a set of buying goals associated with each purchase, and risk is perceived when the consumer realizes that

[3] Bauer, op. cit., p. 390.

he may not be able to reach his buying goals. Furthermore, perceived risk is a function of the uncertainty and the consequences of a buying situation. *Uncertainty* is the consumer's subjective feeling that the consequences of a purchase decision will be unfavorable and *consequences* means the amount at stake that would be lost if the act were not successful. There are psychological, functional, and economic consequences of a purchase decision.[4] Cox's concept is more complex than the original one put forth by Bauer. It is a step in the right direction because it explicitly incorporates more relevant and interrelated components of consumer decision-making.

Some even view the concept of perceived risk as having a chance aspect, in which the emphasis is on probability, and a danger aspect, in which the emphasis is on the severity of negative consequences. Cunningham conceptualized perceived risk as being comprised of uncertainty and consequences.[5] Uncertainty refers to the purchaser's lack of subjective certainty that an event will happen. Consequences refer to the resultant consequences if that certain event does happen. Cunningham captured the comprehensive nature of Cox's concept of perceived risk and refined it so that it is more flexible. Whereas Cox focused on the amount of perceived risk that would result *only* if the consequences were unfavorable, Cunningham avoided this by relating perceived risk to the uncertainty of any event's occurring, favorable or unfavorable, and the consequences that would result if that event occurred.

A second factor complicating the understanding of perceived risk is the terms used in describing it. Traditionally there are four states of nature. *Certainty* is when all states of nature are known and what state of nature will occur when a specific action takes place is also known. *Risk* refers to all the states of nature and the probabilities of given states of nature's occurring. *Uncertainty* is the condition in which all the alternative states of nature are known but the probability of their occurrence is not. *Ignorance* is the condition in which neither all the alternative states of nature nor their associated probabilities are known. Even in this set of definitions uncertainty and ignorance are often interchanged.

In many business situations one encounters conditions of risk, but these are usually limited to the more tangible problems. Consumer behavior is much more complex because it usually occurs in a state of ignorance, in which all possible states of nature are not known. Even for the simplest of choices, all the states of nature are usually beyond

[4] Donald F. Cox, "Risk Handling in Consumer Behavior—An Intensive Study of Two Cases," *Risk Taking and Information Handling in Consumer Behavior*, Donald F. Cox, ed. (Boston: Division of Research, Graduate School of Business Administration, Harvard University, 1967), pp. 36–38.

[5] Scott M. Cunningham, "The Major Dimensions of Perceived Risk," in *Risk Taking and Information Handling in Consumer Behavior*, Donald F. Cox, ed. (Boston: Division of Research, Graduate School of Business Administration, Harvard University, 1967), p. 83.

comprehension and the consumer usually considers only the most obvious consequences. In addition to not knowing all possible consequences, it is rare that the consumer knows the exact probability of a given consequence's happening. He usually feels that a certain consequence "might" happen. Even if the probabilities are available, the consumer is not likely to think in terms of them. This leads us to the third factor causing misunderstanding. In a purchase decision the actual probabilities or risks are irrelevant to a consumer's decision unless he has experienced them before and accepts them as they are. The important consideration of a purchase decision is the amount of risk perceived by the individual consumer and that consumer's subjective evaluation of that amount of perceived risk. The consumer's action will be based on his personal evaluation of the perceived risk, which will not necessarily be the action he "should" take based on the actual probabilities or risks.

In this text the use of the term *perceived risk* will differ from the use of the term *risk* as it applies to a state of nature. To avoid possible confusion, let us say that perceived risk occurs when an individual consumer perceives the possible hazard or chance of loss as the result of a purchase decision. Perceived risk will be a function of uncertainty and consequences. In terms of perceived risk, uncertainty is defined as the subjective uncertainty perceived by the individual consumer of a given event's happening. Consequences are defined as the consequences that will result from a given purchase decision.

Even when the terms have been identified as they were in the preceding paragraph the concept of perceived risk may be confusing because of the following factors. What one person may perceive as outside his tolerable boundary for perceived risk may be well within the next person's boundary. Additionally, one person may perceive a purchase as containing some types of perceived risks, whereas another may encounter other types. Lastly, what one perceives to be risky at some period in time may not be perceived as risky at a future date. Therefore, the concept of perceived risk is elusive because of its highly individualistic nature, its many facets, and its dynamic nature over time.

THE CAUSES OF PERCEIVED RISK

It has been assumed that the consumer is goal oriented. In a purchase decision the consumer tries to identify his buying goals and then match these goals with product offerings. Perceived risk may be caused by any one or a combination of the following factors:

1. The consumer may be uncertain as to what her buying goals are. The buying goals are not identified. Should the consumer purchase a black cocktail dress which would be functional and could be worn on many occasions, or should she purchase a "sexy dress"? Inability to identify buying goals may be the result of uncertainty about:
   a. The nature of the goals. Does she want a functional, versatile dress

that will yield good appearance and economy or does she want a "sexy dress" that will yield excitement and ego enhancement?

b. Goal acceptance levels or levels of aspirations. What will satisfy her goals? Does she just want to be well dressed or does she want to be the best dressed at the party?

c. The relative importance of achieving the goal. Is it more important to be well dressed or to have good furniture?

d. Current degree of goal attainment. Consumers may vary in their certainty concerning the extent of the difference between their current state and their desired goal acceptance level.

2. The consumer may be uncertain as to which purchase (place, product, brand, model, style, size, color, etc.) will best match or satisfy acceptance levels of buying goals. If the consumer wanted to be well dressed, at which store should she purchase her dresses? Or, if the consumer wants a special meal and knows that at a particular restaurant both the prime rib and lobster newburg are excellent, which item will satisfy the consumer more?

3. The consumer may perceive possible adverse consequences if the purchase is made (or is not made) and the result is a failure to satisfy her buying goals. If a "sexy dress" is inappropriate or ineffective, she may be embarrassed. If a laundry product does not perform as advertised she may waste time and/or damage clothes. In addition, in each case she would lose her investment.[6]

The previous factors do not comprise a complete list of the causes of perceived risk. These factors are of a generalized nature and most purchase situations can be included in these broad categories, although there may be specific exceptions. Granbois listed several determinants of perceived risk.[7] They included factors such as the consumer's having little past experience with the purchase decision; the consumer's past experience's being unsatisfactory; the purchase's being discretionary rather than necessary; all alternatives' having both positive and negative consequences; the consumer's knowing that this purchase decision differs from that of an important reference group; and the consumer's anticipating important changes in his economic or political environment. Some would argue that these factors can be classified under the more general classes of perceived risk previously discussed.

THE COMPONENTS OF PERCEIVED RISK

Perceived risk is comprised of uncertainty and consequences as diagrammed in Figure 18-1. As previously stated, uncertainty is the consumer's subjective uncertainty that an event will occur. Usually this can be interpreted in a more specific sense relating to a given purchase decision as the subjective uncertainty of matching the consumer's goals with the purchased product. In addition to matching goals and products, there may also be uncertainty in identifying or choosing the original

---

[6] Cox, "Introduction," op. cit., pp. 5–7.

[7] Donald H. Granbois, "The Role of Communication in the Family Decision-Making Process," in *Consumer Behavior: Selected Readings,* James F. Engel, ed. (Homewood, Ill.: Richard D. Irwin, Inc., 1968), pp. 153–154.

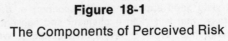

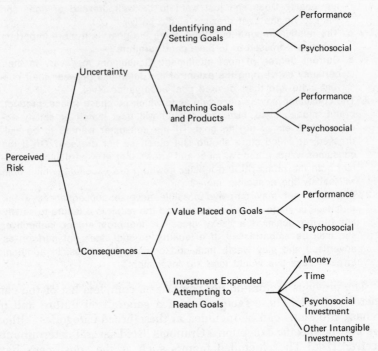

Figure 18-1

The Components of Perceived Risk

buying goals. There are usually two facets to these goals: (1) the consumer will set performance goals that relate to his expectations of the functional ability of the product, and (2) the consumer will set psychosocial goals that relate to how he and his peers will view his purchase decision. Indeed, buying goals may never be precisely defined in the mind of the consumer.

Consequences relate to the performance, the psychosocial, or the economic consequences that will occur after a purchase decision is made. The consequences are a function of the value placed by the consumer on the attainment of his goals and of the investment made in the attempt to attain these goals.

The components of perceived risk are diagrammed in Figure 18-1. These components can be approximated mathematically as follows:

$$PR = f(U, C);$$
$$U = f(g, m); \ g = f(p_{F_g}, p_{S_g}); \ m = f(p_{F_m}, p_{S_m});$$
$$C = f(v, i); \ v = f(p_{r_v}, p_{s_v}); \ i = f(d, t, p_S, O);$$

where:

PR = perceived risk
U = uncertainty

$C =$ consequences
$g =$ identifying and setting goals
$m =$ matching goals and products
$v =$ value placed on goals
$i =$ investment expended attempting to reach goals

and where:

$d =$ money
$t =$ time
$p_s =$ psychosocial investment
$O =$ other intangible investments
All p_{r_i} symbols are psychosocial goals
All P_{s_i} symbols are performance goals

Although the diagram and the mathematical model show each element as a discrete unit, they may be intertwined so that it is hard to distinguish between psychosocial and performance goals. This is easily demonstrated by a simple example. A housewife may demand an electric range with accurate temperature controls (a performance goal) so she can cook a perfect meal (a performance goal) for her dinner guests, which would enhance her image as a good housewife (a psychosocial goal). Therefore, the two types of goals are not always independent.

Because there may be performance risks and psychosocial risks involved, the types of perceived risks may react with each other. Although a consumer may be able to differentiate between perceived performance and psychological risk, it is doubtful that these elements could be specifically quantified. Additionally, even if the performance and psychosocial elements could be quantified separately, these quantities would probably not be additive. The total perceived risk of a purchase decision would then be greatly unequal to the sum of its elements. Or mathematically:

$$PR = f(U, C);$$
$$(U, C) > \Sigma(u, c)$$

where:

$PR =$ perceived risk
$U =$ uncertainty
$C =$ consequence
$u =$ a component of uncertainty
$c =$ a component of consequence

Each element of perceived risk becomes a part that changes the whole of the product. This phenomenon is an elementary perceptual axiom of Gestalt psychology that states that the whole is greater than the sum of its parts. The point to be made is that the purchase decision has to be viewed as a whole, a total system, not a conglomerate of parts.[8]

REACTION TO PERCEIVED RISK

The consumer will react to how he subjectively perceives and evaluates the risk in a purchase decision by taking action based on his evaluation of where the perceived risk is in relation to his acceptable range. If the type or amount of perceived risk is within the consumer's acceptable range, no action to alter the perceived risk will be made. If it is outside his range, he will take action to alter the amount or the type of perceived risk.

The consumer's acceptable range is dependent upon the type and absolute amount of perceived risk and the amount of investment required to modify either the amount or the type of perceived risk. It should be noted that this acceptable range is dynamic and can change over time by product, by person, by situation, and so forth.

Care has been taken to identify an acceptable level of perceived risk in order to incorporate the concept of a range that provides the flexibility to explain situations in which perceived risk is decreased or situations in which it is increased. Most of the research done has been concentrated on the reduction of uncertainty and perceived risk. However, there have been instances in which the consumer tries to increase perceived risks.[9] These instances are explained by the acceptance of a greater uncertainty and more perceived risks in hopes of greater payoffs. Another explanation is that a consumer will increase perceived risk and uncertainty to relieve boredom. Although there are instances of increasing uncertainty and perceived risk, reductions of these factors are most typical of consumer behavior and are the ones this chapter will examine.

METHODS OF REDUCING PERCEIVED RISK

There are basically two methods of reducing perceived risk. Either the uncertainty or the consequences can be reduced. The consumer can reduce uncertainty by increasing certainty. He can do this by seeking additional information. The consumer can reduce the consequences by reducing the amount at stake, which he can do by altering (lowering) his performance and psychological purchase goals. In addition, he may reduce the amount at stake by attempting to reduce the penalties that might be incurred in trying to make the gain and by reducing the means by which the gain is to be made. The consumer usually takes steps to increase certainty rather than reduce the amount at stake or the seriousness of the consequences in handling perceived risk.[10]

[8] Irving S. White, "The Perception of Value in Products," in *On Knowing the Consumer*, Joseph W. Newman, ed. (New York: John Wiley & Sons, Inc., 1966), pp. 90–107.

[9] Cox, "Introduction," op. cit., p. 9.

[10] Ibid., p. 80.

STRATEGIES FOR REDUCING PERCEIVED RISK

Some strategies that the consumer uses to reduce perceived risk are

1. Reliance on past experience and/or the experience of others.
2. Information seeking.
3. Taking precautionary measures.
4. Choice avoidance.
5. Goal avoidance.
6. Delegation of buying responsibility to others who are more competent.
7. Reliance on buying maxims.[11]

In addition, consumers often use methods of leveling and sharpening to reduce perceived risk. Leveling occurs when people distort the meaning by overlooking something in the advertising message. Sharpening occurs when people read into the message additional or unintentional meanings in order to make it conform to their preexisting beliefs. These concepts are closely related to perception and recall and are strategies of risk avoidance and risk assumption.[12]

One interesting application of risk avoidance in marketing is in the area of brand loyalty. The historical explanation of brand loyalty has been that a certain brand pleases the consumer so well that he develops a preference for that product and will not consider others. The concept of perceived risk offers an additional explanation of brand loyalty. Some consumers may not be committed to a particular brand, but they are brand loyal to avoid considering other alternatives.[13] Another study of consumer decision-making over time examined the risk-reducing strategies of information seeking, prepurchase deliberation, and brand loyalty. The findings indicated that information seeking and prepurchase deliberation declined over time and that brand loyalty increased over time.[14] This means simply that the consumer will take action on a product perceived as risky by using strategies of information seeking and prepurchase deliberation. Once the product is within the tolerable range of perceived risk, the consumer will then use the brand loyalty strategy to avoid perceived risk in future purchase decisions.

BUYING SITUATIONS THAT CONTAIN PERCEIVED RISK

It is possible for any purchase decision to contain perceived risk. Initially, it is more obvious that the perceived-risk concept could apply

---

[11] Ibid., p. 610.

[12] John C. Maloney, "Is Advertising Believability Really Important?" in *Consumer Behavior: Selected Readings*, J. F. Engel, ed. (Homewood, Ill.: Richard D. Irwin, Inc., 1968), pp. 153–154

[13] James F. Engel, David T. Kollat, and Roger D. Blackwell, *Consumer Behavior* (New York: Holt, Rinehart & Winston, Inc., 1968), pp. 52–53; also see Cunningham, op. cit., pp. 507–523.

[14] Jagdish N. Sheth and M. Venkatesan, "Risk-Reduction Processes in Repetitive Consumer Behavior," *Journal of Marketing Research*, Vol. 5 (August 1968), pp. 307–310.

to expensive items such as automobiles or major appliances, but the concept may apply equally to small-ticket items. The reason for this is that perceived risk is affected by the economic, performance, and psychosocial consequences of a purchase decision. One must also look beyond the primary consequences to the secondary consequences of the purchase decision. The decision to purchase a car may be perceived as risky because if it turns out to be a lemon the monetary loss, an economic consequence, could be substantial. The decision of a hostess to purchase a deodorant may be perceived as risky because if it fails she would suffer embarrassment, a psychosocial consequence. The secondary consequences may also be a source of perceived risk. If the deodorant does prevent offensive odors but does not stop perspiration stains, then a $300 hostess gown may be ruined (a secondary economic consequence).

As demonstrated by the deodorant example, the cost of the product is only one factor in determining perceived risk. In many purchase decisions the perceived risk generated by the cost of the product is only a small fraction of the perceived risk of the entire purchase decision. One must grasp the idea that psychosocial consequences may be far more important than obvious economic and performance consequences. One should also understand the possibility of secondary economic, performance, and psychosocial consequences. The broad applicability of the concept of perceived risk can be comprehended only after these basic ideas are understood, because the uncertainty of a purchase decision is a function of an unbounded set of possible consequences.

Research has shown that perceived risk applies to a wide range of products, such as headache remedies, fabric softeners, and spaghetti.[15] At the opposite end of the product spectrum there have been several studies showing perceived risk in the purchase of automobiles. Also there is a perceived-risk hierarchy. Some products or categories of products are perceived by most consumers to be more risky than others.[16] Although this phenomenon is apparent, one should think of the consumer as perceiving risk and reacting to this subjective evaluation of it as each purchase decision is encountered. One should not automatically classify a product as being a member of a certain risk category. Perceived risk is individualistic and may vary in intensity from person to person and over time.

Information Handling as a Means of Reducing Perceived Risk

The consumer can reduce perceived risk by reducing the uncertainty or the consequences of the purchase decision. Reducing the

---

[15] Cunningham, op. cit., p. 107.

[16] Ibid.; also see Donald F. Cox and Stuart U. Rich, "Perceived Risk and Consumer Decision Making—The Case of Telephone Shopping," *Journal of Marketing Research*, Vol. 1 (November 1964), pp. 32–39.

uncertainty is preferred by most consumers to reducing the consequences or the amount at stake because they are reluctant to alter their purchase goals once they are set. Most consumers prefer to seek information to reduce the uncertainty and thus the perceived risk of a purchase decision. Perhaps one possible reason that decreasing uncertainty is preferred to reducing the amount at stake is that man has some unsatisfied needs that generate wants and he expresses these wants as purchase goals. Rather than change these goals, which may leave some of his original needs unsatisfied, he prefers to retain the goals and increase the certainty of achieving them through information handling.

INFORMATION HANDLING AND COMMUNICATION

For years communication researchers and advertisers have studied how the audience is influenced and persuaded by information. The process of communication was viewed primarily as a one-way street with the advertisers doing the influencing and the consumers being persuaded. The newer viewpoint on information handling is that consumers participate actively in the communication process. Consumers will acquire, transmit, and process information in relation to their information needs. What the advertisers view as persuasive, the consumer may view as a decision on his part to use the advertiser's information for the purpose of making a better decision. In other words, consumers decide on the sources, type, and amount of information they will use in making a purchase decision. This does not imply that consumers are not passive at times. Rather, the implication is that when consumers have a need for information they will become actively involved in the process of acquiring and evaluating information. Another implication is that consumers are more likely to utilize an advertiser's message when it meets their information needs.

INFORMATION ACQUISITION. Consumer decision-making is a type of problem-solving activity. A problem is perceived by the consumer when information is received that indicates there may be a gap between his goal acceptance level and his existing state. This creates a degree of perceived risk. Not only does information receiving increase the perception of problems, but it also helps solve them. When perceived risk is significant, the consumer will seek additional information to reduce the uncertainty and risk. This process of information receiving or acquisition encompasses the source, the nature, and the amount of information received.

INFORMATION TRANSMISSION. Consumers often take the initiative in transmitting information to others through a process called interpersonal communications or word-of-mouth advertising. Information transmission research is concerned with the reason consumers transmit information, the types and amounts of information they transmit, and the relationship between opinion leaders and followers.

INFORMATION PROCESSING. Information processing refers to the way a consumer evaluates, uses, and stores different kinds of information. The consumer takes the initiative in processing information regardless of the way in which it was obtained—voluntarily or involuntarily. The consumer may be aware of this process or it may occur in his subconsciousness. In each case this process is patterned, systematic, and possibly predictable.[17]

Thus understanding how consumers handle information to reduce perceived risk is important because the use of information is the most widely used and preferred means of altering perceived risk. Instead of being a passive recipient of information, the consumer will take an active role in the communication process. First, the consumer will often take the initiative in information acquisition and transmission, and he will always take the initiative in the processing of information. Second, the processes of information acquisition, processing, and transmission are largely thought to be patterned, rather than random, behavior.

INFORMATION NEEDS. The consumer needs three types of information to make a purchase. First, he must be exposed to some information in order to be aware of the product. Second, there must be some information concerning the product that causes him to be interested. Third, he must have information to evaluate the product.

SOURCES OF INFORMATION. There are three primary sources of information available to the consumer. They are marketer-dominated, consumer-dominated, and neutral sources of information. Marketer-dominated channels of information are advertising, promotion, personal selling, and other aspects of product information over which the marketer has control. Consumer-dominated channels are word-of-mouth advertising and other types of interpersonal sources of information over which the marketer does not have direct control. Neutral sources of information are publications such as *Consumer's Report* and other sources that are not directly controlled by the marketer or the consumer. Now that the types of information sources are known, we need to know which of these sources the customer uses and for what reason.

Marketer-dominated channels provide the consumer with a wide variety of product information that is usually generalized rather than detailed. Although it may become more specific, the initial contact usually lacks specific information. The cost of the information to the consumer is quite low. The major drawback to marketer-dominated channels of information is that the consumer knows the marketer is trying to sell him something. Thus the consumer may ask questions such as "Is all he says true?" or "Is he not telling me the disadvantages about his product that I should know about?"

Consumer-dominated channels of communication provide advice

---

[17] The word *possibly* was added by the author. Although Cox feels the process is predictable, the author differs and thinks it may be only possible to predict.

that may result from the evaluations of a marketer's advertisement or the evaluation of the product by other consumers. Therefore, the consumer will be better able to evaluate the psychosocial and performance consequences with the information characteristic of this channel. The information found in this channel may vary from the simple to the complex because the channel is very flexible in adapting to the individual needs of each consumer. In addition, it is usually perceived by the consumer as being a more trustworthy source of information than the marketer-dominated channel, although the information may not be as accurate. The main disadvantage is that the cost of acquiring information is usually greater in the consumer-dominated channels because of the time spent by the consumer in seeking information.

Neutral channels offer accurate and trustworthy information at a relatively low cost. Like those of marketer-dominated channels, their messages are not as flexible or selective as are those of the consumer-dominated channels. The consumer may not be able to get as specific or as detailed information as he needs.

CONSUMER USE OF INFORMATION SOURCES. Because the consumer must have information to become aware of, to become interested in, and to evaluate a product, what sources are used for what type of information and when? The two-step flow implies that information sources compete with one another. The information-seeking model views the sources as complementary.[18]

Marketer-dominated channels or formal channels of communication may be used to create awareness, to stimulate interest, and to provide information for product evaluation. Consumer-dominated and neutral channels may be used for the same purpose. Let us examine how these channels may be used in a typical product decision. First, a marketer-dominated channel may create an awareness through an advertisement in some type of mass media. This awareness could be either that a product exists or that it is available somewhere. Second, the marketer-dominated channel may have provided enough information to stimulate an interest. Third, the consumer seeks information for evaluating the product through informal channels if the marketer-dominated channels do not satisfy his information needs.

In the evaluation process the consumer may need information about the product—its specifications, features, availability, price, and performance. The marketer may provide the type of information that enables the consumer to make product comparisons. Also, the consumer may need information to evaluate the psychosocial consequences of the purchase decision. This is the weakest point of the marketer-dominated channel and it is the strongest point of the consumer-dominated channel. The informal channel is more trustworthy and influential in providing the information used to evaluate the psychosocial consequences of a purchase decision.

[18] King and Summers, op. cit., p. 251.

Information seeking will occur after the consumer has received the information that created an awareness and stimulated an interest in a product, providing sufficient risk is perceived to justify the cost of information seeking. In many cases the marketer-dominated channels will create an awareness and stimulate an interest, but it will fail to satisfy completely the consumer's information needs for evaluation. Because the formal channels cannot provide adequate information about the product, the consumer must use informal channels as a complementary source of information to complete the evaluation of the product.

The consumer may use informal sources at any time in the awareness-interest-evaluation process. It does seem most probable, however, that the consumer would seek information from informal channels only if the formal sources failed to satisfy his information needs, because information seeking is more costly than information receiving. For most purchase decisions the marketer-dominated channels are most likely to be able to create an awareness and stimulate an interest, but informal channels are more important sources of information in the evaluation stage of the adoption process.[19]

It has been suggested that a consumer will use informal channels of information if the perceived risk is high enough to warrant the cost.[20] Thus those who recognize a high perceived risk would be more likely to use informal channels of information to reduce this risk to a tolerable level.[21] A study of twelve hundred housewives also revealed that risk reduction is not necessarily a continual process or one that occurs with every purchase but is one that may occur at widely separated intervals.[22] Thus for many low-risk products or products whose perceived risk has been reduced to a tolerable level, the consumer may not seek information from informal channels at all.

USE OF INFORMAL CHANNELS. In the two-step flow the opinion leader relays information from the marketer to the group members. The opinion leader, as previously stated, is not merely a relayer of information; in addition, he screens and evaluates the information before he passes it on. The information-seeking model questions whether group members are so passive that they receive only the opinion leader's transmission as is believed by the two-step hypothesis. A number of

[19] Everett M. Rogers, *Diffusion of Innovation* (New York: The Free Press, 1962), p. 99.

[20] Donald F. Cox, "Synthesis-Risk Taking and Information Handling," in *Risk Taking and Information Handling in Consumer Behavior,* Donald F. Cox, ed. (Boston: Division of Research, Graduate School of Business Administration, Harvard University, 1967), pp. 606–610.

[21] Raymond A. Bauer, "Consumer Behavior as Risk Taking," in *Proceedings of the 43rd Conference of the American Marketing Association,* R. S. Hancock, ed. (1960), pp. 389–398.

[22] Cox, "Synthesis-Risk Taking and Information Handling," op. cit., pp. 606–610.

studies show that approximately 50 per cent of the product conversations were initiated not by the opinion leader but by the consumer who was seeking information about the product.[23] This finding refutes the previous implication that the audience is passive. The consumer is active in informal communication channels when his needs are not satisfied by the formal channels. One interesting implication of Cunningham's survey was that a high-risk perceiver may become an opinion leader because he has developed some expertise as a result of his information-seeking activity to reduce his own perceived risk.[24]

THE IMPACT OF WORD-OF-MOUTH ADVERTISING. It has been demonstrated that those receiving favorable word-of-mouth information were four to seven times as likely to buy as those who were not personally influenced.[25] Word-of-mouth advertising is more effective than any other source of information. The usual explanation for the impact of word of mouth is that because it is interpersonal, there is individual or group pressure to comply with the advice given or received. Another reason of at least equal importance for this impact is that consumers engage in word-of-mouth discussion to reduce perceived risk and that this informal channel is particularly valuable as an information source because it is trustworthy and reliable.

The communication process is much more complex than we first believed. Although the two-step flow may be relatively valid in describing a particular phenomenon in the communication process, it does not offer a comprehensive explanation that would include the following important phenomena. First, the communication process is a multistep process. Second, opinion leaders are not as influential or effective as first believed. Third, consumers actively seek and transmit information in informal channels to reduce perceived risk. Fourth, the channels are viewed by the consumer as complementary rather than competitive.

COMMUNICATIONS MODELS: A REVISED LOOK

It is doubtful if any communications model could completely describe the communication process. Communication processes are multidimensional, interrelated, and largely intangible. Then why set upon such a formidable task as constructing a revised model? However mundane and repetitive it may be, the objective is to integrate several of the existing models and known phenomena to yield a more accurate and comprehensive model that will better duplicate the essence of the communication system.

Furthermore, the communication models presented in Chapter 11 depicted communication largely from the point of view of the marketer or the disseminator of information or messages. The model in Figure

[23] Ibid., pp. 182–183.

[24] Cunningham, op. cit., pp. 287–288.

[25] Jagdish N. Sheth, "Perceived Risk and Diffusion of Innovations," in *Insights into Consumer Behavior*, Johan Arndt, ed. (Boston: Allyn & Bacon, Inc., 1968), pp. 173–189.

18-2, however, is an information-seeking model. This model depicts the communication process from the point of view of the consumer decision-maker confronted by perceived risk and, hence, uncertainty.

Before the model is presented, let us digress a bit and discuss two problems that plague and complicate the communication process. First, words do not have meaning in themselves; they depend on people to give them meaning. Therefore, it is not the transfer of words but the transfer of meaning that is the goal of communication. A vivid example of the difference between words and meanings is the vocabulary of the average person, excluding the jargon peculiar to his environment. He can recognize in excess of 600,000 words. Of those he uses approximately 2,000 words daily. By using a dictionary, one finds that the 500 most frequently used words have over 14,000 meanings. This example demonstrates how words can frequently fail to convey the meaning intended in communication with others. This leads us to the second problem that makes the whole communication process so difficult. In the communication process there are three phases of alteration between an intended meaning and the resultant meaning as the communication process takes place. The first phase of degradation occurs as one encodes one's thoughts (meaning) into words. Everyone has felt at one time or another that he could not express himself to his satisfaction. The second phase occurs in the transmission of a message. It involves the inconsistency of what is said with what is heard. All, part, or none of what is said may be heard, and what is heard is received at varying degrees of conscious or subconscious attention. In other words, we may not even be exposed to what is said, or we may not be paying attention to those communications (what is said) to which we are exposed. In either case, we do not hear all of what is said. The third phase of degradation occurs as we decode what we heard into thoughts. What different meanings would different people find in such a statement as, "Too much government is bad for business"? In sum, communication is difficult because words do not have meaning in themselves but depend on people to give them meaning.

THE INFORMATION-SEEKING MODEL: A MASS COMMUNICATIONS MODEL. There are two versions of the information seeking model—one for mass communications and one for personal communications. The mass communications model depicts the firm as it selects cognitions from its reservoir of market knowledge and organizes them into a message or communication. The message transmitted is dependent upon the adequacy of the firm's market knowledge and its ability to express this knowledge in an effective manner. This describes why some advertisements are good and others are poor. The communication is subject to the first phase of degradation as the firm tries to encode its message. The concept of degradation is used because it is more comprehensive than are the terms of noise, amplification, and distortion. Degradation would include all elements or phenomena that would have the effect of changing the meaning of the intended communication.

Because the firm's selection of the various media will affect the market response to its advertised message, this is an important consideration in the transmission stage. The firm wishes to accomplish two objectives. First, it wants to reach the largest number of desired prospects and customers per dollar spent on promotion. Second, it wants those it reaches to hear what is said. At times these two objectives are in conflict because one objective deals with efficiency whereas the other is concerned with effectiveness. The model illustrates these two objectives and the second phase of degradation with the arrow showing an escape of energy from the transmission stage, thus indicating that some of the transmission is not received by anyone and that none or only part of the communication may be received by some. Receiving none or only part of the communication indicates that the medium is to some degree undesirable. Stated again, the second phase of degradation occurs when all that is said is not heard. Therefore, in the transmission stage degradation can take the form of events such as media not reaching a relevant market, of not having the attention of the prospect or the customer reached, and of the technical errors relative to printing and broadcasting.

As the model indicates, opinion leaders are exposed to and receive a greater amount of communication than group members. Not only are they exposed to a greater amount of communication, but they are also exposed to more types and sources of communication than group members.

The third phase of degradation becomes active as the receiver of the message decodes what is heard into cognitions or, in other words, associates meaning with what is heard. Each person assigns his own meaning to the message.

The resultant meaning is dependent on a multitude of interrelated factors, such as past experience, images, values, attitudes, beliefs, environmental factors, and the message source. This is not a comprehensive list but is meant to give the reader an idea of the type of factors that affect perception, interpretation, and the assignment of meaning.

After meanings are associated with a given message, those meanings or cognitions are added to the individual's reservoir of thoughts, which comprise his cognitions, attitudes, beliefs, values, and so forth. The more effective messages will be those that match the individual's reservoir of cognitions, attitudes, beliefs, and values. Messages that attempt to change the individual's purchase behavior will have first to alter his reservoir of cognitions. The effect of one message will alter the total reservoir to only a small extent, and thus any change in purchase behavior is likely to be in only a small degree.

The reservoir is constantly undergoing change. Not only are meanings of messages being added, but also some existing ones are undergoing alteration. They may be forgotten, leveled, sharpened, or discarded, just to name a few of the phenomena that occur in the individual's cognitive system. In the model these phenomena, which

Figure 18-2

The Information Seeking Model: A Mass Communication Model

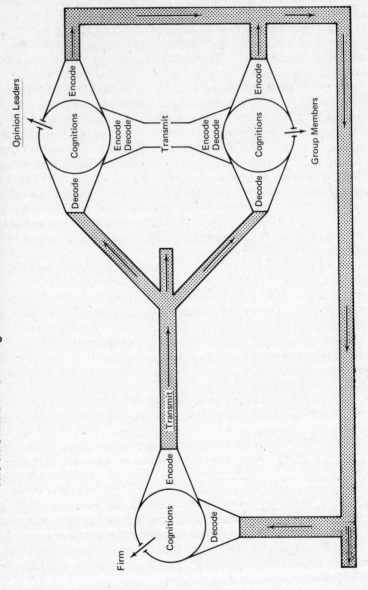

represent an alteration of the original message meanings, are symbolized by the exit opening in the memory cell with an outflowing arrow to represent an energy loss in the system. Some may argue that the alteration that occurs in the individual's memory is the fourth phase of degradation of communication. Additional research is needed in this area before any final conclusions can be drawn. One of the arguments supporting the idea of degradation is that some messages that are greatly in conflict with one's present cognitions or that cause extreme emotional arousal are often discarded, forgotten, or minimized. On the other hand, it may be that the alteration phenomena can be explained in terms of redecoding, encoding, or internal memory-processing independent of the communication process. In that case, there would not be a fourth phase of degradation of the communication process because the alteration, not classified as being one of the three phases that occurred, would be associated with independent internal processing and would not be a part of the communication process.

Because the objective of this model is to depict mass communication processes, the interaction between individuals is not directly discussed. The interaction between opinion leaders and group members is shown, however, to indicate that both the opinion leaders and the group members actively participate in receiving and transmitting data. The audience is no longer the passive recipient of transmitted communications as before. Instead, the audience seeks information to fulfill their information needs. The group member often initiates product discussion in the interactive relationship with the opinion leader. Both transmit and receive information as shown by the interaction dyad. The dyad is open to account for second-phase degradation, similar to that of the formal channel, as the group member and the opinion leader interact.

Consumers consciously or unconsciously encode their thoughts of the firm's message into some response that is transmitted over a feedback or response loop. This encoding of the response is also subject to the first phase of degradation.

Unfortunately, only a small part of the response transmitted over the feedback loop is captured by the firm, as indicated by the small transmission line leading to the firm. The second phase of degradation is usually at its most powerful in the feedback loop because most of the response (what is said) is never sensed (heard) by the antennae of the firm. The trouble lies in the fact that most firms have relatively strong channels of communication for transmitting information but have crudely developed and weak channels for receiving or sensing market response information. Ironically, it seems the firm has a fault that is common in most humans; that is, they like to talk rather than listen. To interject a moral into this analogy, it is more difficult to listen than to talk, but those who do listen effectively are usually more successful than those who do not. Again, to stress this vital point, most of the market response is not detected and this results in an energy loss to the system.

In decoding the market response the firm does happen to capture somehow, the firm faces the same third phase of degradation that the consumer faces. In fact, it may be more difficult for the firm to associate meaning with the market response it has detected because of the nature of the response. Third-phase degradation in the firm's decoding process can take many intentional as well as unintentional forms, but it is beyond the scope of this discussion to treat the implications and organizational problems that could arise from decoding market information.

The final step in the system cycle is the adding of the decoded market information to the firm's reservoir of market knowledge. Many of the phenomena that occur in the human mind are also present in the firm's information system. The most fundamental of these is that the firm can also lose information (energy). To draw another analogy, although a human may have great amounts of information, he may also forget great amounts; likewise, a firm may have an excellent information-gathering and -recording system, but it may have an extremely poor information retrieval system.

Now that the mass communications model is built, the next step is to construct a model of the interpersonal communication process.

THE INFORMATION-SEEKING MODEL: AN INTERPERSONAL COMMUNICATIONS MODEL. The primary function of this model is to represent the communicative process as it exists on a personal basis. Most of the concepts found in the mass communications model are found here. The same logic prevails for this system. Briefly, one draws from a reservoir of cognitions, encodes them, and transmits the message; and the other individual decodes the message and adds it to his reservoir of cognitions. The system is still subject to the three phases of degradation. Loss of energy is represented by the open interaction dyad and the reservoir openings.

The primary difference is the emphasis on the importance of the interactive relationship as indicated by the interaction dyad. The interactive relationship between the participants eliminates the need for a subsidiary feedback loop. This is not to say there is no feedback; instead it emphasizes that the response is more direct and explicit. A second implication of the interaction dyad is that consumers actively participate in the communication process. They are active information-seekers and they often initiate the product conversation by questioning those individuals who can satisfy their information needs. Many times they transmit information to their peers, in support of the trickle-across phenomena. There are many other implications that could be explored. The reader may wish to review some of these by taking another look at previous models and their shortcomings, the studies of communications, and the information-handling viewpoints that were presented in preceding sections of this book.

The revised communication models are designed to incorporate the strengths and minimize the weaknesses of previous models and to tie together many of the concepts and phenomena, both sociopsycho-

Figure 18-3

The Information Seeking Model:
An Interpersonal Communication Model

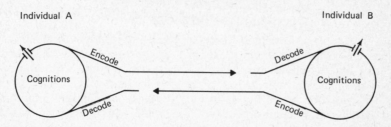

logical and sociocultural, involved in the process of communication. As our understanding of this complex process improves, our ability to predict the probable effectiveness of our communications, as the variables are changed, will increase. Finally, as has been stated, as we understand and are able to predict, steps can be made in controlling the variables of the communications process. The last statement does not imply that the firm will be able to manipulate the consumer. Quite the contrary, it means that the firm will be able to communicate more effectively and efficiently because it understands its market better. In other words, as the firm develops its feedback channels, it will better understand the likes and dislikes of the market. Because of this knowledge the firm will be able to alter its marketing mix to serve the market. The firm will become more effective and efficient because it will be able to encode more effective messages and make better media selections when advertising its products, prices, and places to the consumer.

Now that the process of communication within this new context has been discussed, we shall proceed in the next section with an analysis of the last major aspect of information handling, that of information processing.

Information Processing

Consumers take an active part in the communication process. They always assume the initiative in the processing of information. They must evaluate the information they have received and decide what to use and what to remember. The value of a product the advertiser tries to communicate does not automatically equate with the value the consumer perceives.[26] The consumer is not a passive recipient of a value already innate in a product; he is a selector and organizer of this experience. Thus, because he thinks for himself, the consumer is not passively influenced to change. Although advertisers use many tech-

[26] Irving S. White, "The Perception of Value in Products," in *On Knowing the Consumer*, J. Newman, ed. (New York: John Wiley & Sons Inc.), pp. 90–97.

niques to persuade him, the individual still retains the power of evaluation and decision. The consumer determines the value of a product in relation to his needs; and he decides whether or not and to what degree he will be influenced by the advertiser's message.

CONSUMER DECISION-MAKING THEORIES

The study of how consumers process information is a study of consumer decision-making processes. There are several theories of decision-making processes. Classical economists assume a rational man who bases his decisions on marginal revenue and marginal cost. The scientific method starts by stating a hypothesis or defining a problem and arriving at a conclusion several steps later. Optimizing models use the power of mathematics to manipulate the variables of the problem to yield an optimum answer. The major limitation of these models is the failure to cast light on the subjective processes that form the core of consumer decision-making.

Decision making by bounded rationality views rationality as being limited by inherent psychological and environmental factors. Personal motives and goals become an integral part of the decision-making process. The decision maker knows only a few of the alternatives available to him and what he expects of these is subjective because of incomplete and imperfect information.[27] The decision effort is directed toward satisfying, not maximizing.[28]

The concept of bounded rationality gives us a foundation from which we can take a deeper look into the actual information-processing activity in decision making. This activity is difficult to analyze because it is second nature to the decision maker and is done with relative ease. Additionally, the subject being studied is sure that no amount of analysis will be able to reproduce his processing activity because it is "intuitive."[29] The information-seeking model borrows the concept of bounded rationality. Therefore, it is a departure from most theories that consider the decision maker "rational" because it is primarily concerned with the rationalized subconscious, which they do not consider at all.[30]

METHODS OF PROCESSING INFORMATION

SEARCH PATTERNS. The consumer uses one of two search patterns to obtain and evaluate alternatives. One is a display pattern in which several alternatives are enumerated and expectant outcomes are

[27] R. M. Cyert and J. W. March, *A Behavioral Theory of the Firm* (Englewood Cliffs, N.J.: Prentice-Hall, Inc., 1963), pp. 124–127.

[28] John E. Fleming, "Study of a Business Decision," *California Management Review*, Vol. 9 (Winter 1966), p. 51.

[29] John A. Howard and William M. Morganroth, "Information Processing Model of Executive Decision," *Management Science*, Vol. 14 (March 1968), p. 417.

[30] Robert C. Ferber, "The Role of the Subconscious in Executive Decision Making," *Management Science*, Vol. 13 (April 1967), p. B519.

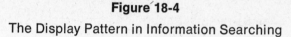

Figure 18-4

The Display Pattern in Information Searching

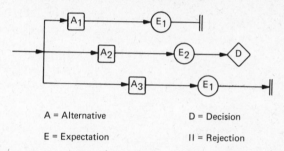

A = Alternative   D = Decision

E = Expectation   II = Rejection

formulated for each. Although the outcome of one of the first alternatives may have been acceptable, the decision maker continues to examine the other courses of action and chooses the best alternative. The concept of the display pattern is shown in Figure 18-4.

The second search pattern, the sequential pattern, is shown in Figure 18-5. The consumer evaluates each alternative before searching for the next. At times this leads to the acceptance of a satisfactory course of action rather than the best one. The primary reason for this is that the decision maker terminates the search process when an acceptable alternative is found.

Both search patterns are similar to the concept of bounded rationality because of the diverse decisions that can be observed, although the sequential pattern is the closer of the two to the concept. Diverse decisions are reached because each man will bring into a problem situation his personality, experience, and aspirations. The development of expectations is highly subjective and relies on subjective appraisals and past experience instead of facts. The sequential pattern is more congruent to the bounded-rationality concept because the limited-search effort and the decision-making effort are directed toward finding a satisfactory solution rather than an optimum solution to the problem.

Green compared the search process by which consumers acquire and use risk-reducing information to a Bayesian model. He found that the consumer does not use all of the information available to him and tends to obtain too little information instead of too much, seemingly because a psychic tension caused by extended searching results in a psychological cost that is added to the monetary cost of the additional information. Thus the total cost of the information is higher than the monetary cost.[31]

---

[31] Paul E. Green, "Consumer Use of Information," *On Knowing the Consumer*, Joseph W. Newman, ed. (New York: John Wiley & Sons, Inc., 1966), pp. 67–80; also see J. T. Lonzetta and V. T. Kanareff, "Information Cost, Amount of Payoff and Level of Aspirations as Determinates of Information Seeking in Decision Making," *Behavioral Science*, Vol. 7 (October 1962), pp. 459–473.

Figure 18-5

The Sequential Pattern in Information Searching

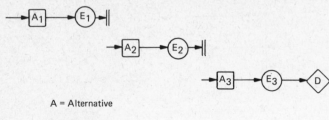

A = Alternative

E = Expectation

D = Decision

II = Rejection

EVALUATION METHODS. That consumers are rational but not in a very deliberative sense is suggested by the bounded-rationality concept.[32] The consumer rank-orders alternatives in an effort-reward combination according to his perceived probability of their occurrence.[33] This is done rather subjectively and crudely.[34] If the consumer rationally ranks alternatives on a crude basis, what processes are necessary to reach this result? How does the consumer evaluate a product?

An important work in the evaluation process is the sorting-rule model.[35] This model assumes that a product is conceived of as an array of cues. This array of cues contains such information as price, color, scent, feel, and friends' and salesmen's opinions. The consumer evaluates a product by using these information cues to make judgments about a product. Some cues will be valued more highly than others, and the higher the value of a given cue, the higher the probability that that cue will be used as a primary basis for evaluating the product. Thus the consumer is selective in using information about a product and will tend to base evaluations primarily on information or cues that are valued highly.

The sorting-rule model suggests that the consumer will follow certain steps. In order to understand how the sorting-rule model is used

[32] Paul E. Green, "Decision Theory and Market Plánning and Research," in *Models, Measurement and Marketing*, Peter Langhoff, ed. (Englewood Cliffs, N.J.: Prentice-Hall, Inc., 1965), pp. 171–196.

[33] Jerome B. Kernan, "Choice Criteria, Decision Behavior and Personality," *Journal of Marketing Research*, Vol. 5 (May 1968), pp. 155–164.

[34] W. T. Tucker, *Foundations for a Theory of Consumer Behavior* (New York: Holt, Rinehart & Winston, Inc., 1967), pp. 133–144.

[35] Adapted from Donald F. Cox, "The Sorting Rule Model of the Consumer Product Evaluation Process," in *Risk Taking and Information Handling in Consumer Behavior*, Donald F. Cox, ed. (Boston: Division of Research, Graduate School of Business Administration, Harvard University, 1967), pp. 324–369.

in the evaluation of a product, assume that the housewife wants to buy a lemon. She will proceed through the following steps:

1. She will establish attribute categories on which the product will be judged. These will be based on the consumer's buying goals or the characteristics of the product. Each attribute will have a set of categories. Assume the attribute under consideration is taste. The attribute categories are sour, bitter, and sweet. The consumer must judge what the lemon's taste will be or of what category of the attribute of taste the lemon will be a member.

2. She will assign values and attributes to each attribute category. The consumer may value a bitter taste more than a sour or sweet taste.

3. She will establish criteria by which the product is defined as being in a particular attribute category. This involves the selection of the cues that are the most important to the consumer. Suppose the consumer chooses color and weight in relation to size.

4. She will establish criterion categories and criterion-attribute relationships. A criterion category is a set of specific cues, similar in nature but varying in degree, that tend to predict the same attribute category. Each of these categories tend to be associated with a particular attribute, such as:
   a. Colors $yellow_1$ to $yellow_{10}$ tend to indicate sweet lemons.
      Colors $yellow_{11}$ to $yellow_{28}$ tend to indicate bitter lemons.
      Colors $yellow_{29}$ to $yellow_{37}$ tend to indicate sour lemons.
   b. Weight/size ratio of 2:1 predicts sweet.
      Weight/size ratio of 3:1 predicts bitter.
      Weight/size ratio of 4:1 predicts sour.

Thus $yellow_{15}$ is a specific cue of the criterion category that tends to indicate bitter lemons.

5. She will assign a predictive value to each criterion-attribute relationship. The consumer may assign a predictive value of .8 on color, and .7 on weight/size to indicate the taste attribute of the lemon. The consumer does this quite subjectively. Although there are probably many determinants making up a consumer's predictive value, it is probably based primarily on past experience. Therefore, in this case, the consumer feels that color is a better indication of taste than is weight/size ratio.

6. She will establish a degree of confidence or confidence value by which each cue can be sorted into a criterion category. If the consumer does not consider herself a good judge of what color of yellow indicates a bitter taste in the lemon, she will assign a low confidence value to the color cue. She may assign a high confidence value to the weight/size ratio because there are scales available that she can use to determine this ratio. This is a different dimension than predictive value. Predictive

value refers to the ability of a cue to predict an attribute. Confidence value is how confident the consumer is in being able to use the predictive cue correctly.

7. She will sort the product into an attribute category. The consumer will try to determine whether the lemon is sour, bitter, or sweet. She will use the criterion category with the highest predictive value to sort the lemon into the attribute category, provided that the cue has a high confidence value. If the cue does not have a high confidence value, the criterion category that has the next highest predictive value and whose cues have a high confidence value will be used to sort the product into the indicated attribute category.

Thus by using the sorting rule the consumer would first attempt to sort the lemon into the sour, bitter, or sweet category on the basis of color because this criterion has the highest predictive value (.8). However, if the consumer is unable to distinguish between the various shades of color and therefore has a low degree of confidence in her ability to choose a color that indicates a bitter lemon, she will then use the weight/size ratio, although it has a lower predictive value (.7), because she can determine the ratio with a high degree of confidence with the store scales. The decision whether the lemon is sour, bitter, or sweet will then be based primarily on the weight/size criterion.

8. She will combine the various judgments already made in order to make a higher-order judgment, such as quality. The consumer may repeat the preceding process for additional attributes such as freshness. Each attribute would then be weighted according to the value or consequence of the respective categories. That value would be multiplied by the subjective probability of receiving that value. The subjective probability of receiving the value will be a function of the predictive value of the criterion category and the confidence value of the cues belonging to the criterion category. For example, the consumer may value freshness twice as highly as bitterness in determining the quality of a lemon, but if the consumer is twice as certain the lemon is bitter as she is certain it is fresh, she may assign the two attributes an equal weight in determining quality.

9. She will validate the judgment made. The consumer will validate the predictive value and the degree of confidence of the criteria with which she categorized the lemon by tasting it.

We shall now discuss the major implications of this model. First, the cues used to make an evaluation are selected on their predictive and confidence values. This is a departure from previous work done in psychology that assumed that evaluations about information were made on the basis of predictive value only.

Second, the relationship between a cue on which an evaluation is made and the attributes on which the decision is made need not be a logical one. This was demonstrated most explicitly by an appliance company that had a successful electric mixer. They insulated it to make it operate more quietly and immediately sales dropped. It was discovered later that the reason for the decline in sales was that consumers interpreted a quieter mixer as being a less powerful one. The company removed the insulation and sales increased. In this classical case sound instead of rated horsepower predicted power, which was illogical.

Third, every cue can be assigned to an attribute category with a predictive value between −1 and +1.

Fourth, the number of cues on which the consumer makes a judgment is a function of the predictive and confidence values assigned to these cues. Thus, one cue can affect the judgment of many attributes of a product. For example, the odor of hosiery influenced judgments about its texture, feel, and wearability. This is one aspect of the halo effect.

Fifth, consumers may vary as to the amount of predictive confidence value assigned to the same cues. For example, the same flavor sherbert was made with various colors. Those who relied on color as a predictor thought different colored sherbet varied in taste. Those who were not misled by the cue conflict placed a lower predictive and/or confidence value on color and based their judgments on flavor, which had higher predictive and/or confidence values.

The sorting-rule model and its implications were supported entirely by an experiment of 414 lower- annd middle-class housewives in Boston.[36] In summary, consumers evaluate or assign an information value to cues based on the cue's predictive value and the cue's confidence value. The consumer will base his evaluation on the cue with the highest predictive value, but he will prefer a high-confidence-value and a low-predictive-value cue to a low-confidence-value and a high-predictive-value cue.

The sorting-rule model differs from other models explaining the use of information in the evaluation process in three ways. First, the predictive value of information is based on the consumer's estimate of the degree of association between the cue and the attribute. The older Brunswick model is based on the ecological validity of the cue.[37] The ecological validity is not always a good predictor of the perceived-information value of a cue because a cue may be perceived as more or less valid than it is. There need be no logical relationship between the cue on which the evaluation is based and the attribute on which the product is evaluated.

[36] For additional implications, see Cox, "The Sorting Rule Model of the Consumer Product Evaluation Process," op. cit., pp. 338–341.

[37] L. Postman and E. C. Tolman, "Brunswick's Probabilistic Functionalism," in *Psychology: A Study of a Science, Study F, Volume 1, Sensory Perceptual and Physiological Foundations*, S. Koch, ed. (New York: McGraw-Hill Book Company, 1959), p. 513.

Second, two dimensions of information value are recognized instead of one. In addition to the predictive-value dimension of a cue, there is another independent dimension called the confidence value of a cue. The confidence value is how certain the consumer is that the cue is what he thinks it is. This explains the phenomenon of cue preference, in which a cue is valued higher or lower than it should be.

Third, with the Brunswick model the consumer assigns weights to the cues in relation to their ecological validity and then bases his decision on the weighted sum or the expected value of the cues in an array.[38] The sorting-rule model states that the consumer will not weight cues in relation to their ecological validity or use a weighted sum of the validity of the array of cues to make a decision. The consumer is more selective in the use of information and uses only cues with the highest information value. The information value is not a simple additive or multiplicative function of predictive and confidence values.

Conclusions

There are few direct applications of risk taking and information handling that the marketer of today will be able to use in his marketing strategy. Instead, the concept of perceived risk is valuable because it ties many of the bits and pieces of consumer behavior together and presents a more unified picture of consumer behavior. In addition to providing a framework for others to build upon, the concept is also valuable because it points out what we do not know. By using the concept of perceived risk we can also see some gaps in current theories of consumer behavior. The information-seeking model of communications resulted because of the shortcomings of previous communications models.

As we learn more about consumer behavior we come to understand that it is more complex than we realized. This knowledge should serve notice to those who grasp for one simple, single law of consumer behavior. As our knowledge increases, we come to the realization that there are few, if any, laws of consumer behavior. We might very well ask whether such a continuation of this type of research is justifiable. Research must be continued so that the frontiers of knowledge will be pushed back. We need the more complex to understand the simpler. As we acquire more knowledge we hopefully will reach a new and higher plateau for recognizing and understanding the needs of consumers and for adapting to and satisfying these needs.

The main finding of the concept of perceived risk is that consumers have a need for information to help them satisfy their consumption needs and that consumers react favorably to and use the information that helps them solve the problems they encounter in satisfying their consumption needs.

[38] F. H. Allport, *Theories of Perception and the Concept of Structure* (New York: John Wiley & Sons, Inc., 1955), p. 259.

Questions for Study, Reflection, and Review

1 Define the concept of perceived risk as it applies to consumer decision-making.

2 What are the possible causes of perceived risk in purchase situations?

3 Identify and discuss the components of perceived risk.

4 Describe the purchase situations in which perceived risk is apt to be most prevalent.

5 Discuss the importance of information processing as a means of reducing perceived risk.

6 What are the various sources of information available to the consumer and how does the consumer use these sources?

7 Comment on the problem of generating a common meaning in the communication process.

8 What are the major differences between the mass communications model and the interpersonal communications model?

9 Distinguish between the two search patterns used by consumers to obtain and evaluate alternatives.

10 Discuss the sorting-rule model and its implications for consumer evaluation of alternatives.

Part VI

Concluding Comments

19

Theory and Metatheory in Consumer Behavior: New Directions and New Research

Introduction

During the preceding eighteen chapters we have examined the various dimensions of consumer behavior, and although our treatment has lacked neither depth nor scope, there are several reasons that this book can be considered an introduction. First of all, in exploring the concepts, generalizations, theory, and examples illustrating how social and behavioral science findings are used for gaining an understanding of consumer behavior, we have presented only sufficient material to enable the reader to construct his own problem designs. Second, this book is an introduction because the field of consumer behavior is so relatively new. We have, figuratively speaking, stepped upon but a few islands of knowledge in what is otherwise an uncharted sea of mystery, ignorance, and misunderstanding. From our humble beginnings and undertakings in this, and the other early works in consumer behavior, will emerge a more cohesive, more scientific understanding of consumer behavior. Yet in many ways the real difficulty in writing this book was not to find enough examples, concepts, generalizations, or theories to fill a book but to determine how much to exclude and how to integrate what was included into some meaningfully patterned whole.

The variety of concepts, generalizations, and theories related to consumer behavior would fill several volumes. Yet it was felt that giving too many generalizations or presenting too many concepts would clutter up the material to the point that the reader would not be able to see the forest for the trees. It is hoped that what has been presented will be useful to students, teachers, researchers, and practitioners. Thus the writer's main purpose has not been to present loosely connected odd pieces of information and disjointed conceptualizations. Although the individual trees may be shown to be particularly useful, our main object has been to present the forest. Given the rapidly exploding stream of information regarding consumer behavior and the amount of reported research results, it is quite difficult for a would-be technologist to keep up to date with everything that may be applicable to the field. This, of course, leads to still another reason for considering this book an introduction. Although a tremendous amount of research has been conducted and although extremely important and unexpected generalizations have been discovered, research in consumer behavior and the behavioral and social sciences continues. Very probably some of the greatest discoveries about ourselves and about ourselves as consumers are still to be made. As in most areas of science and technology, there is a perpetual sense of wonder at how much has already been accomplished. Most importantly, however, it must be stated that for new discoveries in consumer behavior or in the behavioral or social sciences generally to be really effective in improving consumer strategies or facilitating improved market planning, it is essential that all this knowledge be installed in the conscious and subconscious attitudes and behavior of the entire population rather than being confined to the minds of a privileged few. There is always this small hope in the mind of every writer and disseminator of information.

In every effort there does, however, come a time to stop. And we have practically reached that point. Before we do, however, let us reflect upon just a few more ideas. We began this work with a chapter on marketing theory, strategy, and consumer behavior. In the interest of closure it seems only fitting that we return briefly to some of these earlier comments for some final appraisal and review. Finally, in the concluding paragraphs of this brief chapter it would also seem fitting that we look not backward but ahead and comment briefly on the future of consumer behavior as an academic discipline and the trends and directions that the discipline is likely to take in the ensuing years.

THE "SCIENCE" OF CONSUMER BEHAVIOR

The question of whether the study of, or the field of, consumer behavior is a science is something of a moot point. For some years now there has been a continuing discussion, somewhat fruitful but sometimes too contrived, as to whether marketing is a science or an art.[1]

---

[1] For example, see Robert Bartels, "Can Marketing Be a Science?" *Journal of Marketing*, Vol. 15 (January 1951), pp. 319–328; Robert D. Buzzell, "Is Marketing a Science?" *Harvard Business Review*, Vol. 41 (January–February 1963), pp. 32 ff; and Weldon J. Taylor, "Is Marketing a Science Revisited," *Journal of Marketing*, Vol. 29 (July 1965), pp. 49–53.

Yet the issue of whether or not the study of consumer behavior is a science is a rather important one. Even as a recognized academic subject, consumer behavior is very new. Accordingly, students of consumer behavior have to a great extent been preoccupied with keeping abreast of the latest managerial strategies, consumer habits, and inferred buying motives. Only in the past few years have scholars made a concerted effort to *explain* consumer behavior, that is, to step aside from considerations of what, where, when, and how, and to address the more fundamental and, hence, perhaps more scientific question of the "why" of consumer behavior. To this extent at least, the study of consumer behavior has become more "scientific," and is perhaps well on its way to becoming a science. Conant says that science "is a process of fabricating a web of interconnected concepts and conceptual schemes arising from experiments and observations and fruitful of further experiments and observations."[2]

Definitions are always relevant to one's purposes and seldom meet the logician's requirements of accuracy. Certainly the concept of science is so elaborate and so many-faceted that any definition of it will emphasize only selected aspects. Conant's definition is no exception. He chooses to emphasize the *method* by which we arrive at verified knowledge, but he also implies the *logical* priority of theory over data, at least within the *research* context. In its broader and more general sense, the function of science is to establish general principles covering the behavior of empirical regularities or events with which the science in question is concerned and to order these into a system that will adequately represent existing scientific data. Many consumer behavioralists would easily meet this definitional requirement.

CHARACTERISTICS OF SCIENCE. Science manifests certain characteristics and to the degree that a discipline or intellectual effort and inquiry fulfills these characteristics, we have a measure as to whether that discipline or effort is a "science."

1. *Science is propositional.*[3] Science formulates statements of relationship about aspects and properties of nature that have ascertainable truth value. To this end, consumer behavior deals with propositions about certain aspects of human behavior.

2. *Science is empirical.* The propositional characteristic of science rests upon sense data. This means simply that abstract concepts and theories are formulated with a concern for the real world. Formulations are generated in the form of hypothetical solutions to empirical problems. From the hypothetical solution are deduced predictions of other observable phenomena. Observations are then made to test these

---

[2] James B. Conant, *Modern Science and Modern Man* (Garden City, N.Y.: Doubleday & Company, Inc., 1953), pp. 106–107.

[3] The basic source for this list of characteristics is R. G. Francis, *An Introduction to Social Research,* John T. Doby, ed. (Harrisburg, Pa.: Stackpole Books, 1954), pp. 6–9.

predictions. If the outcomes occur as predicted, then the hypothesis is accepted. If the predictions are only partially fulfilled or not at all, then the hypothesis is modified or rejected.

3. *Science is logical.* A system of logic is not a theory; it is instead a system of signs and the rules for their use. Thus the conclusions and inferences of science regarding the acceptance or rejection of propositions are justified by the rules of logic. Modern science consists of a set of symbolic statements that have been given physical interpretations, and these interpreted signs then serve to designate the basic concepts of the theory or theories in question.

4. *Science is operational.* The operational characteristic of science is primarily concerned with the means or steps that one uses to generate or obtain empirical content for the theoretical classes. Most specifically, it is the mathematical formulation of a physical problem.

5. *Science is public.* Science is completely communicable and hence public. The standardized aspect of science and scientific procedures and the symbolic structure of science make it possible for specific studies to be reproduced by others and for previous results to be tested.

6. *Science is problem solving.* In general we mean by problem solving the explanation of an empirical pattern or regularity. Hence the goals of science are fundamentally concerned with the development of new theory and the goals of technology with the application of theory to the problems of living and adaptation.

Given this list of characteristics, it would appear that the study of consumer behavior, or what constitutes the research effort of those who call themselves consumer behavioralists, is science. Of course, the study of consumer behavior is both a science and an art. Perhaps in one sense Jevon's words are simplest: "Science is to know, and art is to do."[4] Yet consumer behavioralists and other scientists do not wish to suppose that science is synonymous with knowledge. In our understanding, science is known, but not all that is known is science.[5]

SCIENCE AND THEORY. It was earlier asserted that the fundamental aim of science is the establishment of laws and theories. These theories are developed to provide explanations of the empirical facts investigated. Research in consumer behavior, as in other sciences or scientific fields, is solidly linked with scientific theory. *Theory* provides the framework within which any research design must be formulated. New formulations must connect logically with existing theory. However, this does not mean that all new formulations must agree with existing ones. It does, however, suggest that they are related in a logical sense and that they are capable of being rejected or affirmed. To grasp why something is as it is requires a theory. To ascertain whether that theory has merit

[4] See the definition of *science* in *Webster's Third New International Dictionary*, unabridged.

[5] See Ray G. Francis, *The Rhetoric of Science* (Minneapolis, Minn.: University of Minnesota Press, 1961), especially pp. 4–6.

requires verification by some objective procedure. The heart of any scientific activity, therefore, rests in the important relationship between theories and the methods used to obtain appropriate evidence for their verification.

THEORY AND METATHEORY IN CONSUMER BEHAVIOR

In the course of our journey across the theoretical islands of thought in consumer behavior, it should have become quite evident that there are many theories of consumer behavior. There are economic theories, sociopsychological theories, and cultural-social theories. In a finer breakdown there are

1. Theories of income.
2. Theories of assets.
3. Theories of motivation.
4. Theories of perception and social perception.
5. Theories of attitudes, values, and beliefs.
6. Theories of group behavior and processes.
7. Theories of interpersonal relations and interpersonal communication.
8. Theories of social influence processes.
9. Theories of balance, congruity, and dissonance.
10. Theories of social learning and interaction.
11. Theories of personality.
12. Theories of culture and symbolic behavior.

Of course, this list is not exhaustive. However, it is illustrative of the wide range of *theoretical* approaches to consumer behavior. We talked at length in Chapter 1 about the role of theory in consumer behavior, about the nature, functions, and kinds of theory and their relevance to consumer behavior analysis.

The problem in consumer behavior may well be that we have too many theories about consumer behavior or, stated another way, that we need a better set of *metatheory* regarding the numerous theories of consumer behavior. A *metatheory* is a theory that deals with the subject of theories. *Webster's Third New International Dictionary* defines metatheory as follows: "A theory concerned with the investigation, analysis, or description of theory itself." To some extent our holistic approach and our cognitive orientation constitute something of a metatheory of consumer behavior; that is, incorporated within a broader theoretical framework are a number of distinct theories or approaches to consumer behavior. Bartels states that, "Metatheory . . . pertain[s] to the *requirements of theory formulation*, with particular reference to the *structure of thought* and to *utilization of language for the communication of meaning*."[6] He further contends that the quality of marketing thought in a discipline, such as consumer behavior, can be facilitated

---

[6] Robert Bartels, *Marketing Theory and Metatheory* (Homewood, Ill.: Richard D. Irwin, Inc., 1970), p. 4.

by the creating and understanding of a metatheory to marketing theory.[7]

Hence, in its broadest context, *metatheory* is defined as: "The investigation, analysis, and description of the technology of: (1) theory building, (2) theory testing, and (3) theory utilization."[8]

Metatheory is thus seen as a framework out of which specific or individual theories of consumer behavior are to be structured, tested, and implemented. Such a framework suggests identifiable guidelines for the development of theories in consumer behavior:

(1) A first requirement which a metatheory makes is that a theory should deal with a specific and definable subject and be related to it throughout. This means that we need to seek some agreement as to what consumer behavior is, and what aspects of human behavior we wish to study, and in what context.

(2) A second axiom of a metatheory for consumer behavior is that theory is built upon basic concepts derived from the concept of the subject and from related scientific disciplines. The interdisciplinary nature of consumer behavior suggests adherence to this axiom.

(3) By subdivision of basic concepts, their range and qualities may be shown in intraconcept differences. An intraconcept difference is a difference in degree as opposed to differences in kind. The concept of perception is related to motivation, but basically they are interconcept differences, i.e., differences in kind. However, effectance motivation and deficiency motivation are intraconcept differences, i.e., differences which are internal and matters of degree rather than kind.

(4) Concepts in a dependent-independent relationship are the basis of explanation or prediction. A presumption of causality is basic to prediction. However, as shown earlier, the causality presumed in the theory of consumer behavior is conceptual rather than physically deterministic. It is a presumed condition in the relationship between two concepts that one is deemed an independent variable, and the other a dependent variable. For example, $B(f)C$ where B = behavior, a dependent variable and C = cognition (knowledge, perception, motivation, and other variables in the psychological field), the independent variable.

(5) Theory based upon presumed relationships is valid to the degree that those relationships have generality. This suggests that isolated incidents of relationships among variables may suggest a theory, but in the actual development of theory a general validity of those relationships is necessary.

(6) Another axiom of metatheory is that, as theory bears the mark of the marketing theorist, individuality and diversity are normal characteristics of theory.

[7] Ibid.

[8] Gerald Zaltman, Reinhard Angelmar, and Christian Pinson, "Metatheory in Consumer Behavior Research," in *Proceedings of the 2nd Annual Conference of the Association for Consumer Research,* 1971, David M. Gardner, ed. (College Park, Md.: University of Maryland, September 1–3, 1971), pp. 476–497, at p. 476.

(7) Finally, the last axiom of metatheory states that all theories of a discipline, however diverse, should be embraceable, implicitly or explicitly, in a general theory, either by grouping or by synthesis.[9]

The reasoning behind the presentation of the concept of a metatheory is that such an awareness of and sensitivity to a thinking methodology involving the investigation, analysis, and description of the many aspects of theory construction may conceivably lead to the more critical evaluation of existing theoretical work in consumer behavior and, hopefully, more sophisticated work in the future development of theoretical aspects of consumer behavior analysis.

Consumer Behavior and Marketing

Before completing this treatise, the author feels one additional compulsion. Consumer behavioralists may need to broaden the scope of their thinking as to what delineates consumer behavior. To the extent that consumer behavior is a part of marketing, the scope that we impute to marketing will affect the range and scope that we impute to consumer behavior. Traditionally we have treated marketing mainly as a business function concerned with the sale of physical products and consumer services. Those with limited vision would insist that this view prevail.[10] However, a more progressive point of view regarding marketing is that of metamarketing, that is, the furthering of organizations, persons, places, and causes.[11] *Metamarketing* means literally "beyond marketing."

Metamarketing infuses all organizations and stems from the fact that all institutions—hospitals, foundations, unions, associations, libraries, museums, government agencies, professional groups, schools, churches, politicians, welfare agencies, and whole countries—face marketinglike tasks.[12]

Metamarketing suggests a much wider scope to marketing activities, and hence it suggests that our concern with consumer behavior may transcend the conventional bounds of a consumer related to product/service activities in the conventional sense of a consumer-retailer dyad or the consumer-manufacturer-marketer relationship.

The more narrow view that is largely confined to product/service marketing may at this time be too restrictive. We have today to think in terms of marketing activities and consumer behavior in

[9] These guidelines are from Bartels, op. cit., pp. 6–13.

[10] See the views of David J. Luck in "Broadening the Concept of Marketing—Too Far," *Journal of Marketing*, Vol. 33 (July, 1969), pp. 53–55; and the reply by Philip Kotler and Sidney J. Levy, "A New Form of Marketing Myopia: Rejoinder to Professor Luck," pp. 55–57.

[11] Philip Kotler, *Marketing Management: Analysis, Planning and Control*, 2nd ed. (Englewood Cliffs, N.J.: Prentice-Hall, Inc., 1972), especially Chapter 24, pp. 867–884.

[12] Ibid., p. 867.

relation to such things as art, music, concerts, and so forth. We have to consider the marketing tasks and the related consumer behavior of such activities as the hospitality industry—restaurants, hotels-motels, convention centers, sporting events, and the whole range of professional business service marketing. As a matter of fact, marketing is such a vital and organic part of all business and semibusiness activity that Kotler has suggested a whole additional, but heretofore largely unrecognized, list of kinds of marketing efforts.

I. *Organization Marketing.* Organization marketing is defined as those activities undertaken by an organization to create, maintain, or alter attitudes and/or behavior of various audiences toward the organization as a whole in order to stimulate exchange. Such marketing in terms of the organization's audience implies a wider scope to consumer behavior. Hence, consumer behavior in such instances is audience behavior.

Examples of organization marketing are provided by this simple listing:
   A) Business Organization Marketing
   B) Government Agency Marketing
      1. NASA
      2. Post Office
      3. TVA
      4. Bonneville Power Administration
   C) Cultural Organization Marketing
      1. Symphony Orchestra Marketing
      2. Community Theatre
      3. University Marketing
   D) Service Organization Marketing
      1. American Medical Association
      2. Church Marketing
      3. Contribution Marketing

II. *Person Marketing.* Person marketing consists of activities undertaken to create, maintain, or alter attitudes toward a person. Examples of such person marketing are provided by the following suggested kinds of such activity.
   A) Political Candidate Marketing
   B) Celebrity Marketing
   C) Credential Marketing—Executive Placement

III. *Place Marketing.* Place marketing involves activities undertaken to create, maintain, or alter attitudes and/or behavior toward places. For example:
   A) Domicile Marketing
   B) Business Site Marketing
   C) Land Investment Marketing
   D) Travel Marketing
   E) Nation Marketing

IV. *Social and Welfare Marketing.* Essentially social marketing involves activities undertaken to create, maintain, or alter attitudes and/or behavior toward an idea or cause, independently of the sponsoring organization or person. Examples are as follows:

A) Population Planning.
B) Welfare Reform.
C) Mental Illness.
D) Conservation and Ecology.
E) Alcoholism.
F) Defensive Driving.[13]

The essence of metamarketing is that marketinglike activities are used in the projection, promotion, or furthering of organizations, persons, places, and causes, as well as business products or services. What is even more important is that in all cases the "seller" is trying to achieve or maintain an *exchange relation* with others through promotional-communicative activities. This implies a rather wide range and scope to consumer behavior analysis. Voters are thus "consumers" of political candidates with varying degrees of "brand" loyalty. Audience members of a given medium are thus "consumers" of the product of that medium. A sick person seeking a doctor is thus a consumer of medical services and his choice of a doctor has strong behavioral implications. A person who buys a ticket to the community's lecture-artist series has probably gone through a decision choice process and has considered this "choice" in relationship to alternative "products" such as new clothes, saving, travel, and so on.

All this further suggests that the study of consumer behavior is not necessarily just a johnny-come-lately discipline. Efforts at voter analysis and behavior, the adoption and diffusion process, communication analysis, and so forth are all really a part of the larger field of consumer behavior analysis.

Finally, the expanded view of consumer behavior that emerges from the concept of metamarketing suggests the validity and usefulness of generalizing behavioral findings in other fields to marketing and, of course, the reverse flow, that of generalizing findings related to consumers in product/service marketing to the expanded range of marketing activities subsumed under metamarketing categories.

Looking Ahead

In art we seek distinction through differentiation, in science through exactness, and in prediction and forecasting through accuracy. Throughout this book we have sought a degree of differentiation and exactness. We should like to attain a high degree of accuracy in our forecast of future events. However, there are many hazards involved in attempting to speculate about the future of any field of inquiry. These hazards appear to be magnified in the case of a field such as consumer behavior that promises to continue to experience a rapid and burgeoning growth in the years to come. However, there are trends

[13] Ibid., pp. 868–882.

underway that appear to be promising and desirable. First of all, it is quite likely that the theories of consumer behavior will continue to play a vital role in its advance as a discipline and perhaps even as a science. It is probably unlikely and even undesirable that any grand theory of consumer behavior will be developed in the near future. The study of consumer behavior includes too diverse a group of relatively young subdisciplines to be accounted for by any single network of hypotheses. It seems that theories will continue to be proposed and that research related to those theories will continue to be generated. It is already inevitable, as consumer behavioralists are confronted with some of the inadequacies of their theories through the difficulties that they experience in testing them, that theory building will become more sophisticated. This sophistication will be in terms of factors such as simplicity of terminology, testability, specificity of predictions and the conditions under which predictions hold, and internal and external theoretical consistency. Empirical testing and model building will most probably serve as a feedback mechanism for theories. Insofar as advances are made in the research methodology, this feedback function of laboratory research will be facilitated.

Surely theories will continue to proliferate if the research that they generate tends to be directed at proving the hypothesis within a given theory, for once that set of hypotheses has run its course. a new theory will be needed and proposed. The comparative testing of theories will not only lead theories to expand to encompass new conditions but will speak to the comparative viability of one theory in relation to another. In due time, of course, the less viable theories will be cast aside and the more tenable ones will survive and become guides for future research, and they will become, in turn, the objects of conceptual modification.

The intention of this book was to posit the theories in consumer behavior in a fashion clear enough to render them understandable and to stimulate the reader to make conceptual comparisons among related theories. It is the author's hope that this goal has been at least reasonably approached. In an even more wistful and idealistic sense, it is the author's hope that this book might help in some small way to stimulate theoretical advances in the field of consumer behavior.

Questions for Study, Reflection, and Review

1 How has the study of consumer behavior become more scientific?
2 Explain the general function of science.
3 Discuss some of the major characteristics of science.
4 Relate the characteristics of science to the study of consumer behavior.
5 Comment on the significance of theory in scientific research.
6 What is metatheory?

7 Discuss the basic guidelines set forth by metatheory for the development of theories.

8 What is metamarketing and what does it encompass?

9 Distinguish between organization marketing, person marketing, and place marketing.

10 Describe the concept of social and welfare marketing.

Index

Social learning approach, 254–59, 284–86. *See also* Groups; Personal influence
Social man, 48–50
Social marketing, 560–61
Social processes, and sociopsychological processes, 466–67
Social system, 369–70
  consumer behavior and, 370–73
Socialization, 361–88
  anticipatory, 373–74
  defined, 363–66
  by family, 428–29
  personal influence and, 373–80
  theories of, 366–73
Sociopsychological processes, and cultural-social process, 466–67
Sorting-rule model of product evaluation, 544–48
Source effect, 326
Standard of living, in the U.S., 27. *See also* Consumption; Income
Stereotyping, 218
Stimulus theories of personality development, 342–43
Structural pluralism, defined, 462, 469
Structure-function theory of family structure, 426
Subcultures
  exploitation of, 36–37
  values of, 477–82
Summated ratings, method of, 288
Superego, 66
Symbolic man approach, 367–68
Symboling behavior, 233
Symbols, goods as, 124, 138–39, 170
Symmetry theory, 137–40
System strain, 138
Systems approach to socialization, 369–73

T

Teleology, 96
Tension
  existential, 74
  holists on, 100
  management of, 54, 372
Tests
  of attitude, 287–91
  by consumer, 544–48

Tests—*Continued*
  of life style, 441–43
  of models, 102–103
  of motivation, 192–93
  of personality and consumer behavior, 351
  of personality traits, 341
Theorizers, 7
Theory
  defined, 5–7
  metatheory and, 557–59
  versus model, 78
  role of, 556–57
Thibaut and Kelley theory of interaction outcomes, 384–86
Thinking, convergent versus divergent, 250–51
Thresholds of sensation, 200–202, 225
Thurstone's equal-appearing interval scale, 288
Time
  dissonance and, 147
  planning, 56
T.O. selling, 31
Tolman's purposive behaviorism, 254–55
Trait approach to personality, 340–41
Transactional approach to perception, 217–22
Transactional theory of communication, 317, 318–20
Trauma, in attitude formation, 299
TUNCA, 42
Twofold judgments, 471
Two-step flow theory of communication, 315–17
Type approach to personality, 341–42

U

Umpire aspect of personality, 336
Unit pricing, 34–35
Unit relations, 135
Universals, cultural, 463–64
Unsolicited goods, 31
Utility
  attitude and, 270–71, 272
  theory of, 59–61